Less managing. More teaching. Greater learning.

 INSTRUCTORS...

Would you like your **students** to show up for class more **prepared**? *(Let's face it, class is much more fun if everyone is engaged and prepared...)*

Want ready-made application-level **interactive assignments,** student progress reporting, and auto-assignment grading? *(Less time grading means more time teaching...)*

Want an **instant view of student or class performance** relative to learning objectives? *(No more wondering if students understand...)*

Need to **collect data and generate reports** required for administration or accreditation? *(Say goodbye to manually tracking student learning outcomes...)*

Want to **record and post your lectures** for students to view online?

 With **McGraw-Hill's *Connect*™ *Management*,**

INSTRUCTORS GET:

- Interactive Applications – **book-specific interactive assignments** that require students to APPLY what they've learned.
- Simple **assignment management,** allowing you to spend more time teaching.
- **Auto-graded** assignments, quizzes, and tests.
- **Detailed Visual Reporting** where student and section results can be viewed and analyzed.
- Sophisticated **online testing** capability.
- A **filtering and reporting** function that allows you to easily assign and report on materials that are correlated to accreditation standards, learning outcomes, and Bloom's taxonomy.
- An easy-to-use **lecture capture** tool.

STUDENTS...

Want an online, **searchable version** of your textbook?

Wish your textbook could be **available online** while you're doing your assignments?

Connect™ Plus Management eBook

If you choose to use *Connect™ Plus Management*, you have an affordable and searchable online version of your book integrated with your other online tools.

Connect™ Plus Management eBook offers features like:

- Topic search
- Direct links from assignments
- Adjustable text size
- Jump to page number
- Print by section

STUDENTS...

Want to get more **value** from your textbook purchase?

Think learning management should be a bit more **interesting**?

Check out the STUDENT RESOURCES section under the *Connect™* Library tab.

Here you'll find a wealth of resources designed to help you achieve your goals in the course. You'll find things like **quizzes, PowerPoints, and Internet activities** to help you study. Every student has different needs, so explore the STUDENT RESOURCES to find the materials best suited to you.

fundamentals of
Human Resource Management

Fourth Edition

Raymond A. Noe
The Ohio State University

John R. Hollenbeck
Michigan State University

Barry Gerhart
University of Wisconsin–Madison

Patrick M. Wright
Cornell University

McGraw-Hill Irwin

FUNDAMENTALS OF HUMAN RESOURCE MANAGEMENT

Published by McGraw-Hill/Irwin, a business unit of The McGraw-Hill Companies, Inc., 1221 Avenue of the Americas, New York, NY 10020. Copyright © 2011, 2009, 2007, 2004 by The McGraw-Hill Companies, Inc. All rights reserved. No part of this publication may be reproduced or distributed in any form or by any means, or stored in a database or retrieval system, without the prior written consent of The McGraw-Hill Companies, Inc., including, but not limited to, in any network or other electronic storage or transmission, or broadcast for distance learning.

Some ancillaries, including electronic and print components, may not be available to customers outside the United States.

This book is printed on acid-free paper.

1 2 3 4 5 6 7 8 9 0 DOW/DOW 1 0 9 8 7 6 5 4 3 2 1 0

ISBN   978-0-07-353046-8
MHID   0-07-353046-8

Vice president and editor-in-chief: *Brent Gordon*
Editorial director: *Paul Ducham*
Publisher: *Doug Hughes*
Executive editor: *John Weimeister*
Director of development: *Ann Torbert*
Development editor: *Sara Knox Hunter*
Editorial assistant: *Heather Darr*
Vice president and director of marketing: *Robin J. Zwettler*
Marketing director: *Amee Mosley*
Executive marketing manager: *Anke Braun Weekes*
Vice president of editing, design, and production: *Sesha Bolisetty*
Project manager: *Dana M. Pauley*
Buyer II: *Debra R. Sylvester*
Interior designer: *Pam Verros*
Senior photo research coordinator: *Jeremy Cheshareck*
Photo researcher: *Ira C. Roberts*
Senior media project manager: *Susan Lombardi*
Media project manager: *Cathy L. Tepper*
Typeface: *10.5/12 Goudy*
Compositor: *Laserwords Private Limited*
Printer: *R. R. Donnelley*

Library of Congress Cataloging-in-Publication Data

Fundamentals of human resource management / Raymond A. Noe . . . [et al.].—4th ed.
    p. cm.
   Includes index.
   ISBN-13: 978-0-07-353046-8 (alk. paper)
   ISBN-10: 0-07-353046-8 (alk. paper)
   1. Personnel management. I. Noe, Raymond A.
HF5549.F86 2011
658.3—dc22

                                     2010029454

In tribute to the lives of Raymond and Mildred Noe
—R.A.N.

To my parents, Harold and Elizabeth, my wife, Patty, and
my children, Jennifer, Marie, Timothy, and Jeffrey
—J.R.H.

To my parents, Robert and Shirley, my wife, Heather,
and my children, Chris and Annie
—B.G.

To my parents, Patricia and Paul, my wife, Mary, and my
sons, Michael and Matthew
—P.M.W.

About the Authors

Raymond A. Noe is the Robert and Anne Hoyt Professor of Management at The Ohio State University. He was previously a professor in the Department of Management at Michigan State University and the Industrial Relations Center of the Carlson School of Management, University of Minnesota. He received his BS in psychology from The Ohio State University and his MA and PhD in psychology from Michigan State University. Professor Noe conducts research and teaches undergraduate as well as MBA and PhD students in human resource management, managerial skills, quantitative methods, human resource information systems, training, employee development, and organizational behavior. He has published articles in the *Academy of Management Journal, Academy of Management Review, Journal of Applied Psychology, Journal of Vocational Behavior,* and *Personnel Psychology.* Professor Noe is currently on the editorial boards of several journals including *Personnel Psychology, Journal of Applied Psychology,* and *Journal of Organizational Behavior.* Professor Noe has received awards for his teaching and research excellence, including the Herbert G. Heneman Distinguished Teaching Award in 1991 and the Ernest J. McCormick Award for Distinguished Early Career Contribution from the Society for Industrial and Organizational Psychology in 1993. He is also a fellow of the Society for Industrial and Organizational Psychology.

John R. Hollenbeck received his PhD in Management from New York University in 1984, and is currently the Eli Broad Professor of Management at the Eli Broad Graduate School of Business Administration at Michigan State University. Dr. Hollenbeck was the first recipient of the Ernest J. McCormick Award for Early Contributions to the field of Industrial and Organizational Psychology in 1992, and is currently a Fellow of the Academy of Management, the American Psychological Association, and the Society of Industrial and Organizational Psychology. He has published over 70 articles and book chapters on the topics of work motivation and group behavior with more than 40 of these appearing in the most highly cited refereed outlets. According to the Institute for Scientific Research, this body of work has been cited over 1,300 times by other researchers. Dr. Hollenbeck was the acting editor at *Organizational Behavior and Human Decision Processes* in 1995, the associate editor at *Decision Sciences* between 1998 and 2004, and the editor of *Personnel Psychology* from 1996 to 2002. He currently serves on the editorial board of the *Academy of Management Journal,* the *Journal of Applied Psychology, Personnel Psychology,* and *Organizational Behavior and Human Decision Processes.* Dr. Hollenbeck's teaching has been recognized with several awards, including the Michigan State University Teacher-Scholar Award in 1987 and the Michigan State University Distinguished Faculty Award in 2006. Within the Broad School of Business, he was awarded the Dorothy Withrow Teaching Award in 2002, the Lewis Quality of Excellence Award in both 2001 and 2004, and Most Outstanding MBA Faculty Award in 2007.

Barry Gerhart is the Bruce R. Ellig Distinguished Chair in Pay and Organizational Effectiveness and Director of the Strategic Human Resources Program at the University of Wisconsin–Madison. He was previously the Frances Hampton Currey Chair in Organizational Studies at the Owen School of Management at Vanderbilt University and Associate Professor and Chairman of the Department of Human Resource Studies, School of Industrial and Labor Relations at Cornell University. He received his BS in psychology from Bowling Green State University in 1979 and his PhD in industrial relations from the University of Wisconsin–Madison in 1985. His research is in the areas of compensation/rewards, staffing, and employee attitudes. Professor Gerhart has worked with a variety of organizations, including TRW, Corning, and Bausch & Lomb. His work has appeared in the *Academy of Management Journal, Industrial Relations, Industrial and Labor Relations Review, Journal of Applied Psychology, Personnel Psychology,* and *Handbook of Industrial and Organizational Psychology,* and he has served on the editorial boards of the *Academy of Management Journal, Industrial and Labor Relations Review,* and the *Journal of Applied Psychology.* He was a corecipient of the 1991 Scholarly Achievement Award, Human Resources Division, Academy of Management.

Patrick M. Wright is Professor of Human Resource Studies and Director of the Center for Advanced Human Resource Studies in the School of Industrial and Labor Relations at Cornell University. He was formerly Associate Professor of Management and Coordinator of the Master of Science in Human Resource Management program in the College of Business Administration and Graduate School of Business at Texas A&M University. He holds a BA in psychology from Wheaton College and an MBA and a PhD in organizational behavior/human resource management from Michigan State University. He teaches, conducts research, and consults in the areas of personnel selection, employee motivation, and strategic human resource management. His research articles have appeared in journals such as the *Academy of Management Journal, Journal of Applied Psychology, Organizational Behavior and Human Decision Process, Journal of Management,* and *Human Resource Management Review.* He has served on the editorial boards of *Journal of Applied Psychology* and *Journal of Management* and also serves as an ad hoc reviewer for *Organizational Behavior* and *Human Decision Processes, Academy of Management Journal,* and *Academy of Management Review.* In addition, he has consulted for a number of organizations, including Whirlpool Corporation, Amoco Oil Company, and the North Carolina State government.

He has co-authored two textbooks, has co-edited a number of special issues of journals dealing with the future of Strategic HRM as well as Corporate Social Responsibility. He has taught in Executive Development programs and has conducted programs and/or consulted for a number of large public and private sector organizations. Dr. Wright served as the Chair of the HR Division of the Academy of Management and on the Board of Directors for SHRM Foundation, World at Work, and Human Resource Planning Society.

Preface

The management of human resources is critical for companies to provide "value" to customers, shareholders, employees, and the community where they are located. Value includes not only profits but also employee growth and satisfaction, creation of new jobs, protection of the environment, and contributions to community programs. All aspects of human resource management including acquiring, preparing, developing, and compensating employees can help companies meet their competitive challenges and create value. Also, effective human resource management requires an awareness of broader contextual issues affecting business such as the economic recession, legal issues, and globalization. Both the popular press and academic research show that effective human resource management practices do result in greater value for shareholders and employees. For example, the human resource management practices at companies such as SAS, Google, Edward Jones, and W. L. Gore help them earn recognition on *Fortune* magazine's list of "The Top 100 Best Companies to Work For." This publicity creates a positive vibe for these companies, helping them attract talented new employees, motivate and retain current employees, and make their services and products more desirable to consumers.

Engaging, Focused, and Applied: Our Approach in *Fundamentals of Human Resource Management*

Following graduation most students will find themselves working in businesses or not-for-profit organizations. Regardless of their position or career aspirations, their role in either directly managing other employees or understanding human resource management practices is critical for ensuring both company and personal success. As a result, *Fundamentals of Human Resource Management* focuses on human resource issues and how HR is used at work. *Fundamentals of Human Resource Management* is applicable to both HR majors and students from other majors or colleges who are taking a human resource course as an elective or a requirement. Our approach to teaching human resource management involves *engaging* the student in learning through the use of examples and best practices, *focusing* them on the important HR issues and concepts, and providing them the opportunity to *apply* what they have learned through end-of-chapter cases and in-chapter features. Students not only learn about best practices but they are actively engaged through the use of cases and decision making. As a result, students will be able to take what they have learned in the course and apply it to solving human resource management problems they will encounter on their jobs.

For example, as described in detail in the guided tour of the book, each chapter includes "Thinking Ethically" which confronts students with ethical issues that occur in managing human resources, "HR Oops!", which highlights human resource management issues that were handled poorly, and several different cases (*BusinessWeek* cases and additional end-of-chapter cases). All of these features encourage students to critically evaluate human resource–related situations and problems that have occurred in companies and apply the chapter concepts.

"Did You Know" boxes are included in each chapter. The information provided in these boxes shows how the issues discussed in the chapter play out in companies. Some examples include what turns off an interviewer, how job satisfaction is slipping, and the top 10 causes of workplace injuries.

Adopters of *Fundamentals* have access to Manager's Hot Seat exercises which include video segments showing scenarios that are critical for HR success including ethics, diversity, working in teams, and the virtual workplace. Students assume the role of manager as they watch the videos and answer questions that appear during the segments—forcing them to make on-the-spot decisions. *Fundamentals of Human Resource Management* also assists students with "how to" perform HR activities such as responding to complaints of harassment, which they are likely to have to address as part of their jobs. Finally, the eHRM boxes show how the Internet and other technologies can be useful in managing human resources on a daily basis.

The author team believes that the focused, engaging, and applied approach distinguishes this book from others that have similar coverage of HR topics. The book has timely coverage of important HR issues, is easy to read, has many features that grab the students' attention, and gets the students actively involved in learning. We would like to thank those of you who have adopted previous editions of *Fundamentals*, and we hope that you will continue to use upcoming editions! For those of you considering *Fundamentals* for adoption, we believe that our approach makes *Fundamentals* your text of choice for human resource management.

Organization

Fundamentals of Human Resource Management includes an introductory chapter (Chapter 1) and five parts.

Chapter 1 discusses why human resource management is an essential element for an organization's success. The chapter introduces human resource management practices and human resource professionals and managers' roles and responsibilities in managing human resources. Also, ethics in human resource management is emphasized.

Part 1 discusses the environmental forces that companies face in trying to effectively use their human resources. These forces include economic, technological, and social trends, employment laws, and work design. Employers typically have more control over work design than development of equal employment law or economic, technological, or social trends, but all affect how employers attract, retain, and motivate human resources. Some of the major trends discussed in Chapter 2 include how workers are trying to find employment and make ends meet as the U.S. economy moves from recession to recovery, greater availability of new and inexpensive technology for human resource management, the growth of human resource management on a global scale, the types of skills needed for today's jobs, and a focus on aligning human resource management with a company's overall strategy. Chapter 3, "Providing Equal Employment Opportunity and a Safe Workplace," presents an overview of the major laws affecting employers in these areas and ways that organizations can develop human resource practices that are in compliance with the laws. Chapter 4, "Analyzing Work and Designing Jobs," shows how jobs and work systems determine the knowledge, skills, and abilities that employees need to provide services or produce products and influence employees' motivation, satisfaction, and safety at work. The process of analyzing and designing jobs is discussed.

Part 2 deals with identifying the types of employees needed, recruiting and choosing them, and training them to perform their jobs. Chapter 5, "Planning for and Recruiting Human Resources," discusses how to develop a human resource plan. The strengths and weaknesses of different employment options for dealing with shortages or excesses of human resources including outsourcing, use of contract workers, and downsizing are emphasized. Strategies for recruiting talented employees including use of electronic recruiting sources such as job boards and blogs are emphasized. Chapter 6, "Selecting Employees and Placing Them in Jobs," emphasizes that selection is a process starting with screening applications and résumés and concluding with a job offer. The chapter takes a look at the most widely used methods for minimizing errors in choosing employees including applications and résumés, employment tests, and interviews. Selection method standards such as reliability and validity are discussed in understandable terms. Chapter 7, "Training Employees," covers the features of effective training systems. Effective training includes not only creating a good learning environment, but managers who encourage employees to use training content in their jobs and employees who are motivated to learn. The advantages and disadvantages of different training methods, including e-learning, are discussed.

Part 3 discusses how to assess employee performance and capitalize on their talents through retention and development. In "Managing Employees' Performance" (Chapter 8), we examine the strengths and weaknesses of different performance management systems including controversial forced distribution or ranking systems. "Developing Employees for Future Success" (Chapter 9) shows the student how assessment, job experiences, formal courses, and mentoring relationships can be used to develop employees for future success. Chapter 10, "Separating and Retaining Employees," discusses how to maximize employee satisfaction and productivity and retain valuable employees as well as how to fairly and humanely separate employees if the need arises because of poor performance or economic conditions.

Part 4 covers rewarding and compensating human resources, including how to design pay structures, recognize good performers, and provide benefits. In Chapter 11, "Establishing a Pay Structure," we discuss how managers weigh the importance and costs of pay to develop a compensation structure and levels of pay for each job given the worth of the jobs, legal requirements, and employee's judgments about the fairness of pay levels. The advantages and disadvantages of different types of incentive pay including merit pay, gainsharing, and stock ownership are discussed in Chapter 12, "Recognizing Employee Contributions with Pay." Chapter 13, "Providing Employee Benefits," highlights the contents of employee benefit packages, the ways that organizations administer benefits, and what companies can do to help employees understand the value of benefits and control benefits costs. The chapter also includes a new section on the Health Care legislation passed by Congress in 2010. The discussion includes a general overview of the Law's provisions as they relate to companies providing health care as an employee benefit.

Part 5 covers other HR goals including collective bargaining and labor relations, managing human resource globally, and creating and maintaining high-performance organizations. "Collective Bargaining and Labor Relations" (Chapter 14) explores human resource activities where employees belong to unions or are seeking to join unions. Traditional issues in labor-management relations such as union structure and membership, the labor organizing process, and contract negotiations are discussed, as well as new ways unions and management are working together in less adversarial and more cooperative relationships. In "Managing Human Resources Globally" (Chapter 15), HR planning, selection, training, and compensating in international settings are discussed. We show how global differences among countries affect decisions about human resources. The role of human resources in creating an organization that achieves a high level of performance for employees, customers, community, shareholders, and managers is the focus of Chapter 16, "Creating and Maintaining High-Performance Organizations." The chapter describes high-performance work systems and the conditions that contribute to high performance and introduces students to the ways to measure the effectiveness of human resource management.

Acknowledgments

The fourth edition of *Fundamentals of Human Resource Management* would not have been possible without the staff of McGraw-Hill/Irwin and Elm Street Publishing Services. John Weimeister, our editor, helped us in developing the vision for the book and gave us the resources we needed to develop a top-of-the-line HRM teaching package. Heather Darr's valuable insights and organizational skills kept the author team on deadline and made the book more visually appealing than the authors could have ever done on their own. Cate Rzasa and Ingrid Benson of Elm Street worked diligently to make sure that the book was interesting, practical, and readable, and remained true to findings of human resource management research. We also thank Amee Mosley for her marketing efforts for this new book.

Our supplement authors deserve thanks for helping us create a first-rate teaching package. Julie Gedro of Empire State College wrote the newly custom-designed *Instructor's Manual* and Les Wiletzky of Pierce College authored the new PowerPoint presentation.

We would like to extend our sincere appreciation to all of the professors who gave of their time to offer their suggestions and insightful comments that helped us to develop and shape this new edition:

Angela D. Boston
The University of Texas–Arlington

Jerry Anthony Carbo II
Fairmont State University

John Despagna
Nassau Community College

Elizabeth Evans
Concordia University Wisconsin

William P. Ferris
Western New England College

Diane Galbraith
Slippery Rock University

Jane Whitney Gibson
Nova Southeastern University

Jean Grube
University of Wisconsin–Madison

Kathy Harris
Northwestern Oklahoma State University

Janet Henquinet
Metropolitan State University, St. Paul

Beth A Livingston
Cornell University

Michael Dane Loflin
Limestone College / York Technical College

Cheryl Macon
Butler College

Ellen Mullen
Iowa State University

Suzy Murray
Piedmont Technical College

Karen J. Smith
Columbia Southern University

Linda Turner
Morrisville State College

William Van Lente
Alliant International University

Nancy Elizabeth Waldeck
University of Toledo

Laura Wolfe
Lousiana State University

We would also like to thank the professors who gave of their time to review the previous editions through various stages of development.

Cheryl Adkins
Longwood University

Jerry Carbo
Fairmont State College

Michelle Alarcon
Hawaii Pacific University

Kevin Carlson
Virginia Tech

Lydia Anderson
Fresno City College

Xiao-Ping Chen
University of Washington

Brenda Anthony
Tallahassee Community College

Sharon Clark
Lebanon Valley College

Barry Armandi
SUNY–Old Westbury

Gary Corona
Florida Community College

Kristin Backhaus
State University of New York at New Paltz

Craig Cowles
Bridgewater State College

Charlene Barker
Spokane Falls Community College

Suzanne Crampton
Grand Valley State University

Melissa Woodard Barringer
University of Massachusetts at Amherst

Denise Daniels
Seattle Pacific University

Wendy Becker
University of Albany

K. Shannon Davis
North Carolina State University

Jerry Bennett
Western Kentucky University

Cedric Dawkins
Ashland University

Tom Bilyeu
Southwestern Illinois College

Tom Diamante
Adelphi University

Genie Black
Arkansas Tech University

Anita Dickson
Northampton Community College

Larry Borgen
Normandale Community College

Robert Ericksen
Craven Community College

Kay Braguglia
Hampton University

Dave Erwin
Athens State University

John Brau
Alvin Community College

Philip Ettman
Westfield State College

Jon Bryan
Bridgewater State College

Angela Farrar
University of Nevada at Las Vegas

Susan Burroughs
Roosevelt University

Ronald Faust
University of Evansville

Tony Cafarelli
Ursuline College

David Foote
Middle Tennessee State University

Lucy Ford
Rutgers University

Coy Jones
The University of Memphis

Wanda Foster
Calumet College of St. Joseph

Gwendolyn Jones
University of Akron

Marty Franklin
Wilkes Community College

Kathleen Jones
University of North Dakota

Rusty Freed
Tarleton State University

Jordan Kaplan
Long Island University

Walter Freytag
University of Washington

Jim Kennedy
Angelina College

Donald Gardner
University of Colorado–Colorado Springs

Shawn Komorn
University of Texas Health Sciences Center

Michael Gavlik
Vanderbilt University

Lee W. Lee
Central Connecticut State University

Treena Gillespie
California State University–Fullerton

Leo Lennon
Webster University

Kris Gossett
Ivy Tech State College

Dan Lybrook
Purdue University

Samuel Hazen
Tarleton State University

Patricia Martinez
University of Texas at San Antonio

James Hess
Ivy Tech State College

Jalane Meloun
Kent State University

Kim Hester
Arkansas State University

Angela Miles
Old Dominion University

Chad Higgins
University of Washington

James Morgan
California State University–Chico

Nancy Higgins
Montgomery College

Vicki Mullenex
Davis & Elkins College

Charles Hill
UC Berkeley

Cliff Olson
Southern Adventist University

Mary Hogue
Kent State University

Laura Paglis
University of Evansville

MaryAnne Hyland
Adelphi University

Teresa Palmer
Illinois State University

Linda Isenhour
University of Central Florida

Jack Partlow
Northern Virginia Community College

Henry Jackson
Delaware County Community College

Dana Partridge
University of Southern Indiana

Pamela Johnson
California State University–Chico

Brooke Quizz
Peirce College

Barbara Rau
University of Wisconsin–Oshkosh

Mike Roberson
Eastern Kentucky University

Foreman Rogers, Jr.
Northwood University

Mary Ellen Rosetti
Hudson Valley Community College

Joseph Salamone
State University of New York at Buffalo

Lucian Spataro
Ohio University

James Tan
University of Wisconsin—Stout

Steven Thomas
Southwest Missouri State University

Alan Tilquist
West Virginia State College

Tom Tudor
University of Arkansas

Fraya Wagner-Marsh
Eastern Michigan University

Richard Wagner
University of Wisconsin–Whitewater

Melissa Waite
SUNY Brockport

Barbara Warschawski
Schenectady County Community College

Gary Waters
Hawaii Pacific University

Bill Waxman
Edison Community College

Steven Wolff
Marist College

John Zietlow
Lee University

John Zummo
York College

Raymond A. Noe
John R. Hollenbeck
Barry Gerhart
Patrick M. Wright

fundamentals of **human**
resource
management

Noe   Hollenbeck   Gerhart   Wright

fundamentals of
Human Resource Management
fourth edition

engaging.
focused.
applied.

The fourth edition of
*Fundamentals of Human
Resource Management*
continues to offer students
a brief introduction to
HRM that is rich with
examples and engaging in
its application.

**Please take a moment to
page through some of the
highlights of this new
edition.**

FEATURES

Students who want to learn more about how human resource management is used in the everyday work environment will find that the fourth edition is engaging, focused, and applied, giving them the HRM knowledge they need to succeed.

WHAT DO I NEED TO KNOW?

Assurance of learning:
- Learning objectives open each chapter.
- Learning objectives are referenced in the page margins where the relevant discussion begins.
- The chapter summary is written around the same learning objectives.
- The student quiz on the textbook OLC and instructor testing questions are tagged to the appropriate objective they cover.

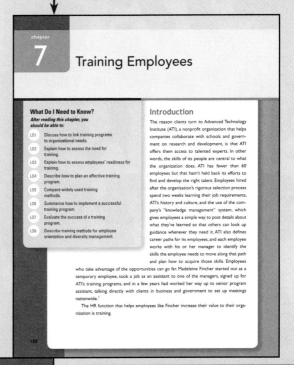

chapter
7   Training Employees

What Do I Need to Know?
After reading this chapter, you should be able to:

LO1   Discuss how to link training programs to organizational needs.

LO2   Explain how to assess the need for training.

LO3   Explain how to assess employees' readiness for training.

LO4   Describe how to plan an effective training program.

LO5   Compare widely used training methods.

LO6   Summarize how to implement a successful training program.

LO7   Evaluate the success of a training program.

LO8   Describe training methods for employee orientation and diversity management.

Introduction
The reason clients turn to Advanced Technology Institute (ATI), a nonprofit organization that helps companies collaborate with schools and government on research and development, is that ATI offers them access to talented experts. In other words, the skills of its people are central to what the organization does. ATI has fewer than 60 employees but that hasn't held back its efforts to find and develop the right talent. Employees hired after the organization's rigorous selection process spend two weeks learning their job requirements, ATI's history and culture, and the use of the company's "knowledge management" system, which gives employees a simple way to post details about what they've learned so that others can look up guidance whenever they need it. ATI also defines career paths for its employees, and each employee works with his or her manager to identify the skills the employee needs to move along that path and plan how to acquire those skills. Employees who take advantage of the opportunities can go far. Madeleine Fincher started out as a temporary employee, took a job as an assistant to one of the managers, signed up for ATI's training programs, and in a few years had worked her way up to senior program assistant, talking directly with clients in business and government to set up meetings nationwide.[1]

The HR function that helps employees like Fincher increase their value to their organization is training.

188

HR Oops!

When Training Crashes

Edy Greenblatt conducts adventure training in which participants experience how a team of four people must work together to put on a performance on the flying trapeze. Everyone learns firsthand how hard it is to listen while swinging high above the ground and wondering if they'll fall.

While Greenblatt has seen her clients learn a lot about teamwork under pressure, she also has seen and heard about the limits of adventure training. She recalls that one team of trainees told her about an earlier outing with a boss whose leadership they doubted. The training exercise only reinforced their doubts.

The boss became terrified and started crying, and the team concluded, "He's the loser he thought he was."

Trainer Linda Henman doesn't even bother recommending adventure learning anymore. She says when groups would spend the morning learning teamwork skills with her, then move to a park for an afternoon of practicing teamwork through wilderness navigation, they would return complaining that the time outside had been wasted. They preferred a focus on work-related issues.

Source: Based on Holly Dolezalek, "Extreme Training," *Training*, January

20, 2010, Business & Company Resource Center, http://galenet.galegroup.com.

Questions

1. Given the criticisms of adventure learning, why do you think it remains an attractive option to some? Would you want to participate in one of these training programs? Why or why not?

2. Imagine that you are an HR manager in a company where an executive wants to sign the sales team up for adventure learning. What steps could you take to increase the likelihood that the effort will benefit the organization?

UPDATED!

HR Oops!

Engage students through examples of companies whose HR department has fallen short. Discussion questions at the end of each example encourage student analysis of the situation. Examples include "When Social Networking Gets Too 'Social,'" "When Training Crashes," and "Programs That Discourage Safety."

Best Practices

Orkin Trains Experts

When people call Orkin, it's generally because they have an unpleasant problem, like ants, cockroaches, or bedbugs. And when people have that kind of problem, they generally just want it to go away. That's where Orkin sees a chance to offer a competitive advantage. As the company's ads say, when you call on Orkin, you "hire an expert."

So where does Orkin get those experts? The company does have a team of entomologists and other scientists with doctorate degrees, but the people who call on homes and companies to get rid of bugs didn't join the company as experts. Rather, they are committed, service-oriented individuals who have taken advantage of the company's extensive training program.

While many employers would say they consider their employees key resources, Orkin backs that claim with training that amounts to "the biggest investment we make in our employees," in the words of David Lamb, Orkin's vice president of learning and media services. New employ-

as well as working with interactive Web-based training materials. The broadcasts originate in a 28,000-square-foot training facility that Orkin built in Atlanta, featuring simulated customer locales: a house, hospital room, restaurant, bar, grocery store, and warehouse. Employees view these realistic setups to understand what they'll need to look for while they're on the job.

After this orientation period, the training continues on the job. Each new employee begins working alongside a certified field trainer, service manager, or branch manager, who observes how the new employee performs. This field trainer quizzes and coaches employees in identifying the particular species of pests they encounter, selecting the best treatment, and explaining their plans to the customer.

Even when employees have learned their job, the training continues. New pests invade, and new treatments are developed, so employees need to continue their training. Orkin's commitment to learning includes inviting entomol-

company's specialists. The forums are recorded, so employees in the field can watch the videos afterward. Orkin also brings in experts from the Centers for Disease Control and Prevention to inform its employees about health risks related to pests, so that employees can share these lessons with their customers. And in a partnership with the Building Owners and Managers Association, Orkin has developed guidelines for preventing and treating pests in the most environmentally friendly ways that have been identified.

All that training supports Orkin's strategy only if the company verifies that it is covering relevant topics. So staff members from the learning and media services department visit field offices to verify that the training is relevant to the actual issues workers are encountering.

Sources: Holly Dolezalek, "Shaper Image," *Training*, November 25, 2009, Business & Company Resource Center, http://galenet.galegroup.com; "Green Pest-Control Checklist Available Online," *Buildings*, January 2009, p. 12; and Orkin, Careers Web page, http://

focus on social responsibility

Best Practices UPDATED!

Engage students through examples of companies where the HR department is working well. Examples include "Verizon Connects with Disabled Workers," "Frito-Lay Takes a Fresh Look at Job Design," and "Room to Bloom and Grow at Four Seasons."

HR How To

DEVELOPING EFFECTIVE CLASSROOM PRESENTATIONS

What separates a boring lecture from an attention-grabbing presentation that helps you learn? Here are some ideas for developing a classroom presentation that gets results:

- *Build rapport and two-way communication from the very beginning.* As participants arrive, introduce yourself, learn names, and show you're interested in the people who are there. Lead off with a question that invites discussion.
- *Remember the real purpose.* The presentation should cover knowledge and skills participants can apply at work, not just facts for them to memorize. As you consider what to include, imagine participants hearing you and asking, "So what? How can I use this?" Then tailor the presentation to answer those questions.
- *Use multimedia as appropriate.* If you can embed relevant music, video clips, or other media into your presentation, the effort can engage participants more fully than just words on a screen.
- *Invite discussion.* The use of discussions helps participants

software: the chance to convey ideas visually. Before you opt for bullet points, think about ways to interest the audience with a photograph or drive a point home with a graph. For example, one of the first slides could be a flow chart showing how the ideas in the presentation are related to each other and to the objectives for the course. As the presentation progresses, you can provide additional images to illustrate which part of the flow you're covering. At the end, another graph (a "concept map") could show relationships among the pieces of knowledge, relating them to each other and to participants' real-world applications.

take the general ideas and apply them to their specific situations. When they get involved in this way, participants not only are more likely to remember what they learned, they also are in a stronger position to use what they learned. If participants don't have questions, the presenter should have some ready—even as simple as a pop quiz about what was just covered.

- *Introduce role playing.* If the topic involves ways that people interact, a role-play is an excellent way for you to demonstrate and for the participants to practice the skills being taught.

Sources: Carmine Gallo, "Improve Your Employee Training Sessions," *BusinessWeek*, February 2, 2010, http://www.businessweek.com; Emanuel Albu, "Presenting Course Outlines in a Flow Chart Format," *T&D*, February 2010, pp. 76–77; and Mark Magnacca, "Do You Have a 'So What' Mindset?" *T&D*, November 2009, pp. 66–67.

HR How To UPDATED!

Engage students through specific steps to create HRM programs and tackle common challenges. Examples include "Putting Compensation into Perspective," "Leading after Layoffs," and "Developing Effective Classroom Presentations."

eHRM

TRAINING GETS MOBILE

Just as the widespread adoption of personal computers brought training to employees' desks, now the greater capabilities of wireless devices are bringing training pretty much anywhere employees can get a signal on their cell phone or PDA. Content can include anything these devices can download: alerts, study aids, audio and video clips, and interactive practices and tests.

For Allison Hickey, director and program manager of consultant Accenture's national security services practices, receiving training on her BlackBerry is huge.

Juggling work and family responsibilities, Hickey had struggled to carve out time to sit down at a computer and complete a training module. The mobile training divides training programs into handy ten-minute chunks that Accenture executives can squeeze in when they step out for a lunch break or while waiting for a boarding call at the airport. At the end of each course is a quiz that participants complete and transmit back to Accenture's learning management system to verify they have learned the mandatory lessons.

Users of mobile learning praise the approach. Employees love the convenience. Merrill Lynch says participants in its mobile learning program complete their courses faster than through traditional e-learning, boosting their personal productivity by saving hours of training time every year.

Sources: Sarah Boehle, "Mobile Training: Don't Leave Home without Your BlackBerry," *Training*, September 21, 2009, Business & Company Resource Center, http://galenet.galegroup.com; and Judy Brown, "Can You Hear Me Now?" *T&D*, February 2010, Business & Company Resource Center, http://galenet.galegroup.com

eHRM UPDATED!

Engage students through examples of how HR departments use technology on a daily basis. Examples include "Talent Management," "Confirming Eligibility with E-Verify," and "Finding a Mentor Online."

Did You Know?

Many Companies Outsource Training Tasks

A recent survey of U.S.-based corporations found that over half were outsourcing the instruction of training courses. Four out of ten said they used outside experts to create custom content.

Source: "Training 2009 Industry Report," *Training*, November/December 2009, pp. 32–36.

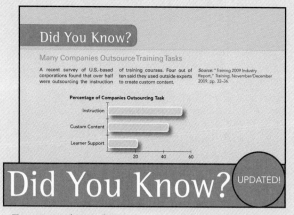

Percentage of Companies Outsourcing Task

Did You Know? UPDATED!

Engage students through interesting statistics related to chapter topics. Examples include "Employees Want More Feedback," "Unpleasant Employees Are Bad for Business," and "Investing in Human Resources."

FEATURES

Focused on ethics. Reviewers indicate that the Thinking Ethically feature, which confronts students in each chapter with an ethical issue regarding managing human resources, is a highlight. This feature has been updated throughout the text.

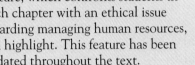

A model that shows how to make jobs more motivating is the Job Characteristics Model, developed by Richard Hackman and Greg Oldham. This model describes jobs in terms of five characteristics:[16]

1. *Skill variety*—The extent to which a job requires a variety of skills to carry out the tasks involved.
2. *Task identity*—The degree to which a job requires completing a "whole" piece of work from beginning to end (for example, building an entire component or resolving a customer's complaint).
3. *Task significance*—The extent to which the job has an important impact on the lives of other people.
4. *Autonomy*—The degree to which the job allows an individual to make decisions about the way the work will be carried out.
5. *Feedback*—The extent to which a person receives clear information about performance effectiveness from the work itself.

As shown in Figure 4.6, the more of each of these characteristics a job has, the more motivating the job will be, according to the Job Characteristics Model. The model predicts that a person with such a job will be more satisfied and will produce more and better work. For example, to increase the meaningfulness of making artery stents (devices that are surgically inserted to promote blood flow), the maker of these products invites its production workers to an annual party, where they meet patients whose lives were saved by the products they helped to manufacture.[17]

Applications of the job characteristics approach to job design include job enlargement, job enrichment, self-managing work teams, flexible work schedules, and telework.

focus on social responsibility

Job Enlargement

In a job design, **job enlargement** refers to broadening the types of tasks performed. The objective of job enlargement is to make jobs less repetitive and more interesting. Spirit AeroSystems improved profitability by enlarging jobs. After the company

Job Enlargement
Broadening the types of tasks performed in a job.

Figure 4.6
Characteristics of a Motivating Job

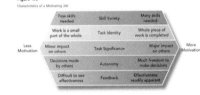

Focused on corporate social responsibility. Throughout the chapters, in-text discussions highlight companies and their commitment to social responsibility and are identified by this icon.

Focused on student resources. The end-of-chapter 'It's a **WRAP!**' box clearly indicates options students have for **R**eviewing, **A**pplying, and **P**racticing the concepts learned in each chapter at www.mhhe.com/noe4e.

Apply the concepts in each chapter through comprehensive review and discussion questions.

REVIEW AND DISCUSSION QUESTIONS

1. Assume you are the manager of a fast-food restaurant. What are the outputs of your work unit? What are the activities required to produce those outputs? What are the inputs?
2. Based on Question 1, consider the cashier's job in the restaurant. What are the outputs, activities, and inputs for that job?
3. Consider the "job" of college student. Perform a job analysis on this job. What tasks are required in the job? What knowledge, skills, and abilities are necessary to perform those tasks? Prepare a job description based on your analysis.
4. Discuss how the following trends are changing the skill requirements for managerial jobs in the United States:
   a. Increasing use of computers and the Internet.
   b. Increasing international competition.
   c. Increasing work-family conflicts.
5. How can a job analysis of each job in the work unit help a supervisor to do his or her job?
6. Consider the job of a customer service representative who fields telephone calls from customers of a retailer that sells online and through catalogs. What measures can an employer take to design this job to make it efficient? What might be some drawbacks or challenges of designing this job for efficiency?
7. How might the job in Question 6 be designed to make it more motivating? How well would these considerations apply to the cashier's job in Question 2?
8. What ergonomic considerations might apply to each of the following jobs? For each job, what kinds of costs would result from addressing ergonomics? What costs might result from failing to address ergonomics?
   a. A computer programmer.
   b. A UPS delivery person.
   c. A child care worker.
9. The chapter said that modern electronics have eliminated the need for a store's cashiers to calculate change due on a purchase. How does this development modify the job description for a cashier? If you were a store manager, how would it affect the skills and qualities of job candidates you would want to hire? Does this change in mental processing requirements affect what you would expect from a cashier? How?
10. Consider a job you hold now or have held recently. Would you want this job to be redesigned to place more emphasis on efficiency, motivation, ergonomics, or mental processing? What changes would you want, and why? (Or why do you not want the job to be redesigned?)

BUSINESSWEEK CASE

Lucky for Cain, Pfizer now lets him punt those tedious and time-consuming tasks to India with the click of a button. PfizerWorks, launched early last year, permits some 4,000 employees to pass off parts of their job to outsiders. You might call it personal outsourcing. With workers in India handling everything from basic market research projects to presentations, professionals such as Cain can focus on higher-value work. "It has really been a godsend," says Cain. "I can send them something in the evening, and the next morning it's waiting for me when I get to the office."

Apply the concepts in each chapter through two cases looking at companies and how their practices illustrate chapter content. These cases can be used in class lecture, and the questions provided at the end of each case are suitable for assignments or discussion.

Case: Jack B. Kelley Drives Home Safety Lessons

Jack B. Kelley, Inc. (JBK) is a trucking company—a common carrier that hauls bulk commodities in tanker trucks for its customers around the United States and parts of Canada. It specializes in transporting compressed gas, liquid carbon dioxide, and a variety of specialized chemicals. It can deliver them on demand or will set up a regular distribution system for repeat loads.

The company defines a three-part corporate vision of being "(1) A great place for our customers"; "(2) A great place for people to work"; and having "(3) The financial strength to accomplish 1 and 2." Especially at a company where most employees drive trucks delivering liquid and gas chemicals, it's clear that safety is important not only for being "a great place" to work but also as a basis for providing the best service to customers and maintaining financial strength. "When drivers operate safely, they take better care of their equipment," notes Mark Davis, JBK's president. And, in fact, safety records are one of the company's basic performance measures.

In support of these corporate objectives, safety training has an important place at JBK. It is the responsibility of Lee Drury, safety director at JBK, who started out with JBK as a trainer and has since put together a team of employees focused on safety.

Safety training begins as soon as the company hires new drivers. Groups of about four or five new employees meet in JBK's corporate training facility for six days of classroom training and hands-on practice.

The first session introduces a variety of topics including the company's drug-use policy, the types of commodities transported, the satellite tracking and communication system installed in the trucks, and the company's history and culture. On the afternoon of the first session, drivers climb into a 15-passenger van to practice using the company's satellite tracking system, which records and reports safety issues such as incidents of speeding or heavy braking, as well as other measures such as the amount of time the truck has been driving and idling. The trainers emphasize that the electronic reporting relieves them of paperwork and helps them become safer drivers, free to concentrate on the road.

… of training begins with lessons on man… e. Then much of the remainder of the … ands-on training in loading and unload… ids and compressed gases. This practice is repeated on each of the remaining days of training. The goal is that by the end of the orientation training, employees will know how to load and unload each product JBK transports for its customers.

The third day of orientation training includes a visit to corporate headquarters, where the new drivers meet employees in the billing department who will handle their paperwork. They also meet Davis, who stresses JBK's commitment to safety. Davis emphasizes that JBK's goals include "zero accidents, zero incidents, and zero personal injuries." During the remaining orientation days, the lessons on handling products are extended and reinforced with further practice. Drivers also learn how to refresh their memory on details by checking the company's online information system.

After the orientation period, JBK's drivers move to their home terminals, where each one is assigned to a driver trainer. There, training continues until the terminal manager and safety director determine that the new driver is fully prepared to work alone safely and professionally. Even then, a regional trainer rides along with the driver on at least one round trip to verify that the driver is handling the job well.

After orientation is behind them, drivers are fully prepared, but training continues to be available. The company provides refresher training to its experienced drivers, as well as the computer system where they can look up information on products they may not handle often.

SOURCES: Charles E. Wilson, "Award-Winning Safety Starts at the Top at Jack B. Kelley Inc.," *Bulk Transporter*, June 1, 2009, Business & Company Resource Center, http://galenet.galegroup.com; Charles E. Wilson, "Safety Should Be a Zero-Sum Program," *Bulk Transporter*, June 1, 2009, Business & Company Resource Center, http://galenet.galegroup.com; and Jack B. Kelley, Inc., "About Us," corporate Web site, www.jackbkelley.com, accessed March 29, 2010.

Questions

1. How is training at Jack B. Kelley related to its organizational needs?
2. If you were involved in preparing JBK's safety training program, how would you assess employees' readiness for training? In what ways can (or does) the company's work environment support the training?
3. Do you think e-learning might be an appropriate training method for JBK's drivers? Why or why not?

BUSINESSWEEK CASE

BusinessWeek The World Is IBM's Classroom

When 10 IBM management trainees piled into a minibus in the Philippines for a weekend tour last October, the last thing they expected was to wind up local heroes. Yet that's what happened in the tiny village of Carmen. After passing a water well project, they learned the effort had stalled because of engineering mistakes and a lack of money. The IMBers decided to do something about it. They organized a meeting of the key people involved in the project and volunteered to pay $250 out of their own pockets for additional building materials. Two weeks later the well was completed. Locals would no longer have to walk four miles for drinkable water. And the trainees learned a lesson in collaborative problem-solving. "You motivate people to take the extra step, you create a shared vision, you divide the labor, and the impact can be big," says Erwin van Overbeek, 40, who runs environmental sustainability projects for IBM clients.

While saving a village well wasn't part of the group agenda for that trip, it's the kind of experience the architects of IBM's Corporate Service Corps had in mind when they launched the initiative last year. Modeled on the U.S. Peace Corps, the program aims to turn IBM employees into global citizens. Last year, IBM selected 300 top management prospects out of 5,400 applicants. It then trained and dispatched them to emerging markets for a month in groups of 8 to 10 to help solve economic and social problems. The goal, says IBM's human resources chief, J. Randall MacDonald, is to help future leaders "understand how the world works, show them how to network, and show them how to work collaboratively with people who are far away."

Like most corporations, IBM trains managers in classrooms, so this represents a dramatic departure. And while other companies encourage employees to volunteer for social service, IBM is the first to use such programs for management training, says Rosabeth Moss Kanter, a professor at Harvard Business School.

The program is growing rapidly. This year some 500 people will participate, and the list of countries will expand from five to nine, including Brazil, India, Malaysia, and South Africa. The teams spend three months before going overseas reading about their host countries, studying the problems they're assigned to work on, and getting to know their teammates via teleconferences and social networking Web sites. On location, they work with local governments, universities, and business groups to do anything from upgrading technology for a government agency to improving public water quality.

Participating in the program is not without its risks. Charlie Ung, a new-media producer from IBM Canada, got malaria while working in Ghana and spent a week in the hospital. Other participants report encounters with wild dogs in Romania. IBM planners deliberately choose out-of-the-way places and bunk the teams in guest houses that lack such amenities as Western food and CNN. "We want them to have a transformative experience, so they're shaken up and walk away feeling they're better equipped to confront the challenges of the 21st century," says Kevin Thompson, the IBMer who conceived of the CSC program and now manages it.

IBM concedes that one month overseas is a short stint, but it believes participants can pick up valuable lessons. Debbie Maconnel, a 45-year-old IT project manager in Lexington, Kentucky, says the trip prompted her to change her management style. She coordinates the activities of 13 people in the United States and 12 in India, Mexico, and China. She used to give assignments to the overseas employees and then leave them on their own. Now she spends more time trying to build a global team.

SOURCE: Excerpted from Steve Hamm, "The World Is IBM's Classroom," *BusinessWeek*, March 12, 2009, http://www.businessweek.com.

Questions

1. Based on the information given but in your own words, what are the training objectives for IBM's Corporate Service Corps? Based on the information given, how well would you say the program is meeting those objectives? What additional measures would help you evaluate the program's success?
2. Which of the training methods described in this chapter are incorporated into the Corporate Service Corps? How well suited are these methods to achieving IBM's objectives?
3. Suggest some ways that IBM can help participants apply on the job what they have learned from their one-month service project.

Here's what our reviewers have said:

"I definitely would say this is the best introduction to HRM text on the market. I find it easy to read and understand, yet it contains the necessary level of knowledge needed to be successful in an entry level HR generalist role." *Jerry Carbo, Fairmont State University*

"The features are outstanding . . . very easy to read and understand and allow for application of the information." *Angela Boston, The University of Texas–Arlington*

"The features are outstanding and add a lot to the book. They keep the book current and give insight to real-life applications." *Jane Gibson, Nova Southeastern University*

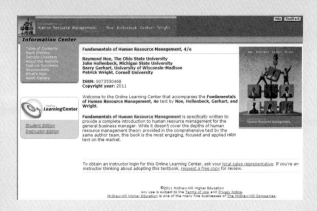

Instructor's Manual

The newly custom-designed Instructor's Manual includes chapter summaries, learning objectives, an extended chapter outline, key terms, description of text boxes, discussion questions, summary of end-of-chapter cases, video notes, and additional activities.

Test Bank

The test bank includes multiple choice, true/false, and essay questions for each chapter. Rationales and page references are also provided for the answers. Available on the Instructor OLC.

EZ Test

McGraw-Hill's EZ Test is a flexible and easy-to use electronic testing program. The program allows instructors to create tests from book specific items. It accommodates a wide range of question types and instructors may add their own questions. Multiple versions of the test can be created and any test can be exported for use with course management systems such as WebCT, BlackBoard, or PageOut. The program is available for Windows and Macintosh environments.

Videos

Videos for each chapter, along with accompanying video cases and quizzes, are located on the OLC and highlight companies and current HRM issues.

PowerPoint

The slides include lecture material, key terms, additional content to expand concepts in the text, hotlinks, and discussion questions. The Power-Point is found on the Instructor Online Learning Center. The PPT also now includes detailed teaching notes.

Online Learning Center

(www.mhhe.com/noefund4e)
This text-specific Web site follows the text chapter by chapter. Students can go online to take
self-grading quizzes, watch video clips and answer discussion questions, read relevant and current HR news, and work through interactive exercises. New to this edition are Small Business Cases; one per chapter located on the Web site. There is a guide linking the PHR/SPHR certification exam with the text. Instructors can also access downloadable supplements such as the Instructor's Manual and Manager's Hot Seat notes. Professors and students can access this content directly through the textbook Web site, through PageOut, or within a course management system (i.e., WebCT or Blackboard).

Self-Assessments and Test Your Knowledge Quizzes

These interactive features provide students with tools to study chapter concepts in a variety of environments, and provide instructors with additional assignments or in-class discussion opportunities. These are premium content features and require a purchased access code.

Manager's Hot Seat

The Manager's Hot Seat is an interactive online feature that allows students to watch as 15 real managers apply their years of experience to confront issues. Students assume the role of the manager as they watch the video and answer multiple choice questions that pop up during the segment—forcing them to make decisions on the spot. Students learn from the manager's mistakes and successes, and then do a report critiquing the manager's approach by defending their reasoning. Reports can be e-mailed or printed out for credit. Manager's Hot Seat is included in the asset Gallery as premium content.

Brief Contents

Contents

Managing Human Resources

What Do I Need to Know?

After reading this chapter, you should be able to:

LO1 Define human resource management, and explain how HRM contributes to an organization's performance.

LO2 Identify the responsibilities of human resource departments.

LO3 Summarize the types of skills needed for human resource management.

LO4 Explain the role of supervisors in human resource management.

LO5 Discuss ethical issues in human resource management.

LO6 Describe typical careers in human resource management.

Introduction

Imagine trying to run a business where you have to replace every employee two or three times a year. If that sounds chaotic, you can sympathize with the challenge facing Rob Cecere when he took the job of regional manager for a group of eight Domino's Pizza stores in New Jersey. In Cecere's region, store managers were quitting after a few months on the job. The lack of consistent leadership at the store level contributed to employee turnover rates of up to 300 percent a year (one position being filled three times in a year). In other words, new managers constantly had to find, hire, and train new workers—and rely on inexperienced people to keep customers happy. Not surprisingly, the stores in Cecere's new territory were failing to meet sales goals.

Cecere made it his top goal to build a stable team of store managers who in turn could retain employees at their stores. He held a meeting with the managers and talked about improving sales, explaining, "It's got to start with people": hiring good people and keeping them on board. He continues to coach his managers, helping them build sales and motivate their workers through training and patience. In doing so, he has the backing of Domino's headquarters. When the company's former chief executive, David Brandon, took charge, he was shocked by the high employee turnover (then 158 percent nationwide), and he made that problem his priority. Brandon doubts the pay rates are what keeps employees with any fast-food company; instead, he emphasizes careful hiring, extensive coaching, and opportunities to earn promotions. In the years since Brandon became CEO, employee turnover at Domino's has fallen. And in New Jersey, Cecere is beginning to see results from his store managers as well.[1]

Figure 1.1

Human Resource Management Practices

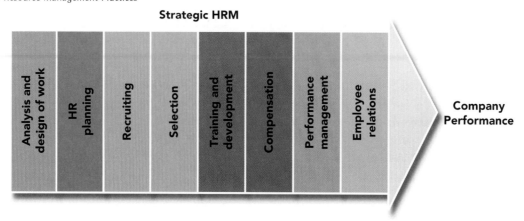

The challenges faced by Domino's are important dimensions of **human resource management (HRM),** the policies, practices, and systems that influence employees' behavior, attitudes, and performance. Many companies refer to HRM as involving "people practices." Figure 1.1 emphasizes that there are several important HRM practices that should support the organization's business strategy: analyzing work and designing jobs, determining how many employees with specific knowledge and skills are needed (human resource planning), attracting potential employees (recruiting), choosing employees (selection), teaching employees how to perform their jobs and preparing them for the future (training and development), evaluating their performance (performance management), rewarding employees (compensation), and creating a positive work environment (employee relations). An organization performs best when all of these practices are managed well. At companies with effective HRM, employees and customers tend to be more satisfied, and the companies tend to be more innovative, have greater productivity, and develop a more favorable reputation in the community.[2]

In this chapter, we introduce the scope of human resource management. We begin by discussing why human resource management is an essential element of an organization's success. We then turn to the elements of managing human resources: the roles and skills needed for effective human resource management. Next, the chapter describes how all managers, not just human resource professionals, participate in the activities related to human resource management. The following section of the chapter addresses some of the ethical issues that arise with regard to human resource management. We then provide an overview of careers in human resource management. The chapter concludes by highlighting the HRM practices covered in the remainder of this book.

Human Resources and Company Performance

Managers and economists traditionally have seen human resource management as a necessary expense, rather than as a source of value to their organizations. Economic value is usually associated with *capital*—cash, equipment, technology, and facilities. However, research has demonstrated that HRM practices can be valuable.[3] Decisions such as whom to hire, what to pay, what training to offer, and how to evaluate employee performance directly affect employees' motivation and ability to provide

Human Resource Management (HRM)
The policies, practices, and systems that influence employees' behavior, attitudes, and performance.

LO1 Define human resource management, and explain how HRM contributes to an organization's performance.

goods and services that customers value. Companies that attempt to increase their competitiveness by investing in new technology and promoting quality throughout the organization also invest in state-of-the-art staffing, training, and compensation practices.[4]

The concept of "human resource management" implies that employees are *resources* of the employer. As a type of resource, **human capital** means the organization's employees, described in terms of their training, experience, judgment, intelligence, relationships, and insight—the employee characteristics that can add economic value to the organization. In other words, whether it manufactures automobiles or forecasts the weather, for an organization to succeed at what it does, it needs employees with certain qualities, such as particular kinds of training and experience. This view means employees in today's organizations are not interchangeable, easily replaced parts of a system but the source of the company's success or failure. By influencing *who* works for the organization and *how* those people work, human resource management therefore contributes to basic measures of an organization's performance such as quality, profitability, and customer satisfaction. Figure 1.2 shows this relationship.

Fabick Caterpillar (CAT), which sells, rents, and repairs Caterpillar construction equipment, demonstrates the importance of human capital to the company's bottom line. Fabick CAT, which serves construction businesses and contractors in Missouri and southern Illinois and pipeline contractors throughout the world, has more than 600 employees in 12 locations. When Doug Fabick inherited the business from his father in 1999, he wondered why it was underperforming many other CAT dealerships in the United States. Fabick studied traditional financial indicators and organizational charts but could find no common thread. He began to think success depended on getting the right people in the right positions and doing *something* to get them passionate about their jobs. Initial assessments of employee attitudes suggested he was right: only 16 percent of employees were "engaged" (fully committed to their work). Fabick began working with managers and employees on such HR practices as developing management talent, selecting new employees with the right skills and abilities to succeed, and training salespeople to develop strong customer relationships. As employees began to feel the company was focused on building on their strengths, their engagement with their work began to rise—and so did Fabick CAT's sales and profits.[5]

Human Capital
An organization's employees, described in terms of their training, experience, judgment, intelligence, relationships, and insight.

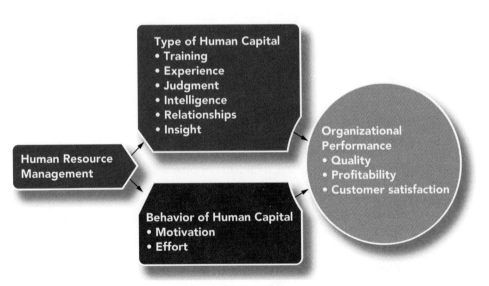

Figure 1.2

Impact of Human Resource Management

At Southwest Airlines, the company's focus is on keeping employees loyal, motivated, trained, and compensated. In turn, there is a low turnover rate and a high rate of customer satisfaction.

Human resource management is critical to the success of organizations because human capital has certain qualities that make it valuable. In terms of business strategy, an organization can succeed if it has a *sustainable competitive advantage* (is better than competitors at something and can hold that advantage over a sustained period of time). Therefore, we can conclude that organizations need the kind of resources that will give them such an advantage. Human resources have these necessary qualities:

- Human resources are *valuable*. High-quality employees provide a needed service as they perform many critical functions.
- Human resources are *rare* in the sense that a person with high levels of the needed skills and knowledge is not common. An organization may spend months looking for a talented and experienced manager or technician.
- Human resources *cannot be imitated*. To imitate human resources at a high-performing competitor, you would have to figure out which employees are providing the advantage and how. Then you would have to recruit people who can do precisely the same thing and set up the systems that enable those people to imitate your competitor.
- Human resources have *no good substitutes*. When people are well trained and highly motivated, they learn, develop their abilities, and care about customers. It is difficult to imagine another resource that can match committed and talented employees.

These qualities imply that human resources have enormous potential. As demonstrated in the "Did You know?" box, an organization realizes this potential through the ways it practices human resource management.

Effective management of human resources can form the foundation of a **high-performance work system**—an organization in which technology, organizational structure, people, and processes all work together to give an organization an advantage in the competitive environment. As technology changes the ways organizations manufacture, transport, communicate, and keep track of information, human resource management must ensure that the organization has the right kinds of people to meet the new challenges. Maintaining a high-performance work system may include development of training programs, recruitment of people with new skill sets, and establishment of rewards for such behaviors as teamwork, flexibility, and learning. In the next chapter, we will see some of the changes that human resource managers are planning for, and Chapter 16 examines high-performance work systems in greater detail.

High-Performance Work System
An organization in which technology, organizational structure, people, and processes all work together to give an organization an advantage in the competitive environment.

LO2 Identify the responsibilities of human resource departments.

Responsibilities of Human Resource Departments

In all but the smallest organizations, a human resource department is responsible for the functions of human resource management. On average, an organization has one HR staff person for every 93 employees served by the department.[6] One way to define the responsibilities of HR departments is to think of HR as a business within the company with three product lines:[7]

1. *Administrative services and transactions*—Handling administrative tasks (for example, hiring employees and answering questions about benefits) efficiently and with a commitment to quality. This requires expertise in the particular tasks.

Engaged, Enabled Employees Deliver Bottom-Line Benefits

Comparing companies where employees are highly engaged (through communication and leadership) and highly enabled (carefully selected for well-designed jobs with adequate resources and training) with low-engagement, low-enablement companies, the Hay Group found big performance differences.

Source: Hay Group, "Tough Decisions in a Downturn Don't Have to Lead to Disengaged Employees," news release, August 13, 2009, http://www.haygroup.com.

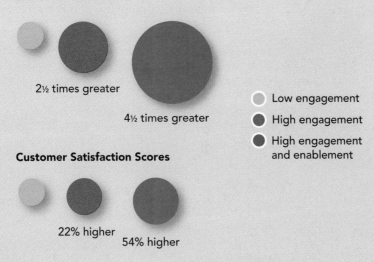

Growth in Revenues

2½ times greater

4½ times greater

○ Low engagement

● High engagement

● High engagement and enablement

Customer Satisfaction Scores

22% higher

54% higher

2. *Business partner services*—Developing effective HR systems that help the organization meet its goals for attracting, keeping, and developing people with the skills it needs. For the systems to be effective, HR people must understand the business so it can understand what the business needs.
3. *Strategic partner*—Contributing to the company's strategy through an understanding of its existing and needed human resources and ways HR practices can give the company a competitive advantage. For strategic ideas to be effective, HR people must understand the business, its industry, and its competitors.

Another way to think of HR responsibilities is in terms of specific activities. Table 1.1 details the responsibilities of human resource departments. These responsibilities include the practices introduced in Figure 1.1 plus two areas of responsibility that support those practices: (1) establishing and administering personnel policies and (2) ensuring compliance with labor laws.

Although the human resource department has responsibility for these areas, many of the tasks may be performed by supervisors or others inside or outside the organization. No two human resource departments have precisely the same roles because of differences in organization sizes and characteristics of the workforce, the industry, and management's values. In some companies, the HR department handles all the activities listed in Table 1.1. In others, it may share the roles and duties with managers of other departments such as finance, operations, or information technology. In some companies, the HR department actively advises top management. In others,

Table 1.1

Responsibilities of HR Departments

FUNCTION	RESPONSIBILITIES
Analysis and design of work	Work analysis; job design; job descriptions
Recruitment and selection	Recruiting; job postings; interviewing; testing; coordinating use of temporary labor
Training and development	Orientation; skills training; career development programs
Performance management	Performance measures; preparation and administration of performance appraisals; discipline
Compensation and benefits	Wage and salary administration; incentive pay; insurance; vacation leave administration; retirement plans; profit sharing; stock plans
Employee relations	Attitude surveys; labor relations; employee handbooks; company publications; labor law compliance; relocation and outplacement services
Personnel policies	Policy creation; policy communication; record keeping; HR information systems
Compliance with laws	Policies to ensure lawful behavior; reporting; posting information; safety inspections; accessibility accommodations
Support for strategy	Human resource planning and forecasting; change management

SOURCE: Based on SHRM-BNA Survey No. 66, "Policy and Practice Forum: Human Resource Activities, Budgets, and Staffs, 2000–2001," *Bulletin to Management,* Bureau of National Affairs Policy and Practice Series (Washington, DC: Bureau of National Affairs, June 28, 2001).

the department responds to top-level management decisions and implements staffing, training, and compensation activities in light of company strategy and policies.

Let's take an overview of the HR functions and some of the options available for carrying them out. Human resource management involves both the selection of which options to use and the activities involved with using those options. Later chapters of the book will explore each function in greater detail.

Analyzing and Designing Jobs

To produce their given product or service (or set of products or services), companies require that a number of tasks be performed. The tasks are grouped together in various combinations to form jobs. Ideally, the tasks should be grouped in ways that help the organization to operate efficiently and to obtain people with the right qualifications to do the jobs well. This function involves the activities of job analysis and job design. **Job analysis** is the process of getting detailed information about jobs. **Job design** is the process of defining the way work will be performed and the tasks that a given job requires.

In general, jobs can vary from having a narrow range of simple tasks to having a broad array of complex tasks requiring multiple skills. At one extreme is a worker on an assembly line at a poultry-processing facility; at the other extreme is a doctor in an emergency room. In the past, many companies have emphasized the use of narrowly defined jobs to increase efficiency. With many simple jobs, a company can easily find workers who can quickly be trained to perform the jobs at relatively low pay. However, greater concern for innovation and quality has shifted the trend to more use of broadly defined jobs. Also, as we will see in Chapters 2 and 4, some organizations assign work even more broadly, to teams instead of individuals.

Job Analysis
The process of getting detailed information about jobs.

Job Design
The process of defining the way work will be performed and the tasks that a given job requires.

Recruiting and Hiring Employees

Based on job analysis and design, an organization can determine the kinds of employees it needs. With this knowledge, it carries out the function of recruiting and hiring employees. **Recruitment** is the process through which the organization seeks applicants for potential employment. **Selection** refers to the process by which the organization attempts to identify applicants with the necessary knowledge, skills, abilities, and other characteristics that will help the organization achieve its goals. An organization makes selection decisions in order to add employees to its workforce, as well as to transfer existing employees to new positions.

Home Depot and other retail stores use in-store kiosks similar to the Career Center shown here to recruit applicants for employment.

Approaches to recruiting and selection involve a variety of alternatives. Some organizations may actively recruit from many external sources, such as Internet job postings, newspaper want-ads, and college recruiting events. Other organizations may rely heavily on promotions from within, applicants referred by current employees, and the availability of in-house people with the necessary skills.

At some organizations the selection process may focus on specific skills, such as experience with a particular programming language or type of equipment. At other organizations, selection may focus on general abilities, such as the ability to work as part of a team or find creative solutions. The focus an organization favors will affect many choices, from the way the organization measures ability, to the questions it asks in interviews, to the places it recruits. Table 1.2 lists the top five qualities that employers say they are looking for in job candidates.

Training and Developing Employees

Although organizations base hiring decisions on candidates' existing qualifications, most organizations provide ways for their employees to broaden or deepen their knowledge, skills, and abilities. To do this, organizations provide for employee training and development. **Training** is a planned effort to enable employees to learn job-related knowledge, skills, and behavior. For example, many organizations offer safety training to teach employees safe work habits. **Development** involves acquiring knowledge, skills, and behavior that improve employees' ability to meet the challenges of a variety of new or existing jobs, including the client and customer demands of those jobs. Development programs often focus on preparing employees for management responsibility. Likewise, if a company plans to set up teams to manufacture products, it might offer a development program to help employees learn the ins and outs of effective teamwork.

Recruitment
The process through which the organization seeks applicants for potential employment.

Selection
The process by which the organization attempts to identify applicants with the necessary knowledge, skills, abilities, and other characteristics that will help the organization achieve its goals.

Training
A planned effort to enable employees to learn job-related knowledge, skills, and behavior.

Development
The acquisition of knowledge, skills, and behaviors that improve an employee's ability to meet changes in job requirements and in customer demands.

Table 1.2

Top Qualities Employers Look For in Employees

1. Interpersonal skills
2. Work ethic
3. Initiative/flexibility
4. Honesty/loyalty
5. Strong communication skills (verbal and written)

SOURCES: "Skills Employers Look for in Employees," articles by Leigh Goessl, Juan Leer, and Sun Meilan at www.helium.com, accessed May 12, 2010, and Dennis Lee, "10 Qualities Interviewers Look For," at www.goldsea.com, accessed May 12, 2010.

Decisions related to training and development include whether the organization will emphasize enabling employees to perform their current jobs, preparing them for future jobs, or both. An organization may offer programs to a few employees in whom the organization wants to invest, or it may have a philosophy of investing in the training of all its workers. Some organizations, especially large ones, may have extensive formal training programs, including classroom sessions and training programs online. Other organizations may prefer a simpler, more flexible approach of encouraging employees to participate in outside training and development programs as needs are identified.

Managing Performance

Managing human resources includes keeping track of how well employees are performing relative to objectives such as job descriptions and goals for a particular position. The process of ensuring that employees' activities and outputs match the organization's goals is called **performance management.** The activities of performance management include specifying the tasks and outcomes of a job that contribute to the organization's success. Then various measures are used to compare the employee's performance over some time period with the desired performance. Often, rewards—the topic of the next section—are developed to encourage good performance.

Performance Management
The process of ensuring that employees' activities and outputs match the organization's goals.

The human resource department may be responsible for developing or obtaining questionnaires and other devices for measuring performance. The performance measures may emphasize observable behaviors (for example, answering the phone by the second ring), outcomes (number of customer complaints and compliments), or both. When the person evaluating performance is not familiar with the details of the job, outcomes tend to be easier to evaluate than specific behaviors.[8] The evaluation may focus on the short term or long term and on individual employees or groups. Typically, the person who completes the evaluation is the employee's supervisor. Often employees also evaluate their own performance, and in some organizations, peers and subordinates participate, too.

Planning and Administering Pay and Benefits

The pay and benefits that employees earn play an important role in motivating them. This is especially true when rewards such as bonuses are linked to the individual's or group's achievements. Decisions about pay and benefits can also support other aspects of an organization's strategy. For example, a company that wants to provide an exceptional level of service or be exceptionally innovative might pay significantly more than competitors in order to attract and keep the best employees. At other companies, a low-cost strategy requires knowledge of industry norms, so that the company does not spend more than it must.

Planning pay and benefits involves many decisions, often complex and based on knowledge of a multitude of legal requirements. An important decision is how much to offer in salary or wages, as opposed to bonuses, commissions, and other performance-related pay. Other decisions involve which benefits to offer, from retirement plans to various kinds of insurance to time off with pay. These pay decisions may also be linked to other decisions and policies aimed at motivating and engaging workers, as described in the "HR How To" box. All such decisions have implications for the organization's bottom line, as well as for employee motivation.

PUTTING COMPENSATION IN PERSPECTIVE

When it comes to attracting, keeping, and motivating workers, a lot of people think first about pay, and certainly getting paid is one important reason we get up and go to work day after day. But to get employees to use all their talents and go the extra mile, companies have to combine decisions about compensation with other efforts at engaging and enabling their people:

- *Link significant differences in pay to high performance—* The best workers should be up for bonuses, promotions, or other measurable rewards. That means compensation budgets should include money set aside for those rewards.
- *Make sure employees know what is expected of them—* This requires a combination of careful job design and thorough communication. HR staff can work with supervisors to spell out what superior performance looks like for each position in the organization.
- *Give employees plenty of feedback, so performance problems can be identified and corrected early on—* HR personnel can work with supervisors by developing and helping them use systems for performance feedback.
- *Make success possible—* That includes matching qualified people to jobs and participating in efforts to eliminate or improve inefficient work processes. Training should be available to help employees fulfill job requirements, update skills, and advance in their careers.
- *Create a positive climate—* When possible, encourage employees to collaborate and take on authority for decision making in the areas for which they are responsible.

Source: Based on William Werhane and Mark Royal, "Engaging and Enabling Employees," *workspan*, October 2009, pp. 39–43.

Administering pay and benefits is another big responsibility. Organizations need systems for keeping track of each employee's earnings and benefits. Employees need information about their health plan, retirement plan, and other benefits. Keeping track of this involves extensive record keeping and reporting to management, employees, the government, and others.

Maintaining Positive Employee Relations

Organizations often depend on human resource professionals to help them maintain positive relations with employees. This function includes preparing and distributing employee handbooks that detail company policies and, in large organizations, company publications such as a monthly newsletter or a Web site on the organization's intranet. Preparing these communications may be a regular task for the human resource department.

The human resource department can also expect to handle certain kinds of communications from individual employees. Employees turn to the HR department for answers to questions about benefits and company policy. If employees feel they have been discriminated against, see safety hazards, or have other problems and are dissatisfied with their supervisor's response, they may turn to the HR department for help. Members of the department should be prepared to address such problems.

In organizations where employees belong to a union, employee relations entail additional responsibilities. The organization periodically conducts collective bargaining to negotiate an employment contract with union members. The HR department maintains communication with union representatives to ensure that problems are resolved as they arise.

Establishing and Administering Personnel Policies

All the human resource activities described so far require fair and consistent decisions, and most require substantial record keeping. Organizations depend on their HR department to help establish policies related to hiring, discipline, promotions, and benefits. For example, with a policy in place that an intoxicated worker will be immediately terminated, the company can handle such a situation more fairly and objectively than if it addressed such incidents on a case-by-case basis. The company depends on its HR professionals to help develop and then communicate the policy to every employee, so that everyone knows its importance. If anyone violates the rule, a supervisor can quickly intervene—confident that the employee knew the consequences and that any other employee would be treated the same way. Not only do such policies promote fair decision making, but they also promote other objectives, such as workplace safety and customer service.

All aspects of human resource management require careful and discreet record keeping, from processing job applications, to performance appraisals, benefits enrollment, and government-mandated reports. Handling records about employees requires accuracy as well as sensitivity to employee privacy. Whether the organization keeps records in file cabinets or on a sophisticated computer information system, it must have methods for ensuring accuracy and for balancing privacy concerns with easy access for those who need information and are authorized to see it.

Ensuring Compliance with Labor Laws

As we will discuss in later chapters, especially Chapter 3, the government has many laws and regulations concerning the treatment of employees. These laws govern such matters as equal employment opportunity, employee safety and health, employee pay and benefits, employee privacy, and job security. Government requirements include filing reports and displaying posters, as well as avoiding unlawful behavior. Most managers depend on human resource professionals to help them keep track of these requirements.

Ensuring compliance with laws requires that human resource personnel keep watch over a rapidly changing legal landscape. For example, the increased use of and access to electronic databases by employees and employers suggest that in the near future legislation will be needed to protect employee privacy rights. Currently, no federal laws outline how to use employee databases in such a way as to protect employees' privacy while also meeting employers' and society's concern for security.

Lawsuits that will continue to influence HRM practices concern job security. Because companies are forced to close facilities and lay off employees because of economic or competitive conditions, cases dealing with the illegal discharge of employees have increased. The issue of "employment at will"—that is, the principle that an employer may terminate employment at any time without notice—will be debated. As the age of the overall workforce increases, as described in the next chapter, the number of cases dealing with age discrimination in layoffs, promotions, and benefits will likely rise. Employers will need to review work rules, recruitment practices, and performance evaluation systems, revising them if necessary to ensure that they do not falsely communicate employment agreements the company does not intend to honor (such as lifetime employment) or discriminate on the basis of age.

Supporting the Organization's Strategy

At one time, human resource management was primarily an administrative function. The HR department focused on filling out forms and processing paperwork. As more organizations have come to appreciate the significance of highly skilled human resources, however, many HR departments have taken on a more active role in supporting the organization's strategy. As a result, today's HR professionals need to understand the organization's business operations, project how business trends might affect the business, reinforce positive aspects

One reason W. L. Gore & Associates is repeatedly named one of the 100 Best Companies to Work for in America is their unusual corporate culture where all employees are known as associates and bosses are not to be found. How do you think this boosts morale in the workplace?

of the organization's culture, develop talent for present and future needs, craft effective HR strategies, and make a case for them to top management.[9] Evidence for greater involvement in strategy is that more corporations' boards of directors are adding HR executives. Hewitt Associates brought onboard William J. Conaty, formerly the head of HR for General Electric, to help with recruiting talented leaders, and VF Corporation's board includes Ursula Fairbairn, former HR head at American Express Company. When VF acquired North Face, Fairbairn used her experience with mergers to help the company communicate effectively with its new employees.[10]

An important element of this responsibility is **human resource planning,** identifying the numbers and types of employees the organization will require in order to meet its objectives. Using these estimates, the human resource department helps the organization forecast its needs for hiring, training, and reassigning employees. Planning also may show that the organization will need fewer employees to meet anticipated needs. In that situation, human resource planning includes how to handle or avoid layoffs.

As part of its strategic role, one of the key contributions HR can make is to engage in evidence-based HR. **Evidence-based HR** refers to demonstrating that human resource practices have a positive influence on the company's profits or key stakeholders (employees, customers, community, shareholders). This practice helps show that the money invested in HR programs is justified and that HRM is contributing to the company's goals and objectives. For example, data collected on the relationship between HR practices and productivity, turnover, accidents, employee attitudes, and medical costs may show that HR functions are as important to the business as finance, accounting, and marketing. The "Best Practices" box describes how Lifespan, a group of hospitals, has benefited from using evidence-based HR.

Often, an organization's strategy requires some type of change—for example, adding, moving, or closing facilities; applying new technology; or entering markets in other regions or countries. Common reactions to change include fear, anger, and confusion. The organization may turn to its human resource department for help in managing the change process. Skilled human resource professionals can apply knowledge of human behavior, along with performance management tools, to help the organization manage change constructively.

Human Resource Planning
Identifying the numbers and types of employees the organization will require to meet its objectives.

Evidence-based HR
Collecting and using data to show that human resource practices have a positive influence on the company's bottom line or key stakeholders.

FOR LIFESPAN, DATA-DRIVEN APPROACH HELPS HR GET BETTER

In a hospital, getting talented employees engaged in their work is more than a matter of profits; it also shapes patients' health and sometimes their lives. So it's no wonder that Lifespan, a group of five New England hospitals with almost 12,000 employees, takes HR very seriously. Lifespan has a formally defined mission statement that emphasizes quality service aimed at improving health, and Lifespan's HR group has its own mission to help the hospitals achieve their goals to be the institution that patients and health workers choose for their health care or jobs.

The HR function uses a methodical approach that starts by figuring out what drives engagement among Lifespan's employees. Every two years, the company uses a contractor called PeopleMetrics to conduct a survey of all Lifespan employees; in

this way, Lifespan learned that at all of its hospitals, employees are most engaged when they perceive that the organization cares for its employees. Based on this and other conclusions from the surveys, HR helps the individual hospital and department management develop action plans for improving the drivers of engagement. In follow-up surveys, Lifespan determines whether it is improving in the targeted areas, as well as watching for improvements in outcomes, such as employee turnover and patient satisfaction and health.

Measurements by People-Metrics found that as employee engagement has improved at Lifespan, so has patient satisfaction and the likelihood that patients will recommend the hospitals to others. The research also found that when employee engagement was higher, fewer

medication errors occurred, and patients were less likely to get hospital-acquired infections. Those improvements in care have an obvious benefit to patients. They also have a bottom-line benefit. Medicare and Medicaid no longer reimburse hospitals for serious preventable events, so avoiding medication errors and preventable infections saves the company money that would be spent to provide services for which it will not be paid. That makes for healthier hospitals—financially speaking—as well as healthier, happier patients.

Sources: Lifespan, "Lifespan Mission Statement" and "Lifespan Statistics," Lifespan Web site, http://www.lifespan.org, accessed February 17, 2010; and PeopleMetrics, "Lifespan Uses Employee Engagement Management (EEM) to Increase Patient Satisfaction," case study, 2009, www.peoplemetrics.com, accessed February 16, 2010.

focus on social responsibility

Corporate Social Responsibility
A company's commitment to meeting the needs of its stakeholders.

Stakeholders
The parties with an interest in the company's success (typically, shareholders, the community, customers, and employees).

Another strategic challenge tackled by a growing number of companies is how to be both profitable and socially responsible. **Corporate social responsibility** describes a company's commitment to meeting the needs of its stakeholders. **Stakeholders** are the parties that have an interest in the company's success; typically, they include shareholders, the community, customers, and employees. Ways to exercise social responsibility include minimizing environmental impact, providing high-quality products and services, and measuring how well the company is meeting stakeholders' needs (e.g., a fair return on investors' capital, safe and reliable products for customers, fair compensation and safe working conditions for employees, and clean air and water for communities). Exercising social responsibility can be strategic when it boosts a company's image with customers, opens access to new markets, and helps attract and retain talented employees. HR departments support this type of strategy by helping establish programs that enable and reward employees for efforts at social responsibility. After General Mills acquired Pillsbury, the Meals Division brought the newly merged team of employees to volunteer for the Perspectives Family Center, which helps families in transition. Meals Division employees have helped by painting child care center rooms, participating in school supply drives, and delivering Christmas trees. Besides helping the community, volunteer efforts such as these strengthen ties among General Mills' employees and help them develop leadership and other skills.[11]

Skills of HRM Professionals

With such varied responsibilities, the human resource department needs to bring together a large pool of skills. These skills fall into the six basic functions shown in Figure 1.3.[12] Members of the HR department need to be:

1. *Credible activists*—means being so well respected in the organization that you can influence the positions taken by managers. HR professionals who are competent in this area have the most influence over the organization's success, but to build this competency, they have to gain credibility by mastering all the others.
2. *Cultural steward*—involves understanding the organization's culture and helping to build and strengthen or change that culture by identifying and expressing its values through words and actions.

LO3 Summarize the types of skills needed for human resource management.

Figure 1.3

Six Competencies for the HR Profession

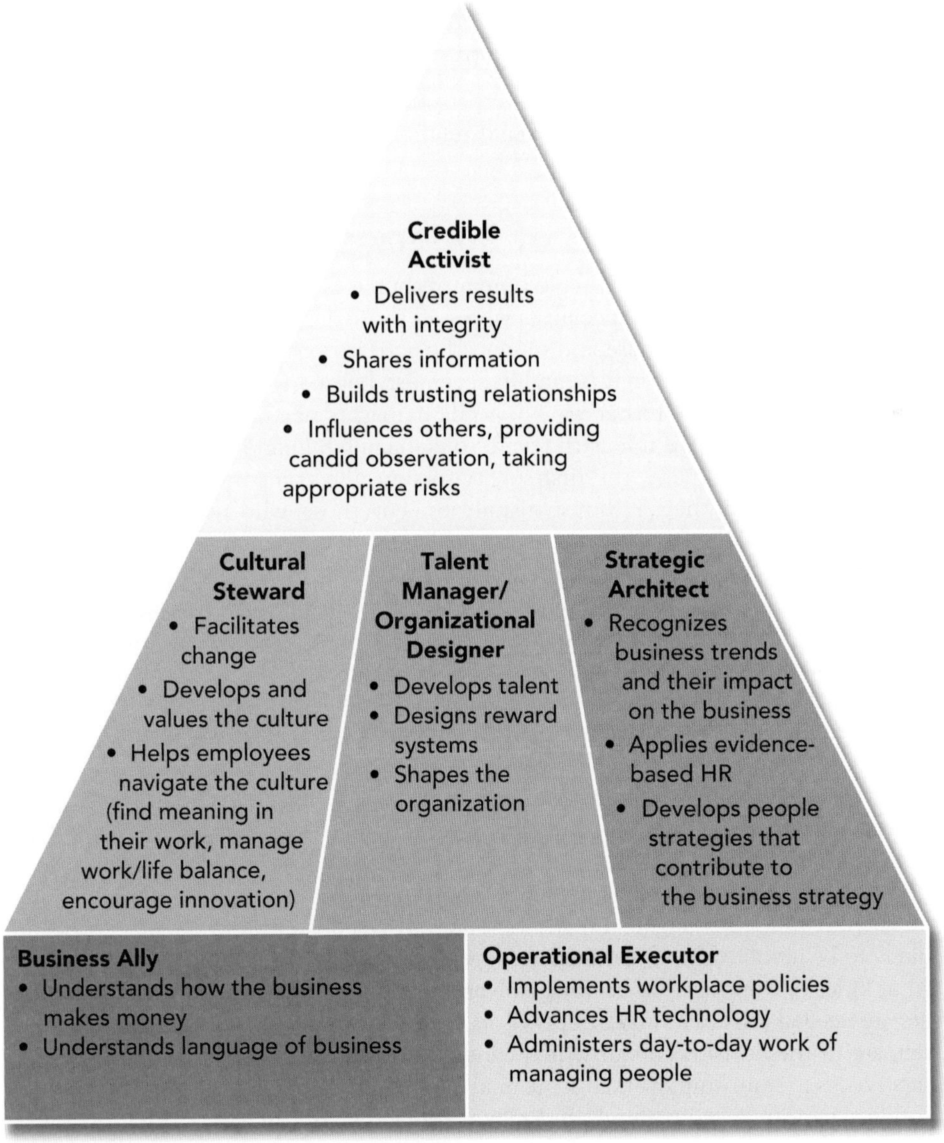

Credible Activist
- Delivers results with integrity
- Shares information
- Builds trusting relationships
- Influences others, providing candid observation, taking appropriate risks

Cultural Steward
- Facilitates change
- Develops and values the culture
- Helps employees navigate the culture (find meaning in their work, manage work/life balance, encourage innovation)

Talent Manager/ Organizational Designer
- Develops talent
- Designs reward systems
- Shapes the organization

Strategic Architect
- Recognizes business trends and their impact on the business
- Applies evidence-based HR
- Develops people strategies that contribute to the business strategy

Business Ally
- Understands how the business makes money
- Understands language of business

Operational Executor
- Implements workplace policies
- Advances HR technology
- Administers day-to-day work of managing people

SOURCE: Based on Robert J. Grossman, "New Competencies for HR," *HR Magazine*, June 2007, p. 60.

3. *Talent manager/organizational designer*—knows the ways that people join the organization and move to different positions within it. To do this effectively requires knowledge of how the organization is structured and how that structure might be adjusted to help it meet its goals for developing and using employees' talents.

4. *Strategy architect*—requires awareness of business trends and an understanding of how they might affect the business, as well as opportunities and threats they might present. A person with this capability spots ways effective management of human resources can help the company seize opportunities and confront threats to the business.

5. *Business allies*—know how the business makes money, who its customers are, and why customers buy what the company sells.

6. *Operational executors*—at the most basic level carry out particular HR functions such as handling the selection, training, or compensation of employees. All of the other HR skills require some ability as operational executor, because this is the level at which policies and transactions deliver results by legally, ethically, and efficiently acquiring, developing, motivating, and deploying human resources.

All of these competencies require interpersonal skills. Successful HR professionals must be able to share information, build relationships, and influence persons inside and outside the company.

HR Responsibilities of Supervisors

LO4 Explain the role of supervisors in human resource management.

Although many organizations have human resource departments, HR activities are by no means limited to the specialists who staff those departments. In large organizations, HR departments advise and support the activities of the other departments. In small organizations, there may be an HR specialist, but many HR activities are carried out by line supervisors. Either way, non-HR managers need to be familiar with the basics of HRM and their role with regard to managing human resources.

At a start-up company, the first supervisors are the company's founders. Not all founders recognize their HR responsibilities, but those who do have a powerful advantage. When the Pennsylvania Historical and Museum Commission had to make budget cuts, the future of the historic U.S. brig *Niagara*, berthed at the Erie Maritime Museum, was in doubt. But a nonprofit, the Flagship Niagara League, stepped forward to take over maintaining the ship and opening it to visitors. That meant the league would have to grow. From a staff of one full-time employee and six part-timers, the league doubled in size to five crew members, five employees in the gift shop, a supervisor, and two administrators. Suddenly, human resource needs couldn't be handled informally. The league's executive director, Bill Sutton, determined that the fastest way to get going would be to find an HR consultant to help the league put in place an entire HR program with all the programs and procedures required to follow legal requirements.[13]

As we will see in later chapters, supervisors typically have responsibilities related to all the HR functions. Figure 1.4 shows some HR responsibilities that supervisors are likely to be involved in. Organizations depend on supervisors to help them determine what kinds of work need to be done (job analysis and design) and how many employees are needed (HR planning). Supervisors typically interview job candidates and participate in the decisions about which candidates to hire. Many organizations expect supervisors to train employees in some or all aspects of the employees' jobs. Supervisors conduct performance appraisals and may recommend pay increases. And, of course, supervisors play a key role in employee relations, because they are most often the voice

Figure 1.4

Supervisors' Involvement in HRM: Common Areas of Involvement

of management for their employees, representing the company on a day-to-day basis. In all these activities, supervisors can participate in HRM by taking into consideration the ways that decisions and policies will affect their employees. Understanding the principles of communication, motivation, and other elements of human behavior can help supervisors inspire the best from the organization's human resources.

Ethics in Human Resource Management

Whenever people's actions affect one another, ethical issues arise, and business decisions are no exception. **Ethics** refers to fundamental principles of right and wrong; ethical behavior is behavior that is consistent with those principles. Business decisions, including HRM decisions, should be ethical, but the evidence suggests that is not always what happens. Recent surveys indicate that the general public and managers do not have positive perceptions of the ethical conduct of U.S. businesses. For example, in a Gallup poll on honesty and ethics in 21 professions, only 12 percent of Americans rated business executives high or very high; three times as many rated them low or very low. And from a global perspective, an international poll of Facebook members found that two-thirds believe individuals do not apply values they hold in their personal lives to their professional activities.[14]

Many ethical issues in the workplace involve human resource management. The recent financial crisis, in which the investment bank Lehman Brothers collapsed, insurance giant AIG survived only with a massive infusion of government funds, and many observers feared that money for loans would dry up altogether, had many causes. Among these, some people believe, were ethical lapses related to compensation and other HR policies. The "HR Oops!" box provides some details about this viewpoint.

LO5 Discuss ethical issues in human resource management.

Ethics
The fundamental principles of right and wrong.

Employee Rights

In the context of ethical human resource management, HR managers must view employees as having basic rights. Such a view reflects ethical principles embodied in the U.S. Constitution and Bill of Rights. A widely adopted understanding of human rights, based on the work of the philosopher Immanuel Kant, as well as the tradition of the Enlightenment, assumes that in a moral universe, every person has certain basic rights:

- *Right of free consent*—People have the right to be treated only as they knowingly and willingly consent to be treated. An example that applies to employees would

HR Oops!

Ethics of a Financial Crisis

One force behind the financial panic that accompanied the bursting of the real estate bubble in 2008 was the trading of risky mortgages that were treated as relatively low-risk investments. Why would otherwise prudent banking and insurance executives do something so foolish? One explanation is that they had financial incentives to do so: performance standards and bonuses that rewarded them for taking chances. For example, banks rewarded loan officers with pay based on the number and size of the loans they made. This system brings in lots of business, but if the compensation system includes no penalty for loans that go bad, there is no incentive to be

careful not to make loans that are too risky.

Another problem comes from cultures that glorify individuals who bring in lots of business. That might sound like a good thing—and in good times, it may well be—but a culture that doesn't glorify prudent decisions that look out for the entire company's long-term interests is likely to fall victim to carelessness and excessive risk at some point. A company may even find that some individuals engage in cheating or questionable activities to boost their star status. Then the company sacrifices its long-term reputation for the glory of a few individual stars.

Source: Wayne F. Cascio and Peter Cappelli, "Lessons from the Financial Services Crisis," *HR Magazine*, January 2009, Business & Company Resource Center, http://galenet.galegroup.com.

Questions

1. What ethical values do you think would be essential for a bank to uphold? Suggest three ways a bank could strengthen those values in its employees through HR policies and practices.
2. Which of the HR skills described in this chapter would be needed to prevent the kinds of problems described in this analysis of the financial crisis?

be that employees should know the nature of the job they are being hired to do; the employer should not deceive them.

- *Right of privacy*—People have the right to do as they wish in their private lives, and they have the right to control what they reveal about private activities. One way an employer respects this right is by keeping employees' personal records confidential.
- *Right of freedom of conscience*—People have the right to refuse to do what violates their moral beliefs, as long as these beliefs reflect commonly accepted norms. A supervisor who demands that an employee do something that is unsafe or environmentally damaging may be violating this right if the task conflicts with the employee's values. (Such behavior could be illegal as well as unethical.)
- *Right of freedom of speech*—People have the right to criticize an organization's ethics, if they do so in good conscience and their criticism does not violate the rights of individuals in the organization. Many organizations address this right by offering hot lines or policies and procedures designed to handle complaints from employees.
- *Right to due process*—If people believe their rights are being violated, they have the right to a fair and impartial hearing. As we will see in Chapter 3, Congress has addressed this right in some circumstances by establishing agencies to hear complaints when employees believe their employer has not provided a fair hearing. For example, the Equal Employment Opportunity Commission may prosecute complaints of discrimination if it believes the employer did not fairly handle the problem.

One way to think about ethics in business is that the morally correct action is the one that minimizes encroachments on and avoids violations of these rights.

Organizations often face situations in which the rights of employees are affected. In particular, the right of privacy of health information has received much attention in recent years. Computerized record keeping and computer networks have greatly increased the ways people can gain (authorized or unauthorized) access to records about individuals. Health-related records can be particularly sensitive. HRM responsibilities include the ever growing challenge of maintaining confidentiality and security of employees health information as required by the Health Insurance Portability and Accountability Act (HIPAA).

Standards for Ethical Behavior

Ethical, successful companies act according to four principles.[15] First, in their relationships with customers, vendors, and clients, ethical and successful companies emphasize mutual benefits. Second, employees assume responsibility for the actions of the company. Third, such companies have a sense of purpose or vision that employees value and use in their day-to-day work. Finally, they emphasize fairness; that is, another person's interests count as much as their own.

Cisco Systems has made a commitment to ensure that every employee takes responsibility for ethical behavior. The computer-networking company spells out its values in a detailed code of conduct that includes maintaining a safe and respectful workplace, avoiding conflicts of interest, exercising social responsibility, and protecting company assets, including proprietary information. All employees are required to follow the requirements of the code; each year, employees are asked to sign an acknowledgment that they have received the latest version of the code, so everyone knows what is expected. That information includes guidelines on how to make an ethical decision, answers to a variety of "what if?" questions aimed at helping employees address particular, sticky situations, and information on where to go for help in resolving ethical conflicts or reporting questionable behavior. Cisco also hired a contractor called The Network to help develop an online ethics training program that would give employees an engaging experience with the topic. The training, styled after *American Idol*, features cartoon characters singing lyrics that describe a variety of workplace ethical dilemmas. Instead of critiquing their vocal style, the cartoon judges offer possible ways to handle the situation described, and employees vote on which judge's answer was best. Then they can see how other employees voted and what the official Cisco policy is. The training program was based on input from human resources and other departments with insights into ethical business policies and practices.[16]

focus on
*social
responsibility*

For human resource practices to be considered ethical, they must satisfy the three basic standards summarized in Figure 1.5.[17] First, HRM practices must result in the greatest good for the largest number of people. Second, employment practices must respect basic human rights of privacy, due process, consent, and free speech. Third, managers must treat employees and customers equitably and fairly. These standards are most vexing when none of the alternatives in a situation meet all three of them. For instance, the supervisor of a clinical laboratory struggled with an ethical conflict when a technologist insisted that she would not perform pregnancy tests from a crisis pregnancy clinic, on the grounds that women who received positive results would have abortions, which would violate the ethical norms of the technologist. The dilemma for the supervisor was how to balance the employee's right to freedom

Figure 1.5

Standards for Identifying
Ethical Practices

of conscience against the laboratory's obligation to serve its customers fairly and to allocate work equitably and efficiently among its employees. Arriving at an ethical solution could require this supervisor to evaluate job requirements carefully. Perhaps redesigning jobs or reassigning employees would enable the technologist to meet her own ethical standards without harming the lab's efficiency—possibly even improving it or expanding some employees' skills. Whether or not such goals are possible, ethics would require the supervisor to be clear and respectful in reviewing the job requirements with the technologist (without critiquing the technologist's personal views) so that this employee can decide whether to remain in her position with the laboratory.[18] The company's human resource staff should be able to help the supervisor carry out these responsibilities.

LO6 Describe typical careers in human resource management.

Careers in Human Resource Management

There are many different types of jobs in the HRM profession. Figure 1.6 shows selected HRM positions and their salaries. The salaries vary depending on education and experience, as well as the type of industry in which the person works. As you can see from Figure 1.6, some positions involve work in specialized areas of HRM such as recruiting, compensation, or employee benefits. Usually, HR generalists make between $50,000 and $80,000, depending on their experience and education level. Generalists usually perform the full range of HRM activities, including recruiting, training, compensation, and employee relations.

The vast majority of HRM professionals have a college degree, and many also have completed postgraduate work. The typical field of study is business (especially human resources or industrial relations), but some HRM professionals have degrees in the social sciences (economics or psychology), the humanities, and law programs. Those who have completed graduate work have master's degrees in HR management, business management, or a similar field. This is important because to be successful in HR, you need to speak the same language as people in the other business functions.

Position

Figure 1.6

Median Salaries for HRM Positions

SOURCE: Based on J. Dooney and E. Esen, "HR Salaries Weaken with the Economy," *HR Magazine's 2009 HR Trendbook* (Alexandria, VA: Society for Human Resource Management, 2009), p. 14.

You have to have credibility as a business leader, so you must be able to understand finance and to build a business case for HR activities.

HR professionals can increase their career opportunities by taking advantage of training and development programs. Valero Energy Corporation encourages its HR managers to earn certificates in general management through a local executive MBA program. The company pays the tuition so its HR leaders will understand business basics well enough to discuss issues like finance and value creation with other managers at Valero.[19]

Some HRM professionals have a professional certification in HRM, but many more are members of professional associations. The primary professional organization for HRM is the Society for Human Resource Management (SHRM). SHRM is the world's largest human resource management association, with more than 250,000 professional and student members throughout the world. SHRM provides education and information services, conferences and seminars, government and media representation, and online services and publications (such as *HR Magazine*). You can visit SHRM's Web site to see their services at **www.shrm.org**.

Organization of This Book

This chapter has provided an overview of human resource management to give you a sense of its scope. In this book, the topics are organized according to the broad areas of human resource management shown in Table 1.3. The numbers in the table refer to the part and chapter numbers.

Part 1 discusses aspects of the human resource environment: trends shaping the field (Chapter 2), legal requirements (Chapter 3), and the work to be done by the

Table 1.3

Topics Covered in This Book

I. The Human Resource Environment
2. Trends in Human Resource Management
3. Providing Equal Employment Opportunity and a Safe Workplace
4. Analyzing Work and Designing Jobs
II. Acquiring and Preparing Human Resources
5. Planning For and Recruiting Human Resources
6. Selecting Employees and Placing Them in Jobs
7. Training Employees
III. Assessing Performance and Developing Employees
8. Managing Employees' Performance
9. Developing Employees for Future Success
10. Separating and Retaining Employees
IV. Compensating Human Resources
11. Establishing a Pay Structure
12. Recognizing Employee Contributions with Pay
13. Providing Employee Benefits
V. Meeting Other HR Goals
14. Collective Bargaining and Labor Relations
15. Managing Human Resources Globally
16. Creating and Maintaining High-Performance Organizations

organization, which is the basis for designing jobs (Chapter 4). Part 2 explores the responsibilities involved in acquiring and preparing human resources: HR planning and recruiting (Chapter 5), selection and placement of employees (Chapter 6), and training (Chapter 7). Part 3 turns to the assessment and development of human resources through performance management (Chapter 8) and employee development (Chapter 9), as well as appropriate ways to handle employee separation when the organization determines it no longer wants or needs certain employees (Chapter 10). Part 4 addresses topics related to compensation: pay structure (Chapter 11), pay to recognize performance (Chapter 12), and benefits (Chapter 13). Part 5 explores special topics faced by HR managers today: human resource management in organizations where employees have or are seeking union representation (Chapter 14), international human resource management (Chapter 15), and high-performance organizations (Chapter 16).

Along with examples highlighting how HRM helps a company maintain high performance, the chapters offer various other features to help you connect the principles to real-world situations. "Best Practices" boxes tell success stories related to the chapter's topic. "HR Oops!" boxes identify situations gone wrong and invite you to find better alternatives. "HR How To" boxes provide details about how to carry out a practice in each HR area. "Did You Know?" boxes are snapshots of interesting statistics related to chapter topics. Many chapters also include an "eHRM" box identifying ways that human resource professionals are applying information technology and the Internet to help their organizations excel in the fast-changing modern world. The "Focus on Social Responsibility" icon provided in the margin identifies in-text examples of companies' commitment to meeting the needs of their stakeholders.

SHRM provides education, information services (such as this conference), seminars, government and media representation, and online services and publications.

thinking ethically

WHO'S RESPONSIBLE FOR YOUR COMPANY'S REPUTATION?

In a recent poll, almost 7 out of 10 Americans rated the reputation of American companies as either "not good" or "terrible." But they did identify some firms they thought had good reputations. Ranked among the best were Microsoft, Johnson & Johnson, and 3M Corporation. Respondents admired companies that focused on quality, were environmentally responsible, and were engaged in activities that helped the needy. Philanthropy by Microsoft's founder, Bill Gates, helped put his company in first place.

Companies that act on a belief they should go beyond legal requirements to demonstrate concern for the environment, labor issues, and human rights are often called "socially responsible." For some companies, an important area of social responsibility is clean water—protecting water resources and/or making clean water available where the companies make or sell their products. The Beck Group, which designs and builds commercial structures, uses its employees to serve as volunteers who build wells (and also schools and other structures) in poor communities in Latin America. The HR department assists in identifying employees with the skills needed for particular projects. Nestlé India teaches hygiene programs and has built wells at village schools near Nestlé factories and in rural areas that supply the company with milk. Along with doing good, Nestlé expects that such efforts help it ensure safe water for its suppliers.

SOURCES: Ronald Alsop, "How Boss's Deeds Buff a Firm's Reputation," *Wall Street Journal*, January 31, 2007, http://online.wsj.com; Beckey Bright, "Managing Corporate Social Responsibility," *Wall Street Journal*, March 3, 2007, http://online.wsj.com; and Aliah D. Wright, "Dive into Clean Water," *HR Magazine*, June 2009, pp. 76–80.

Questions

1. Should social responsibility be a matter of business strategy (deciding whether the practices will boost profits in the long term), ethics (deciding whether the practices are morally right), or both? Why?
2. Review the functions and responsibilities of human resource management, and identify areas where HRM might contribute to social responsibility. In deciding whether to take a socially responsible approach in each of these areas, consider what ethical principles you could apply.

SUMMARY

LO1 Define human resource management, and explain how HRM contributes to an organization's performance.

Human resource management consists of an organization's "people practices"—the policies, practices, and systems that influence employees' behavior, attitudes, and performance. HRM influences who works for the organization and how those people work. These human resources, if well managed, have the potential to be a source of sustainable competitive advantage, contributing to basic objectives such as quality, profits, and customer satisfaction.

LO2 Identify the responsibilities of human resource departments.

By carrying out HR activities or supporting line management, HR departments have responsibility for a variety of functions related to acquiring and managing employees. The HRM process begins with analyzing and designing jobs, then recruiting and selecting employees to fill those jobs. Training and development equip employees to carry out their present jobs and follow a career path in the organization. Performance management ensures that employees' activities and outputs match the organization's goals. Human resource departments also plan and administer the organization's pay and benefits. They carry out activities in support of employee relations, such as communications programs and collective bargaining. Conducting all these activities involves the establishment and administration of personnel policies. Management also depends on human resource professionals for help in ensuring compliance with labor laws, as well as for support for the organization's strategy—for example, human resource planning and change management.

LO3 Summarize the types of skills needed for human resource management.

Human resource management requires substantial human relations skills, including skill in communicating, negotiating, and team development. Human resource professionals also need decision-making skills based on knowledge of the HR field as well as the organization's line of business. Leadership skills are necessary, especially for managing conflict and change. Technical skills of human resource professionals include knowledge of current techniques, applicable laws, and computer systems.

LO4 Explain the role of supervisors in human resource management.

Although many organizations have human resource departments, non-HR managers must be familiar with the basics of HRM and their own role with regard to managing human resources. Supervisors typically have responsibilities related to all the HR functions. Supervisors help analyze work, interview job candidates, participate in selection decisions, provide training, conduct performance appraisals, and recommend pay increases. On a day-to-day basis, supervisors represent the company to their employees, so they also play an important role in employee relations.

LO5 Discuss ethical issues in human resource management.

Like all managers and employees, HR professionals should make decisions consistent with sound ethical principles. Their decisions should result in the greatest good for the largest number of people; respect basic rights of privacy, due process, consent, and free speech; and treat employees and customers equitably and fairly. Some areas in which ethical issues arise include concerns about employee privacy, protection of employee safety, and fairness in employment practices (for example, avoiding discrimination).

LO6 Describe typical careers in human resource management.

Careers in human resource management may involve specialized work in fields such as recruiting, training, or labor relations. HR professionals may also be generalists, performing the full range of HR activities described in this chapter. People in these positions usually have a college degree in business or the social sciences. Human resource management means enhancing communication with employees and concern for their well-being, but it also involves a great deal of paperwork and a variety of non-people skills, as well as knowledge of business and laws.

KEY TERMS

corporate social responsibility, p. 12
development, p. 7
ethics, p. 15
evidence-based HR, p. 11
high-performance work system, p. 4
human capital, p. 3

human resource management (HRM), p. 2
human resource planning, p. 11
job analysis, p. 6
job design, p. 6

performance management, p. 8
recruitment, p. 7
selection, p. 7
stakeholders, p. 12
training, p. 7

REVIEW AND DISCUSSION QUESTIONS

1. How can human resource management contribute to a company's success?
2. Imagine that a small manufacturing company decides to invest in a materials resource planning (MRP) system. This is a computerized information system that improves efficiency by automating such work as planning needs for resources, ordering materials, and scheduling work on the shop floor. The company hopes that with the new MRP system, it can grow by quickly and efficiently processing small orders for a variety of products. Which of the human resource functions are likely to be affected by this change? How can human resource management help the organization carry out this change successfully?
3. What skills are important for success in human resource management? Which of these skills are already strengths of yours? Which would you like to develop?

4. Traditionally, human resource management practices were developed and administered by the company's human resource department. Line managers are now playing a major role in developing and implementing HRM practices. Why do you think non-HR managers are becoming more involved?
5. If you were to start a business, which aspects of human resource management would you want to entrust to specialists? Why?
6. Why do all managers and supervisors need knowledge and skills related to human resource management?
7. Federal law requires that employers not discriminate on the basis of a person's race, sex, national origin, or age over 40. Is this also an ethical requirement? A competitive requirement? Explain.
8. When a restaurant employee slipped on spilled soup and fell, requiring the evening off to recover, the owner

realized that workplace safety was an issue to which she had not devoted much time. A friend warned the owner that if she started creating a lot of safety rules and procedures, she would lose her focus on customers and might jeopardize the future of the restaurant. The safety problem is beginning to feel like an ethical dilemma. Suggest some ways the restaurant owner might address this dilemma. What aspects of human resource management are involved?

9. Does a career in human resource management, based on this chapter's description, appeal to you? Why or why not?

BUSINESSWEEK CASE

BusinessWeek Rebuilding Competitive Advantage

As the U.S. economy moves from recession to recovery, businesses are obsessively focused on risk management, cost containment, supply-chain sustainability, resource efficiency, and maintaining their competitive edge.

Yet a company's success—or lack thereof—in any or all of these areas will be moot unless it recognizes and deals with its vulnerabilities related to retention and succession. Business results will be predicated by an organization's approach to executive talent management.

Bill Conaty, who spent four decades in human resources leadership roles at General Electric (GE), effectively synthesized this agenda. He stated that gaining a decided advantage over the competition starts with attracting the right talent to the organization.

He added that companies must also invest in executive talent development, assessment, and retention because they're just as critical to business performance. The market leaders in any industry recognize that attracting and developing the best executive talent is a continual, institutional priority, no matter what the economic environment, Conaty said. He pointed out that development needs—even for people at the most senior level—are not fatal flaws for a corporation or an individual unless they go unaddressed.

Claudio Fernández-Aráoz of Egon Zehnder International says that despite [today's high] unemployment numbers, companies still need to focus on attracting superior executives because demographics already indicate that the number of managers in the right age bracket for leadership roles will drop by 30 percent in just six years.

"Companies need to beef up their ability to attract great leaders," Fernández-Aráoz contends. "While over the long run companies should focus on becoming more attractive by developing the type of culture, environment and team that outstanding executives want to join, they also need to immediately focus on winning the coming fight for executive talent one leader at a time." And that's not just about money.

Companies can attract superior talent by demonstrating active support for the candidate's interests, describing the role realistically, and involving the hiring manager (not just HR) in closing the deal, he adds. Further, by enlisting the involvement of C-level executives while recruiting for top positions and ensuring that compensation for a new recruit is fair to current employees, companies can more effectively integrate new leaders.

When it comes to assessing executive talent, Sumner Redstone, majority owner and chairman of the board of his family controlled National Amusements, Inc., and majority owner of CBS Corp. and Viacom, told me recently during an exclusive interview that it all comes down to his "Three C's."

"I insist that anyone I'll hire, particularly an executive, bring what I call the 'Three C's.' That's competence, commitment, and the most important one, character," Redstone said. "Without character, I'm not interested in their competence or commitment."

The final piece of building, rebuilding, or maintaining a company's prized management advantage over the competition is retaining the best executives.

Former Medtronic CEO Bill George offers his own advice. To keep your top business leaders onboard, George says you have to challenge them. "Put them in tough jobs. Make them responsible for something. Promote young people; flatten the organization; and give people opportunities to lead right now and they'll stay with you and be true to you."

Exceptional companies, he believes, must reward business leaders for their performance and not simply reward their decision to stay with the company.

SOURCE: Excerpted from Joseph Daniel McCool, "How Companies Rebuild Competitive Advantage," *BusinessWeek*, February 24, 2010, http://www.businessweek.com.

Questions

1. Which functions of human resources management are described in this case? Which are missing? In what ways, if any, are the missing functions relevant to building competitive advantage, too?
2. The writer and people interviewed talk about competitive advantage coming from the qualities of a company's top executives. To what extent do these principles apply to middle managers, supervisors, and nonmanagement employees?

3. Imagine that you are an HR manager in a company that has been struggling to stay profitable during the past two years. Your company's executives have been focused mainly on cutting costs and landing orders. Write a paragraph making the case for why your company's executives should also be concerned about developing talent at this time. Keep in mind that they may not see any money being available for hiring new people or training current employees.

Case: Can The TSA Secure Top-Flight Performance?

If you've flown in the United States recently, you've passed through security checkpoints staffed by the Transportation Security Administration, a federal agency created in November 2001 to protect all modes of transportation. TSA agents are best known for scanning baggage and screening persons headed for gates in the nation's airports. Most travelers appreciate the concern for safety following the 2001 terrorist attacks, but many also grumble about times they have encountered a TSA employee who was unpleasant or seemed capricious in enforcing rules.

For its part, TSA management has been challenged to maintain a workforce that is knowledgeable, well qualified, ethical, and vigilant about identifying risky persons and behavior. Occasional news reports have identified lapses such as items stolen from luggage (perhaps when TSA agents are inspecting checked bags) and claims that security screeners have cheated on tests of their ability to spot smuggled weapons.

In a recent year, TSA received about 1,400 claims each month for lost, stolen, or damaged items, affecting a small share of the 55 million passengers who travel in a month. Occasionally, a TSA employee is implicated in baggage thefts. TSA, like the airlines, tries to avoid such problems by conducting background checks of prospective employees. In addition, policies call for firing any employee caught stealing. The TSA also has tried to minimize the problem through job design: it has been installing automated systems to minimize human contact with most baggage, and it has installed surveillance cameras to monitor agents who search items in baggage.

Cheating on security tests is another problem that raises ethics questions. One report said agents at airports in San Francisco and Jackson, Mississippi, allegedly were tipped off about undercover tests to be conducted. According to the allegations, TSA employees described to screeners the undercover agents, the type of weapons they would attempt to smuggle through checkpoints, and the way the weapons would be hidden.

What is the TSA doing to improve the professionalism of its employees? Many of the efforts involve human resource management. One practice involves the design of jobs. TSA wants employees to see themselves not just as "screeners" who sit in airports but as part of a larger law enforcement effort. So screener job titles were eliminated and replaced with the term *security officers*, and career paths were developed. The agency also improved its training in job tasks such as interpreting X-rays and searching property. It added performance-based pay to its compensation plan, so high-performing employees are rewarded in a practical way. Such changes have helped reduce employee turnover substantially. A survey also found greater job satisfaction among TSA workers.

These improvements are no small achievement, considering that government agencies have tended to lag behind many businesses in creating a focus on high performance. In a government agency, which is not ruled by sales and profits, it can be difficult to develop measurable performance outcomes—measuring what individuals and groups actually achieve, rather than merely tracking their day-to-day activities. As a result, employees may not always see how their individual efforts can help the agency achieve broader goals. Without this vision, they have less incentive to excel.

TSA, part of the Department of Homeland Security (DHS), has tried to become an exception, a performance-oriented government agency. Marta Perez, chief human capital officer of DHS, says TSA defined its overall objective as "to deploy layers of security to protect the traveling public and the nation's transportation system." To achieve that objective, the agency set specific goals for individual airports, including goals to improve the efficiency and effectiveness of airport screening, as well as safety targets. For example, one goal is that the wait time for 80 percent of the passengers going through airport security should be 10 minutes or less. Individuals at each airport have specific goals aimed at achieving the airport's overall goals. According to Perez, the goals help employees and managers talk about what is expected and how they will be evaluated.

SOURCES: Mark Schoeff Jr., "TSA Sees Results from Revamped People Practices," *Workforce Management*, December 11, 2006, p. 20; Bill Trahant, "Realizing a Performance Culture in Federal Agencies," *Public Manager*, Fall 2007, pp. 45–50; Thomas Frank, "Investigation Looks at Airport-Screener Testing," *USA Today*, October 5, 2007, General Reference Center Gold, http://find.galegroup.com; and Kelly Yamanouchi, "Airports Target Luggage Thieves," *Atlanta Journal-Constitution*, October 4, 2009, Business & Company Resource Center, http://galenet.galegroup.com.

Questions

1. Which, if any, of the HR practices described in this case do you think can contribute to greater efficiency and effectiveness of TSA employees? What other practices would you recommend?

2. Which, if any, of the HR practices described in this case do you think can contribute to ethical behavior by TSA employees? What other practices would you recommend?

 IT'S A WRAP! McGraw Hill **connect**

www.mhhe.com/noefund4e is your source for Reviewing, Applying, and Practicing the concepts you learned about in Chapter 1.

Review
- Chapter learning objectives
- Test Your Knowledge: What Do You Know about HRM?

Application
- Manager's Hot Seat segment: "Ethics, Let's Make a Fourth Quarter Deal"
- Video case and quiz: "Creative Corporation"
- Self-Assessments: Do You Have What It Takes for a Career in HR? and Assessing Your Ethical Decision-Making Skills
- Web exercise: Society for Human Resource Management
- Small-business case: Managing HR at a Services Firm

Practice
- Chapter quiz

NOTES

1. Erin White, "To Keep Employees, Domino's Decides It's Not All about Pay," *Wall Street Journal,* February 17, 2005, http://online.wsj.com.
2. A. S. Tsui and L. R. Gomez-Mejia, "Evaluating Human Resource Effectiveness," in *Human Resource Management: Evolving Rules and Responsibilities,* ed. L. Dyer (Washington, DC: BNA Books, 1988), pp. 1187–227; M. A. Hitt, B. W. Keats, and S. M. DeMarie, "Navigating in the New Competitive Landscape: Building Strategic Flexibility and Competitive Advantage in the 21st Century," *Academy of Management Executive* 12, no. 4 (1998), pp. 22–42; J. T. Delaney and M. A. Huselid, "The Impact of Human Resource Management Practices on Perceptions of Organizational Performance," *Academy of Management Journal* 39 (1996), pp. 949–69.
3. W. F. Cascio, *Costing Human Resources: The Financial Impact of Behavior in Organizations,* 3rd ed. (Boston: PWS-Kent, 1991).
4. S. A. Snell and J. W. Dean, "Integrated Manufacturing and Human Resource Management: A Human Capital Perspective," *Academy of Management Journal* 35 (1992), pp. 467–504; M. A. Youndt, S. Snell, J. W. Dean Jr., and D. P. Lepak, "Human Resource Management, Manufacturing Strategy, and Firm Performance," *Academy of Management Journal* 39 (1996), pp. 836–66.
5. J. Robinson, "A Caterpillar Dealer Unearths Employee Engagement," *Gallup Management Journal* (October 12, 2006), http://gmj.gallup.com/content/24874/1/A-Caterpillar-Dealer-Unearths-Employee-Engagement.aspx.
6. F. Hansen, "2006 Data Bank Annual," *Workforce Management,* December 11, 2006, p. 48.
7. E. E. Lawler, "From Human Resource Management to Organizational Effectiveness," *Human Resource Management* 44 (2005), pp. 165–69.
8. S. Snell, "Control Theory in Strategic Human Resource Management: The Mediating Effect of Administrative Information," *Academy of Management Journal* 35 (1992), pp. 292–327.
9. R. Grossman, "New Competencies for HR," *HRMagazine,* June 2007, pp. 58–62; HR Competency Assessment Tools, www.shrm.org/competencies/benefits.asp.
10. Joann S. Lublin, "HR Executives Suddenly Get Hot," *Wall Street Journal,* December 14, 2009, http://online.wsj.com.

11. M. Weinstein, "Charity Begins at Work," *Training,* May 2008, pp. 56–58.

12. Robert J. Grossman, "New Competencies for HR," *HR Magazine,* June 2007, pp. 58–62.

13. Erica Erwin, "Growth of Erie's Flagship Niagara Spurs Need for H.R. Program," *Erie Times-News,* February 8, 2010, Business & Company Resource Center, http://galenet.galegroup.com.

14. Lydia Saad, "Nurses Shine, Bankers Slump in Ethics Ratings," Gallup Poll report, November 24, 2008, www.gallup.com; Angela Monaghan, "Survey Highlights 'Crisis of Ethics,'" *Daily Telegraph,* January 19, 2010, Business & Company Resource Center, http://galenet.galegroup.com.

15. M. Pastin, *The Hard Problems of Management: Gaining the Ethics Edge* (San Francisco: Jossey-Bass, 1986); and T. Thomas, J. Schermerhorn Jr., and J. Dienhart, "Strategic Leadership of Ethical Behavior in Business," *Academy of Management Executive* 18 (2004), pp. 56–66.

16. Cynthia Kincaid, "Corporate Ethics Training: The Right Stuff," *Training,* April 6, 2009, Business & Company Resource Center, http://galenet.galegroup.com; Cisco Systems, *Connecting with Our Values: Code of Business Conduct,* 2009, accessed at http://investor.cisco.com, February 19, 2010.

17. G. F. Cavanaugh, D. Moberg, and M. Velasquez, "The Ethics of Organizational Politics," *Academy of Management Review* 6 (1981), pp. 363–74.

18. Barbara Harty-Golder, "Pregnancy Tests Cause Crisis of Conscience," *Medical Laboratory Observer,* December 2009, Business & Company Resource Center, http://galenet.galegroup.com.

19. Bill Roberts, "Analyze This!" *HR Magazine,* October 2009, pp. 35–41.

The Human Resource Environment

PART ONE

chapter

2

Trends in Human Resource Management

What Do I Need to Know?

After reading this chapter, you should be able to:

LO1 Describe trends in the labor force composition and how they affect human resource management.

LO2 Summarize areas in which human resource management can support the goal of creating a high-performance work system.

LO3 Define employee empowerment, and explain its role in the modern organization.

LO4 Identify ways HR professionals can support organizational strategies for quality, growth, and efficiency.

LO5 Summarize ways in which human resource management can support organizations expanding internationally.

LO6 Discuss how technological developments are affecting human resource management.

LO7 Explain how the nature of the employment relationship is changing.

LO8 Discuss how the need for flexibility affects human resource management.

Introduction

Less than a decade into the 21st century, workers around the world were shaken by economic uncertainty as a banking crisis coupled with crashing real estate values triggered a severe recession. In the United States, unprecedented numbers of layoffs were followed by dire predictions of a "jobless recovery." Experienced workers settled for entry-level jobs while young people wondered how they would find a place for themselves in the workforce. Meanwhile, a revolution in information technology continued to redefine what it means to be "in touch" or "at work." And through it all, many employers and employees have continued to innovate and persevere in meeting these challenges.

One indicator of the extent of the challenge is the growing ranks of unemployed seniors. While many people over age 65 have retired, others by choice or necessity are looking for jobs. For example, Mary Bennett had worked since she was 17 years old but at the age of 80 applied for unemployment benefits for the first time in her life. Work as a coffeepot assembler and waitress enabled her to pay the bills following a divorce, but when she tried retiring at age 70, she found she couldn't afford it after raising seven children. She found a job in a machine shop but was laid off from that company when the economy stalled. So Bennett turned to unemployment benefits and a federal job-training program. "I'm an easy person to teach," she assured a reporter.[1] Situations like Bennett's are of particular interest, because as we will see in this chapter, the proportion of older workers is increasing in the United States.

Examples of the resilience of the American worker come from those who are coping with the economic downturn by combining part-time jobs and contract assignments into enough pay to make ends meet. In Eugene, Oregon, Mike Lockier was laid off from a job as broadcast engineer and has been unable to land a job using his other major skill, computer programming. He hires himself out to do construction and repair jobs during the day and spends evening and nighttime hours answering repair questions submitted to FixYa.com.[2] Dividing hours among part-time shifts reflects various trends, including the shortening of the average workweek in response to lower demand, as well as the growing popularity of Web sites for matching independent contractors with short-term work assignments.

These creative responses to change and uncertainty illustrate the kinds of people and situations that shape the nature of human resource management today. This chapter describes major trends that are affecting human resource management. It begins with an examination of the modern labor force, including trends that are determining who will participate in the workforce of the future. Next is an exploration of the ways HRM can support a number of trends in organizational strategy, from efforts to maintain high-performance work systems to changes in the organization's size and structure. Often, growth includes the use of human resources on a global scale, as more and more organizations hire immigrants or open operations overseas. The chapter then turns to major changes in technology, especially the role of the Internet. As we will explain, the Internet is changing organizations themselves, as well as providing new ways to carry out human resource management. Finally, we explore the changing nature of the employment relationship, in which careers and jobs are becoming more flexible.

Change in the Labor Force

The term *labor force* is a general way to refer to all the people willing and able to work. For an organization, the **internal labor force** consists of the organization's workers— its employees and the people who have contracts to work at the organization. This internal labor force has been drawn from the organization's **external labor market,** that is, individuals who are actively seeking employment. The number and kinds of people in the external labor market determine the kinds of human resources available to an organization (and their cost). Human resource professionals need to be aware of trends in the composition of the external labor market, because these trends affect the organization's options for creating a well-skilled, motivated internal labor force.

An Aging Workforce

In the United States, the Bureau of Labor Statistics (BLS), an agency of the Department of Labor, tracks changes in the composition of the U.S. labor force and forecasts employment trends. The BLS has projected that from 2008 to 2018, the total U.S. civilian labor force will grow from 154 million to

LO1 Describe trends in the labor force composition and how they affect human resource management.

Internal Labor Force
An organization's workers (its employees and the people who have contracts to work at the organization).

External Labor Market
Individuals who are actively seeking employment.

As more and more of the workforce reaches retirement age, some companies have set up mentoring programs between older and younger workers so that knowledge is not lost but passed on. How does the company benefit from these mentoring programs?

Figure 2.1

Age Distribution of U.S. Labor Force, 2008 and 2018

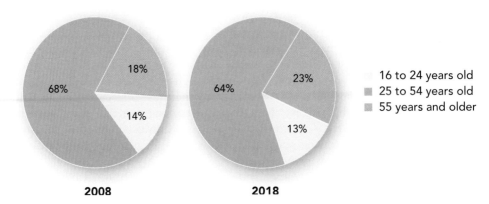

SOURCE: Bureau of Labor Statistics, "Employment Projections: 2008–18," news release, December 10, 2009, www.bls.gov.

167 million workers.[3] This 8.2 percent increase is noticeably lower than the 12.1 percent increase experienced during the previous decade.

Some of the expected change involves the distribution of workers by age. From 2008 to 2018, the fastest-growing age group is expected to be workers 55 and older. The 25- to 44-year-old group will increase its numbers only slightly, so its share of the total workforce will fall. And young workers between the ages of 16 and 24 will actually be fewer in number. This combination of trends will cause the overall workforce to age. Figure 2.1 shows the change in age distribution, as forecast by the Bureau of Labor Statistics, between 2008 and 2018. By 2010, more than half of U.S. workers will be older than 40, and a significant share will be nearing retirement.[4] Human resource professionals will therefore spend much of their time on concerns related to planning retirement, retraining older workers, and motivating workers whose careers have plateaued. Organizations will struggle with ways to control the rising costs of health care and other benefits, and many of tomorrow's managers will supervise employees much older than themselves. At the same time, organizations will have to find ways to attract, retain, and prepare the youth labor force.

Older people want to work, and many say they plan a working retirement. Despite myths to the contrary, worker performance and learning do not suffer as a result of aging.[5] Older employees are willing and able to learn new technology. More older workers are asking to work part-time or for only a few months at a time as a way to transition to full retirement. Employees and companies are redefining the meaning of retirement to include second careers as well as part-time and temporary work assignments. Although recruiting and retaining older workers may present some challenges related to costs of health care and other benefits, companies also are benefiting from these employees' talents and experience.

Borders Group, for example, has adapted hiring and retention practices to capitalize on older workers.[6] Half of book purchases in the United States are made by customers over the age of 45, so the company believes older workers can relate well to these customers. To attract and retain older workers, Borders added medical and dental benefits for part-time workers and began developing a "passport" program in which workers can work half the year at a Borders store in one part of the country and half the year at another location, which accommodates those who want to spend winters in warm climates. Since Borders launched the program, employee turnover has plunged, and the turnover rate among workers over age 50 is one-tenth the turnover of employees under 30.

A Diverse Workforce

Another kind of change affecting the U.S. labor force is that it is growing more diverse in racial, ethnic, and gender terms. As Figure 2.2 shows, the 2018 workforce is expected to be 79 percent white, 12 percent black, and 9 percent Asian and other minorities. The fastest-growing of these categories are Asian and "other groups," because these groups are experiencing immigration and birthrates above the national average. In addition to these racial categories, the ethnic category of Hispanics is growing equally fast, and the Hispanic share of the U.S. labor force is expected to near 18 percent of the total in 2018.[7] Along with greater racial and ethnic diversity, there is also greater gender diversity. More women today, than in the past, are in the paid labor force, and the labor force participation rate for men has been slowly declining. By 2018, the share of women in the civilian labor force is expected to reach about 47 percent.[8]

Figure 2.2

Projected Racial/Ethnic Makeup of the U.S. Workforce, 2018

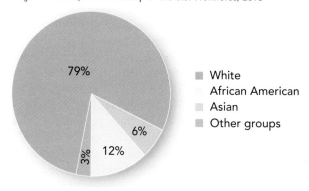

SOURCE: Bureau of Labor Statistics, "Employment Projections: 2008–2018," news release, December 10, 2009, www.bls.gov.

One important source of racial and ethnic diversity is immigration. The U.S. government establishes procedures for foreign nationals to follow if they wish to live and work permanently in the United States, and it sets limits on the number of immigrants who are admitted through these channels. Of the more than 1 million immigrants who come to the United States legally each year, more than six out of ten are relatives of U.S. citizens. Another one-fourth come on work-related visas, some of which are set aside for workers with exceptional qualifications in science, business, or the arts. (About half of the work-related visas go to the immediate relatives of those coming to the United States to work, allowing workers to bring their spouse and children.) The U.S. government also grants temporary work visas to a limited number of highly educated workers, permitting them to work in the United States for a set period of time but not to remain as immigrants. U.S. law requires employers to verify that any job candidate who is not a U.S. citizen has received permission to work in the United States as an immigrant or with a temporary work permit. (This requirement is discussed in Chapter 6.)

Other foreign-born workers in the United States arrived to this country without meeting the legal requirements for immigration or asylum. These individuals, known as undocumented or illegal immigrants, likely number in the millions. While government policy toward immigrants is a matter of heated public debate, the human resource implications have two practical parts. The first involves the supply of and demand for labor. Many U.S. industries, including meatpacking, construction, farming, and services, rely on immigrants to perform demanding work that may be low paid. In other industries, such as computer software development, employers say they have difficulty finding enough qualified U.S. workers to fill technical jobs. These employers are pressing for immigration laws to allow a greater supply of foreign-born workers.

The other HR concern is the need to comply with laws. Recently, Immigration and Customs Enforcement agents have been cracking down on employers who allegedly knew they were employing undocumented immigrants. Businesses that have justified hiring these people on the grounds that they work hard and are needed for the business to continue operating now are facing greater legal risks.[9] Even as some companies are lobbying for changes to immigration laws, the constraints on labor supply force companies to consider a variety of ways to meet their demand for labor, including job redesign (see Chapter 4), higher pay (Chapter 11), and foreign operations (Chapter 15).

The greater diversity of the U.S. labor force challenges employers to create HRM practices that ensure they fully utilize the talents, skills, and values of all employees. As a result, organizations cannot afford to ignore or discount the potential contributions of women and minorities. Employers will have to ensure that employees and HRM systems are free of bias and value the perspectives and experience that women and minorities can contribute to organizational goals such as product quality and customer service. As we will discuss further in the next chapter, managing cultural diversity involves many different activities. These include creating an organizational culture that values diversity, ensuring that HRM systems are bias-free, encouraging career development for women and minorities, promoting knowledge and acceptance of cultural differences, ensuring involvement in education both within and outside the organization, and dealing with employees' resistance to diversity.[10] Figure 2.3 summarizes ways in which HRM can support the management of diversity for organizational success.

Many U.S. companies have already committed themselves to ensuring that they recognize the diversity of their internal labor force and use it to gain a competitive advantage. In a recent survey of HR professionals, most rated workplace diversity as somewhat or extremely important, and 96 percent said "diversity management skills"

Figure 2.3

HRM Practices That Support Diversity Management

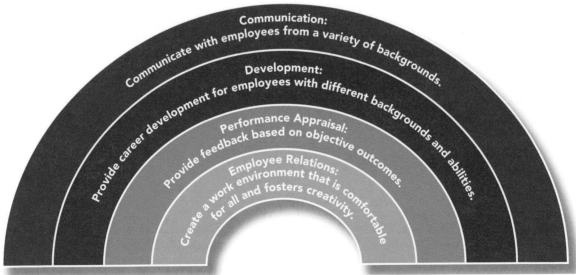

SOURCE: Based on M. Loden and J. B. Rosener, *Workforce America!* (Homewood, IL: Business One Irwin, 1991).

are important for an organization.[11] Respondents also indicated that concern for diversity should go beyond hiring decisions to include ways organizations can benefit from using the contributions of all its employees.

Valuing diversity is part of Safeway's approach to competing with specialty grocers and big-box stores such as Walmart and Target.[12] Safeway invested in programs to attract, develop, and retain its best talent and to position the company as an employer of choice. Although 70 percent of Safeway's customers are women, male leaders had been the norm in the retail grocery industry. Safeway took initiatives to help women, including women of color, advance into management. The CEO speaks regularly with employees about diversity issues, and employees have access to DVDs featuring interviews with successful employees who are women and people of color. The company ensures that all employees who qualify for its Retail Leadership Program, including those who work part-time and have flexible schedules to juggle work and family responsibilities, have the same opportunities for coaching, development, and advancement. A women's leadership network sponsors development meetings between promising women and executives who suggest new job opportunities that can help the women advance to the next level. With these and other efforts, the number of female store managers has risen a dramatic 42 percent, and financial analysts have concluded that the advancement of women and minorities has increased Safeway's sales and earnings.

Throughout this book, we will show how diversity affects HRM practices. For example, from a staffing perspective, it is important to ensure that tests used to select employees are not unfairly biased against minority groups. From the perspective of work design, employees need flexible schedules that allow them to meet nonwork needs. In terms of training, it is clear that employees must be made aware of the damage that stereotypes can do. With regard to compensation, organizations are providing benefits such as elder care and day care as a way to accommodate the needs of a diverse workforce. As we will see later in the chapter, successfully managing diversity is also critical for companies that compete in international markets.

Skill Deficiencies of the Workforce

The increasing use of computers to do routine tasks has shifted the kinds of skills needed for employees in the U.S. economy. Such qualities as physical strength and mastery of a particular piece of machinery are no longer important for many jobs. More employers are looking for mathematical, verbal, and interpersonal skills, such as the ability to solve math or other problems or reach decisions as part of a team. Often, when organizations are looking for technical skills, they are looking for skills related to computers and using the Internet. Today's employees must be able to handle a variety of responsibilities, interact with customers, and think creatively.

To find such employees, most organizations are looking for educational achievements. A college degree is a basic requirement for many jobs today. Competition for qualified college graduates in many fields is intense. At the other extreme, workers with less education often have to settle for low-paying jobs. Some companies are unable to find qualified employees and instead rely on training to correct skill deficiencies.[13] Other companies team up with universities, community colleges, and high schools to design and teach courses ranging from basic reading to design blueprint reading.

Not all the skills employers want require a college education. Employers surveyed by the National Association of Manufacturers report a deficiency in qualified production workers—not just engineers and computer experts. At Whirlpool, for example, production workers need algebra skills to ensure that steel sizes conform to specifications; the company has had to develop training programs to provide those skills.[14] Today's U.S. production jobs rely on intelligence and skills as much as on strength. Workers often must operate sophisticated computer-controlled machinery and monitor quality levels. In some areas, companies and communities have set up apprenticeship and training programs to fix the worker shortage. The gap between skills needed and skills available has decreased U.S. companies' abilities to compete because as a consequence of the deficiency they sometimes lack the capacity to upgrade technology, reorganize work, and empower employees.

High-Performance Work Systems

LO2 Summarize areas in which human resource management can support the goal of creating a high-performance work system.

High-Performance Work Systems Organizations that have the best possible fit between their social system (people and how they interact) and technical system (equipment and processes).

Human resource management is playing an important role in helping organizations gain and keep an advantage over competitors by becoming **high-performance work systems.** These are organizations that have the best possible fit between their social system (people and how they interact) and technical system (equipment and processes).[15] As the nature of the workforce and the technology available to organizations have changed, so have the requirements for creating a high-performance work system. Customers are demanding high quality and customized products, employees are seeking flexible work arrangements, and employers are looking for ways to tap people's creativity and interpersonal skills. Such demands require that organizations make full use of their people's knowledge and skill, and skilled human resource management can help organizations do this.

Among the trends that are occurring in today's high-performance work systems are reliance on knowledge workers, empowerment of employees to make decisions, and use of teamwork. The following sections describe those three trends, and Chapter 16 will explore the ways HRM can support the creation and maintenance of a high-performance work system. HR professionals who keep up with change are well positioned to help create high-performance work systems.

Knowledge Workers

The growth in e-commerce, plus the shift from a manufacturing to a service and information economy, has changed the nature of employees that are most in demand. The Bureau of Labor Statistics forecasts that between 2008 and 2018, most new jobs will be in service occupations, especially food preparation, education, and health services.

The number of service jobs has important implications for human resource management. Research shows that if employees have a favorable view of HRM practices—career opportunities, training, pay, and feedback on performance—they are more likely to provide good service to customers. Therefore, quality HRM for service employees can translate into customer satisfaction.

Besides differences among industries, job growth varies according to the type of job. The "Did You Know?" box lists the 10 occupations expected to gain the most jobs between 2008 and 2018. Of the jobs expected to have the greatest percentage increases, most are related to health care and computers. The fastest-growing occupations are expected to be biomedical engineers, network systems and data communications analysts, home health aides, personal and home care aides, and financial examiners.[16] Many of these occupations require a college degree. In contrast, the

Did You Know?

Top 10 Occupations for Job Growth

The following graph shows the occupations that are expected to add the most new jobs between 2008 and 2018. These jobs require widely different levels of training and responsibility, and pay levels vary considerably.

Source: Bureau of Labor Statistics, "Occupational Employment," *Occupational Outlook Quarterly*, Winter 2009–10, p. 13.

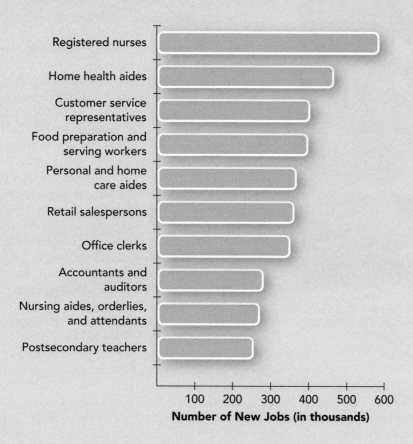

occupations expected to have the largest numerical increases more often require only on-the-job training. (Exceptions are registered nurses and postsecondary teachers.) This means that many companies' HRM departments will need to provide excellent training as well as hiring.

These high-growth jobs are evidence of another trend: The future U.S. labor market will be both a knowledge economy and a service economy.[17] Along with low-education jobs in services like health care and food preparation, there will be many high-education professional and managerial jobs. To meet these human capital needs, companies are increasingly trying to attract, develop, and retain knowledge workers. **Knowledge workers** are employees whose main contribution to the organization is specialized knowledge, such as knowledge of customers, a process, or a profession. Further complicating that challenge, many of these knowledge workers will have to be

Knowledge Workers
Employees whose main contribution to the organization is specialized knowledge, such as knowledge of customers, a process, or a profession.

35

Knowledge workers are employees whose value to their employers stems primarily from what they know. Engineers such as the ones pictured here have in-depth knowledge of their field and are hard to replace because of their special knowledge.

"technoservice" workers who not only know a specialized field such as computer programming or engineering but also must be able to work directly with customers.

Knowledge workers are in a position of power, because they own the knowledge that the company needs in order to produce its products and services, and they must share their knowledge and collaborate with others in order for their employer to succeed. An employer cannot simply order these employees to perform tasks. Managers depend on the employees' willingness to share information. Furthermore, skilled knowledge workers have many job opportunities, even in a slow economy. If they choose, they can leave a company and take their knowledge to another employer. Replacing them may be difficult and time consuming.

As more organizations become knowledge-based, they must promote and capture learning at the level of employees, teams, and the overall organization. At Nissan Motor's U.S. operations, 16 teams each bring together 8 to 16 high-performing salaried employees from different departments.[18] They meet weekly to discuss issues such as quality and diversity, proposing new ideas that can benefit the company. One team looking for ways to save money developed a proposal for working at home. The team conducted a study that showed working at home could improve morale while cutting expenses.

The reliance on knowledge workers also affects organizations' decisions about the kinds of people they are recruiting and selecting.[19] They are shifting away from focusing on specific skills, such as how to operate a particular kind of machinery, and toward a greater emphasis on general cognitive skills (thinking and problem solving) and interpersonal skills. Employers are more interested in evidence that job candidates will excel at working in teams or interacting with customers. These skills also support an employee's ability to gather and share knowledge, helping the organization to innovate and meet customer needs. To the extent that technical skills are important, employers often are most interested in the ability to use information technology, including the Internet and statistical software.

LO3 Define employee empowerment, and explain its role in the modern organization.

Employee Empowerment
Giving employees responsibility and authority to make decisions regarding all aspects of product development or customer service.

Employee Empowerment

To completely benefit from employees' knowledge, organizations need a management style that focuses on developing and empowering employees. **Employee empowerment** means giving employees responsibility and authority to make decisions regarding all aspects of product development or customer service.[20] Employees are then held accountable for products and services. In return, they share the resulting losses and rewards.

HRM practices such as performance management, training, work design, and compensation are important for ensuring the success of employee empowerment. Jobs must be designed to give employees the necessary latitude for making a variety of decisions. Employees must be properly trained to exert their wider authority and use information resources such as the Internet as well as tools for communicating information. Employees also need feedback to help them evaluate their success. Pay and other rewards should reflect employees' authority and be related to successful handling of their responsibility. In addition, for empowerment to succeed, managers must be trained to link employees to resources within and outside the organization, such as customers, co-workers in other departments, and Web sites with needed information. Managers must also encourage employees to interact with staff throughout the organization, must ensure that employees receive the information they need, and must reward cooperation. Finally, empowered employees deliver the best results if they are fully engaged in their work. *Employee engagement*—full involvement in one's work and commitment to one's job and company—is associated with higher productivity, better customer service, and lower turnover.[21]

As with the need for knowledge workers, use of employee empowerment shifts the recruiting focus away from technical skills and toward general cognitive and interpersonal skills. Employees who have responsibility for a final product or service must be able to listen to customers, adapt to changing needs, and creatively solve a variety of problems.

Teamwork

Modern technology places the information that employees need for improving quality and providing customer service right at the point of sale or production. As a result, the employees engaging in selling and producing must also be able to make decisions about how to do their work. Organizations need to set up work in a way that gives employees the authority and ability to make those decisions. One of the most popular ways to increase employee responsibility and control is to assign work to teams. **Teamwork** is the assignment of work to groups of employees with various skills who interact to assemble a product or provide a service. Work teams often assume many activities traditionally reserved for managers, such as selecting new team members, scheduling work, and coordinating work with customers and other units of the organization. Work teams also contribute to total quality by performing inspection and quality-control activities while the product or service is being completed.

In some organizations, technology is enabling teamwork even when workers are at different locations or work at different times. These organizations use *virtual teams*—teams that rely on communications technology such as videoconferences, e-mail, and cell phones to keep in touch and coordinate activities.

Teamwork can motivate employees by making work more interesting and significant. At organizations that rely on teamwork, labor costs may be lower as well. Spurred by such advantages, a number of companies are reorganizing assembly operations—abandoning the assembly line in favor of operations that combine mass production with jobs in which employees perform multiple tasks, use many skills, control the pace of work, and assemble the entire final product.

Witnessing the resulting improvements, companies in the service sector also have moved toward greater use of teamwork. Teamwork was part of the fix for MFS Investment Management, a manager of mutual funds, which was losing clients after several years of poor performance and scandal. MFS brought in a new chief executive, who took the unusual step of organizing analysts into teams responsible for knowing particular industry sectors in which they invested. Instead of focusing on standing out individually because of a particular skill, the analysts pool their knowledge of,

Teamwork
The assignment of work to groups of employees with various skills who interact to assemble a product or provide a service.

say, technology companies. The teamwork is reinforced through HR practices such as basing compensation partly on performance reviews by other team members. The teamwork has helped MFS improve its investment performance and is bringing in new cash from clients.[22]

Focus on Strategy

LO4 Identify ways HR professionals can support organizational strategies for quality, growth, and efficiency.

As we saw in Chapter 1, traditional management thinking treated human resource management primarily as an administrative function, but managers today are beginning to see a more central role for HRM. They are looking at HRM as a means to support a company's *strategy*—its plan for meeting broad goals such as profitability, quality, and market share. This strategic role for HRM has evolved gradually. At many organizations, managers still treat HR professionals primarily as experts in designing and delivering HR systems. But at a growing number of organizations, HR professionals are strategic partners with other managers.

This means they use their knowledge of the business and of human resources to help the organization develop strategies and to align HRM policies and practices with those strategies. To do this, human resource managers must focus on the future as well as the present, and on company goals as well as human resource activities. They may, for example, become experts at analyzing the business impact of HR decisions or at developing and keeping the best talent to support business strategy. An example of an HRM professional who understands this role is Cynthia McCague, director of human resources at Coca-Cola. When McCague took the post, profit growth was stalling, morale was poor, and employee turnover was a major problem. McCague had HR staff conduct a survey of Coke's top 400 managers. Analysis showed that the company lacked a clear direction and shared purpose, and it confirmed the low morale, as well as a focus on short-term performance at the expense of long-term results. Coke put together teams of top leaders to address each of these problems, and then the HR group helped roll out changes such as a mission statement, an improved reward system, and a more useful intranet for sharing company information online. As employees have begun to feel more purposeful, turnover has fallen, attitudes have improved, and the company has begun reporting high sales and stock prices.[23]

The specific ways in which human resource professionals support the organization's strategy vary according to their level of involvement and the nature of the strategy. Strategic issues include emphasis on quality and decisions about growth and efficiency. Human resource management can support these strategies, including efforts such as quality improvement programs, mergers and acquisitions, and restructuring. Decisions to use reengineering and outsourcing can make an organization more efficient and also give rise to many human resource challenges. International expansion presents a wide variety of HRM challenges and opportunities. Figure 2.4 summarizes these strategic issues facing human resource management.

High Quality Standards

Total Quality Management (TQM)
A companywide effort to continually improve the ways people, machines, and systems accomplish work.

To compete in today's economy, companies need to provide high-quality products and services. If companies do not adhere to quality standards, they will have difficulty selling their product or service to vendors, suppliers, or customers. Therefore, many organizations have adopted some form of **total quality management (TQM)**—a

Figure 2.4

Business Strategy: Issues Affecting HRM

companywide effort to continually improve the ways people, machines, and systems accomplish work.[24] TQM has several core values:[25]

- Methods and processes are designed to meet the needs of internal and external customers (that is, whomever the process is intended to serve).
- Every employee in the organization receives training in quality.
- Quality is designed into a product or service so that errors are prevented from occurring, rather than being detected and corrected in an error-prone product or service.
- The organization promotes cooperation with vendors, suppliers, and customers to improve quality and hold down costs.
- Managers measure progress with feedback based on data.

Based on these values, the TQM approach provides guidelines for all the organization's activities, including human resource management. To promote quality, organizations need an environment that supports innovation, creativity, and risk taking to meet customer demands. Problem solving should bring together managers, employees, and customers. Employees should communicate with managers about customer needs. For an example of a company that engages in such practices, see the "Best Practices" box.

Human resource management also supports a strong commitment to quality at Philips Respironics, which makes medical devices that help people with sleep apnea to breathe while sleeping. To improve quality, cost, delivery, safety, and morale, the company develops measurable objectives and assembles employee teams to tackle projects in particular areas. Under the slogan "Enable, Empower, Engage," the emphasis is on inviting and responding to ideas from employees. The Exchange Team is charged with improving the working environment for employees. Groups of five have completed projects such as installing an on-site fitness center and establishing

HR A COMPONENT OF QUALITY AT MESA PRODUCTS

Privately owned Mesa Products Inc., based in Tulsa, Oklahoma, has persistently dedicated itself to quality improvement. The company, which designs, makes, and installs systems to keep underground pipelines and tanks from corroding, decided several years ago to seek a government-sponsored Malcolm Baldrige National Quality Award. To win the Baldrige, companies have to demonstrate excellence in leadership, strategic planning, focus on customers, measurement for use in performance management, focus on the workforce, and management and improvement of work processes, as well as superior results in all its business areas. Competing for the award is a way to keep everyone in the company focused on the real goal, which is improved quality and results.

To hit this target, Mesa geared up by setting goals for better customer service, customer relationships, performance (cycle time and productivity), work environment,

and growth (profits and sales). While HR could help in all these areas through efforts such as job design and reward systems, of particular relevance were the targets for work environment. Mesa's goals included objectives for employee training, job satisfaction, and ethical conduct. These objectives are consistent with the Baldrige requirements for excellence in workforce focus: companies must enable their people to develop their full potential, and they should align their workforce (for example, in terms of staffing and motivation) with corporate objectives.

Meeting the targets wasn't easy. CEO Terry May says that when the Baldrige assessment team delivered its first feedback, "It was somewhat of a wakeup call for me." But May got his people involved in making improvements, and as they persevered over the course of several years, "Our people became more comfortable" with the effort at continual improvement of processes.

The small steps required for these ambitious goals have had a real payoff for Mesa. Sales have soared, profitability is way up, and the company retains a remarkable 100 percent of its key customers. In independent customer satisfaction surveys, Mesa is generally the preferred supplier. And even during the recent economic downturn, Mesa was hiring new engineers.

HR has done its part to contribute to quality. According to surveys of employees in the industry, Mesa's employees are among the most satisfied—an attitude that shows up in the company's low rate of employee turnover.

Sources: Ryan C. Burge, "The Baldrige Journey," *Industrial Engineer,* February 2009, pp. 40–44; Kyle Arnold, "Plenty of Work," *Tulsa World,* March 1, 2009, Business & Company Resource Center, http://galenet.galegroup.com; and Mesa Products, "About Mesa," corporate Web site, http://www.mesaproducts.com, accessed February 25, 2010.

a recycling program. On a typical day, eight new ideas for improvement are being implemented at Philips Respironics. The pace of change may seem exhausting, but employees more often feel energized because they feel heard and because they have a sense that what they do matters.[26]

Mergers and Acquisitions

Often, organizations join forces through mergers (two companies becoming one) and acquisitions (one company buying another). Some mergers and acquisitions result in consolidation within an industry, meaning that two firms in one industry join to hold a greater share of the industry. For example, British Petroleum's acquisition of Amoco Oil represented a consolidation, or reduction of the number of companies in the oil industry. Other mergers and acquisitions cross industry lines. In a merger to form Citigroup, Citicorp combined its banking business with Traveller's Group's insurance business. Furthermore, these deals more frequently take the form of global megamergers, or mergers of big companies based in different countries (as in the case of BP-Amoco).

HRM should have a significant role in carrying out a merger or acquisition. Differences between the businesses involved in the deal make conflict inevitable. Training efforts should therefore include development of skills in conflict resolution. Also, HR professionals have to sort out differences in the two companies' practices with regard to compensation, performance appraisal, and other HR systems. Settling on a consistent structure to meet the combined organization's goals may help to bring employees together.

Downsizing

As shown in Figure 2.5 the number of organizations undergoing downsizing has increased significantly, reaching record highs in 2009.[27] The current economic crisis means that one important question facing companies is how, despite having to reduce the size of their workforce, they can develop a reputation as an employer of choice and engage employees in working toward the goals of the firm. The way companies answer this question will determine how they can compete by meeting the stakeholder needs of their employees.

Downsizing presents a number of challenges and opportunities for HRM. In terms of challenges, the HRM function must "surgically" reduce the workforce by cutting only the workers who are less valuable in their performance. Achieving this is difficult because the best workers are most able (and often willing) to find alternative employment and may leave voluntarily before the organization lays off anyone.

Figure 2.5

Number of Employees Laid Off during the Past Decade

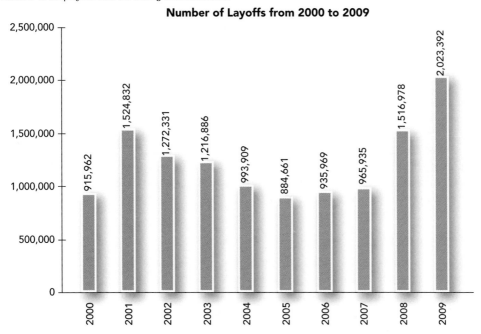

SOURCE: Bureau of Labor Statistics, "Extended Mass Layoffs: Fourth Quarter 2009, Annual Totals 2009," news release, February 17, 2010, www.bls.gov/mls.

Early-retirement programs are humane, but they essentially reduce the workforce with a "grenade" approach—not distinguishing good from poor performers but rather eliminating an entire group of employees. In fact, research indicates that when companies downsize by offering early-retirement programs, they usually end up rehiring to replace essential talent within a year. Often the company does not achieve its cost-cutting goals because it spends 50 to 150 percent of the departing employee's salary in hiring and retraining new workers. Adding to the problem, because layoffs typically involve severance pay, they don't even bring the same dollar-for-dollar benefits of a direct reduction in spending, such as cutting pay rates or hours worked.[28]

Another HRM challenge is to boost the morale of employees who remain after the reduction; this is discussed in greater detail in Chapter 5 and in the "HR How To" box. HR professionals should maintain open communication with remaining employees to build their trust and commitment, rather than withholding information.[29] All employees should be informed why the downsizing is necessary, what costs are to be cut, how long the downsizing will last, and what strategies the organization intends to pursue. Finally, HRM can provide downsized employees with outplacement services to help them find new jobs. Such services are ways an organization can show that it cares about its employees, even though it cannot afford to keep all of them on the payroll.

Reengineering

Rapidly changing customer needs and technology have caused many organizations to rethink the way they get work done. For example, when an organization adopts new technology, its existing processes may no longer result in acceptable quality levels, meet customer expectations for speed, or keep costs to profitable levels. Therefore, many organizations have undertaken **reengineering**—a complete review of the organization's critical work processes to make them more efficient and able to deliver higher quality.

Reengineering
A complete review of the organization's critical work processes to make them more efficient and able to deliver higher quality.

Ideally, reengineering involves reviewing all the processes performed by all the organization's major functions, including production, sales, accounting, and human resources. Therefore, reengineering affects human resource management in two ways. First, the way the HR department itself accomplishes its goals may change dramatically. Second, the fundamental change throughout the organization requires the HR department to help design and implement change so that all employees will be committed to the success of the reengineered organization. Employees may need training for their reengineered jobs. The organization may need to redesign the structure of its pay and benefits to make them more appropriate for its new way of operating. It also may need to recruit employees with a new set of skills. Often, reengineering results in employees being laid off or reassigned to new jobs, as the organization's needs change. HR professionals should also help with this transition, as they do for downsizing.

Outsourcing

Many organizations are increasingly outsourcing business activities. **Outsourcing** refers to the practice of having another company (a vendor, third-party provider, or consultant) provide services. For instance, a manufacturing company might outsource its accounting and transportation functions to businesses that specialize in these activities. Outsourcing gives the company access to in-depth expertise and is often more economical as well.

Outsourcing
The practice of having another company (a vendor, third-party provider, or consultant) provide services.

LEADING AFTER LAYOFFS

Downsizing is a difficult strategy. Besides the obvious pain for those who lose their jobs, there are the unpleasant duties of making the tough decisions and delivering bad news, perhaps while silently second-guessing whether past staffing decisions were less than ideal, given that some of those people are now seen as expendable. Downsizing is also an emotional experience for the employees who remain afterward and are often expected to make do—and even do more—with less.

That situation calls for strong leadership, and HR can play a role:

- Help management craft and communicate positive messages about the company's new vision and priorities.
- Identify how new priorities and strategy call for redesigned jobs, so that the smaller workforce can focus on what's most important. Managers should meet with their employees to review job requirements and consider how they can be met in the smaller organization.
- Make sure expectations for the remaining employees are realistic; a plan to survive with exhausted, stressed-out employees is not a viable plan for success.
- Encourage employees and departments to collaborate and share ideas. This may be the time to revamp evaluation and rewards systems to reward group performance.
- Identify high-potential employees who can take on challenging new assignments that could develop them for advancement.

Sources: Based on Toddi Gutner, "Coping with Aftermath of Layoffs at Your Firm," *Wall Street Journal*, February 3, 2009, http://online.wsj.com; and Eric Krell, "Spreading the Workload," *HR Magazine*, July 2009, Business & Company Resource Center, http://galenet.galegroup.com.

Not only do HR departments help with a transition to outsourcing, but many HR functions are being outsourced. One study suggests that 8 out of 10 companies outsource at least one human resource activity, and a more recent study found that 91 percent of U.S. companies have taken steps to standardize their HR processes to prepare for outsourcing.[30] Cardinal Health, a provider of health care products, services, and technology, signed a contract with ExcellerateHRO to provide administrative functions.[31] HR professionals remaining at Cardinal work in strategic areas such as talent management, organizational effectiveness, and total rewards, while ExcellerateHRO provides routine services.

Expanding into Global Markets

LO5 Summarize ways in which human resource management can support organizations expanding internationally.

Companies are finding that to survive they must compete in international markets as well as fend off foreign competitors' attempts to gain ground in the United States. To meet these challenges, U.S. businesses must develop global markets, keep up with competition from overseas, hire from an international labor pool, and prepare employees for global assignments.

Companies that are successful and widely admired not only operate on a multinational scale, but also have workforces and corporate cultures that reflect their global markets. IBM—which obtains more than two-thirds of its revenues from outside the United States—prepares its employees to work with people in unfamiliar locations by setting up a Service Corps in which teams of employees participate in nonprofit projects in Romania, Turkey, Vietnam, the Philippines, Ghana, and Tanzania. For example, a

focus on *social responsibility*

Figure 2.6

Where Immigrants to the United States Came from in 2008

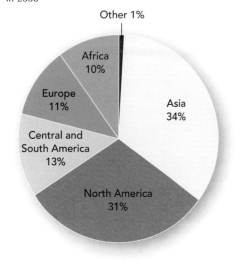

Other 1%

Africa 10%

Europe 11%

Asia 34%

Central and South America 13%

North America 31%

SOURCE: Department of Homeland Security, Office of Immigration Statistics, "U.S. Legal Permanent Residents: 2008," *Annual Flow Report*, March 2009, Table 3, p. 4, www.dhs.gov.

Offshoring
Moving operations from the country where a company is headquartered to a country where pay rates are lower but the necessary skills are available.

software development manager helped a maker of furniture for offices and schools meet its goals to operate more efficiently. While the employees are providing community service in these developing nations, IBM sees the effort also as "a management development exercise for high-potential people," in the words of Randy MacDonald, IBM's senior vice president for human resources. Participants gain skill in understanding cultural differences, communicating effectively, and working as a team.[32]

The Global Workforce

For today's and tomorrow's employers, talent comes from a global workforce. Organizations with international operations hire at least some of their employees in the foreign countries where they operate. In fact, regardless of where their customers are located, more and more organizations are looking overseas to hire talented people willing to work for less pay than the U.S. labor market requires. Intel, for example, has projected that most of its future employees will be hired outside U.S. borders. The efforts to hire workers in other countries are common enough that they have spurred the creation of a popular name for the practice: **offshoring.** Just a few years ago, most offshoring involved big manufacturers building factories in countries with lower labor costs. But today it is so easy to send information and software around the world that even start-ups are hiring overseas. In one study, almost 4 out of 10 new companies employed foreign analysts, marketers, engineers, and other employees. In contrast to computer and printer manufacturer Hewlett-Packard, which hired its first foreign workers 20 years after its founding in 1939, search engine Google employed people outside the United States just three years after its 1998 start.[33]

Hiring in developing nations such as India, Mexico, and Brazil gives employers access to people with potential who are eager to work yet who will accept lower wages than elsewhere in the world. Challenges, however, may include employees' lack of familiarity with technology and corporate practices, as well as political and economic instability in the areas. Important issues that HR experts can help companies weigh include whether workers in the offshore locations can provide the same or better skills, how offshoring will affect motivation and recruitment of employees needed in the United States, and whether managers are well prepared to manage and lead offshore employees. In addition, as offshoring becomes the norm, U.S. employers are finding that many workers in developing nations such as India don't fit the old stereotypes. Young Indian programmers and engineers, for example, may have attitudes and ambitions more like those of their Western counterparts than their parents in many regards.[34]

Even hiring at home may involve selection of employees from other countries. The beginning of the 21st century, like the beginning of the last century, has been a time of significant immigration, with over 1.1 million people obtaining permanent resident status in 2008 alone.[35] Figure 2.6 shows the distribution of immigration by continent of origin. The impact of immigration will be especially large in some regions of the United States, with large shares of immigrants residing in California, New York, Florida, and Texas. About 7 out of 10 foreign-born workers will be Hispanics and Asians.[36]

Employers in tight labor markets—such as those seeking experts in computer science, engineering, and information systems—have been especially likely to recruit international students.

International Assignments

Besides hiring an international workforce, organizations must be prepared to send employees to other countries. This requires HR expertise in selecting employees for international assignments and preparing them for those assignments. Employees who take assignments in other countries are called **expatriates.**

U.S. companies must better prepare employees to work in other countries. The failure rate for U.S. expatriates is greater than that for European and Japanese expatriates.[37] To improve in this area, U.S. companies must carefully select employees to work abroad based on their ability to understand and respect the cultural and business norms of the host country. Qualified candidates also need language skills and technical ability. In Chapter 15, we discuss practices for training employees to understand other cultures.

Expatriates
Employees who take assignments in other countries.

Technological Change in HRM

Advances in computer-related technology have had a major impact on the use of information for managing human resources. Large quantities of employee data (including training records, skills, compensation rates, and benefits usage and cost) can easily be stored on personal computers and manipulated with user-friendly spreadsheets or statistical software. Often these features are combined in a **human resource information system (HRIS),** a computer system used to acquire, store, manipulate, analyze, retrieve, and distribute information related to an organization's human resources.[38] An HRIS can support strategic decision making, help the organization avoid lawsuits, provide data for evaluating programs or policies, and support day-to-day HR decisions. Table 2.1 describes some of the technologies that may be included in an organization's HRIS.

The support of an HRIS can help HR professionals navigate the challenges of today's complex business environment. For example, rapidly changing technology can cause employees' skills to become obsolete. Organizations must therefore carefully monitor their employees' skills and the organization's needed skills. Often the employees and needs are distributed among several locations, perhaps among several

LO6 Discuss how technological developments are affecting human resource management.

Human Resource Information System (HRIS)
A computer system used to acquire, store, manipulate, analyze, retrieve, and distribute information related to an organization's human resources.

TECHNOLOGY	WHAT IT DOES	EXAMPLE
Internet portal	Combines data from several sources into a single site; lets user customize data without programming skills.	A company's manager can track labor costs by work group.
Shared service centers	Consolidate different HR functions into a single location; eliminate redundancy and reduce administrative costs; process all HR transactions at one time.	AlliedSignal combined more than 75 functions, including finance and HR, into a shared service center.
Application service provider (ASP)	Lets companies rent space on a remote computer system and use the system's software to manage its HR activities, including security and upgrades.	KPMG Consulting uses an ASP to host the company's computerized learning program.
Business intelligence	Provides insight into business trends and patterns and helps businesses improve decisions.	Managers use the system to analyze labor costs and productivity among different employee groups.

Table 2.1

New Technologies Influencing HRM

The Internet and e-HRM are helpful for employees who work outside the office because they can receive and share information online easily. The benefits of products such as Blackberrys and other smartphones are enormous, but is it possible to be too accessible?

countries. Sisters of St. Francis Health Services, which operates hospitals in Illinois and Indiana, uses HRIS applications to identify and develop existing and needed employee talent. The organization uses its HRIS for access to performance appraisals and compensation records. Users enter staffing goals and plans, and the HRIS helps them track their progress. For an organization with 17,000 employees, the automation makes it practical to maintain a focus on how staffing, training, and compensation decisions contribute to the group's mission.[39]

The Internet Economy

The way business is conducted has changed rapidly during the past two decades and will continue to do so. Much of the change is related to the widespread adoption of the Internet by businesses and individuals.

The Internet economy creates many HRM challenges.[40] The fast pace of change in information technology requires companies to continually update their skill requirements and then recruit and train people to meet those requirements. The competition for such employees may be stiff and, as described earlier, often involves recruiting on an international scale.

Motivation can also be a challenge. The first Internet-based organizations were small start-up companies founded by young, forward-looking people who saw the potential of a then-new technology. These companies sometimes made up for inexperienced management with a culture based on creativity, enthusiasm, and intense commitment. Policies and procedures sometimes took a backseat to team spirit and workplace fun. But as competition from established companies heated up and as investors withdrew funding, the start-up companies were acquired, went out of business, or had to radically cut back hiring and spending. In this environment, HRM needs to help companies comply with labor laws, motivate employees, and craft human resource policies that seem fair to workers and meet employers' competitive demands.

Electronic Human Resource Management (e-HRM)

Many HRM activities have moved onto the Internet. Electronic HRM applications let employees enroll in and participate in training programs online. Employees can go online to select from items in a benefits package and enroll in the benefits they choose. They can look up answers to HR-related questions and read company news, perhaps downloading it as a podcast. This processing and transmission of digitized HR information is called **electronic human resource management (e-HRM).**

E-HRM has the potential to change all traditional HRM functions. Table 2.2 shows some major implications of e-HRM. For example, employees in different geographic areas can work together. Use of the Internet lets companies search for talent without geographic limitations. Recruiting can include online job postings, applications, and candidate screening from the company's Web site or the Web sites of companies that specialize in online recruiting, such as Monster.com or Yahoo! HotJobs. Employees from different geographic locations can all receive the same training over the company's computer network. The "eHRM" box describes an application for scheduling workers.

Electronic Human Resource Management (e-HRM)
The processing and transmission of digitized HR information, especially using computer networking and the Internet.

HRM PRACTICES	IMPLICATIONS OF e-HRM
Analysis and design of work	Employees in geographically dispersed locations can work together in virtual teams using video, e-mail, and the Internet.
Recruiting	Post job openings online; candidates can apply for jobs online.
Training	Online learning can bring training to employees anywhere, anytime.
Selection	Online simulations, including tests, videos, and e-mail, can measure job candidates' ability to deal with real-life business challenges.
Compensation and benefits	Employees can review salary and bonus information and seek information about and enroll in benefit plans.

Table 2.2

Implications of e-HRM for HRM Practices

Privacy is an important issue in e-HRM. A great deal of HR information is confidential and not suitable for posting on a Web site for everyone to see. One solution is to set up e-HRM on an *intranet,* which is a network that uses Internet tools but limits access to authorized users in the organization. However, to better draw on the Internet's potential, organizations are increasingly replacing intranets with Web portals (Web sites designed to serve as a gateway to the Internet, highlighting links to relevant information).[41] Whether a company uses an intranet or a Web portal, it must ensure that it has sufficient security measures in place to protect employees' privacy.

Sharing of Human Resource Information

Information technology is changing the way HR departments handle record keeping and information sharing. Today, HR employees use technology to automate much of their work in managing employee records and giving employees access to information and enrollment forms for training, benefits, and other programs. As a result, HR employees play a smaller role in maintaining records, and employees now get information through **self-service.** This means employees have online access to information about HR issues such as training, benefits, compensation, and contracts; go online to enroll themselves in programs and services; and provide feedback through online surveys. Today, employees routinely look up workplace policies and information about their benefits online, and they may receive electronic notification when deposits are made directly to their bank accounts.

Self-Service
System in which employees have online access to information about HR issues and go online to enroll themselves in programs and provide feedback through surveys.

For GameStop, a retailer of video games, self-service is the obvious choice. The company's 40,000 employees, who typically are game fans themselves, don't want to bother reading brochures about benefits plans. But if they don't pay attention to what the company offers, the spending on benefits isn't delivering value in terms of motivating workers. So, recognizing that its workers are familiar with and even expect the convenience of online shopping, GameStop started with its 12,900 full-time employees, phoning them with a message to enroll. The employees could simply press 1 to be connected to a benefits counselor. While they chatted, they could view options on a screen in the store or on their home computer. As they made choices, the screen would show the total value of their selected benefits. Then GameStop invited its part-timers to enroll in optional benefits. To reach them, it sent them text messages with links to a Web site where they could view an interactive feature telling them about what was available. The effort not only improved communications, it boosted enrollment in the health plan while enabling GameStop to cut $5 million in benefits granted erroneously.[42]

A growing number of companies are combining employee self-service with management self-service, such as the ability to go online to authorize pay increases,

HIGH-TECH SCHEDULING AT BANK OF THE WEST

Bank of the West, which specializes in commercial lending and small-business accounts, competes with banking giants by using technology to help it offer top-quality service efficiently. A software program called Planet, provided by GMT Corporation, analyzes the needs of the company's 700 branches to create staffing schedules based on seasonal and local usage.

With Planet, banks can analyze personnel needs and staff branches with a basic level of employees. A pool of floating employees is prepared to move from branch to branch as needed. The balanced level of staffing gives customers a good banking experience at any time of year, while the software ensures that schedules are drawn up fairly, automatically taking into account employee preferences and requests for time off.

Employees like the system, because they can easily request time off or make changes to the schedule. While critics have complained that the last-minute, as-needed scheduling can exploit workers, a well-designed system can take their preferences into account. Managers, too, like this kind of scheduling optimization software because it simplifies a difficult task and helps them plan ahead.

Sources: "Case in Point: Bank of the West Bullish on Workforce Optimization Software," *ABA Banking Journal,* July 2007, General Reference Center Gold, http://find.galegroup.com; Global Management Technologies, "Products: Workforce Management," GMT Web site, www.gmt.com, accessed December 7, 2007; and "Kronos for Retail Schedules 1.5 Million Associates," *Computer Technology Journal,* January 29, 2009, p. 275.

approve expenses, and transfer employees to new positions. More sophisticated systems extend management applications to decision making in areas such as compensation and performance management. For example, managers can schedule job interviews or performance appraisals, guided by the system to provide the necessary information and follow every step called for by the company's procedures.[43] To further support management decisions, the company may create an *HR dashboard,* or a display of how the company is performing on specific HR metrics, such as productivity and absenteeism. For example, Cisco Systems helps with talent management by displaying on its HR dashboard how many of its people move and why.[44] The data can help management identify divisions where the managers are successfully developing new talent.

LO7 Explain how the nature of the employment relationship is changing.

Psychological Contract
A description of what an employee expects to contribute in an employment relationship and what the employer will provide the employee in exchange for those contributions.

Change in the Employment Relationship

Technology and the other trends we have described in this chapter require managers at all levels to make rapid changes in response to new opportunities, competitive challenges, and customer demands. These changes are most likely to succeed in flexible, forward-thinking organizations, and the employees who will thrive in such organizations need to be flexible and open to change as well. In this environment, employers and employees have begun to reshape the employment relationship.[45]

A New Psychological Contract

We can think of that relationship in terms of a **psychological contract,** a description of what an employee expects to contribute in an employment relationship and what the employer will provide the employee in exchange for those contributions.[46] Unlike a written sales contract, the psychological contract is not formally put into words.

Instead, it describes unspoken expectations that are widely held by employers and employees. In the traditional version of this psychological contract, organizations expected their employees to contribute time, effort, skills, abilities, and loyalty. In return, the organizations would provide job security and opportunities for promotion.

However, this arrangement is being replaced with a new type of psychological contract.[47] To stay competitive, modern organizations must frequently change the quality, innovation, creativeness, and timeliness of employee contributions and the skills needed to make those contributions. This need has led to organizational restructuring, mergers and acquisitions, layoffs, and longer hours for many employees. Companies demand excellent customer service and high productivity levels. They expect employees to take more responsibility for their own careers, from seeking training to balancing work and family. These expectations result in less job security for employees, who can count on working for several companies over the course of a career. In the federal government's most recent survey of wage and salary workers aged 25 and older, they had been with their present employer for a median of just four years. Workers 55 and older and those in government jobs tended to have much longer tenures.[48] But if four years with a company is typical, that amounts to many employers in the course of one's career.

In exchange for top performance and working longer hours without job security, employees want companies to provide flexible work schedules, comfortable working conditions, more control over how they accomplish work, training and development opportunities, and financial incentives based on how the organization performs. (Figure 2.7 provides a humorous look at an employee who seems to have benefited from this modern psychological contract by obtaining a family friendly work arrangement.) Employees realize that companies cannot provide employment security, so they want *employability*. This means they want their company to provide training and job experiences to help ensure that they can find other employment opportunities.

Figure 2.7

A Family Friendly Work Arrangement

By permission of Dave Coverly and Creators Syndicate, Inc.

Flexibility

The new psychological contract largely results from the HRM challenge of building a committed, productive workforce in turbulent economic conditions—conditions that offer opportunity for financial success but can also quickly turn sour, making every employee expendable. From the organization's perspective, the key to survival in a fast-changing environment is flexibility. Organizations want to be able to change as fast as customer needs and economic conditions change. Flexibility in human resource management includes flexible staffing levels and flexible work schedules.

LO8 Discuss how the need for flexibility affects human resource management.

Flexible Staffing Levels

A flexible workforce is one the organization can quickly reshape and resize to meet its changing needs. To be able to do this without massive hiring and firing

When a Contractor Isn't a Contractor

Signing up contract workers instead of hiring employees can look like a good deal, because the company doesn't have to pay the Social Security, Medicare, and unemployment insurance taxes required for employees on the company's payroll. They also can get around laws designed to protect employees, such as minimum wages. With stiff competition and slow economy, experts say, some companies incorrectly say workers are "contractors."

Although the classification may be a judgment call in some cases, it's not just a matter of opinion. Under the law, workers are employees if someone at the company decides how and when they are to perform their jobs.

Recently, federal and state governments have indicated they are going to crack down with stricter enforcement and tougher penalties on employers who wrongly classify employees as contract workers. The federal government estimates that its part in the crackdown over the next decade will generate $7 billion in taxes that otherwise wouldn't have been collected.

Source: Steven Greenhouse, "U.S. Cracks Down on 'Contractors' as a Tax Dodge," *New York Times*, February 18, 2010.

Questions

1. Why might a company legitimately want to hire contractors rather than employees? How significant do you think the savings on payroll taxes would be for most employers who use contractors?
2. Given that employers may not direct the details of when and how contractors do their work, what HR challenges could result from relying on contractors?

Alternative Work Arrangements
Methods of staffing other than the traditional hiring of full-time employees (for example, use of independent contractors, on-call workers, temporary workers, and contract company workers).

campaigns, organizations are using more alternative work arrangements. **Alternative work arrangements** are methods of staffing other than the traditional hiring of full-time employees. There are a variety of methods, with the following being most common:

- *Independent contractors* are self-employed individuals with multiple clients.
- *On-call workers* are persons who work for an organization only when they are needed.
- *Temporary workers* are employed by a temporary agency; client organizations pay the agency for the services of these workers.
- *Contract company workers* are employed directly by a company for a specific time specified in a written contract.

However, as illustrated by the "HR Oops!" box, employers need to use these options with care.

The Bureau of Labor Statistics estimates that about one-tenth of employed individuals work in alternative employment arrangements.[49] The majority, about 10.3 million, are independent contractors. Another 2.5 million are on-call workers, 1.2 million work for temporary-help agencies, and over 800,000 are workers provided by contract firms. In addition, about 11 percent of noninstitutionalized civilians who are old enough to work have part-time jobs; a majority of them work part-time by choice. Along with 96,000 employees worldwide, Microsoft's workforce includes between 70,000 and 80,000 contingent workers. The majority work for vendors, and roughly 10 percent are temporary employees hired from agencies. Other contingent workers are categorized as interns and visiting researchers. Using contingent workers allows Microsoft to adjust its workforce for particular needs such as landscaping, driving shuttle buses, writing technical documents, and staffing reception desks. Microsoft may bring in contingent workers with technical expertise when it needs help with special projects.[50]

Multitasking has become a way of life for many employees who need to make the most of every minute. This trend is affecting human resource management and the employees it supports.

More workers in alternative employment relationships are choosing these arrangements, but preferences vary. Most independent contractors and contract workers have this type of arrangement by choice. In contrast, temporary agency workers and on-call workers are likely to prefer traditional full-time employment. There is some debate about whether nontraditional employment relationships are good or bad. Some labor analysts argue that alternative work arrangements are substandard jobs featuring low pay, fear of unemployment, poor health insurance and retirement benefits, and dissatisfying work. Others claim that these jobs provide flexibility for companies and employees alike. With alternative work arrangements, organizations can more easily modify the number of their employees. Continually adjusting staffing levels is especially cost-effective for an organization that has fluctuating demand for its products and services. And when an organization downsizes by laying off temporary and part-time employees, the damage to morale among permanent full-time workers is likely to be less severe.

Flexible Work Schedules

The globalization of the world economy and the development of e-commerce have made the notion of a 40-hour workweek obsolete. As a result, companies need to be staffed 24 hours a day, seven days a week. Employees in manufacturing environments and service call centers are being asked to work 12-hour days or to work afternoon or midnight shifts. Similarly, professional employees face long hours and work demands that spill over into their personal lives. E-mail, pagers, and cell phones bombard employees with information and work demands. In the car, on vacation, on planes, and even in the bathroom, employees can be interrupted by work demands. More demanding work results in greater employee stress, less satisfied employees, loss of productivity, and higher turnover—all of which are costly for companies.

Many organizations are taking steps to provide more flexible work schedules, to protect employees' free time, and to more productively use employees' work time. Workers consider flexible schedules a valuable way to ease the pressures and conflicts of trying to balance work and nonwork activities. Employers are using flexible schedules to recruit and retain employees and to increase satisfaction and productivity. For example, Best Buy created its Results-Only Work Environment (ROWE) to give employees control over how, when, and where they get the job done, as long as they achieve the desired results.[51] The idea of this experiment is to let employees focus on productivity, rather than whether they are physically present in a meeting or seated behind their desk at a particular time of day. In divisions that have tried ROWE, employees say they are more engaged at work, are more committed to the company, and have improved their family relationships at the same time.

thinking ethically

THE ETHICS OF OFFSHORING

When companies use offshoring, they are eliminating higher-paid U.S. jobs and replacing them with lower-paid jobs elsewhere. The debate has raged over whether this practice is ethical.

Businesses certainly need to make a profit, and offshoring can help lower costs. One manager who endorses offshoring is George Hefferan, vice president and general counsel for Mindcrest, a legal services firm based in Chicago. According to Hefferan, the company would not even exist if it couldn't hire lawyers in Mumbai and Pune, India. At far lower rates than U.S. attorneys charge, the Indian lawyers review lease agreements and do other routine tasks. This assistance frees employees in Chicago to tackle more complicated assignments.

The downside involves considerations other than profits. In a country where companies routinely offshore important talents, such as engineering innovation, the country may become weaker in those areas. And workers suffer if they lose jobs or have to accept pay cuts to compete with workers in lower-cost areas.

Business owner Valarie King-Bailey once lost her own engineering job to offshoring. King-Bailey then started her own company, OnShore Technology, an information technology (IT) engineering firm. The company now has eight employees and a mission of "keeping technology jobs on America's shores."

SOURCES: Ann Meyer, "U.S. Exit Strategy Splits Employers," *Chicago Tribune*, October 29, 2007, sec. 3, p. 2; and Jamie Eckle, "Career Watch: Ron Hira," *ComputerWorld*, December 21, 2009, p. 28 (interview with Ron Hira).

Questions

1. When a company moves jobs to another country, who benefits? Who loses? Given the mix of winners and losers, do you think offshoring is ethical? Why or why not?
2. Imagine you are an HR manager at a company that is planning to begin offshoring its production or customer service operations. How could you help the company proceed as ethically as possible?

SUMMARY

LO1 Describe trends in the labor force composition and how they affect human resource management.

An organization's internal labor force comes from its external labor market—individuals who are actively seeking employment. In the United States, this labor market is aging and becoming more racially and ethnically diverse. The share of women in the U.S. workforce has grown to nearly half of the total. To compete for talent, organizations must be flexible enough to meet the needs of older workers, possibly redesigning jobs. Organizations must recruit from a diverse population, establish bias-free HR systems, and help employees understand and appreciate cultural differences. Organizations also need employees with skills in decision making, customer service, and teamwork, as well as technical skills. The competition for such talent is intense. Organizations facing a skills shortage often hire employees who lack certain skills, then train them for their jobs.

LO2 Summarize areas in which human resource management can support the goal of creating a high-performance work system.

HRM can help organizations find and keep the best possible fit between their social system and

technical system. Organizations need employees with broad skills and strong motivation. Recruiting and selection decisions are especially important for organizations that rely on knowledge workers. Job design and appropriate systems for assessment and rewards have a central role in supporting employee empowerment and teamwork.

LO3 Define employee empowerment, and explain its role in the modern organization.

Employee empowerment means giving employees responsibility and authority to make decisions regarding all aspects of product development or customer service. The organization holds employees accountable for products and services, and in exchange, the employees share in the rewards (or losses) that result. Selection decisions should provide to the organization people who have the necessary decision-making and interpersonal skills. HRM must design jobs to give employees latitude for decision making and train employees to handle their broad responsibilities. Feedback and rewards must be appropriate for the work of empowered employees. HRM can also play a role in giving employees access to the information they need.

LO4 Identify ways HR professionals can support organizational strategies for quality, growth, and efficiency.

HR professionals should be familiar with the organization's strategy and may even play a role in developing the strategy. Specific HR practices vary according to the type of strategy. Job design is essential for empowering employees to practice total quality management. In organizations planning major changes such as a merger or acquisition, downsizing, or reengineering, HRM must provide leadership for managing the change in a way that includes skillful employee relations and meaningful rewards. HR professionals can bring "people issues" to the attention of the managers leading these changes. They can provide training in conflict-resolution skills, as well as knowledge of the other organization involved in a merger or acquisition. HR professionals also must resolve differences between the companies' HR systems, such as benefits packages and performance appraisals. For a downsizing, the HR department can help to develop voluntary programs to reduce the workforce or can help identify the least valuable employees to lay off. Employee relations can help maintain the morale of employees who remain after a downsizing. In reengineering, the HR department can lead in communicating with employees and providing training. It will also have to prepare new approaches for recruiting and appraising employees that are better suited to the reengineered jobs. Outsourcing presents similar issues related to job design and employee selection.

LO5 Summarize ways in which human resource management can support organizations expanding internationally.

Organizations with international operations hire employees in foreign countries where they operate, so they need knowledge of differences in culture and business practices. Even small businesses discover that qualified candidates include immigrants, because they account for a significant and growing share of the U.S. labor market. HRM needs to understand and train employees to deal with differences in cultures. HRM also must be able to help organizations select and prepare employees for overseas assignments. To support efficiency and growth, HR staff can prepare companies for offshoring, in which operations are moved to lower-wage countries. HR experts can help organizations determine whether workers in offshore locations can provide the same or better skills, how offshoring will affect motivation and recruitment of employees needed in the United States, and whether managers are prepared to manage offshore employees.

LO6 Discuss how technological developments are affecting human resource management.

Information systems have become a tool for more HR professionals, and often these systems are provided through the Internet. The widespread use of the Internet includes HRM applications. Organizations search for talent globally using online job postings and by screening candidates online. Organizations' Web sites feature information directed toward potential employees. Employees may receive training online. At many companies, online information sharing enables employee self-service for many HR needs, from application forms to training modules to information about the details of company policies and benefits. Organizations can now structure work that involves collaboration among employees at different times and places. In such situations, HR professionals must ensure that communications remain effective enough to detect and correct problems when they arise.

LO7 Explain how the nature of the employment relationship is changing.

The employment relationship takes the form of a "psychological contract" that describes what employees and employers expect from the employment relationship. It includes unspoken expectations that are widely held. In the traditional version, organizations expected their employees to contribute time, effort, skills, abilities, and loyalty in exchange for job security and opportunities for promotion. Today, modern organizations' needs are constantly changing, so organizations are requiring top performance and longer work hours but cannot provide job security. Instead, employees are looking for flexible work schedules, comfortable working conditions, greater autonomy, opportunities for training and development, and performance-related financial incentives. For HRM, the changes require planning for flexible staffing levels.

LO8 Discuss how the need for flexibility affects human resource management.

Organizations seek flexibility in staffing levels through alternatives to the traditional employment relationship. They may use outsourcing as well as temporary and contract workers. The use of such workers can affect job design and also the motivation of the organization's permanent employees. Organizations also may seek flexible work schedules, including shortened workweeks. They may offer flexible schedules as a way for employees to adjust work hours to meet personal and family needs. Organizations also may move employees to different jobs to meet changes in demand.

KEY TERMS

alternative work arrangements, p. 50

electronic human resource management (e-HRM), p. 46

employee empowerment, p. 36

expatriates, p. 45

external labor market, p. 29

high-performance work systems, p. 34

human resource information system (HRIS), p. 45

internal labor force, p. 29

knowledge workers, p. 35

offshoring, p. 44

outsourcing, p. 42

psychological contract, p. 48

reengineering, p. 42

self-service, p. 47

teamwork, p. 37

total quality management (TQM), p. 38

REVIEW AND DISCUSSION QUESTIONS

1. How does each of the following labor force trends affect HRM?
   a. Aging of the labor force.
   b. Diversity of the labor force.
   c. Skill deficiencies of the labor force.
2. At many organizations, goals include improving people's performance by relying on knowledge workers, empowering employees, and assigning work to teams. How can HRM support these efforts?
3. Merging, downsizing, and reengineering all can radically change the structure of an organization. Choose one of these changes, and describe HRM's role in making the change succeed. If possible, apply your discussion to an actual merger, downsizing, or reengineering effort that has recently occurred.
4. When an organization decides to operate facilities in other countries, how can HRM practices support this change?
5. Why do organizations outsource HRM functions? How does outsourcing affect the role of human resource professionals? Would you be more attracted to the role of HR professional in an organization that outsources many HR activities or in the outside firm that has the contract to provide the HR services? Why?
6. Suppose you have been hired to manage human resources for a small company that offers business services including customer service calls and business report preparation. The 20-person company has been preparing to expand from serving a few local clients that are well known to the company's owners. The owners believe that their experience and reputation for quality will help them expand to serve more and larger clients. What challenges will you need to prepare the company to meet? How will you begin?
7. What e-HRM resources might you use to meet the challenges in Question 4?
8. What HRM functions could an organization provide through self-service? What are some advantages and disadvantages of using self-service for these functions?
9. How is the employment relationship typical of modern organizations different from the relationship of a generation ago?

BUSINESSWEEK CASE

BusinessWeek   Raises or Rebuilding? A Business Owner's Dilemma

Business is starting to creep upward at some small companies. And employees who have gone without raises or had their salaries cut over the past two years are hoping that more money coming in will lead to a raise in the near future.

But owners who need to rebuild their businesses may not be able to give those raises. They may need to put the revenue toward equipment purchases they've had to put off. Or they may need to travel to more trade shows to prospect for new customers.

It's not an easy decision, especially in a company whose employees have sacrificed for the good of the company.

"It's a really tough call. You have to have a motivated workforce," said Jill McBride, who owns a six-person public relations firm, JZMcBride & Associates, in Cincinnati. She's trying to decide whether to give raises or add staff as business improves.

Human resources consultants advised owners during the recession to be open with employees about business and the challenges that their companies face. It's no different now, when employees are hoping for raises that may not be forthcoming.

McBride said she gave bonuses rather than raises last year but didn't cut anyone's pay or the 401(k) match. And, "we didn't let anyone go."

Now, she's asking, if the company is better off adding a new person who can bring in new business rather than giving out raises.

HR professionals say owners need to be sensitive to the fact that employees who have gone without raises are likely to feel some resentment if they see money going toward equipment or a new hire. So before an owner invests thousands of dollars in, say, a new server, he or she needs to let the staff know that raises won't be forthcoming. And, an owner needs to explain to employees that they stand to ultimately benefit from the purchase.

"If they can tie getting the server to increased productivity or ability to serve customers that will result in a higher level of revenue," employees are likely to accept the boss's decision, said Rick Gibbs, a senior human resources specialist with Administaff, a Houston-based company that provides HR outsourcing.

Likewise, a new employee who can bring in more business will help generate income that can fund those raises.

Gibbs also suggested telling staffers, "we need to get additional business before we loosen up the budget on salaries." In that way, the boss is letting workers know that raises are still a priority, and that as business continues to pick up, they'll be rewarded.

Don Mallo, a vice president at Extensis, a Woodbridge, N.J.–based company that provides HR outsourcing, recommends that owners also explain what other steps the company took before making the wage freeze, for example, what other expenses were cut.

Winbush held such a conversation with his staff, inviting everyone over to his house during the holidays.

"We talked about the growth of the company and where we needed to go and what steps we needed to take," he said. "They didn't take it lightly, but they understood that it was the responsible business thing to do."

SOURCE: Excerpted from Joyce M. Rosenberg, "Raises or Rebuilding? A Business Owner's Dilemma," *BusinessWeek*, February 24, 2010, http://www.businessweek.com.

Questions

1. What human resource trends described in this chapter are behind the situation faced by Jill McBride?
2. What advice to McBride would you add, beyond the recommendations given in this case?
3. Imagine you are a human resources consultant McBride has hired to help her align her HR practices with her growth strategy. Write a proposal of up to three paragraphs, outlining what aspects of human resources you would like to consider as ways to motivate McBride's employees even as she makes cautious moves toward building her business.

Case: Hershey's Sweet Mission

The mission statement of the Hershey Company brings to mind its signature chocolate bars and kisses: "Bringing sweet moments of Hershey happiness to the world every day." Living out that mission, however, comes down to more than candy. The company defines its mission in terms of its relationships with all stakeholders—consumers, employees, business partners (such as suppliers and distributors), shareholders, and the communities in which it operates. With regard to employees, the mission involves "winning with an aligned and empowered organization . . . while having fun."

"Aligned" employees should share values, be clear about how their work contributes to the organization's mission, collaborate effectively, and be selected, equipped, and rewarded for meeting company objectives. These requirements, of course, call upon the skills of human resource management.

With regard to values, Hershey has identified four and communicates them on its Web site:

We are Open to Possibilities by embracing diversity, seeking new approaches and striving for continuous improvement.

We are Growing Together by sharing knowledge and unwrapping human potential in an environment of mutual respect.

We are Making a Difference by leading with integrity and determination to have a positive impact on everything we do.

We are One Hershey, winning together while accepting individual responsibility for our results.

All of these values play into the way Hershey addresses human resource management.

Take, for example, the age distribution of the workforce. When Hershey provided training in characteristics of the different generations of workers, manager Mary Parsons became interested in how this might apply to building a workforce that better embraces this type of diversity and meets the value of "unwrapping human potential." One application of this idea was the creation of a mentoring program for the research and development group. When R&D hires a new "millennial" worker (the generation now in their twenties), it pairs this worker with a more experienced employee from the baby boom. The baby boomers tend to be interested in leaving a legacy, making the world better, so they generally are enthusiastic about mentoring their younger colleagues.

Hershey has also redesigned its performance management system. Appealing to the younger generations' eagerness for challenge, autonomy, and results, the redesign was a bottom-up effort, in which people throughout the company set goals and track progress on projects. The system measures not only business results but whether they are achieved in accordance the Hershey's four core values.

One area in which two generations—baby boomers and millennials—are already aligned is in a desire to have a positive impact on the world. Hershey reflects that with a commitment to social responsibility carried out through involvement in the communities where it is located. In particular, the company supports the Milton Hershey School, which provides care and education to disadvantaged children. Also, through a program called "Dollars for Doers," Hershey contributes cash to charities at which its employees volunteer for at least 100 hours per year.

SOURCES: Mary Parsons, "Generations at Work," *Research-Technology Management*, November–December 2009, pp. 41–44; and Hershey Company, "About the Hershey Company," corporate Web site, http://thehersheycompany.com, accessed February 25, 2010.

Questions

1. Pick any two of the trends described in this chapter, and discuss how Hershey's values result in positioning the company to use those trends to its advantage.
2. Besides the mentorship program, how else might Hershey encourage its younger and older researchers to work together toward company goals? What might be the role of human resource staff in supporting or implementing your ideas?
3. How well does this description of working at Hershey fit with the new "psychological contract" described in this chapter? Explain.

🖨 IT'S A WRAP!   McGraw Hill connect

www.mhhe.com/noefund4e is your source for Reviewing, Applying, and Practicing the concepts you learned about in Chapter 2.

Review
- Chapter learning objectives

Application
- Manager's Hot Seat segment: "Privacy: Burned by the Firewall"
- Video case and quiz: "Best Buy's Clockless Office"
- Self-assessment: Trends in Human Resource Management
- Web exercise: HRM and new technologies
- Small-business case: Radio Flyer Rolls Forward

Practice
- Chapter quiz

NOTES

1. Clare Ansberry, "Elderly Emerge as a New Class of Workers—and the Jobless," *Wall Street Journal*, February 23, 2009, http://online.wsj.com.
2. Sue Shellenbarger, "Recession Tactic: The Mini-Shift," *Wall Street Journal*, February 24, 2010, http://online.wsj.com.
3. Bureau of Labor Statistics (BLS), "Employment Projections: 2008–18," news release, December 10, 2009, http://www.bls.gov/emp.
4. Anne Fisher, "How to Battle the Coming Brain Drain," *Fortune*, March 21, 2005, downloaded from Infotrac at http://web7.infotrac.galegroup.com.
5. N. Lockwood, *The Aging Workforce* (Alexandria, VA: Society for Human Resource Management, 2003).
6. J. Marquez, "Novel Ideas at Borders Lure Older Workers," *Workforce Management*, May 2005, pp. 28, 30.
7. BLS, "Employment Projections: 2008–18."
8. Ibid.
9. For background and examples related to immigration, see U.S. Citizenship and Immigration Services, "How Do I Become a Lawful Permanent Resident while in the United States?" *Services and Benefits: Permanent Resident (Green Card)*, CIS website, www.uscis.gov, accessed March 2,

2010; Federation for American Immigration Reform, "Overview of Annual Immigration," last updated October 2009, www.fairus.org; Center for Immigration Studies, "Legal Immigration," *Topics*, www.cis.org, accessed December 10, 2007; U.S. State Department, "Temporary Workers," June 2007, http://travel.state.gov; Barry Newman, "Immigration Crackdown Targets Bosses This Time," *Wall Street Journal*, February 27, 2007, http://online.wsj.com; and Juliana Barbassa, "Legal Immigrant High-Tech Workers Speak," *Yahoo News*, October 29, 2007, http://news.yahoo.com.

10. T. H. Cox and S. Blake, "Managing Cultural Diversity: Implications for Organizational Competitiveness," *The Executive* 5 (1991), pp. 45–56.

11. "What Is Diversity? Not Many Workplaces Know the Answer," *HR Focus*, May 2008, Business & Company Resource Center, http://galenet.galegroup.com.

12. A. Pomeroy, "Cultivating Female Leaders," *HRMagazine*, February 2007, pp. 44–50.

13. J. Rossi, "The 'Future' of U.S. Manufacturing," *TD*, March 2006, pp. 12–13; and R. Davenport, "Eliminate the Skills Gap," *TD*, February 2006, pp. 26–34.

14. M. Schoeff, "Amid Calls to Bolster U.S. Innovation, Experts Lament Paucity of Basic Math Skills," *Workforce Management*, March 2006, pp. 46–49.

15. J. A. Neal and C. L. Tromley, "From Incremental Change to Retrofit: Creating High-Performance Work Systems," *Academy of Management Executive* 9 (1995), pp. 42–54.

16. Bureau of Labor Statistics, "Occupational Employment," *Occupational Outlook Quarterly*, Winter 2009–10, p. 12.

17. M. Hilton, "Skills for Work in the 21st Century: What Does the Research Tell Us?" *Academy of Management Executive*, November 2008, pp. 63–78.

18. J. Marquez, "Driving Ideas Forward at Nissan," *Workforce Management*, July 17, 2006, p. 28.

19. Art Murray, "Report from the Trenches: Progress and Challenges," *KM World*, February 2010, Business & Company Resource Center, http:// galenet.galegroup.com; and Dan Holtshouse, "The Future of Knowledge Workers," *KM World*, October 2009, Business & Company Resource Center, http://galenet.galegroup.com.

20. T. J. Atchison, "The Employment Relationship: Untied or Re-Tied," *Academy of Management Executive* 5 (1991), pp. 52–62.

21. R. Vance, *Employee Engagement and Commitment* (Alexandria, VA: Society for Human Resource Management, 2006); M. Huselid, "The Impact of Human Resource Management Practices on Turnover, Productivity, and Corporate Financial Performance," *Academy of Management Journal* 38 (1995), pp. 635–72; S. Payne and S. Webber, "Effects of Service Provider Attitudes and Employment Status on Citizenship Behaviors and Customers' Attitudes and Loyalty Behavior," *Journal of Applied Psychology* 91 (2006), pp. 365–68; and J. Hartner, F. Schmidt, and T. Hayes, "Business-Unit Level Relationship between Employee Satisfaction, Employee Engagement, and Business Outcomes: A Meta-analysis," *Journal of Applied Psychology* 87 (2002), pp. 268–79.

22. Rebecca Knight, "Modest Manager Promotes Teamwork," *Financial Times*, August 24, 2009, Business & Company Resource Center, http://galenet.galegroup.com.

23. Associated Press, "Coca-Cola CEO Neville Isdell to Step Down," *CBS News*, December 6, 2007, www.cbsnews.com; Adrienne Fox, "Refreshing a Beverage Company's Culture," *HR Magazine*, November 2007, General Reference Center Gold, http://find.galegroup.com; and Laila Karamally, "Coke's New CEO Focuses on Workers," *Workforce Management*, July 1, 2004, General Reference Center Gold, http://find.galegroup.com.

24. J. R. Jablonski, *Implementing Total Quality Management: An Overview* (San Diego: Pfeiffer, 1991).

25. R. Hodgetts, F. Luthans, and S. Lee, "New Paradigm Organizations: From Total Quality to Learning to World-Class," *Organizational Dynamics*, Winter 1994, pp. 5–19.

26. Steve Minter, "Working Hard So Others Can Breathe Easy," *Industry Week*, January 2010, Business & Company Resource Center, http://galenet.galegroup.com; and Steve Minter, "Diamonds in the Rough," *Industry Week*, January 2010, Business & Company Resource Center, http://galenet.galegroup.com.

27. Bureau of Labor Statistics, "Extended Mass Layoffs in 2009," *The Editor's Desk*, February 23, 2010, http://data.bls.gov.

28. J. Lopez, "Managing: Early-Retirement Offers Lead to Renewed Hiring," *Wall Street Journal*, January 26, 1993, p. B1; Peter Cappelli, "Alternatives to Layoffs," *Human Resource Executive Online*, January 5, 2009, http://www.hreonline.com; and Cali Yost, "Wharton's Dr. Peter Cappelli on Flexible Downsizing," *Fast Company*, January 22, 2009, http://www.fastcompany.com.

29. A. Church, "Organizational Downsizing: What Is the Role of the Practitioner?" *Industrial-Organizational Psychologist* 33, no. 1 (1995), pp. 63–74.

30. S. Caudron, "HR Is Dead, Long Live HR," *Workforce*, January 2003, pp. 26–29; and P. Ketter, "HR Outsourcing Accelerates," *TD*, February 2007, pp. 12–13.

31. M. Schoeff Jr., "Cardinal Health HR to Take More Strategic Role," *Workforce Management*, April 24, 2006, p. 7.

32. S. Deutsch, "Volunteering Abroad to Climb at IBM," *The New York Times*, March 26, 2008, sec. C, p. 4; and C. Hymowitz, "IBM Combines Volunteer Service, Teamwork to Cultivate Emerging Markets," *Wall Street Journal*, August 4, 2008, p. B6.

33. Jim Hopkins, "To Start Up Here, Companies Hire over There," *USA Today*, February 10, 2005, downloaded at www.usatoday.com.

34. S. Hamm, "Young and Impatient in India," *Business-Week*, January 28, 2008, p. 45.

35. Department of Homeland Security, Office of Immigration Statistics, "U.S. Legal Permanent Residents: 2008," *Annual Flow Report*, March 2009, p. 1, http://www.dhs.gov.

36. Bureau of Labor Statistics, "Foreign-Born Workers: Labor Force Characteristics in 2008," news release, March 26, 2009, http://www.bls.gov/eps/.

37. R. L. Tung, "Expatriate Assignments: Enhancing Success and Minimizing Failure," *Academy of Management Executive* 12, no. 4 (1988), pp. 93–106.

38. M. J. Kavanaugh, H. G. Guetal, and S. I. Tannenbaum, *Human Resource Information Systems: Development and Application* (Boston: PWS-Kent, 1990).

39. Halogen Software, "Sisters of St. Francis Health Services, Inc. Selects Halogen as Talent Management Standard," *Internet Wire*, February 11, 2009, Business & Company Resource Center, http://galenet .galegroup.com.

40. This section is based on L. Grensing-Pophal, "Are You Suited for a Dot-Com?" *HR Magazine*, November 2000, pp. 75–80; Leslie A. Weatherly, "HR Technology: Leveraging the Shift to Self-Service," *HR Magazine*, March 2005, downloaded from Infotrac at http://web7.infotrac.galegroup.com.

41. See Weatherly, "HR Technology."

42. Drew Robb, "Get the Benefits Message Out: Web-Based Tools Are Improving Employee Benefits Communication," *HR Magazine*, October 2009, Business & Company Resource Center, http://galenet. galegroup.com.

43. Weatherly, "HR Technology."

44. N. Lockwood, *Maximizing Human Capital: Demonstrating HR Value with Key Performance Indicators* (Alexandria, VA: SHRM Research Quarterly, 2006).

45. J. O'Toole and E. Lawler III, *The New American Workplace* (New York: Palgrave Macmillan, 2006).

46. D. M. Rousseau, "Psychological and Implied Contracts in Organizations," *Employee Rights and Responsibilities Journal* 2 (1989), pp. 121–29.

47. D. Rousseau, "Changing the Deal while Keeping the People," *Academy of Management Executive* 11 (1996), pp. 50–61; and M. A. Cavanaugh and R. Noe, "Antecedents and Consequences of the New Psychological Contract," *Journal of Organizational Behavior* 20 (1999), pp. 323–40.

48. Bureau of Labor Statistics, "Employee Tenure in 2008," news release, September 26, 2008, http://www.bls.gov/cps/.

49. Bureau of Labor Statistics (BLS), "Charting the U.S. Labor Market in 2006," *Current Population Survey*, www.bls.gov, last modified September 28, 2007; BLS, "Alternative Employment Arrangements and Worker Preferences," *Monthly Labor Review: The Editor's Desk*, August 4, 2005, www.bls.gov, last updated August 8, 2005; and BLS, "Independent Contractors in 2005," *Monthly Labor Review: The Editor's Desk*, July 29, 2005, www.bls.gov, last updated August 1, 2005.

50. Benjamin J. Romano, "Microsoft's Other Workers," *Seattle Times*, March 4, 2009, Business & Company Resource Center, http://galenet.galegroup.com.

51. P. Kiger, "Flexibility to the Fullest," *Workforce Management*, September 25, 2006, pp. 1, 16–23.

Providing Equal Employment Opportunity and a Safe Workplace

What Do I Need to Know?

After reading this chapter, you should be able to:

LO1 Explain how the three branches of government regulate human resource management.

LO2 Summarize the major federal laws requiring equal employment opportunity.

LO3 Identify the federal agencies that enforce equal employment opportunity, and describe the role of each.

LO4 Describe ways employers can avoid illegal discrimination and provide reasonable accommodation.

LO5 Define sexual harassment, and tell how employers can eliminate or minimize it.

LO6 Explain employers' duties under the Occupational Safety and Health Act.

LO7 Describe the role of the Occupational Safety and Health Administration.

LO8 Discuss ways employers promote worker safety and health.

Introduction

More than a dozen years ago, the giant consulting and accounting firm Deloitte was urged to look more like its clients. While most Deloitte partners were white men, they were increasingly meeting with men and women of all races and ethnic backgrounds. Those clients were wondering why Deloitte remained so unrepresentative of the U.S. and global workforce.

Deloitte's response has included a women's initiative program, which combines four activities: A mentoring program develops female employees' professional and leadership ability. Women are intentionally placed in speaking engagements and other opportunities to be more visible to Deloitte's clients. Diversity groups for women and minority employees meet to develop a sense of community. And the firm has committed to innovation in the way it welcomes women as employees and as clients.

With regard to racial and ethnic diversity, Deloitte remains a mostly white firm. But recently, Deloitte expanded recruiting efforts beyond the nation's top universities to include community colleges. While some people assume these schools don't attract top students, for many bright, hardworking individuals, they are an affordable way to begin preparing for a career. Deloitte hopes that recruiting at community colleges will introduce the firm to students with high potential who also represent a more diverse pool of talent. Deloitte intends to connect with them early on and guide them toward careers in accounting and management consulting. The company also has a mentoring program that identifies high-potential minority employees and coaches them in navigating the corporate environment.[1] Such efforts will translate into results when clients start to say that Deloitte's people really can relate to them.

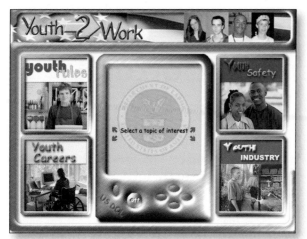

One way the executive branch communicates information about laws is through Web sites like Youth2Work. This site is designed to provide young workers with a safe workplace by making them aware of laws that, for example, restrict the amount of work they can do and the machinery they can operate.

As we saw in Chapter 1, human resource management takes place in the context of the company's goals and society's expectations for how a company should operate. In the United States, the federal government has set some limits on how an organization can practice human resource management. Among these limits are requirements intended to prevent discrimination in hiring and employment practices and to protect the health and safety of workers while they are on the job. Questions about a company's compliance with these requirements can result in lawsuits and negative publicity that often cause serious problems for a company's success and survival. Conversely, a company that skillfully navigates the maze of regulations can gain an advantage over its competitors. A further advantage may go to companies that, like Deloitte, go beyond mere legal compliance to find ways of linking fair employment and worker safety to business goals such as building a workforce that is highly motivated and attuned to customers.

This chapter provides an overview of the ways government bodies regulate equal employment opportunity and workplace safety and health. It introduces you to major laws affecting employers in these areas, as well as the agencies charged with enforcing those laws. The chapter also discusses ways organizations can develop practices that ensure they are in compliance with the laws.

One point to make at the outset is that managers often want a list of dos and don'ts that will keep them out of legal trouble. Some managers rely on strict rules such as "Don't ever ask a female applicant if she is married," rather than learning the reasons behind those rules. Clearly, certain practices are illegal or at least inadvisable, and this chapter will provide guidance on avoiding such practices. However, managers who merely focus on how to avoid breaking the law are not thinking about how to be ethical or how to acquire and use human resources in the best way to carry out the company's mission. This chapter introduces ways to think more creatively and constructively about fair employment and workplace safety.

LO1 Explain how the three branches of government regulate human resource management.

Regulation of Human Resource Management

All three branches of the U.S. government—legislative, executive, and judicial— play an important role in creating a legal environment for human resource management. The legislative branch, which consists of the two houses of Congress, has enacted a number of laws governing human resource activities. Senators and U.S. Representatives generally develop these laws in response to perceived societal needs. For example, during the civil rights movement of the early 1960s, Congress enacted Title VII of the Civil Rights Act to ensure that various minority groups received equal opportunities in many areas of life.

The executive branch, including the many regulatory agencies that the president oversees, is responsible for enforcing the laws passed by Congress. Agencies do this through a variety of actions, from drawing up regulations detailing how to abide by the laws to filing suit against alleged violators. Some federal agencies involved in regulating human resource management include the Equal Employment Opportunity Commission and the Occupational Safety and Health Administration. In addition, the president may issue executive orders, which are directives issued solely by the president, without requiring congressional approval. Some executive orders regulate the activities of organizations that have contracts with the federal government. For example, President Lyndon Johnson signed Executive Order 11246, which requires all federal contractors and subcontractors to engage in affirmative-action programs designed to hire and promote women and minorities. (We will explore the topic of affirmative action later in this chapter.)

The judicial branch, the federal court system, influences employment law by interpreting the law and holding trials concerning violations of the law. The U.S. Supreme Court, at the head of the judicial branch, is the court of final appeal. Decisions made by the Supreme Court are binding; they can be overturned only through laws passed by Congress. The Civil Rights Act of 1991 was partly designed to overturn Supreme Court decisions.

Equal Employment Opportunity

Among the most significant efforts to regulate human resource management are those aimed at achieving **equal employment opportunity (EEO)**—the condition in which all individuals have an equal chance for employment, regardless of their race, color, religion, sex, age, disability, or national origin. The federal government's efforts to create equal employment opportunity include constitutional amendments, legislation, and executive orders, as well as court decisions that interpret the laws. Table 3.1 summarizes major EEO laws discussed in this chapter. These are U.S. laws; equal employment laws in other countries may differ.

Constitutional Amendments

Two amendments to the U.S. Constitution—the Thirteenth and Fourteenth—have implications for human resource management. The Thirteenth Amendment abolished slavery in the United States. Though you might be hard-pressed to cite an example of race-based slavery in the United States today, the Thirteenth Amendment has been applied in cases where discrimination involved the "badges" (symbols) and "incidents" of slavery.

The Fourteenth Amendment forbids the states from taking life, liberty, or property without due process of law and prevents the states from denying equal protection of the laws. Recently it has been applied to the protection of whites in charges of reverse discrimination. In a case that marked the early stages of a move away from race-based quotas, Alan Bakke alleged that as a white man he had been discriminated against in the selection of entrants to the University of California at Davis medical school.[2] The university had set aside 16 of the available 100 places for "disadvantaged" applicants who were members of racial minority groups. Under this quota system, Bakke was able to compete for only 84 positions, whereas a minority applicant was able to compete for all 100. The federal court ruled in favor of Bakke, noting that this quota system had violated white individuals' right to equal protection under the law.

An important point regarding the Fourteenth Amendment is that it applies only to the decisions or actions of the government or of private groups whose activities are

LO2 Summarize the major federal laws requiring equal employment opportunity.

Equal Employment Opportunity (EEO)
The condition in which all individuals have an equal chance for employment, regardless of their race, color, religion, sex, age, disability, or national origin.

Table 3.1

Summary of Major EEO Laws and Regulations

ACT	REQUIREMENTS	COVERS	ENFORCEMENT AGENCY
Thirteenth Amendment	Abolished slavery	All individuals	Court system
Fourteenth Amendment	Provides equal protection for all citizens and requires due process in state action	State actions (e.g., decisions of government organizations)	Court system
Civil Rights Acts (CRAs) of 1866 and 1871 (as amended)	Grant all citizens the right to make, perform, modify, and terminate contracts and enjoy all benefits, terms, and conditions of the contractual relationship	All individuals	Court system
Equal Pay Act of 1963	Requires that men and women performing equal jobs receive equal pay	Employers engaged in interstate commerce	EEOC
Title VII of CRA	Forbids discrimination based on race, color, religion, sex, or national origin	Employers with 15 or more employees working 20 or more weeks per year; labor unions; and employment agencies	EEOC
Age Discrimination in Employment Act of 1967	Prohibits discrimination in employment against individuals 40 years of age and older	Employers with 15 or more employees working 20 or more weeks per year; labor unions; employment agencies; federal government	EEOC
Rehabilitation Act of 1973	Requires affirmative action in the employment of individuals with disabilities	Government agencies; federal contractors and subcontractors with contracts greater than $2,500	OFCCP
Pregnancy Discrimination Act of 1978	Treats discrimination based on pregnancy-related conditions as illegal sex discrimination	All employees covered by Title VII	EEOC
Americans with Disabilities Act of 1990	Prohibits discrimination against individuals with disabilities	Employers with more than 15 employees	EEOC
Executive Order 11246	Requires affirmative action in hiring women and minorities	Federal contractors and subcontractors with contracts greater than $10,000	OFCCP
Civil Rights Act of 1991	Prohibits discrimination (same as Title VII)	Same as Title VII, plus applies Section 1981 to employment discrimination cases	EEOC
Uniformed Services Employment and Reemployment Rights Act of 1994	Requires rehiring of employees who are absent for military service, with training and accommodations as needed	Veterans and members of reserve components	Veterans' Employment and Training Service
Genetic Information Non-discrimination Act of 2008	Prohibits discrimination because of genetic information	Employers with 15 or more employees	EEOC

deemed government actions. Thus, a person could file a claim under the Fourteenth Amendment if he or she had been fired from a state university (a government organization) but not if the person had been fired by a private employer.

Legislation

The periods following the Civil War and during the civil rights movement of the 1960s were times when many voices in society pressed for equal rights for all without regard to a person's race or sex. In response, Congress passed laws designed to provide for equal opportunity. In later years, Congress has passed additional laws that have extended EEO protection more broadly.

Civil Rights Acts of 1866 and 1871

During Reconstruction, Congress passed two Civil Rights Acts to further the Thirteenth Amendment's goal of abolishing slavery. The Civil Rights Act of 1866 granted all persons the same property rights as white citizens, as well as the right to enter into and enforce contracts. Courts have interpreted the latter right as including employment contracts. The Civil Rights Act of 1871 granted all citizens the right to sue in federal court if they feel they have been deprived of some civil right. Although these laws might seem outdated, they are still used because they allow the plaintiff to recover both compensatory and punitive damages (that is, payment to compensate them for their loss plus additional damages to punish the offender).

Equal Pay Act of 1963

Under the Equal Pay Act of 1963, if men and women in an organization are doing equal work, the employer must pay them equally. The act defines *equal* in terms of skill, effort, responsibility, and working conditions. However, the act allows for reasons why men and women performing the same job might be paid differently. If the pay differences result from differences in seniority, merit, quantity or quality of production, or any factor other than sex (such as participating in a training program or working the night shift), then the differences are legal.

Title VII of the Civil Rights Act of 1964

The major law regulating equal employment opportunity in the United States is Title VII of the Civil Rights Act of 1964. Title VII directly resulted from the civil rights movement of the early 1960s, led by such individuals as Dr. Martin Luther King Jr. To ensure that employment opportunities would be based on character or ability rather than on race, Congress wrote and passed Title VII, and President Lyndon Johnson signed it into law in 1964. The law is enforced by the **Equal Employment Opportunity Commission (EEOC),** an agency of the Department of Justice.

Title VII prohibits employers from discriminating against individuals because of their race, color, religion, sex, or national origin. An employer may not use these characteristics as the basis for not hiring someone, for firing someone, or for discriminating against them in the terms of their pay, conditions of employment, or privileges of employment. In addition, an employer may not use these characteristics to limit, segregate, or classify employees or job applicants in any way that would deprive any individual of employment opportunities or otherwise adversely affect his or her status as an employee. The act applies to organizations that employ 15 or

Equal Employment Opportunity Commission (EEOC) Agency of the Department of Justice charged with enforcing Title VII of the Civil Rights Act of 1964 and other antidiscrimination laws.

more persons working 20 or more weeks a year and that are involved in interstate commerce, as well as state and local governments, employment agencies, and labor organizations.

Title VII also states that employers may not retaliate against employees for either "opposing" a perceived illegal employment practice or "participating in a proceeding" related to an alleged illegal employment practice. *Opposition* refers to expressing to someone through proper channels that you believe an illegal employment act has taken place or is taking place. *Participation in a proceeding* refers to testifying in an investigation, hearing, or court proceeding regarding an illegal employment act. The purpose of this provision is to protect employees from employers' threats and other forms of intimidation aimed at discouraging employees from bringing to light acts they believe to be illegal. Companies that violate this prohibition may be liable for punitive damages.

Age Discrimination in Employment Act (ADEA)

One category of employees not covered by Title VII is older workers. Older workers sometimes are concerned that they will be the targets of discrimination, especially when a company is downsizing. Older workers tend to be paid more, so a company that wants to cut labor costs may save by laying off its oldest workers. To counter such discrimination, Congress in 1967 passed the Age Discrimination in Employment Act (ADEA), which prohibits discrimination against workers who are over the age of 40. Similar to Title VII, the ADEA outlaws hiring, firing, setting compensation rates, or other employment decisions based on a person's age being over 40.

Many firms have offered early-retirement incentives as an alternative or supplement to involuntary layoffs. Because this approach to workforce reduction focuses on older employees, who would be eligible for early retirement, it may be in violation of the ADEA. Early-retirement incentives require that participating employees sign an agreement waiving their rights to sue under the ADEA. Courts have tended to uphold the use of early-retirement incentives and waivers as long as the individuals were not coerced into signing the agreements, the agreements were presented in a way the employees could understand (including technical legal requirements such as the ages of discharged and retained employees in the employee's work unit), and the employees had enough time to make a decision.[3] However, the Equal Employment Opportunity Commission recently expanded the interpretation of discriminatory retirement policies when it charged a law firm with having an illegal "age-based retirement policy." According to the charges, Sidley Austin Brown & Wood, based in Chicago, gave more than 30 lawyers older than age 40 notice that their status was being lowered from partner to special counsel or counsel and that they would be expected to leave the firm in a few years. The firm described the action as a way to provide more opportunities for young lawyers, but lawyers who were pressured to retire contended they were forced out as a way to boost profits by replacing highly paid partners with less-experienced, lower-paid lawyers. Sidley Austin settled the suit at a cost of $27.5 million.[4] One practical way to defend against such claims is to establish performance-related criteria for layoffs, rather than age- or salary-related criteria.

Age discrimination complaints make up a large percentage of the complaints filed with the Equal Employment Opportunity Commission, and whenever the economy is slow, the number of complaints grows. For example, as shown in Figure 3.1, the number of age discrimination cases jumped in 2008 and 2009, when many firms were

Figure 3.1

Age Discrimination Complaints, 1994–2009

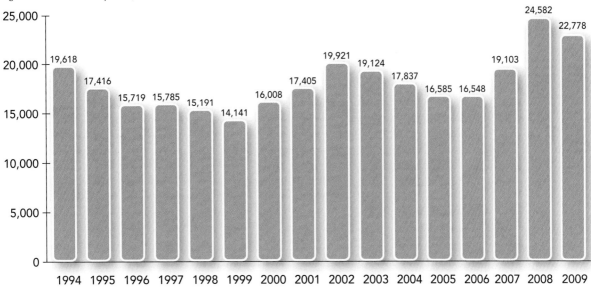

SOURCE: Equal Employment Opportunity Commission, http://www1.eeoc.gov//eeoc/statistics/enforcement/.

downsizing. Another increase in age discrimination claims accompanied the economic slowdown at the beginning of the 2000s.

In today's environment, in which firms are seeking talented individuals to achieve the company's goals, older employees can be a tremendous pool of potential resources. McDonald's recently did some research that suggests just how valuable these resources can be, at least in the fast-food business. The company combined information about employees' ages and engagement with performance data for 635 of its outlets. The data showed that in the restaurants with a higher average age of employees, performance was better across several measures, including cleanliness, sales, customer satisfaction, and number of customer visits. Investigating further, the researchers found that performance was best in restaurants with at least one employee over age 60. Looking into employee attitudes, the researchers found that in these restaurants, there was more of a feeling that the crew was a family, an attitude that might be driving greater commitment to quality.[5]

Vocational Rehabilitation Act of 1973

In 1973, Congress passed the Vocational Rehabilitation Act to enhance employment opportunity for individuals with disabilities. This act covers executive agencies and contractors and subcontractors that receive more than $2,500 annually from the federal government. These organizations must engage in affirmative action for individuals with disabilities. **Affirmative action** is an organization's active effort to find opportunities to hire or promote people in a particular group. Thus, Congress intended this act to encourage employers to recruit qualified individuals with disabilities and to make reasonable accommodations to all those people to become active members of the labor market. The Department of Labor's Employment Standards Administration enforces this act.

Affirmative Action
An organization's active effort to find opportunities to hire or promote people in a particular group.

Vietnam Era Veteran's Readjustment Act of 1974

Similar to the Rehabilitation Act, the Vietnam Era Veteran's Readjustment Act of 1974 requires federal contractors and subcontractors to take affirmative action toward employing veterans of the Vietnam War (those serving between August 5, 1964, and May 7, 1975). The Office of Federal Contract Compliance Procedures, discussed later in this chapter, has authority to enforce this act.

Pregnancy Discrimination Act of 1978

An amendment to Title VII of the Civil Rights Act of 1964, the Pregnancy Discrimination Act of 1978 defines discrimination on the basis of pregnancy, childbirth, or related medical conditions to be a form of illegal sex discrimination. According to the EEOC, this means that employers must treat "women who are pregnant or affected by related conditions . . . in the same manner as other applicants or employees with similar abilities or limitations."[6] For example, an employer may not refuse to hire a woman because she is pregnant. Decisions about work absences or accommodations must be based on the same policies as the organization uses for other disabilities. Benefits, including health insurance, should cover pregnancy and related medical conditions in the same way that it covers other medical conditions.

Americans with Disabilities Act (ADA) of 1990

One of the farthest-reaching acts concerning the management of human resources is the Americans with Disabilities Act. This 1990 law protects individuals with disabilities from being discriminated against in the workplace. It prohibits discrimination based on disability in all employment practices such as job application procedures, hiring, firing, promotions, compensation, and training. Other employment activities

Figure 3.2

Disabilities Associated with Complaints Filed under ADA

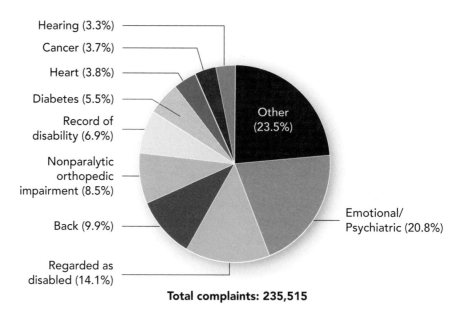

Hearing (3.3%)
Cancer (3.7%)
Heart (3.8%)
Diabetes (5.5%)
Record of disability (6.9%)
Nonparalytic orthopedic impairment (8.5%)
Back (9.9%)
Regarded as disabled (14.1%)
Other (23.5%)
Emotional/ Psychiatric (20.8%)

Total complaints: 235,515

SOURCE: Equal Employment Opportunity Commission, "ADA Charge Data by Impairments/Bases: Receipts," data for 2009, http://www1.eeoc.gov.

Best Practices

VERIZON CONNECTS WITH DISABLED WORKERS

focus on *social responsibility*

Like many companies, Verizon Wireless until recently tackled accommodations for disabled employees purely on a case-by-case basis. But experiences with some disabled employees helped the HR department realize that if it planned ahead for addressing this need, it could do so in a way that saves money and retains employees. So Verizon established policies for helping employees continue working if they become disabled. These policies include short-term leave if an employee needs time to adjust emotional or physically to a new disability, as well as procedures for assessing the need for accommodations and making adjustments to job requirements and the workplace. The aim is to keep valued employees and enabling them to continue meeting their pre-disability performance targets.

Verizon put those policies in action when a supervisor of customer service representatives discovered she had progressive corneal degeneration. As her vision continued to deteriorate, the supervisor became legally blind, although she retained some limited vision. As this employee coped with her vision problems and associated fears, the HR staff swung into action. They brought together company specialists in human resources, information technology, and facilities management in meetings with a disability management consultant to determine what accommodations the supervisor could benefit from and how to set them up. They identified technologies such as computer screen readers and magnification, and they trained the supervisor how to use them. They also adapted her job requirements: instead of using computer graphics to monitor statistics about her employees' performance, the supervisor reviews performance with the traditional method of listening in on calls, observing the representatives in action, and writing up individual reports on the employees. While the supervisor was making these changes, Verizon temporarily reduced the number of employees reporting to her; as she developed her competence with the new tools and procedures, Verizon restored employees to her team. The transition took about six months.

Verizon follows up with its disabled employees and measures the results of its policy. In the first few years of this systematic approach, Verizon estimates that it has spent about $60,000 to accommodate employees and saved $160,000 in what it would have spent to find and train replacements if disabled employees had left the company.

Source: J. Adam Shoemaker, "A 'Welcome Back' for Workers with Disabilities," *HR Magazine,* October 2009, pp. 30–32.

covered by the ADA are employment advertising, recruitment, tenure, layoff, leave, and fringe benefits.

The ADA defines **disability** as a physical or mental impairment that substantially limits one or more major life activities, a record of having such an impairment, or being regarded as having such an impairment. The first part of the definition refers to individuals who have serious disabilities—such as epilepsy, blindness, deafness, or paralysis—that affect their ability to perform Major bodily functions and major life activities such as walking, seeing, performing manual tasks, learning, caring for oneself, and working. The second part refers to individuals who have a history of disability, such as someone who has had cancer but is currently in remission, someone with a history of mental illness, and someone with a history of heart disease. The third part of the definition, "being regarded as having a disability," refers to people's subjective reactions, as in the case of someone who is severely disfigured; an employer might hesitate to hire such a person on the grounds that people will react negatively to such an employee.[7]

Disability
Under the Americans with Disabilities Act, a physical or mental impairment that substantially limits one or more major life activities, a record of having such an impairment, or being regarded as having such an impairment.

The ADA covers specific physiological disabilities such as cosmetic disfigurement and anatomical loss affecting the body's systems. In addition, it covers mental and psychological disorders such as mental retardation, organic brain syndrome, emotional or mental illness, and learning disabilities. Conditions not covered include obesity, substance abuse, eye and hair color, and lefthandedness.[8] Also, if a person needs ordinary eyeglasses or contact lenses to perform each major life activity with little or no difficulty, the person is not considered disabled under the ADA. (In determining whether an impairment is substantially limiting, mitigating measures, such as medicine, hearing aids, and prosthetics, once could be considered but now must be ignored.) Figure 3.2, on page 66, shows the types of disabilities associated with complaints filed under the ADA in 2009.

In contrast to other EEO laws, the ADA goes beyond prohibiting discrimination to require that employers take steps to accommodate individuals covered under the act. If a disabled person is selected to perform a job, the employer (perhaps in consultation with the disabled employee) determines what accommodations are necessary for the employee to perform the job. Examples include using ramps and lifts to make facilities accessible, redesigning job procedures, and providing technology such as TDD lines for hearing-impaired employees. Some employers have feared that accommodations under the ADA would be expensive. However, the Department of Labor has found that two-thirds of accommodations cost less than $500, and many of these cost nothing.[9] As technology advances, the cost of many technologies has been falling. The "Best Practices" box provides an example of a company where accommodating disabilities has been well worth the effort.

Civil Rights Act of 1991

In 1991 Congress broadened the relief available to victims of discrimination by passing a Civil Rights Act (CRA 1991). CRA 1991 amends Title VII of the Civil Rights Act of 1964, as well as the Civil Rights Act of 1866, the Americans with Disabilities Act, and the Age Discrimination in Employment Act of 1967. One major change in EEO law under CRA 1991 has been the addition of compensatory and punitive damages in cases of discrimination under Title VII and the Americans with Disabilities Act. Before CRA 1991, Title VII limited damage claims to *equitable relief*, which courts have defined to include back pay, lost benefits, front pay in some cases, and attorney's fees and costs. CRA 1991 allows judges to award compensatory and punitive damages when the plaintiff proves the discrimination was intentional or reckless. Compensatory damages include such things as future monetary loss, emotional pain, suffering, and loss of enjoyment of life. Punitive damages are a punishment; by requiring violators to pay the plaintiff an amount beyond the actual losses suffered, the courts try to discourage employers from discriminating.

Recognizing that one or a few discrimination cases could put an organization out of business, and so harm many innocent employees, Congress has limited the amount

Table 3.2

Maximum Punitive Damages Allowed under the Civil Rights Act of 1991

EMPLOYER SIZE	DAMAGE LIMIT
14 to 100 employees	$ 50,000
101 to 200 employees	100,000
201 to 500 employees	200,000
More than 500 employees	300,000

of punitive damages. As shown in Table 3.2, the amount of damages depends on the size of the organization charged with discrimination. The limits range from $50,000 per violation at a small company (14 to 100 employees) to $300,000 at a company with more than 500 employees. A company has to pay punitive damages only if it discriminated intentionally or with malice or reckless indifference to the employee's federally protected rights.

Uniformed Services Employment and Reemployment Rights Act of 1994

When members of the armed services were called up following the terrorist attacks of September 2001, a 1994 employment law—the Uniformed Services Employment and Reemployment Rights Act (USERRA)—assumed new significance. Under this law, employers must reemploy workers who left jobs to fulfill military duties for up to five years. When service members return from active

Aric Miller, an Army reservist sergeant, was deployed for service with the 363rd military police unit in Iraq for over a year. When he returned to the states, he was able to resume his job as an elementary school teacher thanks to the 1994 Uniformed Services Employment and Reemployment Rights Act. The act requires employers to reemploy service members in the job they would have held if they had not left to serve in the military. Why is this act important?

duty, the employer must reemploy them in the job they would have held if they had not left to serve in the military, providing them with the same seniority, status, and pay rate they would have earned if their employment had not been interrupted. Disabled veterans also have up to two years to recover from injuries received during their service or training, and employers must make reasonable accommodations for a remaining disability.

Service members also have duties under USERRA. Before leaving for duty, they are to give their employers notice, if possible. After their service, the law sets time limits for applying to be reemployed. Depending on the length of service, these limits range from approximately 2 to 90 days. Veterans with complaints under USERRA can obtain assistance from the Veterans' Employment and Training Service of the Department of Labor.

Genetic Information Nondiscrimination Act of 2008

Thanks to the decoding of the human genome and developments in the fields of genetics and medicine, researchers can now identify more and more genes associated with risks for developing particular diseases or disorders. While learning that you are at risk of, say, colon cancer may be a useful motivator to take precautions, the information opens up some risks as well. For example, what if companies began using genetic screening to identify and avoid hiring job candidates who are at risk of developing costly diseases? Concerns such as this prompted Congress to pass the Genetic Information Nondiscrimination Act (GINA) of 2008.

Under GINA's requirements, companies with 15 or more employees may not use genetic information in making decisions related to the terms, conditions, or privileges of employment—for example, decisions to hire, promote, or lay off a worker. This genetic information includes information about a person's genetic tests, genetic tests of the person's family members, and family medical histories. Furthermore, employers may not intentionally obtain this information, except in certain limited situations (such as an employee voluntarily participating in a wellness program or requesting time off to care for a sick relative). If companies do acquire such information, they must keep the information confidential. The law also forbids harassment of any employee because of that person's genetic information.

Executive Orders

Two executive orders that directly affect human resource management are Executive Order 11246, issued by Lyndon Johnson, and Executive Order 11478, issued by Richard Nixon. Executive Order 11246 prohibits federal contractors and subcontractors from discriminating based on race, color, religion, sex, or national origin. In addition, employers whose contracts meet minimum size requirements must engage in affirmative action to ensure against discrimination. Those receiving more than $10,000 from the federal government must take affirmative action, and those with contracts exceeding $50,000 must develop a written affirmative-action plan for each of their establishments. This plan must be in place within 120 days of the beginning of the contract. This executive order is enforced by the Office of Federal Contract Compliance Procedures.

Executive Order 11478 requires the federal government to base all its employment policies on merit and fitness. It specifies that race, color, sex, religion, and national origin may not be considered. Along with the government, the act covers all contractors and subcontractors doing at least $10,000 worth of business with the federal government. The U.S. Office of Personnel Management is in charge of ensuring that the government is in compliance, and the relevant government agencies are responsible for ensuring the compliance of contractors and subcontractors.

LO3 Identify the federal agencies that enforce equal employment opportunity, and describe the role of each.

The Government's Role in Providing for Equal Employment Opportunity

At a minimum, equal employment opportunity requires that employers comply with EEO laws. To enforce those laws, the executive branch of the federal government uses the Equal Employment Opportunity Commission and the Office of Federal Contract Compliance Procedures.

Equal Employment Opportunity Commission (EEOC)

The Equal Employment Opportunity Commission (EEOC) is responsible for enforcing most of the EEO laws, including Title VII, the Equal Pay Act, and the Americans with Disabilities Act. To do this, the EEOC investigates and resolves complaints about discrimination, gathers information, and issues guidelines.

When individuals believe they have been discriminated against, they may file a complaint with the EEOC or a similar state agency. They must file the complaint within 180 days of the incident. Figure 3.3 illustrates the number of charges filed with the EEOC for different types of discrimination in 2009. Many individuals file more than one type of charge (for instance, both race discrimination and retaliation), so the total number of complaints filed with the EEOC is less than the total of the amounts in each category.

After the EEOC receives a charge of discrimination, it has 60 days to investigate the complaint. If the EEOC either does not believe the complaint to be valid or fails to complete the investigation within 60 days, the individual has the right to

Figure 3.3

Types of Charges Filed with the EEOC

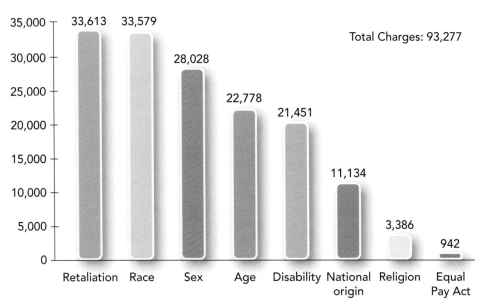

Total Charges: 93,277

SOURCE: Equal Employment Opportunity Commission, "Charge Statistics FY 1997 through FY 2009," www.eeoc.gov, accessed March 2, 2010.

sue in federal court. If the EEOC determines that discrimination has taken place, its representatives will attempt to work with the individual and the employer to try to achieve a reconciliation without a lawsuit. Sometimes the EEOC enters into a consent decree with the discriminating organization. This decree is an agreement between the agency and the organization that the organization will cease certain discriminatory practices and possibly institute additional affirmative-action practices to rectify its history of discrimination. A settlement with the EEOC can be costly, including such remedies as back pay, reinstatement of the employee, and promotions.

If the attempt at a settlement fails, the EEOC has two options. It may issue a "right to sue" letter to the alleged victim. This letter certifies that the agency has investigated the victim's allegations and found them to be valid. The EEOC's other option, which it uses less often, is to aid the alleged victim in bringing suit in federal court.

The EEOC also monitors organizations' hiring practices. Each year organizations that are government contractors or subcontractors or have 100 or more employees must file an Employer Information Report (EEO-1) with the EEOC. The **EEO-1 report** is an online questionnaire requesting the number of employees in each job category (such as managers, professionals, and laborers), broken down by their status as male or female, Hispanic or non-Hispanic, and members of various racial groups. The EEOC analyzes those reports to identify patterns of discrimination, which the agency can then attack through class-action lawsuits. Employers must display EEOC posters detailing employment rights. These posters must be in prominent and accessible locations—for example, in a company's cafeteria or near its time clock. Also, employers should retain copies of documents related to employment decisions—recruitment letters, announcements of jobs, completed job applications, selections for training, and so on. Employers must keep these records for at least six months or until a complaint is resolved, whichever is later.

EEO-1 Report
The EEOC's Employer Information Report, which counts employees sorted by job category, sex, ethnicity, and race.

Besides resolving complaints and suing alleged violators, the EEOC issues guidelines designed to help employers determine when their decisions violate the laws enforced by the EEOC. These guidelines are not laws themselves. However, the courts give great consideration to them when hearing employment discrimination cases. For example, the **Uniform Guidelines on Employee Selection Procedures** is a set of guidelines issued by the EEOC and other government agencies. The guidelines identify ways an organization should develop and administer its system for selecting employees so as not to violate Title VII. The courts often refer to the *Uniform Guidelines* to determine whether a company has engaged in discriminatory conduct. Similarly, in the *Federal Register*, the EEOC has published guidelines providing details about what the agency will consider illegal and legal in the treatment of disabled individuals under the Americans with Disabilities Act.

Uniform Guidelines on Employee Selection Procedures
Guidelines issued by the EEOC and other agencies to identify how an organization should develop and administer its system for selecting employees so as not to violate antidiscrimination laws.

Office of Federal Contract Compliance Procedures (OFCCP)

The **Office of Federal Contract Compliance Procedures (OFCCP)** is the agency responsible for enforcing the executive orders that cover companies doing business with the federal government. As we stated earlier in the chapter, businesses with contracts for more than $50,000 may not discriminate in employment based on race, color, religion, national origin, or sex, and they must have a written affirmative-action plan on file. This plan must include three basic components:

Office of Federal Contract Compliance Procedures (OFCCP)
The agency responsible for enforcing the executive orders that cover companies doing business with the federal government.

1. *Utilization analysis*—A comparison of the race, sex, and ethnic composition of the employer's workforce with that of the available labor supply. The percentages in the employer's workforce should not be greatly lower than the percentages in the labor supply.
2. *Goals and timetables*—The percentages of women and minorities the organization seeks to employ in each job group, and the dates by which the percentages are to be attained. These are meant to be more flexible than quotas, requiring only that the employer have goals and be seeking to achieve the goals.
3. *Action steps*—A plan for how the organization will meet its goals. Besides working toward its goals for hiring women and minorities, the company must take affirmative steps toward hiring Vietnam veterans and individuals with disabilities.

Each year, the OFCCP audits government contractors to ensure they are actively pursuing the goals in their plans. The OFCCP examines the plan and conducts on-site visits to examine how individual employees perceive the company's affirmative-action policies. If the agency finds that a contractor or subcontractor is not complying with the requirements, it has several options. It may notify the EEOC (if there is evidence of a violation of Title VII), advise the Department of Justice to begin criminal proceedings, request that the Secretary of Labor cancel or suspend any current contracts with the company, and forbid the firm from bidding on future contracts. For a company that depends on the federal government for a sizable share of its business, that last penalty is severe.

LO4 Describe ways employers can avoid illegal discrimination and provide reasonable accommodation.

Businesses' Role in Providing for Equal Employment Opportunity

Rare is the business owner or manager who wants to wait for the government to identify that the business has failed to provide for equal employment opportunity. Instead, out of motives ranging from concern for fairness to the desire to avoid costly lawsuits

VIDEO RÉSUMÉS—PERILOUS POLICY?

Internet technology makes it easy for almost anyone to shoot a video and post it online. Some people are applying their technical talents to their own careers by creating video résumés. These résumés let people tell their story creatively and just might set a job applicant apart from the crowd.

The risk is that the technique might also set a candidate apart from the crowd in a harmful way. Employers know they must avoid discrimination based on race, color, national origin, disability, and so on. But if the video shows an applicant from a group the employer is biased against, it might be all too easy for that

employer to think of a reason not to interview the candidate.

On the up side, some experts think a well-executed video résumé can help a person shine. For Pat Woods, whose independent employment agency serves a primarily African American clientele, video résumés are a signal of keeping up with the times, as well as a chance to gain an audience. Video producer Alan Naumann says a professionally made video can be a vehicle for actually showing the job candidate in action—demonstrating skills or interacting with people in the hiring company's customer population.

In a recent survey by Vault.com, 89 percent of employers said they would look at a video résumé. Yet, companies crafting a policy for this use of technology should consider not only the benefits but also the possible drawbacks.

Source: Aysha Hussain, "Do Video Résumés Help or Lead to Discrimination?" *DiversityInc*, June 26, 2007, www.diversityinc.com; Steve Giegerich, "'Cruel' Market Forces Jobs Agent to Improvise," *St. Louis Post-Dispatch*, October 16, 2009, Business & Company Resource Center, http://galenet.galegroup.com; and Alan Naumann, "Résumé or Visumé?" *EventDV*, November 2009, Business & Company Resource Center, http://galenet.galegroup.com.

and settlements, most companies recognize the importance of complying with these laws. Often, management depends on the expertise of human resource professionals to help in identifying how to comply. These professionals can help organizations take steps to avoid discrimination and provide reasonable accommodation.

Avoiding Discrimination

How would you know if you had been discriminated against? Decisions about human resources are so complex that discrimination is often difficult to identify and prove. However, legal scholars and court rulings have arrived at some ways to show evidence of discrimination.

Disparate Treatment

One sign of discrimination is **disparate treatment**—differing treatment of individuals, where the differences are based on the individuals' race, color, religion, sex, national origin, age, or disability status. For example, disparate treatment would include hiring or promoting one person over an equally qualified person because of the individual's race. Or suppose a company fails to hire women with school-age children (claiming the women will be frequently absent) but hires men with school-age children. In that situation, the women are victims of disparate treatment, because they are being treated differently based on their sex. To sustain a claim of discrimination based on disparate treatment, the women would have to prove that the employer intended to discriminate.

Disparate Treatment
Differing treatment of individuals, where the differences are based on the individuals' race, color, religion, sex, national origin, age, or disability status.

To avoid disparate treatment, companies can evaluate the questions and investigations they use in making employment decisions. These should be applied equally. For example, if the company investigates conviction records of job applicants, it should investigate them for all applicants, not just for applicants from certain racial groups. Companies may want to avoid some types of questions altogether. For example, questions about marital status can cause problems, because interviewers may unfairly make different assumptions about men and women. (Common stereotypes about women have been that a married woman is less flexible or more likely to get pregnant than a single woman, in contrast to the assumption that a married man is more stable and committed to his work.)

Evaluating interview questions and decision criteria to make sure they are job related is especially important given that bias is not always intentional or even conscious. Researchers have conducted studies finding differences between what people *say* about how they evaluate others and how people actually *act* on their attitudes. For example, one set of studies applied a statistical method called conjoint analysis, which marketers use to see how consumers value particular packages of product features. In conjoint analysis, subjects indicate their preferences in a whole set of decisions (for example, cars with different features and prices), and researchers analyze the results to determine what various features are worth to the subjects. To mimic hiring decisions, the researchers invited subjects either to participate in a team game or to rate possible jobs they might take, and then described people with various qualities. Subjects selected which candidates they wanted on their team or which job they would take. Although subjects said they didn't care about teammates' weight, they actually sacrificed IQ scores to select thin teammates, and although subjects said they didn't care about their boss's sex, they selected lower-paying offers when the boss was male.[10] These results suggest that even when we doubt we have biases, it may be helpful to use decision-making tools that keep the focus on the most important criteria.

Is disparate treatment ever legal? The courts have held that in some situations, a factor such as sex or race may be a **bona fide occupational qualification (BFOQ)**, that is, a necessary (not merely preferred) qualification for performing a job. A typical example is a job that includes handing out towels in a locker room. Requiring that employees who perform this job in the women's locker room be female is a BFOQ. However, it is very difficult to think of many jobs where criteria such as sex and race are BFOQs. In a widely publicized case from the 1990s, Johnson Controls, a manufacturer of car batteries, instituted a "fetal protection" policy that excluded women of childbearing age from jobs that would expose them to lead, which can cause birth defects. Johnson Controls argued that the policy was intended to provide a safe workplace and that sex was a BFOQ for jobs that involved exposure to lead. However, the Supreme Court disagreed, ruling that BFOQs are limited to policies directly related to a worker's ability to do the job.[11]

Bona Fide Occupational Qualification (BFOQ)
A necessary (not merely preferred) qualification for performing a job.

Disparate Impact

Another way to measure discrimination is by identifying **disparate impact**— a condition in which employment practices are seemingly neutral yet disproportionately exclude a protected group from employment opportunities. In other words, the company's employment practices lack obvious discriminatory content, but they affect one group differently than others. Examples of employment practices that might result in disparate impact include pay, hiring, promotions, or training. A complaint

Disparate Impact
A condition in which employment practices are seemingly neutral yet disproportionately exclude a protected group from employment opportunities.

Example: A new hotel has to hire employees to fill 100 positions. Out of 300 total applicants, 200 are black and the remaining 100 are white. The hotel hires 40 of the black applicants and 60 of the white applicants.

Figure 3.4

Applying the Four-Fifths Rule

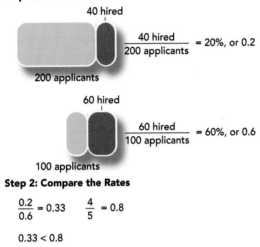

Step 1: Find the Rates

40 hired

$$\frac{40 \text{ hired}}{200 \text{ applicants}} = 20\%, \text{ or } 0.2$$

200 applicants

60 hired

$$\frac{60 \text{ hired}}{100 \text{ applicants}} = 60\%, \text{ or } 0.6$$

100 applicants

Step 2: Compare the Rates

$$\frac{0.2}{0.6} = 0.33 \qquad \frac{4}{5} = 0.8$$

$$0.33 < 0.8$$

The four-fifths requirement is not satisfied, providing evidence of discrimination.

was made by police officers and dispatchers in Jackson, Mississippi, that younger workers were receiving higher-percentage pay increases than the department was granting to older workers. Rather than intending to discriminate on the basis of age, the department was trying to bring starting pay into line with that of other police departments, but the policy had a disparate impact on different age groups.[12] A commonly used test of disparate impact is the **four-fifths rule,** which finds evidence of discrimination if the hiring rate for a minority group is less than four-fifths the hiring rate for the majority group. Keep in mind that this rule of thumb compares *rates* of hiring, not numbers of employees hired. Figure 3.4 illustrates how to apply the four-fifths rule.

If the four-fifths rule is not satisfied, it provides evidence of discrimination. To avoid declarations of practicing illegally, an organization must show that the disparate impact caused by the practice is based on a "business necessity." This is accomplished by showing that the employment practice is related to a legitimate business need or goal. In our example, the city could argue that disparate impact of the pay increases between younger and older police officers and dispatchers was necessary to keep pay within the city's budget. Of course, it is ultimately up to the court to decide if the evidence provided by the organization shows a real business necessity or is illegal. The court will also consider if other practices could have been used that would have met the business need or goal but not resulted in discrimination.

An important distinction between disparate treatment and disparate impact is the role of the employer's intent. Proving disparate treatment in court requires showing that the employer intended the disparate treatment, but a plaintiff need not show intent in the case of disparate impact. It is enough to show that the result of the treatment was unequal. For example, the requirements for some jobs, such as firefighters or pilots, have sometimes included a minimum height. Although the

Four-Fifths Rule
Rule of thumb that finds evidence of discrimination if an organization's hiring rate for a minority group is less than four-fifths the hiring rate for the majority group.

Regina Genwright talks to a voice-activated copier at the American Foundation for the Blind. The copier has a Braille keyboard and is wheelchair-accessible height. Equipment like this can help employers make reasonable accommodation for their disabled employees.

intent may be to identify people who can perform the jobs, an unintended result may be disparate impact on groups that are shorter than average. Women tend to be shorter than men, and people of Asian ancestry tend to be shorter than people of European ancestry.

One way employers can avoid disparate impact is to be sure that employment decisions are really based on relevant, valid measurements. If a job requires a certain amount of strength and stamina, the employer would want measures of strength and stamina, not simply individuals' height and weight. The latter numbers are easier to obtain but more likely to result in charges of discrimination. Assessing validity of a measure can be a highly technical exercise requiring the use of statistics. The essence of such an assessment is to show that test scores or other measurements are significantly related to job performance. In the case of age discrimination, the Supreme Court's recent ruling allows a somewhat easier standard: To justify disparate impact on older employees, the employer must be able to show that the impact results from "reasonable factors other than age."[13] The Jackson police department set up a pay policy to help it recruit new officers, and the Supreme Court considered this plan reasonable.

EEO Policy

Employers can also avoid discrimination and defend against claims of discrimination by establishing and enforcing an EEO policy. The policy should define and prohibit unlawful behaviors, as well as provide procedures for making and investigating complaints. The policy also should require that employees at all levels engage in fair conduct and respectful language. Derogatory language can support a court claim of discrimination.

Affirmative Action and Reverse Discrimination

In the search for ways to avoid discrimination, some organizations have used affirmative-action programs, usually to increase the representation of minorities. In its original form, affirmative action was meant as taking extra effort to attract and retain minority employees. These efforts have included extensively recruiting minority candidates on college campuses, advertising in minority-oriented publications, and providing educational and training opportunities to minorities. However, over the years, many organizations have resorted to quotas, or numerical goals for the proportion of certain minority groups, to ensure that their workforce mirrors the proportions of the labor market. Sometimes these organizations act voluntarily; in other cases, the quotas are imposed by the courts or the EEOC.

Whatever the reasons for these hiring programs, by increasing the proportion of minority or female candidates hired or promoted, they necessarily reduce the proportion of white or male candidates hired or promoted. In many cases, white and/or male individuals have fought against affirmative action and quotas, alleging what is called *reverse discrimination*. In other words, the organizations are allegedly discriminating against white males by preferring women and minorities. Affirmative action remains controversial in the United States. Surveys have found that Americans are least likely to favor affirmative action when programs use quotas.[14]

Figure 3.5

Examples of Reasonable Accommodations under the ADA

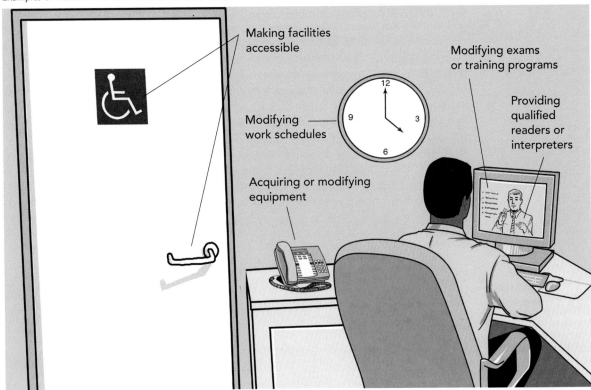

Note: Reasonable accommodations do *not* include hiring an unqualified person, lowering quality standards, or compromising co-workers' safety.

SOURCE: Based on Equal Employment Opportunity Commission, "The ADA: Your Responsibilities as an Employer," modified August 1, 2008, www.eeoc.gov.

Providing Reasonable Accommodation

Especially in situations involving religion and individuals with disabilities, equal employment opportunity may require that an employer make **reasonable accommodation.** In employment law, this term refers to an employer's obligation to do something to enable an otherwise qualified person to perform a job. The Vail Corporation recently settled a case in which a Christian supervisor claimed that the ski resort operator failed to make religious accommodation, because it scheduled her so she had to work during the time of her religious services, even though other employees were available to work during those hours. Under the terms of the settlement, the Vail Corporation agreed to accommodate the employee's religious practices with more flexible scheduling. The company also had to educate its employees on avoiding harassment, because the supervisor's manager and co-workers had created a hostile environment in which she repeatedly felt offended.[15]

In the context of religion, this principle recognizes that for some individuals, religious observations and practices may present a conflict with work duties, dress codes, or company practices. For example, some religions require head coverings, or individuals might need time off to observe the sabbath or other holy days, when the company might have them scheduled to work. When the employee has a legitimate

Reasonable Accommodation
An employer's obligation to do something to enable an otherwise qualified person to perform a job.

religious belief requiring accommodation, the employee should demonstrate this need to the employer. Assuming that it would not present an undue hardship, employers are required to accommodate such religious practices. They may have to adjust schedules so that employees do not have to work on days when their religion forbids it, or they may have to alter dress or grooming requirements.

For employees with disabilities, reasonable accommodations also vary according to the individuals' needs. As shown in Figure 3.5, employers may restructure jobs, make facilities in the workplace more accessible, modify equipment, or reassign an employee to a job that the person can perform. In some situations, a disabled individual may provide his or her own accommodation, which the employer allows, as in the case of a blind worker who brings a guide dog to work.

If accommodating a disability would require significant expense or difficulty, however, the employer may be exempt from the reasonable accommodation requirement (although the employer may have to defend this position in court). An accommodation is considered "reasonable" if it does not impose an undue hardship on the employer, such as an expense that is large in relation to a company's resources.

Preventing Sexual Harassment

LO5 Define sexual harassment, and tell how employers can eliminate or minimize it.

Sexual Harassment
Unwelcome sexual advances as defined by the EEOC.

Based on Title VII's prohibition of sex discrimination, the EEOC defines sexual harassment of employees as unlawful employment discrimination. **Sexual harassment** refers to unwelcome sexual advances. The EEOC has defined the types of behavior and the situations under which this behavior constitutes sexual harassment:

Unwelcome sexual advances, requests for sexual favors, and other verbal or physical contact of a sexual nature constitute sexual harassment when

1. Submission to such conduct is made either explicitly or implicitly a term or condition of an individual's employment,
2. Submission to or rejection of such conduct by an individual is used as the basis for employment decisions affecting such individual, or
3. Such conduct has the purpose or effect of unreasonably interfering with an individual's work performance or creating an intimidating, hostile, or offensive working environment.[16]

Under these guidelines, preventing sexual discrimination includes managing the workplace in a way that does not permit anybody to threaten or intimidate employees through sexual behavior.

In general, the most obvious examples of sexual harassment involve *quid pro quo harassment,* meaning that a person makes a benefit (or punishment) contingent on an employee's submitting to (or rejecting) sexual advances. For example, a manager who promises a raise to an employee who will participate in sexual activities is engaging in quid pro quo harassment. Likewise, it would be sexual harassment to threaten to reassign someone to a less-desirable job if that person refuses sexual favors.

A more subtle, and possibly more pervasive, form of sexual harassment is to create or permit a "hostile working environment." This occurs when someone's behavior in the workplace creates an environment in which it is difficult for someone of a particular sex to work. Common complaints in sexual harassment lawsuits include claims that harassers ran their fingers through the plaintiffs' hair, made suggestive remarks, touched intimate body parts, posted pictures with sexual content in the workplace, and used sexually explicit language or told sex-related jokes. The reason that these behaviors are considered discrimination is that they treat individuals differently based on their sex.

RESPONDING TO COMPLAINTS OF HARASSMENT

When an employee comes to an HR professional with a complaint that he or she has been harassed, that employee is probably already upset, so the HR response can make a huge difference in whether the complaint is resolved successfully or escalates into a lawsuit.

- *Listen with an open mind*—Consider that the employee may be describing a real problem, even if the supposed perpetrator is someone you respect. At the same time, consider that there is possibly another side to the story. So don't say, "That's terrible," unless you know for sure that something terrible really did happen.

- *Don't use legal jargon unless you're a lawyer*—For example, you could ask, "Did anyone else do anything you thought was inappropriate?" That keeps the focus on the facts. But if you ask, "Did anyone else harass you?" you're using a word that defines illegal conduct. Unless harassment is proven, that label could be unfair. Of course, you also shouldn't argue that harassment *didn't* occur. Stick to the facts.

- *Be serious and professional*—Jokes are unlikely to break the tension; more likely, they will signal that you don't take the complaint seriously. Likewise, putting a sympathetic hand on the shoulder of someone who is telling you he or she has been touched inappropriately is just asking for the situation to escalate.

Source: Based on Jonathan A. Segal, "A Sexual Harassment Complaint? Ten Responses to Avoid," *BusinessWeek*, February 12, 2010, http://www.businessweek.com.

Although a large majority of sexual harassment complaints received by the EEOC involve women being harassed by men, a growing share of sexual harassment claims have been filed by men. Some of the men claimed that they were harassed by women, but same-sex harassment also occurs and is illegal. The EEOC recently filed a charge against Boh Bros. Construction Company after investigating a male iron worker's complaint that he had been the victim of male-on-male sexual harassment by the company's site superintendent. According to the iron worker, the superintendent had subjected him to taunts, verbal abuse, and sexual advances.[17]

To ensure a workplace free from sexual harassment, organizations can follow some important steps. First, the organization can develop a policy statement making it very clear that sexual harassment will not be tolerated in the workplace. Second, all employees, new and old, can be trained to identify inappropriate workplace behavior. In addition, the organization can develop a mechanism for reporting sexual harassment in a way that encourages people to speak out. Finally, management can prepare to act promptly to discipline those who engage in sexual harassment, as well as to protect the victims of sexual harassment. The "HR How To" box provides some additional guidance on responding to complaints.

Valuing Diversity

As we mentioned in Chapter 2, the United States is a diverse nation, and becoming more so. In addition, many U.S. companies have customers and operations in more than one country. Managers differ in how they approach the challenges related to this diversity. Some define a diverse workforce as a competitive advantage that brings them a wider pool of talent and greater insight into the needs and behaviors of their diverse customers. These organizations say they have a policy of *valuing diversity*.

The practice of valuing diversity has no single form; it is not written into law or business theory. Organizations that value diversity may practice some form of affirmative action, discussed earlier. They may have policies stating their value of understanding and respecting differences. Organizations may try to hire, reward, and promote employees who demonstrate respect for others. They may sponsor training programs designed to teach employees about differences among groups. Whatever their form, these efforts are intended to make each individual feel respected. Also, these actions can support equal employment opportunity by cultivating an environment in which individuals feel welcome and able to do their best.

Valuing diversity, especially in support of an organization's mission and strategy, need not be limited to the categories protected by law. Root Learning, a management consulting firm in Sylvania, Ohio, believes that effective teamwork starts with a group of individuals who know they bring different strengths to the game. To highlight each employee's uniqueness, Root has caricatures drawn of each employee, showing each person with symbols of his or her talents and hobbies. The caricatures hang on the walls of Root's lobby, where clients and co-workers alike can see the employees as more than stereotypes and learn about what makes each employee special. The goal is for employees to know each other well enough to bring in the right people with the right expertise for a particular project. Other ways in which Root expresses appreciation of individual differences include employee reviews of co-workers' strengths, a budget for employee-selected training goals, and monthly meetings at which employees are encouraged to describe one another's accomplishments.[18]

LO6 Explain employers' duties under the Occupational Safety and Health Act.

Occupational Safety and Health Act (OSH Act)

Occupational Safety and Health Act (OSH Act)
U.S. law authorizing the federal government to establish and enforce occupational safety and health standards for all places of employment engaging in interstate commerce.

Like equal employment opportunity, the protection of employee safety and health is regulated by the government. Through the 1960s, workplace safety was primarily an issue between workers and employers. By 1970, however, roughly 15,000 work-related fatalities occurred every year. That year, Congress enacted the **Occupational Safety and Health Act (OSH Act),** the most comprehensive U.S. law regarding worker safety. The OSH Act authorized the federal government to establish and enforce occupational safety and health standards for all places of employment engaging in interstate commerce.

Occupational Safety and Health Administration (OSHA)
Labor Department agency responsible for inspecting employers, applying safety and health standards, and levying fines for violation.

The OSH Act divided enforcement responsibilities between the Department of Labor and the Department of Health. Under the Department of Labor, the **Occupational Safety and Health Administration (OSHA)** is responsible for inspecting employers, applying safety and health standards, and levying fines for violation. The Department of Health is responsible for conducting research to determine the criteria for specific operations or occupations and for training employers to comply with the act. Much of the research is conducted by the National Institute for Occupational Safety and Health (NIOSH).

LO7 Describe the role of the Occupational Safety and Health Administration.

General and Specific Duties

The main provision of the OSH Act states that each employer has a general duty to furnish each employee a place of employment free from recognized hazards that cause or are likely to cause death or serious physical harm. This is called the act's *general-duty clause.* Employers also must keep records of work-related injuries and illnesses and post an annual summary of these records from February 1 to April 30 in the following year. Figure 3.6 shows a sample of OSHA's Form 300A,

Figure 3.6

OSHA Form 300A: Summary of Work-Related Injuries and Illnesses

OSHA's Form 300A (Rev. 01/2004)

Summary of Work-Related Injuries and Illnesses

Year 20____

U.S. Department of Labor
Occupational Safety and Health Administration
Form approved OMB no. 1218-0176

All establishments covered by Part 1904 must complete this Summary page, even if no work-related injuries or illnesses occurred during the year. Remember to review the Log to verify that the entries are complete and accurate before completing this summary.

Using the Log, count the individual entries you made for each category. Then write the totals below, making sure you've added the entries from every page of the Log. If you had no cases, write "0."

Employees, former employees, and their representatives have the right to review the OSHA Form 300 in its entirety. They also have limited access to the OSHA Form 301 or its equivalent. See 29 CFR Part 1904.35, in OSHA's recordkeeping rule, for further details on the access provisions for these forms.

Number of Cases

Total number of deaths	Total number of cases with days away from work	Total number of cases with job transfer or restriction	Total number of other recordable cases
(G)	(H)	(I)	(J)

Number of Days

Total number of days away from work	Total number of days of job transfer or restriction
(K)	(L)

Injury and Illness Types

Total number of . . .
(M)
(1) Injuries _____
(2) Skin disorders _____
(3) Respiratory conditions _____
(4) Poisonings _____
(5) Hearing loss _____
(6) All other illnesses _____

Post this Summary page from February 1 to April 30 of the year following the year covered by the form.

Public reporting burden for this collection of information is estimated to average 58 minutes per response, including time to review the instructions, search and gather the data needed, and complete and review the collection of information. Persons are not required to respond to the collection of information unless it displays a currently valid OMB control number. If you have any comments about these estimates or any other aspects of this data collection, contact: US Department of Labor, OSHA Office of Statistical Analysis, Room N-3644, 200 Constitution Avenue, NW, Washington, DC 20210. Do not send the completed forms to this office.

Establishment information

Your establishment name _____

Street _____
City _____ State _____ ZIP _____

Industry description (e.g., Manufacture of motor truck trailers) _____

Standard Industrial Classification (SIC), if known (e.g., 3715) _____

OR

North American Industrial Classification (NAICS), if known (e.g., 336212) _____

Employment information (If you don't have these figures, see the Worksheet on the back of this page to estimate.)

Annual average number of employees _____
Total hours worked by all employees last year _____

Sign here

Knowingly falsifying this document may result in a fine.

I certify that I have examined this document and that to the best of my knowledge the entries are true, accurate, and complete.

Company executive _____ Title _____
Phone (   ) _____ Date _____

SOURCE: *The OSHA Recordkeeping Handbook,* U.S. Dept. of Labor, April 1, 2010, http://osha.gov/recordkeeping/new-osha300form1-1-04.pdf.

OSHA is responsible for inspecting businesses, applying safety and health standards, and levying fines for violations. OSHA regulations prohibit notifying employers of inspections in advance.

the annual summary that must be posted, even if no injuries or illnesses occurred.

The act also grants specific rights; for example, employees have the right to:

- Request an inspection.
- Have a representative present at an inspection.
- Have dangerous substances identified.
- Be promptly informed about exposure to hazards and be given access to accurate records regarding exposure.
- Have employer violations posted at the work site.

Although OSHA regulations have a (sometimes justifiable) reputation for being complex, a company can get started in meeting these requirements by visiting OSHA's Web site (www.osha.gov) and looking up resources such as the agency's *Small Business Handbook* and its step-by-step guide called "Compliance Assistance Quick Start."

The Department of Labor recognizes many specific types of hazards, and employers must comply with all the occupational safety and health standards published by NIOSH. For example, NIOSH is currently investigating exposures of workers in nail salons to the vapor from solvents contained in nail products. One part of the investigation includes a study of vented nail tables, which are a type of work table on which customers rest their hands for a manicure. On the vented tables, a downdraft is supposed to pull the vapors away from the technician's face. NIOSH is measuring how effective these tables are at reducing exposure to vapor and will use information from the research to develop educational guidelines for protecting workers in nail salons.[19]

Although NIOSH publishes numerous standards, it is impossible for regulators to anticipate all possible hazards that could occur in the workplace. Thus, the general-duty clause requires employers to be constantly alert for potential sources of harm in the workplace (as defined by the standard of what a reasonably prudent person would do) and to correct them. Information about hazards can come from employees or from outside researchers. A recent study found that health care workers are unusually likely to develop work-related asthma. The researchers found that the disease occurred because the workers were frequently exposed to latex and disinfectants known to cause asthma. They also worked around asthma-aggravating materials, including cleaning products and materials used in renovating buildings. Hospitals and other health care providers can protect their workers from asthma by substituting nonlatex or powder-free gloves for powdered latex gloves. They also can be more selective in their use of disinfectants.[20]

Enforcement of the OSH Act

To enforce the OSH Act, the Occupational Safety and Health Administration conducts inspections. OSHA compliance officers typically arrive at a workplace unannounced; for obvious reasons, OSHA regulations prohibit notifying employers of inspections in advance. After presenting credentials, the compliance officer tells the employer the reasons for the inspection and describes, in a general way, the procedures necessary to conduct the investigation.

An OSHA inspection has four major components. First, the compliance officer reviews the company's records of deaths, injuries, and illnesses. OSHA requires this kind of record keeping at all firms with 11 or more full- or part-time employees. Next, the officer—typically accompanied by a representative of the employer (and perhaps by a representative of the employees)—conducts a "walkaround" tour of the employer's premises. On this tour, the officer notes any conditions that may violate specific published standards or the less specific general-duty clause. The third component of the inspection, employee interviews, may take place during the tour. At this time, anyone who is aware of a violation can bring it to the officer's attention. Finally, in a closing conference, the compliance officer discusses the findings with the employer, noting any violations.

Following an inspection, OSHA gives the employer a reasonable time frame within which to correct the violations identified. If a violation could cause serious injury or death, the officer may seek a restraining order from a U.S. District Court. The restraining order compels the employer to correct the problem immediately. In addition, if an OSHA violation results in citations, the employer must post each citation in a prominent place near the location of the violation.

Besides correcting violations identified during the inspection, employers may have to pay fines. These fines range from $20,000 for violations that result in death of an employee to $1,000 for less-serious violations. Other penalties include criminal charges for falsifying records that are subject to OSHA inspection or for warning an employer of an OSHA inspection without permission from the Department of Labor.

Employee Rights and Responsibilities

Although the OSH Act makes employers responsible for protecting workers from safety and health hazards, employees have responsibilities as well. They have to follow OSHA's safety rules and regulations governing employee behavior. Employees also have a duty to report hazardous conditions.

Along with those responsibilities go certain rights. Employees may file a complaint and request an OSHA inspection of the workplace, and their employers may not retaliate against them for complaining. Employees also have a right to receive information about any hazardous chemicals they handle in the course of their jobs. OSHA's Hazard Communication Standard and many states' **right-to-know laws** require employers to provide employees with information about the health risks associated with exposure to substances considered hazardous. State right-to-know laws may be more stringent than federal standards, so organizations should obtain requirements from their state's health and safety agency, as well as from OSHA.

Under OSHA's Hazard Communication Standard, organizations must have **material safety data sheets (MSDSs)** for chemicals that employees are exposed to. An MSDS is a form that details the hazards associated with a chemical; the chemical's producer or importer is responsible for identifying these hazards and detailing them on the form. Employers must also ensure that all containers of hazardous chemicals are labeled with information about the hazards, and they must train employees in safe handling of the chemicals. Office workers who

Right-to-Know Laws
State laws that require employers to provide employees with information about the health risks associated with exposure to substances considered hazardous.

Material Safety Data Sheets (MSDSs)
Forms on which chemical manufacturers and importers identify the hazards of their chemicals.

Figure 3.7

Rates of Occupational Injuries and Illnesses

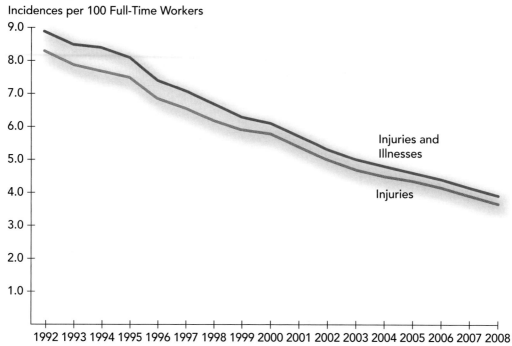

Note: Data do not include fatal work-related injuries and illnesses.

SOURCE: Bureau of Labor Statistics, "Industry, Injury, and Illness Data," www.bls.gov, accessed March 2, 2010.

encounter a chemical infrequently (such as a secretary who occasionally changes the toner in a copier) are not covered by these requirements. In the case of a copy machine, the Hazard Communication Standard would apply to someone whose job involves spending a large part of the day servicing or operating such equipment.

Impact of the OSH Act

The OSH Act has unquestionably succeeded in raising the level of awareness of occupational safety. Yet legislation alone cannot solve all the problems of work site safety. Indeed, the rate of occupational illnesses more than doubled between 1985 and 1990, according to the Bureau of Labor Statistics, while the rate of injuries rose by about 8 percent. However, as depicted in Figure 3.7, both rates have shown an overall downward trend since then.[21]

Many industrial accidents are a product of unsafe behaviors, not unsafe working conditions. Because the act does not directly regulate employee behavior, little behavior change can be expected unless employees are convinced of the standards' importance.[22]

Conforming to the law alone does not necessarily guarantee their employees will be safe, so many employers go beyond the letter of the law. In the next section we examine various kinds of employer-initiated safety awareness programs that comply with OSHA requirements and, in some cases, exceed them.

Employer-Sponsored Safety and Health Programs

LO8 Discuss ways employers promote worker safety and health.

Many employers establish safety awareness programs to go beyond mere compliance with the OSH Act and attempt to instill an emphasis on safety. A safety awareness program has three primary components: identifying and communicating hazards, reinforcing safe practices, and promoting safety internationally.

Identifying and Communicating Job Hazards

Employees, supervisors, and other knowledgeable sources need to sit down and discuss potential problems related to safety. One method for doing this is the **job hazard analysis technique.**[23] With this technique, each job is broken down into basic elements, and each of these is rated for its potential for harm or injury. If there is agreement that some job element has high hazard potential, the group isolates the element and considers possible technological or behavior changes to reduce or eliminate the hazard. The "Did You Know?" box shows the leading causes of injuries at work in 2007.

Job Hazard Analysis Technique
Safety promotion technique that involves breaking down a job into basic elements, then rating each element for its potential for harm or injury.

Another means of isolating unsafe job elements is to study past accidents. The **technic of operations review (TOR)** is an analysis method for determining which specific element of a job led to a past accident.[24] The first step in a TOR analysis is to establish the facts surrounding the incident. To accomplish this, all members of the work group involved in the accident give their initial impressions of what happened. The group must then, through discussion, come to an agreement on the single, systematic failure that most likely contributed to the incident, as well as two or three major secondary factors that contributed to it.

Technic of Operations Review (TOR)
Method of promoting safety by determining which specific element of a job led to a past accident.

United Parcel Service combined job analysis with employee empowerment to reduce injury rates dramatically. Concerned about the many sprains, strains, and other injuries experienced by its workers, UPS set up Comprehensive Health and Safety Process (CHSP) committees that bring together management and nonmanagement employees. Each committee investigates and reports on accidents, conducts audits of facilities and equipment, and advises employees on how to perform their jobs more safely. For example, the committees make sure delivery people know safe practices for lifting packages and backing up trucks. Whenever committee members see someone behaving unsafely, they are required to intervene. Since the CHSP committees began their work, the injury rate at UPS has fallen from over 27 injuries per 200,000 hours worked to just 10.2 injuries per 200,000, well on the way to the company's target injury rate of 3.2 per 200,000 hours.[25]

To communicate with employees about job hazards, managers should talk directly with their employees about safety. Memos also are important, because the written communication helps establish a "paper trail" that can later document a history of the employer's concern regarding the job hazard. Posters, especially if placed near the hazard, serve as a constant reminder, reinforcing other messages.

In communicating risk, managers should recognize that different groups of individuals may constitute different audiences. For example, as women started entering more sectors of the workforce, it became apparent that personal protective equipment designed with men in mind did not always fit women very well. For example, cut-resistant leather gloves designed for men's hands often proved too clumsy and bulky for female workers. Likewise, gloves that are too big can actually make handling of slippery or wet items more dangerous. And when gloves or other equipment doesn't fit properly, workers are less motivated to wear it, losing the equipment's protection altogether.

Did You Know?

Top 10 Causes of Workplace Injuries

Every year, the Liberty Mutual Research Institute for Safety produces the Liberty Mutual Workplace Safety Index, which estimates the direct costs of disabling workplace injuries in the United States. In 2007, serious work-related injuries cost employers $53 billion. The leading cause was overexertion (for example, excessive lifting, pushing, carrying, or throwing), followed by falls on the same level (rather than from a height), and falls to a lower level (such as from a ladder).

Source: Liberty Mutual Research Institute for Safety, "2009 Workplace Safety Index," www.libertymutual.com/researchinstitute, accessed March 2 2010.

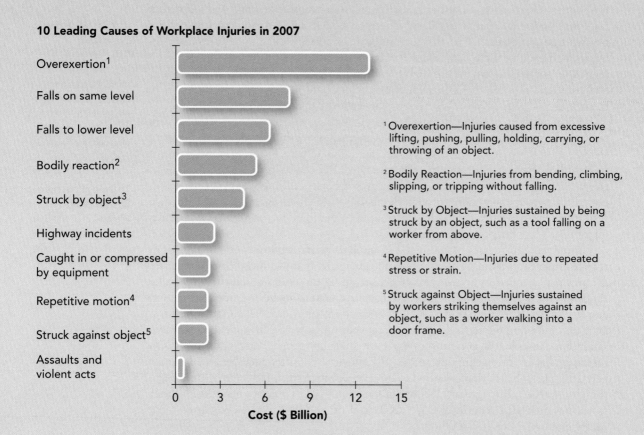

10 Leading Causes of Workplace Injuries in 2007

[1] Overexertion—Injuries caused from excessive lifting, pushing, pulling, holding, carrying, or throwing of an object.

[2] Bodily Reaction—Injuries from bending, climbing, slipping, or tripping without falling.

[3] Struck by Object—Injuries sustained by being struck by an object, such as a tool falling on a worker from above.

[4] Repetitive Motion—Injuries due to repeated stress or strain.

[5] Struck against Object—Injuries sustained by workers striking themselves against an object, such as a worker walking into a door frame.

Fortunately, equipment designers today are becoming more aware of the needs of their customers' female employees, so more sizes and designs are now available.[26]

Other workers who may be at higher risk are at each end of the age spectrum. Older workers tend to have fewer but more severe injuries and take longer to recover. In addition, whereas young workers are more likely to suffer an acute injury such as a cut or burn, older workers are more likely to injure themselves as a result of cumulative trauma, such as repetitive motions, awkward postures, and the use of too much force over and over. Such injuries can often be prevented with careful job design.[27] Organizations may need to make reasonable accommodations in response to their concerns, both to protect their employees and to meet the challenges of an aging workforce, described in Chapter 2. With young workers, the safety challenge is to protect them

HR Oops!

Construction Firm Falls Down on the Training Job

Recently, OSHA fined C. A. Franc, a Valencia, Pennsylvania, construction company, more than half a million dollars for its failure to protect its workers from falls. The investigation came after a worker fell 40 feet from a pitched roof at a Washington, Pennsylvania, work site and died.

According to OSHA, the company failed to provide its roofers with any fall protection. Furthermore, a newly hired worker, a college student, was not trained in hazards or in the safety measures required for roofing work. The agency's penalties included fines for each worker who lacked fall protection plus a fine for failure to train the young employee.

John M. Hermanson, the OSHA administrator for the region noted, "Falls are the leading cause of fatalities in the construction industry. Failure to provide employees with fall protection is unconscionable."

Source: Based on Occupational Safety and Health Administration, "US Department of Labor's OSHA Cites C.A. Franc $539,000 for Willful Fall Hazard Violations following Worker's Death at Washington, Pa., Worksite," news release, February 12, 2010, http://osha.gov.

Questions

1. Do you think college students around age 20 would be more vulnerable to falls during roofing jobs than older employees? Why or why not? How could a roofing company protect these workers from falls?
2. Imagine that C. A. Franc called you in to give human resources advice. The owner points out that these are difficult times for the construction industry, so there is really no budget for training. What advice would you give?

from risk taking. Young workers may be especially eager to please the adults they work with, and they may be more fearful than their older colleagues when safety requires challenging authority. Employees who are new to the workforce may not be aware of the health and safety laws that are supposed to protect them. Research by the National Safety Council indicates that 40 percent of accidents happen to individuals in the 20-to-29 age group and that 48 percent of accidents happen to workers during their first year on the job.[28] The "HR Oops!" box shows the danger of assuming that employees are aware of safety risks on the job.

Reinforcing Safe Practices

To ensure safe behaviors, employers should not only define how to work safely but reinforce the desired behavior. One common technique for reinforcing safe practices is implementing a safety incentive program to reward workers for their support of and commitment to safety goals. Such programs start by focusing on monthly or quarterly goals or by encouraging suggestions for improving safety. Possible goals might include good housekeeping practices, adherence to safety rules, and proper use of protective equipment. Later, the program expands to include more wide-ranging, long-term goals. Typically, the employer distributes prizes in highly public forums, such as company or department meetings. Using merchandise for prizes, instead of cash, provides a lasting symbol of achievement. A good deal of evidence suggests that such incentive programs are effective in reducing the number and cost of injuries.[29]

Besides focusing on specific jobs, organizations can target particular types of injuries or disabilities, especially those for which employees may be at risk. For example, Prevent Blindness America estimates that 2,000 eye injuries occur every day in occupational settings.[30] Organizations can prevent such injuries through a combination of job analysis, written policies, safety training, protective eyewear, rewards and sanctions for safe and unsafe behavior, and management support for the safety effort. Similar practices for preventing other types of injuries are available in trade publications, through the National Safety Council, and on the Web site of the Occupational Safety and Health Administration (www.osha.gov).

Promoting Safety Internationally

Given the increasing focus on international management, organizations also need to consider how to ensure the safety of their employees regardless of the nation in which they operate. Cultural differences may make this more difficult than it seems. For example, a study examined the impact of one standardized corporationwide safety policy on employees in three different countries: the United States, France, and Argentina. The results of this study indicate that employees in the three countries interpreted the policy differently because of cultural differences. The individualistic, control-oriented culture of the United States stressed the role of top management in ensuring safety in a top-down fashion. However, this policy failed to work in Argentina, where the culture is more "collectivist" (emphasizing the group). Argentine employees tend to feel that safety is everyone's joint concern, so the safety programs needed to be defined from the bottom of the organization up.[31]

focus on **social responsibility**

Another challenge in promoting safety internationally is that laws, enforcement practices, and political climates vary from country to country. With the increasing use of offshoring, described in Chapter 2, more companies have operations in countries where labor standards are far less strict than U.S. standards. Managers and employees in these countries may not think the company is serious about protecting workers' health and safety. In that case, strong communication and oversight will be necessary if the company intends to adhere to the ethical principle of valuing its foreign workers' safety as much as the safety of its U.S. workers. The Gap treats this issue as part of its corporate social responsibility. The company views its supply chain as socially sustainable only when working conditions and factory conditions meet acceptable business practices. According to Eva Sage-Gavin, Gap's executive vice president of human resources and corporate communications, "We know that better factory working conditions lead to better factories, and better factories make better products." In addition, Sage-Gavin notes, Gap employees in the United States care about working for a company they view as socially responsible, so these efforts also matter for corporate performance at home.[32]

thinking ethically

DO FAMILY FRIENDLY POLICIES HURT MEN?

As more women have entered the workforce, companies wanting the best talent have moved toward adding more benefits that help mothers in particular juggle the responsibilities of job and family. Part-time work schedules and flexible hours help parents find time to tend to children and—with the aging of the nation's population—help adult children tend to elderly parents. Traditionally, these family responsibilities have been taken up primarily by women.

But as companies add these benefits, some male employees (and some childless women as well) have complained that the company is spending money on benefits that flow to some workers at the expense (at least theoretically) of others. Some men have even complained that fathers don't get assistance with child care or an opportunity to bring their babies to work.

In fact, in the United States, companies do have to extend the same benefits to fathers as to mothers (except, of course, that if a mother is disabled after childbirth, she is the one who gets the disability benefit). But men note that it is women who are more likely to use these benefits, even though studies show that men are experiencing more work–life conflict than male workers did a few decades ago. And as more pregnant women stay on the job, the disparity is as obvious as the bulging bellies.

SOURCES: Sue Shellenbarger, "Do Work-Family Policies Discriminate against Men?" *Wall Street Journal*, February 4, 2010, http://blogs.wsj.com; and Sue Shellenbarger, "Handling the Office Baby Boom," *Wall Street Journal*, January 13, 2010, http://online.wsj.com.

Questions

1. Who, if anyone, suffers when some workers get flexible hours? What would be a fair way to distribute the costs and benefits of flexibility in work schedules?
2. Do employee benefits have to be used equally in order for them to be fair or ethical? Why or why not? If you were in the HR department of a company where some employees were unhappy about this issue, how would you recommend that the company address it?

SUMMARY

LO1 Explain how the three branches of government regulate human resource management.

The legislative branch develops laws such as those governing equal employment opportunity and worker safety and health. The executive branch establishes agencies such as the Equal Employment Opportunity Commission and Occupational Safety and Health Administration to enforce the laws by publishing regulations, filing lawsuits, and performing other activities. The president may also issue executive orders, such as requirements for federal contractors. The judicial branch hears cases related to employment law and interprets the law.

LO2 Summarize the major federal laws requiring equal employment opportunity.

The Civil Rights Acts of 1866 and 1871 grants all persons equal property rights, contract rights, and the right to sue in federal court if they have been deprived of civil rights. The Equal Pay Act of 1963 requires equal pay for men and women who are doing work that is equal in terms of skill, effort, responsibility, and working conditions. Title VII of the Civil Rights Act of 1964 prohibits employment discrimination on the basis of race, color, religion, sex, or national origin. The Age Discrimination in Employment Act prohibits employment discrimination against persons older than 40. The Vocational Rehabilitation Act of 1973 requires that federal contractors engage in affirmative action in the employment of persons with disabilities. The Vietnam Era Veteran's Readjustment Act of 1974 requires affirmative action in employment of veterans who served during the Vietnam War. The Pregnancy Discrimination Act of 1978 treats discrimination based on pregnancy-related conditions as illegal sex discrimination. The Americans with Disabilities Act requires reasonable accommodations for qualified workers with disabilities. The Civil Rights Act of 1991 provides for compensatory and punitive damages in cases of discrimination. The Uniformed Services Employment and Reemployment Rights Act of 1994 requires that employers reemploy service members who left jobs to fulfill military duties. Under the Genetic Information Nondiscrimination Act (GINA) of 2008, employers may not use genetic information in making decisions related to the terms, conditions, or privileges of employment.

LO3 Identify the federal agencies that enforce equal employment opportunity, and describe the role of each.

The Equal Employment Opportunity Commission is responsible for enforcing most of the EEO laws, including Title VII and the Americans with Disabilities Act. It investigates and resolves complaints, gathers information, and issues guidelines. The Office of Federal Contract Compliance Procedures is responsible for enforcing executive orders that call for affirmative action by companies that do business with the federal government. It monitors affirmative-action plans and takes action against companies that fail to comply.

LO4 Describe ways employers can avoid illegal discrimination and provide reasonable accommodation.

Employers can avoid discrimination by avoiding disparate treatment of job applicants and employees, as well as policies that result in disparate impact. Companies can develop and enforce an EEO policy coupled with policies and practices that demonstrate a high value placed on diversity. Affirmative action may correct past discrimination, but quota-based activities can result in charges of reverse discrimination. To provide reasonable accommodation, companies should recognize needs based on individuals' religion or disabilities. Employees may need to make such accommodations as adjusting schedules or dress codes, making the workplace more accessible, or restructuring jobs.

LO5 Define sexual harassment, and tell how employers can eliminate or minimize it.

Sexual harassment is unwelcome sexual advances and related behavior that makes submitting to the conduct a term of employment or the basis for employment decisions or that interferes with an individual's work performance or creates a work environment that is intimidating, hostile, or offensive. Organizations can prevent sexual harassment by developing a policy that defines and forbids it, training employees to recognize and avoid this behavior, and providing a means for employees to complain and be protected.

LO6 Explain employers' duties under the Occupational Safety and Health Act.

Under the Occupational Safety and Health Act, employers have a general duty to provide employees a place of employment free from recognized safety and health hazards. They must inform employees about hazardous substances, maintain and post records of accidents and illnesses, and comply with NIOSH standards about specific occupational hazards.

LO7 Describe the role of the Occupational Safety and Health Administration.

The Occupational Safety and Health Administration publishes regulations and conducts inspections. If OSHA finds violations, it discusses them with the employer and monitors the employer's response in correcting the violation.

LO8 Discuss ways employers promote worker safety and health.

Besides complying with OSHA regulations, employers often establish safety awareness programs designed to instill an emphasis on safety. They may identify and communicate hazards through the job hazard analysis technique or the technic of operations review. They may adapt communications and training to the needs of different employees, such as differences in experience levels or cultural differences from one country to another. Employers may also establish incentive programs to reward safe behavior.

KEY TERMS

affirmative action, p. 65

bona fide occupational qualification (BFOQ), p. 74

disability, p. 67

disparate impact, p. 74

disparate treatment, p. 73

EEO-1 report, p. 71

equal employment opportunity (EEO), p. 61

Equal Employment Opportunity Commission (EEOC), p. 63

four-fifths rule, p. 75

job hazard analysis technique, p. 85

material safety data sheets (MSDSs), p. 83

Occupational Safety and Health Act (OSH Act), p. 80

Occupational Safety and Health Administration (OSHA), p. 80

Office of Federal Contract Compliance Procedures (OFCCP), p. 72

reasonable accommodation, p. 77

right-to-know laws, p. 83

sexual harassment, p. 78

technic of operations review (TOR), p. 85

Uniform Guidelines on Employee Selection Procedures, p. 72

REVIEW AND DISCUSSION QUESTIONS

1. What is the role of each branch of the federal government with regard to equal employment opportunity?

2. For each of the following situations, identify one or more constitutional amendments, laws, or executive orders that might apply.

   a. A veteran of the Vietnam conflict experiences lower-back pain after sitting for extended periods of time. He has applied for promotion to a supervisory position that has traditionally involved spending most of the workday behind a desk.

   b. One of two female workers on a road construction crew complains to her supervisor that she feels uncomfortable during breaks, because the other employees routinely tell off-color jokes.

   c. A manager at an architectural firm receives a call from the local newspaper. The reporter wonders how the firm wishes to respond to calls from two of its employees alleging racial discrimination. About half of the firm's employees (including all of its partners and most of its architects) are white. One of the firm's clients is the federal government.

3. For each situation in the preceding question, what actions, if any, should the organization take?

4. The Americans with Disabilities Act requires that employers make reasonable accommodations for individuals with disabilities. How might this requirement affect law enforcement officers and firefighters?

5. To identify instances of sexual harassment, the courts may use a "reasonable woman" standard of what constitutes offensive behavior. This standard is based on the idea that women and men have different ideas of what behavior is appropriate. What are the implications of this distinction? Do you think this distinction is helpful or harmful? Why?

6. Given that the "reasonable woman" standard referred to in Question 5 is based on women's ideas of what is appropriate, how might an organization with mostly male employees identify and avoid behavior that could be found to be sexual harassment?

7. What are an organization's basic duties under the Occupational Safety and Health Act?

8. OSHA penalties are aimed at employers, rather than employees. How does this affect employee safety?

9. How can organizations motivate employees to promote safety and health in the workplace?

10. For each of the following occupations, identify at least one possible hazard and at least one action employers could take to minimize the risk of an injury or illness related to that hazard.
   a. Worker in a fast-food restaurant
   b. Computer programmer
   c. Truck driver
   d. House painter

BUSINESSWEEK CASE

BusinessWeek Attacked by a Whale

A veteran SeaWorld trainer was rubbing a killer whale from a poolside platform when the 12,000-pound creature reached up, grabbed her ponytail in its mouth and dragged her underwater. Despite workers rushing to her, the trainer was killed.

Horrified visitors who had stuck around after a noontime show watched the animal charge through the pool with the trainer in its jaws. Workers used nets as an alarm sounded, but it was too late. Dawn Brancheau had drowned. It marked the third time the animal had been involved in a human death.

Brancheau's interaction with the whale appeared leisurely and informal at first to audience member Eldon Skaggs. But then, the whale "pulled her under and started swimming around with her," Skaggs told The Associated Press.

Some workers hustled the audience out of the stadium while the others tried to save Brancheau, 40.

Skaggs said he heard that during an earlier show the whale was not responding to directions. Others who attended the earlier show said the whale was behaving like an ornery child.

But [Chuck] Tompkins [head of animal training at all SeaWorld parks] said the whale had performed well in the show and that Dawn was rubbing him down as a reward for doing a good job. "There wasn't anything to indicate that there was a problem," Tompkins told the CBS "Early Show."

Because of his size and the previous deaths, trainers were not supposed to get into the water with Tilikum, and only about a dozen of the park's trainers worked with him. Brancheau had more experience with the 30-year-old whale than most. She was one of the park's most experienced trainers overall.

A SeaWorld spokesman said Tilikum was one of three orcas blamed for killing a trainer in 1991 after the woman lost her balance and fell in the pool at Sealand of the Pacific near Victoria, British Columbia. Steve Huxter, who was head of Sealand's animal care and training department then, said he's surprised it happened again. He says Tilikum was a well-behaved, balanced animal.

Tilikum was also involved in a 1999 death, when the body of a man who had sneaked by SeaWorld security was found draped over him. The man either jumped, fell or was pulled into the frigid water and died of hypothermia, though he was also bruised and scratched by Tilikum.

According to a profile of Brancheau in the *Sentinel* in 2006, she was one of SeaWorld Orlando's leading trainers. Brancheau worked her way into a leadership role at Shamu Stadium during her career with SeaWorld, starting at the Sea Lion & Otter Stadium before spending 10 years working with killer whales, the newspaper said.

Bill Hurley, chief animal officer at the Georgia Aqaurium—the world's largest—said there are inherent dangers to working with orcas, just as there are with driving race cars or piloting jets.

"In the case of a killer whale, if they want your attention or if they're frustrated by something or if they're confused by something, there's only a few ways of handling that," he said. "If you're right near pool's edge and they decide they want a closer interaction during this, certainly they can grab you."

And, he added, "At 12,000 pounds there's not a lot of resisting you're going to do."

SOURCE: Excerpted from Mike Schneider, "Whale Drags Trainer off Platform in Fatal Attack," *BusinessWeek*, February 25, 2010, www.businessweek.com.

Questions

1. React to Bill Hurley's comment that some jobs, like race car driver, are inherently dangerous. Do some employees simply have to accept the risk of death? If so, what is the employer's responsibility, if any, with regard to the safety of such jobs?

2. How can human resource management contribute to a lower risk of death among trainers at a facility such as SeaWorld? Consider the various HR functions, such as employee selection and training, and how they might contribute to this goal.

3. Imagine that you worked in SeaWorld's human resources department when this incident occurred. What are some actions that you would want your department to take at that time or in the months afterward?

Case: Walmart's Discrimination Difficulties

Perhaps it shouldn't be a surprise, since it is the largest private employer in the United States, but Walmart periodically has made headlines because someone has accused the discount retailer of discrimination. For instance, the company not long ago reached a settlement in a federal lawsuit that charged the company with racial discrimination. According to the class-action lawsuit, thousands of black applicants were repeatedly denied jobs as truck drivers over a period of seven years. The settlement requires hiring some of these individuals and notifying others as positions become available. Walmart also promised that it would try harder to recruit minorities.

A more recent settlement involved allegations of discrimination against women. The Equal Employment Opportunity Commission charged the company with turning down female applicants to fill orders in its distribution center in London, Kentucky, even though they were at least as well qualified as the male applicants who were hired. According to the lawsuit, those whose names on job applications were clearly female were not considered for the positions. The basis for the conclusion was that there was a statistically significant pattern of hiring males and turning down females.

A female job applicant added details of her experience: Brenda Overby said an interviewer asked her if she could lift a 150-pound bag of potatoes over her head. She said no, and she recalled later that the interviewer responded that "women weren't needed" to work in the warehouse. Overby went on to find a warehouse job at another company, performing work similar to what Walmart required.

In this settlement, Walmart agreed to pay $11.7 million, most of it to be distributed among the plaintiffs, and to hire women for 50 of the warehouse's order-filling positions, as well as every other position of the next 50 that become available. It also agreed to avoid discrimination, to make hiring decisions based on validated interview questions, and to give its employees training in how to avoid discrimination.

As it faces these challenges among hourly employees, Walmart is also tackling the challenge of bringing more diversity to its management ranks. The company has assembled a women's council consisting of 14 members from each of the retailer's global markets, tasked with finding ways to bring in more female managers. So far, about one-fourth of Walmart's senior managers are women. This statistic is surprising, considering that the company has said about 8 out of 10 Walmart shoppers are women.

SOURCES: "Bias Suit Settlement," *MMR*, July 13, 2009, Business & Company Resource Center, http://galenet.galegroup.com; Equal Employment Opportunity Commission, "Walmart to Pay More than $11.7 Million to Settle EEOC Sex Discrimination Suit," news release, March 1, 2010, http://www1.eeoc.gov; Bill Estep and Dori Hjalmarson, "Wal-Mart Will Pay Millions in Bias Case," *Lexington Herald-Leader*, March 3, 2010, Business & Company Resource Center, http://galenet.galegroup.com; and Matthew Boyle, "Wal-Mart Vows to Promote Women," *BusinessWeek*, June 5, 2009, www.businessweek.com.

Questions

1. According to this case, which employment laws has Walmart been accused of violating? How might it have avoided those charges?

2. Which challenge do you think will be more difficult for Walmart: diversifying its top-management ranks or ending charges of discrimination? Why?

3. Do you think more diversity among its executives would help Walmart avoid problems with discrimination? If so, how? If not, why not?

IT'S A WRAP! connect

www.mhhe.com/noefund4e is your source for Reviewing, Applying, and Practicing the concepts you learned about in Chapter 3.

Review	Application	Practice

Review
- Chapter learning objectives
- Review HR Forms: EEOC Form 100: Employer Information Report and OSHA Form 300A: Summary of Work-Related Injuries and Illnesses
- Test Your Knowledge: Comparing Affirmative Action, Valuing and Managing Diversity

Application
- Manager's Hot Seat segment: "Office Romance: Groping for Answers"
- Video case and quiz: "Working through a Medical Crisis"
- Self-assessments: What Do You Know about Sexual Harassment? and Appreciating and Valuing Diversity
- Web exercise: Equal Employment Opportunity Commission
- Small-business case: Medical-Testing Company Flunks the Fair-Employment Test

Practice
- Chapter quiz

NOTES

1. Roger O. Crockett, "Deloitte's Diversity Push," *BusinessWeek*, October 5, 2009, Business & Company Resource Center, http://galenet.galegroup.com; and Laura Mazzuca Toops, "Work Force Diversity Plus Inclusion Equals True Organizational Innovation," *National Underwriter Property & Casualty Insurance*, November 30, 2009, Business & Company Resource Center, http://galenet.galegroup.com.

2. *Bakke v. Regents of the University of California*, 17 F.E.P.C. 1000 (1978).

3. "Labor Letter," *Wall Street Journal*, August 25, 1987, p. 1; and Bryce G. Murray and E. Frederick Preis Jr., "Age Discrimination in Employment," *Corporate Counselor*, September 1, 2009, Business & Company Resource Center, http://galenet.galegroup.com.

4. Henry Weinstein, "U.S. Charges Law Partnership with Age Bias," *Los Angeles Times*, January 20, 2005, downloaded at Yahoo News, http://story.news.yahoo.com; and Equal Employment Opportunity Commission, "$27.5 Million Consent Decree Resolves EEOC Age Bias Suit against Sidley Austin," news release, www.eeoc.gov/press/ October 5, 2007.

5. Stefan Stern, "The Kids Are Allright but They Need Help," *Financial Times*, February 23, 2010, Business & Company Resource Center, http://galenet.galegroup.com.

6. Equal Employment Opportunity Commission, "Pregnancy Discrimination," *Discrimination by Type: Facts and Guidance*, www.eeoc.gov, modified March 2, 2005.

7. Equal Employment Opportunity Commission, "Facts about the Americans with Disabilities Act," http://www1.eeoc.gov//eeoc/publications/, accessed March 3, 2010; EEOC, "Summary of Key Provisions: EEOC's Notice of Proposed Rulemaking (NPRM) to Implement the ADA Amendments Act of 2008 (ADAAA)," http://www.eeoc.gov/laws/regulations/, accessed March 3, 2010; and EEOC, "Questions and Answers on the Notice of Proposed Rulemaking for the ADA Amendments Act of 2008," www.eeoc.gov/policy/docs/qanda_adaaa_nprm.pdf, accessed March 2, 2010.

8. "ADA Supervisor Training Program: A Must for Any Supervisor Conducting a Legal Job Interview," *Employment Law Update* 7, no. 6 (1992), pp. 1–6; and EEOC "Questions and Answers."

9. U.S. Department of Labor, Office of Disability Employment Policy, "The ADA: Myths and Facts," September 2005, http://www.dol.gov/odep/pubs/.

10. "The Price of Prejudice," *The Economist*, January 15, 2009, http://www.economist.com.

11. *UAW v. Johnson Controls, Inc.*, 499 U.S. 187 (1991).

12. Jan Crawford Greenburg, "Age-Bias Law Expanded," *Chicago Tribune*, March 31, 2005, sec. 1, pp. 1, 17; and Jess Bravin, "Court Expands Age Bias Claims for Work Force," *Wall Street Journal*, March 31, 2005, http://online.wsj.com.

13. Greenburg, "Age-Bias Law Expanded"; and Bravin, "Court Expands Age Bias Claims."

14. D. Kravitz and J. Platania, "Attitudes and Beliefs about Affirmative Action: Effects of Target and of

Respondent Sex and Ethnicity," *Journal of Applied Psychology* 78 (1993), pp. 928–38.

15. Equal Employment Opportunity Commission, "The Vail Corporation Pays $80,000 to Settle EEOC Religious and Sexual Harassment Lawsuit," news release, June 22, 2009, http://www.eeoc.gov.

16. EEOC guideline based on the Civil Rights Act of 1964, Title VII.

17. "Lawsuit Filed in U.S. District Court in Louisiana Accuses Boh Bros. Superintendent of Sexual Harassment," *New Orleans City Business*, September 23, 2009, Business & Company Resource Center, http://galenet.galegroup.com; and Ben Myers, "Two Area Employers in N.O. Face Sexual Harassment Lawsuits," *New Orleans City Business*, November 2, 2009, Business & Company Resource Center, http://galenet.galegroup.com.

18. Kelly K. Spors, "Top Small Workplaces 2009," *Wall Street Journal*, September 28, 2009, http://online.wsj.com.

19. Susan Reutman, "Nail Salon Table Evaluation," *NIOSH Science Blog*, March 10, 2009, http://www.cdc.gov/niosh/blog/.

20. Reuters Limited, "Healthcare Workers Risk Getting Asthma on the Job," *Yahoo News*, March 24, 2005, http://news.yahoo.com.

21. Bureau of Labor Statistics, "Workplace Injuries and Illnesses, 2008," news release, October 29, 2009, http://www.bls.gov/iif/oshsum.htm; and Occupational Health and Safety Administration, "Statement of Labor Secretary Elaine L. Chao on Historic Lows in Workplace Injury and Illness," OSHA Web site, www.osha.gov, December 18, 2001.

22. J. Roughton, "Managing a Safety Program through Job Hazard Analysis," *Professional Safety* 37 (1992), pp. 28–31.

23. Roughton, "Managing a Safety Program."

24. R. G. Hallock and D. A. Weaver, "Controlling Losses and Enhancing Management Systems with TOR Analysis," *Professional Safety* 35 (1990), pp. 24–26.

25. Douglas P. Shuit, "A Left Turn for Safety," *Workforce Management*, March 2005, pp. 49–50.

26. David Shutt, "Protecting the Hands of Working Women," *EHS Today*, October 2009, Business & Company Resource Center, http://galenet.galegroup.com.

27. Cynthia Roth, "Who Is the Older Worker?" *EHS Today*, January 2009, Business & Company Resource Center, http://galenet.galegroup.com.

28. J. F. Mangan, "Hazard Communications: Safety in Knowledge," *Best's Review* 92 (1991), pp. 84–88.

29. R. King, "Active Safety Programs, Education Can Help Prevent Back Injuries," *Occupational Health and Safety* 60 (1991), pp. 49–52.

30. Prevent Blindness America, "2,000 Employees Suffer Work-Related Eye Injuries Every Day in the United States," news release, March 1, 2005, downloaded at www.preventblindness.org.

31. M. Janssens, J. M. Brett, and F. J. Smith, "Confirmatory Cross-Cultural Research: Testing the Viability of a Corporation-wide Safety Policy," *Academy of Management Journal* 38 (1995), pp. 364–82.

32. E. Sage-Gavin and P. Wright, "Corporate Social Responsibility at Gap, Inc.: An Interview with Eva Sage-Gavin," *Human Resource Planning* 30, mar. 1, (2007), pp. 45–48.

4

Analyzing Work and Designing Jobs

What Do I Need to Know?

After reading this chapter, you should be able to:

LO1 Summarize the elements of work flow analysis.

LO2 Describe how work flow is related to an organization's structure.

LO3 Define the elements of a job analysis, and discuss their significance for human resource management.

LO4 Tell how to obtain information for a job analysis.

LO5 Summarize recent trends in job analysis.

LO6 Describe methods for designing a job so that it can be done efficiently.

LO7 Identify approaches to designing a job to make it motivating.

LO8 Explain how organizations apply ergonomics to design safe jobs.

LO9 Discuss how organizations can plan for the mental demands of a job.

Introduction

When brothers Michael and Jack Kennedy started Railroad Associates Corporation, a contracting firm that repairs railways, they wanted an organization that would be both flexible and efficient. So the two owners decided that decision making wouldn't be a managers-only responsibility. In fact, they skipped middle management altogether. Workers at job sites are expected to make their own decisions when questions and problems arise. That means Railroad Associates has to hire workers who are willing and able to take responsibility, and the company has to provide plenty of training. The company also gives employees access to its intranet, where they can look up budgets and schedules for the jobs they're working on. But the company doesn't just expect flexibility *from* its employees; it also offers flexibility *to* them in the form of work schedules employees can adjust when they have commitments outside of work. Once, when a truck driver's daughter needed surgery, Michael Kennedy drove the man's tractor trailer for the week the employee spent taking care of his daughter.[1]

Broad responsibilities, duties like truck driving or construction tasks, and a flexible work schedule—all these are elements of workers' jobs with Railroad Associates. These elements give rise to the types of skills and personalities required for success, and they in turn help to narrow the field of people who will succeed at the company. Consideration of such elements is at the heart of analyzing work, whether in a start-up enterprise, a multinational corporation, or a government agency.

This chapter discusses the analysis and design of work and, in doing so, lays out some considerations that go into making informed decisions about how to create and link jobs. The chapter begins with a look at the big-picture issues related to analyzing work flow and organizational structure. The discussion then turns to the more specific issues of analyzing and designing jobs. Traditionally, job analysis has emphasized the study of existing jobs in order to make decisions such as employee selection, training, and compensation. In contrast, job design has emphasized making jobs more efficient or more motivating. However, as this chapter shows, the two activities are interrelated.

Work Flow in Organizations

LO1 Summarize the elements of work flow analysis.

Informed decisions about jobs take place in the context of the organization's overall work flow. Through the process of **work flow design,** managers analyze the tasks needed to produce a product or service. With this information, they assign these tasks to specific jobs and positions. (A **job** is a set of related duties. A **position** is the set of duties performed by one person. A school has many teaching *positions;* the person filling each of those positions is performing the *job* of teacher.) Basing these decisions on work flow design can lead to better results than the more traditional practice of looking at jobs individually.

Work Flow Design
The process of analyzing the tasks necessary for the production of a product or service.

Job
A set of related duties.

Position
The set of duties (job) performed by a particular person.

Work Flow Analysis

Before designing its work flow, the organization's planners need to analyze what work needs to be done. Figure 4.1 shows the elements of a work flow analysis. For each type of work, such as producing a product line or providing a support service (accounting, legal support, and so on), the analysis identifies the output of the process, the activities involved, and three categories of inputs: raw inputs (materials and information), equipment, and human resources.

Outputs are the products of any work unit, whether a department, team, or individual. An output can be as readily identifiable as a completed purchase order, an employment test, or a hot, juicy hamburger. An output can also be a service, such as transportation, cleaning, or answering questions about employee benefits. Even at an organization that produces tangible goods, such as computers, many employees produce other outputs, such as components of the computers, marketing plans, and building security. Work flow analysis identifies the outputs of particular work units. The analysis considers not only the amount of output but also quality standards. This attention to outputs has only recently gained attention among HRM professionals. However, it gives a clearer view of how to increase the effectiveness of each work unit.

For the outputs identified, work flow analysis then examines the work processes used to generate those outputs. Work processes are the activities that members of a work unit engage in to produce a given output. Every process consists of operating procedures that specify how things should be done at each stage of developing the output. These procedures include all the tasks that must be performed in producing the output. Usually, the analysis breaks down the tasks into those performed by each person in the work unit. This analysis helps with design of efficient work systems by clarifying which tasks are necessary. Typically, when a unit's work load increases, the unit adds people, and when the work load decreases, some members of the unit may busy themselves with unrelated tasks in an effort to appear busy. Without knowledge of work processes, it is more difficult to identify whether the work

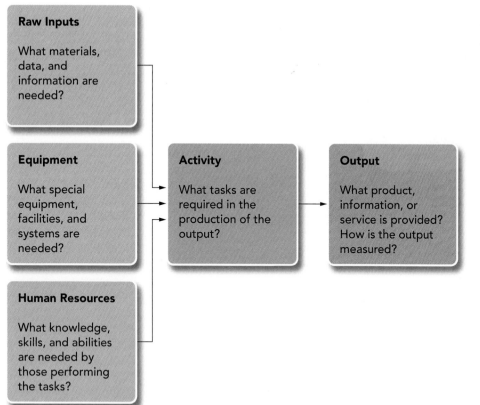

Figure 4.1

Developing a Work Flow Analysis

unit is properly staffed. Knowledge of work processes also can guide staffing changes when work is automated, outsourced, or restructured. At some companies, so much effort has gone into analyzing and refining work processes to improve efficiency that when demand plummeted in the recent recession, layoffs—as great as they were— were less than what the decline in sales would have predicted. For example, the South Carolina manufacturing plant of Parker Hannifin Corporation needs so few people to run the facility and each person is so knowledgeable that the company cannot operate the plant if it lays off any workers. In addition, at companies like surgical-device maker Conmed, work processes have become so flexible that the companies adjust to changes in demand gradually as they occur, rather than piling up inventory and then halting and later resuming production.[2]

The final stage in work flow analysis is to identify the inputs used in the development of the work unit's product. As shown in Figure 4.1, these inputs can be broken down into the raw inputs (materials and knowledge), equipment, and human skills needed to perform the tasks. In the mortgage banking industry, the inputs required for servicing loans increased dramatically after the financial crisis and economic recession made repayment impossible for a wave of borrowers. The federal government launched the Home Affordable Modification Program (HAMP), in which loan servicers—who traditionally handled just the routine transactions of paying off a home loan—were expected to work with borrowers to arrange new deals they could afford. Loan servicers suddenly needed many more people, and these people needed skills in working with the public as well as technical knowledge for determining what borrowers can afford to pay, what their home is worth, and what documents are required to modify a loan

Firefighters work as a team. They and their equipment are the "inputs" (they do the work), and the "output" is an extinguished fire and the rescue of people and pets. In any organization or team, workers need to be cross-trained in several skills to create an effective team. If these firefighters are trained to do any part of the job, the chief can deploy them rapidly as needed.

LO2 Describe how work flow is related to an organization's structure.

under HAMP. The servicers also needed computer software and hardware for processing all the data and documents. The challenge of quickly providing these new inputs is so great that some servicers are simply outsourcing the whole process to specialists.[3]

Work Flow Design and an Organization's Structure

Besides looking at the work flow of each process, it is important to see how the work fits within the context of the organization's structure. Within an organization, units and individuals must cooperate to create outputs. Ideally, the organization's structure brings together the people who must collaborate to efficiently produce the desired outputs. The structure may do this in a way that is highly centralized (that is, with authority concentrated in a few people at the top of the organization) or decentralized (with authority spread among many people). The organization may group jobs according to functions (for example, welding, painting, packaging), or it may set up divisions to focus on products or customer groups.

Although there are an infinite number of ways to combine the elements of an organization's structure, we can make some general observations about structure and work design. If the structure is strongly based on function, workers tend to have low authority and to work alone at highly specialized jobs. Jobs that involve teamwork or broad responsibility tend to require a structure based on divisions other than functions. When the goal is to empower employees, companies therefore need to set up structures and jobs that enable broad responsibility, such as jobs that involve employees in serving a particular group of customers or producing a particular product, rather than performing a narrowly defined function. The organization's structure also affects managers' jobs. Managing a division responsible for a product or customer group tends to require more experience and cognitive (thinking) ability than managing a department that handles a particular function.[4]

Work design often emphasizes the analysis and design of jobs, as described in the remainder of this chapter. Although all of these approaches can succeed, each focuses on one isolated job at a time. These approaches do not necessarily consider how that single job fits into the overall work flow or structure of the organization. To use these techniques effectively, human resource personnel should also understand their organization as a whole. As the "HR Oops!" emphasizes, without this big-picture appreciation, they might redesign a job in a way that makes sense for the particular job but is out of line with the organization's work flow, structure, or strategy.

LO3 Define the elements of a job analysis, and discuss their significance for human resource management.

Job Analysis
The process of getting detailed information about jobs.

Job Analysis

To achieve high-quality performance, organizations have to understand and match job requirements and people. This understanding requires **job analysis,** the process of getting detailed information about jobs. Analyzing jobs and understanding what is required to carry out a job provide essential knowledge for staffing, training, performance appraisal, and many other HR activities. For instance, a supervisor's evaluation of an employee's work should be based on performance relative to job requirements. In very small organizations, line managers may perform a job analysis, but usually the

HR Oops!

An Undefined Job

One way to see the significance of work design and job analysis is to learn from what happens at companies that fail to define jobs. An anonymous employee of a multimedia company told *Entrepreneur* magazine's Scott Gornall about an editor who was given a new job title, "creative manager of content." Unfortunately, the scope of that job was never specified or explained to others in the company.

The new creative manager appointed himself to teach the others how to be more creative. He placed some magazines in a cubicle and called a meeting to announce that, henceforth, that space was the Idea Lab, where employees could go to reflect on ideas. He drew up a flow chart to explain the Idea Lab. He called monthly meetings for idea sharing. His colleagues, unimpressed, felt that he was disturbing their work in order to justify his new responsibilities, whatever they were.

Perhaps in principle, a creative manager of content would have met a real need for this publisher, but because the position and its fit with the organization's objectives were never clearly spelled out, the idea was wasted.

Source: Based on Scott Gornall, "The Superfluous Position," *Entrepreneur*, July 2009, http://www.entrepreneur.com.

Questions

1. Why might management be reluctant to prepare a formal job description for a position like "creative manager of content"? What are the pitfalls of not doing so?
2. What advice about the position would you give to this company's managers?

work is done by a human resource professional. A large company may have a compensation management department that includes job analysts (also called personnel analysts). Organizations may also contract with firms that provide this service.

Job Descriptions

An essential part of job analysis is the creation of job descriptions. A **job description** is a list of the tasks, duties, and responsibilities (TDRs) that a job entails. TDRs are observable actions. For example, a news photographer's job requires the jobholder to use a camera to take photographs. If you were to observe someone in that position for a day, you would almost certainly see some pictures being taken. When a manager attempts to evaluate job performance, it is most important to have detailed information about the work performed in the job (that is, the TDRs). This information makes it possible to determine how well an individual is meeting each job requirement.

A job description typically has the format shown in Figure 4.2. It includes the job title, a brief description of the TDRs, and a list of the essential duties with detailed specifications of the tasks involved in carrying out each duty. Although organizations may modify this format according to their particular needs, all job descriptions within an organization should follow the same format. This helps the organization make consistent decisions about such matters as pay and promotions. It also helps the organization show that it makes human resource decisions fairly.

Whenever the organization creates a new job, it needs to prepare a job description, using a process such as the one detailed in the "HR How To" box on page 101. Job descriptions should then be reviewed periodically (say, once a year) and updated if necessary. Performance appraisals can provide a good opportunity for updating job descriptions, as the employee and supervisor compare what the employee has been doing against the details of the job description.

Job Description
A list of the tasks, duties, and responsibilities (TDRs) that a particular job entails.

99

Figure 4.2

Sample Job Description

> ### TRAIN CREW/SERVICE AT UNION PACIFIC
>
> **OVERVIEW**
> When you work on a Union Pacific train crew, you're working at the very heart of our railroad. Moving trains. Driving trains. Making sure our customers' freight gets delivered safely and on time.
>
> **JOB DESCRIPTION**
> In this entry-level position, you'll start as a Switchperson or Brakeperson, working as on-the-ground traffic control. You don't need any previous railroad experience; we provide all training. These jobs directly lead to becoming a Conductor and a Locomotive Engineer, where you will have a rare opportunity to work on board a moving locomotive. The Conductor is responsible for the train, the freight and the crew. The Locomotive Engineer actually operates the locomotive.
>
> **DUTIES**
> As a Switchperson or Brakeperson, you'll learn to move trains safely in the yards and over the road. You'll be climbing ladders, boarding freight cars, operating track switches, inspecting cars, and using radio communications to control train movement.
>
> **MAJOR TASKS AND RESPONSIBILITIES**
> You won't work a standard 40-hour work week. Train crews are always on-call, even on weekends and holidays. You'll travel with our trains, sometimes spending a day or more away from your home terminal.

SOURCE: Union Pacific Web site, www.unionpacific.jobs/careers/explore/train/train_service.shtml, accessed March 8, 2010.

Organizations should give each newly hired employee a copy of his or her job description. This helps the employee to understand what is expected, but it shouldn't be presented as limiting the employee's commitment to quality and customer satisfaction. Ideally, employees will want to go above and beyond the listed duties when the situation and their abilities call for that. Many job descriptions include the phrase *and other duties as requested* as a way to remind employees not to tell their supervisor, "But that's not part of my job."

Job Specifications

Job Specification
A list of the knowledge, skills, abilities, and other characteristics (KSAOs) that an individual must have to perform a particular job.

Whereas the job description focuses on the activities involved in carrying out a job, a **job specification** looks at the qualities or requirements the person performing the job must possess. It is a list of the knowledge, skills, abilities, and other characteristics (KSAOs) that an individual must have to perform the job. *Knowledge* refers to factual or procedural information that is necessary for successfully performing a task. For example, this course is providing you with knowledge in how to manage human resources. A *skill* is an individual's level of proficiency at performing a particular task—that is, the capability to perform it well. With knowledge and experience, you could

HR How To

WRITING A JOB DESCRIPTION

Preparing a job description begins with gathering information from sources who can identify the details of performing a task—for example, persons already performing the job, the supervisor or team leader, or if the job is new, managers who are creating the new position. Other sources of information may include the company's human resource files, such as past job advertisements and job descriptions, as well as general sources of information about similar jobs, such as O*NET (http://online.onetcenter.org).

Based on the information gathered, the next step is to identify which activities are essential duties of the job. These include mental and physical tasks, as well as any particular methods and equipment to be used in carrying out those tasks. When possible, these should be stated in terms that are broad and goal oriented enough for the person in the position to innovate and improve. For example, "Developing and implementing a system for ordering supplies efficiently" implies a goal (efficiency) as well as a task.

From these sources, the writer of the job description obtains the important elements of the description:

- *Title of the job*—The title should be descriptive and, if appropriate, indicate the job's level in the organization.
- *Administrative information about the job*—The job description may identify a division, department, supervisor's title, date of the analysis, name of the analyst, and other information for administering the company's human resource activities.
- *Statement of the job's purpose*—This should be brief and describe the position in broad terms.

- *Essential duties of the job*—These should be listed in order of importance to successful performance and should include details such as physical requirements (for example, the amount of weight to be lifted), the persons with whom an employee in this job interacts, and the results to be accomplished. This section should include every duty that the job analysis identified as essential.
- *Additional responsibilities*—The job description may state that the position requires additional responsibilities as requested by the supervisor.

Sources: Small Business Administration, "Writing Effective Job Descriptions," *Small Business Planner,* www.sba.gov/smallbusinessplanner/, accessed March 10, 2010; and "How to Write a Job Analysis and Description," *Entrepreneur,* www.entrepreneur.com, accessed March 10, 2010.

acquire skill in the task of preparing job specifications. *Ability,* in contrast to skill, refers to a more general enduring capability that an individual possesses. A person might have the ability to cooperate with others or to write clearly and precisely. Finally, *other characteristics* might be personality traits such as someone's persistence or motivation to achieve. Some jobs also have legal requirements, such as licensing or certification. Figure 4.3 is a set of sample job specifications for the job description in Figure 4.2.

In developing job specifications, it is important to consider all of the elements of KSAOs. As with writing a job description, the information can come from a combination of people performing the job, people supervising or planning for the job, and trained job analysts. Most of the jobs in a grocery warehouse are physically taxing, so to describe positions at a Roanoke County, Virginia, distribution center, Atlas Logistics emphasizes KSAOs related to that challenge. Atlas needs employees who are strong enough to lift 80 pounds and who are willing to spend part of the day working in the freezer area.[5]

In contrast to tasks, duties, and responsibilities, KSAOs are characteristics of people and are not directly observable. They are observable only when individuals are carrying out the TDRs of the job—and afterward, if they can show the product of

Figure 4.3

Sample Job Specifications

TRAIN CREW/SERVICE AT UNION PACIFIC

REQUIREMENTS

You must be at least 18 years old. You must speak and read English because you'll be asked to follow posted bulletins, regulations, rule books, timetables, switch lists, etc. You must pass a reading comprehension test (see sample) to be considered for an interview.

JOB REQUIREMENTS

You must be able to use a computer keyboard, and you must be able to count and compare numbers. (You might, for example, be asked to count the cars on a train during switching.) You must be able to solve problems quickly and react to changing conditions on the job.

You must have strong vision and hearing, including the ability to: see and read hand signals from near and far; distinguish between colors; visually judge the speed and distance of moving objects; see at night; and recognize changes in sounds.

You must also be physically strong: able to push, pull, lift and carry up to 25 pounds frequently; up to 50 pounds occasionally; and up to 83 pounds infrequently. You'll need good balance to regularly step on and off equipment and work from ladders to perform various tasks. And you must be able to walk, sit, stand and stoop comfortably.

You'll be working outdoors in all weather conditions—including snow, ice, rain, cold, and heat—and frequently at elevations more than 12 feet above the ground.

SOURCE: Union Pacific Web site, www.unionpacific.jobs/careers/explore/train/train_service.shtml, accessed March 8, 2010.

their labor. Thus, if someone applied for a job as a news photographer, you could not simply look at the individual to determine whether he or she can spot and take effective photographs. However, you could draw conclusions later about the person's skills by looking at examples of his or her photographs.

Accurate information about KSAOs is especially important for making decisions about who will fill a job. A manager attempting to fill a position needs information about the characteristics required and about the characteristics of each applicant. Interviews and selection decisions should therefore focus on KSAOs.

LO4 Tell how to obtain information for a job analysis.

Sources of Job Information

Information for analyzing an existing job often comes from incumbents, that is, people who currently hold that position in the organization. They are a logical source of information because they are most acquainted with the details of the job. Incumbents should be able to provide very accurate information.

A drawback of relying solely on incumbents' information is that they may have an incentive to exaggerate what they do in order to appear more valuable to the organization. Information from incumbents should therefore be supplemented with information from observers, such as supervisors, who look for a match between what incumbents are doing and what they are supposed to do. Research suggests that supervisors may provide the most accurate estimates of the importance of job duties, while incumbents may be more accurate in reporting information about the actual time spent performing job tasks and safety-related risk factors.[6] For analyzing skill levels, the best source may be external job analysts who have more experience rating a wide range of jobs.[7]

Manpower, an employment services company, uses the O*Net to classify its jobs and track demand nationwide.

The government also provides background information for analyzing jobs. In the 1930s, the U.S. Department of Labor created the *Dictionary of Occupational Titles (DOT)* as a vehicle for helping the new public employment system link the demand for skills and the supply of skills in the U.S. workforce. The *DOT* described over 12,000 jobs, as well as some of the requirements of successful job holders. This system served the United States well for over 60 years, but it became clear to Labor Department officials that jobs in the new economy were so different that the *DOT* no longer served its purpose. The Labor Department therefore introduced a new system, called the Occupational Information Network (O*NET).

Instead of relying on fixed job titles and narrow task descriptions, the O*NET uses a common language that generalizes across jobs to describe the abilities, work styles, work activities, and work context required for 1,000 broadly defined occupations. Users can visit O*NET OnLine (http://online.onetcenter.org) to review jobs' tasks, work styles and context, and requirements including skills, training, and experience. When Boeing prepared to close its plant in Monrovia, California, it used the O*NET's Skills Survey and database to help employees to be laid off identify jobs where they could use their skills elsewhere. Piedmont Natural Gas uses the O*NET to improve selection of entry-level employees, hoping to reduce turnover by ensuring a better match between candidates' KSAOs and the requirements of open positions at Piedmont.[8] Furthermore, although the O*NET was developed to analyze jobs in the U.S. economy, research suggests that its ratings tend to be the same for jobs located in other countries.[9]

focus on social responsibility

Position Analysis Questionnaire

After gathering information, the job analyst uses the information to analyze the job. One of the broadest and best-researched instruments for analyzing jobs is the **Position Analysis Questionnaire (PAQ).** This is a standardized job analysis questionnaire containing 194 items that represent work behaviors, work conditions, and job characteristics that apply to a wide variety of jobs. The questionnaire organizes these items into six sections concerning different aspects of the job:

1. *Information input*—Where and how a worker gets information needed to perform the job.
2. *Mental processes*—The reasoning, decision making, planning, and information-processing activities involved in performing the job.
3. *Work output*—The physical activities, tools, and devices used by the worker to perform the job.

Position Analysis Questionnaire (PAQ)
A standardized job analysis questionnaire containing 194 questions about work behaviors, work conditions, and job characteristics that apply to a wide variety of jobs.

4. *Relationships with other persons*—The relationships with other people required in performing the job.
5. *Job context*—The physical and social contexts where the work is performed.
6. *Other characteristics*—The activities, conditions, and characteristics other than those previously described that are relevant to the job.

The person analyzing a job determines whether each item on the questionnaire applies to the job being analyzed. The analyst rates each item on six scales: extent of use, amount of time, importance to the job, possibility of occurrence, applicability, and special code (special rating scales used with a particular item). The PAQ headquarters uses a computer to score the questionnaire and generate a report that describes the scores on the job dimensions.

Using the PAQ provides an organization with information that helps in comparing jobs, even when they are dissimilar. The PAQ also has the advantage that it considers the whole work process, from inputs through outputs. However, the person who fills out the questionnaire must have college-level reading skills, and the PAQ is meant to be completed only by job analysts trained in this method. In fact, the ratings of job incumbents tend to be less reliable than ratings by supervisors and trained analysts.[10] Also, the descriptions in the PAQ reports are rather abstract, so the reports may not be useful for writing job descriptions or redesigning jobs.

Fleishman Job Analysis System

Fleishman Job Analysis System
Job analysis technique that asks subject-matter experts to evaluate a job in terms of the abilities required to perform the job.

To gather information about worker requirements, the **Fleishman Job Analysis System** asks subject-matter experts (typically job incumbents) to evaluate a job in terms of the abilities required to perform the job.[11] The survey is based on 52 categories of abilities, ranging from written comprehension to deductive reasoning, manual dexterity, stamina, and originality. As in the example in Figure 4.4, the survey items are arranged into a scale for each ability. Each begins with a description of the ability and a comparison to related abilities. Below this is a seven-point scale with phrases describing extemely high and low levels of the ability. The person completing the survey indicates which point on the scale represents the level of the ability required for performing the job being analyzed.

When the survey has been completed in all 52 categories, the results provide a picture of the ability requirements of a job. Such information is especially useful for employee selection, training, and career development.

Importance of Job Analysis

Job analysis is so important to HR managers that it has been called the building block of everything that personnel does.[12] The fact is that almost every human resource management program requires some type of information that is gleaned from job analysis:[13]

- *Work redesign*—Often an organization seeks to redesign work to make it more efficient or to improve quality. The redesign requires detailed information about the existing job(s). In addition, preparing the redesign is similar to analyzing a job that does not yet exist.
- *Human resource planning*—As planners analyze human resource needs and how to meet those needs, they must have accurate information about the levels of skill required in various jobs, so that they can tell what kinds of human resources will be needed.
- *Selection*—To identify the most qualified applicants for various positions, decision makers need to know what tasks the individuals must perform, as well as the necessary knowledge, skills, and abilities.

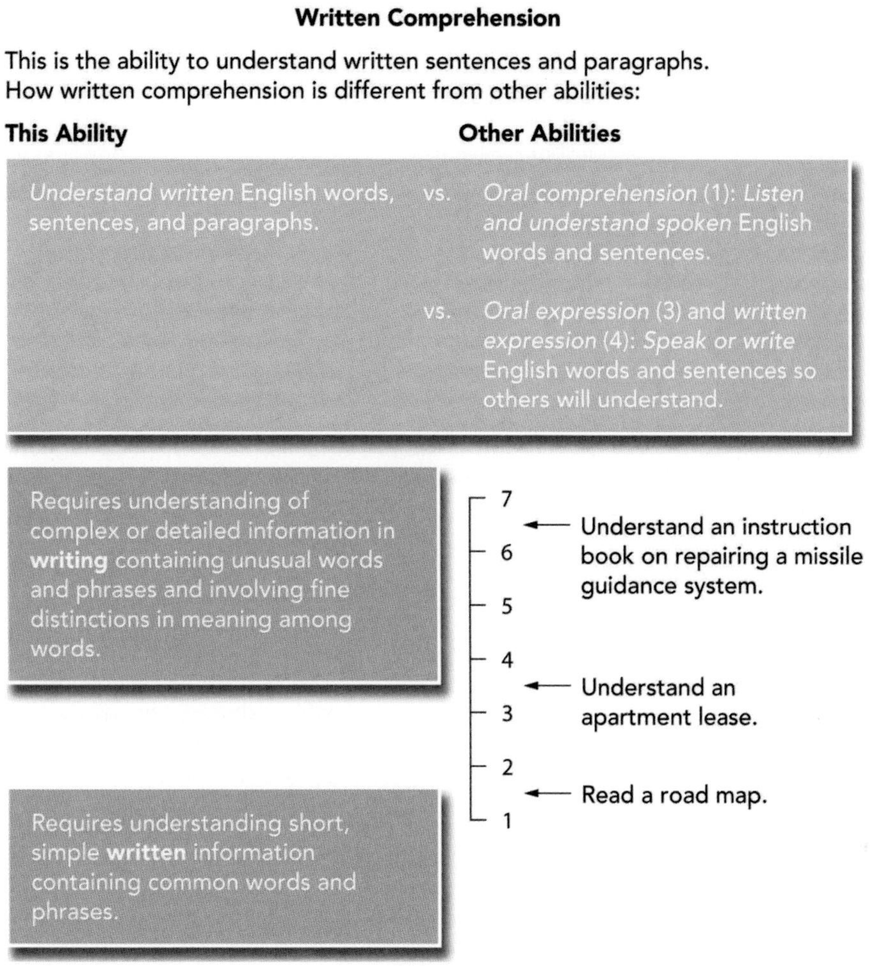

Figure 4.4

Example of an Ability from the Fleishman Job Analysis System

Written Comprehension

This is the ability to understand written sentences and paragraphs. How written comprehension is different from other abilities:

This Ability

Other Abilities

Understand written English words, sentences, and paragraphs.

vs. Oral comprehension (1): Listen and understand spoken English words and sentences.

vs. Oral expression (3) and written expression (4): Speak or write English words and sentences so others will understand.

Requires understanding of complex or detailed information in **writing** containing unusual words and phrases and involving fine distinctions in meaning among words.

7

6 ◄— Understand an instruction book on repairing a missile guidance system.

5

4

3 ◄— Understand an apartment lease.

2

1 ◄— Read a road map.

Requires understanding short, simple **written** information containing common words and phrases.

SOURCE: From E. A. Fleishman and M. D. Mumford, "Evaluating Classifications of Job Behavior: A Construct Validation of the Ability Requirements Scales," *Personnel Psychology* 44 (1991), pp. 423–576. Copyright © 1991 by Blackwell Publishing. Reproduced with permission of Blackwell Publishing via Copyright Clearance Center.

- *Training*—Almost every employee hired by an organization will require training. Any training program requires knowledge of the tasks performed in a job, so that the training is related to the necessary knowledge and skills.
- *Performance appraisal*—An accurate performance appraisal requires information about how well each employee is performing in order to reward employees who perform well and to improve their performance if it is below standard. Job analysis helps in identifying the behaviors and the results associated with effective performance.
- *Career planning*—Matching an individual's skills and aspirations with career opportunities requires that those in charge of career planning know the skill requirements of the various jobs. This allows them to guide individuals into jobs in which they will succeed and be satisfied.
- *Job evaluation*—The process of job evaluation involves assessing the relative dollar value of each job to the organization in order to set up fair pay structures. If employees do not believe pay structures are fair, they will become dissatisfied and may quit, or they will not see much benefit in striving for promotions. To put dollar values on jobs, it is necessary to get information about different jobs and compare them.

FRITO-LAY TAKES A FRESH LOOK AT JOB DESIGN

Frito-Lay's 17,000 route sales representatives (RSRs) play an unglamorous but essential role for the company. Each day, these employees drive trucks loaded with snacks to stores, where they arrange them in displays. The RSRs also talk to managers at the stores to take orders and negotiate for additional selling space. These employees are paid a commission tied to sales volume.

Recently, Frito-Lay was concerned that although RSRs had been meeting goals for sales and profits, high turnover and low productivity were becoming an issue. The company turned to its HR department to uncover the source of the problem. An investigation of compensation found that it was not a strong explanation for the problems. So the department began to analyze the RSR job. This analysis uncovered basic facts:

- The RSR job involves three main tasks: selling, merchandising (setting up displays), and driving and delivery.

- The key to greater sales is getting the best locations for product displays.
- The job is highly structured, with routes laid out each day. Some RSRs have low-volume routes, serving small stores with small trucks. Other RSRs have high-volume routes, serving big stores such as Walmart and driving larger trucks. RSRs on low-volume routes spend more of their day driving. RSRs on high-volume routes spend more of their day with store managers and have support from Frito-Lay employees who deal with buyers at the stores' headquarters.

Frito-Lay's HR analysts concluded that they should investigate whether combining the three types of tasks into one job was productive and whether jobs for the two types of routes should be structured differently.

To find out, the department surveyed RSRs and their supervisors to learn about the employees' backgrounds, motivation,

and satisfaction, linking that information with performance data. Frito-Lay learned that the type of route did indeed make a difference for job design. For the RSRs with low-volume routes, their selling skills—particularly the ability to negotiate additional display space—were most important to their performance. RSRs with more experience in selling tended to perform best in this role. So for these employees, Frito-Lay realized that it needed to emphasize selling skills in its hiring and training. For the high-volume routes, selling was important, but driving mattered more because these RSRs had to deliver all their orders during the early morning. Improving performance of these jobs required redesigning the delivery routes so the RSRs made all their deliveries first and then returned to stores to perform their other tasks later.

Source: Based on Alec Levenson and Tracy Faber, "Count on Productivity Gains," *HR Magazine*, June 2009, pp. 69–74.

Job analysis is also important from a legal standpoint. As we saw in Chapter 3, the government imposes requirements related to equal employment opportunity. Detailed, accurate, objective job specifications help decision makers comply with these regulations by keeping the focus on tasks and abilities. These documents also provide evidence of efforts made to engage in fair employment practices. For example, to enforce the Americans with Disabilities Act, the Equal Employment Opportunity Commission may look at job descriptions to identify the essential functions of a job and determine whether a disabled person could have performed those functions with reasonable accommodations. Likewise, lists of duties in different jobs could be compared to evaluate claims under the Equal Pay Act. However, job descriptions and job specifications are not a substitute for fair employment practices.

Besides helping human resource professionals, job analysis helps supervisors and other managers carry out their duties. Data from job analysis can help managers identify the types of work in their units, as well as provide information about the work flow process, so that managers can evaluate whether work is done in the most efficient way. Job analysis information also supports managers as they make hiring decisions, review performance, and recommend rewards. The "Best Practices" box describes how Frito-Lay used job analysis to help meet the company's productivity goals.

Trends in Job Analysis

LO5 Summarize recent trends in job analysis.

As we noted in the earlier discussion of work flow analysis, organizations are beginning to appreciate the need to analyze jobs in the context of the organization's structure and strategy. In addition, organizations are recognizing that today's workplace must be adaptable and is constantly subject to change. Thus, although we tend to think of "jobs" as something stable, they actually tend to change and evolve over time. Those who occupy or manage jobs often make minor adjustments to match personal preferences or changing conditions.[14] Indeed, although errors in job analysis can have many sources, most inaccuracy is likely to result from job descriptions being outdated. For this reason, job analysis must not only define jobs when they are created, but also detect changes in jobs as time passes.

With global competitive pressure and economic downturns, one corporate change that has affected many organizations is downsizing. Research suggests that successful downsizing efforts almost always entail changes in the nature of jobs, not just their number. Jobs that have survived the downsizing of the most recent recession tend to have a broader scope of responsibilities coupled with less supervision.[15]

These changes in the nature of work and the expanded use of "project-based" organizational structures require the type of broader understanding that comes from an analysis of work flows. Because the work can change rapidly and it is impossible to rewrite job descriptions every week, job descriptions and specifications need to be flexible. At the same time, legal requirements (as discussed in Chapter 3) may discourage organizations from writing flexible job descriptions. This means organizations must balance the need for flexibility with the need for legal documentation. This presents one of the major challenges to be faced by HRM departments in the next decade. Many professionals are meeting this challenge with a greater emphasis on careful job design.

Job Design

LO6 Describe methods for designing a job so that it can be done efficiently.

Although job analysis, as just described, is important for an understanding of existing jobs, organizations also must plan for new jobs and periodically consider whether they should revise existing jobs. When an organization is expanding, supervisors and human resource professionals must help plan for new or growing work units. When an organization is trying to improve quality or efficiency, a review of work units and processes may require a fresh look at how jobs are designed.

These situations call for **job design,** the process of defining how work will be performed and what tasks will be required in a given job, or *job redesign,* a similar process that involves changing an existing job design. To design jobs effectively, a person must thoroughly understand the job itself (through job analysis) and its place in the larger work unit's work flow process (through work flow analysis). Having a detailed knowledge of the tasks performed in the work unit and in the job, a manager then has many alternative ways to design a job. As shown in Figure 4.5, the available

Job Design
The process of defining how work will be performed and what tasks will be required in a given job.

Figure 4.5

Approaches to Job Design

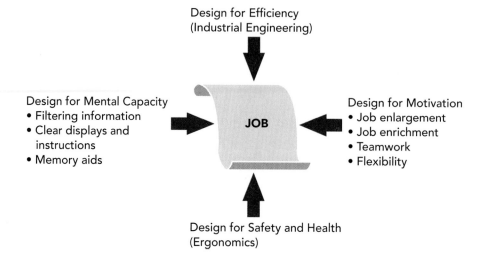

approaches emphasize different aspects of the job: the mechanics of doing a job efficiently, the job's impact on motivation, the use of safe work practices, and the mental demands of the job.

Designing Efficient Jobs

industrial engineering
The study of jobs to find the simplest way to structure work in order to maximize efficiency.

If workers perform tasks as efficiently as possible, not only does the organization benefit from lower costs and greater output per worker, but workers should be less fatigued. This point of view has for years formed the basis of classical **industrial engineering,** which looks for the simplest way to structure work in order to maximize efficiency. Typically, applying industrial engineering to a job reduces the complexity of the work, making it so simple that almost anyone can be trained quickly and easily to perform the job. Such jobs tend to be highly specialized and repetitive.

In practice, the scientific method traditionally seeks the "one best way" to perform a job by performing time-and-motion studies to identify the most efficient movements for workers to make. Once the engineers have identified the most efficient sequence of motions, the organization should select workers based on their ability to do the job, then train them in the details of the "one best way" to perform that job. The company also should offer pay structured to motivate workers to do their best. (Chapters 11 and 12 discuss pay and pay structures.)

Industrial engineering provides measurable and practical benefits. However, a focus on efficiency alone can create jobs that are so simple and repetitive that workers get bored. Workers performing these jobs may feel their work is meaningless. Hence, most organizations combine industrial engineering with other approaches to job design.

Designing Jobs That Motivate

LO7 Identify approaches to designing a job to make it motivating.

Especially when organizations must compete for employees, depend on skilled knowledge workers, or need a workforce that cares about customer satisfaction, a pure focus on efficiency will not achieve human resource objectives. The "Did You Know" box shows that job satisfaction among U.S. employees is declining. To improve job satisfaction, organizations need to design jobs that take into account factors that make jobs motivating and satisfying for employees.

A model that shows how to make jobs more motivating is the Job Characteristics Model, developed by Richard Hackman and Greg Oldham. This model describes jobs in terms of five characteristics:[16]

1. *Skill variety*—The extent to which a job requires a variety of skills to carry out the tasks involved.
2. *Task identity*—The degree to which a job requires completing a "whole" piece of work from beginning to end (for example, building an entire component or resolving a customer's complaint).
3. *Task significance*—The extent to which the job has an important impact on the lives of other people.
4. *Autonomy*—The degree to which the job allows an individual to make decisions about the way the work will be carried out.
5. *Feedback*—The extent to which a person receives clear information about performance effectiveness from the work itself.

As shown in Figure 4.6, the more of each of these characteristics a job has, the more motivating the job will be, according to the Job Characteristics Model. The model predicts that a person with such a job will be more satisfied and will produce more and better work. For example, to increase the meaningfulness of making artery stents (devices that are surgically inserted to promote blood flow), the maker of these products invites its production workers to an annual party, where they meet patients whose lives were saved by the products they helped to manufacture.[17]

Applications of the job characteristics approach to job design include job enlargement, job enrichment, self-managing work teams, flexible work schedules, and telework.

focus on
***social
responsibility***

Job Enlargement

In a job design, **job enlargement** refers to broadening the types of tasks performed. The objective of job enlargement is to make jobs less repetitive and more interesting. Spirit AeroSystems improved profitability by enlarging jobs. After the company

Job Enlargement
Broadening the types of tasks performed in a job.

Figure 4.6

Characteristics of a Motivating Job

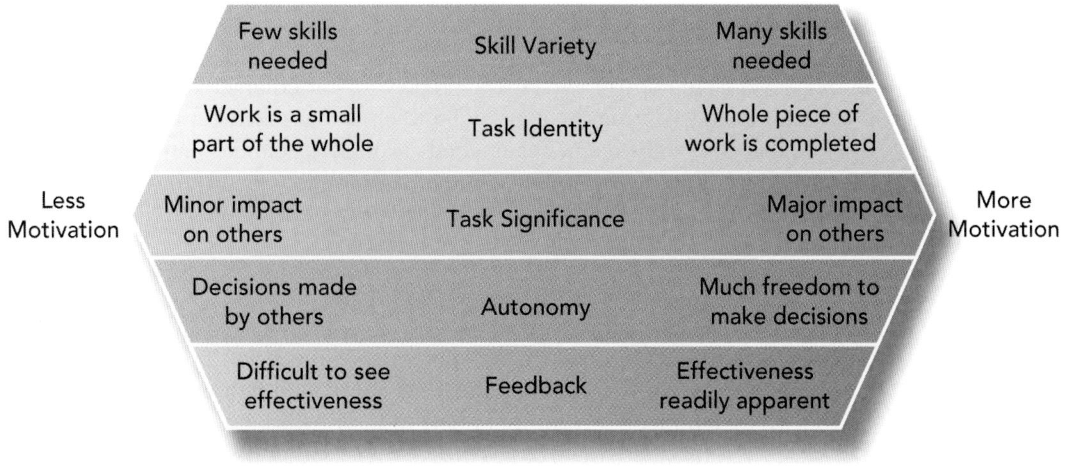

Less Motivation		More Motivation
Few skills needed	**Skill Variety**	Many skills needed
Work is a small part of the whole	**Task Identity**	Whole piece of work is completed
Minor impact on others	**Task Significance**	Major impact on others
Decisions made by others	**Autonomy**	Much freedom to make decisions
Difficult to see effectiveness	**Feedback**	Effectiveness readily apparent

Job Satisfaction Is Slipping

Although many organizations try to design jobs that are motivating, surveys by the Conference Board have found a gradual decline in job satisfaction among U.S. workers since the 1980s. Declines were also measured in satisfaction with particular factors under HR control, such as job design and rewards.

Source: Conference Board, "U.S. Job Satisfaction at Lowest Level in Two Decades," news release, January 5, 2010, http://www.conference-board.org.

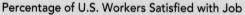

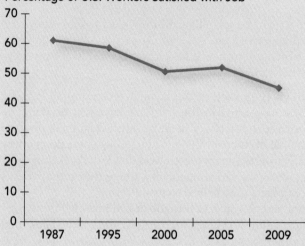

Percentage of U.S. Workers Satisfied with Job

---

bought a manufacturing plant for fuselages and nosecones from Boeing, it rewrote the facility's 160 job classifications and job descriptions to create just 13 enlarged jobs.[18] The effort made work more flexible and efficient, as well as potentially more interesting. Methods of job enlargement include job extension and job rotation.

Job Extension
Enlarging jobs by combining several relatively simple jobs to form a job with a wider range of tasks.

Job extension is enlarging jobs by combining several relatively simple jobs to form a job with a wider range of tasks. An example might be combining the jobs of receptionist, typist, and file clerk into jobs containing all three kinds of work. This approach to job enlargement is relatively simple, but if all the tasks are dull, workers will not necessarily be more motivated by the redesigned job.

Job Rotation
Enlarging jobs by moving employees among several different jobs.

Job rotation does not actually redesign the jobs themselves, but moves employees among several different jobs. This approach to job enlargement is common among production teams. During the course of a week, a team member may carry out each of the jobs handled by the team. Team members might assemble components one day and pack products into cases another day. As with job extension, the enlarged jobs may still consist of repetitive activities, but with greater variation among those activities.

Job Enrichment

Job Enrichment
Empowering workers by adding more decision-making authority to jobs.

The idea of **job enrichment,** or empowering workers by adding more decision-making authority to their jobs, comes from the work of Frederick Herzberg. According to Herzberg's two-factor theory, individuals are motivated more by the intrinsic aspects of work (for example, the meaningfulness of a job) than by extrinsic rewards such as pay. Herzberg identified five factors he associated with motivating jobs: achievement, recognition, growth, responsibility, and performance of the entire job. Thus, ways to enrich a manufacturing job might include giving employees authority to stop production when quality standards are not being met and having each employee perform several tasks to complete a particular stage of the process, rather than dividing up the tasks among the employees. For a salesperson in a store, job enrichment might involve the authority to resolve customer problems, including the authority to decide whether to issue refunds or replace merchandise.

In practice, however, it is important to note that not every worker responds positively to enriched jobs. These jobs are best suited to workers who are flexible and responsive to others; for these workers, enriched jobs can dramatically improve motivation.[19]

Nordstrom empowers its employees to resolve customer problems, which can enhance their job experience.

Self-Managing Work Teams

Instead of merely enriching individual jobs, some organizations empower employees by designing work to be done by self-managing work teams. As described in Chapter 2, these teams have authority for an entire work process or segment. Team members typically have authority to schedule work, hire team members, resolve problems related to the team's performance, and perform other duties traditionally handled by management. Teamwork can give a job such motivating characteristics as autonomy, skill variety, and task identity.

Because team members' responsibilities are great, their jobs usually are defined broadly and include sharing of work assignments. Team members may, at one time or another, perform every duty of the team. The challenge for the organization is to provide enough training so that the team members can learn the necessary skills. Another approach, when teams are responsible for particular work processes or customers, is to assign the team responsibility for the process or customer, then let the team decide which members will carry out which tasks.

A study of work teams at a large financial services company found that the right job design was associated with effective teamwork.[20] In particular, when teams are self-managed and team members are highly involved in decision making, teams are more productive, employees more satisfied, and managers more pleased with performance. Teams also tend to do better when each team member performs a variety of tasks and when team members view their effort as significant.

Flexible Work Schedules

One way in which an organization can give employees some say in how their work is structured is to offer flexible work schedules. Depending on the requirements of the organization and the individual jobs, organizations may be able to be flexible in terms of when employees work. As introduced in Chapter 2, types of flexibility include flextime and job sharing. Figure 4.7 illustrates alternatives to the traditional 40-hour workweek.

Flextime is a scheduling policy in which full-time employees may choose starting and ending times within guidelines specified by the organization. The flextime policy may require that employees be at work between certain hours, say, 10:00 AM and 3:00 PM. Employees work additional hours before or after this period in order to work the full day. One employee might arrive early in the morning in order to leave at 3:00 PM to pick up children after school. Another employee might be a night

Flextime
A scheduling policy in which full-time employees may choose starting and ending times within guidelines specified by the organization.

Figure 4.7

Alternatives to the 8-to-5 Job

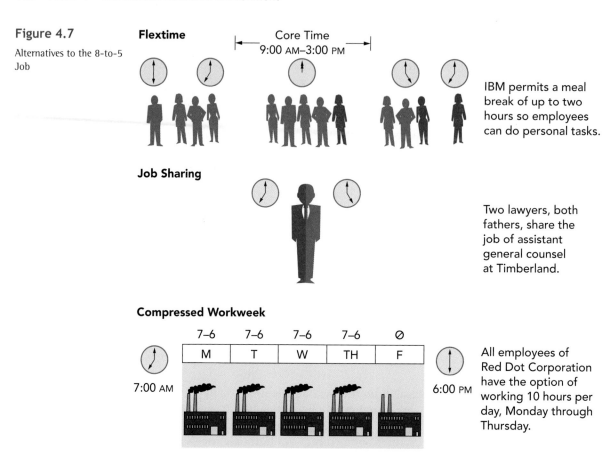

Flextime

Core Time
9:00 AM–3:00 PM

IBM permits a meal break of up to two hours so employees can do personal tasks.

Job Sharing

Two lawyers, both fathers, share the job of assistant general counsel at Timberland.

Compressed Workweek

7–6	7–6	7–6	7–6	∅
M	T	W	TH	F

7:00 AM

6:00 PM

All employees of Red Dot Corporation have the option of working 10 hours per day, Monday through Thursday.

owl who prefers to arrive at 10:00 AM and work until 6:00, 7:00, or even later in the evening. A flextime policy also may enable workers to adjust a particular day's hours in order to make time for doctor's appointments, children's activities, hobbies, or volunteer work. A work schedule that allows time for community and family interests can be extremely motivating for some employees.

Job Sharing
A work option in which two part-time employees carry out the tasks associated with a single job.

Job sharing is a work option in which two part-time employees carry out the tasks associated with a single job. Such arrangements can enable an organization to attract or retain valued employees who want more time to attend school or to care for family members. The job requirements in such an arrangement include the ability to work cooperatively and coordinate the details of one's job with another person.

Although not strictly a form of flexibility on the level of individual employees, another scheduling alternative is the *compressed workweek*. A compressed workweek is a schedule in which full-time workers complete their weekly hours in fewer than five days. For example, instead of working eight hours a day for five days, the employees could complete 40 hours of work in four 10-hour days. This alternative is most common, but some companies use other alternatives, such as scheduling 80 hours over nine days (with a three-day weekend every other week) or reducing the workweek from 40 to 38 or 36 hours. Employees may appreciate the extra days available for leisure, family, or volunteer activities. An organization might even use this schedule to offer a kind of flexibility—for example, letting workers vote whether they want a compressed workweek during the summer months. This type of schedule has a couple of drawbacks, however. One is that employees may become exhausted on the longer workdays. Another is that if the arrangement involves working more than 40 hours during a week, the Fair Labor Standards Act requires the payment of overtime wages to nonsupervisory employees.

Telework

Flexibility can extend to work locations as well as work schedules. Before the Industrial Revolution, most people worked either close to or inside their own homes. Mass production technologies changed all this, separating work life from home life, as people began to travel to centrally located factories and offices. Today, however, skyrocketing prices for office space, combined with drastically reduced prices for portable communication and computing devices, seem ready to reverse this trend. The broad term for doing one's work away from a centrally located office is *telework* or telecommuting.

For employers, advantages of telework include less need for office space and the ability to offer greater flexibility to employees who are disabled or need to be available for children or elderly relatives. The employees using telework arrangements may have less absences from work than employees with similar demands who must commute to work. Telecommuting can also support a strategy of corporate social responsibility because these employees do not produce the greenhouse gas emissions that result from commuting by car. Telework is easiest to implement for people in managerial, professional, or sales jobs, especially those that involve working and communicating on a computer. A telework arrangement is generally difficult to set up for manufacturing workers. Most of the call center representatives for Stanford Federal Credit Union work off-site, an arrangement that saves the organization money because it needs less office space and experiences less absenteeism. The arrangement also is a money saver for employees, who generally cannot afford to live in the credit union's pricey Silicon Valley locale. To make the arrangement work, Stanford Credit Union requires that the reps be experienced and that they set up a quiet, dedicated space for work in their homes.[21]

Given the possible benefits, it is not surprising that telework is a growing trend. A survey by the HR network WorldatWork found 43 percent growth between 2003 and 2008 in the number of U.S. workers who telecommuted at least once a month, reaching about one in four workers in 2008. A separate study by the Consumer Electronics Association found that over one-third of U.S. workers telecommuted at least once a month in 2009. The trend toward telecommuting is much stronger for occasional work at home than for full-time arrangements.[22]

focus on social responsibility

Designing Ergonomic Jobs

The way people use their bodies when they work—whether toting heavy furniture onto a moving van or sitting quietly before a computer screen—affects their physical well-being and may affect how well and how long they can work. The study of the interface between individuals' physiology and the characteristics of the physical work environment is called **ergonomics.** The goal of ergonomics is to minimize physical strain on the worker by structuring the physical work environment around the way the human body works. Ergonomics therefore focuses on outcomes such as reducing physical fatigue, aches and pains, and health complaints. Ergonomic research includes the context in which work takes place, such as the lighting, space, and hours worked.[23]

Ergonomic job design has been applied in redesigning equipment used in jobs that are physically demanding. Such redesign is often aimed at reducing the physical demands of certain jobs so that anyone can perform them. In addition, many interventions focus on redesigning machines and technology—for instance, adjusting

LO8 Explain how organizations apply ergonomics to design safe jobs.

Ergonomics
The study of the interface between individuals' physiology and the characteristics of the physical work environment.

Although employers in all industries are supposed to protect workers under the "general duty" clause, shipyards, nursing homes, grocery stores, and poultry-processing plants are the only four industries for which OSHA has published ergonomic standards.

the height of a computer keyboard to minimize occupational illnesses, such as carpal tunnel syndrome. The design of chairs and desks to fit posture requirements is very important in many office jobs. One study found that having employees participate in an ergonomic redesign effort significantly reduced the number and severity of cumulative trauma disorders (injuries that result from performing the same movement over and over), lost production time, and restricted-duty days.[24]

Ergonomics is about more than buying equipment, as the World Bank discovered when it moved to a new headquarters. To test the impact of ergonomic design, the organization conducted an experiment: one group of employees was given ergonomically designed furniture and worked with a professional ergonomist to set it up so that each employee had correct posture, while a second group simply received the furniture, which these employees set up themselves. Among employees who were experiencing pain and eyestrain at the time of the move, those who worked with the ergonomist had fewer symptoms afterward and also became more productive. The experimenters noted in their report, "Equipment such as an adjustable chair does not add value unless properly adjusted."[25]

The Occupational Safety and Health Administration has a "four-pronged" strategy for encouraging ergonomic job design. The first prong is to issue guidelines (rather than regulations) for specific industries. As of 2010, these guidelines have been issued for the nursing home, grocery store, poultry-processing industries, and for shipyards. Second, OSHA enforces violations of its requirement that employers have a general duty to protect workers from hazards, including ergonomic hazards. Third, OSHA works with industry groups to advise employers in those industries. And finally, OSHA established a National Advisory Committee on Ergonomics to define needs for further research. You can learn more about OSHA's guidelines at the agency's Web site, www.osha.gov.

Designing Jobs That Meet Mental Capabilities and Limitations

LO9 Discuss how organizations can plan for the mental demands of a job.

Just as the human body has capabilities and limitations, addressed by ergonomics, the mind, too, has capabilities and limitations. Besides hiring people with certain mental skills, organizations can design jobs so that they can be accurately and safely performed given the way the brain processes information. Generally, this means reducing the information-processing requirements of a job. In these simpler jobs, workers may be less likely to make mistakes or have accidents. Of course, the simpler jobs also may be less motivating. Research has found that challenging jobs tend to fatigue and dissatisfy workers when they feel little control over their situation, lack social support, and feel motivated mainly to avoid errors. In contrast, they may enjoy the challenges of a difficult job where they have some control and social support, especially if they enjoy learning and are unafraid of making mistakes.[26] Because of this drawback to simplifying jobs, it can be most beneficial to simplify jobs where employees will most appreciate having the mental demands reduced (as in a job that is extremely challenging) or where the costs of errors are severe (as in the job of a surgeon or

"OFFICE" WORK ON THE ROAD

Working on the road used to be the province of truck drivers and salespeople, but today's wireless technology is linking all kinds of employees to their work, whether they're at headquarters, visiting a client site, at home, or en route. For workers behind the wheel, the stakes are high. Research shows that drivers talking on the phone are four times more likely than nonchatters to crash, even if they're using a hands-free headset. When eyes go off the road for text messaging or reading a computer screen, the risks are even worse.

But that hasn't stopped some companies from designing jobs that encourage multitasking on the road. Roto-Rooter Services Company has installed software that lets plumbers use their cell phones to receive job requests, get driving directions, and submit documents such as invoices. Roto-Rooter instructs its drivers not to use the system while driving, but it also expects an immediate response when it puts out a customer request for service. If a plumber doesn't call back, it calls the next plumber on the list, in order to provide responsive customer service.

Sometimes the cost of efficiency is high. An employee for International Paper who was driving while talking on the phone struck another driver, causing injuries that required amputation of the person's arm. The injured driver sued the company on the grounds that it permitted its employees to use cell phones while driving, as long as they used a headset. Confronted with research that compares this multitasking risk to driving while intoxicated, International Paper settled at a cost of $5.2 million.

On a more mundane level, job designers might want to consider studies showing that multitaskers tend to be more distracted, less able to remember new information acquired while multitasking, and less able to pick up the nuances of a conversation. Exxon Mobil and AMEC (an engineering and project management company) have experimented with bans on using cell phones while driving, and both companies reported no loss in productivity among employees who tried the ban.

Source: Based on Matt Richtel, "At 60 M.P.H., Office Work Is a High-Risk Job," *The New York Times,* Business & Company Resource Center, http://galenet.galegroup.com.

air-traffic controller). The "eHRM" box describes the need to reduce errors while driving, which has become part of the job for more and more workers who stay linked to their work through wireless devices.

There are several ways to simplify a job's mental demands. One is to limit the amount of information and memorization that the job requires. Organizations can also provide adequate lighting, easy-to-understand gauges and displays, simple-to-operate equipment, and clear instructions. Often, employees try to simplify some of the mental demands of their own jobs by creating checklists, charts, or other aids. Finally, every job requires some degree of thinking, remembering, and paying attention, so for every job, organizations need to evaluate whether their employees can handle the job's mental demands.

Changes in technology sometimes reduce job demands and errors, but in some cases, technology has made the problem worse. Some employees try to juggle information from several sources at once—say, talking on a cell phone while typing, surfing the Web for information during a team member's business presentation, or repeatedly stopping work on a project to check e-mail or instant messages. In these cases, the cell phone, handheld computer, and e-mail or instant messages are distracting the employees from their primary task. They may convey important information, but they also break the employee's train of thought, reducing performance and increasing the likelihood of errors. The problem may be aggravated by employees downplaying the significance of these interruptions. For example, in a recent survey of workers, only half said they check their e-mail at work more than once an hour, and more than a third said they check every 15 minutes. However, monitoring software on their computers determined that they were actually changing applications to check e-mail up to 30 or 40 times an hour.[27] The sheer volume of e-mail can be a drain on employee time. On average, a person at work sends and receives more than 150 e-mail messages every day, with the number expected to surpass 200 in the next few years. Reading and responding to these messages takes about one-fourth of the average employee's day, more than the time spent in meetings or on the phone.[28]

Information-processing errors also are greater in situations in which one person hands off information to another. Such transmission problems have become a major concern in the field of medicine, because critical information is routinely shared among nurses, doctors, and medical technicians, as well as between hospital employees changing shifts. Problems during shift changes are especially likely as a result of fatigue and burnout among employees with stressful jobs.[29] Some hospitals have coped by introducing a method called SBAR (situation, background, assessment, and recommendation), which standardizes the information delivered at handoff points. In a few seconds, the person handing off the care of a patient gets control of the situation by engaging the listener's attention (situation), relays enough information to establish the context of the problem (background), gives an overall evaluation of the condition (assessment), and makes a specific suggestion about the best action to take next (recommendation). At one hospital that began using the SBAR method, the rate of adverse events (unexpected medical problems causing harm) was reduced by more than half, from 90 to just 40 of every thousand patients treated.[30]

thinking ethically

IS TELECOMMUTING FAIR TO THOSE AT THE OFFICE?

For a growing number of workers who are sick of sitting in rush-hour traffic, the cure is telework, or telecommuting. Employees who embrace telecommuting cite greater flexibility, the chance to take on a new job without relocating, greater work-life flexibility, and the ability to work for stretches uninterrupted by colleagues checking on their weekend activities or inviting them to the break room for birthday cake.

However, not every employee can (or wants to) telecommute, and for those who make the trip to work, telecommuting by others can present some difficulties. Greater flexibility for some employees can make work less flexible for others, who are required to cover certain clients, tasks, or work hours. Supervisors with a last-minute task may find it easier to hand over the work to someone who is on-site. And employees who drive to work each day may feel that telecommuting employees simply have a more comfortable arrangement, which might not seem fair.

SOURCES: Rhymer Rigby, "Employees Feel at Home in the 'Post-Office' World," *Financial Times*, September 8, 2009, Business & Company Resource Center, http://galenet.galegroup.com; Dave Bailey, "How to Gear Up for a Surge in Remote Working," *Computing*, April 2, 2009, Business & Company Resource Center, http://galenet.galegroup.com; and Sam Narisi, "Four Reasons Office Workers Hate Telecommuters," *HR Tech News*, March 6, 2009, http://www.hrtechnews.com.

Questions

1. According to this research, telework benefits some employees at the expense of others. Reviewing the ethical principles from Chapter 1, what can a person ethically do when a course of action benefits some people and hurts others?

2. Imagine that you work in human resource management at a company that has decided to adopt telework as a way to retain valued employees. Suggest ways you can help the company proceed with this plan as ethically as possible.

SUMMARY

LO1 Summarize the elements of work flow analysis.

The analysis identifies the amount and quality of a work unit's outputs, which may be products, parts of products, or services. Next, the analyst determines the work processes required to produce these outputs, breaking down tasks into those performed by each person in the work unit. Finally, the work flow analysis identifies the inputs used to carry out the processes and produce the outputs.

LO2 Describe how work flow is related to an organization's structure.

Within an organization, units and individuals must cooperate to create outputs, and the organization's structure brings people together for this purpose. The structure may be centralized or decentralized, and people may be grouped according to function or into divisions focusing on particular products or customer groups. A functional structure is most appropriate for people who perform highly specialized jobs and hold relatively little authority. Employee empowerment and teamwork succeed best in a divisional structure. Because of these links between structure and types of jobs, considering such issues improves the success of job design.

LO3 Define the elements of a job analysis, and discuss their significance for human resource management.

Job analysis is the process of getting detailed information about jobs. It includes preparation of job descriptions and job specifications. A job description lists the tasks, duties, and responsibilities of a job. Job specifications look at the qualities needed in a person performing the job. They list the knowledge, skills, abilities, and other characteristics that are required for successful performance of a job. Job analysis provides a foundation for carrying out many HRM responsibilities, including work redesign, human resource planning, employee selection and training, performance appraisal, career planning, and job evaluation to determine pay scales.

LO4 Tell how to obtain information for a job analysis.

Information for analyzing an existing job often comes from incumbents and their supervisors. The Labor Department publishes general background information about jobs in the *Dictionary of Occupational Titles* and Occupational Information Network (O*NET). Job analysts, employees, and managers may complete a Position Analysis Questionnaire or fill out a survey for the Fleishman Job Analysis System.

LO5 Summarize recent trends in job analysis.

Because today's workplace requires a high degree of adaptability, job tasks and requirements are subject to constant change. For example, as some organizations downsize, they are defining jobs more broadly, with less supervision of people in those positions. Organizations are also adopting project-based structures and teamwork, which also require flexibility and the ability to handle broad responsibilities.

LO6 Describe methods for designing a job so that it can be done efficiently.

The basic technique for designing efficient jobs is industrial engineering, which looks for the simplest way to structure work to maximize efficiency. Through methods such as time-and-motion studies, the industrial engineer creates jobs that are relatively simple and typically repetitive. These jobs may bore workers because they are so simple.

LO7 Identify approaches to designing a job to make it motivating.

According to the Job Characteristics Model, jobs are more motivating if they have greater skill variety, task identity, task significance, autonomy, and feedback about performance effectiveness. Ways to create such jobs include job enlargement (through job extension or job rotation) and job enrichment. In addition, self-managing work teams offer greater skill variety and task identity. Flexible work schedules and telework offer greater autonomy.

LO8 Explain how organizations apply ergonomics to design safe jobs.

The goal of ergonomics is to minimize physical strain on the worker by structuring the physical work environment around the way the human body works. Ergonomic design may involve modifying equipment to reduce the physical demands of performing certain jobs or redesigning the jobs themselves to reduce strain. Ergonomic design may target work practices associated with injuries.

LO9 Discuss how organizations can plan for the mental demands of a job.

Employers may seek to reduce mental as well as physical strain. The job design may limit the amount of information and memorization involved. Adequate lighting, easy-to-read gauges and displays, simple-to-operate equipment, and clear instructions also can minimize mental strain. Computer software can simplify jobs—for example, by performing calculations or filtering out spam from important e-mail. Finally, organizations can select employees with the necessary abilities to handle a job's mental demands.

KEY TERMS

REVIEW AND DISCUSSION QUESTIONS

1. Assume you are the manager of a fast-food restaurant. What are the outputs of your work unit? What are the activities required to produce those outputs? What are the inputs?

2. Based on Question 1, consider the cashier's job in the restaurant. What are the outputs, activities, and inputs for that job?

3. Consider the "job" of college student. Perform a job analysis on this job. What tasks are required in the job? What knowledge, skills, and abilities are necessary to perform those tasks? Prepare a job description based on your analysis.

4. Discuss how the following trends are changing the skill requirements for managerial jobs in the United States:
   a. Increasing use of computers and the Internet.
   b. Increasing international competition.
   c. Increasing work-family conflicts.

5. How can a job analysis of each job in the work unit help a supervisor to do his or her job?

6. Consider the job of a customer service representative who fields telephone calls from customers of a retailer that sells online and through catalogs. What measures can an employer take to design this job to make it efficient? What might be some drawbacks or challenges of designing this job for efficiency?

7. How might the job in Question 6 be designed to make it more motivating? How well would these considerations apply to the cashier's job in Question 2?

8. What ergonomic considerations might apply to each of the following jobs? For each job, what kinds of costs would result from addressing ergonomics? What costs might result from failing to address ergonomics?
   a. A computer programmer.
   b. A UPS delivery person.
   c. A child care worker.

9. The chapter said that modern electronics have eliminated the need for a store's cashiers to calculate change due on a purchase. How does this development modify the job description for a cashier? If you were a store manager, how would it affect the skills and qualities of job candidates you would want to hire? Does this change in mental processing requirements affect what you would expect from a cashier? How?

10. Consider a job you hold now or have held recently. Would you want this job to be redesigned to place more emphasis on efficiency, motivation, ergonomics, or mental processing? What changes would you want, and why? (Or why do you not want the job to be redesigned?)

BUSINESSWEEK CASE

BusinessWeek Pfizer Outsources Tasks, Not Jobs

David Cain loves his job. Well, most of it anyway. As an executive director for global engineering at Pfizer, Cain finds real satisfaction in assessing environmental real estate risks, managing facilities, and overseeing a multimillion-dollar budget for the pharmaceutical giant. What he doesn't love so much: creating PowerPoint slides and riffling through spreadsheets.

Lucky for Cain, Pfizer now lets him punt those tedious and time-consuming tasks to India with the click of a button. PfizerWorks, launched early last year, permits some 4,000 employees to pass off parts of their job to outsiders. You might call it personal outsourcing. With workers in India handling everything from basic market research projects to presentations, professionals such as Cain can focus on higher-value work. "It has really been a godsend," says Cain. "I can send them something in the evening, and the next morning it's waiting for me when I get to the office."

This novel twist on outsourcing comes at a time when other resources are dwindling. As companies cull people by the thousands—Pfizer itself announced some 8,000 job cuts in January [2009]—those who stay behind are being asked to do more. In a down economy, though, it's especially critical that executives direct their energies to motivating teams, creating new products, and thinking strategically about their next move. "The stakes go up even higher," says David Kreutter, Pfizer's vice president for U.S. commercial operations.

Originally dubbed the Office of the Future, PfizerWorks is partly the by-product of a cost-cutting push that began several years ago. Jordan Cohen, the architect and head of the program, came up with the idea after reading Thomas L. Friedman's book *The World Is Flat* and observing how his own team worked. Cohen recalls seeing one of his recruits, a new father, stay late at the office one night to crunch numbers and search for information on the Web. To Cohen, it didn't seem like time best spent.

Instead of shifting jobs overseas, as companies have done for years, Cohen wanted to find a way to shift tasks. He also felt the program should let employees do one-stop shopping. Instead of setting up a few specialized services, Pfizer employees click a single button on their computer desktop that sends them to the PfizerWorks site. They write up what they need on an online form, which is sent to one of two Indian service-outsourcing firms: Genpact, in Gurgaon, and a unit of Chicago's R. R. Donnelley.

Once a request is received, a team member such as R. R. Donnelley's Biju Kurian in India sets up a call with the Pfizer employee to clarify what's needed and when. The costs involved in each project are charged to the employee's department.

Pfizer is now looking to expand the program to more employees and to a wider array of tasks. While he was introducing a group of Pfizer scientists to the service last year, Cohen says, one of them immediately pointed out its limitations. "I got it, Jordan, we can use this," the researcher said. "But what I really need is a smart guy for a day." He had a point. Some tasks can't easily be broken down into instructions on an online form, Cohen admits, and sometimes employees need an assistant working in the same time zone.

As a result, Pfizer is testing an arrangement with a small Columbus, Ohio-based firm called Pearl Interactive Network. Pearl employs mostly people with physical disabilities who help with such administrative tasks as organizing a marketing team's research documents on a shared server or scheduling meetings. While the partnership is modest and isn't meant to supplant arrangements in India or administrative jobs, Cohen hopes it will make Pfizer staff even more productive.

Although PfizerWorks hasn't quite reached its first anniversary, Cohen estimates that it has already freed up 66,500 hours for employees. Pfizer finds employees are now spending less money on other providers, such as graphic design shops or market research firms. Employees are asked to rate their satisfaction with the finished product. If the score isn't high enough, a department can refuse to pay, which has happened only a handful of times.

SOURCE: Excerpted from Jena McGregor, "Outsourcing Tasks Instead of Jobs," *BusinessWeek*, March 12, 2009, http://www.businessweek.com.

Questions

1. As PfizerWorks is described here, the analysis of work flow and decisions about which tasks to outsource are handled by individual employees, rather than HR teams or outside analysts. What are some advantages and drawbacks of this approach?
2. If you worked in HR for Pfizer, how would you need to adjust job descriptions and requirements to account for employees' ability to outsource tasks?
3. The examples in this case refer to managers and scientists. What positions, if any, at Pfizer should *not* have access to PfizerWorks? Why?

Case: Creative Jobs at W. L. Gore

When the husband-and-wife team of Bill and Vieve Gore founded W. L. Gore & Associates, their aim was not just to make and sell products from high-tech materials. Rather, they believed they could create a thriving, creative organization by giving smart people a chance to fully use their talents and ideas. They believed creativity could be stifled by rigid structure and hierarchy, so they built their company without managers, assigning teams of employees to work on opportunities.

Thus, at W. L. Gore, work flow is often about ideas as well as products. To produce good ideas, the company needs scientists and engineers with a profound understanding of their field of expertise, be it chemistry or the fabrication of a new prototype. At the same time, the company's long-term success requires that it back only ideas that will meet real market needs, so expertise must extend to business knowledge coupled with a willingness to terminate projects that have little chance of success. This pairing of skill sets is especially powerful when an innovation isn't working out because Gore employees are gifted at analyzing the idea to see what aspects can be carried over into new projects, so the company builds on ideas. Also related to business skills, Gore employees must be good at communicating with customers, who can help the company identify needs and assess the value of ideas. This combination of skills is broad because jobs at Gore are broadly defined; in contrast, at many other companies, scientists and engineers communicate mainly with other technical experts, leaving customer communication and market knowledge to the sales force.

The basic principle for organizing work at Gore is the team, established to meet a particular opportunity. Thus, each team includes a variety of functions and areas of expertise. As a result, team members see how different viewpoints are necessary to meet the team's objectives. Teams appoint a leader, so leadership is accountable to the team, rather than to corporate hierarchy.

Team members are expected to balance autonomy in how they work with responsibility for meeting team goals. They also must balance time spent on existing, known business requirements with time spent on ideas for creating value in new ways. To help employees maintain the balance, Gore assigns a "sponsor" to each individual, even the chief executive. The sponsor is someone who has made a commitment to the sponsored employee's success and provides the employee with learning opportunities, such as meeting a customer, building relationships with others in the company, or getting involved in a particular project. Sponsors also advocate for their employees' ideas and help them obtain resources to develop those ideas.

The Gore emphasis on teams provides fertile ground for creative thinking. For example, one of the company's biochemical engineers routinely collaborates with an excellent prototyper to develop innovations. The practice of building, reviewing, and discussing prototypes engages more people in thinking about an idea, so it can be improved and made practical in its early stages. Collaboration across teams and functions is encouraged, too. One employee says he can find an answer to any question from someone in the company in three phone calls or less. Facilities are kept relatively small and incorporate all the functions for a particular line of business, making it easier for employees to know who they work with across various functions. Of course, the company also needs to provide enough lab space and other physical resources. Employees feel reinforced by Gore's culture of trusting them to develop new ideas and tackle big challenges. They report feeling able to create something unique and valuable.

For HR staffers, working for W. L. Gore entails knowing the business unit they support and protecting the organizational culture so carefully laid out by Bill and Vieve Gore. As you might expect, the emphasis is less on forms and structure. When new employees are hired, HR provides them with an orientation and three-day workshop that teaches how work is done at the company. Employees are paired up with their sponsor at the beginning as well. The transition to Gore's culture is tricky for some people who are used to the traditional hierarchy they've experienced at other companies. Some need guidance on how to be influential when they can't rely on their position in a hierarchy.

SOURCES: Debra Ricker France, "Creating Compelling Environments for Innovators," *Research-Technology Management*, November–December 2009, pp. 33–38; and "The World Is Flat," *Personnel Today*, July 22, 2008, Business & Company Resource Center, http://galenet.galegroup.com.

Questions

1. According to the information given, what basic inputs, work activities (processes), and outputs can you identify for work at W. L. Gore?
2. What are some strengths of designing work around teams, as Gore has done? What are some challenges for managing this structure?
3. If you worked in HR for W. L. Gore, what are some knowledge, skills, ability, or other characteristics (KSAOs) you would include in the company's job descriptions?

 IT'S A WRAP!   McGraw-Hill **connect**

www.mhhe.com/noefund4e is your source for **R**eviewing, **A**pplying, and **P**racticing the concepts you learned about in Chapter 4.

Review	**Application**	**Practice**
• Chapter learning objectives	• Manager's Hot Seat segment: "Virtual Workplace: Out of Office Reply"	• Chapter quiz
	• Video case and quiz: "Working Smart"	
	• Self-Assessments Find Your Match: O*NET	
	• Web exercise: Comparative Job Analysis	
	• Small-business case: Inclusivity Defines BraunAbility's Products and Its Jobs	

NOTES

1. Kelly K. Spors, "Top Small Workplaces 2009," *Wall Street Journal*, September 28, 2009, http://online.wsj.com.

2. T. Aeppel and J. Lahart, "Lean Factories Find It Hard to Cut Jobs Even in a Slump," *Wall Street Journal*, March 9, 2009, pp. B2–B3; A. Taylor, "Lean Times: What Caterpillar Can Learn," *Fortune*, January 29, 2009, pp. 35–37; P. Engardio, "Lean and Mean Gets Extreme," *BusinessWeek*, March 23, 2009, pp. 60–62.

3. Jerry DeMuth, "Servicers as Originators," *Mortgage Banking*, November 2009, pp. 38–45.

4. J. R. Hollenbeck, H. Moon, A. Ellis, et al., "Structural Contingency Theory and Individual Differences: Examination of External and Internal Person-Team Fit," *Journal of Applied Psychology* 87 (2002), pp. 599–606.

5. Duncan Adams, "Kroger Distributor Opens Hiring Doors," *Roanoke (VA) Times*, May 7, 2009, Business & Company Resource Center, http://galenet.galegroup.com.

6. A. O'Reilly, "Skill Requirements: Supervisor-Subordinate Conflict," *Personnel Psychology* 26 (1973), pp. 75–80; J. Hazel, J. Madden, and R. Christal, "Agreement between Worker-Supervisor Descriptions of the Worker's Job," *Journal of Industrial Psychology* 2 (1964), pp. 71–79; and A. K. Weyman, "Investigating the Influence of Organizational Role on Perceptions of Risk in Deep Coal Mines," *Journal of Applied Psychology* 88 (2003), pp. 404–12.

7. L. E. Baranowski and L. E. Anderson, "Examining Rater Source Variation in Work Behavior to KSA Linkages," *Personnel Psychology* 58 (2005), pp. 1041–54.

8. National Center for O*NET Development, *O*NET Products at Work*, Winter 2010, accessed at http://www.onetcenter.org/paw.html.

9. P. J. Taylor, W. D. Li, K. Shi, and W. C. Borman, "The Transportability of Job Information across Countries," *Personnel Psychology* 61 (2008), pp. 69–111.

10. *PAQ Newsletter*, August 1989; and E. C. Dierdorff and M. A. Wilson, "A Meta-analysis of Job Analysis Reliability," *Journal of Applied Psychology* 88 (2003), pp. 635–46.

11. E. Fleishman and M. Reilly, *Handbook of Human Abilities* (Palo Alto, CA: Consulting Psychologists Press, 1992); E. Fleishman and M. Mumford, "Ability Requirements Scales," in *The Job Analysis Handbook for Business, Industry, and Government*, ed. S. Gael (New York: Wiley, 1988), pp. 917–35.

12. W. Cascio, *Applied Psychology in Personnel Management*, 4th ed. (Englewood Cliffs, NJ: Prentice Hall, 1991).

13. P. Wright and K. Wexley, "How to Choose the Kind of Job Analysis You Really Need," *Personnel*, May 1985, pp. 51–55.

14. M. K. Lindell, C. S. Clause, C. J. Brandt, and R. S. Landis, "Relationship between Organizational Context and Job Analysis Ratings," *Journal of Applied Psychology* 83 (1998), pp. 769–76.

15. D. S. DeRue, J. R. Hollenbeck, M. D. Johnson, D. R. Ilgen, and D. K. Jundt, "How Different Team Downsizing Approaches Influence Team-Level Adaptation and Performance," *Academy of Management Journal* 51 (2008), pp. 182–96; F. Hanson, "A Leg Up in Down Times," *Workforce Management*, January 19, 2009, p. 14.

16. R. Hackman and G. Oldham, *Work Redesign* (Boston: Addison-Wesley, 1980).

17. W. E. Byrnes, "Making the Job Meaningful All the Way Down the Line," *BusinessWeek*, May 1, 2006, p. 60.

18. S. Holmes, "Soaring Where Boeing Struggled," *BusinessWeek*, February 19, 2007, p. 72.

19. F. W. Bond, P. E. Flaxman, and D. Bunce, "The Influence of Psychological Flexibility on Work Redesign: Mediated Moderation of a Work Reorganization Intervention," *Journal of Applied Psychology* 93 (2008), pp. 645–54.

20. M. A. Campion, G. J. Medsker, and A. C. Higgs, "Relations between Work Group Characteristics and Effectiveness: Implications for Designing Effective Work Groups," *Personnel Psychology* 46 (1993), pp. 823–50.

21. Kevin Jepson, "Call Center Reps Are Out of Site, Top of Mind," *Credit Union Journal*, June 29, 2009, Business & Company Resource Center, http://galenet.galegroup.com.

22. WorldatWork, "Telework Revs Up as More Employers Offer Work Flexibility," news release, February 18, 2009, http://www.worldatwork.org; and "CEA Study: More than One-Third of Employees Teleworking," *Wireless News*, October 16, 2009, Business & Company Resource Center, http://galenet.galegroup.com.

23. See, for example, S. Sonnentag and F. R. H. Zijistra, "Job Characteristics and Off-the-Job Activities as Predictors of Need for Recovery, Well-Being, and

Fatigue," *Journal of Applied Psychology* 91 (2006), pp. 330–50.

24. D. May and C. Schwoerer, "Employee Health by Design: Using Employee Involvement Teams in Ergonomic Job Redesign," *Personnel Psychology* 47 (1994), pp. 861–86.

25. Randy Dotinga, "Takes a Pro to Make Offices Pain-Free," *BusinessWeek,* October 28, 2009, http://www.businessweek.com.

26. N. W. Van Yperen and M. Hagerdoorn, "Do High Job Demands Increase Intrinsic Motivation or Fatigue or Both? The Role of Job Support and Social Control," *Academy of Management Journal* 46 (2003), pp. 339–48; and N. W. Van Yperen and O. Janssen, "Fatigued and Dissatisfied or Fatigued but Satisfied? Goal Orientations and Responses to High Job Demands,"

Academy of Management Journal 45 (2002), pp. 1161–71.

27. Steve Ranger, "Email: The Root of Your Work Stress?" Silicon.com, August 13, 2007, http://hardware.silicon.com/desktops/.

28. Sara Radicati, ed., "Email Statistics Report, 2009–2013" (Palo Alto, CA: Radicati Group, May 2009), http://www.radicati.com.

29. L. E. LaBlanc, J. J. Hox, W. B. Schaufell, T. W. Taris, and M. C. W. Peters, "Take Care! The Evaluation of a Team-Based Burnout Intervention Program for Oncology Health Care Providers," *Journal of Applied Psychology* 92 (2007), pp. 213–27.

30. L. Landro, "Hospitals Combat Errors at the 'Hand-Off,'" *Wall Street Journal,* June 28, 2006, pp. D1–D2.

Acquiring and Preparing Human Resources

PART TWO

chapter

5

Planning for and Recruiting Human Resources

What Do I Need to Know?

After reading this chapter, you should be able to:

LO1 Discuss how to plan for human resources needed to carry out the organization's strategy.

LO2 Determine the labor demand for workers in various job categories.

LO3 Summarize the advantages and disadvantages of ways to eliminate a labor surplus and avoid a labor shortage.

LO4 Describe recruitment policies organizations use to make job vacancies more attractive.

LO5 List and compare sources of job applicants.

LO6 Describe the recruiter's role in the recruitment process, including limits and opportunities.

Introduction

Business news often contains stories of layoffs, as organizations seek cost savings or react to falling demand by cutting their workforce. Recently, automobile manufacturers reported the lowest U.S. sales volume in almost a decade.[1] Expecting slow demand to continue, the companies would not need to build as many vehicles as in the past. Chrysler, for example, announced that it would eliminate shifts at several of its U.S. manufacturing facilities. Such a plan generally involves laying off workers and not replacing any workers who leave voluntarily. In contrast, the situation is far different for accounting firms, which are actively competing to fill entry-level jobs with qualified candidates. Many major accounting firms recruit at colleges and even high schools, seeking interns to establish relationships with high-caliber students even before they are ready to start their careers.[2]

As these two examples show, trends and events that affect the economy also create opportunities and problems in obtaining human resources. When customer demand rises (or falls), organizations may need more (or fewer) employees. When the labor market changes—say, when more people go to college or when a sizable share of the population retires—the supply of qualified workers may grow, shrink, or change in nature. Organizations recently have had difficulty filling information technology jobs because the demand for people with these skills outstrips the supply. To prepare for and respond to these challenges, organizations engage in *human resource planning*—defined in Chapter 1 as identifying the numbers and types of employees the organization will require to meet its objectives.

This chapter describes how organizations carry out human resource planning. In the first part of the chapter, we lay out the steps that go into developing and implementing a human resource plan. Throughout each section, we focus especially on recent trends and practices, including downsizing, employing temporary workers, and outsourcing. The remainder of the chapter explores the process of recruiting. We describe the process by which organizations look for people to fill job vacancies and the usual sources of job candidates. Finally, we discuss the role of recruiters.

The Process of Human Resource Planning

Organizations should carry out human resource planning so as to meet business objectives and gain an advantage over competitors. To do this, organizations need a clear idea of the strengths and weaknesses of their existing internal labor force. They also must know what they want to be doing in the future—what size they want the organization to be, what products and services it should be producing, and so on. This knowledge helps them define the number and kinds of employees they will need. Human resource planning compares the present state of the organization with its goals for the future, then identifies what changes it must make in its human resources to meet those goals. The changes may include downsizing, training existing employees in new skills, or hiring new employees.

These activities give a general view of HR planning. They take place in the human resource planning process shown in Figure 5.1. The process consists of three stages: forecasting, goal setting and strategic planning, and program implementation and evaluation.

Forecasting

The first step in human resource planning is **forecasting,** as shown in the top portion of Figure 5.1. In personnel forecasting, the HR professional tries to determine the supply of and demand for various types of human resources. The primary goal is to predict which areas of the organization will experience labor shortages or surpluses.

L01
Discuss how to plan for human resources needed to carry out the organization's strategy.

Forecasting
The attempts to determine the supply of and demand for various types of human resources to predict areas within the organization where there will be labor shortages or surpluses.

Figure 5.1

Overview of the Human Resource Planning Process

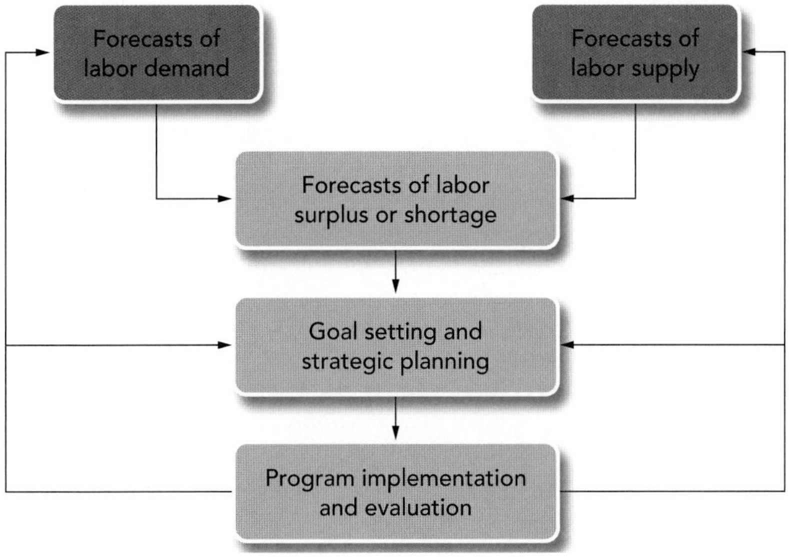

Forecasting supply and demand can use statistical methods or judgment. Statistical methods capture historic trends in a company's demand for labor. Under the right conditions, these methods predict demand and supply more precisely than a human forecaster can using subjective judgment. But many important events in the labor market have no precedent. When such events occur, statistical methods are of little use. To prepare for these situations, the organization must rely on the subjective judgments of experts. Pooling their "best guesses" is an important source of ideas about the future.

Forecasting the Demand for Labor

LO2
Determine the labor demand for workers in various job categories.

Usually, an organization forecasts demand for specific job categories or skill areas. After identifying the relevant job categories or skills, the planner investigates the likely demand for each. The planner must forecast whether the need for people with the necessary skills and experience will increase or decrease. There are several ways of making such forecasts.

Trend Analysis
Constructing and applying statistical models that predict labor demand for the next year, given relatively objective statistics from the previous year.

At the most sophisticated level, an organization might use **trend analysis,** constructing and applying statistical models that predict labor demand for the next year, given relatively objective statistics from the previous year. These statistics are called **leading indicators**—objective measures that accurately predict future labor demand. They might include measures of the economy (such as sales or inventory levels), actions of competitors, changes in technology, and trends in the composition of the workforce and overall population. For example, an industrywide change in prices may signal a problem related to capacity, which in turn may signal a need for more or less labor to correct the capacity problem. Thus, when prices for many manufactured goods fell more than 5 percent in early 2007, it was an indicator that sellers' inventories were getting too large, predicting some of the many job cuts that came in 2008 as orders and production levels fell.[3] On a more detailed scale, Walmart uses past shopping patterns to predict how many employees will be needed to staff shifts in each of its stores on any given day and time.[4]

Leading Indicators
Objective measures that accurately predict future labor demand.

Statistical planning models are useful when there is a long, stable history that can be used to reliably detect relationships among variables. However, these models almost always have to be complemented with subjective judgments of experts. There are simply too many "once-in-a-lifetime" changes to consider, and statistical models cannot capture them.

Determining Labor Supply

Once a company has forecast the demand for labor, it needs an indication of the firm's labor supply. Determining the internal labor supply calls for a detailed analysis of how many people are currently in various job categories or have specific skills within the organization. The planner then modifies this analysis to reflect changes expected in the near future as a result of retirements, promotions, transfers, voluntary turnover, and terminations.

Transitional Matrix
A chart that lists job categories held in one period and shows the proportion of employees in each of those job categories in a future period.

One type of statistical procedure that can be used for this purpose is the analysis of a **transitional matrix.** This is a chart that lists job categories held in one period and shows the proportion of employees in each of those job categories in a future period. It answers two questions: "Where did people who were in each job category go?" and "Where did people now in each job category come from?" Table 5.1 is an example of a transitional matrix.

This example lists job categories for an auto parts manufacturer. The jobs listed at the left were held in 2007; the numbers at the right show what happened to the

Table 5.1

Transitional Matrix: Example for an Auto Parts Manufacturer

2007	2010 (1)	(2)	(3)	(4)	(5)	(6)	(7)	(8)
(1) Sales manager	.95							.05
(2) Sales representative	.05	.60						.35
(3) Sales apprentice		.20	.50					.30
(4) Assistant plant manager				.90	.05			.05
(5) Production manager				.10	.75			.15
(6) Production assembler					.10	.80		.10
(7) Clerical							.70	.30
(8) Not in organization	.00	.20	.50	.00	.10	.20	.30	

people in 2010. The numbers represent proportions. For example, .95 means 95 percent of the people represented by a row in the matrix. The column headings under 2010 refer to the row numbers. The first row is sales managers, so the numbers under column (1) represent people who became sales managers. Reading across the first row, we see that 95 of the people who were sales managers in 2007 are still sales managers in 2010. The other 5 percent correspond to position (8), "Not in organization," meaning the 5 percent of employees who are not still sales managers have left the organization. In the second row are sales representatives. Of those who were sales reps in 2007, 5 percent were promoted to sales manager, 60 percent are still sales reps, and 35 percent have left the organization. In row (3), half (50 percent) of sales apprentices are still in that job, but 20 percent are now sales reps and 30 percent have left the organization. This pattern of jobs shows a career path from sales apprentice to sales representative to sales manager. Of course, not everyone is promoted, and some of the people leave instead.

Reading down the columns provides another kind of information: the sources of employees holding the positions in 2010. In the first column, we see that most sales managers (95 percent) held that same job three years earlier. The other 5 percent were promoted from sales representative positions. Skipping over to column (3), half the sales apprentices on the payroll in 2010 held the same job three years before, and the other half were hired from outside the organization. This suggests that the organization fills sales manager positions primarily through promotions, so planning for this job would focus on preparing sales representatives. In contrast, planning to meet the organization's needs for sales apprentices would emphasize recruitment and selection of new employees.

Matrices such as this one are extremely useful for charting historical trends in the company's supply of labor. More important, if conditions remain somewhat constant, they can also be used to plan for the future. For example, if we believe that that we are going to have a surplus of labor in the production assembler job category in the next three years, we can plan to avoid layoffs. Still, historical

As the average age of many workers in skilled trades grows, the coming demand for workers in many trades is expected to outstrip supply in the United States. There is a potential for employers in some areas to experience a labor shortage because of this. How can HR prepare for this reality? What should be done now to avoid the shortage?

data may not always reliably indicate future trends. Planners need to combine statistical forecasts of labor supply with expert judgments. For example, managers in the organization may see that a new training program will likely increase the number of employees qualified for new openings. Forecasts of labor supply also should take into account the organization's pool of skills. Many organizations include inventories of employees' skills in an HR database. When the organization forecasts that it will need new skills in the future, planners can consult the database to see how many existing employees have those skills.

Besides looking at the labor supply within the organization, the planner should examine trends in the external labor market. The planner should keep abreast of labor market forecasts, including the size of the labor market, the unemployment rate, and the kinds of people who will be in the labor market. For example, we saw in Chapter 2 that the U.S. labor market is aging and that immigration is an important source of new workers. Important sources of data on the external labor market include the *Occupational Outlook Quarterly* and the *Monthly Labor Review*, published by the Labor Department's Bureau of Labor Statistics. Details and news releases are available at the Web site of the Bureau of Labor Statistics (www.bls.gov).

LO3
Summarize the advantages and disadvantages of ways to eliminate a labor surplus and avoid a labor shortage.

Determining Labor Surplus or Shortage

Based on the forecasts for labor demand and supply, the planner can compare the figures to determine whether there will be a shortage or surplus of labor for each job category. Determining expected shortages and surpluses allows the organization to plan how to address these challenges.

Issues related to a labor surplus or shortage can pose serious challenges for the organization. Manufacturers, for example, expect to have difficulty filling skilled-trades positions such as jobs for ironworkers, machinists, plumbers, and welders. Demand for these jobs is strong and is likely to continue as important infrastructure such as bridges and tunnels ages. Also, the average age of tradespeople is rising above 55, and young people tend not to be attracted to these jobs, assuming, often incorrectly, that manufacturing-related jobs will be difficult to find or will not pay well.[5]

Goal Setting and Strategic Planning

The second step in human resource planning is goal setting and strategic planning, as shown in the middle of Figure 5.1. The purpose of setting specific numerical goals is to focus attention on the problem and provide a basis for measuring the organization's success in addressing labor shortages and surpluses. The goals should come directly from the analysis of labor supply and demand. They should include a specific figure indicating what should happen with the job category or skill area and a specific timetable for when the results should be achieved.

For each goal, the organization must choose one or more human resource strategies. A variety of strategies is available for handling expected shortages and surpluses of labor. The top of Table 5.2 shows major options for reducing an expected labor surplus, and the bottom of the table lists options for avoiding an expected labor shortage.

This planning stage is critical. The options differ widely in their expense, speed, and effectiveness. Options for reducing a labor surplus cause differing amounts of human suffering. The options for avoiding a labor shortage differ in terms of how easily the organization can undo the change if it no longer faces a labor shortage. For example, an organization probably would not want to handle every expected labor

Table 5.2

HR Strategies for Addressing a Labor Shortage or Surplus

OPTIONS FOR REDUCING A SURPLUS		
OPTION	**SPEED OF RESULTS**	**AMOUNT OF SUFFERING CAUSED**
Downsizing	Fast	High
Pay reductions	Fast	High
Demotions	Fast	High
Transfers	Fast	Moderate
Work sharing	Fast	Moderate
Hiring freeze	Slow	Low
Natural attrition	Slow	Low
Early retirement	Slow	Low
Retraining	Slow	Low

OPTIONS FOR AVOIDING A SHORTAGE		
OPTION	**SPEED OF RESULTS**	**ABILITY TO CHANGE LATER**
Overtime	Fast	High
Temporary employees	Fast	High
Outsourcing	Fast	High
Retrained transfers	Slow	High
Turnover reductions	Slow	Moderate
New external hires	Slow	Low
Technological innovation	Slow	Low

Core Competency
A set of knowledge and skills that make the organization superior to competitors and create value for customers.

shortage by hiring new employees. The process is relatively slow and involves expenses to find and train new employees. Also, if the shortage becomes a surplus, the organization will have to consider laying off some of the employees. Layoffs involve another set of expenses, such as severance pay, and they are costly in terms of human suffering.

Another consideration in choosing an HR strategy is whether the employees needed will contribute directly to the organization's success. Organizations are most likely to benefit from hiring and retaining employees who provide a **core competency**—that is, a set of knowledge and skills that make the organization superior to competitors and create value for customers. At a store, for example, core competencies include choosing merchandise that shoppers want and providing shoppers with excellent service. For other work that is not a core competency—say, cleaning the store and providing security—the organization may benefit from using HR strategies other than hiring full-time employees.

Organizations try to anticipate labor surpluses far enough ahead that they can freeze hiring and let natural attrition (people leaving on their own) reduce the labor force. Unfortunately for many workers, organizations often stay competitive in a fast-changing environment by responding to a labor surplus with downsizing, which delivers fast results. The impact is painful for those who lose jobs, as well as those left behind to carry on without them. To handle a labor shortage, organizations typically hire temporary employees or use outsourcing. Because downsizing, using temporary employees, and outsourcing are most common, we will look at each of these in greater detail in the following sections.

Cold Stone Creamery employees give their company the competitive advantage with their "entertainment factor." The company is known to seek out employees who like to perform and then "audition" rather than interview potential employees.

Downsizing

Downsizing
The planned elimination of large numbers of personnel with the goal of enhancing the organization's competitiveness.

As we discussed in Chapter 2, **downsizing** is the planned elimination of large numbers of personnel with the goal of enhancing the organization's competitiveness. The primary reason organizations engage in downsizing is to promote future competitiveness. According to surveys, they do this by meeting four objectives:

1. *Reducing costs*—Labor is a large part of a company's total costs, so downsizing is an attractive place to start cutting costs.
2. *Replacing labor with technology*—Closing outdated factories, automating, or introducing other technological changes reduces the need for labor. Often, the labor savings outweigh the cost of the new technology.
3. *Mergers and acquisitions*—When organizations combine, they often need less bureaucratic overhead, so they lay off managers and some professional staff members.
4. *Moving to more economical locations*—Some organizations move from one area of the United States to another, especially from the Northeast and Midwest to the South and the mountain regions of the West. Although the recent recession hit California, Florida, and Texas particularly hard in terms of the number of job losses, the longer-term pattern of job movement to the South and West is expected to continue in the future.[6] McDonald's recently experimented with staffing drive-up service in Michigan by installing a long-distance connection to lower-wage workers in North Dakota, who took down orders and relayed them electronically to the Michigan kitchens.[7] Other moves have shifted jobs to other countries, including Mexico, India, and China, where wages are lower.

Although downsizing has an immediate effect on costs, much of the evidence suggests that it hurts long-term organizational effectiveness. This is especially true for certain kinds of companies, such as those that emphasize research and development and where employees have extensive contact with customers.[8] The negative effect of downsizing was especially high among firms that engaged in high-involvement work practices, such as the use of teams and performance-related pay incentives. As a result, the more a company tries to compete through its human resources, the more layoffs hurt productivity.[9]

Why do so many downsizing efforts fail to meet expectations? There seem to be several reasons. First, although the initial cost savings give a temporary boost to profits, the long-term effects of an improperly managed downsizing effort can be negative. Downsizing leads to a loss of talent, and it often disrupts the social networks through which people are creative and flexible.[10] Unless the downsizing is managed well, employees feel confused, demoralized, and even less willing to stay with the organization. Organizations may not take (or even know) the steps that can counter these reactions—for example, demonstrating how they are treating employees fairly, building confidence in the company's plans for a stronger future, and showing the organization's commitment to behaving responsibly with regard to all its stakeholders, including employees, customers, and the community.[11]

Also, many companies wind up rehiring. Downsizing campaigns often eliminate people who turn out to be irreplaceable. In one survey, 80 percent of the firms that had downsized later replaced some of the very people they had laid off. In one Fortune 100 firm, a bookkeeper making $9 an hour was let go. Later, the company realized she knew many things about the company that no one else knew, so she was hired back as a consultant—for $42 an hour.[12] However, recent trends in employment suggest that companies will not rehire employees for many of the jobs eliminated when they restructured, introduced automation, or moved work to lower-cost regions.[13]

Finally, downsizing efforts often fail because employees who survive the purge become self-absorbed and afraid to take risks. Motivation drops because any hope of future promotions—or any future—with the company dies. Many employees start looking for other employment opportunities. The negative publicity associated with a downsizing campaign can also hurt the company's image in the labor market, so it is harder to recruit employees later.

Many problems with downsizing can be reduced with better planning. Instead of slashing jobs across the board, successful downsizing makes surgical strategic cuts that improve the company's competitive position, and management addresses the problem of employees becoming demoralized. Boeing learned this lesson the hard way in the 1990s, when it reduced its workforce by letting workers choose whether they wanted to accept a buyout package in exchange for leaving. Workers with the most experience (and best prospects elsewhere) were most likely to leave, so when Boeing's orders increased and it needed to rehire later, it was competing in the labor market for the best people. To avoid that situation when it needed to cut 10,000 jobs in 2009, Boeing avoided voluntary reductions and instead required managers to pick which employees' positions would be eliminated.[14]

Reducing Hours

Given the limitations of downsizing, many organizations are more carefully considering other avenues for eliminating a labor surplus (shown in Table 5.2). One alternative seen as a way to spread the burden more fairly is cutting work hours, generally with a corresponding reduction in pay. Besides the thought that this is a more equitable way to weather a slump in demand, companies choose a reduction in work hours because it is less costly than layoffs requiring severance pay, and it is easier to restore the work hours than to hire new employees after a downsizing effort. Window maker Pella, for example, put its employees on a four-day workweek, and Dell Computer offered its employees a chance to take extra (unpaid) days off at the end of the year.[15]

Early-Retirement Programs

Another popular way to reduce a labor surplus is with an early-retirement program. As we discussed in Chapter 2, the average age of the U.S. workforce is increasing. But even though many baby boomers are approaching traditional retirement age, early indications are that this group has no intention of retiring soon.[16] Reasons include improved health of older people, jobs becoming less physically demanding, concerns about the long-term viability of Social Security and pensions, the recent drop in the value of older workers' retirement assets (especially stock funds and home values), and laws against age discrimination. Under the pressures associated with an aging labor force, many employers try to encourage older workers to leave voluntarily by offering a variety of early-retirement incentives. The more lucrative of these programs succeed by some measures. Research suggests that these programs encourage lower-performing older workers to retire.[17] Sometimes they work so well that too many workers retire.

Many organizations are moving from early-retirement programs to phased-retirement programs. In a *phased-retirement program*, the organization can continue to enjoy the experience of older workers while reducing the number of hours that these employees work, as well as the cost of those employees. This option also can give older employees the psychological benefit of easing into retirement, rather than being thrust entirely into a new way of life.[18]

focus on *social responsibility*

Employing Temporary and Contract Workers

While downsizing has been a popular way to reduce a labor surplus, the most widespread methods for eliminating a labor shortage are hiring temporary and contract workers and outsourcing work. Employers may arrange to hire a temporary worker through an agency that specializes in linking employers with people who have the necessary skills. The employer pays the agency, which in turn pays the temporary worker. Employers also may contract directly with individuals, often professionals, to provide a particular service.

To use this source of labor effectively, employers need to overcome some disadvantages. In particular, temporary and contract workers may not be as committed to the organization, so if they work directly with customers, that attitude may spill over and affect customer loyalty. Therefore, many organizations try to use permanent employees in key jobs and use temporary and contract workers in ways that clearly supplement—and do not potentially replace—the permanent employees.[19]

Temporary Workers

As we saw in Chapter 2, the federal government estimated that organizations are using over a million temporary workers. Temporary employment is popular with employers because it gives them flexibility they need to operate efficiently when demand for their products changes rapidly.

In addition to flexibility, temporary employment offers lower costs. Using temporary workers frees the employer from many administrative tasks and financial burdens associated with being the "employer of record." The cost of employee benefits, including health care, pension, life insurance, workers' compensation, and unemployment insurance, can account for 40 percent of payroll expenses for permanent employees. Assuming the agency pays for these benefits, a company using temporary workers may save money even if it pays the agency a higher rate for that worker than the usual wage paid to a permanent employee.

Agencies that provide temporary employees also may handle some of the tasks associated with hiring. Small companies that cannot afford their own testing programs often get employees who have been tested by a temporary agency. Many temporary agencies also train employees before sending them to employers. This reduces employers' training costs and eases the transition for the temporary worker and employer.

Finally, temporary workers may offer value not available from permanent employees. Because the temporary worker has little experience at the employer's organization, this person brings an objective point of view to the organization's problems and procedures. Also, a temporary worker may have a great deal of experience in other organizations that can be applied to the current assignment.

To obtain these benefits, organizations need to overcome the disadvantages associated with temporary workers. For example, tension can develop between temporary and permanent employees. For suggestions on how to address this challenge, see the "HR How To" box.

Employee or Contractor?

Besides using a temporary-employment agency, a company can obtain workers for limited assignments by entering into contracts with them. If the person providing the services is an independent contractor, rather than an employee, the company does not pay employee benefits, such as health insurance and vacations. As with using

USING TEMPORARY EMPLOYEES AND CONTRACTORS

Many full-time employees perceive temporary workers as a threat to their own job security. Such an attitude can interfere with cooperation and, in some cases, lead to outright sabotage if the situation is not well managed.

One way organizations should manage this situation is to complete any downsizing efforts before bringing in temporary or contract workers. Surviving a downsizing is almost like experiencing a death in the family. A decent time interval needs to occur before new temporary workers are introduced. Without the delay, the surviving employees will associate the downsizing effort (which was a threat) with the new temporary employees (who

could be perceived as outsiders brought in to replace old friends). If an upswing in demand follows a downsizing effort, the organization should probably begin meeting its expanded demand for labor by granting overtime to core employees. If the demand persists, the organization will be more certain that the upswing will last and future layoffs will be unnecessary. The extended stretches of overtime will eventually tax the full-time employees, so they will accept using temporary workers to help lessen their load.

The organization may also try to select "nonthreatening" temporary workers, especially those who enjoy temporary assignments for their variety or flexibility.

Many temporary-staffing firms attract people with this outlook.

Organizations that use temporary or contract workers must avoid treating them as second-class citizens. One way to do this is to ensure that the temporary agency provides temporaries with benefits that are comparable with those enjoyed by the organization's permanent workers. For example, one temporary agency, MacTemps, gives its workers long-term health coverage, full disability insurance, and complete dental coverage. This not only reduces the benefit gap between the temporary and permanent workers but also helps attract the best temporary workers in the first place.

temporary employees, the savings can be significant, even if the contractor works at a higher rate of pay.

Consultants at PricewaterhouseCoopers suggest that information technology will make it so practical for contractors and employers to find each other that some contractors will form networks of talented, specialized workers. Instead of competing for full-time talent, companies will simply use contractors from these networks as needed. Companies could even contract for management talent to handle particular projects or solve short-term problems. Charles Grantham of a research group called Work Design Collaborative sees evidence that the main force slowing this trend has been the difficulty of getting and affording health insurance outside of traditional employment. If that barrier is removed, more employees might prefer independent-contractor status.[20]

This strategy carries risks, however. If the person providing the service is a contractor and not an employee, the company is not supposed to directly supervise the worker. The company can tell the contractor what criteria the finished assignment should meet but not, for example, where or what hours to work. This distinction is significant, because under federal law, if the company treats the contractor as an employee, the company has certain legal obligations, described in Part 4, related to matters such as overtime pay and withholding taxes.

When an organization wants to consider using independent contractors as a way to expand its labor force temporarily, human resource professionals can help by alerting the company to the need to verify that the arrangement will meet the legal requirements. A good place to start is with the advice to small businesses at the Internal

Revenue Service Web site (www.irs.gov); search for "independent contractor" to find links to information and guidance. In addition, the organization may need to obtain professional legal advice.

Outsourcing

Outsourcing
Contracting with another organization to perform a broad set of services.

Instead of using a temporary or contract employee to fill a single job, an organization might want a broader set of services. Contracting with another organization to perform a broad set of services is called **outsourcing.** Organizations use outsourcing as a way to operate more efficiently and save money. They choose outsourcing firms that promise to deliver the same or better quality at a lower cost. One reason they can do this is that the outside company specializes in the service and can benefit from economies of scale (the economic principle that producing something in large volume tends to cost less for each additional unit than producing in small volume). This efficiency is often the attraction for outsourcing human resource functions such as payroll. Costs also are lower when the outsourcing firm is located in a part of the world where wages are relatively low. The labor forces of countries such as China, India, Jamaica, and those in Eastern Europe have been creating an abundant supply of labor for unskilled and low-skilled work.

The first uses of outsourcing emphasized manufacturing and routine tasks. However, technological advances in computer networks and transmission have speeded up the outsourcing process and have helped it spread beyond manufacturing areas and low-skilled jobs. For example, DuPont moved legal services associated with its $100 million asbestos case litigation to a team of lawyers working in the Philippines. The work is a combination of routine document handling and legal judgments such as determining the relevance of a document to the case. Salaries for lawyers and paralegals in the Philippines are about one-fifth the cost of their counterparts in the United States.[21]

Outsourcing may be a necessary way to operate as efficiently as competitors, but it does pose challenges. Quality-control problems, security violations, and poor customer service have sometimes wiped out the cost savings attributed to lower wages. To ensure success with an outsourcing strategy, companies should follow these guidelines:

- Learn about what the provider can do for the company, not just the costs. Make sure the company has the necessary skills, including an environment that can meet standards for clear communication, on-time shipping, contract enforcement, fair labor practices, and environmental protection. Some companies are keeping outsourcing work near or inside the United States in order to meet this full set of requirements.[22]
- Do not offshore any work that is proprietary or requires tight security.[23]
- Start small and monitor the work closely, especially in the beginning, when problems are most likely.[24]
- Look for opportunities to outsource work in areas that promote growth, for example, by partnering with experts who can help the organization tap new markets.[25]

Overtime and Expanded Hours

Organizations facing a labor shortage may be reluctant to hire employees, even temporary workers, or to commit to an outsourcing arrangement. Especially if the organization expects the shortage to be temporary, it may prefer an arrangement that is simpler and less costly. Under some conditions, these organizations may try to garner more hours from the existing labor force, asking them to go from part-time to full-time status or to work overtime.

A major downside of overtime is that the employer must pay nonmanagement employees one-and-a-half times their normal wages for work done overtime. Even so, employers see overtime pay as preferable to the costs of hiring and training new employees. The preference is especially strong if the organization doubts that the current higher level of demand for its products will last long.

For a short time at least, many workers appreciate the added compensation for working overtime. Over extended periods, however, employees feel stress and frustration from working long hours. Overtime therefore is best suited for short-term labor shortages.

Implementing and Evaluating the HR Plan

For whatever HR strategies are selected, the final stage of human resource planning involves implementing the strategies and evaluating the outcomes. This stage is represented by the bottom part of Figure 5.1. When implementing the HR strategy, the organization must hold some individual accountable for achieving the goals. That person also must have the authority and resources needed to accomplish those goals. It is also important that this person issue regular progress reports, so the organization can be sure that all activities occur on schedule and that the early results are as expected.

Implementation that ties planning and recruiting to the organization's strategy and to its efforts to develop employees becomes a complete program of *talent management*. As described in the "eHRM" box, today's computer systems have made talent management more practical.

In evaluating the results, the most obvious step is checking whether the organization has succeeded in avoiding labor shortages or surpluses. Along with measuring these numbers, the evaluation should identify which parts of the planning process contributed to success or failure. For example, consider a company where meeting human resource needs requires that employees continually learn new skills. If there is a gap between needed skills and current skill levels, the evaluation should consider whether the problem lies with failure to forecast the needed skills or with implementation. Are employees signing up for training, and is the right kind of training available?

Applying HR Planning to Affirmative Action

As we discussed in Chapter 3, many organizations have a human resource strategy that includes affirmative action to manage diversity or meet government requirements. Meeting affirmative-action goals requires that employers carry out an additional level of human resource planning aimed at those goals. In other words, besides looking at its overall workforce and needs, the organization looks at the representation of subgroups in its labor force—for example, the proportion of women and minorities.

Affirmative-action plans forecast and monitor the proportion of employees who are members of various protected groups (typically, women and racial or ethnic minorities). The planning looks at the representation of these employees in the organization's job categories and career tracks. The planner can compare the proportion of employees who are in each group with the proportion each group represents in the labor market. For example, the organization might note that in a labor market that is 25 percent Hispanic, 60 percent of its customer service personnel are Hispanic. This type of comparison is called a **workforce utilization review.** The organization can use this process to determine whether there is any subgroup whose proportion in the relevant labor market differs substantially from the proportion in the job category.

Workforce Utilization Review
A comparison of the proportion of employees in protected groups with the proportion that each group represents in the relevant labor market.

TALENT MANAGEMENT AT NORTH SHORE–LONG ISLAND JEWISH HEALTH SYSTEM

The North Shore–Long Island Jewish Health System (NS-LI), based in Great Neck, New York, encompasses 15 hospitals. Given the challenges of a tight labor market in the health care industry and the fact that good employees are literally a life-or-death matter in a hospital, the need to manage this talent is intense.

To keep track of its needs and existing resources while planning for the future, NS-LI uses a computerized talent management system from Taleo Corporation. The software gathers information on the organization's HR goals, recruiting efforts, employee performance reviews, and more. Using data from the system, NS-LI is making better hiring decisions that match applicants to jobs, so turnover has fallen. Recruiting ads are delivering better results, because data show which sources provide the best returns in terms of candidates actually hired. The organization is also filling positions faster, now that it can easily find information in the system.

The power of a system like Taleo's is it shows users how HR efforts in one area affect results across all areas—for example, whether recruiting sources are efficiently generating hires of high-performing employees. At one time, software like Taleo's would have been impractical for all but giant corporations. However, greater processing power of today's computers makes the system affordable for even many small businesses.

Source: Mitch Betts, "Talent Management Yields Dramatic ROI," *Computerworld,* November 16, 2009, Business & Company Resource Center, http://galenet.galegroup.com; and Norm Alster, "Taleo Corp., Dublin, California: Demand Stays Strong for Software That Sorts Out Job Applications," *Investor's Business Daily,* January 20, 2010, Business & Company Resource Center, http://galenet.galegroup.com.

If the workforce utilization review indicates that some group—for example, African Americans—makes up 35 percent of the relevant labor market for a job category but that this same group constitutes only 5 percent of the employees actually in the job category at the organization, this is evidence of underutilization. That situation could result from problems in selection or from problems in internal movement (promotions or other movement along a career path). One way to diagnose the situation would be to use transitional matrices, such as the matrix shown in Table 5.1 earlier in this chapter.

The steps in a workforce utilization review are identical to the steps in the HR planning process that were shown in Figure 5.1. The organization must assess current utilization patterns, then forecast how they are likely to change in the near future. If these analyses suggest the organization is underutilizing certain groups and if forecasts suggest this pattern is likely to continue, the organization may need to set goals and timetables for changing. The planning process may identify new strategies for recruitment or selection. The organization carries out these HR strategies and evaluates their success.

LO4
Describe recruitment policies organizations use to make job vacancies more attractive.

Recruiting Human Resources

As the first part of this chapter shows, it is difficult to always predict exactly how many (if any) new employees the organization will have to hire in a given year in a given job category. The role of human resource recruitment is to build a supply of potential new hires that the organization can draw on if the need arises. In human resource management, **recruiting** consists of any practice or activity carried on by the organization with the primary purpose of identifying and attracting potential employees.[26] It thus creates a buffer between planning and the actual selection of new

Recruiting
Any activity carried on by the organization with the primary purpose of identifying and attracting potential employees.

employees (the topic of the next chapter). The goals of recruiting (encouraging qualified people to apply for jobs) and selection (deciding which candidates would be the best fit) are different enough that they are most effective when performed separately, rather than combined as in a job interview that also involves selling candidates on the company.[27]

Because of differences in companies' strategies, they may assign different degrees of importance to recruiting.[28] In general, however, all companies have to make decisions in three areas of recruiting: personnel policies, recruitment sources, and the characteristics and behavior of the recruiter. As shown in Figure 5.2, these aspects of recruiting have different effects on whom the organization ultimately hires. Personnel policies influence the characteristics of the positions to be filled. Recruitment sources influence the kinds of job applicants an organization reaches. And the nature and behavior of the recruiter affect the characteristics of both the vacancies and the applicants. Ultimately, an applicant's decision to accept a job offer—and the organization's decision to make the offer—depend on the match between vacancy characteristics and applicant characteristics.

The remainder of this chapter explores these three aspects of recruiting: personnel policies, recruitment sources, and recruiter traits and behaviors.

Personnel Policies

An organization's *personnel policies* are its decisions about how it will carry out human resource management, including how it will fill job vacancies. These policies influence the nature of the positions that are vacant. According to the research on recruitment, it is clear that characteristics of the vacancy are more important than recruiters or recruiting sources for predicting job choice.[29] Several personnel policies are especially relevant to recruitment:

- *Internal versus external recruiting*—Organizations with policies to "promote from within" try to fill upper-level vacancies by recruiting candidates internally—that is, finding candidates who already work for the organization. Opportunities for advancement make a job more attractive to applicants and employees, as illustrated by the example in the "Best Practices" box. Decisions about internal versus external recruiting affect the nature of jobs, recruitment sources, and the nature of applicants, as we will describe later in the chapter.

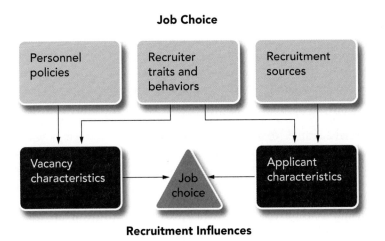

Job Choice

Recruitment Influences

Figure 5.2

Three Aspects of Recruiting

ROOM TO BLOOM AND GROW AT FOUR SEASONS

Four Seasons Hotels and Resorts is known worldwide for its luxurious hotels and impeccable service. Extraordinary service, of course, comes only from extraordinary people, so matching the right people to the right jobs is essential. Employees are enormously proud of the Four Seasons, and for a dozen years, it has been repeatedly named one of *Fortune* magazine's best companies to work for. And where better to find these extraordinary people than from among the company's existing ranks? It's no surprise then that regional marketing director Judith Dumrauf says, "Our culture is to promote from within."

That culture allowed an unusual career path for Elizabeth Knox. After working in hotels while in graduate school, Knox took a job with Four Seasons as director of room service in its Philadelphia hotel. But much as she liked the position, she found that she had little contact with guests, and she missed the interaction. Knox decided she would like to move into the catering end of the business.

Knox approached management with her idea, but there was a problem: she didn't have all the skills she needed for the required office work. In fact, she couldn't type. To learn the skills she would need, she would have to move from her management job to a low-level position and restart from the ground up. Many organizations would discourage such an idea, but Four Seasons gave Knox the green light. She went from manager to administrative assistant, answering phones on the job and practicing how to type after hours. Meanwhile, Knox learned how to plan meetings and parties. Eventually, she was promoted to catering manager.

After six years as a catering manager, Knox won promotion to assistant director of the department. Then her boss, the director, left for another position, and Knox became the acting director. She carried out her responsibilities so enthusiastically that Four Seasons awarded her a prize—a week's vacation at any Four Seasons hotel or resort—for being its best catering manager that year. Soon thereafter, the company appointed Knox the department's permanent director.

Could Four Seasons have found such a dedicated manager from outside its walls? Perhaps. But Knox's wholesale dedication to learning the business would be hard to beat.

Sources: Monica Yant Kinney, "Sidestepping to Move Up," *Philadelphia Inquirer*, March 14, 2010, Business & Company Resource Center, http://galenet.galegroup.com; and David Segal, "Pillow Fights at the Four Seasons," *The New York Times*, June 28, 2009, Business & Company Resource Center, http://galenet.galegroup.com.

Employment at Will
Employment principle that if there is no specific employment contract saying otherwise, the employer or employee may end an employment relationship at any time, regardless of cause.

- *Lead-the-market pay strategies*—Pay is an important job characteristic for almost all applicants. Organizations have a recruiting advantage if their policy is to take a "lead-the-market" approach to pay—that is, pay more than the current market wages for a job. Higher pay can also make up for a job's less desirable features, such as working on a night shift or in dangerous conditions. Organizations that compete for applicants based on pay may use bonuses, stock options, and other forms of pay besides wages and salaries. Chapters 11 and 12 will take a closer look at these and other decisions about pay.

- *Employment-at-will policies*—Within the laws of the state where they are operating, employers have latitude to set polices about their rights in an employment relationship. A widespread policy follows the principle of **employment at will,** which holds that if there is no specific employment contract saying otherwise, the employer or employee may end an employment relationship at any time. An alternative is to establish extensive **due-process policies,** which formally lay out the steps an employee may take to appeal an employer's decision to terminate that employee. An organization's lawyers may advise the company to ensure that all recruitment documents say the employment is "at will," to protect the company from lawsuits about wrongful discharge. Management must decide how to weigh any legal advantages against the impact on recruitment. Job applicants are more attracted to organizations with due-process policies, which imply greater job security and concern for protecting employees, than to organizations with employment-at-will policies.[30]

- *Image advertising*—Besides advertising specific job openings, as discussed in the next section, organizations may advertise themselves as a good place to work in general. Advertising designed to create a generally favorable impression of the organization is called *image advertising*. Image advertising is particularly important for organizations in highly competitive labor markets that perceive themselves as having a bad image.[31] Research suggests that the image of an organization's brand—for example, innovative, dynamic, or fun—influences the degree to which a person feels attracted to the organization.[32] This attraction is especially true if the person's own traits seem to match those of the organization. Also, job applicants seem to be particularly sensitive to issues of diversity and inclusion in image advertising, so organizations should ensure that their image advertisements reflect the broad nature of the labor market from which they intend to recruit.[33]

Image advertising, such as in this campaign to recruit nurses, promotes a whole profession or organization as opposed to a specific job opening. This ad is designed to create a positive impression of the profession, which is now facing a shortage of workers

Recruitment Sources

Another critical element of an organization's recruitment strategy is its decisions about where to look for applicants. The total labor market is enormous and spread over the entire globe. As a practical matter, an organization will draw from a small fraction of that total market. The methods the organization chooses for communicating its labor needs and the audiences it targets will determine the size and nature of the labor market the organization taps to fill its vacant positions.[34] A person who responds to a job advertisement on the Internet is likely to be different from a person responding to a sign hanging outside a factory. The "Did You Know?" box presents some data on sources of recruitment. Each of the major sources from which organizations draw recruits has advantages and disadvantages.

Internal Sources

As we discussed with regard to personnel policies, an organization may emphasize internal or external sources of job applicants. Internal sources are employees who currently hold other positions in the organization. Organizations recruit existing employees through **job posting,** or communicating information about the vacancy on company bulletin boards, in employee publications, on corporate intranets, and anywhere else the organization communicates with employees. Managers also may identify candidates to recommend for vacancies. Policies that emphasize promotions and even lateral moves to achieve broader career experience can give applicants a favorable impression of the organization's jobs. The use of internal sources also affects what kinds of people the organization recruits.

Due-Process Policies
Policies that formally lay out the steps an employee may take to appeal the employer's decision to terminate that employee.

LO5
List and compare sources of job applicants.

Job Posting
The process of communicating information about a job vacancy on company bulletin boards, in employee publications, on corporate intranets, and anywhere else the organization communicates with employees.

Four in Ten Positions Are Filled with Insiders

In a survey of large, well-known businesses, respondents said over one-third of positions are filled with people who already work for the company and accept a promotion or transfer.

Source: Gerry Crispin and Mark Mehler, "CareerXroads 9th Annual Source of Hire Study," February 2010, www.careerxroads.com. (This report includes 2008 data for sources of hire because the authors believe 2009 is not representative.)

Sources of Hire

Note: "Internal movement" refers to jobs filled from employees currently in the company who are referred by managers or receive promotions or transfers; "all external sources" refers to employees found using sources outside the company such as electronic recruiting from company or job Web sites, employment agencies, colleges and universities, walk-in applicants, newspaper ads, and referrals.

For the employer, relying on internal sources offers several advantages.[35] First, it generates applicants who are well known to the organization. In addition, these applicants are relatively knowledgeable about the organization's vacancies, which minimizes the possibility they will have unrealistic expectations about the job. Finally, filling vacancies through internal recruiting is generally cheaper and faster than looking outside the organization.

The value of a strong internal hiring system can be seen in the leadership of North Jersey Federal Credit Union. The credit union's chief executive, Lourdes Cortez, has been with the credit union for more than 20 years, starting out as a teller. From that entry-level position, Cortez worked her way into management. Along the way, she held jobs in almost every department (skipping only accounting) and got to know the organization's members (credit union customers) firsthand. Explaining her strengths, Cortez says, "Having worked my way up at the credit union absolutely gives me a number of different perspectives. I've worked in every department, so I have respect for employees in those positions, and I relate better to membership because I've dealt with them on a one-on-one basis."[36]

External Sources

Despite the advantages of internal recruitment, organizations often have good reasons to recruit externally.[37] For entry-level positions and perhaps for specialized upper-level positions, the organization has no internal recruits from which to draw. Also, bringing in outsiders may expose the organization to new ideas or new ways of doing business. An organization that uses only internal recruitment can wind up with a workforce whose members all think alike and therefore may be poorly suited to innovation.[38]

And finally, companies that are able to grow during a slow economy can gain a competitive edge by hiring the best talent when other organizations are forced to avoid hiring, freeze pay increases, or even lay off talented people.[39] So organizations often recruit through direct applicants and referrals, advertisements, employment agencies, schools, and Web sites. Figure 5.3 shows which of these sources are used most among large companies surveyed.

Direct Applicants and Referrals

Even without a formal effort to reach job applicants, an organization may hear from candidates through direct applicants and referrals. **Direct applicants** are people who apply for a vacancy without prompting from the organization. **Referrals** are people who apply because someone in the organization prompted them to do so. According to the survey results shown in Figure 5.3, the largest share (over one-fourth) of new employees hired by large companies came from referrals, and the next largest share (over 22 percent) came from direct applications made at the employer's

Direct Applicants
People who apply for a vacancy without prompting from the organization.

Referrals
People who apply for a vacancy because someone in the organization prompted them to do so.

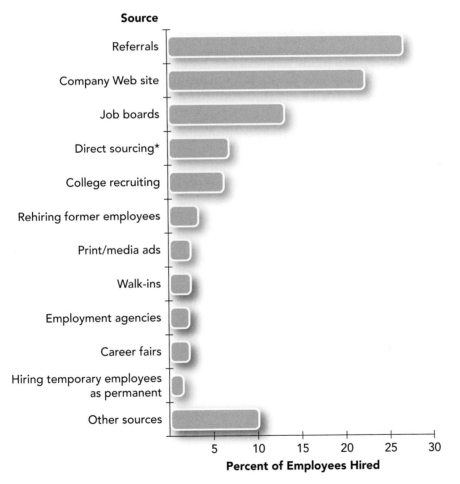

Figure 5.3

External Recruiting Sources

*Direct sourcing includes research by the employer, such as searching internal databases of résumés and social-networking Web sites to identify and contact people who seem to be well-qualified but did not apply.

SOURCE: Gerry Crispin and Mark Mehler, "CareerXroads 9th Annual Source of Hire Study," February 2010, www.careerxroads.com (data for 2009).

Web site.[40] These two sources of recruits share some characteristics that make them excellent pools from which to draw.

One advantage is that many direct applicants are to some extent already "sold" on the organization. Most have done some research and concluded there is enough fit between themselves and the vacant position to warrant submitting an application, a process called *self-selection*, which, when it works, eases the pressure on the organization's recruiting and selection systems. A form of aided self-selection occurs with referrals. Many job seekers look to friends, relatives, and acquaintances to help find employment. Using these social networks not only helps the job seeker but also simplifies recruitment for employers.[41] Current employees (who are familiar with the vacancy as well as the person they are referring) decide that there is a fit between the person and the vacancy, so they convince the person to apply for the job.

An additional benefit of using such sources is that it costs much less than formal recruiting efforts. Considering these combined benefits, referrals and direct applications are among the best sources of new hires. Some employers offer current employees financial incentives for referring applicants who are hired and perform acceptably on the job (for example, if they stay 180 days). Other companies such as Google and SAS play off their good reputations in the labor market to generate direct applications. SAS, a Cary, North Carolina–based developer of business systems, is so well known in the software industry for its generous workplace benefits and challenging assignments that recruiting is a bargain—partly because so many people go to the company looking for jobs and partly because they tend to stick around when they are hired.[42]

The major downside of referrals is that they limit the likelihood of exposing the organization to fresh viewpoints. People tend to refer others who are like themselves. Furthermore, sometimes referrals contribute to hiring practices that are or that appear unfair, an example being **nepotism,** or the hiring of relatives. Employees may resent the hiring and rapid promotion of "the boss's son" or "the boss's daughter," or even the boss's friend.

Nepotism
The practice of hiring relatives.

Advertisements in Newspapers and Magazines

Open almost any newspaper or magazine and you can find advertisements of job openings. These ads typically generate a less desirable group of applicants than direct applications or referrals, and do so at greater expense. However, few employers can fill all their vacancies purely through direct applications and referrals, so they usually need to advertise. An employer can take many steps to increase the effectiveness of recruitment through advertising.

The person designing a job advertisement needs to answer two questions:

What do we need to say?
To whom do we need to say it?

With respect to the first question, an ad should give readers enough information to evaluate the job and its requirements, so they can make a well-informed judgment about their qualifications. Providing enough information may require long advertisements, which cost more. The employer should evaluate the additional costs against the costs of providing too little information: Vague ads generate a huge number of applicants, including many who are not reasonably qualified or would not accept the job if they learned more about it. Reviewing all these applications to eliminate unsuitable applicants is expensive. In practice, the people who write job advertisements tend to overstate the skills and experience required, perhaps generating too few qualified candidates. For example, some have blamed the shortage of qualified engineers in America on job advertising that requires experience with particular processes or software programs, rather than looking for broader abilities that can be transferred to new applications.[43]

Specifying whom to reach with the message helps the advertiser decide where to place the ad. Ads placed in the classified section of local newspapers are relatively inexpensive yet reach many people in a specific geographic area who are currently looking for work (or at least interested enough to be reading the classifieds). On the downside, this medium offers little ability to target skill levels. Typically, many of the people reading classified ads are either over- or underqualified for the position. Also, people who are not looking for work rarely read the classifieds. These people may include candidates the organization could lure from their current employers. For reaching a specific part of the labor market, including certain skill levels and more people who are employed, the organization may get better results from advertising in professional or industry journals. Some employers also advertise on television—particularly cable television.[44]

Electronic Recruiting

In recent years, employers have shifted using their spending on job advertisements away from print ads to online job advertising or a combination of the two. A recent survey by the Conference Board found that the number of online job ads rose by 24 percent over the previous year.[45] Online recruiting generally involves posting career information at company Web sites to address people who are interested in the particular company and posting paid advertisements at career services to attract people who are searching for jobs. Company's are also visiting network sites such as Linked In and Facebook to find job candidates. The "HR Oops!" Box illustrates the potential danger of using social networking sites for recruiting.

Most large companies and many smaller ones make career information available at their Web sites. To make that information easier to find, they may register a domain name with a ".jobs" extension, such as www.starbucks.jobs for a link to information about careers at Starbucks and www.unionpacific.jobs for information about careers at Union Pacific. To be an effective recruiting tool, corporate career information should move beyond generalities, offering descriptions of open positions and an easy way to submit a résumé. One of the best features of this kind of electronic recruiting is the ability to target and attract job candidates whose values match the organization's values and whose skills match the job requirements.[46] Candidates also appreciate an e-mail response that the company has received the résumé—especially a response that gives a timetable about further communications from the company.

Accepting applications at the company Web site is not so successful for smaller and less well-known organizations, because fewer people are likely to visit the Web site. These organizations may get better results by going to the Web sites that are set up to attract job seekers, such as Monster, Yahoo HotJobs, and CareerBuilder, which attract a vast array of applicants. At these sites, job seekers submit standardized résumés. Employers can search the site's database for résumés that include specified key terms, and they can also submit information about their job opportunities, so that job seekers can search that information by key term. With both employers and job seekers submitting information to and conducting searches on them, these sites offer an efficient way to find matches between job seekers and job vacancies. However, a drawback is that the big job Web sites can provide too many leads of

HR Oops!

When Social Networking Gets Too "Social"

Along with inviting applications at Web sites and posting ads on job boards, today's recruiters often visit networking sites like Facebook and LinkedIn to find potential candidates with suitable interests and experience. But sometimes the efforts get awkward.

HR professional Michael Janas, for example, landed an executive job through LinkedIn but thinks recruiters occasionally get sloppy. For example, he has known recruiters to ask early on about a candidate's year of graduation from college, a tactic that could support age discrimination. He also says some recruiters rely too much on easy assumptions about what they see when they need to go deeper into the details of a potential candidate's background.

And, of course, there are the horror stories of people who post information that works against them in a job search. Author and social-media expert Sarah Browne recalls a part-time employee who was being considered for a full-time position. Unfortunately for that employee, he posted a message on Facebook that he'd be unable to attend a party because his boss was so demanding. Instead of giving him the job, the boss fired him later for poor professional judgment.

Source: Based on Julie Vallone, "Job Seekers Employing Social Networking: A Way to Build Connections," *Investor's Business Daily*, December 22, 2009, Business & Company Resource Center, http://galenet.galegroup.com.

Questions

1. What kinds of information do you think recruiters can legitimately expect to learn on a social-networking site? What would they have to learn elsewhere?
2. How do you protect yourself from appearing unprofessional when you use social-networking sites or other public Internet communications?

inferior quality because they are so huge and serve all job seekers and employers, not a select segment.

Because of this limitation of the large Web sites, smaller, more tailored Web sites called "niche boards" focus on certain industries, occupations, or geographic areas. Telecommcareers.net, for example, is a site devoted to, as the name implies, the telecommunications industry. CIO.com, a companion site to *CIO Magazine*, specializes in openings for chief information officers. In addition, companies can improve the effectiveness of online advertising by employing more interactive tools, such as social networking.

Public Employment Agencies

The Social Security Act of 1935 requires that everyone receiving unemployment compensation be registered with a local state employment office. These state employment offices work with the U.S. Employment Service (USES) to try to ensure that unemployed individuals eventually get off state aid and back on employer payrolls. To accomplish this, agencies collect information from the unemployed people about their skills and experience.

Employers can register their job vacancies with their local state employment office, and the agency will try to find someone suitable, using its computerized inventory of local unemployed individuals. The agency refers candidates to the employer at no charge. The organization can interview or test them to see if they are suitable for its vacancies. Besides offering access to job candidates at low cost, public employment agencies can be a useful resource for meeting certain diversity objectives. Laws often mandate that the agencies maintain specialized "desks" for minorities, disabled individuals, and war veterans. Employers that feel they currently are underutilizing any of these subgroups of the labor force may find the agencies to be an excellent source.

The government also provides funding to a variety of local employment agencies. For example, in Virginia, the Frederick County Job Training Agency receives funding from the federal, state, and county governments to help unemployed workers find and prepare for new jobs. When the Von Hoffmann Corporation closed its Frederick plant to consolidate operations in Missouri and Iowa, the 165 employees didn't want to move. A career consultant at the Job Training Agency met with each of them to record their work history and goals. The laid-off workers also can use the agency to visit online job sites, mail résumés at no charge, and participate in classes on writing résumés and interviewing for a job. The Job Training Agency shares a building with the county's Office of Economic Development, in the hope that the development agency, which encourages businesses to locate in the county, can work with it to match employers and workers.[47]

Private Employment Agencies

In contrast to public employment agencies, which primarily serve the blue-collar labor market, private employment agencies provide much the same service for the white-collar labor market. Workers interested in finding a job can sign up with a private employment agency whether or not they are currently unemployed. Another difference between the two types of agencies is that private agencies charge the employers for providing referrals. Therefore, using a private employment agency is more expensive than using a public agency, but the private agency is a more suitable source for certain kinds of applicants.

For managers or professionals, an employer may use the services of a type of private agency called an *executive search firm (ESF)*. People often call these agencies "headhunters" because, unlike other employment agencies, they find new jobs for people almost exclusively already employed. For job candidates, dealing with executive search firms can be sensitive. Typically, executives do not want to advertise their availability, because it could trigger a negative reaction from their current employer. ESFs serve as a buffer, providing confidentiality between the employer and the recruit. That benefit may give an employer access to candidates it cannot recruit in other, more direct ways.

Colleges and Universities

Most colleges and universities have placement services that seek to help their graduates obtain employment. On-campus interviewing is the most important source of recruits for entry-level professional and managerial vacancies.[48] Organizations tend to focus especially on colleges that have strong reputations in areas for which they have critical needs—say, chemical engineering or public accounting.[49] The recruiting strategy at 3M includes concentrating on 25 to 30 selected universities. The company has a commitment to those selected universities and returns to them each year with new job openings. HR professionals make sure that the same person works with the same university year in and year out, to achieve "continuity of contact."[50]

One of the best ways for a company to establish a stronger presence on a campus is with a college internship program. Embassy Suites is one company that participates in such a program. How does this benefit the company and the students at the same time?

Many employers have found that successfully competing for the best students requires more than just signing up prospective graduates for interview slots. One of the best ways to establish a stronger presence on a campus is with a college internship program. Internship programs give an organization early access to potential applicants and let the organization assess their capabilities directly. IBM uses a program called Latin American Grid, in which it partners with colleges in Florida, Mexico, Puerto Rico, and Barcelona by donating hardware and software and collaborating on research. What IBM gets in return is access to a pool of talented Latin American scholars, which it cultivates through mentoring and an internship program. Ultimately, it hires many of them as permanent employees.[51]

Another way of increasing the employer's presence on campus is to participate in university job fairs. In general, a job fair is an event where many employers gather for a short time to meet large numbers of potential job applicants. Although job fairs can be held anywhere (such as at a hotel or convention center), campuses are ideal locations because of the many well-educated, yet unemployed, individuals who are there. Job fairs are an inexpensive means of generating an on-campus presence. They can even provide one-on-one dialogue with potential recruits—dialogue that would be impossible through less interactive media, such as newspaper ads.

Evaluating the Quality of a Source

Yield Ratio
A ratio that expresses the percentage of applicants who successfully move from one stage of the recruitment and selection process to the next.

In general, there are few rules that say what recruitment source is best for a given job vacancy. Therefore, it is wise for employers to monitor the quality of all their recruitment sources. One way to do this is to develop and compare **yield ratios** for each source.[52] A yield ratio expresses the percentage of applicants who successfully move from one stage of the recruitment and selection process to the next. For example, the organization could find the number of candidates interviewed as a percentage of the total number of résumés generated by a given source (that is, number of interviews divided by number of résumés). A high yield ratio (large percentage) means that the source is an effective way to find candidates to interview. By comparing the yield ratios of different recruitment sources, HR professionals can determine which source is the best or most efficient for the type of vacancy.

Another measure of recruitment success is the *cost per hire*. To compute this amount, find the cost of using a particular recruitment source for a particular type of vacancy. Then divide that cost by the number of people hired to fill that type of vacancy. A low cost per hire means that the recruitment source is efficient; it delivers qualified candidates at minimal cost.

To see how HR professionals use these measures, look at the examples in Table 5.3. This table shows the results for a hypothetical organization that used five kinds of recruitment sources to fill a number of vacancies. For each recruitment source, the table shows four yield ratios and the cost per hire. To fill these jobs, the best two sources of recruits were local universities and employee referral programs. Newspaper ads generated the largest number of recruits (500 résumés). However, only 50 were judged acceptable, of which only half accepted employment offers, for a cumulative yield ratio of 25/500, or 5 percent. Recruiting at renowned universities generated highly qualified applicants, but relatively few of them ultimately accepted positions with the organization. Executive search firms produced the highest cumulative yield ratio. These generated only 20 applicants, but all of them accepted interview offers, most were judged acceptable, and 79 percent of these acceptable candidates took jobs with the organization. However, notice the cost per hire. The executive search firms

Table 5.3

Results of a Hypothetical Recruiting Effort

| | RECRUITING SOURCE | | | | | |
	LOCAL UNIVERSITY	RENOWNED UNIVERSITY	EMPLOYEE REFERRALS	NEWSPAPER AD	ONLINE JOB BOARD AD	EXECUTIVE SEARCH FIRMS
Résumés generated	200	400	50	500	7000	20
Interview offers accepted	175	100	45	400	500	20
Yield ratio	**87%**	**25%**	**90%**	**80%**	**7%**	**100%**
Applicants judged acceptable	100	95	40	50	350	19
Yield ratio	**57%**	**95%**	**89%**	**12%**	**70%**	**95%**
Accept employment offers	90	10	35	25	200	15
Yield ratio	**90%**	**11%**	**88%**	**50%**	**57%**	**79%**
Cumulative	**90/200**	**10/400**	**35/50**	**25/500**	**200/7,000**	**15/20**
yield ratio	45%	3%	70%	5%	3%	75%
Cost	$30,000	$50,000	$15,000	$20,000	$5,000	$90,000
Cost per hire	**$333**	**$5,000**	**$428**	**$800**	**$25**	**$6,000**

charged $90,000 for finding these 15 employees, resulting in the largest cost per hire. In contrast, local universities provided modest yield ratios at the lowest cost per hire. Employee referrals provided excellent yield ratios at a slightly higher cost.

Recruiter Traits and Behaviors

LO6
Describe the recruiter's role in the recruitment process, including limits and opportunities.

As we showed in Figure 5.2, the third influence on recruitment outcomes is the recruiter, including this person's characteristics and the way he or she behaves. The recruiter affects the nature of both the job vacancy and the applicants generated. However, the recruiter often becomes involved late in the recruitment process. In many cases, by the time a recruiter meets some applicants, they have already made up their minds about what they desire in a job, what the vacant job has to offer, and their likelihood of receiving a job offer.[53]

Many applicants approach the recruiter with some skepticism. Knowing it is the recruiter's job to sell them on a vacancy, some applicants discount what the recruiter says, in light of what they have heard from other sources, such as friends, magazine articles, and professors. When candidates are already familiar with the company through knowing about its products, the recruiter's impact is especially weak.[54] For these and other reasons, recruiters' characteristics and behaviors seem to have limited impact on applicants' job choices.

Characteristics of the Recruiter

Most organizations must choose whether their recruiters are specialists in human resources or are experts at particular jobs (that is, those who currently hold the same kinds of jobs or supervise people who hold the jobs). According to some studies, applicants perceive HR specialists as less credible and are less attracted to jobs when recruiters are HR specialists.[55] The evidence does not completely discount a positive role for personnel specialists in recruiting. It does indicate, however, that these specialists need to take extra steps to ensure that applicants perceive them as knowledgeable and credible.

In general, applicants respond positively to recruiters whom they perceive as warm and informative. "Warm" means the recruiter seems to care about the applicant and to be enthusiastic about the applicant's potential to contribute to the organization. "Informative" means the recruiter provides the kind of information the applicant is seeking. The evidence of impact of other characteristics of recruiters—including their age, sex, and race—is complex and inconsistent.[56]

Behavior of the Recruiter

Recruiters affect results not only by providing plenty of information, but by providing the right kind of information. Perhaps the most-researched aspect of recruiting is the level of realism in the recruiter's message. Because the recruiter's job is to attract candidates, recruiters may feel pressure to exaggerate the positive qualities of the vacancy and to downplay its negative qualities. Applicants are highly sensitive to negative information. The highest-quality applicants may be less willing to pursue jobs when this type of information comes out.[57] But if the recruiter goes too far in a positive direction, the candidate can be misled and lured into taking a job that has been misrepresented. Then unmet expectations can contribute to a high turnover rate. When recruiters describe jobs unrealistically, people who take those jobs may come to believe that the employer is deceitful.[58]

Realistic Job Preview
Background information about a job's positive and negative qualities.

Many studies have looked at how well **realistic job previews**—background information about jobs' positive and negative qualities—can get around this problem and help organizations minimize turnover among new employees. On the whole, the research suggests that realistic job previews have a weak and inconsistent effect on turnover.[59] Although recruiters can go overboard in selling applicants on the desirability of a job vacancy, there is little support for the belief that informing people about the negative characteristics of a job will "inoculate" them so that the negative features don't cause them to quit.[60]

Finally, for affecting whether people choose to take a job, but even more so, whether they stick with a job, the recruiter seems less important than an organization's personnel policies that directly affect the job's features (pay, security, advancement opportunities, and so on).

Enhancing the Recruiter's Impact

Nevertheless, although recruiters are probably not the most important influence on people's job choices, this does not mean recruiters cannot have an impact. Most recruiters receive little training.[61] If we were to determine what does matter to job candidates, perhaps recruiters could be trained in those areas.

Researchers have tried to find the conditions in which recruiters do make a difference. Such research suggests that an organization can take several steps to increase the positive impact that recruiters have on job candidates:

• Recruiters should provide timely feedback. Applicants dislike delays in feedback. They may draw negative conclusions about the organization (for starters, that the organization doesn't care about their application).

Figure 5.4

Recruits Who Were Offended by Recruiters

_____ has a management training program which the recruiter had gone through. She was talking about the great presentational skills that _____ teaches you, and the woman was barely literate. She was embarrassing. If that was the best they could do, I did not want any part of them. Also, _____ and _____'s recruiters appeared to have real attitude problems. I also thought they were chauvinistic. (arts undergraduate)

I had a very bad campus interview experience . . . the person who came was a last-minute fill-in . . . I think he had a couple of "issues" and was very discourteous during the interview. He was one step away from yawning in my face. . . . The other thing he did was that he kept making these (nothing illegal, mind you) but he kept making these references to the fact that I had been out of my undergraduate and first graduate programs for more than 10 years now. (MBA with 10 years of experience)

One firm I didn't think of talking to initially, but they called me and asked me to talk with them. So I did, and then the recruiter was very, very, rude. Yes, very rude, and I've run into that a couple of times. (engineering graduate)

_____ had set a schedule for me which they deviated from regularly. Times overlapped, and one person kept me too long, which pushed the whole day back. They almost seemed to be saying that it was my fault that I was late for the next one! I guess a lot of what they did just wasn't very professional. Even at the point when I was done, where most companies would have a cab pick you up, I was in the middle of a snowstorm in Chicago and they said, "You can get a cab downstairs." There weren't any cabs. I literally had to walk 12 or 14 blocks with my luggage, trying to find some way to get to the airport. They didn't book me a hotel for the night of the snowstorm so I had to sit in the airport for eight hours trying to get another flight. . . . They wouldn't even reimburse me for the additional plane fare. (industrial relations graduate student)

The guy at the interview made a joke about how nice my nails were and how they were going to ruin them there due to all the tough work. (engineering undergraduate)

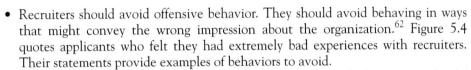

- Recruiters should avoid offensive behavior. They should avoid behaving in ways that might convey the wrong impression about the organization.[62] Figure 5.4 quotes applicants who felt they had extremely bad experiences with recruiters. Their statements provide examples of behaviors to avoid.
- The organization can recruit with teams rather than individual recruiters. Applicants view job experts as more credible than HR specialists, and a team can include both kinds of recruiters. HR specialists on the team provide knowledge about company policies and procedures.

Through such positive behavior, recruiters can give organizations a better chance of competing for talented human resources. In the next chapter, we will describe how an organization selects the candidates who best meet its needs.

thinking ethically

Citizens First?

For years now, U.S. corporations have bemoaned a labor shortage of workers with advanced technical and scientific knowledge. Often, they have sought to fill the talent gap with workers from other countries. Some of these employees come to the United States with an H-1B visa, created to allow companies to hire individuals with exceptional talent. The H-1B program generally does not require employers to exhaust the search for a U.S. citizen before hiring someone with one of these visas.

Many people accepted that practice as a business necessity. But in the recent economic downturn, many high-tech companies have laid off swaths of their workforce. That gives rise to a question: Should companies in the United States be expected to fill positions with U.S. citizens before they should be allowed to look overseas?

Iowa Senator Charles Grassley wrote a letter to Microsoft, calling on the company to give U.S. workers priority. Similarly, Grassley and Vermont Senator Bernie Sanders introduced a bill in Congress forbidding banks that received federal bailout money from hiring workers under the H-1B program. Microsoft's reply to Grassley's letter indicated that it has targeted layoffs based on assessment of its human resource needs in the present and future. In addition, some people question whether favoring U.S. citizens would run afoul of laws requiring equal employment opportunity.

One impact of the economic downturn has been a slowdown in requests to use the program. Until recently, petitions to hire these workers met the 85,000-visa limit almost as soon as the application period opened. But in 2009, when the five-day application period ended, many slots remained available. Meanwhile, the number of graduates in math, engineering, science, and technology in the United States continues to trail far behind projections for the number of people with these skills who are expected to be needed in U.S. jobs.

SOURCES: Ed Frauenheim, "Deep Corporate Staff Cuts Heat Up H-1B Visa Debate," *Workforce Management,* February 5, 2009, http://www.workforce.com; Rebecca Cole, "Applications for Work Visas Tumble," *Chicago Tribune,* April 9, 2009, http://www.chicagotribune.com; and Adrienne Fox, "At Work in 2020," *HR Magazine,* January 2010, Business & Company Resource Center, http://galenet.galegroup.com.

Questions

1. How, if at all, do a company's ethical obligations to employees from its own country differ from its ethical obligations to employees who are citizens of other countries?
2. Should U.S. companies that have laid off U.S. workers try to hire only U.S. workers? Why or why not?
3. For a company making decisions to increase or decrease its workforce, what priority should it give to the following considerations: (a) business advantage; (b) equal employment opportunity; and (c) being a good citizen, caring about the well-being of its country's people? How, if at all, can these considerations be balanced?

SUMMARY

LO1 Discuss how to plan for human resources needed to carry out the organization's strategy.

The first step in human resource planning is personnel forecasting. Through trend analysis and good judgment, the planner tries to determine the supply of and demand for various human resources. Based on whether a surplus or a shortage is expected, the planner sets goals and creates a strategy for achieving those goals. The organization then implements its HR strategy and evaluates the results.

LO2 Determine the labor demand for workers in various job categories.

The planner can look at leading indicators, assuming trends will continue in the future. Mul-

tiple regression can convert several leading indicators into a single prediction of labor needs. Analysis of a transitional matrix can help the planner identify which job categories can be filled internally and where high turnover is likely.

LO3 Summarize the advantages and disadvantages of ways to eliminate a labor surplus and avoid a labor shortage.

To reduce a surplus, downsizing, pay reductions, and demotions deliver fast results but at a high cost in human suffering that may hurt surviving employees' motivation and future recruiting. Also, the organization may lose some of its best employees. Transferring employees and requiring them to share work are also fast methods and the consequences in human suffering are less severe. A hiring freeze or natural attrition is slow to take effect but avoids the pain of layoffs. Early-retirement packages may unfortunately induce the best employees to leave and may be slow to implement; however, they, too, are less painful than layoffs. Retraining can improve the organization's overall pool of human resources and maintain high morale, but it is relatively slow and costly.

To avoid a labor shortage, requiring overtime is the easiest and fastest strategy, which can easily be changed if conditions change. However, overtime may exhaust workers and can hurt morale. Using temporary employees and outsourcing do not build an in-house pool of talent, but by these means staffing levels can be quickly and easily modified. Transferring and retraining employees require investment of time and money, but can enhance the quality of the organization's human resources; however, this may backfire if a labor surplus develops. Hiring new employees is slow and expensive but strengthens the organization if labor needs are expected to expand for the long term. Using technology as a substitute for labor can be slow to implement and costly, but it may improve the organization's long-term performance. New technology and hiring are difficult to reverse if conditions change.

LO4 Describe recruitment policies organizations use to make job vacancies more attractive.

Internal recruiting (promotions from within) generally makes job vacancies more attractive because candidates see opportunities for growth and advancement. Lead-the-market pay strategies make jobs economically desirable. Due-process policies signal that employers are concerned about employee rights. Image advertising can give candidates the impression that the organization is a good place to work.

LO5 List and compare sources of job applicants.

Internal sources, promoted through job postings, generate applicants who are familiar to the organization and motivate other employees by demonstrating opportunities for advancement. However, internal sources are usually insufficient for all of an organization's labor needs. Direct applicants and referrals tend to be inexpensive and to generate applicants who have self-selected; this source risks charges of unfairness, especially in cases of nepotism. Newspaper and magazine advertising reach a wide audience and may generate many applications, although many are likely to be unsuitable. Electronic recruiting gives organizations access to a global labor market, tends to be inexpensive, and allows convenient searching of databases. Public employment agencies are inexpensive and typically have screened applicants. Private employment agencies charge fees but may provide many services. Another inexpensive channel is schools and colleges, which may give the employer access to top-notch entrants to the labor market.

LO6 Describe the recruiter's role in the recruitment process, including limits and opportunities.

Through their behavior and other characteristics, recruiters influence the nature of the job vacancy and the kinds of applicants generated. Applicants tend to perceive job experts as more credible than recruiters who are HR specialists. They tend to react more favorably to recruiters who are warm and informative. Recruiters should not mislead candidates. Realistic job previews are helpful but have a weak and inconsistent effect on job turnover compared with personnel policies and actual job conditions. Recruiters can improve their impact by providing timely feedback, avoiding behavior that contributes to a negative impression of the organization, and teaming up with job experts.

KEY TERMS

core competency, p. 129
direct applicants, p. 141
downsizing, p. 130
due-process policies, p. 138
employment at will, p. 138
forecasting, p. 125

job posting, p. 139
leading indicators, p. 126
nepotism, p. 142
outsourcing, p. 134
realistic job preview, p. 148
recruiting, p. 136

referrals, p. 141
transitional matrix, p. 126
trend analysis, p. 126
workforce utilization review, p. 135
yield ratio, p. 146

REVIEW AND DISCUSSION QUESTIONS

1. Suppose an organization expects a labor shortage to develop in key job areas over the next few years. Recommend general responses the organization could make in each of the following areas:
   a. Recruitment
   b. Training
   c. Compensation (pay and employee benefits)
2. Review the sample transitional matrix shown in Table 5.1. What jobs experience the greatest turnover (employees leaving the organization)? How might an organization with this combination of jobs reduce the turnover?
3. In the same transitional matrix, which jobs seem to rely the most on internal recruitment? Which seem to rely most on external recruitment? Why?
4. Why do organizations combine statistical and judgmental forecasts of labor demand, rather than relying on statistics or judgment alone? Give an example of a situation in which each type of forecast would be inaccurate.
5. Some organizations have detailed affirmative-action plans, complete with goals and timetables, for women and minorities, yet have no formal human resource plan for the organization as a whole. Why might this be the case? What does this practice suggest about the role of human resource management in these organizations?
6. Give an example of a personnel policy that would help attract a larger pool of job candidates. Give an example of a personnel policy that would likely reduce the pool of candidates. Would you expect these policies to influence the quality as well as the number of applicants? Why or why not?
7. Discuss the relative merits of internal versus external recruitment. Give an example of a situation in which each of these approaches might be particularly effective.
8. List the jobs you have held. How were you recruited for each of these? From the organization's perspective, what were some pros and cons of recruiting you through these methods?
9. Recruiting people for jobs that require international assignments is increasingly important for many organizations. Where might an organization go to recruit people interested in such assignments?
10. A large share of HR professionals have rated e-cruiting as their best source of new talent. What qualities of electronic recruiting do you think contribute to this opinion?
11. How can organizations improve the effectiveness of their recruiters?

BUSINESSWEEK CASE

BusinessWeek DirectEmployers Association: New Direction for Online Job Search

Bill Warren founded an early online job board in the 1990s, helped kick-start an industry, and was president of Monster.com, one of the leading Internet career sites. But these days he's not very happy with the results.

So he's taking another crack at it, going after Monster, Career Builder, and similar commercial job sites. Warren is starting a nonprofit job listing system that could lower the costs that employers pay to list positions and make the process easier and more fruitful for applicants.

He has the enthusiastic backing of hundreds of large companies, including IBM Corp., American Express, AT&T Inc. and Johnson & Johnson, the kinds of employers that spend hundreds of thousands of dollars a year searching for new talent.

"This is probably the most significant play that I've seen . . . since the invention of the online job board," said Joshua Akers, vice president of RecruitingBlogs.com, a social networking site for human resources professionals.

The commercial rivals say they are ready for new competition. "We remain confident that we're one of the most cost-effective sources of hiring for recruiters today," said Monster spokesman Matt Henson.

Warren, 68, says that those commercial sites charge employers so much to list openings that the companies don't post all their jobs—leaving potential applicants unaware of opportunities. Warren also believes that the sites push too much advertising on jobseekers and include too many "work at home" scam jobs.

Meanwhile, employers want ways to have a direct relationship with jobseekers. Many say they prefer résumés that are tailored to the positions they're trying to fill, not a generic résumé posted online. As the ranks of the unemployed have doubled to roughly 15 million, recruiters say the response to jobs they post on the boards has gotten overwhelming.

The solution that Warren hopes to launch is being hatched by the DirectEmployers Association, a group formed by more than 500 large companies. Warren is executive director.

The association's plan calls for companies to list jobs under the Internet's ".jobs" domain name to better organize job listings on the Web. For instance, someone can visit ATT.jobs to see all the listings at that company.

DirectEmployers' software will automatically code such listings to make them easily searchable by city or occupation. The association will sort the listings in as many as 30,000 regional ".job" Web addresses, such as "atlanta.jobs." That will help people search for jobs in specific places. The group hopes to add thousands of occupational domain names, such as "engineer.jobs."

Companies that belong to the association pay a $15,000 annual membership fee and will receive prominent placement on the ".jobs" Web sites. Smaller companies can purchase a ".jobs" domain name for about $125 a year and then post jobs for free. They can also work through their state employment agencies, which post jobs online at no charge.

At those prices, the new ".jobs" system could be another online innovation that undercuts what currently exists—much as the invention of job boards themselves undermined newspaper help-wanted ads.

Monster.com's basic rate is $395 per job posting, though it offers volume discounts. Companies also pay to search the résumés that applicants have posted. (Jobseekers can access the sites for free.) Considering that some Fortune 500 companies hire thousands of workers a year, even in tough times, the cost of listing all their open jobs can approach $1 million.

SOURCE: Excerpted from Christopher S. Rugaber, "Pioneer of Online Job Search Starts Over Again," *BusinessWeek*, February 25, 2010, http://www.businessweek.com.

Questions

1. What advantages does this new system from DirectEmployers Association offer to big companies? What advantages does it offer to small companies?
2. How would you expect the introduction of this system to affect employers' use of the various recruiting methods described in this chapter?
3. Imagine you are recruiting for a mechanical engineering job at a small manufacturing company in North Carolina and have decided to post the job opening on this system. What information would you want to include in order to present your position most effectively to desirable candidates?

Case: Apple's Make-vs.-Buy Decision

In a turnaround from a trend in which high-tech (and other) manufacturers have outsourced the making of important components in order to increase efficiency and focus on what they do best, Apple has recently made moves that seem aimed at bringing the design of microchips back in-house. Apple is known for innovative design, and along with that, it tends to keep details of what it makes highly secret. Making chip design a company process, rather than a product to buy, gives Apple more control over the process—and over the secrecy.

Of course, the decision to handle its own development has huge implications for human resource management. The company needs all-new labor forecasts, a larger labor force, and an intense push to bring in technical talent. Recently, Apple has been hiring many new engineers. Products they could be assigned to include microchips that require less power to operate iPhones and iTouch devices, as well as circuitry to improve the graphics displayed in games and videos played on its devices. A top-notch team could, at least in theory, come up with unique improvements that will take rivals by surprise.

One way to acquire a lot of talent fast is to acquire entire companies and make them part of Apple. And that's one move Apple has been making. The company recently acquired P.A. Semi, a start-up company that

designs microchips. Its products could be used to run iPhones and iPods. Observers are guessing that chips developed by P.A. Semi could take the place of chips Apple has been buying from Samsung for its iPhone. Samsung had customized the chips to Apple's specifications. Apple could be worried that a company such as Samsung might intentionally or unintentionally start applying some of Apple's ideas to chips made for competitors' products.

Another bit of evidence about Apple's hunt for talent is visible online at the LinkedIn networking site, where members list their job histories. According to the *Wall Street Journal*, more than 100 people on the site have current job titles at Apple plus past jobs involving microchips. Their prior companies include Intel, Samsung, and Qualcomm. One recent hire was the chief technology officer from Advanced Micro Devices' graphic products group. Furthermore, it's possible to evaluate job openings that Apple has been posting. These have included positions that involve expertise in handwriting recognition technology and microchips used in managing displays.

Apple has been seen at job fairs, too. Its recruiters participated in a job fair for employees who were being laid off at Spansion, a company that makes memory chips and recently declared bankruptcy.

SOURCES: Yukari Iwatani Kane and Don Clark, "In Major Shift, Apple Builds Its Own Team to Design Chips," *Wall Street Journal*, April 30, 2009, http://online.wsj.com; "Apple Turning to Chip Design for Its Innovation," *InformationWeek*, April 30, 2009, Business & Company Resource Center, http://galenet.galegroup.com; and "Apple Increases Investment in British Chip Designer," *InformationWeek*, June 26, 2009, Business & Company Resource Center, http://galenet.galegroup.com.

Questions

1. Given the ideas presented about Apple's strategy, what HR actions would be most suitable for supporting that strategy? (Consider especially the options in Table 5.2.)
2. What challenges would you expect to be most significant for Apple's HR staff in meeting these human resource requirements?
3. What sources of job applicants would you recommend that Apple use to meet the needs described here?

IT'S A WRAP! connect

www.mhhe.com/noefund4e is your source for Reviewing, Applying, and Practicing the concepts you learned about in Chapter 5.

Review
- Chapter learning objectives
- Test Your Knowledge: Recruitment Sources and Stages of the Strategic HRM Process

Application
- Manager's Hot Seat segment: "Diversity: Mediating Morality"
- Video case and quiz: "Balancing Act: Keeping Mothers on a Career Track"
- Self-Assessment: Improving Your Résumé
- Web exercise: Texas Instrument's Fit Check
- Small-business case: For Personal Financial Advisors, a Small Staffing Plan with a Big Impact

Practice
- Chapter quiz

NOTES

1. Rick Popely, "Fewest Vehicles Sold in Nine Years," *Chicago Tribune*, January 4, 2008, sec. 3, pp. 1, 4; and John D. Stoll and Neal E. Boudette, "December Slump in Vehicle Sales Augurs Ill for '08," *Wall Street Journal*, January 4, 2008, http://online.wsj.com.
2. N. Byrnes, "Get 'Em while They're Young," *Business-Week*, May 22, 2006, pp. 86–87; B. Leak, "The Draft Picks Get Younger," *BusinessWeek*, May 8, 2006, p. 96; and A. Singh, "Firms Court New Hires—in High School," *Wall Street Journal*, August 15, 2006, p. B5.
3. P. Coy, "What Falling Prices Tell Us," *BusinessWeek*, February 9, 2009, pp. 24–26.
4. K. Maher, "Wal-Mart Seeks New Flexibility in Worker Shifts," *Wall Street Journal*, January 3, 2007, p. A1.
5. I. Brat, "Where Have All the Welders Gone, as Manufacturing and Repair Boom?" *Wall Street Journal*, August 15, 2006, pp. B2–B3.
6. Bureau of Labor Statistics, "Regional and State Employment and Unemployment Summary," news release, March 10, 2010, http://data.bls.gov; and "Map of USA Shows Projected Job Growth by State,"

San Francisco Chronicle, December 2, 2009, http://www.sfgate.com.
7. J. Schneider, "I'll Take a Big Mac, Fries and Hey How's the Weather in Fargo?" *Lansing State Journal*, January 15, 2009, p. B1.
8. J. P. Guthrie, "Dumb and Dumber: The Impact of Downsizing on Firm Performance as Moderated by Industry Conditions," *Organization Science* 19 (2008), pp. 108–23; and J. McGregor, A. McConnon, and D. Kiley, "Customer Service in a Shrinking Economy," *BusinessWeek*, February 19, 2009, pp. 34–35.
9. C. D. Zatzick and R. D. Iverson, "High-Involvement Management and Workforce Reduction: Competitive Advantage or Disadvantage?" *Academy of Management Journal* 49 (2006), pp. 999–1015.
10. P. P. Shaw, "Network Destruction: The Structural Implications of Downsizing," *Academy of Management Journal* 43 (2000), pp. 101–12.
11. Brenda Kowske, Kyle Lundby, and Rena Rasch, "Turning 'Survive' into 'Thrive': Managing Survivor Engagement in a Downsized Organization," *People & Strategy* 32, no. (4), (2009), pp. 48–56.

12. W. F. Cascio, "Downsizing: What Do We Know? What Have We Learned?" *Academy of Management Executive* 7 (1993), pp. 95–104.

13. Justin Lahart, "Even in a Recovery, Some Jobs Won't Return," *Wall Street Journal*, January 12, 2010, http://online.wsj.com; and Sarah E. Needleman, "Entrepreneurs Prefer to Keep Staffs Lean," *Wall Street Journal*, March 2, 2010, http://online.wsj.com.

14. P. Coy, "Golden Paychecks," *BusinessWeek*, July 2, 2007, p. 13; and J. Weber, "This Time, Old Hands Keep Their Jobs," *BusinessWeek*, February 9, 2009, p. 50.

15. Olga Kharif, "The Rise of the Four-Day Work Week?" *BusinessWeek*, December 18, 2008, http://www.businessweek.com.

16. Adrienne Fox, "At Work in 2020," *HR Magazine*, January 2010, Business & Company Resource Center, http://galenet.galegroup.com.

17. S. Kim and D. Feldman, "Healthy, Wealthy, or Wise: Predicting Actual Acceptances of Early Retirement Incentives at Three Points in Time," *Personnel Psychology* 51 (1998), pp. 623–42.

18. "Schumpeter: How to Survive the Silver Tsunami," *The Economist*, February 6, 2010, Business & Company Resource Center, http://galenet.galegroup.com.

19. S. A. Johnson and B. E. Ashforth, "Externalization of Employment in a Service Environment: The Role of Organizational and Customer Identification," *Journal of Organizational Behavior* 29 (2008), pp. 287–309; and M. Vidal and L. M. Tigges, "Temporary Employment and Strategic Staffing in the Manufacturing Sector," *Industrial Relations* 48 (2009), pp. 55–72.

20. Fox, "At Work in 2020."

21. P. Engardio, "Let's Offshore the Lawyers," *BusinessWeek*, September 18, 2006, pp. 42–43.

22. Steve Minter, "Moving Sourcing Closer to Home," *Industry Week*, September 2009, Business & Company Resource Center, http://galenet.galegroup.com; and Josh Hyatt, "The New Calculus of Offshoring," *CFO*, October 2009, pp. 58–62.

23. A. Tiwana, "Does Firm Modularity Complement Ignorance? A Field Study of Software Outsourcing Alliances," *Strategic Management Journal* 29 (2008), pp. 1241–52.

24. Minter, "Moving Sourcing Closer"; and Hyatt, "The New Calculus of Offshoring."

25. P. Engardio, "The Future of Outsourcing," *BusinessWeek*, January 30, 2006, pp. 50–58.

26. A. E. Barber, *Recruiting Employees* (Thousand Oaks, CA: Sage, 1998).

27. C. K. Stevens, "Antecedents of Interview Interactions, Interviewers' Ratings, and Applicants' Reactions," *Personnel Psychology* 51 (1998), pp. 55–85; A. E. Barber, J. R. Hollenbeck, S. L. Tower, and J. M. Phillips, "The Effects of Interview Focus on Recruitment Effectiveness: A Field Experiment," *Journal of Applied Psychology* 79 (1994), pp. 886–96; and D. S. Chapman and D. I. Zweig, "Developing a Nomological Network for Interview Structure: Antecedents and Consequences of the Structured Selection Interview," *Personnel Psychology* 58 (2005), pp. 673–702.

28. J. D. Olian and S. L. Rynes, "Organizational Staffing: Integrating Practice with Strategy," *Industrial Relations* 23 (1984), pp. 170–83.

29. G. T. Milkovich and J. M. Newman, *Compensation* (Homewood, IL: Richard D. Irwin, 1990).

30. M. Leonard, "Challenges to the Termination-at-Will Doctrine," *Personnel Administrator* 28 (1983), pp. 49–56; C. Schowerer and B. Rosen, "Effects of Employment-at-Will Policies and Compensation Policies on Corporate Image and Job Pursuit Intentions," *Journal of Applied Psychology* 74 (1989), pp. 653–56.

31. S. L. Rynes and A. E. Barber, "Applicant Attraction Strategies: An Organizational Perspective," *Academy of Management Review* 15 (1990), pp. 286–310; and J. A. Breaugh, *Recruitment: Science and Practice* (Boston: PWS-Kent, 1992), p. 34.

32. J. E. Slaughter, M. J. Zickar, S. Highhouse, and D. C. Mohr, "Personality Trait Inferences about Organizations: Development of a Measure and Assessment of Construct Validity," *Journal of Applied Psychology* 89 (2004), pp. 85–103; and D. S. Chapman, K. L. Uggerslev, S. A. Carroll, K. A. Piasentin, and D. A. Jones, "Applicant Attraction to Organizations and Job Choice: A Meta-analytic Review of the Correlates of Recruiting Outcomes," *Journal of Applied Psychology* 90 (2005), pp. 928–44.

33. D. R. Avery, "Reactions to Diversity in Recruitment Advertising—Are Differences in Black and White?" *Journal of Applied Psychology* 88 (2003), pp. 672–79.

34. M. A. Conrad and S. D. Ashworth, "Recruiting Source Effectiveness: A Meta-Analysis and Re-examination of Two Rival Hypotheses," paper presented at the annual meeting of the Society of Industrial/Organizational Psychology, Chicago, 1986.

35. Breaugh, *Recruitment*.

36. Lindsey Siegriest, "You May Never Want to Leave: CEOs Share Their CU Journeys," *Credit Union Times*, September 23, 2009, Business & Company Resource Center, http://galenet.galegroup.com.

37. Breaugh, *Recruitment*, pp. 113–14.

38. R. S. Schuler and S. E. Jackson, "Linking Competitive Strategies with Human Resource Management Practices," *Academy of Management Executive* 1 (1987), pp. 207–19.

39. G. Colvin, "How to Manage Your Business in a Recession," *Fortune*, January 19, 2009, pp. 88–93; M. Orey,

"Hang the Recession, Let's Bulk Up," *BusinessWeek*, February 2, 2009, pp. 80–81; and J. Collins, "How Great Companies Turn Crisis into Opportunity," *Fortune*, February 2, 2009, p. 49.

40. Gerry Crispin and Mark Mehler, "CareerXroads 9th Annual Source of Hire Study," February 2010, www.careerxroads.com.

41. C. R. Wanberg, R. Kanfer, and J. T. Banas, "Predictors and Outcomes of Networking Intensity among Job Seekers," *Journal of Applied Psychology* 85 (2000), pp. 491–503.

42. Patrick J. Kiger, "Burnishing Your Employment Brand: Part 2 of 2," *Workforce Management*, October 22, 2007, downloaded from General Reference Center Gold, http://find.galegroup.com.

43. S. Begley, "Behind 'Shortage' of Engineers: Employers Grow More Choosy," *Wall Street Journal*, November 16, 2005, pp. A1, A12.

44. Breaugh, *Recruitment*, p. 87.

45. Eric Benderoff, "Microsoft Takes on CareerBuilder Stake," *Chicago Tribune*, May 10, 2007, sec. 3, pp. 1, 6.

46. B. Dineen and R. A. Noe, "Effects of Customization on Applicant Decisions and Applicant Pool Characteristics in a Web-Based Recruiting Context," *Journal of Applied Psychology* 94 (2009), pp. 224–34.

47. Amy Joyce, "When a Plant Closes, Job Agency Steps In," *The Washington Post*, January 24, 2005, www. washingtonpost.com.

48. P. Smith, "Sources Used by Employers when Hiring College Grads," *Personnel Journal*, February 1995, p. 25.

49. J. W. Boudreau and S. L. Rynes, "Role of Recruitment in Staffing Utility Analysis," *Journal of Applied Psychology* 70 (1985), pp. 354–66.

50. D. Anfuso, "3M's Staffing Strategy Promotes Productivity and Pride," *Personnel Journal*, February 1995, pp. 28–34.

51. Mark R. Howard, "Lower Profile, Same Impact," *Florida Trend*, March 2010, Business & Company Resource Center, http://galenet.galegroup.com.

52. R. Hawk, *The Recruitment Function* (New York: American Management Association, 1967).

53. C. K. Stevens, "Effects of Preinterview Beliefs on Applicants' Reactions to Campus Interviews," *Academy of Management Journal* 40 (1997), pp. 947–66.

54. C. Collins, "The Interactive Effects of Recruitment Practices and Product Awareness on Job Seekers' Employer Knowledge and Application Behaviors," *Journal of Applied Psychology* 92 (2007), pp. 180–90.

55. M. S. Taylor and T. J. Bergman, "Organizational Recruitment Activities and Applicants' Reactions at Different Stages of the Recruitment Process," *Personnel Psychology* 40 (1984), pp. 261–85; and C. D. Fisher, D. R. Ilgen, and W. D. Hoyer, "Source Credibility, Information Favorability, and Job Offer Acceptance," *Academy of Management Journal* 22 (1979), pp. 94–103.

56. L. M. Graves and G. N. Powell, "The Effect of Sex Similarity on Recruiters' Evaluation of Actual Applicants: A Test of the Similarity-Attraction Paradigm," *Personnel Psychology* 48 (1995), pp. 85–98.

57. R. D. Tretz and T. A. Judge, "Realistic Job Previews: A Test of the Adverse Self-Selection Hypothesis," *Journal of Applied Psychology* 83 (1998), pp. 330–37.

58. P. Hom, R. W. Griffeth, L. E. Palich, and J. S. Bracker, "An Exploratory Investigation into Theoretical Mechanisms Underlying Realistic Job Previews," *Personnel Psychology* 51 (1998), pp. 421–51.

59. G. M. McEvoy and W. F. Cascio, "Strategies for Reducing Employee Turnover: A Meta-Analysis," *Journal of Applied Psychology* 70 (1985), pp. 342–53; and S. L. Premack and J. P. Wanous, "A Meta-Analysis of Realistic Job Preview Experiments," *Journal of Applied Psychology* 70 (1985), pp. 706–19.

60. P. G. Irving and J. P. Meyer, "Reexamination of the Met-Expectations Hypothesis: A Longitudinal Analysis," *Journal of Applied Psychology* 79 (1995), pp. 937–49.

61. R. W. Walters, "It's Time We Become Pros," *Journal of College Placement* 12 (1985), pp. 30–33.

62. S. L. Rynes, R. D. Bretz, and B. Gerhart, "The Importance of Recruitment in Job Choice: A Different Way of Looking," *Personnel Psychology* 44 (1991), pp. 487–522.

6

Selecting Employees and Placing Them in Jobs

What Do I Need to Know?

After reading this chapter, you should be able to:

LO1 Identify the elements of the selection process.

LO2 Define ways to measure the success of a selection method.

LO3 Summarize the government's requirements for employee selection.

LO4 Compare the common methods used for selecting human resources.

LO5 Describe major types of employment tests.

LO6 Discuss how to conduct effective interviews.

LO7 Explain how employers carry out the process of making a selection decision.

Introduction

If you want successful employees, you should hire smart people, right? That's partly true, but a study recently reported in *Forbes* magazine suggests you might want to look for other qualities as well.[1] Using data gathered by the Bureau of Labor Statistics (BLS) over two decades, a Harvard researcher found that she could predict which people would earn the most by looking at their scores on a test that involves assigning codes to words. The test, developed by the armed services to identify people with clerical skills, doesn't require deep thought, just a willingness to try hard and persist until the job is done. When the BLS used this test to gather data on the 12,700 young people it tracked in its study, there was no reward for a high score. Those who did their best probably were inclined to try hard regardless of whether they would be rewarded—what we might call being conscientious. This study suggests that if you want successful employees, you should hire people who are both smart and conscientious.

Hiring decisions are about finding the people who will be a good fit with the job and the organization. Any organization that appreciates the competitive edge provided by good people must take the utmost care in choosing its members. The organization's decisions about selecting personnel are central to its ability to survive, adapt, and grow. Selection decisions become especially critical when organizations face tight labor markets or must compete for talent with other organizations in the same industry. If a competitor keeps getting the best applicants, the remaining companies must make do with who is left.

This chapter will familiarize you with ways to minimize errors in employee selection and placement. The chapter starts by describing the selection process and how to evaluate possible methods for carrying out that process. It then takes an in-depth look at the most widely used methods: applications and résumés, employment tests, and interviews. The chapter ends by describing the process by which organizations arrive at a final selection decision.

Selection Process

LO1 Identify the elements of the selection process.

Personnel Selection
The process through which organizations make decisions about who will or will not be allowed to join the organization.

Through **personnel selection,** organizations make decisions about who will or will not be allowed to join the organization. Selection begins with the candidates identified through recruitment and attempts to reduce their number to the individuals best qualified to perform the available jobs. At the end of the process, the selected individuals are placed in jobs with the organization.

The process of selecting employees varies considerably from organization to organization and from job to job. At most organizations, however, selection includes the steps illustrated in Figure 6.1. First, a human resource professional reviews the applications received to see which meet the basic requirements of the job. For candidates who meet the basic requirements, the organization administers tests and reviews work samples to rate the candidates' abilities. Those with the best abilities are invited to the organization for one or more interviews. Often, supervisors and team members are involved in this stage of the process. By this point, the decision makers are beginning to form opinions about which candidates are most desirable. For the top few candidates, the organization should check references and conduct background checks to verify that the organization's information is correct. Then supervisors, teams, and other decision makers select a person to receive a job offer. In some cases, the candidate may negotiate with the organization regarding salary, benefits, and the like. If the candidate accepts the job, the organization places him or her in that job.

How does an organization decide which of these elements to use and in what order? Some organizations simply repeat a selection process that is familiar. If members of the organization underwent job interviews, they conduct job interviews, asking familiar questions. However, what organizations *should* do is to create a selection process in support of its job descriptions. In Chapter 3, we explained that a job description

Figure 6.1

Steps in the Selection Process

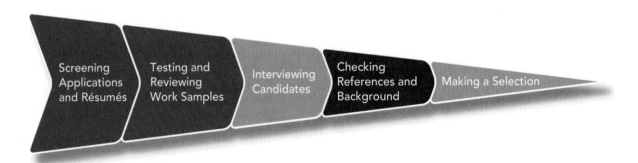

Best Practices

Strategy-Driven Selection for Mike's Carwash

When drivers want to get their cars clean and shiny, the people they deal with won't be corporate management, but employees in entry-level jobs who provide hands-on service. Mike's Carwash doesn't take chances with the positions that provide crucial customer contact. The company is meticulous about how it fills jobs at its three dozen car washes in Indiana and Ohio.

Candidates for jobs at Mike's Carwash take a math test and a personality test. The personality test aims to identify candidates with social and reasoning skills, useful for keeping customers satisfied. Candidates who survive the initial screening are interviewed by at least two managers, who are trained to screen out individuals who raise a red flag, such as a history of frequently quitting jobs. Interviewers look for candidates who exhibit a genuine appreciation of the importance of customers. Drug testing rounds out the screening process. Only about one candidate out of 50 makes it through the whole process and receives a job offer.

Why does Mike's go to so much trouble to hire employees for jobs that are often part-time and seem simple? The answer has to do with how Mike's Carwash competes: exceptional service in a fun atmosphere is what keeps customers driving back again and again. It's a strategy that's symbolized in employees' uniforms: white shirts to convey professionalism plus colorful neckties selected by employees to display a touch of wackiness. In the words of CEO Bill Dahm, "Our two founders . . . always told us that we're truly in the people business. We just happen to wash cars." For that, the company needs to find the best people, train them, and hang on to them for the long term.

With that aim in mind, the rigorous selection process is one piece of a total HR strategy: weekly training videos, monthly prizes for exceptional customer services, a policy of promoting from within, and a tuition reimbursement program to keep employees on the payroll as they advance their education. Together, these strategies support excellent service by building knowledge and experience along with an enthusiastic commitment to customer satisfaction. For example, parents driving into the automatic car wash with nervous children in the backseat are likely to be treated to a smiley face drawn on a window with soap and a clever display of stuffed animals behind a window in the tunnel. These kinds of experiences keep the customers pleased and the business growing.

Sources: Kelly K. Spors, "Top Small Workplaces 2009," *Wall Street Journal*, September 28, 2009, http://online.wsj.com; Tony Jones, "Inner Strength," *Modern Car Care*, April 2008, pp. 48–53; and Mike's Express Carwash Web site, www.mikescarwash.com, accessed March 23, 2010.

---

identifies the knowledge, skills, abilities, and other characteristics required for successfully performing a job. The selection process should be set up in such a way that it lets the organization identify people who have the necessary KSAOs. The Federal Aviation Administration (FAA) has applied these principles to correct a pattern of hiring in which it was selecting many air-traffic controllers who could not pass the certification exam after they had been trained. The FAA began conducting research to learn which employment tests would identify people with the necessary skills: spatial (three-dimensional) thinking, strong memories, and ability to work well under time pressure.[2] For another example of a well-planned selection process, see the "Best Practices" box.

This kind of strategic approach to selection requires ways to measure the effectiveness of selection tools. From science, we have basic standards for this:

- The method provides *reliable* information.
- The method provides *valid* information.

- The information can be *generalized* to apply to the candidates.
- The method offers *high utility* (practical value).
- The selection criteria are *legal*.

Reliability

LO2 Define ways to measure the success of a selection method.

Reliability
The extent to which a measurement is free from random error.

The **reliability** of a type of measurement indicates how free that measurement is from random error.[3] A reliable measurement therefore generates consistent results. Assuming that a person's intelligence is fairly stable over time, a reliable test of intelligence should generate consistent results if the same person takes the test several times. Organizations that construct intelligence tests should be able to provide (and explain) information about the reliability of their tests.

Usually, this information involves statistics such as *correlation coefficients*. These statistics measure the degree to which two sets of numbers are related. A higher correlation coefficient signifies a stronger relationship. At one extreme, a correlation coefficient of 1.0 means a perfect positive relationship—as one set of numbers goes up, so does the other. If you took the same vision test three days in a row, those scores would probably have nearly a perfect correlation. At the other extreme, a correlation of −1.0 means a perfect negative correlation—when one set of numbers goes up, the other goes down. In the middle, a correlation of 0 means there is no correlation at all. For example, the correlation (or relationship) between weather and intelligence would be at or near 0. A reliable test would be one for which scores by the same person (or people with similar attributes) have a correlation close to 1.0.

Validity

Validity
The extent to which performance on a measure (such as a test score) is related to what the measure is designed to assess (such as job performance).

For a selection measure, **validity** describes the extent to which performance on the measure (such as a test score) is related to what the measure is designed to assess (such as job performance). Although we can reliably measure such characteristics as weight and height, these measurements do not provide much information about how a person will perform most kinds of jobs. Thus, for most jobs height and weight provide little validity as selection criteria. One way to determine whether a measure is valid is to compare many people's scores on that measure with their job performance. For example, suppose people who score above 60 words per minute on a keyboarding test consistently get high marks for their performance in data-entry jobs. This observation suggests the keyboarding test is valid for predicting success in that job.

As with reliability, information about the validity of selection methods often uses correlation coefficients. A strong positive (or negative) correlation between a measure and job performance means the measure should be a valid basis for selecting (or rejecting) a candidate. This information is important not only because it helps organizations identify the best employees but also because organizations can demonstrate fair employment practices by showing that their selection process is valid. The federal government's *Uniform Guidelines on Employee Selection Procedures* accept three ways of measuring validity: criterion-related, content, and construct validity.

Criterion-Related Validity
A measure of validity based on showing a substantial correlation between test scores and job performance scores.

Criterion-Related Validity
The first category, **criterion-related validity,** is a measure of validity based on showing a substantial correlation between test scores and job performance scores. In the example in Figure 6.2, a company compares two measures—an intelligence test and

Figure 6.2

Criterion-Related Measurements of a Student's Aptitude

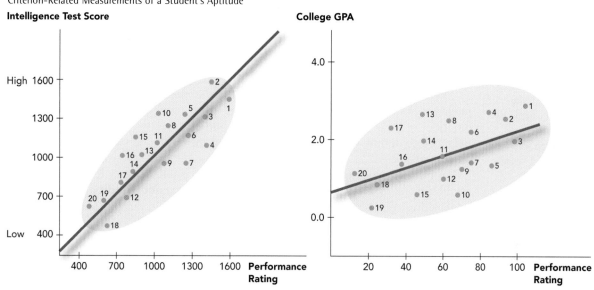

college grade point average—with performance as sales representative. In the left graph, which shows the relationship between the intelligence test scores and job performance, the points for the 20 sales reps fall near the 45-degree line. The correlation coefficient is near .90 (for a perfect 1.0, all the points would be on the 45-degree line). In the graph at the right, the points are scattered more widely. The correlation between college GPA and sales reps' performance is much lower. In this hypothetical example, the intelligence test is more valid than GPA for predicting success at this job.

Two kinds of research are possible for arriving at criterion-related validity:

1. **Predictive validation**—This research uses the test scores of all applicants and looks for a relationship between the scores and future performance. The researcher administers the tests, waits a set period of time, and then measures the performance of the applicants who were hired.
2. **Concurrent validation**—This type of research administers a test to people who currently hold a job, then compares their scores to existing measures of job performance. If the people who score highest on the test also do better on the job, the test is assumed to be valid.

Predictive validation is more time consuming and difficult, but it is the best measure of validity. Job applicants tend to be more motivated to do well on the tests, and their performance on the tests is not influenced by their firsthand experience with the job. Also, the group studied is more likely to include people who perform poorly on the test—a necessary ingredient to accurately validate a test.[4]

Content and Construct Validity

Another way to show validity is to establish **content validity**—that is, consistency between the test items or problems and the kinds of situations or problems that occur on the job. A test that is "content valid" exposes the job applicant to situations that are likely to occur on the job. It tests whether the applicant has the knowledge, skills, or ability to handle such situations. In the case of a company using tests for selecting

Predictive Validation
Research that uses the test scores of all applicants and looks for a relationship between the scores and future performance of the applicants who were hired.

Concurrent Validation
Research that consists of administering a test to people who currently hold a job, then comparing their scores to existing measures of job performance.

Content Validity
Consistency between the test items or problems and the kinds of situations or problems that occur on the job.

a construction superintendent, tests with content validity included organizing a random list of subcontractors into the order they would appear at a construction site and entering a shed to identify construction errors that had intentionally been made for testing purposes.[5] More commonly today, employers use computer role-playing games in which software is created to include situations that occur on the job. The game measures how the candidate reacts to the situations, and then it computes a score based on how closely the candidate's responses match those of an ideal employee.[6]

The usual basis for deciding that a test has content validity is through expert judgment. Experts can rate the test items according to whether they mirror essential functions of the job. Because establishing validity is based on the experts' subjective judgments, content validity is most suitable for measuring behavior that is concrete and observable.

For tests that measure abstract qualities such as intelligence or leadership ability, establishment of validity may have to rely on **construct validity.** This involves establishing that tests really do measure intelligence, leadership ability, or other such "constructs," as well as showing that mastery of this construct is associated with successful performance of the job. For example, if you could show that a test measures something called "mechanical ability," and that people with superior mechanical ability perform well as assemblers, then the test has construct validity for the assembler job. Tests that measure a construct usually measure a combination of behaviors thought to be associated with the construct.

> **Construct Validity**
> Consistency between a high score on a test and high level of a construct such as intelligence or leadership ability, as well as between mastery of this construct and successful performance of the job.

Ability to Generalize

Along with validity in general, we need to know whether a selection method is valid in the context in which the organization wants to use it. A **generalizable** method applies not only to the conditions in which the method was originally developed—job, organization, people, time period, and so on. It also applies to other organizations, jobs, applicants, and so on. In other words, is a selection method that was valid in one context also valid in other contexts?

> **Generalizable**
> Valid in other contexts beyond the context in which the selection method was developed.

Researchers have studied whether tests of intelligence and thinking skills (called *cognitive ability*) can be generalized. The research has supported the idea that these tests are generalizable across many jobs. However, as jobs become more complex, the validity of many of these tests increases. In other words, they are most valid for complex jobs.[7]

> **Utility**
> The extent to which something provides economic value greater than its cost.

NFL teams have been using cognitive tests to select players assuming that intelligence can be generalized to the job requirements of football teams, especially on teams that compete using complex offensive and defensive schemes. What other things, in addition to intelligence, would teams need to look for?

Practical Value

Not only should selection methods such as tests and interview responses accurately predict how well individuals will perform, but they should also produce information that actually benefits the organization. Being valid, reliable, and generalizable adds value to a method. Another consideration is the cost of using the selection method. Selection procedures such as testing and interviewing cost money. They should cost significantly less than the benefits of hiring the new employees. Methods that provide economic value greater than the cost of using them are said to have **utility.**

The choice of a selection method may differ according to the job being filled. If the job involves providing a product or service of high value to the organization, it is worthwhile to spend more to find a top performer. At a company where salespeople are responsible for closing million-dollar deals, the company will be willing to invest more in selection decisions. At a fast-food restaurant, such an investment will not be worthwhile; the employer will prefer faster, simpler ways to select workers who ring up orders, prepare food, and keep the facility clean.

Legal Standards for Selection

As we discussed in Chapter 3, the U.S. government imposes legal limits on selection decisions. The government requires that the selection process be conducted in a way that avoids discrimination and provides access to employees with disabilities. The laws described in Chapter 3 have many applications to the selection process:

LO3 Summarize the government's requirements for employee selection.

- The Civil Rights Act of 1991 and the Age Discrimination in Employment Act of 1967 place requirements on the choice of selection methods. An employer that uses a neutral-appearing selection method that damages a protected group is obligated to show that there is a business necessity for using that method. For example, if an organization uses a test that eliminates many candidates from minority groups, the organization must show that the test is valid for predicting performance of that job. In this context, good performance does not include "customer preference" or "brand image" as a justification for adverse impact. This was a hard lesson for Walgreens when the Equal Employment Opportunity Commission targeted the company with a lawsuit after African American employees complained that the company routinely assigned them to stores that served mainly African Americans. These stores, typically located in cities, tended to be relatively small, generating lower sales, which resulted in lower pay for the employees who worked there.[8]
- The Civil Rights Act of 1991 also prohibits preferential treatment in favor of minority groups. In the case of an organization using a test that tends to reject members of minority groups, the organization may not simply adjust minority applicants' scores upward. Such practices can create an environment that is demotivating to all employees and can lead to government sanctions. Recently, the U.S. Supreme Court found that when the city of New Haven, Connecticut, tried to promote more black candidates by throwing out the results of a test on which white firefighters performed better, the city was unlawfully discriminating against the white firefighters. In that case, the Court majority's reasoning was based on its conclusion that the city could not show that the test was not job related or that there was an equally valid test it could use instead.[9]
- Equal employment opportunity laws affect the kinds of information an organization may gather on application forms and in interviews. As summarized in Table 6.1, the organization may not ask questions that gather information about a person's protected status, even indirectly. For example, requesting the dates a person attended high school and college could indirectly gather information about an applicant's age.
- The Americans with Disabilities Act (ADA) of 1991 requires employers to make "reasonable accommodation" to disabled individuals and restricts many kinds of questions during the selection process.[10] Under the ADA, preemployment questions may not investigate disabilities, but must focus on job performance. An interviewer may ask, "Can you meet the attendance requirements for this job?" but may not ask, "How many days did you miss work last year because you were sick?" Also, the employer may not, in making hiring decisions, use employment physical exams or other tests that could reveal a psychological or physical disability.

Table 6.1

Permissible and Impermissible Questions for Applications and Interviews

PERMISSIBLE QUESTIONS	IMPERMISSIBLE QUESTIONS
What is your full name? Have you ever worked under a different name? [Ask all candidates.]	What was your maiden name? What's the nationality of your name?
If you are hired, can you show proof of age (to meet a legal age requirement)?	How old are you? How would you feel about working for someone younger than you?
Will you need any reasonable accommodation for this hiring process? Are you able to perform this job, with or without reasonable accommodation?	What is your height? Your weight? Do you have any disabilities? Have you been seriously ill? Please provide a photograph of yourself.
What languages do you speak? [Statement that employment is subject to verification of applicant's identity and employment eligibility under immigration laws]	What is your ancestry? Are you a citizen of the United States? Where were you born? How did you learn to speak that language?
What schools have you attended? What degrees have you earned? What was your major?	Is that school affiliated with [religious group]? When did you attend high school? [to learn applicant's age]
Can you meet the requirements of the work schedule? [Ask all candidates.]	What is your religion? What religious holidays do you observe?
Please provide the names of any relatives currently employed by this employer.	What is your marital status? Would you like to be addressed as Mrs., Ms., or Miss? Do you have any children?
Have you ever been convicted of a crime?	Have you ever been arrested?
What organizations or groups do you belong to that you consider relevant to being able to perform this job?	What organizations or groups do you belong to?

Note: This table provides examples and is not intended as a complete listing of permissible and impermissible questions. The examples are based on federal requirements; state laws vary and may affect these examples.

SOURCES: Examples based on Leonard D. Andrew and Richard S. Hobish, eds., "Employment Law Guide for Non-profit Organizations" (Pro Bono Partnership, 2007), Appendix I, http://www.probonopartner.org/PBPGuide/PBPHandbook-32.htm, last modified March 10, 2008; Equal Employment Opportunity Commission, "Prohibited Employment Policies/Practices," http://www1.eeoc.gov, accessed March 19, 2010; and Mississippi University for Women, Vice President of Academic Affairs, "Guide to Legally Permissible Interview Questions," http://www.muw.edu/vpaa/SearchLegalQuestions.pdf, accessed March 19, 2010.

focus on **social** responsibility

Along with equal employment opportunity, organizations must be concerned about candidates' privacy rights. The information gathered during the selection process may include information that employees consider confidential. Confidentiality is a particular concern when job applicants provide information online. Employers should collect data only at secure Web sites, and they may have to be understanding if online applicants are reluctant to provide data such as Social Security numbers, which hackers could use for identity theft.[11] For some jobs, background checks look at candidates' credit history. The Fair Credit Reporting Act requires employers to obtain

CONFIRMING ELIGIBILITY WITH E-VERIFY

One complaint about verifying worker eligibility with Form I-9 is that many months can go by before the federal government finds a mismatch between information on the form and Social Security data. By that point, the company has already invested in training that employee, only to learn it must determine whether the problem is an ineligible worker or simply a typo on the form or in the data.

In an effort to make verification swifter and more accurate, the federal government launched a system called E-Verify. To use the system, employers go online to compare the information on Form I-9 with data in the Social Security Administration database and Department of Homeland Security databases, including information on passports and naturalization (becoming a citizen). More than 95 percent of the time, this electronic verification delivers results within 24 hours.

To use E-Verify, employers must first enroll; using the system is free. Companies that contract to do work for the federal government are required to use E-Verify, but participation for most other companies is voluntary. (Some states require participation.)

Unfortunately, the system has been criticized for inaccuracy. Early complaints were that the system was finding mismatches for legal workers, and the department added databases to reduce that problem. More recently, a test of the system found that it was incorrect 4 percent of the time. By far the majority of mistakes in that test involved failure to catch identity fraud by unauthorized immigrant workers.

Sources: Department of Homeland Security, "Secretary Napolitano Strengthens Employment Verification with Administration's Commitment to E-Verify," news release, July 8, 2009, http://www.dhs.gov; Department of Homeland Security, "E-Verify," last updated March 5, 2010, http://www.dhs.gov; and Louise Radnofsky and Miriam Jordan, "Illegal Workers Slip by System," *Wall Street Journal*, February 25, 2010, http://online.wsj.com.

a candidate's consent before using a third party to check the candidate's credit history or references. If the employer then decides to take an adverse action (such as not hiring) based on the report, the employer must give the applicant a copy of the report and summary of the applicant's rights *before* taking the action.

Another legal requirement is that employers hiring people to work in the United States must ensure that anyone they hire is eligible for employment in this country. Under the **Immigration Reform and Control Act of 1986,** employers must verify and maintain records on the legal rights of applicants to work in the United States. They do this by having applicants fill out the U.S. Citizenship and Immigration Services' Form I-9 and present documents showing their identity and eligibility to work. Employers must complete their portion of each Form I-9, check the applicant's documents, and retain the Form I-9 for at least three years. Employers may (and in some cases must) also use the federal government's electronic system for verifying eligibility to work, as described in the "eHRM" box. At the same time, assuming a person is eligible to work under this law, the law prohibits the employer from discriminating against the person on the basis of national origin or citizenship status.

Immigration Reform and Control Act of 1986
Federal law requiring employers to verify and maintain records on applicants' legal rights to work in the United States.

An important principle of selection is to combine several sources of information about candidates, rather than relying solely on interviews or a single type of testing. The sources should be chosen carefully to relate to the characteristics identified in the job description. When organizations do this, they are increasing the validity of the decision criteria. They are more likely to make hiring decisions that are fair and unbiased. They also are more likely to choose the best candidates.

Job Applications and Résumés

Nearly all employers gather background information on applicants at the beginning of the selection process. The usual ways of gathering background information are by asking applicants to fill out application forms and provide résumés. Organizations also verify the information by checking references and conducting background checks.

Asking job candidates to provide background information is inexpensive. The organization can get reasonably accurate information by combining applications and résumés with background checks and well-designed interviews.[12] A major challenge with applications and résumés is the sheer volume of work they generate for the organization. Human resource departments often are swamped with far more résumés than they can carefully review.

Application Forms

Asking each applicant to fill out an employment application is a low-cost way to gather basic data from many applicants. It also ensures that the organization has certain standard categories of information, such as mailing address and employment history, from each. Figure 6.3 is an example of an application form.

Employers can buy general-purpose application forms from an office supply store, or they can create their own forms to meet unique needs. Either way, employment applications include areas for applicants to provide several types of information:

- *Contact information*—The applicant's name, address, phone number, and e-mail address.
- *Work experience*—Companies the applicant worked for, job titles, and dates of employment.
- *Educational background*—High school, college, and universities attended and degree(s) awarded.
- *Applicant's signature*—Signature following a statement that the applicant has provided true and complete information.

The application form may include other areas for the applicant to provide additional information, such as specific work experiences, technical skills, or memberships in professional or trade groups. Also, including the date on an application is useful for keeping up-to-date records of job applicants. The application form should not request information that could violate equal employment opportunity standards. For example, questions about an applicant's race, marital status, or number of children would be inappropriate.

By reviewing application forms, HR personnel can identify which candidates meet minimum requirements for education and experience. They may be able to rank applicants—for example, giving applicants with 10 years' experience a higher ranking than applicants with 2 years' experience. In this way, the applications enable the organization to narrow the pool of candidates to a number it can afford to test and interview.

Résumés

The usual way that applicants introduce themselves to a potential employer is to submit a résumé. An obvious drawback of this information source is that applicants control the content of the information, as well as the way it is presented. This type of information is therefore biased in favor of the applicant and (although this is

Figure 6.3

Sample Job Application Form

COMPLETE THIS SECTION IF INFORMATION IS NOT INCLUDED ON ATTACHED RESUME

EDUCATION CIRCLE THE HIGHEST GRADE COMPLETED: ELEMENTARY 6 7 8   HIGH SCHOOL 1 2 3 4   COLLEGE 1 2 3 4 5 6 7 8

	NAME(S)	LOCATION(S)	GRADUATED	MAJOR FIELDS OF STUDY AND PRINCIPAL PROFESSOR (OR ADVISOR)	DEGREE(S) RECEIVED	GRADE AVERAGE	CLASS RANK OUT OF
HIGH SCHOOL							
COLLEGE			☐ YES ☐ NO				OVERALL AND MAJOR GPA'S

ACADEMIC HONORS OR OTHER SPECIAL RECOGNITION

FOREIGN LANGUAGES READ   FOREIGN LANGUAGES SPOKEN

HAVE YOU TAKEN THE GMAT, GRE, SAT OR OTHER ACADEMIC ENTRANCE TEST(S) WITHIN THE LAST TEN YEARS?   ☐ YES   ☐ NO
IF YES, LIST TEST(S), DATE(S), AND HIGHEST SCORES).

	DATE TAKEN	SCORES)				
SAT		TOTAL	VERBAL		MATHEMATICAL	
ACT		TOTAL	ENGLISH	READING	MATHEMATICS	SCIENCE
GRE (GENERAL TEST)		TOTAL	VERBAL	QUANTITATIVE	ANALYTICAL	
GMAT		TOTAL	VERBAL	MATH	AWA	
OTHER		TOTAL				

EMPLOYMENT AND MILITARY RECORD
LIST MOST RECENT FIRST. I AGREE TO FURNISH VERIFICATION IF REQUESTED.
ATTACH RESUME. RESPOND BELOW IF INFORMATION IS NOT INCLUDED ON RESUME.

NAME AND ADDRESS OF EMPLOYER	POSITION HELD	PRIMARY RESPONSIBILITIES AND ACCOUNTABILITIES	SALARY		DATES		REASON FOR LEAVING
			START	FINISH	FROM	TO	

ENCIRCLE THOSE EMPLOYERS YOU DO NOT WANT US TO CONTACT
TURN OVER

APPLICATION FOR EMPLOYMENT
An Equal Opportunity Employer

FIRST NAME	MIDDLE NAME	LAST NAME		SOCIAL SECURITY NUMBER
LOCAL	STREET ADDRESS	CITY AND STATE	ZIP CODE	TELEPHONE
PERMANENT	STREET ADDRESS	CITY AND STATE	ZIP CODE	TELEPHONE

ELECTRONIC MAIL ADDRESS

PLEASE ANSWER ALL ITEMS. IF NOT APPLICABLE, WRITE N/A.

ARE YOU A U.S. CITIZEN OR AUTHORIZED TO BE LEGALLY EMPLOYED ON AN ONGOING BASIS IN THE U.S. BASED ON YOUR VISA OR IMMIGRATION STATUS?   ☐ YES   ☐ NO   ARE YOU OVER 18 YEARS OF AGE? YES ☐ NO ☐

DO YOU CURRENTLY HAVE A NONIMMIGRANT U.S. VISA?   ☐ YES   ☐ NO   IF YES, PLEASE SPECIFY:

DO YOU HAVE ANY RELATIVES EMPLOYED HERE?   ☐ NO   ☐ YES
IF YES, GIVE NAME, RELATIONSHIP AND LOCATION WHERE THEY WORK.

DO YOU HAVE ANY RELATIVES EMPLOYED BY THE COMPETITION?   ☐ NO   ☐ YES   WHAT COMPANY?

ARE YOU ABLE TO TRAVEL AS REQUIRED FOR THE POSITION SOUGHT?   ☐ YES   ☐ NO   ARE YOU WILLING TO RELOCATE?   ☐ YES   ☐ NO   IF YES, PLEASE SPECIFY:

ARE THERE GEOGRAPHICAL AREAS WHICH YOU WOULD PREFER OR REFUSE?   ☐ NO   ☐ YES

HAVE YOU EVER BEEN CONVICTED OR PLED GUILTY TO ANY FELONY OR MISDEMEANOR OTHER THAN FOR A MINOR TRAFFIC VIOLATION?   ☐ NO   ☐ YES
IF YES, STATE THE DATE(S) AND LOCATION(S).

WHEN   WHERE   NATURE OF OFFENSE(S)

WORK PREFERENCE

SPECIFIC POSITION FOR WHICH YOU ARE APPLYING   NUMBER OF YEARS OF RELATED EXPERIENCE

LIST COMPUTER SOFTWARE PACKAGES OR PROGRAMMING LANGUAGE SKILLS

STARTING SALARY EXPECTED   DATE AVAILABLE TO START WORK   HOW DID YOU HAPPEN TO APPLY FOR A POSITION HERE?

HAVE YOU EVER WORKED AT, OR APPLIED FOR WORK HERE BEFORE?   ☐ NO   ☐ YES
IF YES, WHEN?   WHERE?

LIST EMPLOYMENT REFERENCES HERE, IF NOT INCLUDED ON ATTACHED RESUME

TURN OVER

Visit the text Web site www.mhhe.com/noefund4e for tips on writing an effective résumé.

unethical) may not even be accurate. However, this inexpensive way to gather information does provide employers with a starting point. Organizations typically use résumés as a basis for deciding which candidates to investigate further.

As with employment applications, an HR staff member reviews the résumés to identify candidates meeting such basic requirements as educational background, related work performed, and types of equipment the person has used. Because résumés are created by the job applicants (or the applicants have at least approved résumés created by someone they hire), they also may provide some insight into how candidates communicate and present themselves. Employers tend to decide against applicants whose résumés are unclear, sloppy, or full of mistakes. On the positive side, résumés may enable applicants to highlight accomplishments that might not show up in the format of an employment application. Review of résumés is most valid when the content of the résumés is evaluated in terms of the elements of a job description.

References

Application forms often ask that applicants provide the names of several references. Applicants provide the names and phone numbers of former employers or others who can vouch for their abilities and past job performance. In some situations, the applicant may provide letters of reference written by those people. It is then up to the organization to have someone contact the references to gather information or verify the accuracy of the information provided by the applicant.

As you might expect, references are not an unbiased source of information. Most applicants are careful to choose references who will say something positive. In addition, former employers and others may be afraid that if they express negative opinions, they will be sued. Their fear is understandable. In a recent case, an employee sued his former supervisor for comments about how the employee had succeeded in overcoming attendance problems related to a struggle with multiple sclerosis. The employee felt that the disclosure of his prior attendance problems was defamatory.[13] (Disclosing his medical condition also would have posed problems for the potential future employer's ability to comply with the Americans with Disabilities Act.) The case, which was settled, shows that even well-intentioned remarks can cause problems.

Usually the organization checks references after it has determined that the applicant is a finalist for the job. Contacting references for all applicants would be time consuming, and it does pose some burden on the people contacted. Part of that burden is the risk of giving information that is seen as too negative or too positive. If the person who is a reference gives negative information, there is a chance the candidate will claim *defamation*, meaning the person damaged the applicant's reputation by making statements that cannot be proved truthful.[14] At the other extreme, if the person gives a glowing statement about a candidate, and the new employer later learns of misdeeds such as sexual misconduct or workplace violence, the new employer might sue the former employer for misrepresentation.[15]

Because such situations occasionally arise, often with much publicity, people who give references tend to give as little information as possible. Most organizations have policies that the human resource department will handle all requests for references and that they will only verify employment dates and sometimes the employee's final salary. In organizations without such a policy, HR professionals should be careful—and train managers to be careful—to stick to observable, job-related behaviors and to avoid broad opinions that may be misinterpreted. In spite of these drawbacks of references, the risks of not learning about significant problems in a candidate's past outweigh the possibility of getting only a little information. Potential employers should check references. In general, the results of this effort will be most valid if the employer contacts many references (if possible, going beyond the list of names provided by the applicant) and speaks with them directly by phone.[16]

Background Checks

A background check is a way to verify that applicants are as they represent themselves to be. Unfortunately, not all candidates are open and honest. Others, even if honest, may find that the Internet makes it easy for potential employers to uncover information that reveals them in an unflattering light and may cost them a job. A recent investigation into the amount of false information on résumés found that it spiked in 2007. Part of the increase came from more efforts to exaggerate or misrepresent facts; but in addition, employers were catching more of this behavior simply by looking up information with Internet search engines like Google.[17]

About 8 out of 10 large companies and over two-thirds of smaller organizations say they conduct criminal background checks. These efforts are affecting more workers, because the slower economy allows many employers to be choosy, the Internet makes searching for convictions easier, and crackdowns on crime have resulted in an estimated 60 percent of American males having been arrested at some point in their lives. An example of one such man is Wally Camis Jr., who told an employment agency he had not been arrested. However, a background check by the agency turned up an incident in the 1980s, when Camis was 18: when two men threatened Camis, he flashed the handle of his hairbrush. He succeeded in convincing them it was a knife, so they told the police they had been assaulted by Camis. He received a no-judgment ruling and agreed to pay a fine; he later served in the Air Force and held several jobs. The issue, according to the employment agency, was that Camis had not been honest about his past. To become employable, Camis had his record expunged—an alternative being sought by a rapidly growing number of individuals convicted of misdemeanors.[18] The fact that the ease and prevalence of background checks are leading to a surge of interest in expungement poses problems for employers concerned about maintaining a safe workplace and avoiding theft. The results of background checks may not be as complete as employers believe.

Another type of background check that has recently drawn greater scrutiny is the use of credit checks. Employers in certain situations, such as processes that involve handling money, are concerned that employees with credit problems will behave less honestly. To avoid hiring such employees, these employers conduct a background check. Also, some employers see good credit as an indicator that a person is responsible. For reasons such as these, the percentage of employers conducting credit checks has risen from 25 percent in 1998 to 47 percent in 2009.[19] But in a time of high unemployment and many home foreclosures, some people see this type of investigation as unfair to people who are desperately trying to find work: the worse their financial situation, the harder the job search becomes. Under federal law, conducting a credit check is legal if the person consents, but some states ban or are considering bans on the practice.

LO5 Describe major types of employment tests.

Employment Tests and Work Samples

When the organization has identified candidates whose applications or résumés indicate they meet basic requirements, the organization continues the selection process with this narrower pool of candidates. Often, the next step is to gather objective data through one or more employment tests. These tests fall into two broad categories:

Aptitude Tests
Tests that assess how well a person can learn or acquire skills and abilities.

1. **Aptitude tests** assess how well a person can learn or acquire skills and abilities. In the realm of employment testing, the best-known aptitude test is the General Aptitude Test Battery (GATB), used by the U.S. Employment Service.
2. **Achievement tests** measure a person's existing knowledge and skills. For example, government agencies conduct civil service examinations to see whether applicants are qualified to perform certain jobs.

Achievement Tests
Tests that measure a person's existing knowledge and skills.

Before using any test, organizations should investigate the test's validity and reliability. Besides asking the testing service to provide this information, it is wise to consult more impartial sources of information, such as the ones identified in Table 6.2.

Physical Ability Tests

Physical strength and endurance play less of a role in the modern workplace than in the past, thanks to the use of automation and modern technology. Even so, many jobs still require certain physical abilities or psychomotor abilities (those connecting brain and body, as in the case of eye-hand coordination). When these abilities are essential to job performance or avoidance of injury, the organization may use physical ability tests. These evaluate one or more of the following areas of physical ability: muscular tension, muscular power, muscular endurance, cardiovascular endurance, flexibility, balance, and coordination.[20]

Although these tests can accurately predict success at certain kinds of jobs, they also tend to exclude women and people with disabilities. As a result, use of physical ability tests can make the organization vulnerable to charges of discrimination. It is therefore important to be certain that the abilities tested for really are essential to job performance or that the absence of these abilities really does create a safety hazard.

Table 6.2

Sources of Information about Employment Tests

Mental Measurements Yearbook	Descriptions and reviews of tests that are commercially available
Principles for the Validation and Use of Personnel Selection Procedures (Society for Industrial and Organizational Psychology)	Guide to help organizations evaluate tests
Standards for Educational and Psychological Tests (American Psychological Association)	Description of standards for testing programs
Tests: A Comprehensive Reference for Assessments in Psychology, Education, and Business	Descriptions of thousands of tests
Test Critiques	Reviews of tests, written by professionals in the field

Cognitive Ability Tests

Although fewer jobs require muscle power today, brainpower is essential for most jobs. Organizations therefore benefit from people who have strong mental abilities. **Cognitive ability tests**—sometimes called "intelligence tests"—are designed to measure such mental abilities as verbal skills (skill in using written and spoken language), quantitative skills (skill in working with numbers), and reasoning ability (skill in thinking through the answer to a problem). Many jobs require all of these cognitive skills, so employers often get valid information from general tests. Many reliable tests are commercially available. The tests are especially valid for complex jobs and for those requiring adaptability in changing circumstances.[21]

The evidence of validity, coupled with the relatively low cost of these tests, makes them appealing, except for one problem: concern about legal issues. These concerns arise from a historical pattern in which use of the tests has had an adverse impact on African Americans. Some organizations responded with *race norming,* establishing different norms for hiring members of different racial groups. Race norming poses its own problems, not the least of which is the negative reputation it bestows on the minority employees selected using a lower standard. In addition, the Civil Rights Act of 1991 forbids the use of race or sex norming. As a result, organizations that want to base selection decisions on cognitive ability must make difficult decisions about how to measure this ability while avoiding legal problems. One possibility is a concept called *banding.* This concept treats a range of scores as being similar, as when an instructor gives the grade of A to any student whose average test score is at least 90. All applicants within a range of scores, or band, are treated as having the same score. Then within the set of "tied" scores, employers give preference to underrepresented groups. This is a controversial practice, and some have questioned its legality.[22]

Cognitive Ability Tests
Tests designed to measure such mental abilities as verbal skills, quantitative skills, and reasoning ability.

Job Performance Tests and Work Samples

Many kinds of jobs require candidates who excel at performing specialized tasks, such as operating a certain machine, handling phone calls from customers, or designing advertising materials. To evaluate candidates for such jobs, the organization may administer tests of the necessary skills. Sometimes the candidates take tests that involve a sample of work, or they may show existing samples of their work. Testing may involve a simulated work setting, perhaps in a testing center or in a computerized "virtual" environment.[23] Examples of job performance tests include tests of keyboarding speed and *in-basket tests*. An in-basket test measures the ability to juggle a variety of demands, as in a manager's job. The candidate is presented with simulated memos and phone messages describing the kinds of problems that confront a person in the job. The candidate has to decide how to respond to these messages and in what order. Examples of jobs for which candidates provide work samples include graphic designers and writers.

Tests for selecting managers may take the form of an **assessment center**—a wide variety of specific selection programs that use multiple selection methods to rate applicants or job incumbents on their management potential. An assessment center typically includes in-basket tests, tests of more general abilities, and personality tests. Combining several assessment methods increases the validity of this approach.

Job performance tests have the advantage of giving applicants a chance to show what they can do, which leads them to feel that the evaluation was fair.[24] The tests also are job specific—that is, tailored to the kind of work done in a specific job. So they have a high level of validity, especially when combined with cognitive ability tests and a highly structured interview.[25] This advantage can become a disadvantage,

Assessment Center
A wide variety of specific selection programs that use multiple selection methods to rate applicants or job incumbents on their management potential.

however, if the organization wants to generalize the results of a test for one job to candidates for other jobs. The tests are more appropriate for identifying candidates who are generally able to solve the problems associated with a job, rather than for identifying which particular skills or traits the individual possesses.[26] Developing different tests for different jobs can become expensive. One way to save money is to prepare computerized tests that can be delivered online to various locations.

Personality Inventories

In some situations, employers may also want to know about candidates' personalities. For example, one way that psychologists think about personality is in terms of the "Big Five" traits: extroversion, adjustment, agreeableness, conscientiousness, and inquisitiveness (explained in Table 6.3). There is evidence that people who score high on conscientiousness tend to excel at work, especially when they also have high cognitive ability.[27] For people-related jobs like sales and management, extroversion and agreeableness also seem to be associated with success.[28] Strong social skills help conscientious people ensure that they get positive recognition for their hard work.[29]

The usual way to identify a candidate's personality traits is to administer one of the personality tests that are commercially available. The employer pays for the use of the test, and the organization that owns the test then scores the responses and provides a report about the test taker's personality. An organization that provides such tests should be able to discuss the test's validity and reliability. Assuming the tests are valid for the organization's jobs, they have advantages. Administering commercially available personality tests is simple, and these tests have generally not violated equal opportunity employment requirements.[30] On the downside, compared with intelligence tests, people are better at "faking" their answers to a personality test to score higher on desirable traits.[31] For example, people tend to score higher on conscientiousness when filling out job-related personality tests than when participating in

People who participate in Google's annual Code Jam—a global programming competition—typically exhibit one of the "Big Five" personality traits.

1. Extroversion	Sociable, gregarious, assertive, talkative, expressive
2. Adjustment	Emotionally stable, nondepressed, secure, content
3. Agreeableness	Courteous, trusting, good-natured, tolerant, cooperative, forgiving
4. Conscientiousness	Dependable, organized, persevering, thorough, achievement-oriented
5. Inquisitiveness	Curious, imaginative, artistically sensitive, broad-minded, playful

Table 6.3

Five Major Personality Dimensions Measured by Personality Inventories

research projects.[32] Ways to address this problem include using trained interviewers rather than surveys, collecting information about the applicant from several sources, and letting applicants know that several sources will be used.[33]

A recent study found that 35 percent of U.S. organizations use personality tests when selecting personnel.[34] One reason is organizations' greater use of teamwork, where personality conflicts can be a significant problem. Traits such as agreeableness and conscientiousness have been associated with effective teamwork.[35] In addition, an organization might try to select team members with similar traits and values in order to promote a strong culture where people work together harmoniously, or they instead might look for a diversity of personalities and values as a way to promote debate and creativity.[36]

Honesty Tests and Drug Tests

No matter what employees' personalities may be like, organizations want employees to be honest and to behave safely. Some organizations are satisfied to assess these qualities based on judgments from reference checks and interviews. Others investigate these characteristics more directly through the use of honesty tests and drug tests.

The most famous kind of honesty test is the polygraph, the so-called lie detector test. However, in 1988 the passage of the Polygraph Act banned the use of polygraphs for screening job candidates. As a result, testing services have developed paper-and-pencil honesty (or integrity) tests. Generally these tests ask applicants directly about their attitudes toward theft and their own experiences with theft. Most of the research into the validity of these tests has been conducted by the testing companies, but evidence suggests they do have some ability to predict such behavior as theft of the employer's property.[37]

As concerns about substance abuse have grown during recent decades, so has the use of drug testing. As a measure of a person's exposure to drugs, chemical testing has high reliability and validity. However, these tests are controversial for several reasons. Some people are concerned that they invade individuals' privacy. Others object from a legal perspective. When all applicants or employees are subject to testing, whether or not they have shown evidence of drug use, the tests might be an unreasonable search and seizure or a violation of due process. Taking urine and blood samples involves invasive procedures, and accusing someone of drug use is a serious matter.

Employers considering the use of drug tests should ensure that their drug-testing programs conform to some general rules:[38]

- Administer the tests systematically to all applicants for the same job.
- Use drug testing for jobs that involve safety hazards.
- Have a report of the results sent to the applicant, along with information about how to appeal the results and be retested if appropriate.
- Respect applicants' privacy by conducting tests in an environment that is not intrusive and keeping results confidential.

focus on
social
responsibility

Another way organizations can avoid some of the problems with drug testing is to replace those tests with impairment testing of employees, also called *fitness-for-duty testing*. These testing programs measure whether a worker is alert and mentally able to perform critical tasks at the time of the test. The test does not investigate the cause of any impairment—whether the employee scores poorly because of illegal drugs, alcohol, prescription drugs, over the counter medicines, or simple fatigue. For example, Bowles-Langley Technology has developed a test that measures alertness by presenting employees with exercises that involve interacting with graphics, much like playing a video game. The test measures various responses including reaction time and hand–eye coordination. For a cost of about $5 or $10 per worker per month, companies can verify that employees such as pilots and truck drivers are able to fly or drive safely. Because the tests can be accessed online, they are available to workers in a variety of situations.[39]

Medical Examinations

Especially for physically demanding jobs, organizations may wish to conduct medical examinations to see that the applicant can meet the job's requirements. Employers may also wish to establish an employee's physical condition at the beginning of employment, so that there is a basis for measuring whether the employee has suffered a work-related disability later on. At the same time, as described in Chapter 3, organizations may not discriminate against individuals with disabilities who could perform a job with reasonable accommodations. Likewise, they may not use a measure of size or strength that discriminates against women, unless those requirements are valid in predicting the ability to perform a job. Furthermore, to protect candidates' privacy, medical exams must be related to job requirements and may not be given until the candidate has received a job offer. Therefore, organizations must be careful in how they use medical examinations. Many organizations make selection decisions first and then conduct the exams to confirm that the employee can handle the job, with any reasonable accommodations required. Limiting the use of medical exams in this way also holds down the cost of what tends to be an expensive process.

LO6 Discuss how to conduct effective interviews.

Interviews

Supervisors and team members most often get involved in the selection process at the stage of employment interviews. These interviews bring together job applicants and representatives of the employer to obtain information and evaluate the applicant's qualifications; The "Did You Know?" box shows some of the ways job applicants create unfavorable impressions with interviewers. While the applicant is providing information, he or she is also forming opinions about what it is like to work for the organization. Most organizations use interviewing as part of the selection process. In fact, this method is used more than any other.

Nondirective Interview
A selection interview in which the interviewer has great discretion in choosing questions to ask each candidate.

Interviewing Techniques

Interview techniques include choices about the type of questions to ask and the number of people who conduct the interview. Several question types are possible:

- In a **nondirective interview,** the interviewer has great discretion in choosing questions. The candidate's reply to one question may suggest other questions to ask. Nondirective interviews typically include open-ended questions about the

Did You Know?

What Turns Off an Interviewer

Interviewers gather information from what job applicants tell them and also from how they behave. Frankly, some behaviors are a turnoff. In a recent survey, HR professionals identified ways that job applicants can kill their prospects.

Source: Based on Diana Middleton, "Avoid These Interview Killers," *Wall Street Journal*, November 14, 2009, http://online.wsj.com.

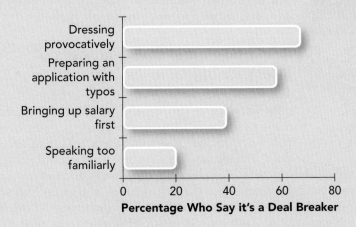

Percentage Who Say it's a Deal Breaker

candidate's strengths, weaknesses, career goals, and work experience. Because these interviews give the interviewer wide latitude, their reliability is not great, and some interviewers ask questions that are not valid or even legal.

- A **structured interview** establishes a set of questions for the interviewer to ask. Ideally, the questions are related to job requirements and cover relevant knowledge, skills, and experiences. The interviewer is supposed to avoid asking questions that are not on the list. Although interviewers may object to being restricted, the results may be more valid and reliable than with a nondirective interview.

- A **situational interview** is a structured interview in which the interviewer describes a situation likely to arise on the job and asks the candidate what he or she would do in that situation. This type of interview may have high validity in predicting job performance.[40]

- A **behavior description interview (BDI)** is a situational interview in which the interviewer asks the candidate to describe how he or she handled a type of situation in the past. Questions about candidates' actual experiences tend to have the highest validity.[41]

The common setup for either a nondirected or structured interview is for an individual (an HR professional or the supervisor for the vacant position) to interview each candidate face to face. However, variations on this approach are possible. In a **panel interview,** several members of the organization meet to interview each candidate. A panel interview gives the candidate a chance to meet more people and see how people interact in that organization. It provides the organization with the judgments of more than one person, to reduce the effect of personal biases in selection

Structured Interview
A selection interview that consists of a predetermined set of questions for the interviewer to ask.

Situational Interview
A structured interview in which the interviewer describes a situation likely to arise on the job, then asks the candidate what he or she would do in that situation.

Behavior Description Interview (BDI)
A structured interview in which the interviewer asks the candidate to describe how he or she handled a type of situation in the past.

175

When interviewing candidates, it's valid to ask about willingness to travel if that is part of the job. Interviewers might ask questions about previous business travel experiences and/or how interviewees handled situations requiring flexibility and self-motivation (qualities that would be an asset in someone who is traveling alone and solving business problems on the road).

Panel Interview
Selection interview in which several members of the organization meet to interview each candidate.

decisions. Panel interviews can be especially appropriate in organizations that use teamwork. At the other extreme, some organizations conduct interviews without any interviewers; they use a computerized interviewing process. The candidate sits at a computer and enters replies to the questions presented by the computer. Such a format eliminates a lot of personal bias—along with the opportunity to see how people interact. Therefore, computer interviews are useful for gathering objective data, rather than assessing people skills.

Advantages and Disadvantages of Interviewing

The wide use of interviewing is not surprising. People naturally want to see prospective employees firsthand. As we noted in Chapter 1, the top qualities that employers seek in new hires include communication skills and interpersonal skills. Talking face to face can provide evidence of these skills. Interviews can give insights into candidates' personalities and interpersonal styles. They are more valid, however, when they focus on job knowledge and skill. Interviews also provide a means to check the accuracy of information on the applicant's résumé or job application. Asking applicants to elaborate about their experiences and offer details reduces the likelihood of a candidate being able to invent a work history.[42]

Despite these benefits, interviewing is not necessarily the most accurate basis for making a selection decision. Research has shown that interviews can be unreliable, low in validity,[43] and biased against a number of different groups.[44] Interviews are also costly. They require that at least one person devote time to interviewing each candidate, and the applicants typically have to be brought to one geographic location. Interviews are also subjective, so they place the organization at greater risk of discrimination complaints by applicants who were not hired, especially if those individuals were asked questions not entirely related to the job. The Supreme Court has held that subjective selection methods like interviews must be validated, using methods that provide criterion-related or content validation.[45]

Organizations can avoid some of these pitfalls.[46] Human resource staff should keep the interviews narrow, structured, and standardized. The interview should focus on accomplishing a few goals, so that at the end of the interview, the organization has ratings on several observable measures, such as ability to express ideas. The interview should not try to measure abilities and skills—for example, intelligence—that tests can measure better. As noted earlier, situational interviews are especially effective for doing this. Organizations can prevent problems related to subjectivity by training interviewers and using more than one person to conduct interviews. Training typically includes focusing on the recording of observable facts, rather than on making subjective judgments, as well as developing interviewers' awareness of their biases.[47] Using a structured system for taking notes is helpful for limiting subjectivity and helping the interviewer remember and justify an evaluation later.[48] Finally, to address costs of interviewing, many organizations videotape interviews and send the tapes (rather than the applicants) from department to department. The above "HR How To" box provides more specific guidelines for successful interviewing.

INTERVIEWING EFFECTIVELY

Interviewing is one HR function that almost all managers are involved with at some point. Here are some tips for conducting interviews that identify the best candidates:

- *Be prepared*—Make sure the place where you interview is accessible and comfortable for you and the candidate. Read the candidate's résumé and other paperwork ahead of time, to avoid asking for information that has already been provided. Prepare a list of questions, as well as information about the company's history, culture, and other details the candidate might be interested in knowing.
- *Put the applicant at ease*— A nervous or cautious job candidate may not show his or her best qualities. Express your appreciation for the candidate's time, and let the person know you're glad to meet him

or her. Briefly explain what to expect during the interview.
- *Ask about past behaviors*— Talking about specific events makes it harder for a candidate to focus on guessing what the interviewer wants to hear, and the answers give clues about what the candidate will do in new situations. For example, depending on the type of job, you might ask, "Please tell me about a time when you received a customer complaint and how you handled it," or "This job involves tight deadlines; could you tell me about a time when you faced a difficult deadline?"
- *Listen*—The interview information is only as good as the interviewer's ability to gather it. Let the candidate do most of the talking, and pay attention to what is being said and not said. If a candidate sounds vague or too good to be true,

ask follow-up questions to gather details.
- *Take notes*—As much as you can without distracting yourself or the candidate, jot down notes to remind you of key points. Also schedule 5 or 10 minutes after each interview for writing down your impressions.
- At the end of the interview, make sure the candidate knows what to expect next— for example, a phone call or additional interviews within the next week.

Sources: U.S. Department of Commerce, Minority Business Development Agency, "Tips on How to Successfully Interview Job Candidates," November 17, 2009, www.mbda.gov; University of South Carolina Division of Human Resources, "Tips on Interviewing University Job Applicants," http://hr.sc.edu, accessed March 23, 2010; and Dun & Bradstreet, "How to Conduct an Effective Employee Interview," Small Business Solutions, http://smallbusiness.dnb.com, accessed March 23, 2010.

Preparing to Interview

Organizations can reap the greatest benefits from interviewing if they prepare carefully. A well-planned interview should be standardized, comfortable for the participants, and focused on the job and the organization. The interviewer should have a quiet place in which to conduct interviews without interruption. This person should be trained in how to ask objective questions, what subject matter to avoid, and how to detect and handle his or her own personal biases or other distractions in order to fairly evaluate candidates.

The interviewer should have enough documents to conduct a complete interview. These should include a list of the questions to be asked in a structured interview, with plenty of space for recording the responses. When the questions are prepared, it is also helpful to determine how the answers will be scored. For example, if questions ask how interviewees would handle certain situations, consider what responses are best in terms of meeting job requirements. If the job requires someone who motivates others, then a response that shows motivating behavior would receive a higher score. The interviewer also should have a copy of the interviewee's employment application and résumé to review before the interview and refer to during the interview. If possible, the interviewer should also have printed information about the organization and the job. Near the beginning of the interview, it is a good idea to go over the job specifications, organizational policies, and so on, so that the interviewee has a clearer understanding of the organization's needs.

The interviewer should schedule enough time to review the job requirements, discuss the interview questions, and give the interviewee a chance to ask questions. To close, the interviewer should thank the candidate for coming and provide information about what to expect—for example, that the organization will contact a few finalists within the next two weeks or that a decision will be made by the end of the week.

Selection Decisions

After reviewing applications, scoring tests, conducting interviews, and checking references, the organization needs to make decisions about which candidates to place in which jobs. In practice, most organizations find more than one qualified candidate to fill an open position. The selection decision typically combines ranking based on objective criteria along with subjective judgments about which candidate will make the greatest contribution.

How Organizations Select Employees

The selection decision should not be a simple matter of whom the supervisor likes best or which candidate will take the lowest offer. Also, as the "HR Oops!" box emphasizes, job candidates, confidence does not necessarily mean they are competent. Rather, the people making the selection should look for the best fit between candidate and position. In general, the person's performance will result from a combination of ability and motivation. Often, the selection is a choice among a few people who possess the basic qualifications. The decision makers therefore have to decide which of those people have the best combination of ability and motivation to fit in the position and in the organization as a whole.

Multiple-Hurdle Model
Process of arriving at a selection decision by eliminating some candidates at each stage of the selection process.

The usual process for arriving at a selection decision is to gradually narrow the pool of candidates for each job. This approach, called the **multiple-hurdle model,** is based on a process such as the one shown earlier in Figure 6.1. Each stage of the process is a hurdle, and candidates who overcome a hurdle continue to the next stage of the process. For example, the organization reviews applications and/or résumés of all candidates, conducts some tests on those who meet minimum requirements, conducts initial interviews with those who had the highest test scores, follows up with additional interviews or testing, and then selects a candidate from the few who survived this process. Another, more expensive alternative is to take most applicants through all steps of the process and then to review all the scores to find the most desirable candidates. With this alternative, decision makers may use a **compensatory model,** in which a very high score on one type of assessment can make up for a low score on another.

Compensatory Model
Process of arriving at a selection decision in which a very high score on one type of assessment can make up for a low score on another.

Whether the organization uses a multiple-hurdle model or conducts the same assessments on all candidates, the decision maker(s) needs criteria for choosing among qualified candidates. An obvious strategy is to select the candidates who score highest on tests and interviews. However, employee performance depends on motivation as well as ability. It is possible that a candidate who scores very high on an ability test might be "overqualified"—that is, the employee might be bored by the job the organization needs to fill, and a less-able employee might actually be a better fit. Similarly, a highly motivated person might learn some kinds of jobs very quickly,

HR Oops!

Style over Substance

Employers intend to pick the candidates who will perform the best on the job, but often they may be picking the candidates who perform best in the job *interview*. According to an experiment conducted at the University of California at Berkeley, people assume candidates are competent when they behave with confidence, whether or not they actually demonstrate competence.

In the experiment, people were assigned to teams of four to solve math problems. The team members gave leadership roles to the member who dominated the group by speaking with confidence, declaring opinions more often, and using body language that signaled certainty. Whether or not that team member had the best math skills, the team members rated that person as highly competent.

Applying that experiment to employee selection, it's important for an interviewer to sort out whether a candidate is simply speaking with confidence or actually providing evidence of competent behavior. Unless the job requirements focus on an ability to inspire confidence, the candidate's assertive behavior may not be the most important trait to measure. Instead, the employer probably needs to base the selection decision on more objective criteria.

Source: Based on Caitlin McDevitt, "The Competence-Confidence Disconnect," *Inc.*, April 24, 2009, www.inc.com.

Questions

1. For what kinds of jobs would it be relevant to look for a candidate who behaves confidently in a job interview?
2. When conducting job interviews, how can you increase the likelihood that you are evaluating relevant job skills, not just deciding who is most persuasive?

potentially outperforming someone who has the necessary skills. Furthermore, some organizations have policies of developing employees for career paths in the organization. Such organizations might place less emphasis on the skills needed for a particular job and more emphasis on hiring candidates who share the organization's values, show that they have the people skills to work with others in the organization, and are able to learn the skills needed for advancement.

Finally, organizations have choices about who will make the decision. Usually a supervisor makes the final decision, often alone. This person may couple knowledge of the job with a judgment about who will fit in best with others in the department. The decision could also be made by a human resource professional using standardized, objective criteria. Especially in organizations that use teamwork, selection decisions may be made by a work team or other panel of decision makers.

Communicating the Decision

The human resource department is often responsible for notifying applicants about the results of the selection process. When a candidate has been selected, the organization should communicate the offer to the candidate. The offer should include the job responsibilities, work schedule, rate of pay, starting date, and other relevant details. If placement in a job requires that the applicant pass a physical examination, the offer should state that contingency. The person communicating the offer should also indicate a date by which the candidate should reply with an acceptance or rejection of the offer. For some jobs, such as management and professional positions, the candidate and organization may negotiate pay, benefits, and work arrangements before they arrive at a final employment agreement.

The person who communicates this decision should keep accurate records of who was contacted, when, and for which position, as well as of the candidate's reply. The HR department and the supervisor also should be in close communication about the job offer. When an applicant accepts a job offer, the HR department must notify the supervisor, so that he or she can be prepared for the new employee's arrival.

thinking ethically

TAINTED BY ASSOCIATION

In a scandal involving fraud worth tens of billions of dollars, Bernard Madoff admitted to authorities that he had involved investors in an extensive Ponzi scheme—promising steady, favorable returns but using funds invested by new clients to pay phony returns to older clients. Eventually, a plunging stock market made the scheme impossible to maintain; it finally unraveled when Madoff was turned in to authorities by his sons and confessed to fraud.

The fallout extended well beyond losses to investors. Employees of Bernard L. Madoff Investment Securities lost their jobs when the firm became insolvent. About 200 people had worked for the firm, and when Surge Trading bought its remaining assets, only about 30 stayed on. Now those who lost their jobs are struggling to rebuild their careers in spite of having a notorious name on their résumés. The association with Madoff is a red flag whether or not they were involved in the illegal and unethical behavior.

Eleanor Squillari was Madoff's assistant. Concluding that she would never find another job in the finance industry, she attended beauty school in the hopes of being able to land a job in a hair salon. Elaine Solomon is still trying to figure out what she can do next. She had been assistant to Peter Madoff, brother of Bernard and the firm's chief compliance officer. Now no one has interest in hiring her.

SOURCE: Based on Aaron Lucchetti, "Not Exactly a Résumé Highlight: Madoff Work," *Wall Street Journal*, December 8, 2009, http://online.wsj.com.

Questions

1. Imagine that you work in the HR department of a financial services company. How would you react to an application from a highly skilled employee with experience at Bernard Madoff's firm? How much would it matter whether you believe the person knew what was going on? How, if at all, would your response change if you worked for a manufacturer?

2. What ethical criteria should you apply to making selection decisions involving people who once worked for Bernard Madoff (or some other firm with ethics or legal problems in its history)?

3. How important is it to you to work only for organizations with high ethical standards? Why does it (or doesn't it) matter to you?

SUMMARY

LO1 Identify the elements of the selection process.

Selection typically begins with a review of candidates' employment applications and résumés. The organization administers tests to candidates who meet basic requirements, and qualified candidates undergo one or more interviews. Organizations check references and conduct background checks to verify the accuracy of information provided by candidates. A candidate is selected to fill each vacant position. Candidates who accept offers are placed in the positions for which they were selected.

LO2 Define ways to measure the success of a selection method.

One criterion is reliability, which indicates the method is free from random error, so that measurements are consistent. A selection method should also be valid, meaning that performance on the measure (such as a test score) is related to what the measure is designed to assess (such as job performance). Criterion-related validity shows a correlation between test scores and job performance scores. Content validity shows consistency between the test items or problems and the kinds of situations or problems that occur on the job. Construct validity establishes that the test actually measures a specified construct, such as intelligence or leadership ability, which is presumed to be associated with success on the job. A selection method also should be generalizable, so that it applies to more than one specific situation. Each selection method should have utility, meaning it provides economic value greater than its cost. Finally, selection methods should meet the legal requirements for employment decisions.

LO3   Summarize the government's requirements for employee selection.

The selection process must be conducted in a way that avoids discrimination and provides access to persons with disabilities. This means selection methods must be valid for job performance, and scores may not be adjusted to discriminate against or give preference to any group. Questions may not gather information about a person's membership in a protected class, such as race, sex, or religion, nor may the employer investigate a person's disability status. Employers must respect candidates' privacy rights and ensure that they keep personal information confidential. They must obtain consent before conducting background checks and notify candidates about adverse decisions made as a result of background checks.

LO4   Compare the common methods used for selecting human resources.

Nearly all organizations gather information through employment applications and résumés. These methods are inexpensive, and an application form standardizes basic information received from all applicants. The information is not necessarily reliable, because each applicant provides the information. These methods are most valid when evaluated in terms of the criteria in a job description. References and background checks help to verify the accuracy of the information. Employment tests and work samples are more objective. To be legal, any test must measure abilities that actually are associated with successful job performance. Employment tests range from general to specific. General-purpose tests are relatively inexpensive and simple to administer. Tests should be selected to be related to successful job performance and avoid charges of discrimination. Interviews are widely used to obtain information about a candidate's interpersonal and communication skills and to gather more detailed information about a candidate's background. Structured interviews are more valid than unstructured ones. Situational interviews provide greater validity than general questions. Interviews are costly and may introduce bias into the selection process. Organizations can minimize the drawbacks through preparation and training.

LO5   Describe major types of employment tests.

Physical ability tests measure strength, endurance, psychomotor abilities, and other physical abilities. They can be accurate but can discriminate and are not always job related. Cognitive ability tests, or intelligence tests, tend to be valid, especially for complex jobs and those requiring adaptability. They are a relatively low-cost way to predict job performance but have been challenged as discriminatory. Job performance tests tend to be valid but are not always generalizable. Using a wide variety of job performance tests can be expensive. Personality tests measure personality traits such as extroversion and adjustment. Research supports their validity for appropriate job situations, especially for individuals who score high on conscientiousness, extroversion, and agreeableness. These tests are relatively simple to administer and generally meet legal requirements. Organizations may use paper-and-pencil honesty tests, which can predict certain behaviors, including employee theft. Organizations may not use polygraphs to screen job candidates. Organizations may also administer drug tests (if all candidates are tested and drug use can be an on-the-job safety hazard). A more job-related approach is to use impairment testing. Passing a medical examination may be a condition of employment, but to avoid discrimination against persons with disabilities, organizations usually administer a medical exam only after making a job offer.

LO6   Discuss how to conduct effective interviews.

Interviews should be narrow, structured, and standardized. Interviewers should identify job requirements and create a list of questions related to the requirements. Interviewers should be trained to recognize their own personal biases and conduct objective interviews. Panel interviews can reduce problems related to interviewer bias. Interviewers should put candidates at ease in a comfortable place that is free of distractions. Questions should ask for descriptions of relevant experiences and job-related behaviors. The interviewers also should be prepared to provide information about the job and the organization.

LO7   Explain how employers carry out the process of making a selection decision.

The organization should focus on the objective of finding the person who will be the best fit with the job and organization. This includes an assessment of ability and motivation. Decision makers may use a multiple-hurdle model in which each stage of the selection process eliminates some of the candidates from consideration at the following stages. At the final stage, only a few candidates remain, and the selection decision determines which of these few is the best fit. An alternative is a compensatory model, in which all candidates are evaluated with all methods. A candidate who scores poorly with one method may be selected if he or she scores very high on another measure.

KEY TERMS

achievement tests, p. 170

aptitude tests, p. 170

assessment center, p. 171

behavior description interview (BDI), p. 175

cognitive ability tests, p. 171

compensatory model, p. 178

concurrent validation, p. 161

construct validity, p. 162

content validity, p. 161

criterion-related validity, p. 160

generalizable, p. 162

Immigration Reform and Control Act of 1986, p. 165

multiple-hurdle model, p. 178

nondirective interview, p. 174

panel interview, p. 175

personnel selection, p. 158

predictive validation, p. 161

reliability, p. 160

situational interview, p. 175

structured interview, p. 175

utility, p. 162

validity, p. 160

REVIEW AND DISCUSSION QUESTIONS

1. What activities are involved in the selection process? Think of the last time you were hired for a job. Which of those activities were used in selecting you? Should the organization that hired you have used other methods as well?
2. Why should the selection process be adapted to fit the organization's job descriptions?
3. Choose two of the selection methods identified in this chapter. Describe how you can compare them in terms of reliability, validity, ability to generalize, utility, and compliance with the law.
4. Why does predictive validation provide better information than concurrent validation? Why is this type of validation more difficult?
5. How do U.S. laws affect organizations' use of each of the employment tests? Interviews?
6. Suppose your organization needs to hire several computer programmers, and you are reviewing résumés you obtained from an online service. What kinds of information will you want to gather from the "work experience" portion of these résumés? What kinds of information will you want to gather from the "education" portion of these résumés? What methods would you use for verifying or exploring this information? Why would you use those methods?
7. For each of the following jobs, select the two kinds of tests you think would be most important to include in the selection process. Explain why you chose those tests.

   a. City bus driver
   b. Insurance salesperson
   c. Member of a team that sells complex high-tech equipment to manufacturers
   d. Member of a team that makes a component of the equipment in (c)

8. Suppose you are a human resource professional at a large retail chain. You want to improve the company's hiring process by creating standard designs for interviews, so that every time someone is interviewed for a particular job category, that person answers the same questions. You also want to make sure the questions asked are relevant to the job and maintain equal employment opportunity. Think of three questions to include in interviews for each of the following jobs. For each question, state why you think it should be included.

   a. Cashier at one of the company's stores
   b. Buyer of the stores' teen clothing line
   c. Accounts payable clerk at company headquarters

9. How can organizations improve the quality of their interviewing so that interviews provide valid information?
10. Some organizations set up a selection process that is long and complex. In some people's opinion, this kind of selection process not only is more valid but also has symbolic value. What can the use of a long, complex selection process symbolize to job seekers? How do you think this would affect the organization's ability to attract the best employees?

BUSINESSWEEK CASE

BusinessWeek Limits on Credit Checks

It's hard enough to find a job in this economy, and now some people are facing another hurdle: Potential employers are holding their credit histories against them.

Sixty percent of employers recently surveyed by the Society for Human Resources Management said they run credit checks on at least some job applicants, compared with 42 percent in a somewhat similar survey in 2006.

Employers say such checks give them valuable information about an applicant's honesty and sense of responsibility. But lawmakers in at least 16 states from South Carolina to Oregon have proposed outlawing most credit checks, saying the practice traps people in debt because their past financial problems prevent them from finding work.

Wisconsin state Rep. Kim Hixson drafted a bill in his state shortly after hearing from Terry Becker, an auto mechanic who struggled to find work. Becker said it all started with medical bills that piled up when his now 10-year-old son began having seizures as a toddler. In the first year alone, Becker ran up $25,000 in medical debt. Over a four and half months period, he was turned down for at least eight positions for which he had authorized the employer to conduct a credit check, Becker said. He said one potential employer told him, "If your credit is bad, then you'll steal from me."

"I was in deep depression. I had lost a business, I was behind on my bills and I was unable to get a job," he said.

Hixson calls what happened to Becker discrimination based on credit history and said his bill would ban it. "If somebody is trying to get a job as a truck driver or a trainer in a gym, what does your credit history have to do with your ability to do that job?" Hixson asked. He said he knows of no research that shows a person with a bad credit history is going to perform poorly.

Under federal law, prospective employers must get written permission from applicants to run a credit check on them. But consumer advocates say most job applicants do not feel they are in a position to say no.

Even though more companies are using credit checks, only 13 percent perform them on all potential hires, according to the Society for Human Resources Management's most recent survey. Mike Aitken, the group's director of government affairs, said a blanket ban could remove a tool employers can use to help them make good hiring decisions.

Aitken pointed to a 2008 survey by the Association of Certified Fraud Examiners that found the two most common red flags for employees who commit workplace fraud are living beyond their means and having difficulty meeting financial obligations. The same survey estimated American companies lost $994 billion to workplace fraud in 2008.

Aitken said someone who cannot pay his or her bills on time may not be more likely to steal, but might not have the maturity or sense of responsibility to handle a job like processing payroll checks.

Becker, the Milton, Wisconsin, resident with bad credit, has found work dismantling cars at an auto recycling company that did not ask to run a credit check. He worries, though, about friends in the auto industry who are looking for work and coming up empty-handed because of credit problems.

"It just seems like once you fall behind, you're behind," he said. "It's really hard to get back on the right financial track."

SOURCE: Excerpted from Kathleen Miller, "States May Ban Credit Checks on Job Applicants," *BusinessWeek*, March 1, 2010, www.businessweek.com.

Questions

1. How well do you think credit checks meet the effectiveness criteria of (a) reliability; (b) validity; (c) ability to generalize results; (d) high utility; and (e) legality?
2. For what kinds of jobs might a credit check be a useful selection method? For what kinds of jobs would it be unhelpful, inappropriate, or unethical?
3. Imagine that you are an HR manager at a company operating in a state where credit checks of job applicants have been banned. What other selection methods could you use to pick honest and responsible employees?

Case: When Recruiting on Campus Is Too Costly

Everyone's tightening belts these days, and HR budgets are by no means exempt from the cost-cutting efforts. Even during lean times, many companies are hiring, but they are trying to pick the best people while trying to keep expenses down. For some companies, that includes thinking twice about flying or driving to college campuses to interview prospective employees.

That doesn't mean recruiters have stopped communicating with students. In more and more cases, it does mean the conversation may take place over a distance, using state-of-the-art technology. The interview setup can

be as simple as two laptops loaded with Skype software, which allows phone calls and webcam images to be transmitted over the Internet. Or it may involve thousands of dollars' worth of videoconferencing equipment for a more natural approach.

At Liberty Mutual Group, recruiting director Ann Nowak visits a few schools where the company has strong relationships and has found a good pool of talent. But she says, "Sometimes I get inquiries from very strong candidates in the top 10 percent of their class" at other schools, and she doesn't want them to slip away. Although the insurance company is growing and hiring sales representatives, Nowak can't afford to fly across the country for a handful of interviews, so she has set up an online recruiting and selection system. Students at distant schools can view online presentations about the kinds of positions the company has available. And when an interested prospect seems like he or she might be a good match, Nowak can use Web-based interviewing to narrow her choices. The company invites those who survive the cut to fly to headquarters for an interview.

Anheuser-Busch InBev is another company that recruits on college campuses. Elatia Abate, the company's global director of recruitment and strategy, picked a few schools she deemed worthy of visits. Career counselors at other schools wanted her to interview their students as well, but there wasn't room in the budget. Lean operations have been a hallmark of the brewing company since Belgium's InBev acquired St. Louis–based Anheuser-Busch. However, for candidates whose background looks interesting, Abate will conduct video interviews.

One way schools avoid getting passed by is to subscribe to a service called InterviewStream. For a few thousand dollars a year, the Bethlehem, Pennsylvania, company sets up a system that allows recruiters to conduct live interviews online. Or they can develop an automated process in which the InterviewStream system delivers each candidate a series of questions and records a video of the candidate's responses. To conduct this method, the company sends the job candidate an e-mail message inviting him or her to click on a link to a Web site that plays a video of the interviewer asking prerecorded questions. The company using the InterviewStream service chooses which questions will be asked and whether to give candidates the option to review and edit their responses. A webcam on the candidate's computer records the interview, which is then made available for the company's hiring people to review whenever they like.

SOURCES: Diana Middleton, "Non-Campus Recruiting," *Wall Street Journal*, February 23, 2010, http://onliune.wsj.com; Jeremiah McWilliams, "Drastic Changes, No Apologies," *St. Louis Post-Dispatch*, November 15, 2009, Business & Company Resource Center, http://galenet.galegroup.com; "Liberty Mutual Adds Reps, Offices in Massachusetts," *Professional Services Close-Up*, April 3, 2009, Business & Company Resource Center, http://galenet.galgroup.com; and Darren Dahl, "Recruiting: Tapping the Talent Pool," *Inc.*, April 1, 2009, www.inc.com.

Questions

1. Under what conditions would it be practical for a company to send recruiters to college campuses to interview prospective employees, and when would it be impractical? What kinds of companies would you expect to see on your college campus? What kinds would you *not* expect to see?

2. Compare in-person interviewing with video or online interviewing in terms of the effectiveness criteria (reliability, validity, ability to generalize results, utility, and legality). Which method is superior? Why?

3. Why do you think Liberty Mutual adds a face-to-face interview of candidates who did well in their online interview? Do you think it's worthwhile to fly a candidate across the country before making a selection decision? Why or why not? What additional information, if any, could be gained from the effort?

🖨 IT'S A WRAP!   Mc Graw Hill **connect**

www.mhhe.com/noefund4e is your source for Reviewing, Applying, and Practicing the concepts you learned about in Chapter 6.

Review
- Chapter learning objectives
- Test Your Knowledge: Reliability and Validity

Application
- Manager's Hot Seat segment: "Diversity in Hiring: Candidate Conundrum"
- Video case and quiz: "Using Interviews to Recruit the Right People"
- Self-Assessments: Assessing How Personality Type Impacts Your Goal Setting Skills and Analyzing Behavioral Interviews
- Web exercise: National Association of Convenience Stores Employee Selection Tool
- Small-business case: Kinaxis Chooses Sales Reps with Personality

Practice
- Chapter quiz

NOTES

1. Ian Ayres and Barry Nalebuff, "For the Love of the Game," *Forbes*, March 12, 2007, downloaded from General Reference Center Gold, http://find.galegroup.com.

2. Scott McCartney, "The Air-Traffic Cops Go to School," *Wall Street Journal*, March 29, 2005, http://online.wsj.com.

3. J. C. Nunnally, *Psychometric Theory* (New York: McGraw-Hill, 1978).

4. N. Schmitt, R. Z. Gooding, R. A. Noe, and M. Kirsch, "Meta-Analysis of Validity Studies Published between 1964 and 1982 and the Investigation of Study Characteristics," *Personnel Psychology* 37 (1984), pp. 407–22.

5. D. D. Robinson, "Content-Oriented Personnel Selection in a Small Business Setting," *Personnel Psychology* 34 (1981), pp. 77–87.

6. M. V. Rafter, "Assessment Providers Scoring Well," *Workforce Management*, January 19, 2009, pp. 24–25.

7. F. L. Schmidt and J. E. Hunter, "The Future of Criterion-Related Validity," *Personnel Psychology* 33 (1980), pp. 41–60; F. L. Schmidt, J. E. Hunter, and K. Pearlman, "Task Differences as Moderators of Aptitude Test Validity: A Red Herring," *Journal of Applied Psychology* 66 (1982), pp. 166–85; and R. L. Gutenberg, R. D. Arvey, H. G. Osburn, and R. P. Jeanneret, "Moderating Effects of Decision-Making/Information Processing Dimensions on Test Validities," *Journal of Applied Psychology* 68 (1983), pp. 600–8.

8. M. Schoeff, "Walgreen Suit Reflects EEOC's Latest Strategy," *Workforce Management*, March 16, 2007, p. 8.

9. Steve Blackstone, "Supreme Court Rules in Favor of White Firefighters in New Haven Case," *Firehouse*, September 2009, Business & Company Resource Center, http://galenet.galegroup.com; and "U.S. Supreme Court Finds 'Reverse' Racial Discrimination Claim Has Merit; Scales Back Use of Preferences," *Mondaq Business Briefing*, September 27, 2009, Business & Company Resource Center, http://galenet.galegroup.com.

10. B. S. Murphy, "EEOC Gives Guidance on Legal and Illegal Inquiries under ADA," *Personnel Journal*, August 1994, p. 26.

11. Perri Capell, "When Applying for Jobs Online, You Can Skip Certain Questions," *Career Journal*, October 9, 2007, www.careerjournal.com.

12. T. W. Dougherty, D. B. Turban, and J. C. Callender, "Confirming First Impressions in the Employment Interview: A Field Study of Interviewer Behavior," *Journal of Applied Psychology* 79 (1994), pp. 659–65.

13. Judy Greenwald, "Layoffs May Spark Defamation Suits," *Business Insurance*, June 1, 2009, Business & Company Resource Center, http://galenet.galegroup.com.

14. A. Ryan and M. Lasek, "Negligent Hiring and Defamation: Areas of Liability Related to Preemployment Inquiries," *Personnel Psychology* 44 (1991), pp. 293–319.

15. A. Long, "Addressing the Cloud over Employee References: A Survey of Recently Enacted State Legislation," *William and Mary Law Review* 39 (October 1997), pp. 177–228.

16. J. S. Lublin, "Bulletproofing Your References in the Hunt for a New Job," *Wall Street Journal*, April 7, 2009, p. C1.

17. C. Tuna, "How to Spot Résumé Fraud," *Wall Street Journal*, November 13, 2008, p. C1.

18. Douglas Belkin, "More Job Seekers Scramble to Erase Their Criminal Past," *Wall Street Journal*, November 12, 2009, http://online.wsj.com.

19. Kristen McNamara, "Bad Credit Derails Job Seekers," *Wall Street Journal*, March 16, 2010, http://online.wsj.com.

20. L. C. Buffardi, E. A. Fleishman, R. A. Morath, and P. M. McCarthy, "Relationships between Ability Requirements and Human Errors in Job Tasks," *Journal of Applied Psychology* 85 (2000), pp. 551–64; J. Hogan, "Structure of Physical Performance in Occupational Tasks," *Journal of Applied Psychology* 76 (1991), pp. 495–507.

21. J. F. Salagado, N. Anderson, S. Moscoso, C. Bertuas, and F. De Fruyt, "International Validity Generalization of GMA and Cognitive Abilities: A European Community Meta-analysis," *Personnel Psychology* 56 (2003), pp. 573–605; M. J. Ree, J. A. Earles, and M. S. Teachout, "Predicting Job Performance: Not Much More than *g*," *Journal of Applied Psychology* 79 (1994), pp. 518–24; L. S. Gottfredson, "The *g* Factor in Employment," *Journal of Vocational Behavior* 29 (1986), pp. 293–96; J. E. Hunter and R. H. Hunter, "Validity and Utility of Alternative Predictors of Job Performance," *Psychological Bulletin* 96 (1984), pp. 72–98; Gutenberg et al., "Moderating Effects of Decision-Making/Information Processing Dimensions on Test Validities"; F. L. Schmidt, J. G. Berner, and J. E. Hunter, "Racial Differences in Validity of Employment Tests: Reality or Illusion," *Journal of Applied Psychology* 58 (1974), pp. 5–6; and J. A. LePine, J. A. Colquitt, and A. Erez, "Adaptability to Changing Task Contexts: Effects of General Cognitive Ability,

Conscientiousness, and Openness to Experience," *Personnel Psychology* 53 (2000), pp. 563–93.

22. D. A. Kravitz and S. L. Klineberg, "Reactions to Versions of Affirmative Action among Whites, Blacks, and Hispanics," *Journal of Applied Psychology* (2000), pp. 597–611.

23. See, for example, C. Winkler, "Job Tryouts Go Virtual," *HRMagazine*, September 2006, pp. 10–15.

24. D. J. Schleiger, V. Venkataramani, F. P. Morgeson, and M. A. Campion, "So You Didn't Get the Job . . . Now What Do You Think? Examining Opportunity to Perform Fairness Perceptions," *Personnel Psychology* 59 (2006), pp. 559–90.

25. F. L. Schmidt and J. E. Hunter, "The Validity and Utility of Selection Methods in Personnel Psychology: Practical and Theoretical Implications of 85 Years of Research Findings," *Psychological Bulletin* 124 (1998), pp. 262–74.

26. W. Arthur, E. A. Day, T. L. McNelly, and P. S. Edens, "Meta-Analysis of the Criterion-Related Validity of Assessment Center Dimensions," *Personnel Psychology* 56 (2003), pp. 125–54; and C. E. Lance, T. A. Lambert, A. G. Gewin, F. Lievens, and J. M. Conway, "Revised Estimates of Dimension and Exercise Variance Components in Assessment Center Postexercise Dimension Ratings," *Journal of Applied Psychology* 89 (2004), pp. 377–85.

27. N. M. Dudley, K. A. Orvis, J. E. Lebieki, and J. M. Cortina, "A Meta-analytic Investigation of Conscientiousness in the Prediction of Job Performance: Examining the Intercorrelation and the Incremental Validity of Narrow Traits," *Journal of Applied Psychology* 91 (2006), pp. 40–57; W. S. Dunn, M. K. Mount, M. R. Barrick, and D. S. Ones, "Relative Importance of Personality and General Mental Ability on Managers' Judgments of Applicant Qualifications," *Journal of Applied Psychology* 79 (1995), pp. 500–9; P. M. Wright, K. M. Kacmar, G. C. McMahan, and K. Deleeuw, "$P = f(M \times A)$: Cognitive Ability as a Moderator of the Relationship between Personality and Job Performance," *Journal of Management* 21 (1995), pp. 1129–39.

28. M. Mount, M. R. Barrick, and J. P. Strauss, "Validity of Observer Ratings of the Big Five Personality Factors," *Journal of Applied Psychology* 79 (1994), pp. 272–80.

29. L. A. Witt and G. R. Ferris, "Social Skill as Moderator of the Conscientiousness–Performance Relationship: Convergent Results across Four Studies," *Journal of Applied Psychology* 88 (2003), pp. 809–20.

30. L. Joel, *Every Employee's Guide to the Law* (New York: Pantheon, 1993).

31. N. Schmitt and F. L. Oswald, "The Impact of Corrections for Faking on the Validity of Non-cognitive Measures in Selection Contexts," *Journal of Applied Psychology* (2006), pp. 613–21.

32. S. A. Birkland, T. M. Manson, J. L. Kisamore, M. T. Brannick, and M. A. Smith, "Faking on Personality Measures," *International Journal of Selection and Assessment* 14 (December 2006), pp. 317–35.

33. C. H. Van Iddekinge, P. H. Raymark, and P. L. Roth, "Assessing Personality with a Structured Employment Interview: Construct-Related Validity and Susceptibility to Response Inflation," *Journal of Applied Psychology* 90 (2005), pp. 536–52; R. Mueller-Hanson, E. D. Heggestad, and G. C. Thornton, "Faking and Selection: Considering the Use of Personality from Select-In and Select-Out Perspectives," *Journal of Applied Psychology* 88 (2003), pp. 348–55; and N. L. Vasilopoulos, J. M. Cucina, and J. M. McElreath, "Do Warnings of Response Verification Moderate the Relationship between Personality and Cognitive Ability?" *Journal of Applied Psychology* 90 (2005), pp. 306–22.

34. E. Freudenheim, "Personality Testing Controversial, but Poised to Take Off," *Workforce Management*, August 14, 2006, p. 38.

35. V. Knight, "Personality Tests as Hiring Tools," *Wall Street Journal*, March 15, 2006, p. B1; G. L. Steward, I. S. Fulmer, and M. R. Barrick, "An Exploration of Member Roles as a Multilevel Linking Mechanism for Individual Traits and Team Outcomes," *Personnel Psychology* 58 (2005), pp. 343–65; and M. Mount, R. Ilies, and E. Johnson, "Relationship of Personality Traits and Counterproductive Work Behaviors: The Mediation Effects of Job Satisfaction," *Personnel Psychology* 59 (2006), pp. 591–622.

36. A. Hedger, "Employee Screening: Common Challenges, Smart Solutions," *Workforce Management*, March 17, 2008, pp. 39–46; and J. Welch and S. Welch, "Team Building: Right and Wrong," *BusinessWeek*, November 24, 2008, p. 130.

37. D. S. Ones, C. Viswesvaran, and F. L. Schmidt, "Comprehensive Meta-analysis of Integrity Test Validities: Findings and Implications for Personnel Selection and Theories of Job Performance," *Journal of Applied Psychology* 78 (1993), pp. 679–703; and H. J. Bernardin and D. K. Cooke, "Validity of an Honesty Test in Predicting Theft among Convenience Store Employees," *Academy of Management Journal* 36 (1993), pp. 1079–1106.

38. K. R. Murphy, G. C. Thornton, and D. H. Reynolds, "College Students' Attitudes toward Drug Test Programs," *Personnel Psychology* 43 (1990), pp. 615–31; and M. E. Paronto, D. M. Truxillo, T. N. Bauer, and M. C. Leo, "Drug Testing, Drug Treatment, and Marijuana Use: A Fairness Perspective," *Journal of Applied Psychology* 87 (2002), pp. 1159–66.

39. Bowles-Langley Technology, "Industrial Safety," corporate Web site, http://bowles-langley.com, accessed March 22, 2010; and Bowles-Langley Technology, "Exhausted—Don't Drive That Tanker," news release, January 16, 2006, http://bowles-langley.com.

40. M. A. McDaniel, F. P. Morgeson, E. G. Finnegan, M. A. Campion, and E. P. Braverman, "Use of Situational Judgment Tests to Predict Job Performance: A Clarification of the Literature," *Journal of Applied Psychology* 86 (2001), pp. 730–40; and J. Clavenger, G. M. Perreira, D. Weichmann, N. Schmitt, and V. S. Harvey, "Incremental Validity of Situational Judgment Tests," *Journal of Applied Psychology* 86 (2001), pp. 410–17.

41. M. A. Campion, J. E. Campion, and J. P. Hudson, "Structured Interviewing: A Note of Incremental Validity and Alternative Question Types," *Journal of Applied Psychology* 79 (1994), pp. 998–1002; E. D. Pulakos and N. Schmitt, "Experience-Based and Situational Interview Questions: Studies of Validity," *Personnel Psychology* 48 (1995), pp. 289–308; and A. P. J. Ellis, B. J. West, A. M. Ryan, and R. P. DeShon, "The Use of Impression Management Tactics in Structured Interviews: A Function of Question Type?" *Journal of Applied Psychology* 87 (2002), pp. 1200–8.

42. N. Schmitt, F. L. Oswald, B. H. Kim, M. A. Gillespie, L. J. Ramsey, and T. Y Yoo, "The Impact of Elaboration on Socially Desirable Responding and the Validity of Biodata Measures," *Journal of Applied Psychology* 88 (2003), pp. 979–88; and N. Schmitt and C. Kunce, "The Effects of Required Elaboration of Answers to Biodata Questions," *Personnel Psychology* 55 (2002), pp. 569–87.

43. Hunter and Hunter, "Validity and Utility of Alternative Predictors of Job Performance."

44. R. Pingitore, B. L. Dugoni, R. S. Tindale, and B. Spring, "Bias against Overweight Job Applicants in a Simulated Interview," *Journal of Applied Psychology* 79 (1994), pp. 184–90.

45. *Watson v. Fort Worth Bank and Trust,* 108 Supreme Court 2791 (1988).

46. M. A. McDaniel, D. L. Whetzel, F. L. Schmidt, and S. D. Maurer, "The Validity of Employment Interviews: A Comprehensive Review and Meta-Analysis," *Journal of Applied Psychology* 79 (1994), pp. 599–616; and A. I. Huffcutt and W. A. Arthur, "Hunter and Hunter (1984) Revisited: Interview Validity for Entry-Level Jobs," *Journal of Applied Psychology* 79 (1994), pp. 184–90.

47. Y. Ganzach, A. N. Kluger, and N. Klayman, "Making Decisions from an Interview: Expert Measurement and Mechanical Combination," *Personnel Psychology* 53 (2000), pp. 1–21; and G. Stasser and W. Titus, "Effects of Information Load and Percentage of Shared Information on the Dissemination of Unshared Information during Group Discussion," *Journal of Personality and Social Psychology* 53 (1987), pp. 81–93.

48. C. H. Middendorf and T. H. Macan, "Note-Taking in the Interview: Effects on Recall and Judgments," *Journal of Applied Psychology* 87 (2002), pp. 293–303.

Training Employees

Introduction

The reason clients turn to Advanced Technology Institute (ATI), a nonprofit organization that helps companies collaborate with schools and government on research and development, is that ATI offers them access to talented experts. In other words, the skills of its people are central to what the organization does. ATI has fewer than 60 employees but that hasn't held back its efforts to find and develop the right talent. Employees hired after the organization's rigorous selection process spend two weeks learning their job requirements, ATI's history and culture, and the use of the company's "knowledge management" system, which gives employees a simple way to post details about what they've learned so that others can look up guidance whenever they need it. ATI also defines career paths for its employees, and each employee works with his or her manager to identify the skills the employee needs to move along that path and plan how to acquire those skills. Employees who take advantage of the opportunities can go far. Madeleine Fincher started out as a temporary employee, took a job as an assistant to one of the managers, signed up for ATI's training programs, and in a few years had worked her way up to senior program assistant, talking directly with clients in business and government to set up meetings nationwide.[1]

The HR function that helps employees like Fincher increase their value to their organization is training.

Training consists of an organization's planned efforts to help employees acquire job-related knowledge, skills, abilities, and behaviors, with the goal of applying these on the job. A training program may range from formal classes to one-on-one mentoring, and it may take place on the job or at remote locations. No matter what its form, training can benefit the organization when it is linked to organizational needs and when it motivates employees.

This chapter describes how to plan and carry out an effective training program. We begin by discussing how to develop effective training in the context of the organization's strategy. Next, we discuss how organizations assess employees' training needs. We then review training methods and the process of evaluating a training program. The chapter concludes by discussing some special applications of training: orientation of new employees and the management of diversity.

Training Linked to Organizational Needs

The nature of the modern business environment makes training more important today than it ever has been. Rapid change, especially in the area of technology, requires that employees continually learn new skills. The new psychological contract, described in Chapter 2, has created the expectation that employees invest in their own career development, which requires learning opportunities. Growing reliance on teamwork creates a demand for the ability to solve problems in teams, an ability that often requires formal training. Finally, the diversity of the U.S. population, coupled with the globalization of business, requires that employees be able to work well with people who are different from them. Successful organizations often take the lead in developing this ability.

With training so essential in modern organizations, it is important to provide training that is effective. An effective training program actually teaches what it is designed to teach, and it teaches skills and behaviors that will help the organization achieve its goals. To achieve those goals, HR professionals approach training through **instructional design**—a process of systematically developing training to meet specified needs.[2]

A complete instructional design process includes the steps shown in Figure 7.1. It begins with an assessment of the needs for training—what the organization requires that its people learn. Next, the organization ensures that employees are ready for training in terms of their attitudes, motivation, basic skills, and work environment. The third step is to plan the training program, including the program's objectives, instructors, and methods. The organization then implements the program. Finally, evaluating the results of the training provides feedback for planning future training programs.

To carry out this process more efficiently and effectively, a growing number of organizations are using a **learning management system (LMS),** a computer application that automates the administration, development, and delivery of a company's training programs.[3]

Training
An organization's planned efforts to help employees acquire job-related knowledge, skills, abilities, and behaviors, with the goal of applying these on the job.

LO1 Discuss how to link training programs to organizational needs.

Instructional Design
A process of systematically developing training to meet specified needs.

Figure 7.1

Stages of Instructional Design

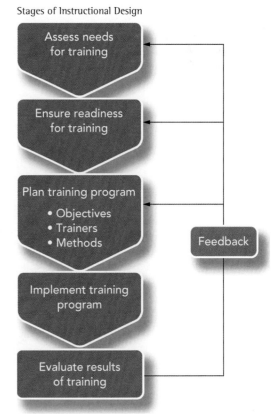

Learning Management System (LMS)
A computer application that automates the administration, development, and delivery of training programs.

Managers and employees can use the LMS to identify training needs and enroll in courses. LMSs can make training programs more widely available and help companies reduce travel and other costs by providing online training. Administrative tools let managers track course enrollments and program completion. The system can be linked to the organization's performance management system to plan for and manage training needs, training outcomes, and associated rewards together.

Needs Assessment

Instructional design logically should begin with a **needs assessment,** the process of evaluating the organization, individual employees, and employees' tasks to determine what kinds of training, if any, are necessary. As this definition indicates, the needs assessment answers questions in three broad areas:[4]

LO2 Explain how to assess the need for training.

1. *Organization*—What is the context in which training will occur?
2. *Person*—Who needs training?
3. *Task*—What subjects should the training cover?

The answers to these questions provide the basis for planning an effective training program.

Needs Assessment
The process of evaluating the organization, individual employees, and employees' tasks to determine what kinds of training, if any, are necessary.

A variety of conditions may prompt an organization to conduct a needs assessment. Management may observe that some employees lack basic skills or are performing poorly. Decisions to produce new products, apply new technology, or design new jobs should prompt a needs assessment because these changes tend to require new

Pfizer employees go through a representative training phase which teaches them about different Pfizer products and how to market them. Workers typically need to be trained in several processes to work in flexible manufacturing.

skills. The decision to conduct a needs assessment also may be prompted by outside forces, such as customer requests or legal requirements.

The outcome of the needs assessment is a set of decisions about how to address the issues that prompted the needs assessment. These decisions do not necessarily include a training program, because some issues should be resolved through methods other than training. For example, suppose a company uses delivery trucks to transport anesthetic gases to medical facilities, and a driver of one of these trucks mistakenly hooks up the supply line of a mild anesthetic from the truck to the hospital's oxygen system, contaminating the hospital's oxygen supply. This performance problem prompts a needs assessment. Whether or not the hospital decides to provide more training will depend partly on the reasons the driver erred. The driver may have hooked up the supply lines incorrectly because of a lack of knowledge about the appropriate line hookup, anger over a request for a pay raise being denied, or mislabeled valves for connecting the supply lines. Out of these three possibilities, only the lack of knowledge can be corrected through training. Other outcomes of a needs assessment might include plans for better rewards to improve motivation, better hiring decisions, and better safety precautions.

The remainder of this chapter discusses needs assessment and then what the organization should do when assessment indicates a need for training. The possibilities for action include offering existing training programs to more employees; buying or developing new training programs; and improving existing training programs. Before we consider the available training options, let's examine the elements of the needs assessment in more detail.

Organization Analysis

Usually, the needs assessment begins with the **organization analysis.** This is a process for determining the appropriateness of training by evaluating the characteristics of the organization. The organization analysis looks at training needs in light of the organization's strategy, resources available for training, and management's support for training activities.

Organization Analysis
A process for determining the appropriateness of training by evaluating the characteristics of the organization.

Training needs will vary depending on whether the organization's strategy is based on growing or shrinking its personnel, whether it is seeking to serve a broad customer base or focusing on the specific needs of a narrow market segment, and various other strategic scenarios. An organization that concentrates on serving a niche market may need to continually update its workforce on a specialized skills set. A company that is cutting costs with a downsizing strategy may need to train employees who will be laid off in job search skills. The employees who remain following the downsizing may need cross-training so that they can handle a wider variety of responsibilities. For an example of a company where a commitment to training supports corporate strategy, see the "Best Practices" box.

Anyone planning a training program must consider whether the organization has the budget, time, and expertise for training. For example, if the company is installing computer-based manufacturing equipment in one of its plants, it can ensure that it has the necessary computer-literate employees in one of three ways. If it has the technical experts on its staff, they can train the employees affected by the change. Or the company may use testing to determine which of its employees are already computer literate and then replace or reassign employees who lack the necessary skills. The third choice is to purchase training from an outside individual or organization.

Best Practices

Orkin Trains Experts

focus on **social** responsibility

When people call Orkin, it's generally because they have an unpleasant problem, like ants, cockroaches, or bedbugs. And when people have that kind of problem, they generally just want it to go away. That's where Orkin sees a chance to offer a competitive advantage. As the company's ads say, when you call on Orkin, you "hire an expert."

So where does Orkin get those experts? The company does have a team of entomologists and other scientists with doctorate degrees, but the people who call on homes and companies to get rid of bugs didn't join the company as experts. Rather, they are committed, service-oriented individuals who have taken advantage of the company's extensive training program.

While many employers would say they consider their employees key resources, Orkin backs that claim with training that amounts to "the biggest investment we make in our employees," in the words of David Lamb, Orkin's vice president of learning and media services. New employees participate in three weeks of training that includes watching satellite broadcasts of classes as well as working with interactive Web-based training materials. The broadcasts originate in a 28,000-square-foot training facility that Orkin built in Atlanta, featuring simulated customer locales: a house, hospital room, restaurant, bar, grocery store, and warehouse. Employees view these realistic setups to understand what they'll need to look for while they're on the job.

After this orientation period, the training continues on the job. Each new employee begins working alongside a certified field trainer, service manager, or branch manager, who observes how the new employee performs. This field trainer quizzes and coaches employees in identifying the particular species of pests they encounter, selecting the best treatment, and explaining their plans to the customer.

Even when employees have learned their job, the training continues. New pests invade, and new treatments are developed, so employees need to continue their training. Orkin's commitment to learning includes inviting entomology professors from major universities to annual meetings, where they can share new ideas with the company's specialists. The forums are recorded, so employees in the field can watch the videos afterward. Orkin also brings in experts from the Centers for Disease Control and Prevention to inform its employees about health risks related to pests, so that employees can share these lessons with their customers. And in a partnership with the Building Owners and Managers Association, Orkin has developed guidelines for preventing and treating pests in the most environmentally friendly ways that have been identified.

All that training supports Orkin's strategy only if the company verifies that it is covering relevant topics. So staff members from the learning and media services department visit field offices to verify that the training is relevant to the actual issues workers are encountering.

Sources: Holly Dolezalek, "Shaper Image," *Training,* November 25, 2009, Business & Company Resource Center, http://galenet.galegroup.com; "Green Pest-Control Checklist Available Online," *Buildings,* January 2009, p. 12; and Orkin, Careers Web page, http://careers.orkin.com, accessed March 29, 2010.

Even if training fits the organization's strategy and budget, it can be viable only if the organization is willing to support the investment in training. Managers increase the success of training when they support it through such actions as helping trainees see how they can use their newly learned knowledge, skills, and behaviors on the job.[5] Conversely, the managers will be most likely to support training if the people planning it can show that it will solve a significant problem or result in a significant improvement, relative to its cost. Managers appreciate training proposals with specific goals, timetables, budgets, and methods for measuring success.

Person Analysis

Following the organizational assessment, needs assessment turns to the remaining areas of analysis: person and task. The **person analysis** is a process for determining individuals' needs and readiness for training. It involves answering several questions:

Person Analysis
A process of determining individuals' needs and readiness for training.

- Do performance deficiencies result from a lack of knowledge, skill, or ability? (If so, training is appropriate; if not, other solutions are more relevant.)
- Who needs training?
- Are these employees ready for training?

The answers to these questions help the manager identify whether training is appropriate and which employees need training. In certain situations, such as the introduction of a new technology or service, all employees may need training. However, when needs assessment is conducted in response to a performance problem, training is not always the best solution.

The person analysis is therefore critical when training is considered in response to a performance problem. In assessing the need for training, the manager should identify all the variables that can influence performance. The primary variables are the person's ability and skills, his or her attitudes and motivation, the organization's input (including clear directions, necessary resources, and freedom from interference and distractions), performance feedback (including praise and performance standards), and positive consequences to motivate good performance. Of these variables, only ability and skills can be affected by training. Therefore, before planning a training program, it is important to be sure that any performance problem results from a deficiency in knowledge and skills. Otherwise, training dollars will be wasted, because the training is unlikely to have much effect on performance.

The person analysis also should determine whether employees are ready to undergo training. In other words, the employees to receive training not only should require additional knowledge and skill, but must be willing and able to learn. (After our discussion of the needs assessment, we will explore the topic of employee readiness in greater detail.)

Task Analysis

The third area of needs assessment is **task analysis,** the process of identifying the tasks, knowledge, skills, and behaviors that training should emphasize. Usually, task analysis is conducted along with person analysis. Understanding shortcomings in performance usually requires knowledge about the tasks and work environment as well as the employee.

Task Analysis
The process of identifying and analyzing tasks to be trained for.

To carry out the task analysis, the HR professional looks at the conditions in which tasks are performed. These conditions include the equipment and environment of the job, time constraints (for example, deadlines), safety considerations, and performance standards. These observations form the basis for a description of work activities, or the tasks required by the person's job. For a selected job, the analyst interviews employees and their supervisors to prepare a list of tasks performed in that job. Then the analyst validates the list by showing it to employees, supervisors, and other subject-matter experts and asking them to complete a questionnaire about the importance, frequency, and difficulty of the tasks. Table 7.1 is an example of a task analysis questionnaire for an electrical maintenance worker. For each task listed, the subject-matter expert uses the scales to rate the task's importance, frequency, and difficulty.

Table 7.1

Sample Items from a Task Analysis Questionnaire

Job: Electrical Maintenance Worker

Task Performance Ratings

Task #s	Task Description	Frequency of Performance	Importance	Difficulty
199-264	Replace a light bulb	0 1 2 3 4 5	0 1 2 3 4 5	0 1 2 3 4 5
199-265	Replace an electrical outlet	0 1 2 3 4 5	0 1 2 3 4 5	0 1 2 3 4 5
199-266	Install a light fixture	0 1 2 3 4 5	0 1 2 3 4 5	0 1 2 3 4 5
199-267	Replace a light switch	0 1 2 3 4 5	0 1 2 3 4 5	0 1 2 3 4 5
199-268	Install a new circuit breaker	0 1 2 3 4 5	0 1 2 3 4 5	0 1 2 3 4 5

Frequency of Performance	Importance	Difficulty
0=never 5=often	1=negligible 5=extremely high	1=easiest 5=most difficult

SOURCE: From E. F. Holton III and C. Bailey, "Top-to-Bottom Curriculum Redesign," *Training and Development*, March 1995, pp. 40–44. Copyright © 1995 by *American Society for Training and Development*. Reproduced with permission of *American Society for Training and Development* via Copyright Clearance Center.

The information from these questionnaires is the basis for determining which tasks will be the focus of the training. The person or committee conducting the needs assessment must decide what levels of importance, frequency, and difficulty signal a need for training. Logically, training is most needed for tasks that are important, frequent, and at least moderately difficult. For each of these tasks, the analysts must identify the knowledge, skills, and abilities required to perform the task. This information usually comes from interviews with subject-matter experts, such as employees who currently hold the job.

LO3 Explain how to assess employees' readiness for training.

Readiness for Training A combination of employee characteristics and positive work environment that permit training.

Readiness for Training

Effective training requires not only a program that addresses real needs, but also a condition of employee readiness. **Readiness for training** is a combination of employee characteristics and positive work environment that permit training. The necessary employee characteristics include ability to learn the subject matter, favorable attitudes toward the training, and motivation to learn. A positive work environment is one that encourages learning and avoids interfering with the training program.

Employee Readiness Characteristics

To be ready to learn, employees need basic learning skills, especially *cognitive ability*, which includes being able to use written and spoken language, solve math problems, and use logic to solve problems. Ideally, the selection process identified job candidates with enough cognitive ability to handle not only the requirements for doing a job but also the training associated with that job. However, recent forecasts of the skill levels of the U.S. workforce indicate that many companies will have to work with employees who lack basic skills.[6] For example, they may have to provide literacy training or access to classes teaching basic skills before some employees can participate in job-related training.

Employees learn more from training programs when they are highly motivated to learn—that is, when they really want to learn the content of the training program.[7] Employees tend to feel this way if they believe they are able to learn, see potential benefits from the training program, are aware of their need to learn, see a fit between the training and their career goals, and have the basic skills needed for participating in the program. Managers can influence a ready attitude in a variety of ways. For example, they can provide feedback that encourages employees, establishes rewards for learning, and communicates with employees about the organization's career paths and future needs.

Work Environment

Readiness for training also depends on two broad characteristics of the work environment: situational constraints and social support.[8] *Situational constraints* are the limits on training's effectiveness that arise from the situation or the conditions within the organization. Constraints can include a lack of money for training, lack of time for training or practicing, and failure to provide proper tools and materials for learning or applying the lessons of training. Conversely, trainees are likely to apply what they learn if the organization gives them opportunities to use their new skills and if it rewards them for doing so.[9]

Social support refers to the ways the organization's people encourage training, including giving trainees praise and encouraging words, sharing information about participating in training programs, and expressing positive attitudes toward the organization's training programs. Table 7.2 summarizes some ways in which managers can support training.

Support can also come from employees' peers. The organization can formally provide peer support by establishing groups of employees who meet regularly to discuss their progress. For example, group members can share how they coped with challenges related to what they learned. Schlumberger, which provides oil field services,

Understand the content of the training.
Know how training relates to what you need employees to do.
In performance appraisals, evaluate employees on how they apply training to their jobs.
Support employees' use of training when they return to work.
Ensure that employees have the equipment and technology needed to use training.
Prior to training, discuss with employees how they plan to use training.
Recognize newly trained employees who use training content.
Give employees release time from their work to attend training.
Explain to employees why they have been asked to attend training.
Give employees feedback related to skills or behavior they are trying to develop.

Table 7.2

What Managers Should Do to Support Training

SOURCE: Based on A. Rossett, "That Was a Great Class, but …" *Training and Development*, July 1997, p. 21.

sets up online "communities of practice," where geologists, physicists, managers, engineers, and other employees around the world can trade knowledge to solve problems.[10] Another way to encourage peer support is for the human resource department or others to publish a newsletter with articles relevant to training, perhaps including interviews with employees who successfully applied new skills. Finally, the organization can assign experienced employees as mentors to trainees, providing advice and support.

Planning the Training Program

LO4 Describe how to plan an effective training program.

Decisions about training are often the responsibility of a specialist in the organization's training or human resources department. When the needs assessment indicates a need for training and employees are ready to learn, the person responsible for training should plan a training program that directly relates to the needs identified. Planning begins with establishing objectives for the training program. Based on those objectives, the planner decides who will provide the training, what topics the training will cover, what training methods to use, and how to evaluate the training.

Objectives of the Program

Formally establishing objectives for the training program has several benefits. First, a training program based on clear objectives will be more focused and more likely to succeed. In addition, when trainers know the objectives, they can communicate them to the employees participating in the program. Employees learn best when they know what the training is supposed to accomplish. Finally, down the road, establishing objectives provides a basis for measuring whether the program succeeded, as we will discuss later in this chapter.

Effective training objectives have several characteristics:

- They include a statement of what the employee is expected to do, the quality or level of performance that is acceptable, and the conditions under which the employee is to apply what he or she learned (for instance, physical conditions, mental stresses, or equipment failure).[11]
- They include performance standards that are measurable.
- They identify the resources needed to carry out the desired performance or outcome. Successful training requires employees to learn but also employers to provide the necessary resources.

A related issue at the outset is who will participate in the training program. Some training programs are developed for all employees of the organization or all members of a team. Other training programs identify individuals who lack desirable skills or have potential to be promoted, then provide training in the areas of need that are identified for the particular employees. When deciding whom to include in training, the organization has to avoid illegal discrimination. The organization should not—intentionally or unintentionally—exclude members of protected groups, such as women, minorities, and older employees. During the training, all participants should receive equal treatment, such as equal opportunities for practice. In addition, the training program should provide reasonable accommodation for trainees with disabilities. The kinds of accommodations that are appropriate will vary according to

Many Companies Outsource Training Tasks

A recent survey of U.S.-based corporations found that over half were outsourcing the instruction of training courses. Four out of ten said they used outside experts to create custom content.

Source: "Training 2009 Industry Report," *Training,* November/December 2009, pp. 32–36.

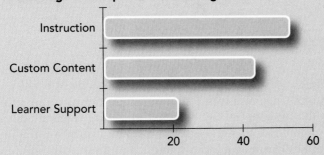

Percentage of Companies Outsourcing Task

the type of training and type of disability. One employee might need an interpreter, whereas another might need to have classroom instruction provided in a location accessible to wheelchairs.

In-House or Contracted Out?

An organization can provide an effective training program, even if it lacks expertise in training. As shown in the "Did You Know?" box, many organizations use outside experts to develop and instruct training courses. Many companies and consultants provide training services to organizations. Community colleges often work with employers to train employees in a variety of skills.

To select a training service, an organization can mail several vendors a *request for proposal (RFP)*, which is a document outlining the type of service needed, the type and number of references needed, the number of employees to be trained, the date by which the training is to be completed, and the date by which proposals should be received. A complete RFP also indicates funding for the project and the process by which the organization will determine its level of satisfaction. Putting together a request for proposal is time consuming but worthwhile because it helps the organization clarify its objectives, compare vendors, and measure results.

Vendors that believe they are able to provide the services outlined in the RFP submit proposals that provide the types of information requested. The organization reviews the proposals to eliminate any vendors that do not meet requirements and to compare the vendors that do qualify. They check references and select a candidate, based on the proposal and the vendor's answers to questions about its experience, work samples, and evidence that its training programs meet objectives.

The cost of purchasing training from a contractor can vary substantially. In general, it is much costlier to purchase specialized training that is tailored to the organization's unique requirements than to participate in a seminar or training course that teaches general skills or knowledge. Preparing a specialized training program can require a significant investment of time for material the consultant won't be able to sell to other clients. Not surprisingly then, in tight economic times, companies have been shrinking the proportion of their training dollars spent on programs prepared by contractors. This has helped them lower the cost per hour of their training programs.[12]

Even in organizations that send employees to outside training programs, someone in the organization may be responsible for coordinating the overall training program. Called *training administration*, this is typically the responsibility of a human resources professional. Training administration includes activities before, during, and after training sessions.

Choice of Training Methods

Whether the organization prepares its own training programs or buys training from other organizations, it is important to verify that the content of the training relates directly to the training objectives. Relevance to the organization's needs and objectives ensures that training money is well spent. Tying training content closely to objectives also improves trainees' learning, because it increases the likelihood that the training will be meaningful and helpful.

After deciding on the goals and content of the training program, planners must decide how the training will be conducted. As we will describe in the next section, a wide variety of methods is available. Training methods fall into the broad categories described in Table 7.3: presentation, hands-on, and group-building methods.

Training programs may use these methods alone or in combination. In general, the methods used should be suitable for the course content and the learning abilities of the participants. The following section explores the options in greater detail.

LO5 Compare widely used training methods.

Training Methods

A wide variety of methods is available for conducting training. Figure 7.2 shows the percentage of learner hours delivered to employees by each of several methods: instructor-led classrooms, online self-study, virtual classrooms, and other methods, including workbooks and videos. These other methods are being phased out at most companies as more and more training moves to Internet applications. As a result, today most training programs are taking place in a virtual or face-to-face classroom or using a combination of instructor-led and technology-based methods (blended methods).[13]

Table 7.3

Categories of Training Methods

METHOD	TECHNIQUES	APPLICATIONS
Presentation methods: trainees receive information provided by others	Lectures, workbooks, CD-ROMs, DVDs, podcasts, Web sites	Conveying facts or comparing alternatives
Hands-on methods: trainees are actively involved in trying out skills	On-the-job training, simulations, role-plays, computer games	Teaching specific skills; showing how skills are related to job or how to handle interpersonal issues
Group-building methods: trainees share ideas and experiences, build group identities, learn about interpersonal relationships and the group	Group discussions, experiential programs, team training	Establishing teams or work groups; managing performance of teams or work groups

Percentage of Student Hours Delivered by Each Training Method

- Instructor-Led Classroom
- Blended (Combination of Methods)
- Online or Computer-Based
- Virtual Classroom/Webcast
- Social Network or Mobile

Figure 7.2

Use of Instructional Methods

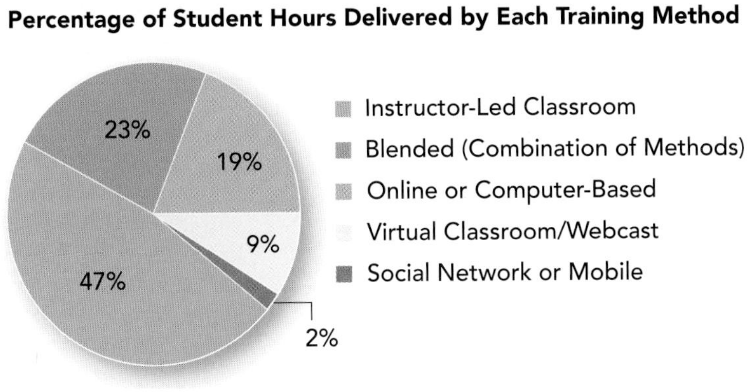

SOURCE: "*Training* 2009 Industry Report," *Training*, November/December 2009, pp. 32–36.

Classroom Instruction

At school, we tend to associate learning with classroom instruction, and that type of training is most widely used in the workplace, too. Classroom instruction typically involves a trainer lecturing a group. Trainers often supplement lectures with slides, discussions, case studies, question-and-answer sessions, and role playing. Actively involving trainees enhances learning.

When the course objectives call for presenting information on a specific topic to many trainees, classroom instruction is one of the least expensive and least time-consuming ways to accomplish that goal. Learning will be more effective if trainers enhance lectures with job-related examples and opportunities for hands-on learning. For more ideas on creating presentations that meet course objectives, see the "HR How To" box.

Modern technology has expanded the notion of the classroom to classes of trainees scattered in various locations. With *distance learning*, trainees at different locations attend programs online, using their computers to view lectures, participate in discussions, and share documents. Technology applications in distance learning may include videoconferencing, e-mail, instant messaging, document-sharing software, and Web cameras. General Mills uses these virtual classrooms at its smaller facilities, where offering a class on site is not cost-effective. Employees can sign up for online courses about specific products, general technical skills, and work functions such as maintenance procedures.[14]

Distance learning provides many of the benefits of classroom training without the cost and time of travel to a shared classroom. The major disadvantage of distance learning is that interaction between the trainer and audience may be limited. To overcome this hurdle, distance learning usually provides a communications link between trainees and trainer. Also, on-site instructors or facilitators should be available to answer questions and moderate question-and-answer sessions.

Audiovisual Training

Presentation methods need not require trainees to attend a class. Trainees can also work independently, using course material prepared on CDs and DVDs or in workbooks. Audiovisual techniques such as overhead transparencies, PowerPoint or other presentation software, and videos or audio clips can also supplement classroom instruction.

DEVELOPING EFFECTIVE CLASSROOM PRESENTATIONS

What separates a boring lecture from an attention-grabbing presentation that helps you learn? Here are some ideas for developing a classroom presentation that gets results:

- *Build rapport and two-way communication from the very beginning.* As participants arrive, introduce yourself, learn names, and show you're interested in the people who are there. Lead off with a question that invites discussion.
- *Remember the real purpose.* The presentation should cover knowledge and skills participants can apply at work, not just facts for them to memorize. As you consider what to include, imagine participants hearing you and asking, "So what? How can I use this?" Then tailor the presentation to answer those questions.
- *Use PowerPoint thoughtfully.* It's easy to write a list of key points, but that doesn't take advantage of the major strength of presentation

software: the chance to convey ideas visually. Before you opt for bullet points, think about ways to interest the audience with a photograph or drive a point home with a graph. For example, one of the first slides could be a flow chart showing how the ideas in the presentation are related to each other and to the objectives for the course. As the presentation progresses, you can provide additional images to illustrate which part of the flow you're covering. At the end, another graph (a "concept map") could show relationships among the pieces of knowledge, relating them to each other and to participants' real-world applications.

- *Use multimedia as appropriate.* If you can embed relevant music, video clips, or other media into your presentation, the effort can engage participants more fully than just words on a screen.
- *Invite discussion.* The use of discussions helps participants

take the general ideas and apply them to their specific situations. When they get involved in this way, participants not only are more likely to remember what they learned, they also are in a stronger position to *use* what they learned. If participants don't have questions, the presenter should have some ready—even as simple as a pop quiz about what was just covered.

- *Introduce role playing.* If the topic involves ways that people interact, a role-play is an excellent way for you to demonstrate and for the participants to practice the skills being taught.

Sources: Carmine Gallo, "Improve Your Employee Training Sessions," *BusinessWeek,* February 2, 2010, http://www.businessweek.com; Emanuel Albu, "Presenting Course Outlines in a Flow Chart Format," *T&D,* February 2010, pp. 76–77; and Mark Magnacca, "Do You Have a 'So What' Mindset?" *T&D,* November 2009, pp. 66–67.

Some technologies make audiovisual training available as podcasts on portable devices such as PDAs and iPods or other portable audio players. As video-enabled devices become more widespread, the use of video files is likely to grow. At Capital One, employees enrolled in training courses receive iPods. They can download programs on topics such as leadership, conflict management, and customer service. To make the audio programs more engaging, some are written in the format of a radio call-in show. In classroom programs, role-play and other exercises are recorded and then made available for download to trainees' iPods.[15] Challenges of using podcasts for learning include ensuring that employees know when and how to use the technology, encouraging collaboration and interaction among trainees, and ensuring that employees can obtain the necessary downloads from their particular location and with their mobile device.[16]

Users of audiovisual training often have some control over the presentation. They can review material and may be able to slow down or speed up the lesson. Videos can show situations and equipment that cannot be easily demonstrated in a classroom. Another advantage of audiovisual presentations is that they give trainees a consistent presentation, not affected by an individual trainer's goals and skills. The problems associated with these methods may include their trying to present too much material, poorly written dialogue, overuse of features such as humor or music, and drama that distracts from the key points. A well-written and carefully produced video can overcome these problems.

Computer-Based Training

Although almost all organizations use classroom training, new technologies are gaining in popularity as technology improves and becomes cheaper. With computer-based training, participants receive course materials and instruction distributed over the Internet or on CD-ROM. Often, these materials are interactive, so participants can answer questions and try out techniques, with course materials adjusted according to participants' responses. Online training programs may allow trainees to submit questions via e-mail and to participate in online discussions. Multimedia capabilities enable computers to provide sounds, images, and video presentations, along with text.

Mobile technology is useful not only for entertainment, but can also be used for employees who travel and need to be in touch with the office. iPods and Smartphones also give employees the ability to listen to and participate in training programs at their own leisure.

Computer-based training is generally less expensive than putting an instructor in a classroom of trainees.[17] The low cost to deliver information gives the company flexibility in scheduling training, so that it can fit around work requirements. Training can be delivered in smaller doses, so material is easier to remember. Trainees often appreciate the multimedia capabilities, which appeal to several senses, and the chance to learn from experts anywhere in the world. Finally, it is easier to customize computer-based training for individual learners.

Current applications of computer-based training can extend its benefits:

- **E-learning** involves receiving training via the Internet or the organization's intranet, typically through some combination of Web-based training modules, distance learning, and virtual classrooms. E-learning uses electronic networks for delivering and sharing information, and it offers tools and information for helping trainees improve performance. Training programs may include links to other online information resources and to trainees and experts for collaboration on problem solving. The e-learning system may also process enrollments, test and evaluate participants, and monitor progress. Ritz Camera Centers uses e-learning to build selling skills and keep employees up-to-date on product information. With employees widely dispersed among its stores and working different hours, e-learning makes training available to everyone and verifies (through online quizzes at the end of each module) that employees are learning.[18]

  E-Learning
  Receiving training via the Internet or the organization's intranet.

- *Electronic performance support systems (EPSSs)* provide access to skills training, information, and expert advice when a problem occurs on the job.[19] As employees need to learn new skills, they can use the EPSS, which gives them access to the particular information they need, such as detailed instructions on how to perform an unfamiliar task. Using an EPSS is faster and more relevant than attending classes, even classes offered online.

TRAINING GETS MOBILE

Just as the widespread adoption of personal computers brought training to employees' desks, now the greater capabilities of wireless devices are bringing training pretty much anywhere employees can get a signal on their cell phone or PDA. Content can include anything these devices can download: alerts, study aids, audio and video clips, and interactive practices and tests.

For Allison Hickey, director and program manager of consultant Accenture's national security services practices, receiving training on her BlackBerry is huge.

Juggling work and family responsibilities, Hickey had struggled to carve out time to sit down at a computer and complete a training module. The mobile training divides training programs into handy ten-minute chunks that Accenture executives can squeeze in when they step out for a lunch break or while waiting for a boarding call at the airport. At the end of each course is a quiz that participants complete and transmit back to Accenture's learning management system to verify they have learned the mandatory lessons.

Users of mobile learning praise the approach. Employees love the convenience. Merrill Lynch says participants in its mobile learning program complete their courses faster than through traditional e-learning, boosting their personal productivity by saving hours of training time every year.

Sources: Sarah Boehle, "Mobile Training: Don't Leave Home without Your BlackBerry," *Training*, September 21, 2009, Business & Company Resource Center, http://galenet.galegroup.com; and Judy Brown, "Can You Hear Me Now?" *T&D*, February 2010, Business & Company Resource Center, http://galenet.galegroup.com.

The best e-learning combines the advantages of the Internet with the principles of a good learning environment. It takes advantage of the Web's dynamic nature and ability to use many positive learning features, including hyperlinks to other training sites and content, control by the trainee, and ability for trainees to collaborate.

On-the-Job Training

On-the-job Training (OJT)
Training methods in which a person with job experience and skill guides trainees in practicing job skills at the workplace.

Apprenticeship
A work-study training method that teaches job skills through a combination of on-the-job training and classroom training.

Although people often associate training with classrooms, much learning occurs while employees are performing their jobs. **On-the-job training (OJT)** refers to training methods in which a person with job experience and skill guides trainees in practicing job skills at the workplace. This type of training takes various forms, including apprenticeships and internships.

An **apprenticeship** is a work-study training method that teaches job skills through a combination of structured on-the-job training and classroom training. The OJT component of an apprenticeship involves the apprentice assisting a certified tradesperson (a journeyman) at the work site. Typically, the classroom training is provided by local trade schools, high schools, and community colleges. Government requirements for an apprenticeship program vary by occupation, but programs generally range from one to six years, with each year including 2,000 hours of on-the-job training plus at least 144 hours of classroom instruction.[20] Some apprenticeship programs are sponsored by individual companies, others by employee unions. As shown in the left column of Table 7.4, most apprenticeship programs are in the skilled trades, such as plumbing, carpentry, and electrical work. For trainees, a major advantage of apprenticeship is the ability to earn an income while learning a trade. In addition, training through an apprenticeship is usually effective because it involves hands-on learning and extensive practice. At its manufacturing facility in Toledo, Ohio, Libbey

APPRENTICESHIP	INTERNSHIP
Bricklayer	Accountant
Carpenter	Doctor
Electrician	Journalist
Plumber	Lawyer
Printer	Nurse
Welder	

Table 7.4

Typical Jobs for Apprentices and Interns

Glass has apprenticeship programs in mold making, machine repair, millwrighting, and maintenance repair.[21] The program develops employees who are open to change, enables Libbey to use employees rather than outsource work, helps the company attract ambitious workers, and lets the company tailor training and work experiences to meet its specific needs.

An **internship** is on-the-job learning sponsored by an educational institution as a component of an academic program. The sponsoring school works with local employers to place students in positions where they can gain experience related to their area of study. For example, Indiana University–Purdue University Fort Wayne (IPFW) has partnered with Sweetwater Sound to expand IPFW's music technology program. Sweetwater, which combines recording services at its headquarters with a giant music retailing business, offers internships to juniors and seniors in the music technology program. In addition, IPFW and Sweetwater share facilities, and experts from Sweetwater serve as adjunct professors, teaching film scoring, recording arts, and other courses.[22] Many internships prepare students for professions such as those listed in the right column of Table 7.4.

Internship
On-the-job learning sponsored by an educational institution as a component of an academic program.

To be effective, OJT programs should include several characteristics:

- The organization should issue a policy statement describing the purpose of OJT and emphasizing the organization's support for it.
- The organization should specify who is accountable for conducting OJT. This accountability should be included in the relevant job descriptions.
- The organization should review OJT practices at companies in similar industries.
- Managers and peers should be trained in OJT principles.
- Employees who conduct OJT should have access to lesson plans, checklists, procedure manuals, training manuals, learning contracts, and progress report forms.
- Before conducting OJT with an employee, the organization should assess the employee's level of basic skills.[23]

Simulations

A **simulation** is a training method that represents a real-life situation, with trainees making decisions resulting in outcomes that mirror what would happen on the job. Simulations enable trainees to see the impact of their decisions in an artificial, risk-free environment. They are used for teaching production and process skills as well as management and interpersonal skills. Simulations used in training include call centers stocked with phones and reference materials, as well as mockups of houses used for training cable installers.

Simulators must have elements identical to those found in the work environment. The simulator needs to respond exactly as equipment would under the conditions and

Simulation
A training method that represents a real-life situation, with trainees making decisions resulting in outcomes that mirror what would happen on the job.

response given by the trainee. For this reason, simulators are expensive to develop and need constant updating as new information about the work environment becomes available. Still, they are an excellent training method when the risks of a mistake on the job are great. Trainees do not have to be afraid of the impact of wrong decisions when using the simulator, as they would be with on-the-job training. Also, trainees tend to be enthusiastic about this type of learning and to learn quickly, and the lessons are generally related very closely to job performance. Given these benefits, this training method is likely to become more widespread as its development costs fall into a range more companies can afford.[24]

Avatars
Computer depictions of trainees, which the trainees manipulate in an online role-play.

When simulations are conducted online, trainees often participate by creating **avatars,** or computer depictions of themselves, which they manipulate onscreen to play roles as workers or other participants in a job-related situation. Stapoil, a Norwegian oil company, has an oil platform in Second Life that allows trainees' avatars to walk around it. Stapoil uses the oil platform for safety training. It catches fire, and employees have to find lifeboats to exit the platform safely.[25]

Virtual Reality
A computer-based technology that provides an interactive, three-dimensional learning experience.

Virtual reality is a computer-based technology that provides an interactive, three-dimensional learning experience. Using specialized equipment or viewing the virtual model on a computer screen, trainees move through the simulated environment and interact with its components. Devices relay information from the environment to the trainees' senses. For example, audio interfaces, gloves that provide a sense of touch, treadmills, or motion platforms create a realistic but artificial environment. Devices also communicate information about the trainee's movements to a computer.

focus on
social
responsibility

Virtual reality applications are as diverse as surgery and welding.[26] In the simulated environment being constructed at the Jump Trading Simulation and Conference Education Center at OSF Saint Francis Medical Center in Peoria, Illinois, doctors will manipulate computerized surgical instruments as they practice new procedures on mannequins. In industry, students learning to weld can practice with a virtual welding system called VRTEX 360, which uses monitors on a virtual welding gun and helmet to gather data for feedback after training exercises are complete. The VRTEX 360 not only offers a safe and economical alternative to real welding projects, but it also is eco-friendly, because it reduces consumption of electricity and welding materials.

Business Games and Case Studies

Training programs use business games and case studies to develop employees' management skills. A case study is a detailed description of a situation that trainees study and discuss. Cases are designed to develop higher-order thinking skills, such as the ability to analyze and evaluate information. They also can be a safe way to encourage trainees to take appropriate risks, by giving them practice in weighing and acting on uncertain outcomes. There are many sources of case studies, including Harvard Business School, the Darden Business School at the University of Virginia, and McGraw-Hill publishing company.

With business games, trainees gather information, analyze it, and make decisions that influence the outcome of the game. For instance, managers at NetApp participated in a game where they assumed the roles of the top executives of an imaginary company (modeled after NetApp). Five-person teams competed to produce the greatest sales and profits as the game presented them with one challenge after another. At the end of the simulation, the participants discussed the impact of the decisions they had made along the way.[27] Games stimulate learning because they actively involve participants and mimic the competitive nature of business. A realistic game may be more meaningful to trainees than presentation techniques such as classroom instruction.

Training with case studies and games requires that participants come together to discuss the cases or the progress of the game. This requires face-to-face or electronic meetings. Also, participants must be willing to be actively involved in analyzing the situation and defending their decisions.

Behavior Modeling

Research suggests that one of the most effective ways to teach interpersonal skills is through behavior modeling.[28] This involves training sessions in which participants observe other people demonstrating the desired behavior, then have opportunities to practice the behavior themselves. For example, a training program could involve several days of four-hour sessions, each focusing on one interpersonal skill, such as communicating or coaching. At the beginning of each session, participants hear the reasons for using the key behaviors; then they watch a video of a model performing the key behaviors. They practice through role-playing and receive feedback about their performance. In addition, they evaluate the performance of the model in the video and discuss how they can apply the behavior on the job.

Experiential Programs

To develop teamwork and leadership skills, some organizations enroll their employees in a form of training called **experiential programs.** In experiential programs, participants learn concepts and then apply them by simulating the behaviors involved and analyzing the activity, connecting it with real-life situations.[29] In France, some businesses are signing up their managers to attend cooking schools, where they whip up a gourmet meal together. Jacques Bally, who works for a school run by one of France's top chefs, says cooking is a great way to learn teamwork: "It's like in any squad, everyone is responsible for playing their part; they have their own tasks but a common objective—and if they want to eat in the end, then they have to get the meal ready."[30]

Experiential training programs should follow several guidelines. A program should be related to a specific business problem. Participants should feel challenged and move outside their comfort zones but within limits that keep their motivation strong and help them understand the purpose of the program.

One form of experiential program, called **adventure learning,** uses challenging, structured outdoor activities, which may include difficult sports such as dogsledding or mountain climbing. Other activities may be structured tasks like climbing walls, completing rope courses, climbing ladders, or making "trust falls" (in which each trainee stands on a table and falls backward into the arms of other group members).

The impact of adventure learning programs has not been rigorously tested, but participants report they gained a greater understanding of themselves and the ways they interact with their co-workers. One key to the success of such programs may be that the organization insist that entire work groups participate together. This encourages people to see, discuss, and correct the kinds of behavior that keep the group from performing well. The "HR Oops!" box shows one potential limitation of adventure learning.

Experiential Programs
Training programs in which participants learn concepts and apply them by simulating behaviors involved and analyzing the activity, connecting it with real-life situations.

Adventure Learning
A teamwork and leadership training program based on the use of challenging, structured outdoor activities.

One of the most important features of organizations today is teamwork. Experiential programs include team-building exercises like wall climbing and rafting to help build trust and cooperation among employees.

Before requiring employees to participate in experiential programs, the organization should consider the possible drawbacks. Because these programs are usually physically demanding and often require participants to touch each other, companies face certain risks. Some employees may be injured or may feel that they were sexually harassed or that their privacy was invaded. Also, the Americans with Disabilities Act (discussed in Chapter 3) raises questions about requiring employees with disabilities to participate in physically demanding training experiences.

Team Training

Cross-Training
Team training in which team members understand and practice each other's skills so that they are prepared to step in and take another member's place.

A possible alternative to experiential programs is team training, which coordinates the performance of individuals who work together to achieve a common goal. An organization may benefit from providing such training to groups when group members must share information and group performance depends on the performance of the individual group members. Examples include the military, nuclear power plants, and commercial airlines. In those work settings, much work is performed by crews, groups, or teams. Success depends on individuals' coordinating their activities to make decisions, perhaps in dangerous situations.

Ways to conduct team training include cross-training and coordination training.[31] In **cross-training,** team members understand and practice each other's skills so that they are prepared to step in and take another member's place. In a factory, for example, production workers could be cross-trained to handle all phases of assembly. This enables the company to move them to the positions where they are most needed to complete an order on time.

Coordination Training
Team training that teaches the team how to share information and make decisions to obtain the best team performance.

Coordination training trains the team in how to share information and decisions to obtain the best team performance. This type of training is especially important for commercial aviation and surgical teams. Both of these kinds of teams must

HR Oops!

When Training Crashes

Edy Greenblatt conducts adventure training in which participants experience how a team of four people must work together to put on a performance on the flying trapeze. Everyone learns firsthand how hard it is to listen while swinging high above the ground and wondering if they'll fall.

While Greenblatt has seen her clients learn a lot about teamwork under pressure, she also has seen and heard about the limits of adventure training. She recalls that one team of trainees told her about an earlier outing with a boss whose leadership they doubted. The training exercise only reinforced their doubts.

The boss became terrified and started crying, and the team concluded, "He's the loser we thought he was."

Trainer Linda Henman doesn't even bother recommending adventure learning anymore. She says when groups would spend the morning learning teamwork skills with her, then move to a park for an afternoon of practicing teamwork through wilderness navigation, they would return complaining that the time outside had been wasted. They preferred a focus on work-related issues.

Source: Based on Holly Dolezalek, "Extreme Training," *Training*, January 20, 2010, Business & Company Resource Center, http://galenet.galegroup.com.

Questions

1. Given the criticisms of adventure learning, why do you think it remains an attractive option to some? Would you want to participate in one of these training programs? Why or why not?

2. Imagine that you are an HR manager in a company where an executive wants to sign the sales team up for adventure learning. What steps could you take to increase the likelihood that the effort will benefit the organization?

---

monitor different aspects of equipment and the environment at the same time sharing information to make the most effective decisions regarding patient care or aircraft safety and performance.

To improve the performance of its ramp employees, United Airlines arranged for them to attend Pit Instruction & Training, near Charlotte, North Carolina. The training program uses a quarter-mile racetrack and pit road to train NASCAR pit crews, but it also provides team training to companies that want their teams to work as efficiently together as a NASCAR pit crew. In United's training program, the ramp workers actually work on race cars—changing tires, filling gas tanks, and so on. The trainers take videos, time them, and deliver feedback on their performance as they face challenges such as staff shortages or a parking spot strewn with lug nuts. The goal is for the ramp workers to develop skills in organizing, communicating, and standardizing their work.[32]

Training may also target the skills needed by the teams' leaders. **Team leader training** refers to training people in the skills necessary for team leadership. For example, the training may be aimed at helping team leaders learn to resolve conflicts or coordinate activities.

Team Leader Training Training in the skills necessary for effectively leading the organization's teams.

Action Learning

Another form of group building is **action learning.** In this type of training, teams or work groups get an actual problem, work on solving it and commit to an action plan, and are accountable for carrying out the plan.[33] Ideally, the project is one for which the efforts and results will be visible not only to participants but also to others

Action Learning Training in which teams get an actual problem, work on solving it and commit to an action plan, and are accountable for carrying it out.

in the organization. The visibility and impact of the task are intended to make participation exciting, relevant, and engaging. At General Electric, action learning has included projects aimed at analyzing the market potential of various countries with fast-developing markets. To heighten the learning, organizations can get their best leaders involved as mentors and coaches to the participants.

The effectiveness of action learning has not been formally evaluated. This type of training seems to result in a great deal of learning, however, and employees are able to apply what they learn because action learning involves actual problems the organization is facing. The group approach also helps teams identify behaviors that interfere with problem solving.

LO6 Summarize how to implement a successful training program.

Implementing the Training Program: Principles of Learning

Learning permanently changes behavior. For employees to acquire knowledge and skills in the training program and apply what they have learned in their jobs, the training program must be implemented in a way that applies what we know about how people learn. Researchers have identified a number of ways employees learn best.[34] Table 7.5 summarizes ways that training can best encourage learning. In general, effective training communicates learning objectives clearly, presents information in distinctive and memorable ways, and helps trainees link the subject matter to their jobs.

Employees are most likely to learn when training is linked to their current job experiences and tasks.[35] There are a number of ways trainers can make this link. Training sessions should present material using familiar concepts, terms, and examples. As far as possible, the training context—such as the physical setting or the images presented on a computer—should mirror the work environment. Along with physical elements, the context should include emotional elements. In the earlier example of training store personnel to handle upset customers, the physical context is more relevant if it includes trainees acting out scenarios of personnel dealing with unhappy customers. The role-play interaction between trainees adds emotional realism and further enhances learning.

To fully understand and remember the content of the training, employees need a chance to demonstrate and practice what they have learned. Trainers should provide ways to actively involve the trainees, have them practice repeatedly, and have them complete tasks within a time that is appropriate in light of the learning objectives. Practice requires physically carrying out the desired behaviors, not just describing them. Practice sessions could include role-playing interactions, filling out relevant forms, or operating machinery or equipment to be used on the job. The more the trainee practices these activities, the more comfortable he or she will be in applying the skills on the job. People tend to benefit most from practice that occurs over several sessions, rather than one long practice session.[36] For complex tasks, it may be most effective to practice a few skills or behaviors at a time, then combine them in later practice sessions.

Trainees need to understand whether or not they are succeeding. Therefore, training sessions should offer feedback. Effective feedback focuses on specific behaviors and is delivered as soon as possible after the trainees practice or demonstrate what they have learned.[37] One way to do this is to videotape trainees, then show the video while indicating specific behaviors that do or do not match the desired outcomes of

Table 7.5

Ways That Training Helps Employees Learn

TRAINING ACTIVITY	WAYS TO PROVIDE TRAINING ACTIVITY
Communicate the learning objective.	Demonstrate the performance to be expected. Give examples of questions to be answered.
Use distinctive, attention-getting messages.	Emphasize key points. Use pictures, not just words.
Limit the content of training.	Group lengthy material into chunks. Provide a visual image of the course material. Provide opportunities to repeat and practice material.
Guide trainees as they learn.	Use words as reminders about sequence of activities. Use words and pictures to relate concepts to one another and to their context. Prompt trainees to evaluate whether they understand and are using effective tactics to learn the material.
Elaborate on the subject.	Present the material in different contexts and settings. Relate new ideas to previously learned concepts. Practice in a variety of contexts and settings.
Provide memory cues.	Suggest memory aids. Use familiar sounds or rhymes as memory cues.
Transfer course content to the workplace.	Design the learning environment so that it has elements in common with the workplace. Require learners to develop action plans that apply training content to their jobs. Use words that link the course to the workplace.
Provide feedback about performance.	Tell trainees how accurately and quickly they are performing their new skill. Show how trainees have met the objectives of the training.

SOURCES: Adapted from R. M. Gagne, "Learning Processes and Instruction," *Training Research Journal 1* (1995/96), pp. 17–28; and Traci Sitzmann, "Self-Regulating Online Course Engagement," *T&D*, March 2010, Business & Company Resource Center, http://galenet.galegroup.com.

the training. Feedback should include praise when trainees show they have learned material, as well as guidance on how to improve.

Well-designed training helps people remember the content. Training programs need to break information into chunks that people can remember. Research suggests that people can attend to no more than four to five items at a time. If a concept or procedure involves more than five items, the training program should deliver information in shorter sessions or chunks.[38] Other ways to make information more memorable include presenting it with visual images and practicing some tasks enough that they become automatic.

Written materials should have an appropriate reading level. A simple way to assess **readability**—the difficulty level of written materials—is to look at the words being used and at the length of sentences. In general, it is easiest to read short sentences and simple, standard words. If training materials are too difficult to understand, several adjustments can help. The basic approach is to rewrite the material looking for ways to simplify it.

Readability
The difficulty level of written materials.

- Substitute simple, concrete words for unfamiliar or abstract words.
- Divide long sentences into two or more short sentences.
- Divide long paragraphs into two or more short paragraphs.
- Add checklists (like this one) and illustrations to clarify the text.

Figure 7.3

Measures of Training Success

Another approach is to substitute video, hands-on learning, or other nonwritten methods for some of the written material. A longer-term solution is to use tests to identify employees who need training to improve their reading levels and to provide that training first.

Measuring Results of Training

After a training program ends, or at intervals during an ongoing training program, organizations should ensure that the training is meeting objectives. The stage to prepare for evaluating a training program is when the program is being developed. Along with designing course objectives and content, the planner should identify how to measure achievement of objectives. Depending on the objectives, the evaluation can use one or more of the measures shown in Figure 7.3: trainee satisfaction with the program, knowledge or abilities gained, use of new skills and behavior on the job (transfer of training), and improvements in individual and organizational performance. The usual way to measure whether participants have acquired information is to administer tests on paper or electronically. Trainers or supervisors can observe whether participants demonstrate the desired skills and behaviors. Surveys measure changes in attitude. Changes in company performance have a variety of measures, many of which organizations keep track of for preparing performance appraisals, annual reports, and other routine documents in order to demonstrate the final measure of success shown in Figure 7.3: return on investment.

Evaluation Methods

Transfer of Training
On-the-job use of knowledge, skills, and behaviors learned in training.

Evaluation of training should look for **transfer of training,** or on-the-job use of knowledge, skills, and behaviors learned in training. Transfer of training requires that employees actually learn the content of the training program and that the necessary conditions are in place for employees to apply what they learned. Thus, the assessment can look at whether employees have an opportunity to perform the skills related to the training. The organization can measure this by asking employees three questions about specific training-related tasks:

1. Do you perform the task?
2. How many times do you perform the task?
3. To what extent do you perform difficult and challenging learned tasks?

Frequent performance of difficult training-related tasks would signal great opportunity to perform. If there is low opportunity to perform, the organization should conduct further needs assessment and reevaluate readiness to learn. Perhaps the organization does not fully support the training activities in general or the employee's supervisor does not provide opportunities to apply new skills. Lack of transfer can also mean that employees have not learned the course material. The organization might offer a refresher course to give trainees more practice. Another reason for poor transfer of training is that the content of the training may not be important for the employee's job.

Assessment of training also should evaluate training *outcomes*, that is, what (if anything) has changed as a result of the training. The relevant training outcomes are the ones related to the organization's goals for the training and its overall performance. Possible outcomes include the following:

- Information such as facts, techniques, and procedures that trainees can recall after the training.
- Skills that trainees can demonstrate in tests or on the job.
- Trainee and supervisor satisfaction with the training program.
- Changes in attitude related to the content of the training (for example, concern for safety or tolerance of diversity).
- Improvements in individual, group, or company performance (for example, greater customer satisfaction, more sales, fewer defects).

Training is a significant part of many organizations' budgets. Therefore, economic measures are an important way to evaluate the success of a training program. Businesses that invest in training want to achieve a high *return on investment*—the monetary benefits of the investment compared to the amount invested, expressed as a percentage. For example, IBM's e-learning program for new managers, Basic Blue, costs $8,708 per manager.[39] The company has measured an improvement in each new manager's performance worth $415,000. That gives IBM a benefit of $415,000 − $8,708 = $406,292 for each manager. This is an extremely large return on investment: $406,292/$8,708 = 46.65, or 4,665 percent! In other words, for every $1 IBM invests in Basic Blue, it receives almost $47.

For any of these methods, the most accurate but most costly way to evaluate the training program is to measure performance, knowledge, or attitudes among all employees before the training and then train only part of the employees. After the training is complete, the performance, knowledge, or attitudes are again measured, and the trained group is compared with the untrained group. A simpler but less accurate way to assess the training is to conduct the pretest and posttest on all trainees, comparing their performance, knowledge, or attitudes before and after the training. This form of measurement does not rule out the possibility that change resulted from something other than training (for example, a change in the compensation system). The simplest approach is to use only a posttest. Use of only a posttest can show if trainees have reached a specified level of competency, knowledge, or skill. Of course, this type of measurement does not enable accurate comparisons, but it may be sufficient, depending on the cost and purpose of the training.

Applying the Evaluation

The purpose of evaluating training is to help with future decisions about the organization's training programs. Using the evaluation, the organization may identify a need to modify the training and gain information about the kinds of changes needed. The organization may decide to expand on successful areas of training and cut back on training that has not delivered significant benefits.

At the Mayo Clinic, evaluation of training for new managers helped the organization select the most cost-effective method. Mayo had determined that new managers needed training in management skills. Coaching would be more expensive than classes, but would it be more effective? The organization tried both forms of training with two test groups of managers. Then it assessed trainees' satisfaction with the program and the managers' knowledge and performance after the program. There was no statistically significant difference in these measures between the two groups, so Mayo decided to proceed with the less costly method, classroom training.[40]

LO8 Describe training methods for employee orientation and diversity management.

Applications of Training

Two training applications that have become widespread among U.S. companies are orientation of new employees and training in how to manage workforce diversity.

Orientation of New Employees

Orientation
Training designed to prepare employees to perform their jobs effectively, learn about their organization, and establish work relationships.

Many employees receive their first training during their first days on the job. This training is the organization's **orientation** program—its training designed to prepare employees to perform their job effectively, learn about the organization, and establish work relationships. Organizations provide for orientation because, no matter how realistic the information provided during employment interviews and site visits, people feel shock and surprise when they start a new job.[41] Also, employees need to become familiar with job tasks and learn the details of the organization's practices, policies, and procedures.

The objectives of orientation programs include making new employees familiar with the organization's rules, policies, and procedures. Table 7.6 summarizes the content of a typical orientation program. Such a program provides information about the overall company and about the department in which the new employee will be working. The topics include social as well as technical aspects of the job. Miscellaneous information helps employees from out of town learn about the surrounding community.

At Randstad North America, a staffing services company, orientation for new staffing agents takes place over 16 weeks. To get basic facts about their job, new employees use online resources, while classroom instruction focuses on understanding the Randstad culture. District managers give presentations on the company's culture, job

Table 7.6

Content of a Typical Orientation Program

Company-level information
Company overview (e.g., values, history, mission)
Key policies and procedures
Compensation
Employee benefits and services
Safety and accident prevention
Employee and union relations
Physical facilities
Economic factors
Customer relations

Department-level information
Department functions and philosophy
Job duties and responsibilities
Policies, procedures, rules, and regulations
Performance expectations
Tour of department
Introduction to department employees

Miscellaneous
Community
Housing
Family adjustment

SOURCE: J. L. Schwarz and M. A. Weslowski, "Employee Orientation: What Employers Should Know," *Journal of Contemporary Business Issues*, Fall 1995, p. 48. Used with permission.

expectations, selling, performance, and bonus plans. Trainees shadow more experienced co-workers, and managers provide coaching. The company credits this orientation program with enabling agents to increase sales by $4 million.[42]

Orientation programs may combine various training methods such as printed and audiovisual materials, classroom instruction, on-the-job training, and e-learning. Decisions about how to conduct the orientation depend on the type of material to be covered and the number of new employees, among other factors.

Diversity Training

In response to Equal Employment Opportunity laws and market forces, many organizations today are concerned about managing diversity—creating an environment that allows all employees to contribute to organizational goals and experience personal growth. This kind of environment includes access to jobs as well as fair and positive treatment of all employees. Chapter 3 described how organizations manage diversity by complying with the law. Besides these efforts, many organizations provide training designed to teach employees attitudes and behaviors that support the management of diversity, such as appreciation of cultural differences and avoidance of behaviors that isolate or intimidate others.

Diversity Training
Training designed to change employee attitudes about diversity and/or develop skills needed to work with a diverse workforce.

Training designed to change employee attitudes about diversity and/or develop skills needed to work with a diverse workforce is called **diversity training.** These programs generally emphasize either attitude awareness and change or behavior change.

Programs that focus on attitudes have objectives to increase participants' awareness of cultural and ethnic differences, as well as differences in personal characteristics and physical characteristics (such as disabilities). These programs are based on the assumption that people who become aware of differences and their stereotypes about those differences will be able to avoid letting stereotypes influence their interactions with people. Many of these programs use video and experiential exercises to increase employees' awareness of the negative emotional and performance effects of stereotypes and resulting behaviors on members of minority groups. A risk of these programs—especially when they define diversity mainly in terms of race, ethnicity, and sex—is that they may alienate white male employees, who conclude that if the company values diversity more, it values them less.[43] Diversity training is more likely to get everyone onboard if it emphasizes respecting and valuing all the organization's employees in order to bring out the best work from everyone to open up the best opportunities for everyone.

Programs that focus on behavior aim at changing the organizational policies and individual behaviors that inhibit employees' personal growth and productivity. Sometimes these programs identify incidents that discourage employees from working up to their potential. Employees work in

Diversity training programs, like the one conducted by Harvard Pilgrim Health Care, are designed to teach employees attitudes and behaviors that support the management of diversity. Why is it important for companies to provide this type of training?

groups to discuss specific promotion opportunities or management practices that they believe were handled unfairly. Another approach starts with the assumption that all individuals differ in various ways and teaches skills for constructively handling the communication barriers, conflicts, and misunderstandings that necessarily arise when different people try to work together.[44] Trainees may be more positive about receiving this type of training than other kinds of diversity training. Finally, some organizations provide diversity training in the form of *cultural immersion*, sending employees directly into communities where they have to interact with persons from different cultures, races, and nationalities. Participants might talk with community members, work in community organizations, or learn about events that are significant to the community they visit. Pepsi addresses behavior change at the highest level of the organization. Senior executives are assigned to be sponsors for specific employee groups, including African Americans, Latinos, Asians, women, white males, women of color, disabled employees, and employees who are gay, lesbian, or transgendered. The executives are responsible for understanding the needs of their assigned group, for identifying talent, and for mentoring at least three of these employees.[45]

Although many organizations have used diversity training, few have provided programs lasting more than a day, and few have researched their long-term effectiveness.[46] The little research that exists on the subject has provided no support for a direct link between diversity programs and business success, but there is evidence that some characteristics make diversity training more effective.[47] Most important, the training should be tied to business objectives, such as understanding customers. The support and involvement of top management, and the involvement of managers at all levels, also are important. Diversity training should emphasize learning behaviors and skills, not blaming employees. Finally, the program should help employees see how they can apply their new skills on the job, deliver rewards for performance, be tied to organizational policies and practices that value diversity, and include a way to measure the success of the training.

An example of a company that gets it right is Sodexho USA, a food and facilities management company, which provides diversity training at all levels. Senior executives participate in classroom training reinforced with community involvement and mentoring relationships. They learn how valuing diversity helps the company meet business challenges, and they are assessed for meeting targets to hire and promote a diverse group of employees, as well as for participation in training, mentoring, and community outreach. Managers can participate in learning labs that address topics such as cross-cultural communications and generational differences in the workplace. Employees have opportunities to learn diversity-related skills relevant to their jobs, such as how to sell to diverse clients or how to recruit diverse employees. Significantly, Sodexho also makes an effort to measure the results of these programs. It has found, for example, that its mentoring program has made a measurable difference in the productivity and retention of female employees and employees of color.[48]

focus on
social
responsibility

thinking ethically

TRAINING EMPLOYEES TO RESPECT PRIVACY

Many employees deal with information that requires a respect for someone's privacy. Examples include employees who process data related to patients' or employees' health, clients' financial matters, and corporate secrets, such as a new product under development. Employees also need to identify appropriate boundaries with one another: for instance, when, if ever, is it OK for one employee to read another's e-mail messages without permission? The answers to such questions must meet ethical (and sometimes legal) requirements. For example, some companies have fired employees for sending e-mail that is "inappropriate" but haven't clarified for their employees how to measure appropriateness—or even that the company monitors e-mail.

To help employees identify situations requiring protection of others' privacy and to teach them how to handle those situations appropriately, some companies provide training in privacy matters. For instance, hospitals may train employees to notice, report, and prevent situations where carelessness with computers or paper makes it possible that the privacy of patients' data was compromised. Employees responsible for a company's information system need policies and guidance for identifying and communicating the boundaries between employees' privacy rights and the organization's right to know what its employees' are doing and communicating.

At Claremont Savings Bank, training in privacy begins at employee orientation. That training program includes case studies of actual situations involving customers' privacy. To reinforce those lessons, the human resource department for the New Hampshire bank uses real-world privacy examples in ongoing communications with the bank's employees. In addition, every year, Claremont's board of directors reviews and approves the bank's privacy policy, and then the HR department communicates with employees to describe any changes or areas needing reinforcement.

SOURCES: Eric Krell, "Privacy Matters," *HR Magazine*, February 2010, Business & Company Resource Center, http://galenet.galegroup.com; Jay Cline, "Privacy Training Gone Awry," *Computerworld*, February 8, 2010, Business & Company Resource Center, http://galenet.galegroup.com; and "Security: Employees Are Key," *Health Management Technology*, January 2010, Business & Company Resource Center, http://galenet.galegroup.com.

Questions

1. In general, what skills and abilities do employees need for making ethical decisions about privacy? What else to they need besides skills and abilities?
2. Suppose you became responsible for providing training in privacy at Claremont Savings Bank. Describe the training methods you think would be most effective, and explain why you chose those methods.
3. Suppose you work in a company's human resource department, and a rumor has reached you that one of the employees during her lunch hour sent out an e-mail to a few friends, describing an embarrassing but not illegal situation she had been in over the weekend. Someone from the company's IT department came to you with the news. What should be your response to this situation? Where in the company are ethical (or legal) issues that should be addressed? How will you address them?

SUMMARY

LO1 Discuss how to link training programs to organizational needs.

Organizations need to establish training programs that are effective. In other words, they teach what they are designed to teach, and they teach skills and behaviors that will help the organization achieve its goals. Organizations create such programs through instructional design. This process begins with a needs assessment. The organization then ensures readiness for training, including employee characteristics and organizational support. Next, the organization plans a training program, implements the program, and evaluates the results.

LO2 Explain how to assess the need for training.

Needs assessment consists of an organization analysis, person analysis, and task analysis. The organization analysis determines the appropriateness of training by evaluating the characteristics of the organization, including its strategy, resources, and management support. The person analysis determines individuals' needs and readiness for training. The task analysis identifies the tasks, knowledge, skills, and behaviors that training should emphasize. It is based on examination of the conditions in which tasks are performed, including equipment and environment of the job, time constraints, safety considerations, and performance standards.

LO3 Explain how to assess employees' readiness for training.

Readiness for training is a combination of employee characteristics and positive work environment that permit training. The necessary employee characteristics include ability to learn the subject matter, favorable attitudes toward the training, and motivation to learn. A positive work environment avoids situational constraints such as lack of money and time. In a positive environment, both peers and management support training.

LO4 Describe how to plan an effective training program.

Planning begins with establishing objectives for the training program. These should define an expected performance or outcome, the desired level of performance, and the conditions under which the performance should occur. Based on the objectives, the planner decides who will provide the training, what topics the training will cover, what training methods to use, and how to evaluate the training. Even when organizations purchase outside training, someone in the organization, usually a member of the HR department, often is responsible for training administration. The training methods selected should be related to the objectives and content of the training program. Training methods may include presentation methods, hands-on methods, or group-building methods.

LO5 Compare widely used training methods.

Classroom instruction is most widely used and is one of the least expensive and least time-consuming ways to present information on a specific topic to many trainees. It also allows for group interaction and may include hands-on practice. Audiovisual and computer-based training need not require that trainees attend a class, so organizations can reduce time and money spent on training. Computer-based training may be interactive and may provide for group interaction. On-the-job training methods such as apprenticeships and internships give trainees firsthand experiences. A simulation represents a real-life situation, enabling trainees to see the effects of their decisions without dangerous or expensive consequences. Business games and case studies are other methods for practicing decision-making skills. Participants need to come together in one location or collaborate online. Behavior modeling gives trainees a chance to observe desired behaviors, so this technique can be effective for teaching interpersonal skills. Experiential and adventure learning programs provide an opportunity for group members to interact in challenging circumstances but may exclude members with disabilities. Team training focuses a team on achievement of a common goal.

Action learning offers relevance, because the training focuses on an actual work-related problem.

LO6 Summarize how to implement a successful training program.

Implementation should apply principles of learning. In general, effective training communicates learning objectives, presents information in distinctive and memorable ways, and helps trainees link the subject matter to their jobs. Employees are most likely to learn when training is linked to job experiences and tasks. Employees learn best when they demonstrate or practice what they have learned and when they receive feedback that helps them improve. Trainees remember information better when it is broken into small chunks, presented with visual images, and practiced many times. Written materials should be easily readable by trainees.

LO7 Evaluate the success of a training program.

Evaluation of training should look for transfer of training by measuring whether employees are performing the tasks taught in the training program. Assessment of training also should evaluate training outcomes, such as change in attitude, ability to perform a new skill, and recall of facts or behaviors taught in the training program. Training should result in improvement in the group's or organization's outcomes, such as customer satisfaction or sales. An economic measure of training success is return on investment.

LO8 Describe training methods for employee orientation and diversity management.

Employee orientation is training designed to prepare employees to perform their job effectively, learn about the organization, and establish work relationships. Organizations provide for orientation because, no matter how realistic the information provided during employment interviews and site visits, people feel shock and surprise when they start a new job, and they need to learn the details of how to perform the job. A typical orientation program includes information about the overall company and the department in which the new employee will be working, covering social as well as technical aspects of the job. Orientation programs may combine several training methods, from printed materials to on-the-job training to e-learning. Diversity training is designed to change employee attitudes about diversity and/or develop skills needed to work with a diverse workforce. Evidence regarding these programs suggests that diversity training is most effective if it is tied to business objectives, has management support, emphasizes behaviors and skills, and is tied to organizational policies and practices that value diversity, including a way to measure success.

KEY TERMS

REVIEW AND DISCUSSION QUESTIONS

1. "Melinda!" bellowed Toran to the company's HR specialist, "I've got a problem, and you've got to solve it. I can't get people in this plant to work together as a team. As if I don't have enough trouble with our competitors and our past-due accounts, now I have to put up with running a zoo. You're responsible for seeing that the staff gets along. I want a training proposal on my desk by Monday." Assume you are Melinda.
   a. Is training the solution to this problem? How can you determine the need for training?
   b. Summarize how you would conduct a needs assessment.

2. How should an organization assess readiness for learning? In Question 1, how do Toran's comments suggest readiness (or lack of readiness) for learning?

3. Assume you are the human resource manager of a small seafood company. The general manager has told you that customers have begun complaining about the quality of your company's fresh fish. Currently, training consists of senior fish cleaners showing new employees how to perform the job. Assuming your needs assessment indicates a need for training, how would you plan a training program? What steps should you take in planning the program?

4. Many organizations turn to e-learning as a less-expensive alternative to classroom training. What are some other advantages of substituting e-learning for classroom training? What are some disadvantages?

5. Suppose the managers in your organization tend to avoid delegating projects to the people in their groups. As a result, they rarely meet their goals. A training needs analysis indicates that an appropriate solution is training in management skills. You have identified two outside training programs that are consistent with your goals. One program involves experiential programs, and the other is an interactive computer program. What are the strengths and weaknesses of each technique? Which would you choose? Why?

6. Consider your current job or a job you recently held. What types of training did you receive for the job? What types of training would you like to receive? Why?

7. A manufacturing company employs several maintenance employees. When a problem occurs with the equipment, a maintenance employee receives a description of the symptoms and is supposed to locate and fix the source of the problem. The company recently installed a new, complex electronics system. To prepare its maintenance workers, the company provided classroom training. The trainer displayed electrical drawings of system components and posed problems about the system. The trainer would point to a component in a drawing and ask, "What would happen if this component were faulty?" Trainees would study the diagrams, describe the likely symptoms, and discuss how to repair the problem. If you were responsible for this company's training, how would you evaluate the success of this training program?

8. In Question 7, suppose the maintenance supervisor has complained that trainees are having difficulty trouble-shooting problems with the new electronics system. They are spending a great deal of time on problems with the system and coming to the supervisor with frequent questions that show a lack of understanding. The supervisor is convinced that the employees are motivated to learn the system, and they are well qualified. What do you think might be the problems with the current training program?

What recommendations can you make for improving the program?

9. Who should be involved in orientation of new employees? Why would it not be appropriate to provide employee orientation purely online?

10. Why do organizations provide diversity training? What kinds of goals are most suitable for such training?

BUSINESSWEEK CASE

BusinessWeek The World Is IBM's Classroom

When 10 IBM management trainees piled into a minibus in the Philippines for a weekend tour last October, the last thing they expected was to wind up local heroes. Yet that's what happened in the tiny village of Carmen. After passing a water well project, they learned the effort had stalled because of engineering mistakes and a lack of money. The IBMers decided to do something about it. They organized a meeting of the key people involved in the project and volunteered to pay $250 out of their own pockets for additional building materials. Two weeks later the well was completed. Locals would no longer have to walk four miles for drinkable water. And the trainees learned a lesson in collaborative problem-solving. "You motivate people to take the extra step, you create a shared vision, you divide the labor, and the impact can be big," says Erwin van Overbeek, 40, who runs environmental sustainability projects for IBM clients.

While saving a village well wasn't part of the group agenda for that trip, it's the kind of experience the architects of IBM's Corporate Service Corps had in mind when they launched the initiative last year. Modeled on the U.S. Peace Corps, the program aims to turn IBM employees into global citizens. Last year, IBM selected 300 top management prospects out of 5,400 applicants. It then trained and dispatched them to emerging markets for a month in groups of 8 to 10 to help solve economic and social problems. The goal, says IBM's human resources chief, J. Randall MacDonald, is to help future leaders "understand how the world works, show them how to network, and show them how to work collaboratively with people who are far away."

Like most corporations, IBM trains managers in classrooms, so this represents a dramatic departure. And while other companies encourage employees to volunteer for social service, IBM is the first to use such programs for management training, says Rosabeth Moss Kanter, a professor at Harvard Business School.

The program is growing rapidly. This year some 500 people will participate, and the list of countries will expand from five to nine, including Brazil, India, Malaysia, and South Africa. The teams spend three months before going overseas reading about their host countries, studying the problems they're assigned to work on, and getting to know their teammates via teleconferences and social networking Web sites. On location, they work with local governments, universities, and business groups to do anything from upgrading technology for a government agency to improving public water quality.

Participating in the program is not without its risks. Charlie Ung, a new-media producer from IBM Canada, got malaria while working in Ghana and spent a week in the hospital. Other participants report encounters with wild dogs in Romania. IBM planners deliberately choose out-of-the-way places and bunk the teams in guest houses that lack such amenities as Western food and CNN. "We want them to have a transformative experience, so they're shaken up and walk away feeling they're better equipped to confront the challenges of the 21st century," says Kevin Thompson, the IBMer who conceived of the CSC program and now manages it.

IBM concedes that one month overseas is a short stint, but it believes participants can pick up valuable lessons. Debbie Maconnel, a 45-year-old IT project manager in Lexington, Kentucky, says the trip prompted her to change her management style. She coordinates the activities of 13 people in the United States and 12 in India, Mexico, and China. She used to give assignments to the overseas employees and then leave them on their own. Now she spends more time trying to build a global team.

SOURCE: Excerpted from Steve Hamm, "The World Is IBM's Classroom," *BusinessWeek*, March 12, 2009, http://www.businessweek.com.

Questions

1. Based on the information given but in your own words, what are the training objectives for IBM's Corporate Service Corps? Based on the information given, how well would you say the program is meeting those objectives? What additional measures would help you evaluate the program's success?

2. Which of the training methods described in this chapter are incorporated into the Corporate Service Corps? How well suited are these methods to achieving IBM's objectives?

3. Suggest some ways that IBM can help participants apply on the job what they have learned from their one-month service project.

Case: Jack B. Kelley Drives Home Safety Lessons

Jack B. Kelley, Inc. (JBK) is a trucking company—a common carrier that hauls bulk commodities in tanker trucks for its customers around the United States and parts of Canada. It specializes in transporting compressed gas, liquid carbon dioxide, and a variety of specialized chemicals. It can deliver them on demand or will set up a regular distribution system for repeat loads.

The company defines a three-part corporate vision of being "(1) A great place for our customers"; "(2) A great place for people to work"; and having "(3) The financial strength to accomplish 1 and 2." Especially at a company where most employees drive trucks delivering liquid and gas chemicals, it's clear that safety is important not only for being "a great place" to work but also as a basis for providing the best service to customers and maintaining financial strength. "When drivers operate safely, they take better care of their equipment," notes Mark Davis, JBK's president. And, in fact, safety records are one of the company's basic performance measures.

In support of these corporate objectives, safety training has an important place at JBK. It is the responsibility of Lee Drury, safety director at JBK, who started out with JBK as a trainer and has since put together a team of employees focused on safety.

Safety training begins as soon as the company hires new drivers. Groups of about four or five new employees meet in JBK's corporate training facility for six days of classroom training and hands-on practice.

The first session introduces a variety of topics including the company's drug-use policy, the types of commodities transported, the satellite tracking and communication system installed in the trucks, and the company's history and culture. On the afternoon of the first session, drivers climb into a 15-passenger van to practice using the company's satellite tracking system, which records and reports safety issues such as incidents of speeding or heavy braking, as well as other measures such as the amount of time the truck has been driving and idling. The trainers emphasize that the electronic reporting relieves them of paperwork and helps them become safer drivers, free to concentrate on the road.

The second day of training begins with lessons on managing driver fatigue. Then much of the remainder of the day is devoted to hands-on training in loading and unloading cryogenic liquids and compressed gases. This practice is repeated on each of the remaining days of training. The goal is that by the end of the orientation training, employees will know how to load and unload each product JBK transports for its customers.

The third day of orientation training includes a visit to corporate headquarters, where the new drivers meet employees in the billing department who will handle their paperwork. They also meet Davis, who stresses JBK's commitment to safety. Davis emphasizes that JBK's goals include "zero accidents, zero incidents, and zero personal injuries." During the remaining orientation days, the lessons on handling products are extended and reinforced with further practice. Drivers also learn how to refresh their memory on details by checking the company's online information system.

After the orientation period, JBK's drivers move to their home terminals, where each one is assigned to a driver trainer. There, training continues until the terminal manager and safety director determine that the new driver is fully prepared to work alone safely and professionally. Even then, a regional trainer rides along with the driver on at least one round trip to verify that the driver is handling the job well.

After orientation is behind them, drivers are fully prepared, but training continues to be available. The company provides refresher training to its experienced drivers, as well as the computer system where they can look up information on products they may not handle often.

SOURCES: Charles E. Wilson, "Award-Winning Safety Starts at the Top at Jack B. Kelley Inc.," *Bulk Transporter,* June 1, 2009, Business & Company Resource Center, http://galenet.galegroup.com; Charles E. Wilson, "Safety Should Be a Zero-Sum Program," *Bulk Transporter,* June 1, 2009, Business & Company Resource Center, http://galenet.galegroup.com; and Jack B. Kelley, Inc., "About Us," corporate Web site, www.jackbkelley.com, accessed March 29, 2010.

Questions

1. How is training at Jack B. Kelley related to its organizational needs?
2. If you were involved in preparing JBK's safety training program, how would you assess employees' readiness for training? In what ways can (or does) the company's work environment support the training?
3. Do you think e-learning might be an appropriate training method for JBK's drivers? Why or why not?

www.mhhe.com/noefund4e is your source for Reviewing, Applying, and Practicing the concepts you learned about in Chapter 7.

Review
- Chapter learning objectives
- Test Your Knowledge: Training Methods

Application
- Manager's Hot Seat segment: "Working in Teams: Cross-Functional Dysfunction"
- Video case and quiz: "Johnson & Johnson eUniversity"
- Self-Assessment: Evaluate Your Own Training Needs
- Web exercise: Online Learning Courses
- Small-business case: How Nick's Pizza Delivers Training Results

Practice
- Chapter quiz

NOTES

1. Kelly K. Spors, "Top Small Workplaces 2009," *Wall Street Journal,* September 28, 2009, http://online.wsj.com.

2. R. Noe, *Employee Training and Development,* 4th ed. (New York: Irwin/McGraw-Hill, 2008).

3. Ryann K. Ellis, *A Field Guide to Learning Management Systems,* Learning Circuits (American Society for Training & Development, 2009), accessed at http://www.astd.org.

4. I. L. Goldstein, E. P. Braverman, and H. Goldstein, "Needs Assessment," in *Developing Human Resources,* ed. K. N. Wexley (Washington, DC: Bureau of National Affairs, 1991), pp. 5-35–5-75.

5. J. Z. Rouillier and I. L. Goldstein, "Determinants of the Climate for Transfer of Training" (presented at Society of Industrial/Organizational Psychology meetings, St. Louis, MO, 1991); J. S. Russell, J. R. Terborg, and M. L. Powers, "Organizational Performance and Organizational Level Training and Support," *Personnel Psychology* 38 (1985), pp. 849–63; and H. Baumgartel, G. J. Sullivan, and L. E. Dunn, "How Organizational Climate and Personality Affect the Payoff from Advanced Management Training Sessions," *Kansas Business Review* 5 (1978), pp. 1–10.

6. Jill Casner-Lotto et al., *Are They Really Ready to Work?* (New York: Conference Board; Washington, DC: Corporate Voices for Working Families; Tucson, AZ: Partnership for 21st Century Skills; Alexandria, VA: Society for Human Resource Management, 2006), available at www.infoedge.com; R. Davenport, "Eliminate the Skills Gap," *T&D,* February 2006, pp. 26–34; and M. Schoeff, "Amid Calls to Bolster U.S. Innovation, Experts Lament Paucity of Basic Math Skills," *Workforce Management,* March 2006, pp. 46–49.

7. R. A. Noe, "Trainees' Attributes and Attitudes: Neglected Influences on Training Effectiveness," *Academy of Management Review* 11 (1986), pp. 736–49; T. T. Baldwin, R. T. Magjuka, and B. T. Loher, "The Perils of Participation: Effects of Choice on Trainee Motivation and Learning," *Personnel Psychology* 44 (1991), pp. 51–66; and S. I. Tannenbaum, J. E. Mathieu, E. Salas, and J. A. Cannon-Bowers, "Meeting Trainees' Expectations: The Influence of Training Fulfillment on the Development of Commitment, Self-Efficacy, and Motivation," *Journal of Applied Psychology* 76 (1991), pp. 759–69.

8. L. H. Peters, E. J. O'Connor, and J. R. Eulberg, "Situational Constraints: Sources, Consequences, and Future Considerations," in *Research in Personnel and Human Resource Management,* eds. K. M. Rowland and G. R. Ferris (Greenwich, CT: JAI Press, 1985), vol. 3, pp. 79–114; E. J. O'Connor, L. H. Peters, A. Pooyan, J. Weekley, B. Frank, and B. Erenkranz, "Situational Constraints' Effects on Performance, Affective Reactions, and Turnover: A Field Replication and Extension," *Journal of Applied Psychology* 69 (1984), pp. 663–72; D. J. Cohen, "What Motivates Trainees?" *Training and Development Journal,* November 1990, pp. 91–93; and Russell, Terborg, and Powers, "Organizational Performance."

9. J. B. Tracey, S. I. Trannenbaum, and M. J. Kavanaugh, "Applying Trade Skills on the Job: The Importance of the Work Environment," *Journal of Applied*

Psychology 80 (1995), pp. 239–52; P. E. Tesluk, J. L. Farr, J. E. Mathieu, and R. J. Vance, "Generalization of Employee Involvement Training to the Job Setting: Individuals and Situational Effects," *Personnel Psychology* 48 (1995), pp. 607–32; and J. K. Ford, M. A. Quinones, D. J. Sego, and J. S. Sorra, "Factors Affecting the Opportunity to Perform Trained Tasks on the Job," *Personnel Psychology* 45 (1992), pp. 511–27.

10. S. Allen, "Water Cooler Wisdom," *Training*, August 2005, pp. 30–34.

11. B. Mager, *Preparing Instructional Objectives*, 2nd ed. (Belmont, CA: Lake, 1984); and B. J. Smith and B. L. Delahaye, *How to Be an Effective Trainer*, 2nd ed. (New York: Wiley, 1987).

12. Andrew Paradise, "Learning Remains Steady during the Downturn," *T&D*, November 2009, pp. 44–49.

13. "*Training* 2009 Industry Report," *Training*, November/December 2009, pp. 32–36.

14. "Training Top 100 Best Practices 2006: General Mills," *Training*, March 2006, p. 61.

15. M. Weinstein, "Ready or Not, Here Comes Podcasting," *Training*, January 2006, pp. 22–23; D. Sussman, "Now Hear This," *T&D*, September 2005, pp. 53–54; and J. Pont, "Employee Training on iPod Playlist," *Workforce Management*, August 2005, p. 18.

16. E. Wagner and P. Wilson, "Disconnected," *T&D*, December 2005, pp. 40–43.

17. Gail Dutton, "Training Tech Check," *Training*, January 12, 2009, Business & Company Resource Center, http://galenet.galegroup.com.

18. S. Murphy, "Ritz Camera Focuses on Web-Based Teaching Tools," *Tech Talk Tuesday*, December 23, 2008, newsletter available at www.chainstoreage.com.

19. American Society for Training and Development, *Learning Circuits: Glossary*, http://www.astd.org/LC/glossary.htm, accessed March 26, 2010.

20. U.S. Department of Labor, Employment and Training Administration, "Registered Apprenticeship: Employers," http://www.doleta.gov, last updated January 7, 2010.

21. M. Rowh, "The Rise of the Apprentice," *Human Resource Executive*, January 2006, pp. 38–43.

22. Ashley Smith, "Sweetwater Joins IPFW for Music Tech Degree," *News-Sentinel (Fort Wayne, Ind.)*, February 19, 2010, Business & Company Resource Center, http://galenet.galegroup.com; Indiana University–Purdue University Fort Wayne, "IPFW and Sweetwater Announce New Music Technology Program," news release, February 19, 2010, www.ipfw.edu; and Sweetwater Productions Web site, http://productions.sweetwater.com, accessed March 30, 2010.

23. W. J. Rothwell and H. C. Kanzanas, "Planned OJT Is Productive OJT," *Training and Development Journal*, October 1990, pp. 53–56.

24. Matt Bolch, "Games People Play," *Training*, December 7, 2009, Business & Company Resource Center, http://galenet.galegroup.com; C. Cornell, "Better than the Real Thing?" *Human Resource Executive*, August 2005, pp. 34–37; and S. Boehle, "Simulations: The Next Generation of E-Learning," *Training*, January 2005, pp. 22–31.

25. H. Dolezalek, "Virtual Vision," *Training*, October 2007, pp. 40–46.

26. Ryan Ori, "OSF, Medical College Receive $25 Million Donation," *Journal Star (Peoria, Ill.)*, February 28, 2010, Business & Company Resource Center, http://galenet.galegroup.com; and "Welding Simulation Software Enhances Training Efforts," *Product News Network*, November 23, 2009, Business & Company Resource Center," http://galenet.galegroup.com.

27. P. Dvorak, "Theory and Practice: Simulation Shows What It Is Like to Be the Boss," *Wall Street Journal*, March 31, 2008, p. B7.

28. G. P. Latham and L. M. Saari, "Application of Social Learning Theory to Training Supervisors through Behavior Modeling," *Journal of Applied Psychology* 64 (1979), pp. 239–46.

29. D. Brown and D. Harvey, *An Experiential Approach to Organizational Development* (Englewood Cliffs, NJ: Prentice Hall, 2000); and Larissa Jõgi, review of *The Handbook of Experiential Learning and Management Education*, eds. Michael Reynolds and Russ Vince, *Studies in the Education of Adults* 40 no. 2 (Autumn 2008): pp. 232–234, accessed at OCLC FirstSearch, http://newfirstsearch.oclc.org.

30. K. Willsher, "French Firms Drop Bungee for Bouillon," *Guardian Unlimited*, February 25, 2005, www.guardian.co.uk.

31. C. Clements, R. J. Wagner, and C. C. Roland, "The Ins and Outs of Experiential Training," *Training and Development*, February 1995, pp. 52–56.

32. S. Carey, "Racing to Improve," *Wall Street Journal*, March 24, 2006, pp. B1, B6.

33. Marshall Goldsmith, "Diving Head-First into Action Learning," *BusinessWeek*, June 10, 2008, http://www.businessweek.com (interview with Chris Cappy).

34. C. E. Schneier, "Training and Development Programs: What Learning Theory and Research Have to Offer," *Personnel Journal*, April 1974, pp. 288–93; M. Knowles, "Adult Learning," in *Training and Development Handbook*, 3rd ed., ed. R. L. Craig (New York: McGraw-Hill, 1987), pp. 168–79; B. J. Smith and B. L. Delahaye, *How to Be an Effective Trainer*, 2nd ed. (New York: Wiley, 1987); and Traci Sitzmann, "Self-Regulating Online Course Engagement," *T&D*,

March 2010, Business & Company Resource Center, http://galenet.galegroup.com.

35. K. A. Smith-Jentsch, F. G. Jentsch, S. C. Payne, and E. Salas, "Can Pretraining Experiences Explain Individual Differences in Learning?" *Journal of Applied Psychology* 81 (1996), pp. 110–16.

36. W. McGehee and P. W. Thayer, *Training in Business and Industry* (New York: Wiley, 1961).

37. R. M. Gagne and K. L. Medsker, *The Condition of Learning* (Fort Worth, TX: Harcourt-Brace, 1996).

38. J. C. Naylor and G. D. Briggs, "The Effects of Task Complexity and Task Organization on the Relative Efficiency of Part and Whole Training Methods," *Journal of Experimental Psychology* 65 (1963), pp. 217–24.

39. K. Mantyla, *Blended E-Learning* (Alexandria, VA: ASTD, 2001).

40. D. Sussman, "Strong Medicine Required," *T&D*, November 2005, pp. 34–38.

41. M. R. Louis, "Surprise and Sense Making: What Newcomers Experience in Entering Unfamiliar Organizational Settings," *Administrative Science Quarterly* 25 (1980), pp. 226–51.

42. D. Sussman, "Getting Up to Speed," *T&D*, December 2005, pp. 49–51.

43. Jarik Conrad, "Don't Derail Your Diversity Training," *Employee Benefit News*, January 1, 2009, Business & Company Resource Center, http://galenet.galegroup.com; Holly Dolezalek, "The Path to Inclusion," *Training*, May 1, 2008, www.managesmarter.com; and A. Aparna, "Why Diversity Training Doesn't Work ... Right Now," *T&D*, November 2008, pp. 52–57.

44. Dolezalek, "The Path to Inclusion"; Stanley F. Slater, Robert A. Weigand, and Thomas J. Zwirlein, "The Business Case for Commitment to Diversity," *Business Horizons* 51 no. 3 (May/June 2008), OCLC FirstSearch, http://newfirstsearch.oclc.org; and Sangeeta Gupta, "Mine the Potential of Multicultural Teams," *HR Magazine*, October 2008, OCLC FirstSearch, http://newfirstsearch.oclc.org.

45. C. Terhune, "Pepsi, Vowing Diversity Isn't Just Image Polish, Seeks Inclusive Culture," *Wall Street Journal*, April 19, 2005, p. B1.

46. S. Rynes and B. Rosen, "A Field Study of Factors Affecting the Adoption and Perceived Success of Diversity Training," *Personnel Psychology* 48 (1995), pp. 247–70.

47. Conrad, "Don't Derail Your Diversity Training"; Dolezalek, "The Path to Inclusion"; and Aparna Nancherta, "Nobody's Perfect: Diversity Training Study Finds Common Flaws," *T&D*, May 2008, OCLC FirstSearch, http://newfirstsearch.oclc.org.

48. Dolezalek, "The Path to Inclusion."

Assessing Performance and Developing Employees

PART THREE

Managing Employees' Performance

What Do I Need to Know?

After reading this chapter, you should be able to:

LO1   Identify the activities involved in performance management.

LO2   Discuss the purposes of performance management systems.

LO3   Define five criteria for measuring the effectiveness of a performance management system.

LO4   Compare the major methods for measuring performance.

LO5   Describe major sources of performance information in terms of their advantages and disadvantages.

LO6   Define types of rating errors, and explain how to minimize them.

LO7   Explain how to provide performance feedback effectively.

LO8   Summarize ways to produce improvement in unsatisfactory performance.

LO9   Discuss legal and ethical issues that affect performance management.

Introduction

The Zoological Society of San Diego had a problem. Its employees often didn't know whether they were doing a good job. Even worse, the organization didn't have a consistent method to rate job performance, and managers faced no consequences if they did not give formal appraisals. To remedy the situation, the Zoological Society set up a formal system so that each employee has individual goals that are tied to the organization's objectives, such as visitor satisfaction and revenue. Managers use a Web-based computer system to rate employees on their progress in meeting goals and on specific areas of competence, such as teamwork and communications. Employees use online journals to record their accomplishments, so managers have easy access to that data. Managers must rate employees twice a year and then discuss the reports face-to-face with each employee. Employees appreciate the clear feedback—and the raises they get if they perform well.[1]

Setting goals, rating performance, and discussing performance, as the Zoological Society's managers do, are all parts of performance management. **Performance management** is the process through which managers ensure that employees' activities and outputs contribute to the organization's goals. This process requires knowing what activities and outputs are desired, observing whether they occur, and providing feedback to help employees meet expectations. In the course of providing feedback, managers and employees may identify performance problems and establish ways to resolve those problems.

In this chapter we examine a variety of approaches to performance management. We begin by describing the activities involved in managing performance, then discuss the purpose of carrying out this process. Next, we discuss specific approaches to performance management, including the strengths and weaknesses of each approach. We also look at various sources of performance information. The next section explores the kinds of errors that commonly occur during the assessment of performance, as well as ways to reduce those errors. Then we describe ways of giving performance feedback effectively and intervening when performance must improve. Finally, we summarize legal and ethical issues affecting performance management.

Performance Management
The process through which managers ensure that employees' activities and outputs contribute to the organization's goals.

The Process of Performance Management

Although many employees have come to dread the annual "performance appraisal" meeting, at which a boss picks apart the employee's behaviors and apparent attitudes from the past year, performance management can potentially deliver many benefits. Effective performance management can tell top performers that they are valued, encourage communication between managers and their employees, establish uniform standards for evaluating employees, and help the organization identify its strongest and weakest performers. Consultant Dick Grote asserts that performance appraisals, properly done, meet an "ethical obligation of leadership" by providing information that all members of an organization want to know so they can succeed: "What is it you expect of me? How am I doing at meeting your expectations?"[2]

LO1 Identify the activities involved in performance management.

To meet these objectives, performance management includes several activities. As shown in Figure 8.1, these are defining performance, measuring performance, and feeding back performance information. First, the organization specifies which aspects of performance are relevant to the organization. These decisions are based on the job analysis, described in Chapter 4. Next, the organization measures the relevant aspects of performance by conducting performance appraisals. Finally, through performance feedback sessions, managers give employees information about their performance so they can adjust their behavior to meet the organization's goals. When there are performance problems, the feedback session should include efforts to identify and resolve the underlying problems. In addition, performance feedback can come through the organization's rewards, as described in Chapter 12. Using this performance management process helps managers and employees focus on the organization's goals.

Computer software and Internet-based performance management systems are available to help managers at various stages of the performance management process. Software can help managers customize performance measurement forms. The manager uses the software to establish a set of performance standards for each job. The manager rates each employee according to the predetermined standards, and the software provides a report that compares the employee's performance to the standards and identifies the employee's strengths and weaknesses. Other software offers help with diagnosing performance problems. This type of software

Figure 8.1

Stages of the Performance Management Process

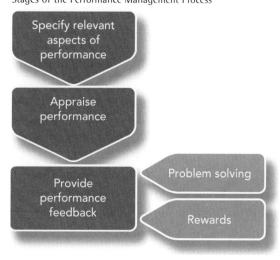

Specify relevant aspects of performance

Appraise performance

Provide performance feedback

Problem solving

Rewards

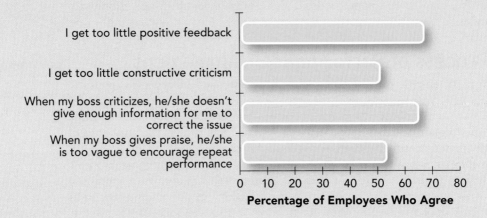
asks questions—for example, Does the employee work under time pressure? The answers suggest reasons for performance problems and ways the manager can help the employee improve.

LO2 Discuss the purposes of performance management systems.

Purposes of Performance Management

Organizations establish performance management systems to meet three broad purposes: strategic, administrative, and developmental. *Strategic purpose* means effective performance management helps the organization achieve its business objectives. It does this by helping to link employees' behavior with the organization's goals. Performance management starts with defining what the organization expects from each employee. It measures each employee's performance to identify where those expectations are and are not being met. This enables the organization to take corrective action, such as training, incentives, or discipline. Performance management can achieve its strategic purpose only when measurements are truly linked to the organization's goals and when the goals and feedback about performance are communicated to employees. Just Born, the company that makes Peeps and Mike and Ike candy, meets the strategic purpose of performance management. Its system has employees and managers meet to agree on several personal objectives through which each employee will help meet the objectives of his or her department. Together, they identify whatever training the employee needs and meet regularly to discuss the employee's progress in meeting the objectives.[3]

The *administrative purpose* of a performance management system refers to the ways in which organizations use the system to provide information for day-to-day decisions about salary, benefits, and recognition programs. Performance management can also support decision making related to employee retention, termination for poor behavior, and hiring or layoffs. Because performance management supports these administrative decisions, the information in a performance appraisal can have a great impact on the future of individual employees. Managers recognize this, which is the reason they may feel uncomfortable conducting performance appraisals when the appraisal information is negative and, therefore, likely to lead to a layoff, disappointing pay increase, or other negative outcome.

Finally, performance management has a *developmental purpose,* meaning that it serves as a basis for developing employees' knowledge and skills. Even employees who are meeting expectations can become more valuable when they hear and discuss performance feedback. Effective performance feedback makes employees aware of their strengths and of the areas in which they can improve. Discussing areas in which employees fall short can help the employees and their manager uncover the source of problems and identify steps for improvement. Although discussing weaknesses may feel uncomfortable, it is necessary when performance management has a developmental purpose.

Criteria for Effective Performance Management

LO3 Define five criteria for measuring the effectiveness of a performance management system.

In Chapter 6, we saw that there are many ways to predict performance of a job candidate. Similarly, there are many ways to measure the performance of an employee. For performance management to achieve its goals, its methods for measuring performance must be good. Selecting these measures is a critical part of planning a performance management system. Several criteria determine the effectiveness of performance measures:

- *Fit with strategy*—A performance management system should aim at achieving employee behavior and attitudes that support the organization's strategy, goals, and culture. If a company emphasizes customer service, then its performance management system should define the kinds of behavior that contribute to good customer service. Performance appraisals should measure whether employees are engaging in those behaviors. Feedback should help employees improve in those areas. When an organization's strategy changes, human resource personnel should help managers assess how the performance management system should change to serve the new strategy.
- *Validity*—As we discussed in Chapter 6, *validity* is the extent to which a measurement tool actually measures what it is intended to measure. In the case of performance appraisal, validity refers to whether the appraisal measures all the relevant aspects of performance and omits irrelevant aspects of performance. Figure 8.2 shows

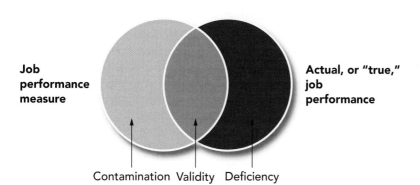

Figure 8.2

Contamination and Deficiency of a Job Performance Measure

MINING FOR GOLD: RATING EMPLOYEES WITH DATA MINING

When performance appraisals rely heavily on managers' ratings of their employees, concerns arise about whether managers' opinions are too subjective to be valid and reliable. Some companies have looked for more objective kinds of data. A few have begun applying a method called data mining—using computers to sift through massive amounts of data generated by networked computers, looking for patterns.

A relatively new idea is to look for patterns in "social networks," that is, the patterns of people that individuals interact with on a regular basis. Software collects data about employees' online interactions, such as e-mail traffic, address books, and buddy lists, and measures the amount and frequency of contacts among employees. It creates maps showing the extent to which each employee (represented by a circle) interacts (lines on the map) with each other employee. The software also looks at outcomes, such as the sales volume or billable hours produced by each employee, in order to hunt for relationships between social activity and business outcomes.

For example, a study of consultants at IBM found that those who communicate extensively with their manager produce more revenue (through billable hours) than other consultants. In contrast, if consultants have weak ties with many managers (perhaps trying to satisfy many superiors), they tend to earn less than average. Microsoft uses a similar type of analysis to identify which employees are "superconnectors," busily sharing ideas with others, and which are "bottlenecks," where information flow stops. The presumption is that the superconnectors are most valuable to the organization.

Counting worker interactions certainly is more objective than asking a manager to rate someone's communications skills. The question, of course, is whether this type of data mining is an effective performance measure. For example, is the number of e-mails a person sends and receives a valid measure of the extent of that person's communications? Will people in the organization accept it as a performance measure? And would informing employees that they are expected to send frequent electronic messages help them produce more or better-quality work?

Sources: Stephen Baker, "Putting a Price on Social Connections," *BusinessWeek,* April 8, 2009, www.businessweek.com; and Stephen Baker, "Data Mining Moves to Human Resources," *BusinessWeek,* March 12, 2009, www.businessweek.com.

two sets of information. The circle on the left represents all the information in a performance appraisal; the circle on the right represents all relevant measures of job performance. The overlap of the circles contains the valid information. Information that is gathered but irrelevant is "contamination." Comparing salespeople based on how many calls they make to customers could be a contaminated measure. Making a lot of calls does not necessarily improve sales or customer satisfaction, unless every salesperson makes only well-planned calls. Information that is not gathered but is relevant represents a deficiency of the performance measure. For example, suppose a company measures whether employees have good attendance records but not whether they work efficiently. This limited performance appraisal is unlikely to provide a full picture of employees' contribution to the company. Performance measures should minimize both contamination and deficiency.

- *Reliability*—With regard to a performance measure, reliability describes the consistency of the results that the performance measure will deliver. *Interrater reliability* is consistency of results when more than one person measures performance. Simply asking a supervisor to rate an employee's performance on a scale of 1 to 5 would likely have low interrater reliability; the rating will differ depending on who is scoring the employees. *Test-retest reliability* refers to consistency of results over time. If a performance measure lacks test-retest reliability, determining whether an employee's performance has truly changed over time will be impossible.

- *Acceptability*—Whether or not a measure is valid and reliable, it must meet the practical standard of being acceptable to the people who use it. For example, the people who use a performance measure must believe that it is not too time consuming. Likewise, if employees believe the measure is unfair, they will not use the feedback as a basis for improving their performance.
- *Specific feedback*—A performance measure should specifically tell employees what is expected of them and how they can meet those expectations. Being specific helps performance management meet the goals of supporting strategy and developing employees. If a measure does not specify what an employee must do to help the organization achieve its goals, it does not support the strategy. If the measure fails to point out employees' performance problems, they will not know how to improve.

Methods for Measuring Performance

Organizations have developed a wide variety of methods for measuring performance. Some methods rank each employee to compare employees' performance. Other methods break down the evaluation into ratings of individual attributes, behaviors, or results. Many organizations use a measurement system that includes a variety of the preceding measures, as in the case of applying total quality management to performance management. Table 8.1 compares these methods in terms of our criteria for effective performance management.

LO4 Compare the major methods for measuring performance.

Making Comparisons

The performance appraisal method may require the rater to compare one individual's performance with that of others. This method involves some form of ranking, in which some employees are best, some are average, and others are worst. The usual techniques for making comparisons are simple ranking, forced distribution, and paired comparison.

Simple ranking requires managers to rank employees in their group from the highest performer to the poorest performer. In a variation of this approach, *alternation ranking,* the manager works from a list of employees. First, the manager decides which employee is best and crosses that person's name off the list. From the remaining names, the manager selects the worst employee and crosses off that name. The process continues with the manager selecting the second best, second worst, third best, and so on, until all the employees have been ranked. The major downside of ranking involves validity. To state a performance measure as broadly as "best" or "worst" doesn't define what exactly is good or bad about the person's contribution to the organization. Ranking therefore raises questions about fairness.

Another way to compare employees' performance is with the **forced-distribution method.** This type of performance measurement assigns a certain percentage of employees to each category in a set of categories. For example, the organization might establish the following percentages and categories:

- Exceptional—5 percent
- Exceeds standards—25 percent

Simple Ranking
Method of performance measurement that requires managers to rank employees in their group from the highest performer to the poorest performer.

Forced-Distribution Method
Method of performance measurement that assigns a certain percentage of employees to each category in a set of categories.

Table 8.1

Basic Approaches to Performance Measurement

APPROACH	FIT WITH STRATEGY	VALIDITY	RELIABILITY	ACCEPTABILITY	SPECIFICITY
			CRITERIA		
Comparative	Poor, unless manager takes time to make link	Can be high if ratings are done carefully	Depends on rater, but usually no measure of agreement used	Moderate; easy to develop and use but resistant to normative standard	Very low
Attribute	Usually low; requires manager to make link	Usually low; can be fine if developed carefully	Usually low; can be improved by specific definitions of attributes	High; easy to develop and use	Very low
Behavioral	Can be quite high	Usually high; minimizes contamination and deficiency	Usually high	Moderate; difficult to develop, but accepted well for use	Very high
Results	Very high	Usually high; can be both contaminated and deficient	High; main problem can be test–retest— depends on timing of measure	High; usually developed with input from those to be evaluated	High regarding results, but low regarding behaviors necessary to achieve them
Quality	Very high	High, but can be both contaminated and deficient	High	High; usually developed with input from those to be evaluated	High regarding results, but low regarding behaviors necessary to achieve them

- Meets standards—55 percent
- Room for improvement—10 percent
- Not acceptable—5 percent

The manager completing the performance appraisal would rate 5 percent of his or her employees as exceptional, 25 percent as exceeding standards, and so on. A forced-distribution approach works best if the members of a group really do vary this much in terms of their performance. It overcomes the temptation to rate everyone high in order to avoid conflict. Research simulating some features of forced rankings found that they improved performance when combined with goals and rewards, especially in the first few years, when the system eliminated the poorest performers.[4] However, a manager who does very well at selecting, motivating, and training employees will have a group of high performers. This manager would have difficulty assigning employees to the bottom categories. In that situation, saying that some employees require improvement or are "not acceptable" not only will be inaccurate, but will hurt morale.

Paired-Comparison Method
Method of performance measurement that compares each employee with each other employee to establish rankings.

Another variation on rankings is the **paired-comparison method.** This approach involves comparing each employee with each other employee to establish rankings. Suppose a manager has five employees, Allen, Barbara, Caitlin, David, and Edgar. The manager compares Allen's performance to Barbara's and assigns one point to whichever employee is the higher performer. Then the manager compares Allen's performance to Caitlin's, then to David's, and finally to Edgar's. The manager repeats this process with Barbara, comparing her performance to Caitlin's, David's, and Edgar's. When the manager has compared every pair of employees, the manager counts the number of points for each employee. The employee with the most points is considered the top-ranked employee. Clearly, this method is time consuming if a group has more than a handful of employees. For a group of 15, the manager must make 105 comparisons.

In spite of the drawbacks, ranking employees offers some benefits. It counteracts the tendency to avoid controversy by rating everyone favorably or near the center of the scale. Also, if some managers tend to evaluate behavior more strictly (or more leniently) than others, a ranking system can erase that tendency from performance scores. Therefore, ranking systems can be useful for supporting decisions about how to distribute pay raises or layoffs. Some ranking systems are easy to use, which makes them acceptable to the managers who use them. A major drawback of rankings is that they often are not linked to the organization's goals. Also, a simple ranking system leaves the basis for the ranking open to interpretation. In that case, the rankings are not helpful for employee development and may hurt morale or result in legal challenges.

Rating Individuals

Instead of focusing on arranging a group of employees from best to worst, performance measurement can look at each employee's performance relative to a uniform set of standards. The measurement may evaluate employees in terms of attributes (characteristics or traits) believed desirable. Or the measurements may identify whether employees have *behaved* in desirable ways, such as closing sales or completing assignments. For both approaches, the performance management system must identify the desired attributes or behaviors, then provide a form on which the manager can rate the employee in terms of those attributes or behaviors. Typically, the form includes a rating scale, such as a scale from 1 to 5, where 1 is the worst performance and 5 is the best.

Rating Attributes

The most widely used method for rating attributes is the **graphic rating scale.** This method lists traits and provides a rating scale for each trait. The employer uses the scale to indicate the extent to which the employee being rated displays the traits. The rating scale may provide points to circle (as on a scale going from 1 for poor to 5 for excellent), or it may provide a line representing a range of scores, with the manager marking a place along the line. Figure 8.3 shows an example of a graphic rating scale that uses a set of ratings from 1 to 5. A drawback of this approach is that it leaves to the particular manager the decisions about what is "excellent knowledge" or "commendable judgment" or "poor interpersonal skills." The result is low reliability, because managers are likely to arrive at different judgments.

To get around this problem, some organizations use **mixed-standard scales,** which use several statements describing each trait to produce a final score for that trait. The manager scores the employee in terms of how the employee compares to

Graphic Rating Scale
Method of performance measurement that lists traits and provides a rating scale for each trait; the employer uses the scale to indicate the extent to which an employee displays each trait.

Mixed-Standard Scales
Method of performance measurement that uses several statements describing each trait to produce a final score for that trait.

Figure 8.3

Example of a Graphic Rating Scale

The following areas of performance are significant to most positions. Indicate your assessment of performance on each dimension by circling the appropriate rating.

PERFORMANCE DIMENSION	RATING				
	DISTINGUISHED	EXCELLENT	COMMENDABLE	ADEQUATE	POOR
Knowledge	5	4	3	2	1
Communication	5	4	3	2	1
Judgment	5	4	3	2	1
Managerial skill	5	4	3	2	1
Quality performance	5	4	3	2	1
Teamwork	5	4	3	2	1
Interpersonal skills	5	4	3	2	1
Initiative	5	4	3	2	1
Creativity	5	4	3	2	1
Problem solving	5	4	3	2	1

each statement. Consider the sample mixed-standard scale in Figure 8.4. To create this scale, the organization determined that the relevant traits are initiative, intelligence, and relations with others. For each trait, sentences were written to describe a person having a high level of that trait, a medium level, and a low level. The sentences for the traits were rearranged so that the nine statements about the three traits are mixed together. The manager who uses this scale reads each sentence, then indicates whether the employee performs above (+), at (0), or below (−) the level described. The key in the middle section of Figure 8.4 tells how to use the pluses, zeros, and minuses to score performance. Someone who excels at every level of performance (pluses for high, medium, and low performance) receives a score of 7 for that trait. Someone who fails to live up to every description of performance (minuses for high, medium, and low) receives a score of 1 for that trait. The bottom of Figure 8.4 calculates the scores for the ratings used in this example.

Rating attributes is the most popular way to measure performance in organizations. In general, attribute-based performance methods are easy to develop and can be applied to a wide variety of jobs and organizations. If the organization is careful to identify which attributes are associated with high performance, and to define them carefully on the appraisal form, these methods can be reliable and valid. However, appraisal forms often fail to meet this standard. In addition, measurement of attributes is rarely linked to the organization's strategy. Furthermore, employees tend perhaps rightly to be defensive about receiving a mere numerical rating on some attribute. How would you feel if you were told you scored 2 on a 5-point scale of initiative or communication skill? The number might seem arbitrary, and it doesn't tell you how to improve.

An employee's performance measurement differs from job to job. For example, a car dealer's performance is measured by the dollar amount of sales, the number of new customers, and customer satisfaction surveys. How would the performance measurements of a car dealer differ from those of a company CEO?

Figure 8.4

Example of a Mixed-Standard Scale

Three traits being assessed:	Levels of performance in statements:
Initiative (INTV)	High (H)
Intelligence (INTG)	Medium (M)
Relations with others (RWO)	Low (L)

Instructions: Please indicate next to each statement whether the employee's performance is above (+), equal to (0), or below (−) the statement.

INTV	H	1. This employee is a real self-starter. The employee always takes the initiative and his/her superior never has to prod this individual.		+
INTG	M	2. While perhaps this employee is not a genius, s/he is a lot more intelligent than many people I know.		+
RWO	L	3. This employee has a tendency to get into unnecessary conflicts with other people.		0
INTV	M	4. While generally this employee shows initiative, occasionally his/her superior must prod him/her to complete work.		+
INTG	L	5. Although this employee is slower than some in understanding things, and may take a bit longer in learning new things, s/he is of average intelligence.		+
RWO	H	6. This employee is on good terms with everyone. S/he can get along with people even when s/he does not agree with them.		−
INTV	L	7. This employee has a bit of a tendency to sit around and wait for directions.		+
INTG	H	8. This employee is extremely intelligent, and s/he learns very rapidly.		−
RWO	M	9. This employee gets along with most people. Only very occasionally does s/he have conflicts with others on the job, and these are likely to be minor.		−

Scoring Key:

STATEMENTS			SCORE
HIGH	MEDIUM	LOW	
+	+	+	7
0	+	+	6
−	+	+	5
−	0	+	4
−	−	+	3
−	−	0	2
−	−	−	1

Example score from preceding ratings:

	STATEMENTS			SCORE
	HIGH	MEDIUM	LOW	
Initiative	+	+	+	7
Intelligence	0	+	+	6
Relations with others	−	−	0	2

Rating Behaviors

One way to overcome the drawbacks of rating attributes is to measure employees' behavior. To rate behaviors, the organization begins by defining which behaviors are associated with success on the job. Which kinds of employee behavior help the organization achieve its goals? The appraisal form asks the manager to rate an employee in terms of each of the identified behaviors.

One way to rate behaviors is with the **critical-incident method.** This approach requires managers to keep a record of specific examples of the employee acting in ways that are either effective or ineffective. Here's an example of a critical incident in the performance evaluation of an appliance repairperson:

Critical-Incident Method
Method of performance measurement based on managers' records of specific examples of the employee acting in ways that are either effective or ineffective.

> A customer called in about a refrigerator that was not cooling and was making a clicking noise every few minutes. The technician prediagnosed the cause of the problem and checked his truck for the necessary parts. When he found he did not have them, he checked the parts out from inventory so that the customer's refrigerator would be repaired on his first visit and the customer would be satisfied promptly.

This incident provides evidence of the employee's knowledge of refrigerator repair and concern for efficiency and customer satisfaction. Evaluating performance in this specific way gives employees feedback about what they do well and what they do poorly. The manager can also relate the incidents to how the employee is helping the company achieve its goals. Keeping a daily or weekly log of critical incidents requires significant effort, however, and managers may resist this requirement. Also, critical incidents may be unique, so they may not support comparisons among employees.

Behaviorally Anchored Rating Scale (BARS)
Method of performance measurement that rates behavior in terms of a scale showing specific statements of behavior that describe different levels of performance.

A **behaviorally anchored rating scale (BARS)** builds on the critical-incidents approach. The BARS method is intended to define performance dimensions specifically, using statements of behavior that describe different levels of performance.[5] (The statements are "anchors" of the performance levels.) The scale in Figure 8.5 shows various performance levels for the behavior of "preparing for duty." The statement at the top (rating 7) describes the highest level of preparing for duty. The statement at the bottom describes behavior associated with poor performance. These statements are based on data about past performance. The organization gathers many critical incidents representing effective and ineffective performance, then classifies them from most to least effective. When experts about the job agree the statements clearly represent levels of performance, they are used as anchors to guide the rater. Although BARS can improve interrater reliability, this method can bias the manager's memory. The statements used as anchors can help managers remember similar behaviors, at the expense of other critical incidents.[6]

Behavioral Observation Scale (BOS)
A variation of a BARS which uses all behaviors necessary for effective performance to rate performance at a task.

A **behavioral observation scale (BOS)** is a variation of a BARS. Like a BARS, a BOS is developed from critical incidents.[7] However, while a BARS discards many examples in creating the rating scale, a BOS uses many of them to define all behaviors necessary for effective performance (or behaviors that signal ineffective performance). As a result, a BOS may use 15 behaviors to define levels of performance. Also, a BOS asks the manager to rate the frequency with which the employee has exhibited the behavior during the rating period. These ratings are averaged to compute an overall performance rating. Figure 8.6 provides a simplified example of a BOS for measuring the behavior "overcoming resistance to change."

A major drawback of this method is the amount of information required. A BOS can have 80 or more behaviors, and the manager must remember how often the employee exhibited each behavior in a 6- to 12-month rating period. This is taxing enough for one employee, but managers often must rate 10 or more employees. Even so, compared to BARS and graphic rating scales, managers and employees have said they prefer BOS for ease of use, providing feedback, maintaining objectivity, and suggesting training needs.[8]

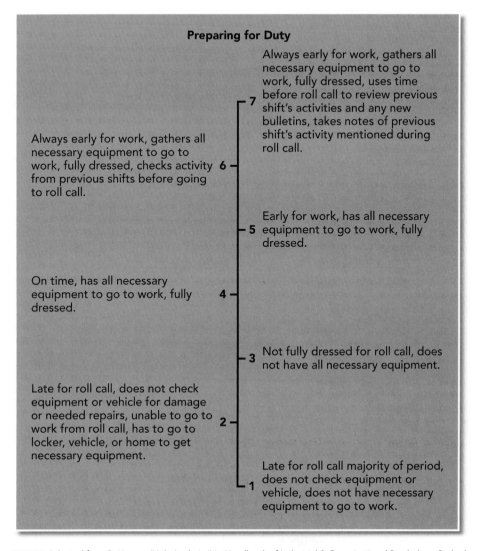

Figure 8.5

Task-BARS Rating
Dimension: Patrol Officer

Preparing for Duty

7 — Always early for work, gathers all necessary equipment to go to work, fully dressed, uses time before roll call to review previous shift's activities and any new bulletins, takes notes of previous shift's activity mentioned during roll call.

Always early for work, gathers all necessary equipment to go to work, fully dressed, checks activity 6 — from previous shifts before going to roll call.

5 — Early for work, has all necessary equipment to go to work, fully dressed.

On time, has all necessary equipment to go to work, fully 4 — dressed.

3 — Not fully dressed for roll call, does not have all necessary equipment.

Late for roll call, does not check equipment or vehicle for damage or needed repairs, unable to go to 2 — work from roll call, has to go to locker, vehicle, or home to get necessary equipment.

1 — Late for roll call majority of period, does not check equipment or vehicle, does not have necessary equipment to go to work.

SOURCE: Adapted from R. Harvey, "Job Analysis," in *Handbook of Industrial & Organizational Psychology,* 2nd ed., eds, M. Dunnette and L. Hough (Palo Alto, CA: Consulting Psychologists Press, 1991), p. 138.

Another approach to assessment builds directly on a branch of psychology called *behaviorism*, which holds that individuals' future behavior is determined by their past experiences—specifically, the ways in which past behaviors have been reinforced. People tend to repeat behaviors that have been rewarded in the past. Providing feedback and reinforcement can therefore modify individuals' future behavior. Applied to behavior in organizations, **organizational behavior modification (OBM)** is a plan for managing the behavior of employees through a formal system of feedback and reinforcement. Specific OBM techniques vary, but most have four components:[9]

1. Define a set of key behaviors necessary for job performance.
2. Use a measurement system to assess whether the employee exhibits the key behaviors.

Organizational Behavior Modification (OBM)
A plan for managing the behavior of employees through a formal system of feedback and reinforcement.

Figure 8.6

Example of a Behavioral Observation Scale

Overcoming resistance to Change					
Directions: Rate the frequency of each behavior from 1 (Almost Never) to 5 (Almost Always).					
	Almost Never				Almost Always
1. Describes the details of the change to employees.	1	2	3	4	5
2. Explains why the change is necessary.	1	2	3	4	5
3. Discusses how the change will affect the employee.	1	2	3	4	5
4. Listens to the employee's concerns.	1	2	3	4	5
5. Asks the employee for help in making the change work.	1	2	3	4	5
6. If necessary, specifies the date for a follow-up meeting to respond to the employee's concerns.	1	2	3	4	5

Score: Total number of points = _____

Performance

Points	Performance Rating
6–10	Below adequate
11–15	Adequate
16–20	Full
21–25	Excellent
26–30	Superior

Scores are set by management.

3. Inform employees of the key behaviors, perhaps in terms of goals for how often to exhibit the behaviors.
4. Provide feedback and reinforcement based on employees' behavior.

OBM techniques have been used in a variety of settings. For example, a community mental health agency used OBM to increase the rates and timeliness of critical job behaviors by showing employees the connection between job behaviors and the agency's accomplishments.[10] This process identified job behaviors related to administration, record keeping, and service provided to clients. Feedback and reinforcement improved staff performance. OBM also increased the frequency of safety behaviors in a processing plant.[11]

Behavioral approaches such as organizational behavior modification and rating scales can be very effective. These methods can link the company's goals to the specific behavior required to achieve those goals. Behavioral methods also can generate specific feedback, along with guidance in areas requiring improvements. As a result, these methods tend to be valid. The people to be measured often help in developing the measures, so acceptance tends to be high as well. When raters are well trained, reliability also tends to be high. However, behavioral methods do not work as well for complex jobs in which it is difficult to see a link between behavior and results or there is more than one good way to achieve success.[12]

Measuring Results

Performance measurement can focus on managing the objective, measurable results of a job or work group. Results might include sales, costs, or productivity (output per worker or per dollar spent on production), among many possible measures. Two of the most popular methods for measuring results are measurement of productivity and management by objectives.

Productivity is an important measure of success, because getting more done with a smaller amount of resources (money or people) increases the company's profits. Productivity usually refers to the output of production workers, but it can be used more generally as a performance measure. To do this, the organization identifies the products—set of activities or objectives—it expects a group or individual to accomplish. At a repair shop, for instance, a product might be something like "quality of repair." The next step is to define how to measure production of these products. For quality of repair, the repair shop could track the percentage of items returned because they still do not work after a repair and the percentage of quality-control inspections passed. For each measure, the organization decides what level of performance is desired. Finally, the organization sets up a system for tracking these measures and giving employees feedback about their performance in terms of these measures. This type of performance measurement can be time consuming to set up, but research suggests it can improve productivity.[13]

Management by objectives (MBO) is a system in which people at each level of the organization set goals in a process that flows from top to bottom, so employees at all levels are contributing to the organization's overall goals. These goals become the standards for evaluating each employee's performance. An MBO system has three components:[14]

1. Goals are specific, difficult, and objective. The goals listed in the second column of Table 8.2 provide two examples for a bank.
2. Managers and their employees work together to set the goals.
3. The manager gives objective feedback through the rating period to monitor progress toward the goals. The two right-hand columns in Table 8.2 are examples of feedback given after one year.

MBO can have a very positive effect on an organization's performance. In 70 studies of MBO's performance, 68 showed that productivity improved.[15] The productivity gains tended to be greatest when top management was highly committed to MBO. Also, because staff members are involved in setting goals, it is likely that MBO systems effectively link individual employees' performance with the organization's overall goals.

Management by Objectives (MBO) A system in which people at each level of the organization set goals in a process that flows from top to bottom, so employees at all levels are contributing to the organization's overall goals; these goals become the standards for evaluating each employee's performance.

Table 8.2

Management by Objectives: Two Objectives for a Bank

KEY RESULT AREA	OBJECTIVE	% COMPLETE	ACTUAL PERFORMANCE
Loan portfolio management	Increase portfolio value by 10% over the next 12 months	90	Increased portfolio value by 9% over the past 12 months
Sales	Generate fee income of $30,000 over the next 12 months	150	Generated fee income of $45,000 over the past 12 months

In general, evaluation of results can be less subjective than other kinds of perfor-mance measurement. This makes measuring results highly acceptable to employees and managers alike. Results-oriented performance measurement is also relatively easy to link to the organization's goals. However, measuring results has problems with validity, because results may be affected by circumstances beyond each employee's performance. Also, if the organization measures only final results, it may fail to mea-sure significant aspects of performance that are not directly related to those results. If individuals focus only on aspects of performance that are measured, they may neglect significant skills or behaviors. For example, if the organization measures only produc-tivity, employees may not be concerned enough with customer service. The outcome may be high efficiency (costs are low) but low effectiveness (sales are low, too).[16] Finally, focusing strictly on results does not provide guidance on how to improve.

Total Quality Management

The principles of *total quality management*, introduced in Chapter 2, provide methods for performance measurement and management. Total quality management (TQM) differs from traditional performance measurement in that it assesses both individual performance and the system within which the individual works. This assessment is a process through which employees and their customers work together to set standards and measure performance, with the overall goal being to improve customer satisfac-tion. In this sense, an employee's customers may be inside or outside the organization; a "customer" is whoever uses the goods or services produced by the employee. The

Coaches provide feedback to their team just as managers provide feedback to their employees. Feedback is important so that individuals know what they are doing well and what areas they may need to work on.

feedback aims at helping employees continuously improve the satisfaction of their customers. The focus on continuously improving customer satisfaction is intended to avoid the pitfall of rating individuals on outcomes, such as sales or profits, over which they do not have complete control.

With TQM, performance measurement essentially combines measurements of attributes and results. The feedback in TQM is of two kinds: (1) subjective feedback from managers, peers, and customers about the employee's personal qualities such as cooperation and initiative; and (2) objective feedback based on the work process. The second kind of feedback comes from a variety of methods called *statistical quality control*. These methods use charts to detail causes of problems, measures of performance, or relationships between work-related variables. Employees are responsible for tracking these measures to identify areas where they can avoid or correct problems. Because of the focus on systems, this feedback may result in changes to a work process, rather than assuming that a performance problem is the fault of an employee. The TQM system's focus has practical benefits, but it does not serve as well to support decisions about work assignments, training, or compensation.

Sources of Performance Information

All the methods of performance measurement require decisions about who will collect and analyze the performance information. To qualify for this task, a person should have an understanding of the job requirements and the opportunity to see the employee doing the job. The traditional approach is for managers to gather information about their employees' performance and arrive at performance ratings. However, many sources are possible. Possibilities of information sources include managers, peers, subordinates, self, and customers.

Using just one person as a source of information poses certain problems. People tend to like some people more than others, and those feelings can bias how an employee's efforts are perceived. Also, one person is likely to see an employee in a limited number of situations. A supervisor, for example, cannot see how an employee behaves when the supervisor is not watching—for example, when a service technician is at the customer's facility. To get as complete an assessment as possible, some organizations combine information from most or all of the possible sources, in what is called a **360-degree performance appraisal**.

Managers

The most-used source of performance information is the employee's manager. For example, at YMCA of Greater Rochester, New York, managers rate the performance of the organization's 2,900 employees. The YMCA also reviews the managers' performance in evaluating employees. The vice president of human resources and the chief operating officer go over each performance appraisal together. When they identify reports in which feedback is vague or seems to be the first conversation a manager and employee have had about an issue, they work with the manager to improve the reviewing process.[17]

It is usually safe for organizations to assume that supervisors have extensive knowledge of the job requirements and that they have enough opportunity to observe their employees. In other words, managers possess the basic qualifications for this responsibility. Another advantage of using managers to evaluate performance is that they have an incentive to provide accurate and helpful feedback, because their own

360-Degree Performance Appraisal
Performance measurement that combines information from the employee's managers, peers, subordinates, self, and customers.

Performance management is critical for executing a talent management system and involves one-on-one contact with managers to ensure that proper training and development are taking place.

success depends so much on their employees' performance.[18] Finally, when managers try to observe employee behavior or discuss performance issues in the feedback session, their feedback can improve performance, and employees tend to perceive the appraisal as accurate.[19]

Still, in some situations, problems can occur with using supervisors as the source of performance information. For employees in some jobs, the supervisor does not have enough opportunity to observe the employee performing job duties. A sales manager with many outside salespeople cannot be with the salespeople on many visits to customers. Even if the sales manager does make a point of traveling with salespeople for a few days, they are likely to be on their best behavior while the manager is there. The manager cannot observe how they perform at other times.

Peers

Another source of performance information is the employee's peers or co-workers. Peers are an excellent source of information about performance in a job where the supervisor does not often observe the employee. Examples include law enforcement and sales. For these and other jobs, peers may have the most opportunity to observe the employee in day-to-day activities. Peers have expert knowledge of job requirements. They also bring a different perspective to the evaluation and can provide extremely valid assessments of performance.[20]

Peer evaluations obviously have some potential disadvantages. Friendships (or rivalries) have the potential to bias ratings. Research, however, has provided little evidence that this is a problem.[21] Another disadvantage is that when the evaluations are done to support administrative decisions, peers are uncomfortable with rating employees for decisions that may affect themselves. Generally, peers are more favorable toward participating in reviews to be used for employee development.[22]

Subordinates

For evaluating the performance of managers, subordinates are an especially valuable source of information. Subordinates—the people reporting to the manager—often have the best chance to see how well a manager treats employees. Dell, for example, asks employees to rate their manager in terms of measures such as whether the employee receives ongoing performance feedback and whether the supervisor "is effective at managing people."[23]

Subordinate evaluations have some potential problems because of the power relationships involved. Subordinates are reluctant to say negative things about the person to whom they report; they prefer to provide feedback anonymously. Managers, however, have a more positive reaction to this type of feedback when the subordinates are identified. When feedback forms require that the subordinates identify themselves, they tend to give the manager higher ratings.[24] Another problem is that when managers receive ratings from their subordinates, the employees have more power, so managers tend to emphasize employee satisfaction, even at the expense of productivity. This issue arises primarily when the evaluations are used for administrative decisions. Therefore, as with peer evaluations, subordinate evaluations are most appropriate for developmental purposes. To protect employees, the process should be anonymous and use at least three employees to rate each manager.

Self

No one has a greater chance to observe the employee's behavior on the job than does the employee himself or herself. Self-ratings are rarely used alone, but they can contribute valuable information. A common approach is to have employees evaluate their own performance before the feedback session. This activity gets employees thinking about their performance. Areas of disagreement between the self-appraisal and other evaluations can be fruitful topics for the feedback session. YMCA of Greater Rochester introduced self-appraisals in response to complaints that ratings by the managers weren't an effective tool for employee development. Employees report that the opportunity to give examples of their successes and request training has sparked more helpful conversations with their managers. Managers, in turn, feel that the employee-provided information makes the evaluation process easier.[25]

The obvious problem with self-ratings is that individuals have a tendency to inflate assessments of their performance. Especially if the ratings will be used for administrative decisions, exaggerating one's contributions has practical benefits. Also, social psychologists have found that, in general, people tend to blame outside circumstances for their failures while taking a large part of the credit for their successes. Supervisors can soften this tendency by providing frequent feedback, but because people tend to perceive situations this way, self-appraisals are not appropriate as the basis for administrative decisions.[26]

Customers

Services are often produced and consumed on the spot, so the customer is often the only person who directly observes the service performance and may be the best source of performance information. Many companies in service industries have introduced customer evaluations of employee performance. Marriott Corporation provides a customer satisfaction card in every room and mails surveys to a random sample of its hotel customers. Whirlpool's Consumer Services Division conducts mail and telephone surveys of customers after factory technicians have serviced their appliances. These surveys allow the company to evaluate an individual technician's customer-service behaviors while in the customer's home. The "Best Practices" box provides another example of a company that effectively uses customer feedback to support better employee performance.

Using customer evaluations of employee performance is appropriate in two situations.[27] The first is when an employee's job requires direct service to the customer or linking the customer to other services within the organization. Second, customer evaluations are appropriate when the organization is interested in gathering information to determine what products and services the customer wants. That is, customer evaluations contribute to the organization's goals by enabling HRM to support the organization's marketing activities. In this regard, customer evaluations are useful both for evaluating an employee's performance and for helping to determine whether

Best Practices

CUSTOMER FEEDBACK FUELS CUSTOMER SATISFACTION AT UNITED COMMUNITY BANK

United Community Bank (UCB), which describes itself as the "third-largest traditional bank holding company in Georgia," has employees in over a hundred facilities throughout Georgia, North Carolina, and Tennessee. To fulfill the bank's mission of providing high-quality financial services to its communities, UCB's management knows the bank needs highly qualified, well-motivated employees with a commitment to customer service.

In support of this strategy, UCB's performance measures include feedback from customers. UCB contracts with a research company known as Customer Service Profiles to obtain data on customer satisfaction. The organization contacts customers who have used particular services and obtains their impressions about the quality of service they received from the bank's employees.

The reason the customer service data provide feedback in support of employee development is that the bank uses the research as part of a complete process of goal setting and coaching. UCB set performance standards for how to satisfy customers, and it informs employees about what customers want from people in their position at the bank.

In general, customer responses are used as a coaching tool. Employees discuss evaluations with their supervisor. If a customer reports dissatisfaction with a particular employee, the discussion focuses on how the employee can do his or her job better in the future. In the unusual case of an employee who has a pattern of poor scores, the performance information would make its way into the organization's formal performance review process. But typically, says Craig Metz,

UCB's vice president of marketing, employees "want to know what they can do to improve."

The drive to use customer evaluations as a tool for measuring employee performance and coaching employees bears fruit. Customer Service Profiles measures overall customer satisfaction with UCB and other banks. While banks typically score between 70 and 79 percent out of a perfect 100, UCB routinely scores in the high nineties.

Sources: Melanie Scarborough, "Managed Assets," *Community Banker,* January 2010, Business & Company Resource Center, http://galenet.galegroup.com; and United Community Bank, "About Us," corporate Web site, www.ucbi.com, accessed April 2, 2010.

the organization can improve customer service by making changes in HRM activities such as training or compensation.

The weakness of customer surveys for performance measurement is their expense. The expenses of a traditional survey can add up to hundreds of dollars to evaluate one individual. Many organizations therefore limit the information gathering to short periods once a year.

LO6 Define types of rating errors, and explain how to minimize them.

Errors in Performance Measurement

As we noted in the previous section, one reason for gathering information from several sources is that performance measurements are not completely objective, and errors can occur. People observe behavior, and they have no practical way of knowing all the circumstances, intentions, and outcomes related to that behavior, so they interpret what they see. In doing so, observers make a number of judgment calls, and in some situations may even distort information on purpose. Therefore, fairness in rating performance and interpreting performance appraisals requires that managers understand the kinds of distortions that commonly occur.

Types of Rating Errors

Several kinds of errors and biases commonly influence performance measurements:

- People often tend to give a higher evaluation to people they consider similar to themselves. Most of us think of ourselves as effective, so if others are like us, they must be effective, too. Research has demonstrated that this effect is strong. Unfortunately, it is sometimes wrong, and when similarity is based on characteristics such as race or sex, the decisions may be discriminatory.[28]
- If the rater compares an individual, not against an objective standard, but against other employees, *contrast errors* occur. A competent performer who works with exceptional people may be rated lower than competent, simply because of the contrast.
- Raters make *distributional errors* when they tend to use only one part of a rating scale. The error is called *leniency* when the reviewer rates everyone near the top, *strictness* when the rater favors lower rankings, and *central tendency* when the rater puts everyone near the middle of the scale. Distributional errors make it difficult to compare employees rated by the same person. Also, if different raters make different kinds of distributional errors, scores by these raters cannot be compared.
- Raters often let their opinion of one quality color their opinion of others. For example, someone who speaks well might be seen as helpful or talented in other areas, simply because of the overall good impression created by this one quality. Or someone who is occasionally tardy might be seen as lacking in motivation. When the bias is in a favorable direction, this is called the *halo error*. When it involves negative ratings, it is called the *horns error*. Halo error can mistakenly tell employees they don't need to improve in any area, while horns error can cause employees to feel frustrated and defensive.

Ways to Reduce Errors

Usually people make these errors unintentionally, especially when the criteria for measuring performance are not very specific. Raters can be trained how to avoid rating errors.[29] Prospective raters watch videos whose scripts or storylines are designed to lead them to make specific rating errors. After rating the fictional employees in the videos, raters discuss their rating decisions and how such errors affected their rating decisions. Training programs offer tips for avoiding the errors in the future.

Another training method for raters focuses on the complex nature of employee performance.[30] Raters learn to look at many aspects of performance that deserve their attention. Actual examples of performance are studied to bring out various performance dimensions and the standards for those dimensions. This training aims to help raters evaluate employees' performance more thoroughly and accurately.

Political Behavior in Performance Appraisals

Unintentional errors are not the only cause of inaccurate performance measurement. Sometimes the people rating performance distort an evaluation on purpose to advance their personal goals. This kind of appraisal politics is unhealthy especially because the resulting feedback does not focus on helping employees contribute to the organization's goals. High-performing employees who are rated unfairly will become frustrated, and low-performing employees who are overrated will be rewarded rather than encouraged to improve. Therefore, organizations try to identify and discourage appraisal politics.

Several characteristics of appraisal systems and company culture tend to encourage appraisal politics. Appraisal politics are most likely to occur when raters are accountable to the employee being rated, the goals of rating are not compatible with one another, performance appraisal is directly linked to highly desirable rewards, top executives tolerate or ignore distorted ratings, and senior employees tell newcomers company "folklore" that includes stories about distorted ratings.

Political behavior occurs in every organization. Organizations can minimize appraisal politics by establishing an appraisal system that is fair. One technique is to hold a **calibration meeting,** a gathering at which managers discuss employee performance ratings and provide evidence supporting their ratings with the goal of eliminating the influence of rating errors. As they discuss ratings and the ways they arrive at ratings, managers may identify undervalued employees, notice whether they are much harsher or more lenient than other managers, and help each other focus on how well ratings are associated with relevant performance outcomes. For example, when consultant Dick Grote leads calibration meetings for his clients, he often displays flip charts, one for each rating on a scale, and gives each manager a different-colored Post-it Note pad. On their Post-It Notes, the managers write the names of each employee they rate, and they attach a note for the rating they would give that employee. The distribution of colors on the flip charts provides visually strong information about how the different managers think about their employees. A cluster of green notes on "outstanding" and yellow notes on "meets expectations" would suggest that one manager is a much tougher rater than others, and they could then discuss how they arrive at these different conclusions.[31] The organization can also help managers give accurate and fair appraisals by training them to use the appraisal process, encouraging them to recognize accomplishments that the employees themselves have not identified, and fostering a climate of openness in which employees feel they can be honest about their weaknesses.[32]

focus on *social responsibility*

Calibration Meeting
Meeting at which managers discuss employee performance ratings and provide evidence supporting their ratings with the goal of eliminating the influence of rating errors.

Giving Performance Feedback

LO7 Explain how to provide performance feedback effectively.

Once the manager and others have measured an employee's performance, this information must be given to the employee. Only after the employee has received feedback can he or she begin to plan how to correct any shortcomings. Although the feedback stage of performance management is essential, it is uncomfortable to managers and employees. Delivering feedback feels to the manager as if he or she is standing in judgment of others—a role few people enjoy. Receiving criticism feels even worse. Fortunately, managers can do much to smooth the feedback process and make it effective.

Scheduling Performance Feedback

Performance feedback should be a regular, expected management activity. The custom or policy at many organizations is to give formal performance feedback once a year. But annual feedback is not enough. One reason is that managers are responsible for correcting performance deficiencies as soon as they occur. If the manager notices a problem with an employee's behavior in June, but the annual appraisal is scheduled for November, the employee will miss months of opportunities for improvement.

Another reason for frequent performance feedback is that feedback is most effective when the information does not surprise the employee. If an employee has to wait for up to a year to learn what the manager thinks of his work, the employee will wonder whether he is meeting expectations. Employees should instead receive feedback so often that they know what the manager will say during their annual performance review.

Finally, employees have indicated that they are motivated and directed by regular feedback; they want to know if they are on the right track. Managers have found that young employees in particular are looking for frequent and candid performance feedback from their managers.[33] In response, Ernst & Young created an online "Feedback Zone," where employees can request or submit performance feedback at any time beyond the formal evaluations required twice a year.

Preparing for a Feedback Session

Managers should be well prepared for each formal feedback session. The manager should create the right context for the meeting. The location should be neutral. If the manager's office is the site of unpleasant conversations, a conference room may be more appropriate. In announcing the meeting to an employee, the manager should describe it as a

When giving performance feedback, do it in an appropriate meeting place. Meet in a setting that is neutral and free of distractions. What other factors are important for a feedback session?

chance to discuss the role of the employee, the role of the manager, and the relationship between them. Managers should also say (and believe) that they would like the meeting to be an open dialogue. As discussed in the "HR How To" box, the content of the feedback session and the type of language used can determine the success of this meeting.

Managers should also enable the employee to be well prepared. The manager should ask the employee to complete a self-assessment ahead of time. The self-assessment requires employees to think about their performance over the past rating period and to be aware of their strengths and weaknesses, so they can participate more fully in the discussion. Even though employees may tend to overstate their accomplishments, the self-assessment can help the manager and employee identify areas for discussion. When the purpose of the assessment is to define areas for development, employees may actually understate their performance. Also, differences between the manager's and the employee's rating may be fruitful areas for discussion.

Conducting the Feedback Session

During the feedback session, managers can take any of three approaches. In the "tell-and-sell" approach, managers tell the employees their ratings and then justify those ratings. In the "tell-and-listen" approach, managers tell employees their ratings and then let the employees explain their side of the story. In the "problem-solving" approach, managers and employees work together to solve performance problems in an atmosphere of respect and encouragement. Not surprisingly, research demonstrates that the problem-solving approach is superior. Perhaps surprisingly, most managers rely on the tell-and-sell approach.[34] Managers can improve employee satisfaction with the feedback process by letting employees voice their opinions and discuss performance goals.[35]

HR How To

DISCUSSING EMPLOYEE PERFORMANCE

Employees and managers often dread feedback sessions, because they expect some level of criticism, and criticism feels uncomfortable. However, there are ways to structure communication about employee performance so that it feels more constructive.

Most important, ensure that communication flows in both directions. It should begin with clear expectations laid out—sometimes in detail—well before the feedback session, so that employees have a fair chance to succeed. Employees should know what "fair" and "outstanding" performance look like, if those are the terms used in rating their performance. Employees should be so clear about what is desired that during the time leading up to the meeting, they can be gathering examples of situations in which they met or exceeded expectations. Managers also should be gathering these examples. The meeting should allow enough time for both participants to present, discuss, and learn from the

examples they have identified. Based on what this discussion reveals, the employee or manager should discuss revising goals, setting new goals, or figuring out how to meet unfulfilled goals.

Discussions should consider how the employee's actions have (or have not) been contributing to the employee's, group's, and company's business objectives. This helps the conversation move away from vague discussion of personality toward goal-oriented, objective performance measures.

When an employee's performance falls below expectations, the manager should prepare ahead of time to be sure the facts of the situation are clear and complete. The employee and manager should discuss the problem before the manager writes conclusions on the appraisal form, to ensure that the report will be fair. Whether performance is disappointing or delightful, the manager should be direct and clear in discussing it, focusing on observable behaviors.

The discussion should include plans for the future. The manager should hear the employee's ideas about what he or she needs to continue improving his or her contributions to the organization. The manager should consider a variety of possible needs, including further training or coaching, removing obstacles to high performance, and adopting employee suggestions to improve work processes. Ending with an action plan takes some of the sting out of criticism—and helps employees apply praise in a way that makes them more valuable.

Sources: Christine V. Bonavita, "The Importance of Performance Evaluations," *Employment Law Strategist*, March 1, 2009, Business & Company Resource Center, http://galenet.galegroup.com; "Boost the Value of Performance Reviews," *HR Focus*, December 2009, Business & Company Resource Center, http://galenet.galegroup.com; and Carolyn Heinze, "Fair Appraisals," *Systems Contractor News*, July 2009, Business & Company Resource Center, http://galenet.galegroup.com.

The content of the feedback should emphasize behavior, not personalities. For example, "You did not meet the deadline" can open a conversation about what needs to change, but "You're not motivated" may make the employee feel defensive and angry. As the "HR Oops!" box shows, even employees who are told they are meeting performance goals may not see this as a compliment. The feedback session should end with goal setting and a decision about when to follow up.

LO8 Summarize ways to produce improvement in unsatisfactory performance.

Finding Solutions to Performance Problems

When performance evaluation indicates that an employee's performance is below standard, the feedback process should launch an effort to correct the problem. Even when the employee is meeting current standards, the feedback session may identify areas in which the employee can improve in order to contribute more to the organization in a current or future job. In sum, the final, feedback stage of performance

HR Oops!

We're All Above Average

For all the worries about delivering criticism, it turns out that poor performance isn't the only problem: employees don't want to hear they're doing their jobs if it means they sound "average." Although the very idea of average would imply that many employees rate near the middle, and the very idea of goal setting would be that you want employees to meet a challenge, managers and HR experts report that most employees think they're *above* average and *exceed* expectations.

Penny Wilson, director of corporate learning and development at Talecris Biotherapeutics, suggests that HR departments "could do a better job of explaining that 'meets' is a good rating, and that we need those solid performers."

But John Lewison, director of human resources at MDRC, says that over his career at six different companies, "I've seen every word used for every category. And no matter what you do, people figure out pretty quickly what 'average' is and don't want to be in that category."

Part of the problem may be that the use of forced-distribution methods and links between appraisals and compensation have created a climate in which employees are afraid they won't be rewarded (or will be let go) if they get anything but a stellar review.

Source: Based on Adrienne Fox, "Curing What Ails Performance Reviews," *HR Magazine,* January 2009, pp. 52–56.

Questions

1. If an employee receives performance feedback that implies the employee is "average" or has met (but not exceeded) expectations, how would you expect the employee to react to the feedback during an appraisal interview? How well would this feedback affect the strategic and developmental purposes of performance management?
2. How could performance appraisals or feedback interviews be modified to address employees' resistance to being considered average?

---

management involves identifying areas for improvement and ways to improve performance in those areas.

As shown in Figure 8.7, the most effective way to improve performance varies according to the employee's ability and motivation. In general, when employees have high levels of ability and motivation, they perform at or above standards. But when they lack ability, motivation, or both, corrective action is needed. The type of action called for depends on what the employee lacks:

- *Lack of ability*—When a motivated employee lacks knowledge, skills, or abilities in some area, the manager may offer coaching, training, and more detailed feedback. Sometimes it is appropriate to restructure the job so the employee can handle it.
- *Lack of motivation*—Managers with an unmotivated employee can explore ways to demonstrate that the employee is being treated fairly and rewarded adequately. The solution may be as simple as more positive feedback (praise). Employees may need a referral for counseling or help with stress management.
- *Lack of both*—Performance may improve if the manager directs the employee's attention to the significance of the problem by withholding rewards or providing specific feedback. If the employee does not respond, the manager may have to demote or terminate the employee.

As a rule, employees who combine high ability with high motivation are solid performers. As Figure 8.7 indicates, managers should by no means ignore these employees

Figure 8.7

Improving Performance

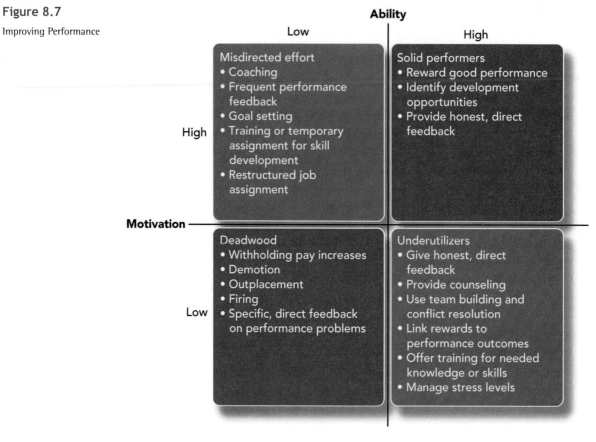

SOURCE: Based on M. London, *Job Feedback* (Mahwah, NJ: Lawrence Erlbaum Associates, 1997), pp. 96–97. Used by permission.

on the grounds of leaving well enough alone. Rather, such employees are likely to appreciate opportunities for further development. Rewards and direct feedback help to maintain these employees' high motivation levels.

LO9 Discuss legal and ethical issues that affect performance management.

Legal and Ethical Issues in Performance Management

In developing and using performance management systems, human resource professionals need to ensure that these systems meet legal requirements, such as the avoidance of discrimination. In addition, performance management systems should meet ethical standards, such as protection of employees' privacy.

Legal Requirements for Performance Management

Because performance measures play a central role in decisions about pay, promotions, and discipline, employment-related lawsuits often challenge an organization's performance management system. Lawsuits related to performance management usually involve charges of discrimination or unjust dismissal.

Discrimination claims often allege that the performance management system discriminated against employees on the basis of their race or sex. Many performance measures are subjective, and measurement errors, such as those described earlier in the chapter, can easily occur. The Supreme Court has held that the selection guidelines in the federal government's *Uniform Guidelines on Employee Selection Procedures* also apply to performance measurement.[36] In general, these guidelines (discussed in Chapters 3 and 6) require that organizations avoid using criteria such as race and age as a basis for employment decisions. This requires overcoming widespread rating errors. A substantial body of evidence has shown that white and black raters tend to give higher ratings to members of their own racial group, even after rater training.[37] In addition, evidence suggests that this tendency is strongest when one group is only a small percentage of the total work group. When the vast majority of the group is male, females receive lower ratings; when the minority is male, males receive lower ratings.[38]

With regard to lawsuits filed on the grounds of unjust dismissal, the usual claim is that the person was dismissed for reasons besides the ones that the employer states. Suppose an employee who works for a defense contractor discloses that the company defrauded the government. If the company fires the employee, the employee might argue that the firing was a way to punish the employee for blowing the whistle. In this type of situation, courts generally focus on the employer's performance management system, looking to see whether the firing could have been based on poor performance. To defend itself, the employer would need a performance management system that provides evidence to support its employment decisions.

To protect against both kinds of lawsuits, it is important to have a legally defensible performance management system.[39] Such a system would be based on valid job analyses, as described in Chapter 4, with the requirements for job success clearly communicated to employees. Performance measurement should evaluate behaviors or results, rather than traits. The organization should use multiple raters (including self-appraisals) and train raters in how to use the system. The organization should provide for a review of all performance ratings by upper-level managers and set up a system for employees to appeal when they believe they were evaluated unfairly. Along with feedback, the system should include a process for coaching or training employees to help them improve, rather than simply dismissing poor performers.

Electronic Monitoring and Employee Privacy

Computer technology now supports many performance management systems. Organizations often store records of employees' performance ratings, disciplinary actions, and work-rule violations in electronic databases. Many companies use computers to monitor productivity and other performance measures electronically. Meijer, a retail supercenter offering groceries and 40 other departments, is one of several retailers using software designed to improve the efficiency of cashiers. The store's computer times how long it takes to complete each customer transaction, taking into account the kinds of merchandise being purchased as well as whether customers are paying with cash, credit, gifts cards, or store credit. Each week the cashiers receive scores. If a cashier falls below the baseline score too many times, he or she may be carefully monitored by a manager, moved to a lower-paying job, or even be let go. Meijer reports that the system has helped managers identify and coach slow cashiers, but cashiers have complained that it forces them to hurry customers along, rather than pay attention to them and help them through the checkout line.[40] Whether customers win depends on whether they prefer a speedy cashier or a friendly one.

Although electronic monitoring can improve productivity, it also generates privacy concerns. Critics point out that an employer should not monitor employees when it has no reason to believe anything is wrong. They complain that monitoring systems threaten to make the workplace an electronic sweatshop in which employees are treated as robots, robbing them of dignity. Some note that employees' performance should be measured by accomplishments, not just time spent at a desk or workbench. Electronic systems should not be a substitute for careful management. When monitoring is necessary, managers should communicate the reasons for using it. Monitoring may be used more positively to gather information for coaching employees and helping them develop their skills. Finally, organizations must protect the privacy of performance measurements, as they must do with other employee records.

thinking ethically

DID WE GET BURNED BY SHORT-TERM GOALS?

In 2008, the business world and government leaders were in shock. Lehman Brothers, an investment bank with a 150-year history, folded, investment giant Merrill Lynch seemed poised to follow, and only a massive bailout by the U.S. government saved AIG, a huge insurance company. It appeared that the entire financial system could collapse, effectively bringing commerce to a halt.

As we slowly recover from the economic slump that followed these events, many are asking what caused the crisis, hoping to prevent such events from recurring. The picture is complicated, but observers place some of the blame at the feet of management, including human resource management.

One source of trouble seems to have been performance management in the mortgage lending industry. Lending companies set goals based on what would help them grow in the near term: make more and more loans to homebuyers. To back up that strategy, they measured the performance of loan officers (who approve loans) and mortgage brokers (who bring together borrowers and lenders) by counting the number of loans they made and adding up the total dollars in those deals. The more loans these employees made, the more money they earned. There were no rewards for turning down risky borrowers or penalties for making bad loans, because the lenders typically sold the loan contracts to other financial companies. When the "bubble" of fast-rising housing prices burst and the slowing economy caused many borrowers to lose jobs, the loan deals went bad on a massive scale, fueling the financial crisis.

SOURCE: Based on Wayne F. Cascio and Peter Cappelli, "Lessons from the Financial Services Crisis," *HR Magazine*, January 2009, Business & Company Resource Center, http://galenet.galegroup.com.

Questions

1. If performance management practices at mortgage companies helped the companies earn impressive profits for a time, would you rate that as a business success? An ethical success? Why or why not?

2. If those same practices made mortgage companies more vulnerable after the real estate bubble burst and the financial crisis occurred, would you rate that as a business failure? An ethical failure? Why or why not?

3. In general, how could performance management at mortgage brokers be adjusted so that the companies treat their employees, customers, investors, and communities more ethically? Explain whether you think your recommendations would help or hurt the companies.

SUMMARY

LO1 Identify the activities involved in performance management.

Performance management is the process through which managers ensure that employees' activities and outputs contribute to the organization's goals. The organization begins by specifying which aspects of performance are relevant to the organization. Next, the organization measures the relevant aspects of performance through performance appraisal. Finally, in performance feedback sessions, managers provide employees with information about their performance so they can adjust their behavior to meet the organization's goals. Feedback includes efforts to identify and solve problems.

LO2 Discuss the purposes of performance management systems.

Organizations establish performance management systems to meet three broad purposes. Effective performance management helps the organization with strategic purposes, that is, meeting business objectives. It does this by helping to link employees' behavior with the organization's goals. The administrative purpose of performance management is to provide information for day-to-day decisions about salary, benefits, recognition, and retention or termination. The developmental purpose of performance management is using the system as a basis for developing employees' knowledge and skills.

LO3 Define five criteria for measuring the effectiveness of a performance management system.

Performance measures should fit with the organization's strategy by supporting its goals and culture. Performance measures should be valid, so they measure all the relevant aspects of performance and do not measure irrelevant aspects of performance. These measures should also provide interrater and test-retest reliability, so that appraisals are consistent among raters and over time. Performance measurement systems should be acceptable to the people who use them or receive feedback from them. Finally, a performance measure should specifically tell employees what is expected of them and how they can meet those expectations.

LO4 Compare the major methods for measuring performance.

Performance measurement may use ranking systems such as simple ranking, forced distribution, or paired comparisons to compare one individual's performance with that of other employees. These methods may be time-consuming, and they will be seen as unfair if actual performance is not distributed in the same way as the ranking system requires. However, ranking counteracts some forms of rater bias and helps distinguish employees for administrative decisions. Other approaches involve rating employees' attributes, behaviors, or outcomes. Rating attributes is relatively simple but not always valid, unless attributes are specifically defined. Rating behaviors requires a great deal of information, but these methods can be very effective. They can link behaviors to goals, and ratings by trained raters may be highly reliable. Rating results, such as

productivity or achievement of objectives, tends to be less subjective than other kinds of rating, making this approach highly acceptable. Validity may be a problem because of factors outside the employee's control. This method also tends not to provide much basis for determining how to improve. Focusing on quality can provide practical benefits but is not as useful for administrative and developmental decisions.

LO5 Describe major sources of performance information in terms of their advantages and disadvantages.

Performance information may come from an employee's self-appraisal and from appraisals by the employee's supervisor, employees, peers, and customers. Using only one source makes the appraisal more subjective. Organizations may combine many sources into a 360-degree performance appraisal. Gathering information from each employee's manager may produce accurate information, unless the supervisor has little opportunity to observe the employee. Peers are an excellent source of information about performance in a job where the supervisor does not often observe the employee. Disadvantages are that friendships (or rivalries) may bias ratings and peers may be uncomfortable with the role of rating a friend. Subordinates often have the best chance to see how a manager treats employees. Employees may be reluctant to contribute honest opinions about a supervisor unless they can provide information anonymously. Self-appraisals may be biased, but they do come from the person with the most knowledge of the employee's behavior on the job, and they provide a basis for discussion in feedback sessions, opening up fruitful comparisons and areas of disagreement between the self-appraisal and other appraisals. Customers may be an excellent source of performance information, although obtaining customer feedback tends to be expensive.

LO6 Define types of rating errors, and explain how to minimize them.

People observe behavior often without a practical way of knowing all the relevant circumstances and outcomes, so they necessarily interpret what they see. A common tendency is to give higher evaluations to people we consider similar to ourselves. Other errors involve using only part of the rating scale: Giving all employees ratings at the high end of the scale is called leniency error. Rating everyone at the low end of the scale is called strictness error. Rating all employees at or near the middle is called central tendency. The halo error refers to rating employees positively in all areas because of strong performance observed in one area. The horns error is rating employees negatively in all areas because of weak performance observed in one area. Ways to reduce rater error are training raters to be aware of their tendencies to make rating errors and training them to be sensitive to the complex nature of employee performance so they will consider many aspects of performance in greater depth. Politics also may influence ratings. Organizations can minimize appraisal politics by establishing a fair appraisal system and bringing managers together to discuss ratings in calibration meetings.

LO7   Explain how to provide performance feedback effectively.

Performance feedback should be a regular, scheduled management activity, so that employees can correct problems as soon as they occur. Managers should prepare by establishing a neutral location, emphasizing that the feedback session will be a chance for discussion, and asking the employee to prepare a self-assessment. During the feedback session, managers should strive for a problem-solving approach and encourage employees to voice their opinions and discuss performance goals. The manager should look for opportunities to praise and should limit criticism. The discussion should focus on behavior and results rather than on personalities.

LO8   Summarize ways to produce improvement in unsatisfactory performance.

For an employee who is motivated but lacks ability, the manager should provide coaching and training, give detailed feedback about performance, and consider restructuring the job. For an employee who has ability but lacks motivation, the manager should investigate whether outside problems are a distraction and if so, refer the employee for help. If the problem has to do with the employee's not feeling appreciated or rewarded, the manager should try to deliver more praise and evaluate whether additional pay and other rewards are appropriate. For an employee lacking both ability and motivation, the manager should consider whether the employee is a good fit for the position. Specific feedback or withholding rewards may spur improvement, or the employee may have to be demoted or terminated. Solid employees who are high in ability and motivation will continue so and may be able to contribute even more if the manager provides appropriate direct feedback, rewards, and opportunities for development.

LO9   Discuss legal and ethical issues that affect performance management.

Lawsuits related to performance management usually involve charges of discrimination or unjust dismissal. Managers must make sure that performance management systems and decisions treat employees equally, without regard to their race, sex, or other protected status. Organizations can do this by establishing and using valid performance measures and by training raters to evaluate performance accurately. A system is more likely to be legally defensible if it is based on behaviors and results, rather than on traits, and if multiple raters evaluate each person's performance. The system should include a process for coaching or training employees to help them improve, rather than simply dismissing poor performers. An ethical issue of performance management is the use of electronic monitoring. This type of performance measurement provides detailed, accurate information, but employees may find it demoralizing, degrading, and stressful. They are more likely to accept it if the organization explains its purpose, links it to help in improving performance, and keeps the performance data private.

KEY TERMS

360-degree performance appraisal, p. 239

behavioral observation scale (BOS), p. 234

behaviorally anchored rating scale (BARS), p. 234

calibration meeting, p. 244

critical-incident method, p. 234

forced-distribution method, p. 229

graphic rating scale, p. 231

management by objectives (MBO), p. 237

mixed-standard scales, p. 231

organizational behavior modification (OBM), p. 235

paired-comparison method, p. 230

performance management, p. 224

simple ranking, p. 229

REVIEW AND DISCUSSION QUESTIONS

1. How does a complete performance management system differ from the use of annual performance appraisals?
2. Give two examples of an administrative decision that would be based on performance management information. Give two examples of developmental decisions based on this type of information.
3. How can involving employees in the creation of performance standards improve the effectiveness of a performance management system? (Consider the criteria for effectiveness listed in the chapter.)
4. Consider how you might rate the performance of three instructors from whom you are currently taking a course. (If you are currently taking only one or two courses, consider this course and two you recently completed.)
   a. Would it be harder to *rate* the instructors' performance or to *rank* their performance? Why?
   b. Write three items to use in rating the instructors— one each to rate them in terms of an attribute, a behavior, and an outcome.
   c. Which measure in (*b*) do you think is most valid? Most reliable? Why?
   d. Many colleges use questionnaires to gather data from students about their instructors' performance. Would it be appropriate to use the data for administrative decisions? Developmental decisions? Other decisions? Why or why not?
5. Imagine that a pet supply store is establishing a new performance management system to help employees provide better customer service. Management needs to decide who should participate in measuring the performance of each of the store's salespeople. From what sources should the store gather information? Why?
6. Would the same sources be appropriate if the store in Question 5 used the performance appraisals to support decisions about which employees to promote? Explain.
7. Suppose you were recently promoted to a supervisory job in a company where you have worked for two years. You genuinely like almost all your co-workers, who now report to you. The only exception is one employee, who dresses more formally than the others and frequently tells jokes that embarrass you and the other workers. Given your preexisting feelings for the employees, how can you measure their performance fairly and effectively?
8. Continuing the example in Question 7, imagine that you are preparing for your first performance feedback session. You want the feedback to be effective—that is, you want the feedback to result in improved performance. List five or six steps you can take to achieve your goal.
9. Besides giving employees feedback, what steps can a manager take to improve employees' performance?
10. Suppose you are a human resource professional helping to improve the performance management system of a company that sells and services office equipment. The company operates a call center that takes calls from customers who are having problems with their equipment. Call center employees are supposed to verify that the problem is not one the customer can easily handle (for example, equipment that will not operate because it has come unplugged). Then, if the problem is not resolved over the phone, the employees arrange for service technicians to visit the customer. The company can charge the customer only if a service technician visits, so performance management of the call center employees focuses on productivity—how quickly they can complete a call and move on to the next caller. To measure this performance efficiently and accurately, the company uses electronic monitoring.
    a. How would you expect the employees to react to the electronic monitoring? How might the organization address the employees' concerns?
    b. Besides productivity in terms of number of calls, what other performance measures should the performance management system include?
    c. How should the organization gather information about the other performance measures?

BUSINESSWEEK CASE

BusinessWeek Performance Review Takes a Page from Facebook

In the world of Facebook or Twitter, people love to hear feedback about what they're up to. But sit them down for a performance review, and suddenly the experience becomes traumatic.

Now companies are taking a page from social networking sites to make the performance evaluation process more fun and useful. Accenture has developed a Facebook-style program called Performance Multiplier in which, among other things, employees post status updates, photos, and two or three weekly goals that can be viewed by fellow staffers. Even more immediate: new software from a Toronto startup called Rypple that lets people post Twitter-length questions about their performance in exchange for anonymous feedback. Companies ranging from sandwich chain Great Harvest Bread Company to Firefox developer Mozilla have signed on as clients.

Such initiatives upend the dreaded rite of annual reviews by making performance feedback a much more real-time and ongoing process. Stanford University management professor Robert Sutton argues that performance reviews "mostly suck" because they're conceived from the top rather than designed with employees' needs in mind. "If you have regular conversations with people, and they know where they stand, then the performance evaluation is maybe unnecessary," says Sutton.

What Rypple's and Accenture's tools do is create a process in which evaluations become dynamic—and more democratic. Rypple, for example, gives employees the chance to post brief, 140-character questions, such as "What did you think of my presentation?" or "How can I run meetings better?" The queries are e-mailed to managers, peers, or anyone else the user selects. Short anonymous responses are then aggregated and sent back, providing a quick-and-dirty 360-degree review. The basic service is free. But corporate clients can pay for a premium version that includes tech support, extra security, and analysis of which topics figure highest in employee posts. Rypple's co-founders have also launched software called TouchBase that's meant to replace the standard annual review with quick monthly surveys and discussions.

Accenture's software, which it's using internally and hoping to sell to outside clients, is more about motivating employees than it is about measuring them. With help from management guru Marcus Buckingham, the consultancy's product has a similar look and feel to other corporate social networks. The major difference is that users are expected to post brief goals for the week on their profile page, as well as a couple for each quarter. If they don't, the lack of goals is visible to their managers, who are also alerted of the omission by e-mail. By prompting people to document and adjust their goals constantly, Accenture hopes the formal discussion will improve. "You don't have to desperately re-create examples of what you've done," says Buckingham. Typically, "managers and employees are scrambling to fill [evaluation forms] out in the 24 hours before HR calls saying 'where's yours?'"

If having your performance goals posted for the world to see sounds a bit Orwellian, consider this: Rypple reports that some two-thirds of the questions posted on its service come from managers wanting feedback about business questions or their own performance. The biggest payoff of these social-network-style tools may prove to be better performance by the boss.

SOURCE: Jena McGregor, "Performance Review Takes a Page from Facebook," *BusinessWeek*, March 12, 2009, www.businessweek.com.

Questions

1. Based on the information given, discuss how well Performance Multiplier and Rypple meet the criteria for effective performance management: fit with strategy, validity, reliability, acceptability, and specific feedback.
2. How suitable would these tools be for fulfilling the strategic, administrative, and developmental purposes of performance management?
3. Think of a job you currently hold, used to have, or would like to have. Imagine that this employer introduced Performance Multiplier or Rypple to your workplace. Describe one area of your performance you would like to seek feedback about, and identify which people you would ask to provide that feedback. What concerns, if any, would you have about using this system to seek feedback about your performance?

Case: When Good Reviews Go Bad

Based on her performance reviews at Merrill Lynch, Kathleen Bostjancic was amazing, at least for a few years. In one appraisal report, her boss said Bostjancic "continues to deliver top-caliber product," and he wrote, "Her judgment is impeccable." After three years, her pay more than doubled to reflect her apparent value to the company.

Then something changed; Bostjancic noticed the difference around the time she took a maternity leave. Her economist boss phoned and asked her to take on a newly created position, Washington policy analyst. But when she returned to work with a plan for the position, her plan was rejected, and tension grew. A year later, Bostjancic's boss issued a memo advising her that her work must "improve dramatically." Seven months later, she was told that she was being laid off in a downsizing effort; the company hired a replacement two months afterward.

A former Citigroup employee also recalls that good reviews before maternity leave didn't do much to help her situation when she returned to work. Wan Li says one performance appraisal after another reported that she was exceeding expectations. Then as she neared maternity leave, she was transferred from a key job in the Structured Trade Finance Group to a support position that would (Li recalls being told) be "more manageable" for her. Upon her return from maternity leave, Li tried to transfer from her temporary support post to a revenue-generating job, but she was instead transferred to another support role. Three years later, following a second maternity leave, Li received a call announcing that her job had been eliminated in a "restructuring."

At Bank of Tokyo-Mitsubishi, Paula Best was progressing well in her career. She was responsible for securities lending and apparently handled the responsibility well enough that the bank added management of international lending to the scope of her job. Best thought she should be made a vice president, like the other employees who reported to the department manager of securities lending. What was holding back her promotion? It wasn't her performance, according to the appraisals; she was rated at the level of "Achieves +," and Best recalls that her vice president promised her a promotion. After two more years and still no promotion, Best, who is African American, complained to the bank's personnel department and then to the Equal Employment Opportunity Commission that she believed she was a victim of sex and race discrimination. Soon thereafter, Best and four other employees in her department were laid off.

How could three employees with glowing performance appraisals be laid off by the institutions that once seemed to value them? Of course, one possibility is that the recent financial crisis required all of these institutions to make hard choices among many valued employees. It's also possible that the three women's performance deteriorated in the time after their last favorable review. Two of the three employers have publicly claimed that their decisions were justified. Merrill Lynch has said that Bostjancic's manager treated her appropriately after her maternity leave; Bank of Tokyo says it fully investigated Best's complaints and

found that management had made appropriate decisions, given her level of responsibility.

Whether or not these decisions were justified, they have proved costly in terms of negative publicity and legal actions. Bostjancic filed a discrimination lawsuit, which is ongoing as of this writing. Li filed a discrimination lawsuit against Citigroup, which was settled to avoid further expense. Best is part of a class-action lawsuit filed against Bank of Tokyo. Meanwhile, among the hundreds of thousands of financial-industry jobs lost in the financial crisis, almost three-quarters of the layoffs have involved women. Notable examples include Zoe Cruz, who had been co-president at Morgan Stanley, and Erin Callan, formerly chief financial officer at Lehman Brothers. The impact is especially dramatic in top-level jobs, where women were already scarce. In one recent survey of executives across industries, 19 percent of women said they'd been laid off in the past two years, compared with 6 percent of male executives.

SOURCES: Anita Raghavan, "Terminated: Why the Women of Wall Street Are Disappearing," *Forbes*, March 16, 2009, Business & Company Resource Center, http://galenet.galegroup.com; Alan Kline and Rebecca Sausner, "Taking Charge in Turbulent Times," *US Banker*, October 1, 2009, Business & Company Resource Center, http://galenet.galegroup.com; and Geraldine Fabrikant, "Bank of America Hires Former Top Citigroup Executive," *The New York Times*, August 4, 2009, Business & Company Resource Center, http://galenet.galegroup.com.

Questions

1. Which purposes of performance management did the appraisals described in this case fulfill? Which purposes did they *not* fulfill?
2. How can managers and HR departments minimize the likelihood of disputes arising over whether employees are continuing to perform at the same level?
3. If you had been in the HR departments of the companies described in this case, and the employees had come to you with their concerns, what would you have done in each situation?

 IT'S A WRAP!   Mc Graw Hill   **connect**

www.mhhe.com/noefund4e is your source for Reviewing, Applying, and Practicing the concepts you learned about in Chapter 8.

Review
- Chapter learning objectives
- Test Your Knowledge: Appraisal Methods and Potential Errors in the Rating Process

Application
- Manager's Hot Seat segment: "Project Management: Steering the Committee"
- Video case and quiz: "Now Who's Boss?"
- Self-Assessment: Conduct an Assessment of Your Job or Project
- Web exercise: Visit HRNet
- Small-business case: Appraisals Matter at Meadow Hills Veterinary Center

Practice
- Chapter quiz

NOTES

1. T. Henneman, "Employee Performance Management: What's Gnu at the Zoo?" *Workforce Management Online,* September 2006, http://www.workforce.com.
2. Carolyn Heinze, "Fair Appraisals," *Systems Contractor News,* July 2009, Business & Company Resource Center, http://galenet.galegroup.com.
3. M. Sallie-Dosunmu, "Born to Grow," *T&D,* May 2006, pp. 33–37.
4. S. Scullen, P. Bergey, and L. Aiman-Smith, "Forced Choice Distribution Systems and the Improvement of Workforce Potential: A Baseline Simulation," *Personnel Psychology* 58 (2005), pp. 1–32.
5. P. Smith and L. Kendall, "Retranslation of Expectations: An Approach to the Construction of Unambiguous Anchors for Rating Scales," *Journal of Applied Psychology* 47 (1963), pp. 149–55.
6. K. Murphy and J. Constans, "Behavioral Anchors as a Source of Bias in Rating," *Journal of Applied Psychology* 72 (1987), pp. 573–77; M. Piotrowski, J. Barnes-Farrel, and F. Estig, "Behaviorally Anchored Bias: A Replication and Extension of Murphy and Constans," *Journal of Applied Psychology* 74 (1989), pp. 823–26.
7. G. Latham and K. Wexley, *Increasing Productivity through Performance Appraisal* (Boston: Addison-Wesley, 1981).
8. U. Wiersma and G. Latham, "The Practicality of Behavioral Observation Scales, Behavioral Expectation Scales, and Trait Scales," *Personnel Psychology* 39 (1986), pp. 619–28.
9. D. C. Anderson, C. Crowell, J. Sucec, K. Gilligan, and M. Wikoff, "Behavior Management of Client Contacts in a Real Estate Brokerage: Getting Agents to Sell More," *Journal of Organizational Behavior Management* 4 (2001), pp. 580–90; and F. Luthans and R. Kreitner, *Organizational Behavior Modification and Beyond* (Glenview, IL: Scott-Foresman, 1975).
10. K. L. Langeland, C. M. Jones, and T. C. Mawhinney, "Improving Staff Performance in a Community Mental Health Setting: Job Analysis, Training, Goal Setting, Feedback, and Years of Data," *Journal of Organizational Behavior Management* 18 (1998), pp. 21–43.
11. J. Komaki, R. Collins, and P. Penn, "The Role of Performance Antecedents and Consequences in Work Motivation," *Journal of Applied Psychology* 67 (1982), pp. 334–40.
12. S. Snell, "Control Theory in Strategic Human Resource Management: The Mediating Effect of Administrative Information," *Academy of Management Journal* 35 (1992), pp. 292–327.
13. R. Pritchard, S. Jones, P. Roth, K. Stuebing, and S. Ekeberg, "The Evaluation of an Integrated Approach to Measuring Organizational Productivity," *Personnel Psychology* 42 (1989), pp. 69–115.
14. G. Odiorne, *MOBII: A System of Managerial Leadership for the 80s* (Belmont, CA: Pitman, 1986).
15. R. Rodgers and J. Hunter, "Impact of Management by Objectives on Organizational Productivity," *Journal of Applied Psychology* 76 (1991), pp. 322–26.
16. P. Wright, J. George, S. Farnsworth, and G. McMahan, "Productivity and Extra-role Behavior: The Effects of Goals and Incentives on Spontaneous Helping," *Journal of Applied Psychology* 78, no. 3 (1993), pp. 374–81.
17. Adrienne Fox, "Curing What Ails Performance Reviews," *HR Magazine,* January 2009, pp. 52–56.
18. R. Heneman, K. Wexley, and M. Moore, "Performance Rating Accuracy: A Critical Review," *Journal of Business Research* 15 (1987), pp. 431–48.
19. T. Becker and R. Klimoski, "A Field Study of the Relationship between the Organizational Feedback Environment and Performance," *Personnel Psychology* 42 (1989), pp. 343–58; H. M. Findley, W. F. Giles, and K. W. Mossholder, "Performance Appraisal and Systems Facets: Relationships with Contextual Performance," *Journal of Applied Psychology* 85 (2000), pp. 634–40.
20. K. Wexley and R. Klimoski, "Performance Appraisal: An Update," in *Research in Personnel and Human Resource Management,* vol. 2, ed. K. Rowland and G. Ferris (Greenwich, CT: JAI Press, 1984).
21. F. Landy and J. Farr, *The Measurement of Work Performance: Methods, Theory, and Applications* (New York: Academic Press, 1983).
22. G. McEvoy and P. Buller, "User Acceptance of Peer Appraisals in an Industrial Setting," *Personnel Psychology* 40 (1987), pp. 785–97.
23. A. Pomeroy, "Agent of Change," *HRMagazine,* May 2005, pp. 52–56.
24. D. Antonioni, "The Effects of Feedback Accountability on Upward Appraisal Ratings," *Personnel Psychology* 47 (1994), pp. 349–56.
25. Fox, "Curing What Ails Performance Reviews," p. 55.
26. H. Heidemeier and K. Moser, "Self-Other Agreement in Job Performance Rating: A Meta-Analytic Test of a Process Model," *Journal of Applied Psychology* 94 (2008), pp. 353–70.
27. J. Bernardin, C. Hagan, J. Kane, and P. Villanova, "Effective Performance Management: A Focus on Precision, Customers, and Situational Constraints," in *Performance Appraisal: State of the Art in Practice,*

ed. J. W. Smither (San Francisco: Jossey-Bass, 1998), pp. 3–48.

28. K. Wexley and W. Nemeroff, "Effects of Racial Prejudice, Race of Applicant, and Biographical Similarity on Interviewer Evaluations of Job Applicants," *Journal of Social and Behavioral Sciences* 20 (1974), pp. 66–78.

29. D. Smith, "Training Programs for Performance Appraisal: A Review," *Academy of Management Review* 11 (1986), pp. 22–40; and G. Latham, K. Wexley, and E. Pursell, "Training Managers to Minimize Rating Errors in the Observation of Behavior," *Journal of Applied Psychology* 60 (1975), pp. 550–55.

30. E. Pulakos, "A Comparison of Rater Training Programs: Error Training and Accuracy Training," *Journal of Applied Psychology* 69 (1984), pp. 581–88.

31. J. Sammer, "Calibrating Consistency," *HR Magazine*, January 2008, pp. 73–75; and Fox, "Curing What Ails Performance Reviews," pp. 55–56.

32. S. W. J. Kozlowski, G. T. Chao, and R. F. Morrison, "Games Raters Play: Politics, Strategies, and Impression Management in Performance Appraisal," in *Performance Appraisal: State of the Art in Practice*, pp. 163–205; and C. Rosen, P. Levy, and R. Hall, "Placing Perceptions of Politics in the Context of the Feedback Environment, Employee Attitudes, and Job Performance," *Journal of Applied Psychology* 91 (2006), pp. 211–20.

33. B. Hite, "Employers Rethink How They Give Feedback," *Wall Street Journal*, October 13, 2008, p. B5.

34. K. Wexley, V. Singh, and G. Yukl, "Subordinate Participation in Three Types of Appraisal Interviews," *Journal of Applied Psychology* 58 (1973), pp. 54–57; K. Wexley, "Appraisal Interview," in *Performance Assessment*, ed. R. A. Berk (Baltimore: Johns Hopkins University Press, 1986), pp. 167–85; B. D. Cawley, L. M. Keeping, and P. E. Levy, "Participation in the Performance Appraisal Process and Employee Reactions: A Meta-analytic Review of Field Investigations," *Journal of Applied Psychology* 83, no. 3 (1998), pp. 615–63; H. Aguinis,

Performance Management (Upper Saddle River, NJ: Pearson Prentice-Hall, 2007); and C. Lee, "Feedback, Not Appraisal," *HR Magazine*, November 2006, pp. 111–14.

35. D. Cederblom, "The Performance Appraisal Interview: A Review, Implications, and Suggestions," *Academy of Management Review* 7 (1982), pp. 219–27; B. D. Cawley, L. M. Keeping, and P. E. Levy, "Participation in the Performance Appraisal Process and Employee Reactions: A Meta-analytic Review of Field Investigations," *Journal of Applied Psychology* 83, no. 3 (1998), pp. 615–63; and W. Giles and K. Mossholder, "Employee Reactions to Contextual and Session Components of Performance Appraisal," *Journal of Applied Psychology* 75 (1990), pp. 371–77.

36. *Brito v. Zia Co.*, 478 F.2d 1200 (10th Cir. 1973).

37. K. Kraiger and J. Ford, "A Meta-Analysis of Ratee Race Effects in Performance Rating," *Journal of Applied Psychology* 70 (1985), pp. 56–65.

38. P. Sackett, C. DuBois, and A. Noe, "Tokenism in Performance Evaluation: The Effects of Work Group Representation on Male-Female and White-Black Differences in Performance Ratings," *Journal of Applied Psychology* 76 (1991), pp. 263–67.

39. G. Barrett and M. Kernan, "Performance Appraisal and Terminations: A Review of Court Decisions since *Brito v. Zia* with Implications for Personnel Practices," *Personnel Psychology* 40 (1987), pp. 489–503; H. Feild and W. Holley, "The Relationship of Performance Appraisal System Characteristics to Verdicts in Selected Employment Discrimination Cases," *Academy of Management Journal* 25 (1982), pp. 392–406; J. M. Werner and M. C. Bolino, "Explaining U.S. Courts of Appeals Decisions Involving Performance Appraisal: Accuracy, Fairness, and Validation," *Personnel Psychology* 50 (1997), pp. 1–24; and Christine V. Bonavita, "The Importance of Performance Evaluations," *Employment Law Strategist*, March 1, 2009, Business & Company Resource Center, http://galenet.galegroup.com.

40. V. O'Connell, "Stores Count Seconds to Cut Labor Costs," *Wall Street Journal*, November 17, 2008, pp. A1, A15.

Developing Employees for Future Success

What Do I Need to Know?

After reading this chapter, you should be able to:

LO1 Discuss how development is related to training and careers.

LO2 Identify the methods organizations use for employee development.

LO3 Describe how organizations use assessment of personality type, work behaviors, and job performance to plan employee development.

LO4 Explain how job experiences can be used for developing skills.

LO5 Summarize principles of successful mentoring programs.

LO6 Tell how managers and peers develop employees through coaching.

LO7 Identify the steps in the process of career management.

LO8 Discuss how organizations are meeting the challenges of the "glass ceiling," succession planning, and dysfunctional managers.

Introduction

As we noted in Chapter 1, employees' commitment to their organization depends on how their managers treat them. To "win the war for talent" managers must be able to identify high-potential employees, make sure the organization uses the talents of these people, and reassure them of their value so that they do not become dissatisfied and leave the organization. Managers also must be able to listen. Although new employees need strong direction, they expect to be able to think independently and be treated with respect. In all these ways, managers provide for **employee development**—the combination of formal education, job experiences, relationships, and assessment of personality and abilities to help employees prepare for the future of their careers. Human resource management establishes a process for employee development that prepares employees to help the organization meet its goals.

This chapter explores the purpose and activities of employee development. We begin by discussing the relationships among development, training, and career management. Next, we look at development approaches, including formal education, assessment, job experiences, and interpersonal relationships. The chapter emphasizes the types of skills, knowledge, and behaviors that are strengthened by each development method, so employees and their managers can choose appropriate methods when planning for development. The third section of the chapter describes the steps of the career management process, emphasizing the responsibilities of employee and employer at each step of the process. The chapter concludes with a discussion of special challenges related to employee development—the so-called glass ceiling, succession planning, and dysfunctional managers.

Training, Development, and Career Management

Organizations and their employees must constantly expand their knowledge, skills, and behavior to meet customer needs and compete in today's demanding and rapidly changing business environment. More and more companies operate internationally, requiring that employees understand different cultures and customs. More companies organize work in terms of projects or customers, rather than specialized functions, so employees need to acquire a broad range of technical and interpersonal skills. Many companies expect employees at all levels to perform roles once reserved for management. Modern organizations are expected to provide development opportunities to employees without regard to their sex, race, ethnic background, or age so that they have equal opportunity for advancement. In this climate, organizations are placing greater emphasis on training and development. To do this, organizations must understand development's relationship to training and career management.

Employee Development The combination of formal education, job experiences, relationships, and assessment of personality and abilities to help employees prepare for the future of their careers.

LO1 Discuss how development is related to training and careers.

Development and Training

The definition of development indicates that it is future oriented. Development implies learning that is not necessarily related to the employee's current job.[1] Instead, it prepares employees for other jobs or positions in the organization and increases their ability to move into jobs that may not yet exist.[2] Development also may help employees prepare for changes in responsibilities and requirements in their current jobs, such as changes resulting from new technology, work designs, or customers.

In contrast, training traditionally focuses on helping employees improve performance of their current jobs. Many organizations have focused on linking training programs to business goals. In these organizations, the distinction between training and development is more blurred. Table 9.1 summarizes the traditional differences.

Development for Careers

The concept of a career has changed in recent years. In the traditional view, a career consists of a sequence of positions within an occupation or organization.[3] For example, an academic career might begin with a position as a university's adjunct professor. It continues with appointment to faculty positions as assistant professor, then associate professor, and finally full professor. An engineer might start as a staff engineer, then with greater experience earn promotions to the positions of advisory engineer, senior engineer, and vice president of engineering. In these examples, the career resembles a set of stairs from the bottom of a profession or organization to the top.

Recently, however, changes such as downsizing and restructuring have become the norm, so the concept of a career has become more fluid. Today's employees are more

	TRAINING	DEVELOPMENT
Focus	Current	Future
Use of work experiences	Low	High
Goal	Preparation for current job	Preparation for changes
Participation	Required	Voluntary

Table 9.1

Training versus Development

Protean Career
A career that frequently changes based on changes in the person's interests, abilities, and values and in the work environment.

likely to have a **protean career,** one that frequently changes based on changes in the person's interests, abilities, and values and in the work environment. For example, an engineer might decide to take a sabbatical from her job to become a manager with Engineers without Borders, so she can develop managerial skills and decide whether she likes managing. As in this example, employees in protean careers take responsibility for managing their careers. This practice is consistent with the modern *psychological contract* described in Chapter 2. Employees look for organizations to provide, not job security and a career ladder to climb, but instead development opportunities and flexible work arrangements.

To remain marketable, employees must continually develop new skills. Fewer of today's careers involve repetitive tasks, and more rely on an expanding base of knowledge.[4] Jobs are less likely to last a lifetime, so employees have to prepare for newly created positions. Beyond knowing job requirements, employees need to understand the business in which they are working and be able to cultivate valuable relationships with co-workers, managers, suppliers, and customers. They also need to follow trends in their field and industry, so they can apply technology and knowledge that will match emerging priorities and needs. Learning such skills requires useful job experiences as well as effective training programs.

These relationships and experiences often take an employee along a career path that is far different from the traditional steps upward through an organization or profession. Although such careers will not disappear, more employees will follow a spiral career path in which they cross the boundaries between specialties and organizations. As organizations provide for employee development (and as employees take control of their own careers), they will need to (1) determine their interests, skills, and weaknesses and (2) seek development experiences involving jobs, relationships, and formal courses. As discussed later in the chapter, organizations can meet these needs through a system for *career management* or *development planning*. Career management helps employees select development activities that prepare them to meet their career goals. It helps employers select development activities in line with their human resource needs.

LO2 Identify the methods organizations use for employee development.

Approaches to Employee Development

Children's Healthcare of Atlanta, a medical organization specializing in pediatric care, focuses development efforts on high-performing employees who have the potential to become managers. These employees complete a full day of assessment that includes taking a personality test and participating in a business simulation in which they take the role of managers. Each year they also attend five workshops, where they learn about leading change, developing a business strategy, and creating a personal vision. They work in teams to solve a practical problem affecting Children's, and they receive coaching to help them set and achieve their own goals.[5]

The many approaches to employee development fall into four broad categories: formal education, assessment, job experiences, and interpersonal relationships.[6] Figure 9.1 summarizes these four methods. Many organizations combine these approaches, as in the previous example of Children's Healthcare.

Formal Education

Organizations may support employee development through a variety of formal educational programs, either at the workplace or off-site. These may include workshops designed specifically for the organization's employees, short courses offered by consultants or universities, university programs offered to employees who live on campus during the program, and executive MBA programs (which enroll managers to meet on weekends or evenings to earn a master's degree in business administration). These programs may involve lectures by business experts, business games and simulations, experiential programs, and meetings with customers. Chapter 7 described most of these training methods, including their pros and cons.

Many companies, including Bank of Montreal and General Electric, operate training and development centers that offer seminars and longer-term programs. The Bank of Montreal operates its own Institute for Learning, featuring classrooms, a presentation hall, and guest accommodations for out-of-town employees. Programs include training in management leadership, risk management, and project management, as well as courses toward an MBA degree.[7] General Electric has one of the oldest and best-known management development centers, the

Figure 9.1

Four Approaches to Employee Development

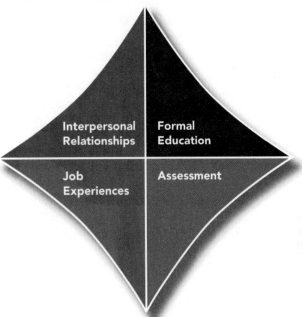

John F. Welch Leadership Center in Crotonville, New York. Each year, GE managers choose employees with high performance and potential and send them to Crotonville for management development programs combining coursework and job experiences.[8]

Independent institutions offering executive education include Harvard, the Wharton School of Business, the University of Michigan, and the Center for Creative Leadership. A growing number of companies and universities are using distance learning (discussed in Chapter 7) to reach executive audiences. For example, Duke University's Fuqua School of Business offers an electronic executive MBA program. Besides attending traditional classes, students use personal computers to view lectures on CD-ROM, download study aids, discuss lectures, and work on team projects online.

Another trend in executive education is for employers and the education provider to create short courses with content designed specifically for the audience. MetLife worked with Babson College to develop a course in which faculty members discuss business principles and then invite corporate executives to discuss how the principles work in MetLife and the insurance industry. Small teams of class participants work on related class projects and develop recommendations for company executives. MetLife has implemented 82 percent of these projects.[9]

LO3 Describe how organizations use assessment of personality type, work behaviors, and job performance to plan employee development.

Assessment

Another way to provide for employee development is **assessment**—collecting information and providing feedback to employees about their behavior, communication style, or skills.[10] Information for assessment may come from the employees, their peers, managers, and customers. The most frequent uses of assessment are to identify employees with managerial potential to measure current managers' strengths and weaknesses. Organizations also use assessment to identify managers with potential to

Assessment
Collecting information and providing feedback to employees about their behavior, communication style, or skills.

One way to develop employees is to begin with an assessment which may consist of assigning an activity to a team and seeing who brings what skills and strengths to the team. How can this assessment help employees?

move into higher-level executive positions. Organizations that assign work to teams may use assessment to identify the strengths and weaknesses of individual team members and the effects of the team members' decision-making and communication styles on the team's productivity.

For assessment to support development, the information must be shared with the employee being assessed. Along with that assessment information, the employee needs suggestions for correcting skill weaknesses and for using skills already learned. The suggestions might be to participate in training courses or develop skills through new job experiences. Based on the assessment information and available development opportunities, employees should develop action plans to guide their efforts at self-improvement.

Organizations vary in the methods and sources of information they use in developmental assessment (see the "Did You Know?" box). Many organizations appraise performance. Organizations with sophisticated development systems use psychological tests to measure employees' skills, personality types, and communication styles. They may collect self, peer, and manager ratings of employees' behavior and style of working with others. The tools used for these assessment methods include the Myers-Briggs Type Indicator, assessment centers, the Benchmarks assessment, performance appraisal, and 360-degree feedback. Edward Jones assesses the leadership potential of financial advisers working outside its St. Louis headquarters by combining personality assessment with peer appraisals. Employees and their managers receive the results, which are used to evaluate whether employees have the behaviors and personality required for a leadership role at headquarters.[11]

Myers-Briggs Type Indicator®

Myers-Briggs Type Indicator (MBTI)®
Psychological test that identifies individuals' preferences for source of energy, means of information gathering, way of decision making, and lifestyle, providing information for team building and leadership development.

The most popular psychological inventory for employee development is the **Myers-Briggs Type Indicator (MBTI)®**. This assessment identifies individuals' preferences for source of energy, means of information gathering, way of decision making, and lifestyle. The assessment consists of more than 100 questions about how the person feels or prefers to behave in different situations (such as "Are you usually a good 'mixer' or rather quiet and reserved?"). The assessment describes these individuals' preferences in the four areas:

1. The *energy* dichotomy indicates where individuals gain interpersonal strength and vitality, measured as their degree of introversion or extroversion. Extroverted types (E) gain energy through interpersonal relationships. Introverted types (I) gain energy by focusing on inner thoughts and feelings.
2. The *information-gathering* dichotomy relates to the preparations individuals make before making decisions. Individuals with a Sensing (S) preference tend to gather the facts and details to prepare for a decision. Intuitive types (N) tend to focus less on the facts and more on possibilities and relationships among them.

Developmental Assessment Often an Unmet Need

If you want to give your company an edge over the competition, try developing your new managers. According to a recent study by the Institute for Corporate Productivity, few companies provide developmental assessments when employees are promoted to management jobs. Among those that do, most rely on performance appraisals and 360-degree feedback.

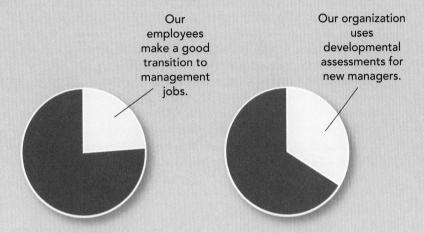

Our employees make a good transition to management jobs.

Our organization uses developmental assessments for new managers.

Sources: Aparna Nancherla, "Mismanaged Transitions: Many Organizations Provide Little or No Guidance for Newly Promoted Employees," *T + D*, October 2009, Business & Company Resource Center, http://galenet.galegroup.com; and Institute for Corporate Productivity, "Most Employers Are Ineffective at Supporting New Managers," news release, August 10, 2009, www.i4cp.com.

3. In *decision making*, individuals differ in the amount of consideration they give to their own and others' values and feelings, as opposed to the hard facts of a situation. Individuals with a Thinking (T) preference try always to be objective in making decisions. Individuals with a Feeling (F) preference tend to evaluate the impact of the alternatives on others, as well as their own feelings; they are more subjective.

4. The *lifestyle* dichotomy describes an individual's tendency to be either flexible or structured. Individuals with a Judging (J) preference focus on goals, establish deadlines, and prefer to be conclusive. Individuals with a Perceiving (P) preference enjoy surprises, are comfortable with changing a decision, and dislike deadlines.

The alternatives for each of the four dichotomies result in 16 possible combinations. Of course people are likely to be mixtures of these types, but the point of the assessment is that certain types predominate in individuals.

As a result of their psychological types, people develop strengths and weaknesses. For example, individuals who are Introverted, Sensing, Thinking, and Judging (known as ISTJs) tend to be serious, quiet, practical, orderly, and logical. They can organize tasks, be decisive, and follow through on plans and goals. But because they do not have the opposite preferences (Extroversion, Intuition, Feeling, and Perceiving),

ISTJs have several weaknesses. They may have difficulty responding to unexpected opportunities, appear to their colleagues to be too task-oriented or impersonal, and make decisions too fast.

Applying this kind of information about employees' preferences or tendencies helps organizations understand the communication, motivation, teamwork, work styles, and leadership of the people in their groups. For example, salespeople or executives who want to communicate better can apply what they learn about their own personality styles and the way other people perceive them. For team development, the MBTI can help teams match team members with assignments based on their preferences and thus improve problem solving.[12] The team could assign brainstorming (idea-generating) tasks to employees with an Intuitive preference and evaluation of the ideas to employees with a Sensing preference.

Research on the validity, reliability, and effectiveness of the MBTI is inconclusive.[13] People who take the MBTI find it a positive experience and say it helps them change their behavior. However, MBTI scores are not necessarily stable over time. Studies in which the MBTI was administered at two different times found that as few as one-fourth of those who took the assessment were classified as exactly the same type the second time. Still, the MBTI is a valuable tool for understanding communication styles and the ways people prefer to interact with others. It is not appropriate for measuring job performance, however, or as the only means of evaluating promotion potential.

Assessment Centers

Assessment Center
An assessment process in which multiple raters or evaluators (assessors) evaluate employees' performance on a number of exercises, usually as they work in a group at an off-site location.

At an **assessment center,** multiple raters or evaluators (assessors) evaluate employees' performance on a number of exercises.[14] An assessment center is usually an off-site location such as a conference center. Usually 6 to 12 employees participate at one time. The primary use of assessment centers is to identify whether employees have the personality characteristics, administrative skills, and interpersonal skills needed for managerial jobs. Organizations also use them to determine whether employees have the skills needed for working in teams.

Leaderless Group Discussion
An assessment center exercise in which a team of five to seven employees is assigned a problem and must work together to solve it within a certain time period.

The types of exercises used in assessment centers include leaderless group discussions, interviews, in-baskets, and role-plays.[15] In a **leaderless group discussion,** a team of five to seven employees is assigned a problem and must work together to solve it within a certain time period. The problem may involve buying and selling supplies, nominating a subordinate for an award, or assembling a product. Interview questions typically cover each employee's work and personal experiences, skill strengths and weaknesses, and career plans. In-basket exercises, discussed as a selection method in Chapter 6, simulate the administrative tasks of a manager's job, using a pile of documents for the employee to handle. In role-plays, the participant takes the part of a manager or employee in a situation involving the skills to be assessed. For example, a participant might be given the role of a manager who must discuss performance problems with an employee, played by someone who works for the assessment center. Other exercises in assessment centers might include interest and aptitude tests to evaluate an employee's vocabulary, general mental ability, and reasoning skills. Personality tests may be used to determine employees' ability to get along with others, tolerance for uncertainty, and other traits related to success as a manager or team member.

The assessors are usually managers who have been trained to look for employee behaviors that are related to the skills being assessed. Typically, each assessor observes and records one or two employees' behaviors in each exercise. The assessors review their notes and rate each employee's level of skills (for example, 5 = high level of leadership skills, 1 = low level of leadership skills). After all the employees have completed the exercises, the assessors discuss their observations of each employee. They compare their ratings and try to agree on each employee's rating for each of the skills.

As we mentioned in Chapter 6, research suggests that assessment center ratings are valid for predicting performance, salary level, and career advancement.[16] Assessment centers may also be useful for development because of the feedback that participants receive about their attitudes, skill strengths, and weaknesses.[17]

Benchmarks

A development method that focuses on measuring management skills is an instrument called **Benchmarks.** This measurement tool gathers ratings of a manager's use of skills associated with success in managing. The items measured by Benchmarks are based on research into the lessons that executives learn in critical events of their careers.[18] Items measure the 16 skills and perspectives listed in Table 9.2, including how well managers deal with subordinates, acquire resources, and create a productive work climate. Research has found that managers who have these skills are more likely to receive positive performance evaluations, be considered promotable, and be promoted.[19]

To provide a complete picture of managers' skills, the managers' supervisors, their peers, and the managers themselves all complete the instrument. The results include

Benchmarks
A measurement tool that gathers ratings of a manager's use of skills associated with success in managing.

Table 9.2

Skills Related to Success as a Manager

Resourcefulness	Can think strategically, engage in flexible problem solving, and work effectively with higher management.
Doing whatever it takes	Has perseverance and focus in the face of obstacles.
Being a quick study	Quickly masters new technical and business knowledge.
Building and mending relationships	Knows how to build and maintain working relationships with co-workers and external parties.
Leading subordinates	Delegates to subordinates effectively, broadens their opportunities, and acts with fairness toward them.
Compassion and sensitivity	Shows genuine interest in others and sensitivity to subordinates' needs.
Straightforwardness and composure	Is honorable and steadfast.
Setting a developmental climate	Provides a challenging climate to encourage subordinates' development.
Confronting problem subordinates	Acts decisively and fairly when dealing with problem subordinates.
Team orientation	Accomplishes tasks through managing others.
Balance between personal life and work	Balances work priorities with personal life so that neither is neglected.
Decisiveness	Prefers quick and approximate actions to slow and precise ones in many management situations.
Self-awareness	Has an accurate picture of strengths and weaknesses and is willing to improve.
Hiring talented staff	Hires talented people for the team.
Putting people at ease	Displays warmth and a good sense of humor.
Acting with flexibility	Can behave in ways that are often seen as opposites.

SOURCE: Adapted with permission from C. D. McCauley, M. M. Lombardo, and C. J. Usher, "Diagnosing Management Development Needs: An Instrument Based on How Managers Develop," *Journal of Management* 15 (1989), pp. 389–403.

a summary report, which the organization provides to the manager so he or she can see the self-ratings in comparison to the ratings by others. Also available with this method is a development guide containing examples of experiences that enhance each skill and ways successful managers use the skill.

Performance Appraisals and 360-Degree Feedback

As we stated in Chapter 8, *performance appraisal* is the process of measuring employees' performance. This information can be useful for employee development under certain conditions.[20] The appraisal system must tell employees specifically about their performance problems and ways to improve their performance. Employees must gain a clear understanding of the differences between current performance and expected performance. The appraisal process must identify causes of the performance discrepancy and develop plans for improving performance. Managers must be trained to deliver frequent performance feedback and must monitor employees' progress in carrying out their action plans.

A recent trend in performance appraisals, also discussed in Chapter 8, is *360-degree feedback*—performance measurement by the employee's supervisor, peers, employees, and customers. Often the feedback involves rating the individual in terms of work-related behaviors. For development purposes, the rater would identify an area of behavior as a strength of that employee or an area requiring further development. The results presented to the employee show how he or she was rated on each item and how self-evaluations differ from other raters' evaluations. The individual reviews the results, seeks clarification from the raters, and sets specific development goals based on the strengths and weaknesses identified.[21]

In an interesting twist on commonly held beliefs about personal development, Tom Rath and Barrie Conchie of the Gallup Organization studied business leaders and concluded that correcting weaknesses does not make an individual a great leader. Rather, they advocate using assessment information to identify personal strengths, then further developing and building those strengths to become a more effective leader. They note that Brad Anderson of Best Buy, Wendy Kopp of Teach for America, Simon Cooper of the Ritz-Carlton Hotel Company, and Mervyn Davies of Standard Chartered Bank are all excellent leaders who rely on different talents to lead. Extending that idea, Rath and Couchie recommend that managers learn to identify and focus on their employees' strengths as a way to help them become more effective. Rather than building well-rounded leaders, this application of assessment information aims to build well-rounded teams of individuals who together possess strengths related to executing plans, influencing others, building relationships, and thinking strategically.[22]

There are several benefits of 360-degree feedback. Organizations collect multiple perspectives of managers' performance, allowing employees to compare their own personal evaluations with the views of others. This method also establishes formal communications about behaviors and skill ratings between employees and their internal and external customers. Several studies have shown that performance improves and behavior changes as a result of participating in upward feedback and 360-degree feedback systems.[23] The change is greatest in people who received lower ratings from others than what they gave themselves. The 360-degree feedback system is most likely to be effective if the rating instrument enables reliable or consistent ratings, assesses behaviors or skills that are job related, and is easy to use. And in an analysis of the impact of 360-degree feedback on leadership, the assessments were most beneficial if the leaders were coached on how to build on the strengths that were identified.[24]

CHALLENGES NOURISH EMPLOYEES' GROWTH AT RAINFOREST ALLIANCE

focus on *social responsibility*

The Rainforest Alliance is an international nonprofit organization based in New York City and active in more than 70 countries. It works with business, local nonprofit groups, and international development agencies to establish standards for sustainable use of natural resources. Companies that agree to abide by the standards can obtain permission to display the Rainforest Alliance certification on their packaging and advertisements, thereby attracting customers who are concerned about the planet's long-term well-being.

At an organization with such an idealistic mission, one would expect that employees are highly motivated to make a difference. In the words of Helena Albuquerque, the organization's director of human resources, people at the Rainforest Alliance "share a common sense of purpose, a collaborative spirit, and the determination to truly make the world a better place." As an employer, the

Rainforest Alliance builds on this advantage by giving employees opportunities to develop their careers by tackling big challenges.

Career development through experiences is an opportunity that many organizations reserve for a few management employees on the fast track. But at Rainforest Alliance, even new hires are trusted with these assignments. Junior employees are invited to conferences and to executive-level meetings. They also can launch and eventually lead research projects in topics they care about. An example is Julie Baroody, who was originally hired as executive assistant to Tensie Whelan, the organization's executive director. Baroody was interested in the topic of climate change, so her quickly growing responsibilities included conducting research. Two promotions later, Baroody was the coordinator of the Rainforest Alliance's climate initiative, representing the organization at conferences around the world.

The Rainforest Alliance's global presence also presents impressive opportunities for career development. More than half of the organization's people work outside the United States, and through an internship program U.S. employees can sign up to work in foreign offices. Those assignments offer chances to get firsthand experience with the organization's core activities and issues.

Thanks to this developmental approach to management, it's not just the environment that's thriving because of the Rainforest Alliance. So are the careers of the group's more than 250 employees.

Sources: Kelly K. Spors, "Top Small Workplaces 2008," *Wall Street Journal*, February 22, 2009, http://online.wsj.com; Rainforest Alliance, "Rainforest Alliance a 'Top Small Work Place,'" *Rainforest Matters*, November 2008, www.rainforest-alliance.org; and Rainforest Alliance, "What We Do," corporate Web site, www.rainforest-alliance.org, accessed April 7, 2010.

There are potential limitations of 360-degree feedback. This method demands a significant amount of time for raters to complete the evaluations. If raters, especially subordinates or peers, provide negative feedback, some managers might try to identify and punish them. A facilitator is needed to help interpret results. Finally, simply delivering ratings to a manager does not provide ways for the manager to act on the feedback (for example, development planning, meeting with raters, or taking courses). As noted earlier, any form of assessment should be accompanied by suggestions for improvement and development of an action plan.

Job Experiences

Most employee development occurs through **job experiences**[25]—the combination of relationships, problems, demands, tasks, and other features of an employee's jobs. Using job experiences for employee development assumes that development is most

LO4 Explain how job experiences can be used for developing skills.

Job Experiences
The combination of relationships, problems, demands, tasks, and other features of an employee's jobs.

likely to occur when the employee's skills and experiences do not entirely match the skills required for the employee's current job. To succeed, employees must stretch their skills. In other words, they must learn new skills, apply their skills and knowledge in new ways, and master new experiences.[26] For example, companies that want to prepare employees to expand overseas markets are assigning them to a variety of international jobs. To learn how a small company successfully uses job experiences to develop employees, see the "Best Practices" box.

Most of what we know about development through job experiences comes from a series of studies conducted by the Center for Creative Leadership.[27] These studies asked executives to identify key career events that made a difference in their managerial styles and the lessons they learned from these experiences. The key events included job assignments (such as fixing a failed operation), interpersonal relationships (getting along with supervisors), and types of transitions (situations in which the manager at first lacked the necessary background). Through job experiences like these, managers learn how to handle common challenges, prove themselves, lead change, handle pressure, and influence others.

The usefulness of job experiences for employee development varies depending on whether the employee views the experiences as positive or negative sources of stress. When employees view job experiences as positive stressors, the experiences challenge them and stimulate learning. When they view job experiences as negative stressors, employees may suffer from high levels of harmful stress. Of the job demands studied, managers were most likely to experience negative stress from creating change and overcoming obstacles (adverse business conditions, lack of management support, lack of personal support, or a difficult boss). Research suggests that all of the job demands except obstacles are related to learning.[28] Organizations should offer job experiences that are most likely to increase learning, and they should consider the consequences of situations that involve negative stress.

Although the research on development through job experiences has focused on managers, line employees also can learn through job experiences. Organizations may, for example, use job experiences to develop skills needed for teamwork, including conflict resolution, data analysis, and customer service. These experiences may occur when forming a team and when employees switch roles within a team.

Various job assignments can provide for employee development. The organization may enlarge the employee's current job or move the employee to different jobs. Lateral moves include job rotation, transfer, or temporary assignment to another organization. The organization may also use downward moves or promotions as a source of job experience. Figure 9.2 summarizes these alternatives.

Job Enlargement

As Chapter 4 stated in the context of job design, *job enlargement* involves adding challenges or new responsibilities to employees' current jobs. Examples include completing a special project, switching roles within a work team, or researching new ways to serve customers. An engineering employee might join a task force developing new career paths for technical employees. The work on the project could give the engineer a leadership role through which the engineer learns about the company's career development system while also practicing leadership skills to help the task force reach its goals. In this way, job enlargement not only makes a job more interesting but also creates an opportunity for employees to develop new skills.

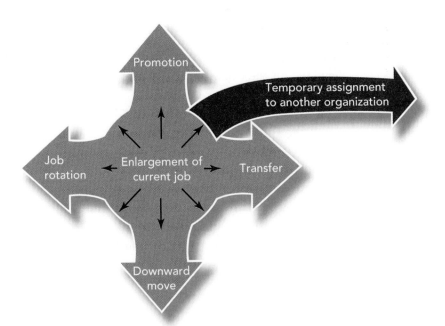

Figure 9.2

How Job Experiences
Are Used for Employee
Development

Job Rotation

Another job design technique that can be applied to employee development is *job rotation*, moving employees through a series of job assignments in one or more functional areas. The job rotation program for Tata Consultancy Services sends employees from its headquarters in India on 18- to 24-month assignments to its operations in China, Hungary, and South America. The program helps the company develop expertise in the cultures of the 42 countries where Tata operates. And when employees return to India, they typically work on similar kinds of projects, so they bring home and share lessons they gained from their overseas assignments.[29]

Job rotation helps employees gain an appreciation for the company's goals, increases their understanding of different company functions, develops a network of contacts, and improves problem-solving and decision-making skills.[30] Job rotation also helps employees increase their salary and earn promotions faster. However, job rotation poses some problems for employees and the organization. Knowing they will be rotated to another job may give the employees a short-term perspective on problems and their solutions. Employees may feel less satisfied and motivated because they have difficulty developing specialized skills and leave the position too soon to fulfill any challenging assignments. The rotation of employees through a department may hurt productivity and increase the workload of those who remain after employees are rotated out. Job rotation is most likely to succeed when it meets certain conditions:[31]

- The organization establishes and communicates clear policies about which positions are eligible for job rotation. Job rotation for nonmanagement employees as well as managers can be beneficial, depending on the program's objectives.
- Employees and their managers understand and agree on the expectations for the job rotation, including which skills are to be developed.
- Goals for the program support business goals. These might include exposing high-potential employees to a variety of business units, customers, or geographic areas

in preparation for management positions or rotating an experienced, talented employee through several business units to mentor or coach employees.

- The rotation schedule is realistic, taking into account how long employees will need to become familiar with their new position, as well as how much time is needed for employees to complete the assignments.
- Top management is committed to the program's success.
- Someone is responsible for measuring whether the program is meeting its goals.

Transfers, Promotions, and Downward Moves

Transfer
Assignment of an employee to a position in a different area of the company, usually in a lateral move.

Most companies use upward, downward, and lateral moves as an option for employee development. In a **transfer,** the organization assigns an employee to a position in a different area of the company. Transfers do not necessarily increase job responsibilities or compensation. They are usually lateral moves, that is, moves to a job with a similar level of responsibility. They may involve relocation to another part of the country or even to another country.

Relocation can be stressful because of the demands of moving, especially when family members are affected. People have to find new housing, shopping, health care, and leisure facilities, and they often lack the support of nearby friends and family. These stresses come at the same time the employee must learn the expectations and responsibilities associated with the new position. Because transfers can provoke anxiety, many companies have difficulty getting employees to accept them. Employees most willing to accept transfers tend to be those with high career ambitions and beliefs that the organization offers a promising future and that accepting the transfer will help the company succeed.[32]

Downward Move
Assignment of an employee to a position with less responsibility and authority.

A **downward move** occurs when an employee is given less responsibility and authority. The organization may demote an employee because of poor performance or move the employee to a lower-level position in another function so that the employee can develop different skills. The temporary cross-functional move is the most common way to use downward moves for employee development. For example, engineers who want to move into management often take lower-level positions, such as shift supervisor, to develop their management skills.

Many employees have difficulty associating transfers and downward moves with development; these changes may feel more like forms of punishment. Employees often decide to leave an organization rather than accept such a change, and then the organization must bear the costs of replacing those employees. Employees will be more likely to accept transfers and downward moves as development opportunities if the organization provides information about the change and its possible benefits and involves the employee in planning the change. Employees are also more likely to be positive about such a recommendation if the organization provides clear performance objectives and frequent feedback. Employers can encourage an

Working outside one's home country is the most important job experience that can develop an employee for a career in the global economy.

employee to relocate by providing financial assistance with the move, information about the new location and job, and help for family members, such as identifying schools, child care and elder care options, and job search assistance for the employee's spouse.[33]

A **promotion** involves moving an employee into a position with greater challenges, more responsibility, and more authority than in the previous job. Usually promotions include pay increases. Because promotions improve the person's pay, status, and feelings of accomplishment, employees are more willing to accept promotions than lateral or downward moves. Even so, employers can increase the likelihood that employees will accept promotions by providing the same kind of information and assistance that are used to support transfers and downward moves. Organizations can more easily offer promotions if they are profitable and growing. In other conditions, opportunities for promoting employees may be limited.

> **Promotion**
> Assignment of an employee to a position with greater challenges, more responsibility, and more authority than in the previous job, usually accompanied by a pay increase.

Temporary Assignments with Other Organizations

In some cases, an employer may benefit from the skills an employee can learn at another organization. The employer may encourage the employee to participate in an **externship**—a full-time temporary position at another organization. Externships are an attractive option for employees in analytical positions, who otherwise might solve the same kinds of problems over and over, becoming bored as they miss out on exposure to challenging new ideas and techniques. GE Money uses this type of development for its analysts in Shanghai and Bangalore. It loans them out for temporary assignments to other business units. Through these externships, the company makes the employees' expertise available to many parts of the company at the same time it keeps them more engaged because they see many ways they contribute to the company's success. And, of course, these employees are challenged to learn as they apply their skills to a more diverse set of business problems.[34]

> **Externship**
> Employee development through a full-time temporary position at another organization.

Temporary assignments can include a **sabbatical**—a leave of absence from an organization to renew or develop skills. Employees on sabbatical often receive full pay and benefits. Sabbaticals let employees get away from the day-to-day stresses of their jobs and acquire new skills and perspectives. Sabbaticals also allow employees more time for personal pursuits such as writing a book or spending more time with family members. Tamara Woodbury used a sabbatical from her job as executive director of the Girl Scouts–Arizona Cactus-Pine Council to study organization theory at the Society of Organizational Learning Institute in Halifax, Nova Scotia. She then devoted four weeks to relaxation and writing in her cabin in Flagstaff, Arizona. The time to study and reflect prepared Woodbury to re-evaluate and restructure the council so that the way it operates is more consistent with its mission.[35] How employees spend their sabbaticals varies from company to company. Some employees may work for a nonprofit service agency; others may study at a college or university or travel and work on special projects in non-U.S. subsidiaries of the company.

> **Sabbatical**
> A leave of absence from an organization to renew or develop skills.

Interpersonal Relationships

Employees can also develop skills and increase their knowledge about the organization and its customers by interacting with a more experienced organization member. Two types of relationships used for employee development are mentoring and coaching.

LO5 Summarize principles of successful mentoring programs.

Mentor
An experienced, productive senior employee who helps develop a less-experienced employee (a protégé).

Mentors

A **mentor** is an experienced, productive senior employee who helps develop a less experienced employee, called the *protégé*. Most mentoring relationships develop informally as a result of interests or values shared by the mentor and protégé. According to research, the employees most likely to seek and attract a mentor have certain personality characteristics: emotional stability, ability to adapt their behavior to the situation, and high needs for power and achievement.[36] Mentoring relationships also can develop as part of the organization's planned effort to bring together successful senior employees with less-experienced employees.

One major advantage of formal mentoring programs is that they ensure access to mentors for all employees, regardless of gender or race. A mentoring program also can ensure that high-potential employees are matched with wise, experienced mentors in key areas—and that mentors in positions of authority are hearing about the real-life challenges of the organization's employees.[37] However, in an artificially created relationship, mentors may have difficulty providing counseling and coaching.[38] To overcome this limitation, mentors and protégés should spend time discussing their work styles, personalities, and backgrounds; these conversations help build the trust that is needed for both parties to be comfortable with their relationship.[39] Mentoring programs tend to be most successful when they are voluntary and participants understand the details of the program. Rewarding managers for employee development is also important, because it signals that mentoring and other development activities are worthwhile. In addition, the organization should carefully select mentors based on their interpersonal and technical skills, train them for the role, and evaluate whether the program has met its objectives.[40]

Information technology can help organizations meet some of these guidelines. For example, videoconferencing may be a good substitute if the mentor and protégé cannot meet face-to-face. Databases can store information about potential mentors' characteristics, and the protégé can use a search engine to locate mentors who best match the qualities he or she is looking for. The "eHRM" box describes how online databases are making successful mentorships more readily available at Xerox.

Mentors and protégés can both benefit from a mentoring relationship. Protégés receive career support, including coaching, protection, sponsorship, challenging assignments, and visibility among the organization's managers. They also receive benefits of a positive relationship—a friend and role model who accepts them, has a positive opinion toward them, and gives them a chance to talk about their worries. Employees with mentors are also more likely to be promoted, earn higher salaries, and have more influence within their organization.[41] Acting as a mentor gives managers a chance to develop their interpersonal skills and increase their feelings that they are contributing something important to the organization. Working with a technically trained protégé on matters such as new research in the field may also increase the mentor's technical knowledge.

So that more employees can benefit from mentoring, some organizations use *group mentoring programs*, which assign four to six protégés to a successful senior employee. A potential advantage of group mentoring is that protégés can learn from each other as well as from the mentor. The leader helps protégés understand the organization, guides them in analyzing their experiences, and helps them clarify career directions. Each member of the group may complete specific assignments, or the group may work together on a problem or issue.

FINDING A MENTOR ONLINE

More than two decades ago, female employees at Xerox wanted to ensure they were taking full advantage of opportunities to advance their careers, so they formed what the company calls a "caucus group"—an organization of dues-paying members that provides programs for career development for a specific group of employees. The group, called The Women's Alliance (TWA), wanted a formal mentoring program, but in their initial efforts, they discovered that the work of matching employees with mentors possessing the right set of interests, skills, and experiences was enormously time consuming.

What saved the TWA mentoring program was online database technology. The group set up Web-based software that makes matching mentors and protégés a self-service operation. Participants fill out an online profile detailing their educational and work background and interests, as well as their goals for participating in the program. The profile also includes information about each participant's geographic location and community-service activities. Once an employee's profile is complete, the individual can use the database to search for a possible mentor by using drop-down menus to select the desired skills, experience, and background. The software returns a set of matching mentor profiles, and the would-be protégé selects one of them. The system generates an e-mail message to that person. The potential mentor reviews the requesting employee's profile and either accepts or rejects the request.

The mentoring program has been received enthusiastically by the women of Xerox. In a recent count, 175 employees were participating. The software is easy to administer and inexpensive enough that the caucus group's dues cover its cost. Based on that success, other Xerox caucus groups, including groups for Asian, Hispanic, and African American employees, have expressed interest in using the system. Thanks to online self-service and the commitment of the women's group, mentoring is spreading at Xerox.

Source: Based on Beth N. Carvin, "The Great Mentor Match," *T + D*, January 2009, OCLC FirstSearch, http://newfirstsearch.oclc.org.

Coaching

A **coach** is a peer or manager who works with an employee to motivate the employee, help him or her develop skills, and provide reinforcement and feedback. Coaches may play one or more of three roles:[42]

LO6 Tell how managers and peers develop employees through coaching.

1. Working one-on-one with an employee, as when giving feedback.
2. Helping employees learn for themselves—for example, helping them find experts and teaching them to obtain feedback from others.
3. Providing resources such as mentors, courses, or job experiences.

Linda Miller, a coaching specialist at the Ken Blanchard Companies, describes the coach's role in terms of two contrasting managers with whom she has worked.[43] The first of these, a manager at a retailing company, had a supervisor who was not a coach. The retail manager's boss was nervous that if his employees learned too much, he wouldn't be as valuable. So he limited the retail manager's experiences until she became so frustrated she began to look for another job. In contrast, at a financial-services business, a manager had a reputation for developing his employees. According to Miller, this manager's strength was coaching: "He knew exactly how much time

Coach
A peer or manager who works with an employee to motivate the employee, help him or her develop skills, and provide reinforcement and feedback.

COACHING EMPLOYEES

Human resource managers may be called upon to coach HR employees or to coach other employees in HR-related skills. In fact, modeling "coach-like" behavior by coaching managers can inspire them to try coaching their employees. Here are some guidelines for effective coaching:

- Listen carefully to learn the client's goals. Then listen for gaps between where the employee is now in a situation and where the employee wants to be. Coaching typically will need to focus on how to close those gaps.
- Instead of giving advice or telling others what to do, ask questions that help people think through the situation themselves. By refraining from

solving problems yourself, you're giving others a chance to develop and see their own problem-solving skills.

- Keep in mind that what works for one person may not work as well for another. Because of individual differences, the person you coach may want to handle a situation differently than you would—and that person's idea might actually work best for that person, given his or her strengths and weaknesses. So instead of focusing on what you would do, focus on building the other person's strengths and passions.
- To the extent that you control the situation, give the person you are coaching enough freedom to try out his or her ideas. If some of the ideas don't

work, ask more questions to help the person figure out what went wrong and come up with new ideas for next time.

- Maintain confidentiality in the coaching relationship. You need to have candid conversations, and these happen only if the person being coached trusts you to keep private conversations private.

Sources: Ken Blanchard Companies, "Why Aren't Managers More Coachlike?" *Ignite,* September 2009, www.kenblanchard.com; Mark Nyman and Liz Thach, "Coaching: A Leadership Development Option," *Supervision,* February 2009, Business & Company Resource Center, http://galenet.galegroup.com; and Marshall Goldsmith, "What to Know about Coaching Your Successor," *BusinessWeek,* April 7, 2010, www.businessweek.com.

it would take for him to develop the person until the person would get recognized by the company and promoted into a new position," and he came to think of this development as his legacy to the company. In other words, the coach knows that his or her great value is the ability to make other employees more valuable.

Research suggests that coaching helps managers improve by identifying areas for improvement and setting goals.[44] Coaching is most likely to succeed if coaches are empathetic, supportive, practical, and self-confident but don't act infallible or try to tell others what to do.[45] To benefit from coaching, employees need to be open-minded and interested in the process. The "HR How To" box provides more guidance in coaching employees.

LO7 Identify the steps in the process of career management.

Systems for Career Management

Employee development is most likely to meet the organization's needs if it is part of a human resource system of career management. In practice, organizations' career management systems vary. Some rely heavily on informal relationships, while others are sophisticated programs. As shown in Figure 9.3, a basic career management system involves four steps: data gathering, feedback, goal setting, and action planning and follow-up. Ways to make this system more effective include gathering data in areas associated with success, keeping feedback confidential and specific, involving

Figure 9.3

Steps in the Career Management Process

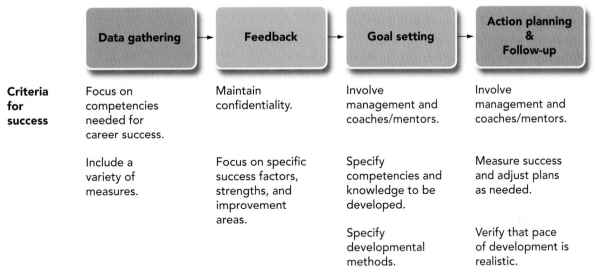

Data gathering	Feedback	Goal setting	Action planning & Follow-up
Criteria for success — Focus on competencies needed for career success.	Maintain confidentiality.	Involve management and coaches/mentors.	Involve management and coaches/mentors.
Include a variety of measures.	Focus on specific success factors, strengths, and improvement areas.	Specify competencies and knowledge to be developed.	Measure success and adjust plans as needed.
		Specify developmental methods.	Verify that pace of development is realistic.

higher-level management in planning and follow-up, and crafting action plans that are realistic and targeted to building expertise needed for the person's career path.[46] Human resource professionals can also contribute to the system's success by ensuring that it is linked to other HR practices such as performance management, training, and recruiting.

Data Gathering

In discussing the methods of employee development, we highlighted several assessment tools. Such tools may be applied to data gathering, the first step in the career management process. **Self-assessment** refers to the use of information by employees to determine their career interests, values, aptitudes, and behavioral tendencies. The employee's responsibility is to identify opportunities and personal areas needing improvement. The organization's responsibility is to provide assessment information for identifying strengths, weaknesses, interests, and values.

Self-assessment tools often include psychological tests such as the Myers-Briggs Type Indicator (described earlier in the chapter), the Strong-Campbell Interest Inventory, and the Self-Directed Search. The Strong-Campbell inventory helps employees identify their occupational and job interests. The Self-Directed Search identifies employees' preferences for working in different kinds of environments—sales, counseling, and so on. Tests may also help employees identify the relative values they place on work and leisure activities. Self-assessment tools can include exercises such as the one in Figure 9.4. This type of exercise helps an employee consider his or her current career status, future plans, and the fit between the career and the employee's current situation and resources. Some organizations provide counselors to help employees in the self-assessment process and to interpret the results of psychological tests. Completing the self-assessment can help employees identify a development need. Such a need can result from gaps between current skills or interests and the type of work or position the employee has or wants.

Self-Assessment
The use of information by employees to determine their career interests, values, aptitudes, behavioral tendencies, and development needs.

Figure 9.4

Sample Self-Assessment Exercise

Step 1: Where am I?
Examine current position of life and career.
Think about your life from past and present to the future. Draw a time line to represent important events.

Step 2: Who am I?
Examine different roles.
Using 3" × 5" cards, write down one answer per card to the question "Who am I?"

Step 3: Where would I like to be, and what would I like to happen?
Begin setting goals.
Consider your life from present to future. Write an autobiography answering these questions:
• What do you want to have accomplished?
• What milestones do you want to achieve?
• What do you want to be remembered for?

Step 4: An ideal year in the future
Identify resources needed.
Consider a one-year period in the future. Answer these questions:
• If you had unlimited resources, what would you do?
• What would the ideal environment look like?
• Does the ideal environment match Step 3?

Step 5: An ideal job
Create current goal.
In the present, think about an ideal job for you with your available resources. Describe your role, resources, and type of training or education needed.

Step 6: Career by objective inventory
Summarize current situation.
• What gets you excited each day?
• What do you do well? What are you known for?
• What do you need to achieve your goals?
• What could interfere with reaching your goals?
• What should you do now to move toward reaching your goals?
• What is your long-term career objective?

SOURCE: Based on J. E. McMahon and S. K. Merman, "Career Development," in *The ASTD Training and Development Handbook*, 4th ed., ed. R. L. Craig (New York: McGraw-Hill, 1996), pp. 679–97. Reproduced with permission.

Verizon Wireless provides an online tool that lets employees assess their current skills and abilities in order to see how well prepared they are for job openings throughout the company. Employees can use the assessment to identify capabilities they lack and to learn what they can do to develop skills through training, job experience, or enrolling in an academic program.[47]

Feedback

Feedback
Information employers give employees about their skills and knowledge and where these assets fit into the organization's plans.

In the next step of career management, **feedback,** employees receive information about their skills and knowledge and where these assets fit into the organization's plans. The employee's responsibility is to identify what skills she or he could realistically develop in light of the opportunities available. The organization's responsibility is to communicate the performance evaluation and the opportunities available to the employee, given the organization's long-range plans. Opportunities might include promotions and transfers.

Usually the employer conducts the reality check as part of a performance appraisal or as the feedback stage of performance management. In well-developed career management systems, the manager may hold separate discussions for performance feedback and career development.

Caterpillar's performance management process includes regular discussions between employees and their managers. To facilitate the discussion, each employee completes a data sheet that serves as an internal résumé. The data sheet includes information about the employee's skills, education, academic degrees, languages spoken, and previous positions. The manager's role is to indicate whether the employee is ready for a new job, whether the job will be a promotion or lateral move, and what education or training the employee needs to be ready for the move. The discussion covers what opportunities are available for the employee, where the employee wants to go next in the organization, and what preparation is needed for that move.[48]

Goal Setting

Based on the information from the self-assessment and reality check, the employee sets short- and long-term career objectives. These goals usually involve one or more of the following categories:

- Desired positions, such as becoming sales manager within three years.
- Level of skill to apply—for example, to use one's budgeting skills to improve the unit's cash flow problems.
- Work setting—for example, to move to corporate marketing within two years.
- Skill acquisition, such as learning how to use the company's human resource information system.

As in these examples, the goals should be specific, and they should include a date by which the goal is to be achieved. It is the employee's responsibility to identify the goal and the method of determining her or his progress toward that goal.

Usually the employee discusses the goals with his or her manager. The organization's responsibilities are to ensure that the goal is specific, challenging, and attainable and to help the employee reach the goal. At candy maker Just Born, employees involved in the company's Career Development Process define future job interests, identify the necessary experiences for obtaining those jobs, and set short- and long-term goals. Each employee discusses these goals with his or her manager, who can suggest changes or support the goals as written.[49]

Action Planning and Follow-Up

During the final step, employees prepare an action plan for how they will achieve their short- and long-term career goals. The employee is responsible for identifying the steps and timetable to reach the goals. The employer should identify resources needed, including courses, work experiences, and relationships. The employee and the manager should meet in the future to discuss progress toward career goals.

Action plans may involve any one or a combination of the development methods discussed earlier in the chapter—training, assessment, job experiences, or the help of a mentor or coach. The approach used depends on the particular developmental needs and career objectives. For example, suppose the program manager in an information systems department uses feedback from performance appraisals to determine that he needs greater knowledge of project management software. The manager plans to increase that knowledge by reading articles (formal education), meeting with software vendors, and contacting the vendors' customers to ask them about the software they have used (job experiences). The manager and his supervisor agree that six months will be the target date for achieving the higher level of knowledge through these activities.

The outcome of action planning often takes the form of a career development plan. Figure 9.5 is an example of a development plan for a product manager. Development plans usually include descriptions of strengths and weaknesses, career goals, and development activities for reaching each goal.

Figure 9.5

Career Development Plan

Name: _____ **Title:** Project Manager **Immediate Manager:** _____

Competencies
Please identify your three greatest strengths and areas for improvement.
Strengths
- Strategic thinking and execution (confidence, command skills, action orientation)
- Results orientation (competence, motivating others, perseverance)
- Spirit for winning (building team spirit, customer focus, respect colleagues)

Areas for Improvement
- Patience (tolerance of people or processes and sensitivity to pacing)
- Written communications (ability to write clearly and succinctly)
- Overly ambitious (too much focus on successful completion of projects rather than developing relationships with individuals involved in the projects)

Career Goals
Please describe your overall career goals.
- **Long-term:** Accept positions of increased responsibility to a level of general manager (or beyond). The areas of specific interest include but are not limited to product and brand management, technology and development, strategic planning, and marketing.
- **Short-term:** Continue to improve my skills in marketing and brand management while utilizing my skills in product management, strategic planning, and global relations.

Next Assignments
Identify potential next assignments (including timing) that would help you develop toward your career goals.
- Manager or director level in planning, development, product, or brand management. Timing estimated to be Spring 2011.

Training and Development Needs
List both training and development activities that will either help you develop in your current assignment or provide overall career development.
- Master's degree classes will allow me to practice and improve my written communications skills. The dynamics of my current position, teamwork, and reliance on other individuals allow me to practice patience and to focus on individual team members' needs along with the success of the projects.

Employee _____ **Date** _____
Immediate Manager _____ **Date** _____
Mentor _____ **Date** _____

Development-Related Challenges

A well-designed system for employee development can help organizations face three widespread challenges: the glass ceiling, succession planning, and dysfunctional behavior by managers.

Indra Nooyi became the first woman CEO of PepsiCo in 2006. Her success at the company gives her the distinction of being one of the women to break through the glass ceiling.

The Glass Ceiling

As we mentioned in Chapter 1, women and minorities are rare in the top level of U.S. corporations. Observers of this situation have noted that it looks as if an invisible barrier is keeping women and minorities from reaching the top jobs, a barrier that has come to be known as the **glass ceiling.** For example, a recent census of the board membership of *Fortune* 500 companies found that just 15.6 percent of their officers were women, and 74 of the companies had no female corporate officers.[50]

The glass ceiling is likely caused by a lack of access to training programs, appropriate developmental job experiences, and developmental relationships such as mentoring.[51] With regard to developmental relationships, women and minorities often have trouble finding mentors. They may not participate in the organization's, profession's, or community's "old boys' network." Also, managers in the organization may prefer to interact with people who have similar status or may avoid interacting with certain people because of discomfort or negative stereotypes.[52]

Organizations can use development systems to help break through the glass ceiling. Managers making developmental assignments need to carefully consider whether stereotypes are influencing the types of assignments men and women receive. A formal process for regularly identifying development needs and creating action plans can make these decisions more objective.

An organization that is actively working to eliminate the glass ceiling is LeasePlan USA, where management was concerned that although most employees were female, most of the top managers were male. LeasePlan hired a consultant to develop a program that focuses on skill assessment, career guidance, and tips on communications. The program also features networking events and a panel discussion with female executives from other companies. Since the company launched the program, many of the participants have been promoted, and almost half of the top managers are women. Even women who haven't made it into management report feeling more satisfied and engaged with their jobs.[53]

LO8 Discuss how organizations are meeting the challenges of the "glass ceiling," succession planning, and dysfunctional managers.

Glass Ceiling Circumstances resembling an invisible barrier that keep most women and minorities from attaining the top jobs in organizations.

focus on *social responsibility*

Succession Planning

Organizations have always had to prepare for the retirement of their leaders, but the need is more intense than ever. The aging of the workforce means that a greater share of employees are reaching retirement age. Many organizations are fueling the trend by downsizing through early-retirement programs. As positions at the top of organizations become vacant, many organizations have determined that their middle managers are fewer and often unprepared for top-level responsibility. This situation has raised awareness of the need for **succession planning**—the process of identifying and tracking high-potential employees who will be able to fill top management positions when they become vacant.

Succession Planning The process of identifying and tracking high-potential employees who will be able to fill top management positions when they become vacant.

HR Oops!

Succession Planning for Top Execs

By any definition, the role of chief executive officer is crucial. The person in this top position is expected to set the tone and direction for the whole organization. If something happens that causes a company to lose its CEO, no one is in charge unless there's a plan for someone to take over immediately. So every company has a succession plan for at least the CEO, right?

Surprisingly, the answer is no. Beverly Behan, who consults with boards of directors on this issue, says often they have just a vague idea about a replacement: a list of some high-potential managers and a list of who is supposed to phone whom in the event of an emergency. A phone tree is a handy tool, but it's no substitute for a leader.

This embarrassing situation came to light recently at Bank of America. In the wake of the financial crisis, rumors swirled that CEO Ken Lewis would be pressured to leave the bank. The board even removed him from the post of chairman, suggesting some lack of confidence. Still, when Lewis announced his retirement, weeks passed without the board naming a replacement. Evidently, if the board had discussed a succession plan, it hadn't reached a final decision on who would get the job.

Being caught without a succession plan when the company needs one is, at best, a real embarrassment. Perhaps it feels too frightening or awkward to contemplate something bad taking away the leader. But as the Bank of America example reminds us, leadership changes.

Questions

1. The evidence presented here implies that Bank of America's board of directors lacked a succession plan for CEO even when the directors had concerns about the current CEO. Why might it be difficult to engage in succession planning during a crisis? Why might it be necessary?

2. Imagine that you are an HR executive. How would you make the case to your company's board of directors to create a specific succession plan for the company's top executives? If they are uncomfortable with the conversation, how would you overcome objections to the topic?

Source: Based on Beverly Behan, "Lesson from BofA: Avoiding a Succession Debacle," *BusinessWeek,* October 6, 2009, www.businessweek .com.

Succession planning offers several benefits.[54] It forces senior management to regularly and thoughtfully review the company's leadership talent. It ensures that top-level management talent is available. It provides a set of development experiences that managers must complete to be considered for top management positions, so the organization does not promote managers before they are ready. Succession planning systems also help attract and retain ambitious managerial employees by providing development opportunities. Although succession planning is important, the "HR Oops!" box suggests that not all companies take it seriously.

Succession planning focuses on *high-potential employees,* that is, employees the organization believes can succeed in higher-level business positions such as general manager of a business unit, director of a function (such as marketing or finance), or chief executive officer.[55] A typical approach to development of high-potential employees is to have them complete an individual development program including education, executive mentoring and coaching, and rotation through job assignments. Job assignments are based on the successful career paths of the managers whom the high-potential employees are preparing to replace. High-potential employees may also receive special assignments, such as making presentations and serving on committees and task forces.

Research shows that an effective program for developing high-potential employees has three stages:[56]

1. *Selection of high-potential employees*—Organizations may select outstanding performers and employees who have completed elite academic programs, such as earning a master's degree in business administration from a prestigious university. They may also use the results of psychological tests such as assessment centers.
2. *Developmental experiences*—As employees participate in developmental experiences, the organization identifies those who succeed in the experiences. The organization looks for employees who continue to show qualities associated with success in top jobs, such as communication skills, leadership talent, and willingness to make sacrifices for the organization. In today's high-performance business environment, these assessments should measure whether participants in the program are demonstrating an ability to lead and delivering results that contribute to the company's success. Employees who display these qualities continue to be considered high-potential employees.
3. *Active involvement with the CEO*—High-potential employees seen by top management as fitting into the organization's culture and having personality characteristics necessary for representing the company become actively involved with the chief executive officer. The CEO exposes these employees to the organization's key people and gives them a greater understanding of the organization's culture. The development of high-potential employees is a slow process. Reaching stage 3 may take 15 to 20 years.

Figure 9.6 breaks this process into seven steps. It begins with identifying the positions to be planned for and the employees to be included in the plan. Planning should also include establishing position requirements and deciding how to measure employees' potential for being able to fill those requirements. The organization also needs to develop a process for reviewing the existing talent. The next step is to link succession planning with other human resource systems. Finally, the organization needs a way to provide employees with feedback about career paths available to them and how well they are progressing toward their goals.

A good example of succession planning is the effort at First State Bank & Trust, based in Fremont, Nebraska. When Ronald Kranz was president and Charles Johannsen was executive vice president, the two men took personality tests to identify their leadership strengths. Seeing similar leadership traits in the two, the bank's board of directors confirmed Johannsen

Figure 9.6

Process for Developing a Succession Plan
SOURCE: Based on B. Dowell, "Succession Planning," in *Implementing Organizational Interventions*, ed. J. Hedge and E. Pulaskos (San Francisco: Jossey-Bass, 2002), pp. 78–109.

- Identify Positions to Plan For
- Identify Employees to Include
- Define Job Requirements
- Measure Employee Potential
- Review and Plan to Meet Development Needs
- Link Succession Planning with Other HR Systems
- Provide Feedback to Employees

as Kranz's eventual successor, and Johannsen embarked on development activities in the areas he wanted to strengthen for his future role. Later, Kranz began working part-time so that Johannsen could begin practicing the responsibilities of the president's job. Now with Johannsen in the president's position and Kranz continuing as board chairman, they are engaged in planning for Johannsen's successor. In addition, First State evaluates its junior and middle managers to see that they are well trained and have opportunities to work with senior managers and prepare for greater responsibility.[57]

Dysfunctional Managers

A manager who is otherwise competent may engage in some behaviors that make him or her ineffective or even "toxic"—someone who stifles good ideas and drives away employees. These dysfunctional behaviors include insensitivity to others, inability to be a team player, arrogance, poor conflict-management skills, inability to meet business objectives, and inability to adapt to change.[58] For example, a manager who has strong technical knowledge but is abrasive and discourages employees from contributing their ideas is likely to have difficulty motivating employees and may alienate people inside and outside the organization.

When a manager is an otherwise valuable employee and is willing to improve, the organization may try to help him or her change the dysfunctional behavior. The usual ways to provide this type of development include assessment, training, and counseling. Development programs for managers with dysfunctional behavior may also include specialized programs such as one called Individual Coaching for Effectiveness (ICE). The ICE program includes diagnosis, coaching, and support activities tailored to each manager's needs.[59] Psychologists conduct the diagnosis, coach and counsel the manager, and develop action plans for implementing new skills on the job. Research suggests that managers who participate in programs like ICE improve their skills and are less likely to be terminated.[60] One possible conclusion is that organizations can benefit from offering development opportunities to valuable employees with performance problems, not just to star performers.

thinking ethically

DEVELOPING ETHICAL EMPLOYEES

Ethical leadership is critical for employees in many settings. For example, in an industrial environment, ethical leadership of safety programs puts employees' well-being ahead of short-term cost savings. And in the accounting profession, high ethical standards are essential for preserving the firm's reputation. Therefore, organizations have an interest in developing ethical leaders, who in turn foster ethical behavior among all employees.

Jim Spigener, a safety consultant, recalls working with a chief executive whose son had recently become a civil engineer for a construction company. Spigener asked his client whether he hoped that the construction company's CEO placed the same value on his employees' safety that the client placed on his own employees' safety. The startled client replied that he hoped his son's CEO had higher standards. In this way, Spigener was coaching his CEO client to think about safety in a new, personal way—hoping that the client, in his role as a leader, would begin to express this new understanding to others at the company.

Many accounting firms use mentoring relationships to foster commitment to integrity and ethical decision making. Ernst & Young, for example, matches newly hired staff members with mentors and has set up a system where the staff can post comments about the mentoring and coaching behaviors they observe. One of the most important ways mentors can develop ethical behavior is by modeling that behavior themselves.

Mentors also try to help employees sort out the nuances of how to behave ethically amidst the real-world challenges of time pressures and office politics.

SOURCES: Jim Spigener, "Leaders Who 'Get' Safety: Values and Personality Shape Personal Ethics," *Industrial Safety & Hygiene News*, October 2009, Business & Company Resource Center, http://galenet.galegroup.com.; and Robert Gagnon, "More than a Legacy," *CA Magazine*, September 2009, Business & Company Resource Center, http://galenet.galegroup.com.

Questions

1. Compare the example of the safety consultant coaching a CEO with the example of Ernst &

Young mentoring accountants. How are these development approaches similar and different?
2. Besides coaches or mentors, what other resources could an organization provide to develop ethical employees? Which of these do you think would be most effective, and why?
3. Can an organization "develop" ethical employees, or is it just a matter of hiring people who are already ethical? How much effort should an organization put into developing strengths in the area of ethics?

SUMMARY

LO1 Discuss how development is related to training and careers.

Employee development is the combination of formal education, job experiences, relationships, and assessment of personality and abilities to help employees prepare for the future of their careers. Training is more focused on improving performance in the current job, but training programs may support employee development. In modern organizations, the concept of a career is fluid—a protean career that changes along with changes in a person's interests, abilities, and values and changes in the work environment. To plan and prepare for a protean career requires active career management, which includes planning for employee development.

LO2 Identify the methods organizations use for employee development.

Organizations may use formal educational programs at the workplace or off-site, such as workshops, university courses and degree programs, company-sponsored training, or programs offered by independent institutions. Organizations may use the assessment process to help employees identify strengths and areas requiring further development. Assessment can help the organization identify employees with managerial potential or identify areas in which teams need to develop. Job experiences help employees develop by stretching their skills as they meet new challenges. Interpersonal relationships with a more experienced member of the organization—often in the role of mentor or coach—can help employees develop their understanding of the organization and its customers.

LO3 Describe how organizations use assessment of personality type, work behaviors, and job performance to plan employee development.

Organizations collect information and provide feedback to employees about their behavior, communication style, and skills. The information may come from the employees, their peers, managers, and customers. Many organizations use performance appraisals as a source of assessment information. Appraisals may take the form of 360-degree feedback. Some organizations use psychological tests designed for this purpose, including the Myers-Briggs Type Indicator and the Benchmarks assessment. Assessment centers combine a variety of methods to provide assessment information. Managers must share the assessments, along with suggestions for improvement.

LO4 Explain how job experiences can be used for developing skills.

Job experiences contribute to development through a combination of relationships, problems, demands, tasks, and other features of an employee's jobs. The assumption is that development is most likely to occur when the employee's skills and experiences do not entirely match the skills required for the employee's current job, so employees must stretch to meet the demands of the new assignment. The impact varies according to whether the employee views the experience as a positive or negative source of stress. Job experiences that support employee development may include job enlargement, job rotations, transfers, promotions, downward moves, and temporary assignments with other organizations.

LO5 Summarize principles of successful mentoring programs.

A mentor is an experienced, productive senior employee who helps develop a less-experienced employee. Although most mentoring relationships develop informally, organizations can link mentoring to development goals by establishing a formal mentoring program. A formal program also provides a basis for ensuring that all eligible employees are included. Mentoring programs tend to be most successful when they are voluntary and participants understand the details of the program. The organization should reward managers for employee development, carefully select mentors based on interpersonal and technical skills, train them for the role, and evaluate whether the program has met its objectives.

LO6 Tell how managers and peers develop employees through coaching.

A coach is a peer or manager who works with an employee to motivate the employee, help him or her develop skills, and provide reinforcement and feedback. Coaches should be prepared to take on one or more of three roles: working one-on-one with an employee, helping employees learn for themselves, and providing resources, such as mentors, courses, or job experiences.

LO7 Identify the steps in the process of career management.

First, during data gathering employees use information to determine their career interests, values, aptitudes, and behavioral tendencies, looking for opportunities and areas needing improvement. Data gathering tools often include psychological tests or exercises that ask about career status and plans. The second step is feedback, during which the organization communicates information about the employee's skills and knowledge and how these fit into the organization's plan. The employee then sets goals and discusses them with his or her manager, who ensures that the goals are specific, challenging, and attainable. Finally, the employee works with his or her manager to create an action plan and follow-up for development activities that will help the employee achieve the goals.

LO8 Discuss how organizations are meeting the challenges of the "glass ceiling," succession planning, and dysfunctional managers.

The glass ceiling is a barrier that has been observed preventing women and minorities from achieving top jobs in an organization. Development programs can ensure that these employees receive access to development resources such as coaches, mentors, and developmental job assignments. Succession planning ensures that the organization prepares qualified employees to fill management jobs as managers retire. It focuses on applying employee development to high-potential employees. Effective succession planning includes methods for selecting these employees, providing them with developmental experiences, and getting the CEO actively involved with employees who display qualities associated with success as they participate in the developmental activities. For dysfunctional managers who have the potential to contribute to the organization, the organization may offer development targeted at correcting the areas of dysfunction. Typically, the process includes collecting information about the manager's personality, skills, and interests; providing feedback, training, and counseling; and ensuring that the manager can apply new, functional behaviors on the job.

KEY TERMS

assessment, p. 261
assessment center, p. 264
Benchmarks, p. 265
coach, p. 273
downward move, p. 270
employee development, p. 258
externship, p. 271

feedback, p. 276
glass ceiling, p. 279
job experiences, p. 267
leaderless group discussion, p. 264
mentor, p. 272
Myers-Briggs Type Indicator (MBTI), p. 262

promotion, p. 271
protean career, p. 260
sabbatical, p. 271
self-assessment, p. 275
succession planning, p. 279
transfer, p. 270

REVIEW AND DISCUSSION QUESTIONS

1. How does development differ from training? How does development support career management in modern organizations?

2. What are the four broad categories of development methods? Why might it be beneficial to combine all of these methods into a formal development program?

3. Recommend a development method for each of the following situations, and explain why you chose that method.
   a. An employee recently promoted to the job of plant supervisor is having difficulty motivating employees to meet quality standards.
   b. A sales manager annoys salespeople by dictating every detail of their work.
   c. An employee has excellent leadership skills but lacks knowledge of the financial side of business.
   d. An organization is planning to organize its production workers into teams for the first time.

4. A company that markets sophisticated business management software systems uses sales teams to help customers define needs and to create systems that meet those needs. The teams include programmers, salespeople who specialize in client industries, and software designers. Occasionally sales are lost as a result of conflict or communication problems among team members. The company wants to improve the effectiveness of these teams, and it wants to begin with assessment. How can the teams use 360-degree feedback and psychological tests to develop?

5. In an organization that wants to use work experiences as a method of employee development, what basic options are available? Which of these options would be most attractive to you as an employee? Why?

6. Many employees are unwilling to relocate because they like their current community and family members prefer not to move. Yet preparation for management requires that employees develop new skills, strengthen areas of weakness, and be exposed to new aspects of the organization's business. How can an organization change an employee's current job to develop management skills?

7. Many people feel that mentoring relationships should occur naturally, in situations where senior managers feel inclined to play that role. What are some advantages of setting up a formal mentoring program, rather than letting senior managers decide how and whom to help?

8. What are the three roles of a coach? How is a coach different from a mentor? What are some advantages of using someone outside the organization as a coach? Some disadvantages?

9. Why should organizations be interested in helping employees plan their careers? What benefits can companies gain? What are the risks?

10. What are the manager's roles in a career management system? Which role do you think is most difficult for the typical manager? Which is the easiest role? List reasons why managers might resist becoming involved in career management.

11. What is the glass ceiling? What are the possible consequences to an organization that has a glass ceiling? How can employee development break the glass ceiling? Can succession planning help? Explain.

12. Why might an organization benefit from giving employee development opportunities to a dysfunctional manager, rather than simply dismissing the manager? Do these reasons apply to nonmanagement employees as well?

BUSINESSWEEK CASE

BusinessWeek   How GE and Zappos Develop Great Leaders

At first glance, Zappos.com, the online retailer, appears to have little in common with General Electric, the multinational conglomerate. Hit hard by the recession, GE is in the throes of scaling down its financial services subsidiary, GE Capital, by an estimated 40 percent. Zappos, on the other hand, is tapping into changing consumer habits and ramping up for 30 percent growth over the next 12 months.

Yet surprisingly, these two organizations with their rapidly shifting environments face similar challenges in motivating and engaging their employees. For Zappos, it's about creating and maintaining passion in a call-center culture. For GE, it's about keeping people engaged in a changing climate.

Named among the 20 Best Companies for Leadership in a recent BusinessWeek.com/Hay Group survey, both GE and Zappos put a premium on selecting, developing, and retaining strong leaders at every level. What sets them and the other companies on the list apart, however, is not just their emphasis on good leadership, but also how they approach it. They carefully tailor their developing leaders to fit their unique business strategies and organizational cultures.

In the survey, respondents were asked about their companies' current focus. Among all the respondents, 65.1 percent said "positioning for the future." Among the Best Companies for Leadership, the figure was 81.9 percent. Executives at the Best Companies for Leadership confirmed this in follow-up interviews. "Our culture is committed to leadership development," says Jayne Johnson, GE's director of leadership education. "Crotonville [the site of GE's corporate university] opened in 1956. Today more than ever, we need our leaders going to Crotonville. It's these very leaders who will make us successful today and in the future."

GE identifies talented leaders early on and places them in stretch assignments, often before they think they're ready, according to Johnson. "And we support them, with over $1 billion a year in structured training. But today, change is such a continual force that even we at GE are taking a fresh look at how to develop talent."

At Zappos, a challenge is developing leaders at a pace that will accommodate the company's growth. "We are projecting 30 percent growth in 2010," says Rebecca Ratner, the online retailer's director of human resources. "We will need more supervisors. How can we best integrate them into the company in terms of how they treat employees?" Noting that Zappos managers spend "10 percent to 20 percent of their time doing team building outside the office, our challenge is figuring out how to assimilate people into what we do."

For anyone coming in from the outside, she says, it's not a typical recruitment process, where they meet with three or four people before either being hired or rejected. "What we do instead is spend seven to 10 hours over four occasions at happy hours, team building events, or other things outside the office. We can see them and they can see us." The process seems to be good for retention. "In 2009, we will have a 20 percent turnover rate," says Ratner. That's impressive for call-center employees. What keeps people at Zappos? "We pay 100 percent of employee benefits," says Ratner. But there's something more, something Zappos calls its "wow factor."

Says Ratner: "We can't ask someone to wow a customer if they haven't been wowed by us." In fact, Zappos is so eager to wow employees and make sure who they hire is really committed that the company offers people $3,000 after they've been trained to walk away if they feel they and Zappos aren't a good fit. Ratner is quick to point out that almost no one takes the $3,000 walk-away money. But many trainees return for more Zappos training to become managers and supervisors. Ratner admits that one of her big concerns is how to keep the wow factor alive as the company adds more people and ramps up its leadership development.

SOURCE: Excerpted from Patricia O'Connell, "How Companies Develop Great Leaders," *BusinessWeek*, February 16, 2010, www.businessweek.com.

Questions

1. Which approaches to employee development are mentioned in this case for Zappos? Which are mentioned for General Electric?
2. These two companies are both well respected and successful but have very different cultures: Zappos is modern and fun, while GE is a huge, competitive, traditional company. How would you expect the cultural differences to affect the choice of developmental methods at the two companies?
3. For each of the companies, name one challenge the company is facing, recommend a form of employee development, and explain how it could help the company meet the challenge you identified.

Case: How Leaders Flourish at Gunderson Lutheran Health System

With nearly 7,000 employees working in its hospital, multispecialty medical practice, and more than three dozen clinics, the Gunderson Lutheran Health System has a tremendous amount of talent in an industry where talent can be a life-or-death situation. The challenge for the La Crosse, Wisconsin, organization is to develop that talent in a way that brings out the best in people in a complex environment. That challenge is especially intense considering that many types of health care professionals are already in short supply, and the demand is expected to increase assuming that the federal government's health care reform legislation gives more people access to services.

To meet the challenge, Gunderson for the past few years has been formally assessing its talent needs and planning for employee development. The effort began in 2001, when the human resource department began researching best practices and trying out development practices on the organization's top leaders. Two years later, Gunderson launched a Talent Development Review Group, whose members included the chief medical officer, senior vice president of business services, chief learning officer, and an internal consultant for talent development. This group is responsible for developing a team of leaders, implementing development programs, and ensuring that high-potential employees are receiving developmental resources.

The effort begins with a definition of the qualities Gunderson requires of its leaders. Based on two years of research, the Review Group determined that the organization's leaders need to have specific skills in operations, finance, vision, strategic thinking, team building, staff development, change management, performance management, and leadership. These needs are arranged into tiers defining which skills are needed at which level of the organization. They also are incorporated into various HRM tools: details of job descriptions, questions in job interviews, measures in performance appraisals, and topics of developmental programs.

Beginning when Gunderson rolled out the development program in 2003, the organization began identifying high-potential employees to participate. Employees are selected as potential leaders in four areas: physician executives, physician administrators, administrative executives, and administrative leaders at the level of directors. Selection is based on assessments that determine whether candidates have the leadership competencies that were identified by the team. To participate in the development program, these candidates also must demonstrate that they are interested in career advancement and committed to the developmental process.

The selected participants then undergo an assessment, using several measures. A behavioral interview and an instrument called the Hogan Potential Report assess leadership potential, and 360-degree feedback looks for what the team calls "potential blind spots." Personality is assessed with the Myers-Briggs Type Indicator, and values are measured with the Hogan Values Report. Gunderson's chief learning officer and the talent development consultant were trained to interpret the data, and they provide a summary of the results to each employee. They work with the rest of the Review Group to develop ideas for closing gaps between the assessment results and the leadership requirements for each employee in the development program.

To create action plans, Gunderson offers a variety of development methods. These include stretch assignments, job rotations, coaching, mentoring, continuing education, committee appointments, and meetings with top executives to discuss strategic issues. Each plan specifies measures of success, and performance is tracked in terms of accomplishing those goals as well as through additional 360-degree reviews and assessments of leadership competencies.

In the years since Gunderson introduced this program, dozens of employees have begun this formal process of career development in all of the leadership areas. Some of them have already moved into director and senior leadership roles. An example is Deb Rislow, who entered the program as an information systems director. She was originally identified as an employee with strong analytical skills, a commitment to excellence, and skill at putting ideas into action. Her original goal was to get the organization's paperwork into an electronic system. Through challenging assignments and increased access to organizational leaders, Rislow advanced her goal while developing her leadership skills. She moved up through the organization to a position of chief information officer, overseeing 900 employees. The success story is not just about individual employees' successes, of course. Developing employees also strengthens the whole organization, which recently was named one of the top 100 hospitals in the nation based on criteria including patient outcomes, patient satisfaction, and profitability.

SOURCES: Nancy Noelke, "Leverage the Present to Build the Future," *HR Magazine*, March 2009, pp. 34–36; and "Meriter Is Named Top 100 Hospital in the Country," *Wisconsin State Journal*, March 30, 2010, Business & Company Resource Center, http://galenet.galegroup.com.

Questions

1. How well does Gunderson's development program follow the career management process described in Figure 9.3? Identify any elements of that system that are missing.

2. What measures would you recommend for determining the success of Gunderson's developmental effort? Discuss how well these are aligned with the organization's goals.

3. Of the developmental methods described in this chapter, which do you think would be most appropriate for developing leadership skills? Which of these does Gunderson use? Which should the organization add or drop from its program, and why?

www.mhhe.com/noefund4e is your source for **R**eviewing, **A**pplying, and **P**racticing the concepts you learned about in Chapter 9.

Review
- Chapter learning objectives
- Test Your Knowledge: Mentoring

Application
- Manager's Hot Seat segment: "Personal Disclosure: Confession Coincidence"
- Video case and quiz: "Patagonia"
- Self-Assessment: Employee Development
- Web exercise: Leadership programs at GE
- Small-business case: A Three-Month Break from Little Tokyo Service Center

Practice
- Chapter quiz

NOTES

1. M. London, *Managing the Training Enterprise* (San Francisco: Jossey-Bass, 1989) and D. Day, *Developing Leadership Talent* (Alexandria, VA: SHRM Foundation, 2007).

2. R. W. Pace, P. C. Smith, and G. E. Mills, *Human Resource Development* (Englewood Cliffs, NJ: Prentice Hall, 1991); W. Fitzgerald, "Training versus Development," *Training and Development Journal*, May 1992, pp. 81–84; R. A. Noe, S. L. Wilk, E. J. Mullen, and J. E. Wanek, "Employee Development: Issues in Construct Definition and Investigation of Antecedents," in *Improving Training Effectiveness in Work Organizations*, ed. J. K. Ford (Mahwah, NJ: Lawrence Erlbaum, 1997), pp. 153–89.

3. J. H. Greenhaus and G. A. Callanan, *Career Management*, 2nd ed. (Fort Worth, TX: Dryden Press, 1994); and D. Hall, *Careers in and out of Organizations* (Thousand Oaks, CA: Sage, 2002).

4. M. B. Arthur, P. H. Claman, and R. J. DeFillippi, "Intelligent Enterprise, Intelligent Careers," *Academy of Management Executive* 9 (1995), pp. 7–20; and Dan Schawbel, "Upping Your Value at Work," *BusinessWeek*, December 18, 2009, www.businessweek.com.

5. M. Weinstein, "Teaching the Top," *Training*, February 2005, pp. 30–33.

6. R. Noe, *Employee Training and Development*, 5th ed. (New York: McGraw-Hill Irwin, 2010).

7. C. Waxer, "Bank of Montreal Opens Its Checkbook in the Name of Employee Development," *Workforce Management*, October 24, 2005, pp. 46–48.

8. R. Knight, "GE's Corporate Boot Camp cum Talent Spotting Venue," *Financial Times Business Education*, March 20, 2006, p. 2; J. Durett, "GE Hones Its Leaders at Crotonville," *Training*, May 2006, pp. 25–27;

and General Electric, "Undergraduate Leadership Programs" and "Masters and MBA Leadership Programs," GE careers Web site, www.gecareers.com, accessed April 6, 2009.

9. I. Speizer, "Custom Fit," *Workforce Management*, March 2005, pp. 57–63.

10. A. Howard and D. W. Bray, *Managerial Lives in Transition: Advancing Age and Changing Times* (New York: Guilford, 1988); J. Bolt, *Executive Development* (New York: Harper Business, 1989); J. R. Hinrichs and G. P. Hollenbeck, "Leadership Development," in *Developing Human Resources* ed. K. N. Wexley (Washington, DC: BNA Books, 1991), pp. 5-221–5-237; and Day, *Developing Leadership Talent*.

11. M. Weinstein, "Personalities and Performance," *Training*, July/August 2008, pp. 36–40.

12. A. Thorne and H. Gough, *Portraits of Type* (Palo Alto, CA: Consulting Psychologists Press, 1993).

13. D. Druckman and R. A. Bjork, eds., *In the Mind's Eye: Enhancing Human Performance* (Washington, DC: National Academy Press, 1991); M. H. McCaulley, "The Myers-Briggs Type Indicator and Leadership," in *Measures of Leadership*, eds. K. E. Clark and M. B. Clark (West Orange, NJ: Leadership Library of America, 1990), pp. 381–418.

14. G. C. Thornton III and W. C. Byham, *Assessment Centers and Managerial Performance* (New York: Academic Press, 1982); L. F. Schoenfeldt and J. A. Steger, "Identification and Development of Management Talent," in *Research in Personnel and Human Resource Management*, eds. K. N. Rowland and G. Ferris (Greenwich, CT: JAI Press, 1989), vol. 7, pp. 151–81.

15. Thornton and Byham, *Assessment Centers and Managerial Performance*.

16. P. G. W. Jansen and B. A. M. Stoop, "The Dynamics of Assessment Center Validity: Results of a Seven-Year Study," *Journal of Applied Psychology* 86 (2001), pp. 741–53; and D. Chan, "Criterion and Construct Validation of an Assessment Centre," *Journal of Occupational and Organizational Psychology* 69 (1996), pp. 167–81.

17. R. G. Jones and M. D. Whitmore, "Evaluating Developmental Assessment Centers as Interventions," *Personnel Psychology* 48 (1995), pp. 377–88.

18. C. D. McCauley and M. M. Lombardo, "Benchmarks: An Instrument for Diagnosing Managerial Strengths and Weaknesses," in *Measures of Leadership*, pp. 535–45; and Center for Creative Leadership, "Benchmarks®—Overview," www.ccl.org, accessed March 28, 2006.

19. C. D. McCauley, M. M. Lombardo, and C. J. Usher, "Diagnosing Management Development Needs: An Instrument Based on How Managers Develop," *Journal of Management* 15 (1989), pp. 389–403.

20. S. B. Silverman, "Individual Development through Performance Appraisal," in *Developing Human Resources*, pp. 5-120–5-151.

21. J. F. Brett and L. E. Atwater, "360-Degree Feedback: Accuracy, Reactions, and Perceptions of Usefulness," *Journal of Applied Psychology* 86 (2001), pp. 930–42; Marshall Goldsmith, "How to Increase Your Leadership Effectiveness," *BusinessWeek*, November 20, 2009, www.businessweek.com; and Brenda Bence, "Would You Want to Work for You?" *Supervision*, February 2010, Business & Company Resource Center, http://galenet.galegroup.com.

22. Jennifer Robison, "The Strengths of Leadership," *Gallup Management Journal*, February 26, 2009, Business & Company Resource Center, http://galenet.galegroup.com (interview with Tom Rath and Barry Conchie).

23. L. Atwater, P. Roush, and A. Fischthal, "The Influence of Upward Feedback on Self- and Follower Ratings of Leadership," *Personnel Psychology* 48 (1995), pp. 35–59; J. F. Hazucha, S. A. Hezlett, and R. J. Schneider, "The Impact of 360-Degree Feedback on Management Skill Development," *Human Resource Management* 32 (1993), pp. 325–51; J. W. Smither, M. London, N. Vasilopoulos, R. R. Reilly, R. E. Millsap, and N. Salvemini, "An Examination of the Effects of an Upward Feedback Program over Time," *Personnel Psychology* 48 (1995), pp. 1–34; J. Smither and A. Walker, "Are the Characteristics of Narrative Comments Related to Improvements in Multirater Feedback Ratings over Time?" *Journal of Applied Psychology* 89 (2004), pp. 575–81; and J. Smither, M. London, and R. Reilly, "Does Performance Improve Following Multisource Feedback? A Theoretical Model, Meta-analysis, and Review of Empirical Findings," *Personnel Psychology* 58 (2005), pp. 33–66.

24. John H. Zenger and Scott Edinger, "Demand Inspiring Leadership," *Financial Executive*, July–August 2009, Business & Company Resource Center, http://galenet.galegroup.com.

25. M. W. McCall Jr., *High Flyers* (Boston: Harvard Business School Press, 1998).

26. R. S. Snell, "Congenial Ways of Learning: So Near yet So Far," *Journal of Management Development* 9 (1990), pp. 17–23.

27. M. McCall, M. Lombardo, and A. Morrison, *Lessons of Experience* (Lexington, MA: Lexington Books, 1988); M. W. McCall, "Developing Executives through Work Experiences," *Human Resource Planning* 11 (1988), pp. 1–11; M. N. Ruderman, P. J. Ohlott, and C. D. McCauley, "Assessing Opportunities for Leadership Development," in *Measures of Leadership*, pp. 547–62; and C. D. McCauley, L. J. Estman, and P. J. Ohlott, "Linking Management Selection and Development through Stretch Assignments," *Human Resource Management* 34 (1995), pp. 93–115.

28. C. D. McCauley, M. N. Ruderman, P. J. Ohlott, and J. E. Morrow, "Assessing the Developmental Components of Managerial Jobs," *Journal of Applied Psychology* 79 (1994), pp. 544–60.

29. M. Weinstein, "Foreign but Familiar," *Training*, January 2009, pp. 20–23.

30. M. London, *Developing Managers* (San Francisco: Jossey-Bass, 1985); M. A. Camion, L. Cheraskin, and M. J. Stevens, "Career-Related Antecedents and Outcomes of Job Rotation," *Academy of Management Journal* 37 (1994), pp. 1518–42; and London, *Managing the Training Enterprise*.

31. Margaret Fiester, "Job Rotation, Total Rewards, Measuring Value," *HR Magazine*, August 2008, Business & Company Resource Center, http://galenet.galegroup.com; and "Energize and Enhance Employee Value with Job Rotation," *HR Focus*, January 2008, OCLC FirstSearch, http://newfirstsearch.oclc.org.

32. R. A. Noe, B. D. Steffy, and A. E. Barber, "An Investigation of the Factors Influencing Employees' Willingness to Accept Mobility Opportunities," *Personnel Psychology* 41 (1988), pp. 559–80; S. Gould and L. E. Penley, "A Study of the Correlates of Willingness to Relocate," *Academy of Management Journal* 28 (1984), pp. 472–78; J. Landau and T. H. Hammer, "Clerical Employees' Perceptions of Intraorganizational Career Opportunities," *Academy of Management Journal* 29 (1986), pp. 385–405; and J. M. Brett and A. H. Reilly, "On the Road Again: Predicting the Job Transfer Decision," *Journal of Applied Psychology* 73 (1988), pp. 614–20.

33. J. M. Brett, "Job Transfer and Well-Being," *Journal of Applied Psychology* 67 (1992), pp. 450–63; F. J. Minor, L. A. Slade, and R. A. Myers, "Career Transitions in Changing Times," in *Contemporary Career Development Issues*, eds. R. F. Morrison and J. Adams (Hillsdale, NJ: Lawrence Erlbaum, 1991), pp. 109–20; C. C. Pinder and K. G. Schroeder, "Time to Proficiency Following Job Transfers," *Academy of Management Journal* 30 (1987), pp. 336–53; and Kate Plourd, "To Get the Best Gig, Expand Your Repertoire," *CFO*, September 2008, Business & Company Resource Center, http://galenet.galegroup.com.

34. Thomas H. Davenport, Jeanne G. Harris, and Robert Morison, *Analytics at Work: Smarter Decisions, Better Results* (Boston: Harvard Business Press, 2010), excerpted in *CIO Insight*, March 16, 2010, www.cioinsight.com.

35. Deborah S. Linnell and Tim Wolfred, *Creative Disruption: Sabbaticals for Capacity Building and Leadership Development in the Nonprofit Sector* (CompassPoint Nonprofit Services, 2009), p. 16, accessed at www.compasspoint.org.

36. D. B. Turban and T. W. Dougherty, "Role of Protégé Personality in Receipt of Mentoring and Career Success," *Academy of Management Journal* 37 (1994), pp. 688–702; and E. A. Fagenson, "Mentoring: Who Needs It? A Comparison of Protégés' and Nonprotégés' Needs for Power, Achievement, Affiliation, and Autonomy," *Journal of Vocational Behavior* 41 (1992), pp. 48–60.

37. A. H. Geiger, "Measures for Mentors," *Training and Development Journal*, February 1992, pp. 65–67; Beth N. Carvin, "The Great Mentor Match," *T + D*, January 2009, OCLC FirstSearch, http://newfirstsearch.oclc.org; and Pamela Craig, "Looking for Help at Work? Get a Mentor," *BusinessWeek*, March 2, 2010, www.businessweek.com.

38. K. E. Kram, *Mentoring at Work: Developmental Relationships in Organizational Life* (Glenview, IL: Scott-Foresman, 1985); L. L. Phillips-Jones, "Establishing a Formalized Mentoring Program," *Training and Development Journal* 2 (1983), pp. 38–42; K. Kram, "Phases of the Mentoring Relationship," *Academy of Management Journal* 26 (1983), pp. 608–25; G. T. Chao, P. M. Walz, and P. D. Gardner, "Formal and Informal Mentorships: A Comparison of Mentoring Functions and Contrasts with Nonmentored Counterparts," *Personnel Psychology* 45 (1992), pp. 619–36; and C. Wanberg, E. Welsh, and S. Hezlett, "Mentoring Research: A Review and Dynamic Process Model," in *Research in Personnel and Human Resources Management*, eds. J. Martocchio and G. Ferris (New York: Elsevier Science, 2003), pp. 39–124.

39. E. White, "Making Mentorships Work," *Wall Street Journal*, October 23, 2007, p. B11; E. Holmes, "Career Mentors Today Seem Short on Advice but Give a Mean Tour," *Wall Street Journal*, August 28, 2007, p. B1; and J. Sandburg, "With Bad Mentors It's Better to Break Up than to Make Up," *Wall Street Journal*, March 18, 2008, p. B1.

40. L. Eby, M. Butts, A. Lockwood, and A. Simon, "Protégés' Negative Mentoring Experiences: Construct Development and Nomological Validation," *Personnel Psychology* 57 (2004), pp. 411–47; and M. Boyle, "Most Mentoring Programs Stink—but Yours Doesn't Have To," *Training*, August 2005, pp. 12–15.

41. R. A. Noe, D. B. Greenberger, and S. Wang, "Mentoring: What We Know and Where We Might Go," in *Research in Personnel and Human Resources Management*, eds. G. Ferris and J. Martocchio (New York: Elsevier Science, 2002), vol. 21, pp. 129–74; and T. D. Allen, L. T. Eby, M. L. Poteet, E. Lentz, and L. Lima, "Career Benefits Associated with Mentoring for Protégés: A Meta-Analysis," *Journal of Applied Psychology* 89 (2004), pp. 127–36.

42. D. B. Peterson and M. D. Hicks, *Leader as Coach* (Minneapolis: Personnel Decisions, 1996).

43. Ken Blanchard Companies, "Why Aren't Managers More Coach-like?" *Ignite*, September 2009, www.kenblanchard.com.

44. J. Smither, M. London, R. Flautt, Y. Vargas, and L. Kucine, "Can Working with an Executive Coach Improve Multisource Ratings over Time? A Quasi-experimental Field Study," *Personnel Psychology* 56 (2003), pp. 23–44.

45. J. Toto, "Untapped World of Peer Coaching," *T + D*, April 2006, pp. 69–71.

46. Rajiv L. Gupta and Karol M. Wasylyshyn, "Developing World Class Leaders: The Rohm and Haas Story," *People & Strategy*, December 2009, pp. 36–41; and Kathleen Koster, "This Too Shall Pass," *Employee Benefit News*, July 1, 2009, Business & Company Resource Center, http://galenet.galegroup.com.

47. B. Yovovich, "Golden Opportunities," *Human Resource Executive*, August 2008, pp. 30–34.

48. S. Needleman, "New Career, Same Employer," *Wall Street Journal*, April 21, 2008, p. B9.

49. M. Sallie-Dosunmu, "Born to Grow," *T&D*, May 2006, pp. 34–37.

50. Catalyst, "2007 Census: Corporate Offices and Top Earners," Catalyst Web site, www.catalystwomen.org, accessed February 1, 2008.

51. P. J. Ohlott, M. N. Ruderman, and C. D. McCauley, "Gender Differences in Managers' Developmental Job Experiences," *Academy of Management*

Journal 37 (1994), pp. 46–67; L. A. Mainiero, "Getting Anointed for Advancement: The Case of Executive Women," *Academy of Management Executive* 8 (1994), pp. 53–67; and P. Tharenov, S. Latimer, and D. Conroy, "How Do You Make It to the Top? An Examination of Influences on Women's and Men's Managerial Advancements," *Academy of Management Journal* 37 (1994), pp. 899–931.

52. U.S. Department of Labor, *A Report on the Glass Ceiling Initiative* (Washington, DC: Labor Department, 1991); R. A. Noe, "Women and Mentoring: A Review and Research Agenda," *Academy of Management Review* 13 (1988), pp. 65–78; B. R. Ragins and J. L. Cotton, "Easier Said than Done: Gender Differences in Perceived Barriers to Gaining a Mentor," *Academy of Management Journal* 34 (1991), pp. 939–51; and Jesse Washington, "Study: Networking Hinders Black Women Execs," *Yahoo News*, January 7, 2009, http://news.yahoo.com.

53. C. Tuna, "Initiative Moves Women up Corporate Ladder," *Wall Street Journal*, October 20, 2008, p. B4.

54. W. J. Rothwell, *Effective Succession Planning*, 2nd ed. (New York: AMACOM, 2001).

55. B. E. Dowell, "Succession Planning," in *Implementing Organizational Interventions*, eds. J. Hedge and E. D. Pulakos (San Francisco: Jossey-Bass, 2002), pp. 78–109.

56. C. B. Derr, C. Jones, and E. L. Toomey, "Managing High-Potential Employees: Current Practices in Thirty-Three U.S. Corporations," *Human Resource Management* 27 (1988), pp. 273–90; K. M. Nowack, "The Secrets of Succession," *Training and Development* 48 (1994), pp. 49–54; and "2009 Trends in Review: What Do You Know?" *T + D*, December 2009, pp. 33–39.

57. Apryl Motley, "Filling Their Shoes," *Community Banker*, January 2010, Business & Company Resource Center, http://galenet.galegroup.com.

58. M. W. McCall Jr. and M. M. Lombardo, "Off the Track: Why and How Successful Executives Get Derailed," *Technical Report*, no. 21 (Greensboro, NC: Center for Creative Leadership, 1983); and E. V. Veslo and J. B. Leslie, "Why Executives Derail: Perspectives across Time and Cultures," *Academy of Management Executive* 9 (1995), pp. 62–72.

59. L. W. Hellervik, J. F. Hazucha, and R. J. Schneider, "Behavior Change: Models, Methods, and a Review of Evidence," in *Handbook of Industrial and Organizational Psychology*, 2nd ed., eds. M. D. Dunnette and L. M. Hough (Palo Alto, CA: Consulting Psychologists Press, 1992), vol. 3, pp. 823–99.

60. D. B. Peterson, "Measuring and Evaluating Change in Executive and Managerial Development," paper presented at the annual conference of the Society for Industrial and Organizational Psychology, Miami, 1990.

Separating and Retaining Employees

What Do I Need to Know?

After reading this chapter, you should be able to:

LO1 Distinguish between involuntary and voluntary turnover, and describe their effects on an organization.

LO2 Discuss how employees determine whether the organization treats them fairly.

LO3 Identify legal requirements for employee discipline.

LO4 Summarize ways in which organizations can fairly discipline employees.

LO5 Explain how job dissatisfaction affects employee behavior.

LO6 Describe how organizations contribute to employees' job satisfaction and retain key employees.

Introduction

Keeping productive employees can be a challenge when work and family demands collide. Recently, *Wall Street Journal* reporters talked to some of the nation's top female executives about their career success, and one issue that came up repeatedly was time pressure. Although work and family obligations have caused many women to rethink promising careers, the women who were interviewed had found ways to cope and prosper. Melanie Healey, president of Global Health and Feminine Care at Procter & Gamble, recalled that she had her first child while working in Mexico for an executive who routinely put in 16-hour days. At Healey's request, she and her boss agreed on a set of goals for her to accomplish on her own terms, while leaving each evening at six o'clock. In the end, Healey was so successful that her boss tried to recruit her when he left for a position at another company.

Sheryl Sandberg, a Google vice president, encountered a similar situation from the manager's perspective. A top employee was expecting a baby, and Sandberg encouraged her to stay with the company, opening a discussion on how to make that happen. The woman said that what would matter would be for Sandberg to stop sending her e-mail late at night. If 11:30 P.M. was the best time for Sandberg to work, she needed to realize that a response could wait until the next day.[1] Such efforts to communicate and establish a flexible work environment can be essential for retaining high-performing employees.

Every organization recognizes that it needs satisfied, loyal customers. In addition, success requires satisfied, loyal employees. Research provides evidence that retaining employees helps retain customers and increase sales.[2] Organizations with low turnover and satisfied employees tend to perform better.[3] On the other side of the coin, organizations have to act when an employee's performance consistently falls short. Sometimes terminating a poor performer is the only way to show fairness, ensure quality, and maintain customer satisfaction.

This chapter explores the dual challenges of separating and retaining employees. We begin by distinguishing involuntary and voluntary turnover, describing how each affects the organization. Next we explore the separation process, including ways to manage this process fairly. Finally, we discuss measures the organization can take to encourage employees to stay. These topics provide a transition between Parts 3 and 4. The previous chapters in Part 3 considered how to assess and improve performance, and this chapter describes measures to take depending on whether performance is high or low. Part 4 discusses pay and benefits, both of which play an important role in employee retention.

Managing Voluntary and Involuntary Turnover

Organizations must try to ensure that good performers want to stay with the organization and that employees whose performance is chronically low are encouraged—or forced—to leave. Both of these challenges involve *employee turnover*, that is, employees leaving the organization. When the organization initiates the turnover (often with employees who would prefer to stay), the result is **involuntary turnover.** Examples include terminating an employee for drug use or laying off employees during a downturn. Most organizations use the word *termination* to refer only to a discharge related to a discipline problem, but some organizations call any involuntary turnover a termination. When the employees initiate the turnover (often when the organization would prefer to keep them), it is **voluntary turnover.** Employees may leave to retire or to take a job with a different organization.

In general, organizations try to avoid the need for involuntary turnover and to minimize voluntary turnover, especially among top performers. Both kinds of turnover are costly, as summarized in Table 10.1. Replacing workers is expensive, and new employees need time to learn their jobs and build teamwork skills.[4] In addition, people today are more ready to sue a former employer if they feel they were unfairly discharged. The prospect of workplace violence also raises the risk associated with discharging employees. Effective human resource management can help the organization minimize both kinds of turnover, as well as carry it out effectively when necessary. Despite a company's best efforts at personnel selection, training, and compensation, some employees will fail to meet performance requirements or will violate company policies. When this happens, organizations need to apply a discipline program that could ultimately lead to discharging the individual.

LO1 Distinguish between involuntary and voluntary turnover, and describe their effects on an organization.

Involuntary Turnover
Turnover initiated by an employer (often with employees who would prefer to stay).

Voluntary Turnover
Turnover initiated by employees (often when the organization would prefer to keep them).

INVOLUNTARY TURNOVER	VOLUNTARY TURNOVER
Recruiting, selecting, and training replacements	Recruiting, selecting, and training replacements
Lost productivity	Lost productivity
Lawsuits	Loss of talented employees
Workplace violence	

Table 10.1

Costs Associated with Turnover

HR Oops!

Most Valued, Least Loyal

During the recent economic downturn, as companies scrambled to cut costs wherever they could, many hoped they could count on their top talent to stick around in spite of the belt tightening—after all, they should be grateful to have a job.

Some evidence suggests that this hope may have been misplaced. Worse, the most valuable employees seem to be the ones who are least grateful for the chance to stay with their employers through hard times. According to a survey by the Corporate Executive Board, the percentage of senior executives "willing to go above and beyond what is expected" fell by more than half since before the financial crisis. The same survey found that one-fourth of employees identified by their employers as having high potential were planning to quit their job within the year. Similarly, an annual survey of employees conducted by Watson Wyatt Worldwide and WorldatWork found that employees' commitment to their employers has fallen, with the largest drop registered among the highest performers.

Part of the problem may be a false hope that companies can meet employees' desires inexpensively. In a survey by Spherion Corporation, employers said workers' satisfaction depended most on a positive work environment and good relationships with supervisors. Employees, however, said they cared most about pay and benefits.

Sources: Patricia O'Connell, "Don't Let Top Talent Get Away," *Yahoo News*, February 2, 2009, http://news.yahoo.com; and Sarah E. Needleman, "Businesses Mount Efforts to Retain Valued Employees," *Wall Street Journal*, November 16, 2009, http://online.wsj.com.

Questions

1. What would be the costs to an organization of losing top executives or high-potential employees as the economy improves?
2. How do you think a company can keep top performers onboard if little money is available for raises and bonuses, at least in the near term?

For a number of reasons, discharging employees can be very difficult. First, the decision has legal aspects that can affect the organization. Historically, if the organization and employee do not have a specific employment contract, the employer or employee may end the employment relationship at any time. This is the *employment-at-will doctrine*, described in Chapter 5. This doctrine has eroded significantly, however. Employees who have been terminated sometimes sue their employers for wrongful discharge. Some judges have considered that employment at will is limited where managers make statements that amount to an implied contract; a discharge also can be found illegal if it violates a law (such as antidiscrimination laws) or public policy (for example, firing an employee for refusing to do something illegal).[5] In a typical lawsuit for wrongful discharge, the former employee tries to establish that the discharge violated either an implied agreement or public policy. Most employers settle these claims out of court. Even though few former employees win wrongful-discharge suits, and employers usually win when they appeal, the cost of defending the lawsuit can be hundreds of thousands of dollars.[6]

Along with the financial risks of dismissing an employee, there are issues of personal safety. Distressing as it is that some former employees go to the courts, far worse are the employees who react to a termination decision with violence. Violence in the workplace has become a major organizational problem. Although any number of organizational actions or decisions may incite violence among employees, the "nothing else to lose" aspect of an employee's dismissal makes the situation dangerous, especially when the nature of the work adds other risk factors.[7]

Retaining top performers is not always easy either, and recent trends have made this more difficult than ever. Today's psychological contract, in which workers feel responsibility for their own careers rather than loyalty to a particular employer, makes voluntary turnover more likely. Also, competing organizations are constantly looking at each other's top performers; when the labor market tightened, "poaching talent" became an art form.[8] In fact, as the "HR Oops" box illustrates, not even an economic downturn takes away the challenges.

Employee Separation

Because of the critical financial and personal risks associated with employee dismissal, it is easy to see why organizations must develop a standardized, systematic approach to discipline and discharge. These decisions should not be left solely to the discretion of individual managers or supervisors. Policies that can lead to employee separation should be based on principles of justice and law, and they should allow for various ways to intervene.

Principles of Justice

The sensitivity of a system for disciplining and possibly terminating employees is obvious, and it is critical that the system be seen as fair. Employees form conclusions about the system's fairness based on the system's outcomes and procedures and the way managers treat employees when carrying out those procedures. Figure 10.1 summarizes these principles as outcome fairness, procedural justice, and interactional justice. Outcome fairness involves the ends of a discipline process, while procedural and interactional justice focus on the means to those ends. Not only is behavior ethical that is in accord with these principles, but research has also linked the last two categories of justice with employee satisfaction and productivity.[9]

People's perception of **outcome fairness** depends on their judgment that the consequences of a decision to employees are just. As shown in Figure 10.1, one

LO2 Discuss how employees determine whether the organization treats them fairly.

Outcome Fairness
A judgment that the consequences given to employees are just.

Figure 10.1

Principles of Justice

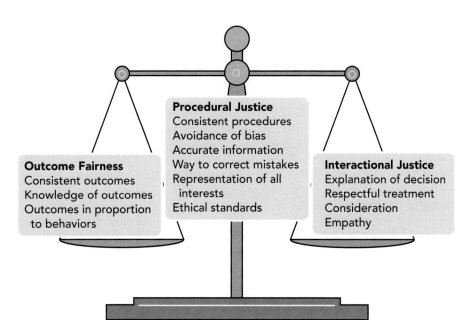

Outcome Fairness
Consistent outcomes
Knowledge of outcomes
Outcomes in proportion to behaviors

Procedural Justice
Consistent procedures
Avoidance of bias
Accurate information
Way to correct mistakes
Representation of all interests
Ethical standards

Interactional Justice
Explanation of decision
Respectful treatment
Consideration
Empathy

employee's consequences should be consistent with other employees' consequences. Suppose several employees went out to lunch, returned drunk, and were reprimanded. A few weeks later, another employee was fired for being drunk at work. Employees might well conclude that outcomes are not fair because they are inconsistent. Another basis for outcome fairness is that everyone should know what to expect. Organizations promote outcome fairness when they clearly communicate policies regarding the consequences of inappropriate behavior. Finally, the outcome should be proportionate to the behavior. Terminating an employee for being late to work, especially if this is the first time the employee is late, would seem out of proportion to the offense in most situations. Employees' sense of outcome fairness usually would reserve loss of a job for the most serious offenses.

Procedural Justice
A judgment that fair methods were used to determine the consequences an employee receives.

People's perception of **procedural justice** is their judgment that fair methods were used to determine the consequences an employee receives. Figure 10.1 shows six principles that determine whether people perceive procedures as fair. The procedures should be consistent from one person to another, and the manager using them should suppress any personal biases. The procedures should be based on accurate information, not rumors or falsehoods. The procedures should also be correctable, meaning the system includes safeguards, such as channels for appealing a decision or correcting errors. The procedures should take into account the concerns of all the groups affected—for example, by gathering information from employees, customers, and managers. Finally, the procedures should be consistent with prevailing ethical standards, such as concerns for privacy and honesty.

Interactional Justice
A judgment that the organization carried out its actions in a way that took the employee's feelings into account.

A perception of **interactional justice** is a judgment that the organization carried out its actions in a way that took the employee's feelings into account. It is a judgment about the ways that managers interact with their employees. A disciplinary action meets the standards of interactional justice if the manager explains to the employee how the action is procedurally just. The manager should listen to the employee. The manager should also treat the employee with dignity and respect and should empathize with the employee's feelings. Even when a manager discharges an employee for doing something wrong, the manager can speak politely and state the reasons for the action. These efforts to achieve interactional justice are especially important when managing an employee who has a high level of hostility and is at greater risk of responding with violence.[10]

LO3 Identify legal requirements for employee discipline.

Legal Requirements

The law gives employers wide latitude in hiring and firing, but employers must meet certain requirements. They must avoid wrongful discharge and illegal discrimination. They also must meet standards related to employees' privacy and adequate notice of layoffs.

Wrongful Discharge

As we noted earlier in the chapter, discipline practices must avoid the charge of wrongful discharge. First, this means the discharge may not violate an implied agreement. Terminating an employee may violate an implied agreement if the employer had promised the employee job security or if the action is inconsistent with company policies. An example might be that an organization has stated that an employee with an unexcused absence will receive a warning for the first violation, but an angry supervisor fires an employee for being absent on the day of an important meeting.

Another reason a discharge may be considered wrongful is that it violates public policy. Violations of public policy include terminating the employee for refusing to do something illegal, unethical, or unsafe. Suppose an employee refuses to dump chemicals into the sewer system; firing that employee could be a violation of public policy. It is also a violation of public policy to terminate an employee for doing what the law requires—for example, cooperating with a government investigation, reporting illegal behavior by the employer, or reporting for jury duty.

HR professionals can help organizations avoid (and defend against) charges of wrongful discharge by establishing and communicating policies for handling misbehavior. They should define unacceptable behaviors and identify how the organization will respond to them. Managers should follow these procedures consistently and document precisely the reasons for disciplinary action. In addition, the organization should train managers to avoid making promises that imply job security (for example, "As long as you keep up that level of performance, you'll have a job with us"). Finally, in writing and reviewing employee handbooks, HR professionals should avoid any statements that could be interpreted as employment contracts. When there is any doubt about a statement, the organization should seek legal advice.

Discrimination

Another benefit of a formal discipline policy is that it helps the organization comply with equal employment opportunity requirements. As in other employment matters, employers must make decisions without regard to individuals' age, sex, race, or other protected status. If two employees steal from the employer but one is disciplined more harshly than the other, the employee who receives the harsher punishment could look for the cause in his or her being of a particular race, country of origin, or some other group. Evenhanded, carefully documented discipline can avoid such claims.

Employees' Privacy

The courts also have long protected individuals' privacy in many situations. At the same time, employers have legitimate reasons for learning about some personal matters, especially when behavior outside the workplace can affect productivity, workplace safety, and employee morale. Employers therefore need to ensure that the information they gather and use is relevant to these matters. For example, safety and security make it legitimate to require drug testing of all employees holding jobs such as police officer, firefighter, and airline flight crew.[11] (Governments at the federal, state, and local levels have many laws affecting drug-testing programs, so it is wise to get legal advice before planning such tests.)

Privacy issues also surface when employers wish to search or monitor employees on the job. An employer that suspects theft, drug use, or other misdeeds on the job may wish to search employees for evidence. In general, random searches of areas such as desks, lockers, toolboxes, and communications

Organizations such as day care facilities and schools must protect employees' right to privacy in their lives and on the job while balancing the need to protect children from harm.

Table 10.2

Measures for Protecting Employees' Privacy

Ensure that information is relevant.
Publicize information-gathering policies and consequences.
Request consent before gathering information.
Treat employees consistently.
Conduct searches discreetly.
Share information only with those who need it.

such as e-mails are permissible, so long as the employer can justify that there is probable cause for the search and the organization has work rules that provide for searches.[12] Employers can act fairly and minimize the likelihood of a lawsuit by publicizing the search policy, applying it consistently, asking for the employee's consent before the search begins, and conducting the search discreetly. Also, when a search is a random check, it is important to clarify that no one has been accused of misdeeds.[13]

No matter how sensitively the organization gathers information leading to disciplinary actions, it should also consider privacy issues when deciding who will see the information.[14] In general, it is advisable to share the information only with people who have a business need to see it—for example, the employee's supervisor, union officials, and in some cases, co-workers. Letting outsiders know the reasons for terminating an employee can embarrass the employee, who might file a defamation lawsuit. HR professionals can help organizations avoid such lawsuits by working with managers to determine fact-based explanations and to decide who needs to see these explanations.

Table 10.2 summarizes these measures for protecting employees' privacy.

LO4 Summarize ways in which organizations can fairly discipline employees.

Notification of Layoffs

Sometimes terminations are necessary not because of individuals' misdeeds, but because the organization determines that for economic reasons it must close a facility. An organization that plans such broad-scale layoffs may be subject to the Workers' Adjustment Retraining and Notification Act. This federal law requires that organizations with more than 100 employees give 60 days' notice before any closing or layoff that will affect at least 50 full-time employees. If employers covered by this law do not give notice to the employees (and their union, if applicable), they may have to provide back pay and fringe benefits and pay penalties as well. Several states and cities have similar laws, and the federal law contains a number of exemptions. Therefore, it is important to seek legal advice before implementing a plant closing.

Hot-Stove Rule
Principle of discipline that says discipline should be like a hot stove, giving clear warning and following up with consistent, objective, immediate consequences.

Progressive Discipline

Organizations look for methods of handling problem behavior that are fair, legal, and effective. A popular principle for responding effectively is the **hot-stove rule.** According to this principle, discipline should be like a hot stove: The glowing or burning stove gives warning not to touch. Anyone who ignores the warning will be burned. The stove has no feelings to influence which people it burns, and it delivers the same burn to any touch. Finally, the burn is immediate. Like the hot stove, an organization's discipline should give warning and have consequences that are consistent, objective, and immediate.

Progressive Discipline
A formal discipline process in which the consequences become more serious if the employee repeats the offense.

The principles of justice suggest that the organization prepare for problems by establishing a formal discipline process in which the consequences become more serious if the employee repeats the offense. Such a system is called **progressive discipline.**

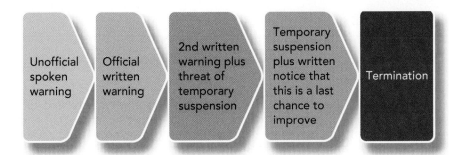

Figure 10.2

Progressive Discipline
Responses

A typical progressive discipline system identifies and communicates unacceptable behaviors and responds to a series of offenses with the actions shown in Figure 10.2— spoken and then written warnings, temporary suspension, and finally, termination. This process fulfills the purpose of discipline by teaching employees what is expected of them and creating a situation in which employees must try to do what is expected. It seeks to prevent misbehavior (by publishing rules) and to correct, rather than merely punish, misbehavior.

Such procedures may seem exasperatingly slow, especially when the employee's misdeeds hurt the team's performance. In the end, however, if an employee must be discharged, careful use of the procedure increases other employees' belief that the organization is fair and reduces the likelihood that the problem employee will sue (or at least that the employee will win in court). For situations in which misbehavior is dangerous, the organization may establish a stricter policy, even terminating an employee for the first offense. In that case, it is especially important to communicate the procedure—not only to ensure fairness but also to prevent the dangerous misbehavior.

Creating a formal discipline process is a primary responsibility of the human resource department. The HR professional should consult with supervisors and managers to identify unacceptable behaviors and establish rules and consequences for violating the rules. The rules should cover disciplinary problems such as the following behaviors encountered in many organizations:

- Tardiness
- Absenteeism
- Unsafe work practices
- Poor quantity or quality of work
- Sexual harassment of co-workers
- Coming to work impaired by alcohol or drugs
- Theft of company property
- Cyberslacking (conducting personal business online during work hours)

For each infraction, the HR professional would identify a series of responses, such as those in Figure 10.2. In addition, the organization must communicate these rules and consequences in writing to every employee. Ways of publishing rules include presenting them in an employee handbook, posting them on the company's intranet, and displaying them on a bulletin board. Supervisors should be familiar with the rules, so that they can discuss them with employees and apply them consistently.

Along with rules and a progression of consequences for violating the rules, a progressive discipline system should have requirements for documenting the rules, offenses, and responses. For issuing an unofficial warning about a less-serious

ELECTRONIC MONITORING OF EMPLOYEE ACTIVITY

For a variety of possible misdeeds, from stealing merchandise to misusing company computers, organizations guard their well-being and make discipline more objective by installing electronic methods of monitoring employees' activities. At Wendy's and Chili's restaurant franchises, managers have installed fingerprint scanners on cash registers. These link each transaction to a specific employee. In restaurants using the scanners, theft has fallen, and so has conflict between employees who had engaged in arguments about who rang up which transactions. IBM installed tracking technology in its computers, enabling the company to locate laptops that had been stolen (or falsely reported stolen by employees).

Increasingly sophisticated software for tracking expenses has been used to monitor fraud associated with business travel and entertainment. A company called Concur Technology has developed expense-reporting software that scours data files to uncover double expense recording (such as two executives asking to be reimbursed for the same restaurant bill), unauthorized travel upgrades (first-class airline tickets), or unusual trends or spikes in account activity.

Companies' computer systems can employ software to keep track of which computers are being used by which employees and for what activities. Coupled with clearly communicated rules for employee conduct, this information can provide a defensible basis for disciplining employees. In one case, an employee sued a hospital for wrongfully discharging her. The employee's case was dismissed after the hospital demonstrated some damning evidence: A computer virus had been introduced to the hospital system on a computer in the emergency room's admitting department, the location of the plaintiff's job. On the day the virus had been introduced, the employee—in violation of the company's policy—had spent seven hours of her eight-hour shift online, visiting hundreds of Web sites that were unrelated to her job responsibilities. The employee had acknowledged receiving and understanding the hospital's computer policy, so the mediator reviewing the case found that the employee's dismissal could stand. Without the electronic monitoring, it would have been much harder for the hospital to verify what the employee had been doing that day, and it would have been much easier for the employee to continue using work time as an opportunity for surfing the Web.

Sources: S. E. Needleman, "Businesses Say Theft by Their Workers Is Up," *Wall Street Journal,* December 2008, pp. C2–C2; S. Covel, "Small Businesses Face More Fraud in Downturn," *Wall Street Journal,* February 19, 2009, p. C2; M. Conlin, "To Catch a Corporate Thief," *BusinessWeek,* February 16, 2009, p. 52; and N. Kamm, "Bodyguard for Electronic Information: Protect Electronic Information with a Current Policy," *HR Magazine,* January 2010, Business & Company Resource Center, http://galenet.galegroup.com.

offense, it may be enough to have a witness present. Even then, a written record would be helpful in case the employee repeats the offense in the future. The organization should provide a document for managers to file, recording the nature and date of the offense, the specific improvement expected, and the consequences of the offense. It is also helpful to indicate how the offense affects the performance of the individual employee, others in the group, or the organization as a whole. These documents are important for demonstrating to a problem employee why he or she has been suspended or terminated. They also back up the organization's actions if it should have to defend a lawsuit. Following the hot-stove rule, the supervisor should complete and discuss the documentation immediately after becoming aware of the offense. A copy of the records should be placed in the employee's personnel file. The organization may have a policy of removing records of warnings after a period such as six months, on the grounds that the employee has learned from the experience.

As we noted in the earlier discussion of procedural justice, the discipline system should provide an opportunity to hear every point of view and to correct errors. Before discussing and filing records of misbehavior, it is important for the supervisor to investigate the incident. The employee should be made aware of what he or she is said to have done wrong and should have an opportunity to present his or her version of events. Anyone who witnessed the misdeed also should have a chance to describe what happened. In general, employees who belong to a union have a right to the presence of a union representative during a formal investigation interview if they request representation.[15] A method of gathering objective performance data, such as the electronic methods described in the "eHRM" box, also supports the fairness of the discipline system.

Besides developing these policies, HR professionals have a role in carrying out progressive discipline.[16] In meetings to announce disciplinary actions, it is wise to include two representatives of the organization. Usually, the employee's supervisor presents the information, and a representative from the HR department acts as a witness. This person can help the meeting stay on track and, if necessary, can later confirm what happened during the meeting. Especially at the termination stage of the process, the employee may be angry, so it is helpful to be straightforward but polite. The supervisor should state the reason for the meeting, the nature of the problem behavior, and the consequences. Listening to the employee is important, but because an investigation was already conducted, there is no purpose to arguing. When an employee is suspended or terminated, the organization should designate a person to escort the employee from the building to protect the organization's people and property.

Alternative Dispute Resolution

Sometimes problems are easier to solve when an impartial person helps to create the solution. Therefore, at various points in the discipline process, the employee or organization might want to bring in someone to help with problem solving. Rather than turning to the courts every time an outsider is desired, more and more organizations are using **alternative dispute resolution (ADR).** A variety of ADR techniques show promise for resolving disputes in a timely, constructive, cost-effective manner.

In general, a system for alternative dispute resolution proceeds through the four stages shown in Figure 10.3:

1. **Open-door policy**—Based on the expectation that two people in conflict should first try to arrive at a settlement together, the organization has a policy of making managers available to hear complaints. Typically, the first "open door" is that of the employee's immediate supervisor, and if the employee does not get a resolution from that person, the employee may appeal to managers at higher levels. This policy works only to the degree that managers who hear complaints listen and are able to act.
2. **Peer review**—If the people in conflict cannot reach an agreement, they take their conflict to a panel composed of representatives from the organization at the same levels as the people in the dispute. The panel hears the case and tries to help the parties arrive at a settlement. To set up a panel to hear disputes as they arise, the organization may assign managers to positions on the panel and have employees elect nonmanagement panel members.
3. **Mediation**—If the peer review does not lead to a settlement, a neutral party from outside the organization hears the case and tries to help the people in conflict arrive at a settlement. The process is not binding, meaning the mediator cannot force a solution.

Alternative Dispute Resolution (ADR)
Methods of solving a problem by bringing in an impartial outsider but not using the court system.

Open-Door Policy
An organization's policy of making managers available to hear complaints.

Peer Review
Process for resolving disputes by taking them to a panel composed of representatives from the organization at the same levels as the people in the dispute.

Mediation
Nonbinding process in which a neutral party from outside the organization hears the case and tries to help the people in conflict arrive at a settlement.

Figure 10.3

Typical Stages of
Alternative Dispute
Resolution

Arbitration
Binding process in
which a professional
arbitrator from outside
the organization
(usually a lawyer or
judge) hears the case
and resolves it by
making a decision.

4. **Arbitration**—If mediation fails, a professional arbitrator from outside the organization hears the case and resolves it by making a decision. Most arbitrators are experienced employment lawyers or retired judges. The employee and employer both have to accept this person's decision.

Each stage reflects a somewhat broader involvement of people outside the dispute. The hope is that the conflict will be resolved at earlier stages, where the costs, time, and embarrassing publicity are lowest. However, even the arbitration stage tends to be much faster, simpler, and more private than a lawsuit.[17]

Professional mediators report that the opportunity to air both sides of a dispute before an objective third party is not merely efficient but also powerful. Vicky Wells, founder of Splash Management Consultancy, and Eve Pienaar, a mediator with ADR Group, both set a rule that one participant may not interrupt the other, forcing all parties to focus on the perspective and emotions of each person. They find that this process, however painful, breaks down barriers and opens the way to a solution. Another professional mediator, John Sturrock, says that after one mediation process, the executive involved told him, "I now see these people in the other team as human beings."[18]

Employee Assistance Programs

While ADR is effective in dealing with problems related to performance and disputes between people at work, many of the problems that lead an organization to want to terminate an employee involve drug or alcohol abuse. In these cases, the organization's discipline program should also incorporate an **employee assistance program (EAP).** An EAP is a referral service that employees can use to seek professional treatment for emotional problems or substance abuse. EAPs began in the 1950s with a focus on treating alcoholism, and in the 1980s they expanded into drug treatment. Today, many are now fully integrated into employers' overall health benefits plans, where they refer employees to covered mental health services.

Employee Assistance Program (EAP)
A referral service that employees can use to seek professional treatment for emotional problems or substance abuse.

EAPs vary widely, but most share some basic elements. First, the programs are usually identified in official documents published by the employer, such as employee handbooks. Supervisors (and union representatives when workers belong to a union) are trained to use the referral service for employees whom they suspect of having health-related problems. The organization also trains employees to use the system to refer themselves when necessary. The organization regularly evaluates the costs and benefits of the program, usually once a year.

The variations among EAPs make evaluating these programs especially important. For example, the treatment for alcoholism varies widely, including hospitalization and participation in Alcoholics Anonymous (AA). General Electric performed an experiment to compare the outcomes of these treatments, and it found that employees who were hospitalized tended to fare the best in a two-year follow-up.[19] Programs that work can make a significant difference for individual employees and for the organization as a whole. Research into depressed employees found that a large majority who use EAP services reported improvements in their condition. In addition, they reported that after using the services, their productivity increased by an average of six hours per week.[20]

Outplacement Counseling

An employee who has been discharged is likely to feel angry and confused about what to do next. If the person feels there is nothing to lose and nowhere else to turn, the potential for violence or a lawsuit is greater than most organizations are willing to tolerate. This concern is one reason many organizations provide **outplacement counseling,** which tries to help dismissed employees manage the transition from one job to another. Organizations also may address ongoing poor performance with discussion about whether the employee is a good fit for the current job. Rather than simply firing the poor performer, the supervisor may encourage this person to think about leaving. In this situation, the availability of outplacement counseling may help the employee decide to look for another job. This approach may protect the dignity of the employee who leaves and promote a sense of fairness.

Outplacement Counseling
A service in which professionals try to help dismissed employees manage the transition from one job to another.

Some organizations have their own staff for conducting outplacement counseling. Other organizations have contracts with outside providers to help with individual cases. Either way, the goals for outplacement programs are to help the former employee address the psychological issues associated with losing a job—grief, depression, and fear—while at the same time helping the person find a new job.

The number of companies offering outplacement counseling has increased dramatically in recent years. This was most evident in the recession of 2008, when the percentage of employers offering this service was 55 percent, compared with just 39 percent during the 2001 recession.[21] In the case of a recession, outplacement counselors may assure the laid-off employees that they have valuable talents but the company could not afford them. In other situations, the message may be that there was a mismatch between an individual and the job. Either way, asking employees to leave is a setback for the employee and for the company. Retaining people who can contribute knowledge and talent is essential to business success. Therefore, the remainder of this chapter explores issues related to retaining employees.

Job Withdrawal

Organizations need employees who are fully engaged and committed to their work. Therefore, retaining employees goes beyond preventing them from quitting. The organization needs to prevent a broader negative condition, called **job withdrawal**— or a set of behaviors with which employees try to avoid the work situation physically, mentally, or emotionally. Job withdrawal results when circumstances such as the nature of the job, supervisors and co-workers, pay levels, or the employee's own disposition cause the employee to become dissatisfied with the job. As shown in Figure 10.4, this job dissatisfaction produces job withdrawal. Job withdrawal may take the form of behavior change, physical job withdrawal, or psychological withdrawal. Some researchers believe employees engage in the three forms of withdrawal behavior in that order, while others think they select from these behaviors to address the particular sources of job dissatisfaction they experience.[22] Although the specifics of these models vary, the consensus is that withdrawal behaviors are related to one another and are at least partially caused by job dissatisfaction.[23]

Job Withdrawal
A set of behaviors with which employees try to avoid the work situation physically, mentally, or emotionally.

Figure 10.4

Job Withdrawal Process

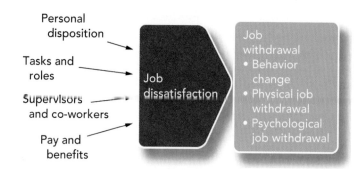

L05 Explain how job dissatisfaction affects employee behavior.

Job Dissatisfaction

Many aspects of people and organizations can cause job dissatisfaction, and managers and HR professionals need to be aware of them because correcting them can increase job satisfaction and prevent job withdrawal. The causes of job dissatisfaction identified in Figure 10.4 fall into four categories: personal dispositions, tasks and roles, supervisors and co-workers, and pay and benefits.

Personal Dispositions

Job dissatisfaction is a feeling experienced by individuals, so it is not surprising that many researchers have studied individual personality differences to see if some kinds of people are more disposed to be dissatisfied with their jobs. In general, job turnover (and presumably dissatisfaction leading up to it) is higher among employees who are low in emotional stability, conscientiousness, and agreeableness.[24] In addition, two other personal qualities associated with job satisfaction are negative affectivity and negative self-evaluations.

Negative affectivity means pervasive low levels of satisfaction with all aspects of life, compared with other people's feelings. People with negative affectivity experience feelings such as anger, contempt, disgust, guilt, fear, and nervousness more than other people do, at work and away. They tend to focus on the negative aspects of themselves and others.[25] Not surprisingly, people with negative affectivity tend to be dissatisfied with their jobs, even after changing employers or occupations.[26]

Core self-evaluations are bottom-line opinions individuals have of themselves and may be positive or negative. People with a positive core self-evaluation have high self-esteem, believe in their ability to accomplish their goals, and are emotionally stable. They also tend to experience job satisfaction.[27] Part of the reason for their satisfaction is that they tend to seek out and obtain jobs with desirable characteristics, and when they are in a situation they dislike, they are more likely to seek change in socially acceptable ways.[28] In contrast, people with negative core self-evaluations tend to blame other people for their problems, including their dissatisfying jobs. They are less likely to work toward change; they either do nothing or act aggressively toward the people they blame.[29]

Tasks and Roles

Role
The set of behaviors that people expect of a person in a particular job.

As a predictor of job dissatisfaction, nothing surpasses the nature of the task itself.[30] Many aspects of a task have been linked to dissatisfaction. Of particular significance are the complexity of the task, the degree of physical strain and exertion required, and the value the employee places on the task.[31] In general, employees (especially women) are bored and dissatisfied with simple, repetitive jobs.[32] People also are more dissatisfied with jobs requiring a great deal of physical strain and exertion. Because automation has removed much of the physical strain associated with jobs, employers often overlook this consideration. Still, many jobs remain physically demanding. Finally, employees feel dissatisfied if their work is not related to something they value.

Employees not only perform specific tasks but also have roles within the organization.[33] A person's **role** consists of the set of behaviors that people expect of a person in that job. These expected behaviors include the formally defined duties of the job but also much more. Sometimes things get complicated or confusing. Co-workers, supervisors, and customers have expectations for how the employee should behave often going far beyond a formal job description and having a large impact on the employee's work satisfaction. Several role-related sources of dissatisfaction are the following:

- **Role ambiguity** is uncertainty about what the organization and others expect from the employee in terms of what to do or how to do it. Employees suffer when they are unclear about work methods, scheduling, and performance criteria, perhaps because others hold different ideas about these. Employees particularly want to know how the organization will evaluate their performance. When they aren't sure, they become dissatisfied.[34]

- **Role conflict** is an employee's recognition that demands of the job are incompatible or contradictory; a person cannot meet all the demands. For example, a company might bring together employees from different functions to work on a team to develop a new product. Team members feel role conflict when they realize that their team leader and functional manager have conflicting expectations of them. Also, many employees may feel conflict between work roles and family roles. A role conflict may be triggered by an organization's request that an employee take an assignment overseas. Foreign assignments can be highly disruptive to family members, and the resulting role conflict is the top reason that people quit overseas assignments.[35]

- **Role overload** results when too many expectations or demands are placed on a person. (The opposite situation is *role underload.*) After an organization downsizes, it may expect so much of the remaining employees that they experience role overload.

Supervisors and Co-workers

Negative behavior by managers and peers in the workplace can produce tremendous dissatisfaction. Often much of the responsibility for positive

Role Ambiguity
Uncertainty about what the organization expects from the employee in terms of what to do or how to do it.

Role Conflict
An employee's recognition that demands of the job are incompatible or contradictory.

Role Overload
A state in which too many expectations or demands are placed on a person.

Military reservists who are sent overseas often experience role conflict among *three* roles: soldier, family member, and civilian employee. Overseas assignments often intensify role conflicts.

Unpleasant Employees Are Bad for Business

Researchers asked employees how they react when their co-workers are rude and nasty. The results showed consequences for just about every basic measure of work:

Source: Based on Christine Porath and Christine Pearson, "How Toxic Colleagues Corrode Performance," *Harvard Business Review*, April 2009, p. 24.

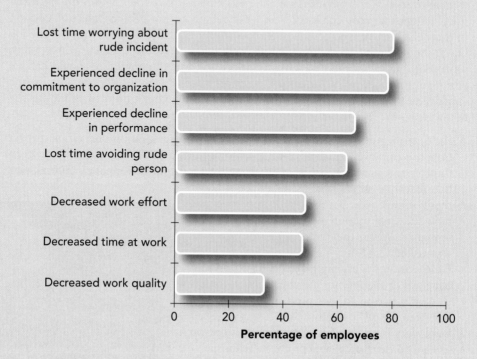

Percentage of employees

- Lost time worrying about rude incident
- Experienced decline in commitment to organization
- Experienced decline in performance
- Lost time avoiding rude person
- Decreased work effort
- Decreased time at work
- Decreased work quality

relationships is placed on direct supervisors, but in a recent survey by Towers Perrin (now part of Towers Watson), employees said that the leadership and visibility of senior managers play an even greater role in their level of engagement with their work.[36] Employees want some evidence that the company's leaders care about them, so they are more likely to be dissatisfied if management is distant and unresponsive.

In other cases, conflicts between employees left unaddressed by management may cause job dissatisfaction severe enough to lead to withdrawal or departure. Research suggests that turnover is higher when employees do not feel that their values and beliefs fit with their work group's values and beliefs.[37] Furthermore, as illustrated in the "Did You Know?" box, uncivil behavior by co-workers generates unhappiness that manifests in a variety of ways.[38]

Pay and Benefits

For all the concern with positive relationships and interesting work, it is important to keep in mind that employees definitely care about their earnings. A job is the primary source of income and financial security for most people. Pay also is an indicator of status within the organization and in society at large, so it contributes to some people's self-worth. For all these reasons, satisfaction with pay is significant for retaining employees. Decisions about pay and benefits are so important and complex that the chapters of the next part of this book are devoted to this topic.

With regard to job satisfaction, the pay level—that is, the amount of income associated with each job—is especially important. Employers seeking to lure away another organization's employees often do so by offering higher pay. Benefits, such as insurance and vacation time, are also important, but employees often have difficulty measuring their worth. Therefore, although benefits influence job satisfaction, employees may not always consider them as much as pay itself.

Behavior Change

A reasonable expectation is that an employee's first response to dissatisfaction would be to try to change the conditions that generate the dissatisfaction. As the employee tries to bring about changes in policy or personnel, the efforts may involve confrontation and conflict with the employee's supervisor. In an organization where employees are represented by a union, as we will discuss in Chapter 14, more grievances may be filed.

From the manager's point of view, the complaints, confrontations, and grievances may feel threatening. On closer inspection, however, this is an opportunity for the manager to learn about and solve a potentially important problem. At Kimpton Hotels and Restaurants, recurring complaints signaled a need for better communication. The chain of boutique hotels was committed to using more environmentally friendly products, so it purchased a line of low-foaming cleaning supplies. However, looking for suds, employees thought they needed to add more soap to the solution, and they began to complain about the skin irritations that followed. After managers provided more information about the products and how to use them, the employees discovered that the products were actually easier on their skin and sinuses as well as the environment. Now they are again happy and proud to work for a company committed to environmental sustainability.[39]

focus on ***social responsibility***

In this example, the result was positive because the organization responded to legitimate concerns. When employees cannot work with management to make changes, they may look for help from outside the organization. Some employees may engage in *whistle-blowing*, taking their charges to the media in the hope that if the public learns about the situation, the organization will be forced to change. From the organization's point of view, whistle-blowing is harmful because of the negative publicity.

Another way employees may go outside the organization for help is to file a lawsuit. This way to force change is available if the employee is disputing policies on the grounds that they violate state and federal laws, such as those forbidding employment discrimination or requiring safe working conditions. Defending a lawsuit is costly, both financially and in terms of the employer's image, whether the organization wins or loses. Most employers would prefer to avoid lawsuits and whistle-blowing. Keeping employees satisfied is one way to do this.

Physical Job Withdrawal

If behavior change has failed or seems impossible, a dissatisfied worker may physically withdraw from the job. Options for physically leaving a job range from arriving late to calling in sick, requesting a transfer, or leaving the organization altogether. Even while they are on the job, employees may withdraw by not actually working. All these options are costly to the employer.

Finding a new job is rarely easy and can take months, so employees often are cautious about quitting. Employees who would like to quit may be late for work. Tardiness is costly because late employees are not contributing for part of the day. Especially when work is done by teams, the tardiness creates difficulties that spill over and affect the entire team's ability to work. Absenteeism is even more of a problem. In a recent survey of 455 companies, the total costs of absences were equivalent to 36 percent of payroll costs. The impact was most severe for hourly union workers: in today's lean operations, when one worker stays home, the company has to bring in a replacement, often at overtime rates.[40]

An employee who is dissatisfied because of circumstances related to the specific job—for example, an unpleasant workplace or unfair supervisor—may be able to resolve that problem with a job transfer. If the source of the dissatisfaction is organizational policies or practices, such as low pay scales, the employee may leave the organization altogether. These forms of physical job withdrawal contribute to high turnover rates for the department or organization. As a result, the organization faces the costs of replacing the employees, (often tens of thousands of dollars per employee) as well as lost productivity until replacement employees learn the jobs.[41]

Organizations need to be concerned with their overall turnover rates as well as the nature of the turnover in terms of who is staying and who is leaving. For example, companies' top performers tend to be among the hardest employees to keep.[42] Also, among managers, women and minorities often have higher turnover rates. Many leave because they see little opportunity for promotions. Chapter 9 discussed how organizations are addressing this problem through career management and efforts to break the glass ceiling.

Psychological Withdrawal

Employees need not leave the company in order to withdraw from their jobs. Especially if they have been unable to find another job, they may psychologically remove themselves. They are physically at work, but their minds are elsewhere.

Psychological withdrawal can take several forms. If an employee is primarily dissatisfied with the job itself, the employee may display a very low level of job involvement. **Job involvement** is the degree to which people identify themselves with their jobs. People with a high level of job involvement consider their work an important part of their life. Doing well at work contributes to their sense of who they are (their *self-concept*). For a dissatisfied employee with low job involvement, performing well or poorly does not affect the person's self-concept.

When an employee is dissatisfied with the organization as a whole, the person's organizational commitment may be low. **Organizational commitment** is the degree to which an employee identifies with the organization and is willing to put forth effort on its behalf.[43] Employees with high organizational commitment will stretch themselves to help the organization through difficult times. Employees with low organizational commitment are likely to leave at the first opportunity for a better job. They have a strong intention to leave, so like employees with low job involvement, they are hard to motivate.

Job Satisfaction

Clearly, organizations want to prevent withdrawal behaviors. As we saw in Figure 10.4, the driving force behind job withdrawal is dissatisfaction. To prevent job withdrawal, organizations therefore need to promote **job satisfaction,** a pleasant

---

Job Involvement
The degree to which people identify themselves with their jobs.

Organizational Commitment
The degree to which an employee identifies with the organization and is willing to put forth effort on its behalf.

LO6 Describe how organizations contribute to employees' job satisfaction and retain key employees.

Job Satisfaction
A pleasant feeling resulting from the perception that one's job fulfills or allows for the fulfillment of one's important job values.

HR How To

CREATING A POSITIVE WORK ENVIRONMENT

The relatively new fields of positive psychology and positive organizational behavior have contributed to the idea that individuals and organizations not only can work on problems but also can take steps that favor the creation of a happy outlook and upbeat workplace. Critics suspect that these kinds of approaches merely sugarcoat miserable situations, but used appropriately, some techniques can make work a more satisfying place. Here are some tips that HR professionals might want to consider:

- Bring in a "happiness coach." Trainers with expertise in positive psychology can teach methods such as meditation and the practice and expression of gratitude.
- When confronted with news, dilemmas, and changes, start with the assumption that the situation is not necessarily bad (or good). Define setbacks as learning experiences. Keeping an open mind can help you and your team identify more alternatives and opportunities.
- Look for employee behaviors to praise, and coach managers to do the same. Use performance feedback to identify strengths employees can build on, not just weaknesses to correct.
- Use selection and development tools that match employees' talents to positions and career paths in the organization.
- Structure work so employees can see why it matters and so they have enough control over their time to engage in activities they care about. Define how the organization contributes to society, and express that mission to employees.
- Ask for ideas from employees, and listen to their ideas.
- Model positive behavior by demonstrating compassion, forgiveness, and gratitude.

Sources: Sue Shellenbarger, "Thinking Happy Thoughts at Work," *Wall Street Journal,* January 27, 2010, http://online.wsj.com; Chet Taranowski, "Advocating for a Positive Workplace," *Journal of Employee Assistance,* January 2009, Business & Company Resource Center, http://galenet.galegroup.com; Ann Pace, "Unleashing Positivity in the Workplace," *T + D,* January 2010, Business & Company Resource Center, http://galenet.galegroup.com; and Stacey Burling, "Psychologists Converge on Philadelphia to Study Happiness," *Philadelphia Inquirer,* June 21, 2009, Business & Company Resource Center, http://galenet.galegroup.com.

feeling resulting from the perception that one's job fulfills or allows for the fulfillment of one's important job values.[44] Several aspects of job satisfaction are:

- Job satisfaction is related to a person's values, defined as "what a person consciously or unconsciously desires to obtain."
- Different employees have different views of which values are important, so the same circumstances can produce different levels of job satisfaction.
- Job satisfaction is based on perception, not always on an objective and complete measurement of the situation. Each person compares the job situation to his or her values, and people are likely to differ in what they perceive. The "HR How To" box describes some ways organizations are trying to contribute to positive perceptions.

In sum, values, perceptions, and ideas of what is important are the three components of job satisfaction. People will be satisfied with their jobs as long as they perceive that their jobs meet their important values. As shown in Figure 10.5, organizations can contribute to job satisfaction by addressing the four sources of job dissatisfaction we identified earlier: personal dispositions, job tasks and roles, supervisors and co-workers, and pay and benefits.

Figure 10.5

Increasing Job Satisfaction

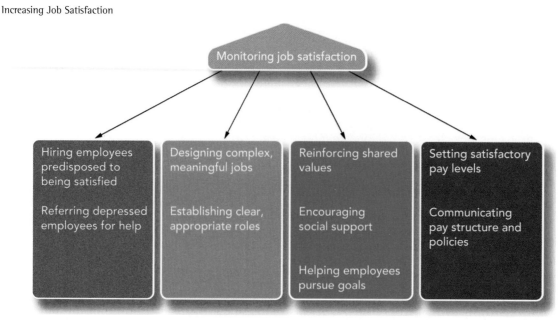

Personal Dispositions

In our discussion of job withdrawal, we noted that sometimes personal qualities of the employee, such as negative affectivity and negative core self-evaluation, are associated with job dissatisfaction. This linkage suggests employee selection in the first instance plays a role in raising overall levels of employee satisfaction. People making the selection decisions should look for evidence of whether employees are predisposed to being satisfied.[45] Interviews should explore employees' satisfaction with past jobs. If an applicant says he was dissatisfied with his past six jobs, what makes the employer think the person won't be dissatisfied with the organization's vacant position?

Employers also should recognize that dissatisfaction with other facets of life can spill over into the workplace. A worker who is having problems with a family member may attribute some of the negative feelings to the job or organization. Of course, managers should not try to become clinical psychologists for their employees and applicants. Still, when employees express negativity and dissatisfaction in many areas, managers should consider that the employee may be clinically depressed.[46] The manager should suggest that the employee contact the organization's employee assistance program or his or her physician. Depression is a common condition, but most cases can be managed with proper care. As a reasonable accommodation under the Americans with Disabilities Act, the employer may need to grant the employee time off or a flexible schedule to accommodate treatment.

Tasks and Roles

Organizations can improve job satisfaction by making jobs more complex and meaningful, as we discussed in Chapter 4. Some of the methods available for this approach to job design are job enrichment and job rotation. Organizations also can increase satisfaction by developing clear and appropriate job roles.

Job Complexity

Not only can job design add to enriching complexity, but employees themselves sometimes take measures to make their work more interesting. Some employees bring personal music players with headsets to work, so they can listen to music or radio shows while they are working. Many supervisors disapprove, worrying that the headsets will interfere with the employees' ability to provide good customer service. However, in simple jobs with minimal customer contact (like processing paperwork or entering data into computers), research suggests that personal headsets can improve performance. One study examined the use of stereo headsets by workers in 32 jobs at a large retailing company. The stereo-using group outperformed the no-stereo group on simple jobs (like invoice processor) but performed worse than the stereo-free group on complex jobs (such as accountant).[47]

Meaningful Work

When it comes to generating satisfaction, the most important aspect of work is the degree to which it is meaningfully related to workers' core values. People sign on to help charitable causes for little or no pay simply because of the value they place on making a difference in the world. Applying this, some employers took on charitable projects when a slowing economy left their employees with too little to do. An Austin advertising agency called Door Number 3 assigned otherwise idle employees to take on work donated to charities such as Habitat for Humanity and the Austin Humane Society. Not only do these projects help the community, but they help employees develop their creative talents and feel proud of what they accomplish. Door Number 3 benefits by hanging on to talented people who otherwise might leave.[48]

focus on
*social
responsibility*

A similar kind of motivation can exist in businesses. Genentech, for example, focuses on developing and testing "big ideas" related to life-and-death treatments in health care. The company selects employees who have a passion for this type of challenge, and it gives them wide latitude to pursue their goals. This approach has helped Genentech attract top scientists and dramatically increase its revenues.[49]

Clear and Appropriate Roles

Organizations can do much to avoid role-related sources of dissatisfaction. They can define roles, clearly spelling out work methods, schedules, and performance measures. They can be realistic about the number of hours required to complete job requirements. When jobs require overtime hours, the employer must be prepared to comply with laws requiring overtime pay, as well as to help employees manage the conflict between work and family roles.

To help employees manage role conflict, employers have turned to a number of family-friendly policies. These policies may include provisions for child care, elder care, flexible work schedules, job sharing, telecommuting, and extended parental leaves. Although these programs create some headaches for managers in terms of scheduling work and reporting requirements, they increase employees' commitment to the organization.[50] Organizations with family-friendly policies also have enjoyed improvements in performance, especially at companies that employ a large percentage of women.[51] Chapter 13 discusses such benefits in greater detail.

Organizations should also pay attention to the fit between job titles and roles, especially as more and more Americans feel overworked. One consequence of this perception is lawsuits seeking overtime pay. The Fair Labor Standards Act exempts managers and professionals from its requirement that the company pay

Appropriate tasks and roles include safety precautions, especially when work could involve risks to workers' health and safety.

Role Analysis Technique
A process of formally identifying expectations associated with a role.

overtime to employees who work more than a 40-hour week. Increasingly, employees are complaining that they have been misclassified as managers and should be treated as nonexempt workers. Their job titles sound like managerial jobs, but their day-to-day activities involve no supervision. IBM, for example, recently reclassified more than 7,500 technical support workers following settlement of a lawsuit charging they had illegally been denied overtime pay. The company had considered them exempt because they are highly skilled professionals, but the employees argued their jobs did not give them enough decision-making authority or creative latitude for that classification.[52]

Because role problems rank just behind job problems in creating job dissatisfaction, some interventions aim directly at role elements. One of these is the **role analysis technique,** a process of formally identifying expectations associated with a role. The technique follows the steps shown in Figure 10.6. The *role occupant* (the person who fills a role) and each member of the person's *role set* (people who directly interact with this employee) each write down their expectations for the role. They meet to discuss their expectations and develop a preliminary list of the role's duties and behaviors, trying to resolve any conflicts among expectations. Next, the role occupant lists what he or she expects of others in the set, and the group meets again to reach a consensus on these expectations. Finally, the group modifies its preliminary list and reaches a consensus on the occupant's role. This process may uncover instances of overload and underload, and the group tries to trade off requirements to develop more balanced roles.

Supervisors and Co-workers

The two primary sets of people in an organization who affect job satisfaction are co-workers and supervisors. A person may be satisfied with these people for one of three reasons:

1. The people share the same values, attitudes, and philosophies. Most individuals find this very important, and many organizations try to foster a culture of shared values. Even when this does not occur across the whole organization, values shared between workers and their supervisor can increase satisfaction.[53]
2. The co-workers and supervisor may provide social support, meaning they are sympathetic and caring. Social support greatly increases job satisfaction, whether the support comes from supervisors or co-workers.[54] Turnover is also lower among employees who experience support from other members of the organization.[55]
3. The co-workers or supervisor may help the person attain some valued outcome. For example, they can help a new employee figure out what goals to pursue and how to achieve them.[56]

Because a supportive environment reduces dissatisfaction, many organizations foster team building both on and off the job (such as with softball or bowling leagues). The idea is that playing together as a team will strengthen ties among group members and develop relationships in which individuals feel supported by one another. Organizations also are developing their managers' mentoring skills and helping to set up these beneficial relationships.[57] (Mentoring was described in Chapter 9.) At Lockheed Martin, turnover plummeted among jobs targeted by a mentoring program.[58]

Pay and Benefits

Organizations recognize the importance of pay in their negotiations with job candidates. HR professionals can support their organizations in this area by repeatedly monitoring pay levels in their industry and for the professions or trades they employ. As we noted in Chapter 5 and will discuss further in Chapter 11, organizations make decisions about whether to match or exceed the industry averages. Also, HR professionals can increase job satisfaction by communicating to employees the value of their benefits.

Two other aspects of pay satisfaction influence job satisfaction. One is satisfaction with pay structure—the way the organization assigns different pay levels to different levels and job categories. A manager of a sales force, for example, might be satisfied with her pay level until she discovers that some of the sales representatives she supervises are earning more than she is. The other important aspect of pay satisfaction is pay raises. People generally expect that their pay will increase over time. They will be satisfied if their expectations are met or dissatisfied if raises fall short of expectations. HR professionals can contribute to these sources of job satisfaction by helping to communicate the reasoning behind the organization's pay structure and pay raises. For example, sometimes economic conditions force an organization to limit pay raises. If employees understand the circumstances (and recognize that the same conditions are likely to be affecting other employers), they may feel less dissatisfied.

Monitoring Job Satisfaction

Employers can better retain employees if they are aware of satisfaction levels, so they can make changes if employees are dissatisfied. The "Best Practices" box applies how monitoring job satisfaction contributed to improving employee engagement at Campbell Soup Company. The usual way to measure job satisfaction is with some kind of survey. A systematic, ongoing program of employee surveys should be part of the organization's human resource strategy. This program allows the organization to monitor trends and prevent voluntary turnover. For example, if satisfaction with promotion opportunities has been falling over several years, the trend may signal a need for better career management (a topic of Chapter 9). An organizational change, such as a merger, also might have important consequences for job satisfaction. In addition, ongoing surveys give the organization a way to measure whether policies adopted to improve job satisfaction and employee retention are working. Organizations can also compare results from different departments to identify groups with successful practices that may apply elsewhere in the organization. Another benefit is that some scales provide data that organizations can use to compare themselves to others in the same industry. This information will be valuable for creating and reviewing human resource policies that enable organizations to attract and retain employees in a competitive job market.

Figure 10.6

Steps in the Role Analysis Technique

Members of role set write expectations for role

Members of role set discuss expectations

Preliminary list of role's duties and behaviors

Role occupant lists expectations for others in role set

Members of role set discuss expectations and reach consensus on occupant's role

Modified list of role's duties and behaviors

Co-worker relationships can contribute to job satisfaction, and organizations therefore try to provide opportunities to build positive relationships. Would a strong sense of teamwork and friendship help you enjoy your work more?

HOW CAMPBELL SOUP STIRRED UP EMPLOYEE SATISFACTION

About a decade ago, Campbell Soup Company hired Douglas R. Conant to turn around a company with disappointing sales and a declining stock price. In Conant's view, a big part of the company's problem wasn't marketing; it was employee engagement. Applying the motto "You can't win in the marketplace unless you win in the workplace," Conant set out to identify and fix whatever in the workplace was keeping employees from giving their all.

An important starting point was to use annual assessments of employee engagement. The company decided to use a survey called Q^{12}, developed by Gallup to assess employees' attitudes with the answers to a dozen questions. Each year the survey goes to thousands of employees representing about one-third of the company's workforce. The resulting measure of employee engagement is one of the key performance measures that Conant focuses on to measure the company's overall success.

The initial results were disappointing, even shocking. Compared with all the clients tracked by Gallup, Campbell had many work groups ranked in the bottom quartile. The global leadership team scored almost that low. But the company held managers responsible for improving the scores (engagement scores are a part of everyone's performance appraisals), so they met with employees to craft plans for improvement. Not all could meet the challenge: of the company's top 350 managers, 300 were replaced. As managers and employees saw that the company was serious about changing, those who remained got excited and began to feel accountable to one another.

A lesson that the company learned from early surveys was that managers are the most important factor leading to employee engagement at Campbell. The company zeroed in on this factor in its later surveys by adding more questions about managers, such as whether they give effective feedback and

link employees' objectives to the company's strategy.

One of Conant's tactics for building trust and inspiring employees is to connect with them on a personal level. He makes a practice of literally walking around the company's headquarters every day, stopping to talk to the people he encounters. Especially when times are difficult, Conant believes, the physical presence of the leader can give people confidence. He takes an active role in mentoring employees and fostering diversity, trying to model the behavior he wants to see in others.

Sources: Jennifer Robison, "Saving Campbell Soup Company," *Gallup Management Journal*, February 11, 2010, http://gmj.gallup.com (interview with Douglas R. Conant); Jennifer Robison, "When Campbell Was in the Soup," *Gallup Management Journal*, March 4, 2010, http://gmj.gallup.com (interview with Douglas R. Conant); and Leigh Rivenbark, "Tools of Engagement," *HR Magazine*, February 2010, Business & Company Resource Center, http://galenet.galegroup.com.

Finally, conducting surveys gives employees a chance to be heard, so the practice itself can contribute to employee satisfaction.

To obtain a survey instrument, an excellent place to begin is with one of the many established scales. The validity and reliability of many satisfaction scales have been tested, so it is possible to compare the survey instruments. The main reason for the organization to create its own scale would be that it wants to measure satisfaction with aspects of work that are specific to the organization (such as satisfaction with a particular health plan).

A widely used measure of job satisfaction is the Job Descriptive Index (JDI). The JDI emphasizes specific aspects of satisfaction—pay, the work itself, supervision, co-workers, and promotions. Figure 10.7 shows several items from the JDI scale. Other scales measure general satisfaction, using broad questions such as "All in all, how satisfied are you with your job?"[59] Some scales avoid language altogether, relying on pictures. The faces scale in Figure 10.8 is an example of this type of measure. Other

Instructions: Think of your present work. What is it like most of time? In the blank beside each word given below, write

____Y____ for "Yes" if it describes your work

____N____ for "No" if it does NOT describe your work

____?____ if you cannot decide

Work Itself	**Pay**	**Promotion Opportunities**
_____ Routine	_____ Less than I deserve	_____ Dead-end job
_____ Satisfying	_____ Highly paid	_____ Unfair policies
_____ Good	_____ Insecure	_____ Based on ability

Supervision	**Co-workers**
_____ Impolite	_____ Intelligent
_____ Praises good work	_____ Responsible
_____ Doesn't supervise enough	_____ Boring

SOURCE: W. K. Balzar, D. C. Smith, D. E. Kravitz, S. E. Lovell, K. B. Paul, B. A. Reilly, and C. E. Reilly, *User's Manual for the Job Descriptive Index (JDI)* (Bowling Green, OH: Bowling Green State University, 1990).

Figure 10.7

Example of Job Descriptive Index (JDI)

scales exist for measuring more specific aspects of satisfaction. For example, the Pay Satisfaction Questionnaire (PSQ) measures satisfaction with specific aspects of pay, such as pay levels, structure, and raises.[60]

Along with administering surveys, more organizations are analyzing basic HR data to look for patterns in employee retention and turnover. The results may confirm expectations or generate surprises that merit further investigation. Either way, they can help HR departments and managers determine which efforts deliver the best return. Thrivent Financial for Lutherans has combined data on employee turnover with data on work experience. The Minneapolis-based company was surprised to discover that employees with *less* prior experience in customer service were more likely to stay with the company. In Pennsylvania, a food service company called Wawa looked at data on employee turnover, wages, and hours worked. Wawa found that turnover among clerks had less to do with wage rates and more to do with limited opportunities for a full-time schedule. The company reduced turnover by adjusting work schedules so that more employees could be scheduled to work at least 30 hours per week.[61]

In spite of surveys and other efforts to retain employees, some employees inevitably will leave the organization. This presents another opportunity to gather information for retaining employees: the **exit interview**—a meeting of the departing employee with the employee's supervisor and/or a human resource specialist to discuss the employee's reasons for leaving. A well-conducted exit interview can uncover reasons why employees leave and perhaps set the stage for some of them to return. HR professionals can help make exit interviews more successful by arranging for the

Exit Interview
A meeting of a departing employee with the employee's supervisor and/or a human resource specialist to discuss the employee's reasons for leaving.

Figure 10.8

Example of a Simplified, Nonverbal Measure of Job Satisfaction

Job Satisfaction from the Faces Scale
Consider all aspects of your job. Circle the face that best describes your feelings about your job in general.

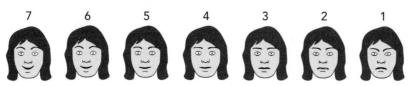

SOURCE: From R. B. Dunham and J. B. Herman, *Journal of Applied Psychology* 60 (1975), pp. 629–31. Reprinted with permission.

employee to talk to someone from the HR department (rather than the departing employee's supervisor) in a neutral location or over the phone.[62] Questions should start out open-ended and general, to give the employee a chance to name the source of the dissatisfaction or explain why leaving is attractive.

A recruiter armed with information about what caused a specific person to leave may be able to negotiate a return when the situation changes. And when several exiting employees give similar reasons for leaving, management should consider whether this indicates a need for change. In the war for talent, the best way to manage retention is to engage in a battle for every valued employee, even when it looks as if the battle has been lost.

thinking ethically

KEEPING EMPLOYEES WHEN YOU CAN'T KEEP PROMISES

When American International Group (AIG) got into financial trouble with risky investments gone bad, the federal government came to the rescue, making loans aimed at limiting the spread of the financial crisis. AIG embarked on the complex process of restructuring the company so that it could return to profitability and repay the loans, but meanwhile the public was furious about the bailout and the bonuses paid to AIG executives in spite of the company's collapse.

Imagine the human resource management challenge facing that company. Employees—many of them involved in the company's insurance business unrelated to the financial fiasco—are embarrassed, afraid, and doubtful they will be able to ever enjoy the career path, pay, and benefits they had expected, even if they keep their jobs.

While AIG's situation is notorious and extreme, from an HR perspective, it is only a more intense version of a situation that faces many employers when they run into financial difficulties. To lure the most talented people, companies look at their financial situation and offer pay, benefits, and working conditions they can afford. They may discuss promotion opportunities based on the company's expected growth. Whether or not

the company makes promises in a strict legal sense, employees look around and see opportunities they once believed in beginning to disappear. Employers typically respond by urging employees to work harder, make do with less, and trust management's reassurance that the difficult times will pass.

SOURCES: Stephen A. Miles and Nathan Bennett, "The Changing Employer-Employee Relationship," *BusinessWeek*, March 31, 2009, www.businessweek.com; and American International Group, "Restructuring" and "About AIG," www.aigcorporate.com, accessed April 19, 2010.

Questions

1. When a seemingly secure job or a job with opportunities for advancement becomes an insecure job at a shrinking company, has the employer broken a promise? Why or why not?
2. What ethical obligations, if any, does a company have to employees when it falls on hard times? In what ways, if any, are those obligations different if the hard times are the result of managers' or employees' unethical conduct?
3. How can a company such as AIG apply principles of fairness to employees during downsizing and restructuring? What impact do you think those efforts would have on employee retention?

SUMMARY

LO1 Distinguish between involuntary and voluntary turnover, and describe their effects on an organization.

Involuntary turnover occurs when the organization requires employees to leave, often when they would prefer to stay. Voluntary turnover occurs when employees initiate the turnover, often when the organization would prefer to keep them. Both are costly because of the need to recruit, hire, and

train replacements. Involuntary turnover can also result in lawsuits and even violence.

LO2 Discuss how employees determine whether the organization treats them fairly.

Employees draw conclusions based on the outcomes of decisions regarding them, the procedures applied, and the way managers treat employees when carrying out those procedures. Outcome fairness is a judgment that the consequences are just. The consequences should be consistent, expected, and in proportion to the significance of the behavior. Procedural justice is a judgment that fair methods were used to determine the consequences. The procedures should be consistent, unbiased, based on accurate information, and correctable. They should take into account the viewpoints of everyone involved, and they should be consistent with prevailing ethical standards. Interactional justice is a judgment that the organization carried out its actions in a way that took the employee's feelings into account—for example, by listening to the employee and treating the employee with dignity.

LO3 Identify legal requirements for employee discipline.

Employee discipline should not result in wrongful discharge, such as a termination that violates an implied contract or public policy. Discipline should be administered evenhandedly, without discrimination. Discipline should respect individual employees' privacy. Searches and surveillance should be for a legitimate business purpose, and employees should know about and consent to them. Reasons behind disciplinary actions should be shared only with those who need to know them. When termination is part of a plant closing, employees should receive the legally required notice, if applicable.

LO4 Summarize ways in which organizations can fairly discipline employees.

Discipline should follow the principles of the hot-stove rule, meaning discipline should give warning and have consequences that are consistent, objective, and immediate. A system that can meet these requirements is progressive discipline, in which rules are established and communicated, and increasingly severe consequences follow each violation of the rules. Usually, consequences range from a spoken warning through written warnings, suspension, and termination. These actions should be documented in writing. Organizations also may

resolve problems through alternative dispute resolution, including an open-door policy, peer review, mediation, and arbitration. When performance problems seem to result from substance abuse or mental illness, the manager may refer the employee to an employee assistance program. When a manager terminates an employee or encourages an employee to leave, outplacement counseling may smooth the process.

LO5 Explain how job dissatisfaction affects employee behavior.

Circumstances involving the nature of a job, supervisors and co-workers, pay levels, or the employee's own disposition may produce job dissatisfaction. When employees become dissatisfied, they may engage in job withdrawal. This may include behavior change, as employees try to bring about changes in policy and personnel through inside action or through whistle-blowing or lawsuits. Physical job withdrawal may range from tardiness and absenteeism to job transfer or leaving the organization altogether. Especially when employees cannot find another job, they may psychologically withdraw by displaying low levels of job involvement and organizational commitment.

LO6 Describe how organizations contribute to employees' job satisfaction and retain key employees.

Organizations can try to identify and select employees who have personal dispositions associated with job satisfaction. They can make jobs more complex and meaningful—for example, through job enrichment and job rotation. They can use methods such as the role analysis technique to make roles clear and appropriate. They can reinforce shared values and encourage social support among employees. They can try to establish satisfactory pay levels and communicate with employees about pay structure and pay raises. Monitoring job satisfaction helps organizations identify which of these actions are likely to be most beneficial.

KEY TERMS

alternative dispute resolution (ADR), p. 301
arbitration, p. 302
employee assistance program (EAP), p. 302
exit interview, p. 315
hot-stove rule, p. 298
interactional justice, p. 296
involuntary turnover, p. 293

job involvement, p. 308
job satisfaction, p. 308
job withdrawal, p. 303
mediation, p. 301
open-door policy, p. 301
organizational commitment, p. 308
outcome fairness, p. 295
outplacement counseling, p. 303
peer review, p. 301

procedural justice, p. 296
progressive discipline, p. 298
role, p. 304
role ambiguity, p. 304
role analysis technique, p. 312
role conflict, p. 304
role overload, p. 304
voluntary turnover, p. 293

REVIEW AND DISCUSSION QUESTIONS

1. Give an example of voluntary turnover and an example of involuntary turnover. Why should organizations try to reduce both kinds of turnover?

2. A member of a restaurant's serving staff is chronically late to work. From the organization's point of view, what fairness issues are involved in deciding how to handle this situation? In what ways might the employee's and other servers' ideas of fairness be different?

3. For the situation in Question 2, how would a formal discipline policy help the organization address issues of fairness?

4. The progressive discipline process described in this chapter is meant to be fair and understandable, but it tends to be slow. Try to think of two or three offenses that should result in immediate discharge, rather than follow all the steps of progressive discipline. Explain why you selected these offenses. If the dismissed employee sued, do you think the organization would be able to defend its action in court?

5. A risk of disciplining employees is that some employees retaliate. To avoid that risk, what organizational policies might encourage low-performing employees to leave while encouraging high-performing employees to stay? (Consider the sources of employee satisfaction and dissatisfaction discussed in this chapter.)

6. List forms of behavior that can signal job withdrawal. Choose one of the behaviors you listed, and describe how you would respond if an otherwise valuable employee whom you supervised engaged in this kind of behavior.

7. What are the four factors that influence an employee's job dissatisfaction (or satisfaction)? Which of these do you think an employer can most easily change? Which would be the most expensive to change?

8. The section on principles of justice used noncompete agreements as an example. How would you expect the use of noncompete agreements to affect voluntary turnover? How might the use of these agreements affect job withdrawal and job satisfaction? Besides requiring noncompete agreements, how could an organization reduce the likelihood of employees leaving to work for competitors? Would these other methods have a better effect on employee satisfaction?

9. Consider your current job or a job you recently held. Overall, were you satisfied or dissatisfied with that job? How did your level of satisfaction or dissatisfaction affect your behavior on the job? Is your own experience consistent with this chapter's models of job withdrawal and job satisfaction?

10. Suppose you are an HR professional who convinced your company's management to conduct a survey of employee satisfaction. Your budget was limited, and you could not afford a test that went into great detail. Rather, you investigated overall job satisfaction and learned that it is low, especially among employees in three departments. You know that management is concerned about spending a lot for HR programs because sales are in a slump, but you want to address the issue of low job satisfaction. Suggest some ways you might begin to make a difference, even with a small budget. How will you convince management to try your ideas?

11. Why are exit interviews important? Should an organization care about the opinions of people who are leaving? How are those opinions relevant to employee separation and retention?

BUSINESSWEEK CASE

BusinessWeek ## How the MGM Grand Maintains Employee Engagement

When Gamal Aziz became president of MGM Grand Hotel & Casino in 2001, Las Vegas was on a roll—and so was the MGM Grand. The 5,000-room hotel was ringing up $175 million a year. The challenge for Aziz: to take something good and make it even better.

Under Aziz, revenue zoomed, and the MGM Grand became the second-most profitable hotel on the strip after the Bellagio. Some credit goes, of course, to a $400 million spruce-up of the hotel in which 36 restaurants were opened or remodeled and Cirque du Soleil was brought in as a headlining act.

But ask Aziz what was the single-most important factor in the jump, and he won't talk about twirling acrobats or signature dishes such as free-range quail stuffed with foie gras. His answer is: the employees. Now with times getting tougher in Las Vegas as tourism drops and gambling revenues fall, Aziz says his people have become even more critical to the company's success.

"Employee engagement in times of difficulties and severe economic climate is far more profoundly important now," says Aziz. "Employees are willing to give their all when they are well treated, appreciated. And the ability to unlock that potential is a competitive distinction. . . . It's their decisions, their actions, their attitude that really makes the difference between [us and] a company that has its employees just punching the clock and trying to get through the day."

But Aziz, like all managers, is under pressure to justify every cost. Although his hotel is still running 96 percent occupied, groups are canceling, and those that do come are spending much less per visit. That's forced Aziz to economize on some of these successful programs. He still does regular employee appreciation dinners for top performers, but he's spending about half as much this year as last. He's started recruiting managers from sister properties to attend his MGM Grand University as a way to defray the costs of training his own top managers. And he's put on hold one program training next-generation line managers.

Aziz shares with employees the challenges he's facing. Employees, the CEO says, were what got the hotel to the next level, and they are the key to pulling through hard times. "We will get through this, we will survive," says Aziz. "Once we get through this, the employees will be the ones who have gotten us through."

When Aziz arrived in 2001, he sought out rank-and-file insight into the hotel and how it could improve. A survey of the hotel's 10,000 employees made clear that very little was being communicated to the staff about the events going on in the hotel on a daily basis, including such basics as who was staying there, and what the hotel had to offer those particular guests. Employees sometimes didn't even know what conventions were at the hotel.

Aziz came up with a simple fix. There is a short meeting now at the start of every shift in which every employee is given a rundown of what's happening in the hotel that day. It's a simple concept, but rolled out across 10,000 employees a day, it's a major undertaking.

In his recent book *Closing the Engagement Gap*, Towers Perrin Managing Director Don Lowman highlights many

MGM programs, including the MGM Grand University that offers dozens of classes on an invitation-only basis for high achievers. The MGM Grand Leadership Institute is a 24-week program for executives. And REACH! is the hotel's six-month course on basic supervisory skills for ambitious hourly workers. This investment in the staff, along with recognition dinners and other rewards, have led to more than 90 percent of MGM Grand employees saying they are satisfied with the jobs, and 89 percent saying their work has special meaning.

In the book, Lowman cites a finding from the firm's survey of tens of thousands of employees in six countries: that the number-one thing that engages employees is senior management's interest in their well-being. Visiting the MGM Grand, Lowman says he found evidence of that connection in spades. Aziz was impressive, Lowman says, for his tendency to ask questions and listen to the answers.

SOURCE: Excerpted from Nanette Byrnes, "The Issue: Maintaining Employee Engagement," *BusinessWeek*, January 16, 2009, www.businessweek.com.

Questions

1. How did the MGM Grand use employee surveys to enhance employee engagement? Besides the applications described, how else could surveys support employee satisfaction and retention at the hotel/casino?
2. In meetings held at the beginning of each shift, employees receive information that helps them provide superior service because they know more about their guests. How could that information also contribute to employee satisfaction and retention?
3. Because of a decline in revenues, the MGM Grand scaled back spending on some employee recognition and development programs. Suggest a few less-costly ways the organization could strengthen employee retention in lean times.

Case: Texas Roadhouse Won't Skimp on Making Employees Happy

When demand falls, where management cuts spending says a lot about what drives success at a company. At the Texas Roadhouse restaurant chain, the economic downturn cut into sales, and the company responded by slowing the pace at which it opened new units. Spending to promote job involvement and organizational commitment remained intact.

That decision reflects priorities held and expressed at the top of the organization. CEO G. J. Hart has said, "If we take care of our employees, they will take care of our customers." Mark Simpson, an HR manager with the

unusual title Senior Director of Legendary People, makes the point in similar language: "We believe that if we love our employees, they're going to love our guests."

How does Texas Roadhouse show the love? The company looks for ways to recognize employees and bring them together to have fun: Before each shift, employees in a restaurant gather for an "alley rally" to get motivated. Competitions include a yearly chance for an employee to win $20,000 for being the chain's best meat cutter. The company gives managers $500 in "fun money" they use to host events such as barbecues or outings for employees.

One event that has drawn national attention is Texas Roadhouse's annual motivational conference. The company invites about a thousand employees, managers, and vendors to bring their spouses to a four-day conference as a way to recognize and reward its best people. While some companies were canceling their retreats during the recent recession, Texas Roadhouse employees were assembling at the Ritz Carlton in San Francisco, where a 25-foot inflatable armadillo outside the hotel advertised their presence. Activities combined team building, charity work, and fun.

The charitable aspect of the annual conference is more than an add-on. CEO Hart says the company typically devotes about a million dollars' worth of labor and materials to community service during each conference. At the San Francisco conference, participants worked on building Habitat for Humanity homes, stuffing USO care packages, and serving food at a community center. Besides demonstrating a commitment to its community, Texas Roadhouse includes these efforts because, the CEO says, "it changes people's hearts." This fits his vision that his restaurant chain should not merely be a place to serve meat but should be about "making a difference and creating a legacy."

A reporter for CNBC criticized Hart for wasting $2 million on luxuries during lean times. Hart replied that the effort to inspire employees was precisely the kind of investment that enables his company to succeed. In fact, he later told another reporter, "During times like [this recession] when everyone is feeling the pinch, it is even more important to recognize and reward folks." The company had no plans to cancel its next retreat, to be held at New York City's Waldorf-Astoria.

The business results at Texas Roadhouse suggest that Hart may be on to something. For example, turnover among the company's on-site recruiters tumbled by two-thirds after the company put in place a program to recognize and reward these employees. Meat cutters are an important way the company differentiates itself in terms of quality by having steaks freshly cut on-site rather than being prepackaged and shipped to the restaurants.

SOURCES: Lisa Jennings, "A Happy Staff Can Soup Up Sales, Satisfy Customers," *Nation's Restaurant News*, September 21, 2009, pp. 1, 18; Gary M. Stern, "Closing Out Opulent Retreats," *Investor's Business Daily*, March 15, 2010, Business & Company Resource Center, http://galent.galegroup.com; and Rachel Eccles, "All Fired Up," *Corporate Meetings & Incentives*, September 1, 2009, Business & Company Resource Center, http://galenet.galegroup.com (interview with G. J. Hart).

Questions

1. Voluntary turnover is a significant challenge in the restaurant business. Why do you think restaurant employees might quit jobs more than employees in many other industries? Why would employee retention be an important advantage in the restaurant business?

2. According to this case, what methods does Texas Roadhouse use to promote employee retention? Suggest a few other methods the company might use and why they would be effective at Texas Roadhouse.

3. What is your response to criticism that companies shouldn't send employees on lavish retreats when the economy is slow? Under what conditions would a lavish retreat help a company, and when would it be harmful to the business? Under what conditions would the retreat be ethical or unethical? Based on your criteria, explain whether Texas Roadhouse seems to have made a good decision in conducting its motivational retreats.

 IT'S A WRAP!   connect

www.mhhe.com/noefund4e is your source for Reviewing, Applying, and Practicing the concepts you learned about in Chapter 10.

Review
- Chapter learning objectives
- Test Your Knowledge: Styles of Handling Conflict

Application
- Manager's Hot Seat segment: "Whistle-Blowing: Code Red or Red Ink?"
- Video case and quiz: "Finding and Keeping the Best Employees at SAS"
- Self-Assessments: Take a sample employee survey and answer the assessment, "What Is Your Preferred Conflict Handling Style"
- Web exercise: Cyberspace and Employee Satisfaction
- Small-business case: Looking to Show Appreciation at Datotel

Practice
- Chapter quiz

NOTES

1. "View from the Top," *Wall Street Journal*, November 19, 2007, http://online.wsj.com; and Carol Hymowitz, "Women Get Better at Forming Networks to Help Their Climb," *Wall Street Journal*, November 19, 2007, http://online.wsj.com.

2. J. D. Shaw, M. K. Duffy, J. L. Johnson, and D. E. Lockhart, "Turnover, Social Capital Losses, and Performance," *Academy of Management Journal* 48 (2005), pp. 594–606; and R. Batt, "Managing Customer Services: Human Resource Practices, Quit Rates, and Sales Growth," *Academy of Management Journal* 45 (2002), pp. 587–97.

3. D. J. Koys, "The Effects of Employee Satisfaction, Organizational Citizenship Behavior, and Turnover on Organizational Effectiveness: A Unit-Level Longitudinal Study," *Personnel Psychology* 54 (2001), pp. 101–14; Batt, "Managing Customer Services"; and M. Boyle, "Happy People, Happy Returns," *Fortune*, January 22, 2007, p. 100.

4. K. M. Kacmer, M. C. Andrews, D. L. Van Rooy, R. C. Steilberg, and S. Cerrone, "Sure Everyone Can Be Replaced . . . but at What Cost? Turnover as a Predictor of Unit-Level Performance," *Academy of Management Journal* 49 (2006), pp. 133–44; J. D. Shaw, N. Gupta, and J. E. Delery, "Alternative Conceptualizations of the Relationship between Voluntary Turnover and Organizational Performance," *Academy of Management Journal* 48 (2005), pp. 50–68; and J. Lublin, "Keeping Clients by Keeping Workers," *Wall Street Journal*, November 20, 2006, p. B1.

5. Lorrie Willey, "The Public Policy Exception to Employment at Will: Balancing Employer's Right and the Public Interest," *Journal of Legal, Ethical and Regulatory Issues* 12 no. 1 (2009), pp. 55–72; and Mitch Baker, "Commentary: 'At Will' Firing Shouldn't Lack a Reason," *Daily Journal of Commerce*, Portland, January 17, 2008, Business & Company Resource Center, http://galenet.galegroup.com.

6. M. Orey, "Fear of Firing," *BusinessWeek*, April 23, 2007, pp. 52–62.

7. M. M. Le Blanc and K. Kelloway, "Predictors and Outcomes of Workplace Violence and Aggression," *Journal of Applied Psychology*, 87, 2002, pp. 444–53.

8. F. Hanson, "'Poaching' Can Be Pricey, but Benefits May Outweigh Costs," *Workforce Management*, January 30, 2006, pp. 37–39.

9. B. J. Tepper, "Relationship among Supervisors' and Subordinates' Procedural Justice Perceptions and Organizational Citizenship Behaviors," *Academy of Management Journal* 46 (2003), pp. 97–105; T. Simons and Q. Roberson, "Why Managers Should Care about Fairness: The Effects of Aggregate Justice Perception on Organizational Outcomes," *Journal of Applied Psychology* 88 (2003), pp. 432–43; C. M. Holmvall and D. R. Bobocel, "What Fair Procedures Say about Me: Self-Construals and Reactions to Procedural Fairness," *Organizational Behavior and Human Decision Processes* 105 (2008), pp. 147–68; and K. K. Spors, "If You Fire People, Don't Be a Jerk about It," *Wall Street Journal*, December 22, 2008, pp. C1–C2.

10. T. A. Judge, B. A. Scott, and R. Ilies, "Hostility, Job Attitudes and Workplace Deviance: A Test of a Multilevel Model," *Journal of Applied Psychology* 91 (2006), pp. 126–38.

11. *Harmon v. Thornburgh*, CA, DC No. 88-5265 (July 30, 1989); *Treasury Employees Union v. Von Raab*, U.S. Sup. Ct. No. 86-18796 (March 21, 1989); *City of Annapolis v. United Food & Commercial Workers Local 400*, Md. Ct. App. No. 38 (November 6, 1989); *Skinner v. Railway Labor Executives Association*, U.S. Sup. Ct. No. 87-1555 (March 21, 1989); and *Bluestein v. Skinner*, 908 F 451, 9th Cir. (1990).

12. D. J. Hoekstra, "Workplace Searches: A Legal Overview," *Labor Law Journal* 47, no. 2 (February 1996), pp. 127–38; Bill Wortel and Christy Phanthavong, "Tips for Drafting Employee Handbooks," *Employment Law Strategist*, May 1, 2009, Business & Company Resource Center, http://galenet.galegroup.com; and Dionne Searcey, "Some Courts Raise Bar on Reading Employee Email," *Wall Street Journal*, November 19, 2009, http://online.wsj.com.

13. G. Henshaw and K. Youmans, "Employee Privacy in the Workplace and an Employer's Right to Conduct Workplace Searches and Surveillance," *SHRM Legal Report*, Spring 1990, pp. 1–5; B. K. Repa, *Your Rights in the Workplace* (Berkeley, CA: Nolo Press, 1997).

14. J. Schramm, "Privacy at Work," *HRMagazine*, April 2005, downloaded from Infotrac at http://web1.infotrac.galegroup.com; M. Denis and J. Andes, "Defamation—Do You Tell Employees Why a Coworker Was Discharged?" *Employee Relations Law Journal* 16, no. 4 (Spring 1991), pp. 469–79; R. S. Soderstrom and J. R. Murray, "Defamation in Employment: Suits by At-Will Employees," *FICC Quarterly*, Summer 1992, pp. 395–426; and "Keeping Pandora's Box Closed: Best Practices in Maintaining Personnel Records," *Mondaq Business Briefing*, June 8, 2009, Business & Company Resource Center, http://galenet.galegroup.com.

15. N. Orkin and M. Heise, "Weingarten through the Looking Glass," *Labor Law Journal* 48, no. 3 (March 1997), pp. 157–63.

16. K. Karl and C. Sutton, "A Review of Expert Advice on Employment Termination Practices: The Experts Don't Always Agree," in *Dysfunctional Behavior in Organizations*, eds. R. Griffin, A. O'Leary-Kelly, and J. Collins (Stanford, CT: JAI Press, 1998).

17. Steven Adler, "Arbitration Prevents Court Fights," *Record (Bergen County, NJ)*, February 18, 2010, Business & Company Resource Center, http://galenet. galegroup.com.

18. Louise Tickle, "Work: Can't We Talk about This?" *Guardian (London)*, October 31, 2009, Business & Company Resource Center, http://galenet.galegroup.com.

19. S. Johnson, "Results, Relapse Rates Add to Cost of Non-Hospital Treatment," *Employee Benefit Plan Review* 46 (1992), pp. 15–16.

20. George A. Brymer, "Trapped Workers: Nowhere to Run?" *Journal of Employee Assistance*, 1st Quarter 2010, pp. 11–13.

21. S. E. Needleman, "More Employers Help the Laid Off Find Jobs," *Wall Street Journal*, April 1, 2009, p. C1.

22. D. W. Baruch, "Why They Terminate," *Journal of Consulting Psychology* 8 (1944), pp. 35–46; J. G. Rosse, "Relations among Lateness, Absence and Turnover: Is There a Progression of Withdrawal?" *Human Relations* 41 (1988), pp. 517–31; C. Hulin, "Adaptation, Persistence and Commitment in Organizations," in *Handbook of Industrial & Organizational Psychology*, 2nd ed., eds. M. D. Dunnette and L. M. Hough (Palo Alto, CA: Consulting Psychologists Press, 1991), pp. 443–50; and E. R. Burris, J. R. Detert, and D. S. Chiaburu, "Quitting before Leaving: The Mediating Effects of Psychological Attachment and Detachment on Voice," *Journal of Applied Psychology* 93 (2008), pp. 912–22.

23. D. A. Harrison, D. A. Newman, and P. L. Roth, "How Important Are Job Attitudes? Meta-analytic Comparisons of Integrative Behavioral Outcomes and Time Sequences," *Academy of Management Journal* 49 (2006), pp. 305–25.

24. R. D. Zimmerman, "Understanding the Impact of Personality Traits on Individuals' Turnover Decisions: A Meta-analysis," *Personnel Psychology* 61 (2008), pp. 309–348.

25. T. A. Judge, E. A. Locke, C. C. Durham, and A. N. Kluger, "Dispositional Effects on Job and Life Satisfaction: The Role of Core Evaluations," *Journal of Applied Psychology* 83 (1998), pp. 17–34.

26. B. M. Staw, N. E. Bell, and J. A. Clausen, "The Dispositional Approach to Job Attitudes: A Lifetime Longitudinal Test," *Administrative Science Quarterly* 31 (1986), pp. 56–78; B. M. Staw and J. Ross, "Stability in the Midst of Change: A Dispositional Approach to Job Attitudes," *Journal of Applied Psychology* 70 (1985), pp. 469–80; and R. P. Steel and J. R. Rentsch, "The Dispositional Model of Job Attitudes Revisited: Findings of a 10-Year Study," *Journal of Applied Psychology* 82 (1997), pp. 873–79.

27. T. A. Judge and J. E. Bono, "Relationship of Core Self-Evaluation Traits—Self-Esteem, Generalized Self-Efficacy, Locus of Control, and Emotional Stability—with Job Satisfaction and Job Performance: A Meta-Analysis," *Journal of Applied Psychology* 86 (2001), pp. 80–92.

28. T. A. Judge, J. E. Bono, and E. A. Locke, "Personality and Job Satisfaction: The Mediating Role of Job Characteristics," *Journal of Applied Psychology* 85 (2000), pp. 237–49.

29. S. C. Douglas and M. J. Martinko, "Exploring the Role of Individual Differences in the Prediction of Workplace Aggression," *Journal of Applied Psychology* 86 (2001), pp. 547–59.

30. B. A. Gerhart, "How Important Are Dispositional Factors as Determinants of Job Satisfaction? Implications for Job Design and Other Personnel Programs," *Journal of Applied Psychology* 72 (1987), pp. 493–502.

31. E. F. Stone and H. G. Gueutal, "An Empirical Derivation of the Dimensions along Which Characteristics of Jobs Are Perceived," *Academy of Management Journal* 28 (1985), pp. 376–96.

32. L. W. Porter and R. M. Steers, "Organizational Work and Personal Factors in Employee Absenteeism and Turnover," *Psychological Bulletin* 80 (1973), pp. 151–76; and S. Melamed, I. Ben-Avi, J. Luz, and M. S. Green, "Objective and Subjective Work Monotony: Effects on Job Satisfaction, Psychological Distress, and Absenteeism in Blue Collar Workers," *Journal of Applied Psychology* 80 (1995), pp. 29–42.

33. D. R. Ilgen and J. R. Hollenbeck, "The Structure of Work: Job Design and Roles," in *Handbook of Industrial & Organizational Psychology*, 2nd ed.

34. J. A. Breaugh and J. P. Colihan, "Measuring Facets of Job Ambiguity: Construct Validity Evidence," *Journal of Applied Psychology* 79 (1994), pp. 191–201.

35. M. A. Shaffer and D. A. Harrison, "Expatriates' Psychological Withdrawal from Interpersonal Assignments: Work, Non-work, and Family Influences," *Personnel Psychology* 51 (1998), pp. 87–118.

36. Towers Perrin, "Debunking Workforce Myths," executive summary of Towers Perrin's Global Workforce Study, March 2008, www.towersperrin.com; and Susan Meisinger, "Management Holds Key to Employee Engagement," *HR Magazine*, February 2008, Business & Company Resource Center, http://galenet.galegroup.com.

37. J. M. Sacco and N. Schmitt, "A Dynamic Multi-level Model of Demographic Diversity and Misfit Effects," *Journal of Applied Psychology* 90 (2005), pp. 203–31; and R. E. Ployhart, J. A. Weekley, and K. Baughman, "The Structure and Function of Human Capital Emergence: A Multilevel Examination of the Attraction–Selection–Attrition Model," *Academy of Management Journal* 49 (2006), pp. 661–77.

38. S. Lim, L. M. Cortina, and V. J. Magley, "Personal and Work-Group Incivility: Impact on Work and Health Outcomes," *Journal of Applied Psychology* 93 (2008), pp. 95–107.

39. Holly LaFon, "Business That Makes a Difference," *Success*, November 2009, pp. 46–48.

40. James Detar, "Tracking the Cost of Employee Absenteeism," *Investor's Business Daily*, March 29, 2010, Business & Company Resource Center, http://galenet.galegroup.com.

41. J. Banks, "Turnover Costs," *Workforce Management*, June 23, 2008, p. 22.

42. J. Sullivan, "Not All Turnover Is Equal," *Workforce Management*, May 21, 2007, p. 42.

43. R. T. Mowday, R. M. Steers, and L. W. Porter, "The Measurement of Organizational Commitment," *Journal of Vocational Behavior* 14 (1979), pp. 224–47.

44. E. A. Locke, "The Nature and Causes of Job Dissatisfaction," in *The Handbook of Industrial & Organizational Psychology*, ed. M. D. Dunnette (Chicago: Rand McNally, 1976), pp. 901–69.

45. N. A. Bowling, T. A. Beehr, S. H. Wagner, and T. M. Libkuman, "Adaptation-Level Theory, Opponent Process Theory, and Dispositions: An Integrated Approach to the Stability of Job Satisfaction," *Journal of Applied Psychology* 90 (2005), pp. 1044–53.

46. Brymer, "Trapped Workers"; Arielle Kass, "Employers Need to Be Mindful of Privacy," *Crain's Cleveland Business*, February 22, 2010, Business & Company Resource Center, http://galenet.galegroup.com.

47. G. R. Oldham, A. Cummings, L. J. Mischel, J. M. Schmidtke, and J. Zhou, "Listen While You Work? Quasi-experimental Relations between Personal-Stereo Headset Use and Employee Work Responses," *Journal of Applied Psychology* 80 (1995), pp. 547–64.

48. Kasey Wehrum, "Using Charitable Donations to Motivate Employees," *Inc.*, November 2009, www.inc.com.

49. B. Morris, "The Best Place to Work Now," *Fortune*, January 20, 2006, pp. 79–86.

50. Mary Shapiro, Cynthia Ingols, Stacy Blake-Beard, and Regina O'Neill, "Canaries in the Mine Shaft: Women Signaling a New Career Model," *People & Strategy*, 32 no. 3 (2009), pp. 52–59; and Susan Seitel, "Research We Don't Hear About," *WFC Resources Newsbrief*, August 2009, Business & Company Resource Center, http://galenet.galegroup.com.

51. J. E. Perry-Smith, "Work Family Human Resource Bundles and Perceived Organizational Performance," *Academy of Management Journal* 43 (2000), pp. 801–15; and M. M. Arthur, "Share Price Reactions to Work-Family Initiatives: An Institutional Perspective," *Academy of Management Journal* 46 (2003), pp. 497–505.

52. Brian Bergstein, "IBM Riles Employees with Base Pay Cuts," *Yahoo News*, January 23, 2008, http://news.yahoo.com.

53. B. M. Meglino, E. C. Ravlin, and C. L. Adkins, "A Work Values Approach to Corporate Culture: A Field Test of the Value Congruence Process and Its Relationship to Individual Outcomes," *Journal of Applied Psychology* 74 (1989), pp. 424–33.

54. G. C. Ganster, M. R. Fusilier, and B. T. Mayes, "Role of Social Support in the Experience of Stress at Work," *Journal of Applied Psychology* 71 (1986), pp. 102–11.

55. R. Eisenberger, F. Stinghamber, C. Vandenberghe, I. L. Sucharski, and L. Rhoades, "Perceived Supervisor Support: Contributions to Perceived Organizational Support and Employee Retention," *Journal of Applied Psychology* 87 (2002), pp. 565–73.

56. R. T. Keller, "A Test of the Path-Goal Theory of Leadership with Need for Clarity as a Moderator in Research and Development Organizations," *Journal of Applied Psychology* 74 (1989), pp. 208–12.

57. S. C. Payne and A. H. Huffman, "A Longitudinal Examination of the Influence of Mentoring on Organizational Commitment and Turnover," *Academy of Management Journal* 48 (2005), pp. 158–68.

58. A. Fisher, "Have You Outgrown Your Job?" *Fortune*, August 21, 2006, pp. 46–54.

59. R. P. Quinn and G. L. Staines, *The 1977 Quality of Employment Survey* (Ann Arbor, MI: Survey Research Center, Institute for Social Research, University of Michigan, 1979).

60. T. Judge and T. Welbourne, "A Confirmatory Investigation of the Dimensionality of the Pay Satisfaction Questionnaire," *Journal of Applied Psychology* 79 (1994), pp. 461–66.

61. Bill Roberts, "Analyze This!" *HR Magazine*, October 2009, pp. 35–41.

62. Terence F. Shea, "Getting the Last Word," *HR Magazine*, January 2010, Business & Company Resource Center, http://galenet.galegroup.com; and L. M. Sixel, "Keeping Top Talent Has Employers Worried," *Houston Chronicle*, March 14, 2010, Business & Company Resource Center, http://galenet.galegroup.com.

Compensating Human Resources

PART FOUR

Establishing a Pay Structure

What Do I Need to Know?

After reading this chapter, you should be able to:

LO1 Identify the kinds of decisions involved in establishing a pay structure.

LO2 Summarize legal requirements for pay policies.

LO3 Discuss how economic forces influence decisions about pay.

LO4 Describe how employees evaluate the fairness of a pay structure.

LO5 Explain how organizations design pay structures related to jobs.

LO6 Describe alternatives to job-based pay.

LO7 Summarize how to ensure that pay is actually in line with the pay structure.

LO8 Discuss issues related to paying employees serving in the military and paying executives.

Introduction

Competition among law firms to get the best new lawyers has been so stiff that salaries have been rising year after year. Traditionally, firms pay them according to their years out of school; the longer the associates have been working, the more they earn. So when a company raises associate salaries, it is raising them for everyone—an expensive move. Recently, however, some law firms have broken that mold and are tying pay more closely to what each associate contributes to the firm. For example, in San Diego, the firm Luce, Forward, Hamilton & Scripps set up 14 pay levels related to the associate's productivity (some work more hours than others) and practice area (some types of legal work are more profitable than others). Some recruiters question whether the new system will seem less fair, identifying some lawyers as having a less-valuable practice. The firm argues that its pay levels offer a wider range of opportunities for lawyers who might prefer to work fewer hours or in a less-profitable area. With the new system, hiring these lawyers becomes affordable.[1]

From the employer's point of view, pay is a powerful tool for meeting the organization's goals. Pay has a large impact on employee attitudes and behaviors. It influences which kinds of employees are attracted to (and remain with) the organization. By rewarding certain behaviors, it can align employees' interests with the organization's goals. Employees care about policies affecting earnings because the policies affect the employees' income and standard of living. Besides the level of pay, employees care about its fairness compared with what others earn. Also, employees consider pay a sign of status and success. They attach great importance to pay decisions when they evaluate their relationship with their employer. For these reasons, organizations must carefully manage and communicate decisions about pay.

At the same time, pay is a major cost. Its share of total costs varies widely from one industry or company to another. At the low end, the wholesaling industry spends over 5 percent of revenues on payroll expenses. At the other extreme, transportation, entertainment, and health care companies spend more than 25 percent to almost 40 percent of revenues on payroll.[2] Managers have to keep this cost reasonable.

This chapter describes how managers weigh the importance and costs of pay to arrive at a structure for compensation and levels of pay for different jobs. We first define the basic decisions in terms of pay structure and pay level. Next, we look at several considerations that influence these decisions: legal requirements related to pay, economic forces, the nature of the organization's jobs, and employees' judgments about the fairness of pay levels. We describe methods for evaluating jobs and market data to arrive at a pay structure. We then summarize alternatives to the usual focus on jobs. The chapter closes with a look at two issues of current importance—pay for employees on leave to serve in the military and pay for executives.

Decisions about Pay

Because pay is important both in its effect on employees and on account of its cost, organizations need to plan what they will pay employees in each job. An unplanned approach, in which each employee's pay is independently negotiated, will likely result in unfairness, dissatisfaction, and rates that are either overly expensive or so low that positions are hard to fill. Organizations therefore make decisions about two aspects of pay structure: job structure and pay level. **Job structure** consists of the relative pay for different jobs within the organization. It establishes relative pay among different functions and different levels of responsibility. For example, job structure defines the difference in pay between an entry-level accountant and an entry-level assembler, as well as the difference between an entry-level accountant, the accounting department manager, and the organization's comptroller. **Pay level** is the average amount (including wages, salaries, and bonuses) the organization pays for a particular job. Together, job structure and pay levels establish a **pay structure** that helps the organization achieve goals related to employee motivation, cost control, and the ability to attract and retain talented human resources. These decisions are supplemented with choices about payroll methods such as the ones described in the "eHRM" box.

The organization's job structure and pay levels are policies of the organization, rather than the amount a particular employee earns. For example, an organization's pay structure could include the range of pay that a person may earn in the job of entry-level accountant. An individual accountant could be earning an amount anywhere within that range. Typically, the amount a person earns depends on the individual's qualifications, accomplishments, and experience. The individual's pay may also depend partly on how well the organization performs. This chapter focuses on the organization's decisions about pay structure, and the next chapter will explore decisions that affect the amount of pay an individual earns.

Especially in an organization with hundreds or thousands of employees, it would be impractical for managers and the human resource department to make an entirely unique decision about each employee's pay. The decision would have to weigh so many factors that this approach would be expensive, difficult, and often unsatisfactory. Establishing a pay structure simplifies the process of making

LO1 Identify the kinds of decisions involved in establishing a pay structure.

Job Structure
The relative pay for different jobs within the organization.

Pay Level
The average amount (including wages, salaries, and bonuses) the organization pays for a particular job.

Pay Structure
The pay policy resulting from job structure and pay-level decisions.

PAYING EMPLOYEES ELECTRONICALLY

focus on
social
responsibility

Walmart recently began implementing a system to pay all of its Walmart and Sam's Club workers in the United States electronically. While management and professional employees have long participated in electronic payment programs where funds are automatically deposited in each employee's checking account on payday, low-wage employees such as sales clerks do not always have checking accounts.

Walmart's solution was to team up with First Data Management Company to provide hourly employees with MasterCard Paycards. These cards look like credit cards,

but instead of being linked to credit, these accounts are funded by the employee's pay. Instead of receiving a paper check that they have to cash, employees have funds automatically credited to their Paycard. Employees can shop with their cards, get cash at an ATM, or use their cards to make a purchase with cash back. Because the funds are deposited electronically, an employee gets paid immediately on payday, even if the employee isn't at work that day. Employees also can opt for direct deposit if they have a bank account.

Walmart instituted the electronic payroll program as part of its

effort to make the company more environmentally friendly. Because the company has over a million employees, it saves a substantial amount of paper by not stuffing paychecks into envelopes.

Sources: "Walmart Launches Associate Electronic Pay Program," *Progressive Grocer,* September 4, 2009, Business & Company Resource Center, http:// galenet.galegroup.com; "With 1.4 Million Employees, Wal-Mart Puts Payroll Cards on the Map," *Digital Transactions,* September 3, 2009, www .digitaltransactions.net; and First Data, "First Data: Money Network," corporate website, www.firstdata.com, accessed April 21, 2010.

decisions about individual employees' pay by grouping together employees with similar jobs. As shown in Figure 11.1, human resource professionals develop this pay structure based on legal requirements, market forces, and the organization's goals, such as attracting a high-quality workforce and meeting principles of fairness.

Figure 11.1

Issues in Developing a Pay Structure

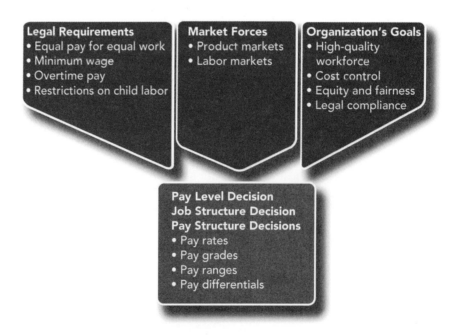

Legal Requirements
• Equal pay for equal work
• Minimum wage
• Overtime pay
• Restrictions on child labor

Market Forces
• Product markets
• Labor markets

Organization's Goals
• High-quality workforce
• Cost control
• Equity and fairness
• Legal compliance

Pay Level Decision
Job Structure Decision
Pay Structure Decisions
• Pay rates
• Pay grades
• Pay ranges
• Pay differentials

Legal Requirements for Pay

LO2 Summarize legal requirements for pay policies.

Government regulation affects pay structure in the areas of equal employment opportunity, minimum wages, pay for overtime, and prevailing wages for federal contractors. All of an organization's decisions about pay should comply with the applicable laws.

Equal Employment Opportunity

Under the laws governing Equal Employment Opportunity, described in Chapter 3, employers may not base differences in pay on an employee's age, sex, race, or other protected status. Any differences in pay must instead be tied to such business-related considerations as job responsibilities or performance. The goal is for employers to provide *equal pay for equal work*. Job descriptions, job structures, and pay structures can help organizations demonstrate that they are upholding these laws.

These laws do not guarantee equal pay for men and women, whites and minorities, or any other groups, because so many legitimate factors, from education to choice of occupation, affect a person's earnings. In fact, numbers show that women and racial minorities in the United States tend to earn less than white men. Among full-time workers in 2008, women on average earned 80 cents for every dollar earned by men. Among male employees, black workers earned 85 cents for every dollar earned by white workers, and Hispanic workers earned just 76 cents (the racial gap among Black and Hispanic female employees is greater, at 76 and 66 cents per dollar, respectively).[3] Even when these figures are adjusted to take into account education, experience, and occupation, the earnings gap does not completely close.[4]

One explanation for historical lower pay for women has been that employers have undervalued work performed by women—in particular, placing a lower value on occupations traditionally dominated by women. Some policy makers have proposed a remedy for this called equal pay for *comparable worth*. This policy uses job evaluation (described later in the chapter) to establish the worth of an organization's jobs in terms of such criteria as their difficulty and their importance to the organization. The employer then compares the evaluation points awarded to each job with the pay for each job. If jobs have the same number of evaluation points, they should be paid equally. If they are not, pay of the lower-paid job is raised to meet the goal of comparable worth.

Comparable-worth policies are controversial. From an economic standpoint, the obvious drawback of such a policy is that raising pay for some jobs places the employer at an economic disadvantage relative to employers that pay the market rate. In addition, a free-market economy assumes people will take differences in pay into account when they choose a career. The courts allow organizations to defend themselves against claims of discrimination by showing that they pay the going market rate.[5] Businesses are reluctant to place themselves at an economic disadvantage, but many state governments adjust pay to achieve equal pay for comparable worth. Also, at both private and government organizations, policies designed to shatter the "glass ceiling" (discussed in Chapter 9) can help to address the problem of unequal pay.

Two employees who do the same job cannot be paid different wages because of gender, race, or age. It would be illegal to pay these two employees differently because one is male and the other is female. Only if there are differences in their experience, skills, seniority, or job performance are there legal reasons why their pay might be different.

Minimum Wage

Minimum Wage
The lowest amount that employers may pay under federal or state law, stated as an amount of pay per hour.

In the United States, employers must pay at least the **minimum wage** established by law. (A *wage* is the rate of pay per hour.) At the federal level, the 1938 **Fair Labor Standards Act (FLSA)** establishes a minimum wage that is $7.25 per hour as of July 2009. The FLSA also permits a lower "training wage," which employers may pay to workers under the age of 20 for a period of up to 90 days. This subminimum wage is approximately 85 percent of the minimum wage. Some states have laws specifying minimum wages; in these states, employers must pay whichever rate is higher.

From the standpoint of social policy, an issue related to the minimum wage is that it tends to be lower than the earnings required for a full-time worker to rise above the poverty level. A number of cities have therefore passed laws requiring a so-called *living wage*, essentially a minimum wage based on the cost of living in a particular region.

Fair Labor Standards Act (FLSA)
Federal law that establishes a minimum wage and requirements for overtime pay and child labor.

Overtime Pay

Another requirement of the FLSA is that employers must pay higher wages for overtime, defined as hours worked beyond 40 hours per week. The overtime rate under the FLSA is one and a half times the employee's usual hourly rate, including any bonuses and piece-rate payments (amounts paid per item produced). The overtime rate applies to the hours worked beyond 40 in one week. Time worked includes not only hours spent on production or sales but also time on such activities as attending required classes, cleaning up the work site, or traveling between work sites. Figure 11.2 shows how this applies to an employee who works 50 hours to earn a base rate of $10 per hour plus a weekly bonus of $30. The overtime pay is based on the base pay ($400) plus the bonus ($30), for a rate of $10.75 per hour. For each of the 10 hours of overtime, the employee would earn $16.13, so the overtime pay is $161.30 ($16.13 times 10). When employees are paid per unit produced or when they receive a monthly or quarterly bonus, those payments must be converted into wages per hour, so that the employer can include these amounts when figuring the correct overtime rate.

Overtime pay is required, whether or not the employer specifically asked or expected the employee to work more than 40 hours.[6] In other words, if the employer knows the

Figure 11.2

Computing Overtime Pay

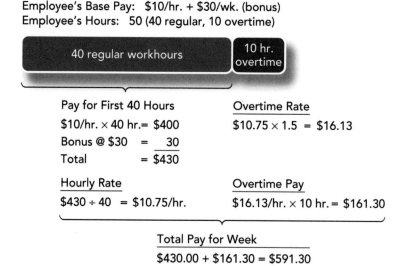

Employee's Base Pay: $10/hr. + $30/wk. (bonus)
Employee's Hours: 50 (40 regular, 10 overtime)

40 regular workhours   10 hr. overtime

Pay for First 40 Hours   Overtime Rate
$10/hr. × 40 hr.= $400 $10.75 × 1.5 = $16.13
Bonus @ $30   =   30
Total   = $430

Hourly Rate   Overtime Pay
$430 ÷ 40 = $10.75/hr. $16.13/hr. × 10 hr. = $161.30

Total Pay for Week
$430.00 + $161.30 = $591.30

Booting Up Your Computer Is Work, Too

Qwest Communications recently got in trouble when employees in its call center sued for unpaid overtime. Employees said they weren't being paid for starting work before their shifts officially began. Why did they do that? In some cases, they said, their managers asked them to come in before the start of their shift and start up their computers. In other cases, their daily job requirements were so challenging that the only way to meet the goals was for the computers to be up and running when their shift began.

Qwest defended itself on the grounds that it had a policy forbidding employees to work off the time clock. But the judge in the case said the company's actual practices, not the policy, were what the jury would need to consider.

Companies that don't want to pay overtime rates for booting up computers have to build that work into employees' scheduled activities.

Questions

1. Why do you think the managers at Qwest didn't seem to think of getting computers started as part of the employees' work?
2. How could HR professionals prevent this sort of misunderstanding?

Source: Based on "Workers Coming in Early to Fire Up Their Computers? You Must Pay Them," *HR Specialist: Employment Law*, March 2010, Business & Company Resource Center, http://galenet.galegroup.com.

---

employee is working overtime but does not pay time and a half, the employer may be violating the FLSA (see the "HR Oops!" box for an example).

Not everyone is eligible for overtime pay. Under the FLSA, executive, professional, administrative, and highly compensated white-collar employees are considered **exempt employees,** meaning employers need not pay them one and a half times their regular pay for working more than 40 hours per week. Exempt status depends on the employee's job responsibilities, salary level (at least $455 per week), and "salary basis," meaning that the employee is paid a given amount regardless of the number of hours worked or quality of the work.[7] Paying an employee on a salary basis means the organization expects that this person can manage his or her own time to get the work done, so the employer may deduct from the employee's pay only in certain limited circumstances, such as disciplinary action or for unpaid leave for personal reasons. Additional exceptions apply to certain occupations, including outside salespersons, teachers, and computer professionals (if they earn at least $27.63 per hour). Thus, the standards are fairly complicated. For more details about the standards for exempt employees, contact the Labor Department's Wage and Hour Division or refer to its Web site at www.dol.gov/whd.

Exempt Employees
Managers, outside salespeople, and any other employees not covered by the FLSA requirement for overtime pay.

Any employee who is not in one of the exempt categories is called a **nonexempt employee.** Most workers paid on an hourly basis are nonexempt and therefore subject to the laws governing overtime pay. However, paying a salary does not necessarily mean a job is exempt.

Nonexempt Employees
Employees covered by the FLSA requirements for overtime pay.

Child Labor

In the early years of the Industrial Revolution, employers could pay low wages by hiring children. The FLSA now sharply restricts the use of child labor, with the aim of protecting children's health, safety, and educational opportunities.[8] The restrictions apply to children younger than 18. Under the FLSA, children aged 16 and 17 may not be employed in hazardous occupations defined by the Department of Labor, such as mining, meatpacking, and certain kinds of manufacturing using heavy machinery. Children aged 14 and 15 may work only outside school hours, in jobs defined as non-hazardous, and for limited time periods. A child under age 14 may not be employed in any work associated with interstate commerce, except work performed in a non-hazardous job for a business entirely owned by the child's parent or guardian. A few additional exemptions from this ban include acting, babysitting, and delivering newspapers to consumers.

Besides the FLSA, state laws also restrict the use of child labor. Many states have laws requiring working papers or work permits for minors, and many states restrict the number of hours or times of day that minors aged 16 and older may work. Before hiring any workers under the age of 18, employers must ensure they are complying with the child labor laws of their state, as well as the FLSA requirements for their industry.

Prevailing Wages

Two additional federal laws, the Davis-Bacon Act of 1931 and the Walsh-Healy Public Contracts Act of 1936, govern pay policies of federal contractors. Under these laws, federal contractors must pay their employees at rates at least equal to the prevailing wages in the area. The calculation of prevailing rates must be based on 30 percent of the local labor force. Typically, the rates are based on relevant union contracts. Pay earned by union members tends to be higher than the pay of nonunion workers in similar jobs, so the effect of these laws is to raise the lower limit of pay an employer can offer.

These laws do not cover all companies. Davis-Bacon covers construction contractors that receive more than $2,000 in federal money. Walsh-Healy covers all government contractors receiving $10,000 or more in federal funds.

LO3 Discuss how economic forces influence decisions about pay.

Economic Influences on Pay

An organization cannot make spending decisions independent of the economy. Organizations must keep costs low enough that they can sell their products profitably, yet they must be able to attract workers in a competitive labor market. Decisions about how to respond to the economic forces of product markets and labor markets limit an organization's choices about pay structure.

Product Markets

The organization's *product market* includes organizations that offer competing goods and services. In other words, the organizations in a product market are competing to serve the same customers. To succeed in their product markets, organizations must be able to sell their goods and services at a quantity and price that will bring them a sufficient profit. They may try to win customers by being superior in a number of areas, including quality, customer service, and price. An important influence on price is the cost to produce the goods and services for sale. As we mentioned earlier, the cost of labor is a significant part of an organization's costs.

If an organization's labor costs are higher than those of its competitors, it will be under pressure to charge more than competitors charge for similar products. If one company spends $50 in labor costs to make a product and its competitor spends only

$35, the second company will be more profitable unless the first company can justify a higher price to customers. This is one reason U.S. automakers have had difficulty competing against Japanese companies. The labor-related expenses per vehicle for a U.S. company have been as much as $1,000 higher than for Japanese car makers operating in the United States. As that competitive disadvantage contributed to slower sales, U.S. producers have persuaded unions to let them reduce hourly labor costs, bringing them much closer in line with Japanese car makers.[9]

Product markets place an upper limit on the pay an organization will offer. This upper limit is most important when labor costs are a large part of an organization's total costs and when the organization's customers place great importance on price. Organizations that want to lure top-quality employees by offering generous salaries therefore have to find ways to automate routine activities (so that labor is a smaller part of total costs) or to persuade customers that high quality is worth a premium price. Organizations under pressure to cut labor costs may respond by reducing staff levels, freezing pay levels, postponing hiring decisions, or requiring employees to bear more of the cost of benefits such as insurance premiums.

Labor Markets

Besides competing to sell their products, organizations must compete to obtain human resources in *labor markets*. In general, workers prefer higher-paying jobs and avoid employers that offer less money for the same type of job. In this way, competition for labor establishes the minimum an organization must pay to hire an employee for a particular job. If an organization pays less than the minimum, employees will look for jobs with other organizations.

An organization's competitors in labor markets typically include companies with similar products and companies in other industries that hire similar employees. For example, a truck transportation firm would want to know the pay earned by truck drivers at competing firms as well as truck drivers for manufacturers that do their own shipping, drivers for moving and storage companies, and drivers for stores that provide delivery services. In setting pay levels for its bookkeepers and administrative assistants, the company would probably define its labor market differently, because bookkeepers and administrative assistants work for most kinds of businesses. The company would likely look for data on the earnings of bookkeepers and administrative assistants in the region. For all these jobs, the company wants to know what others are paying so that it will pay enough to attract and keep qualified employees. The "Did You Know?" box compares average pay levels for some broad occupational categories in the United States.

There is a strong demand for nurses in the labor market. What this means for hospitals is that they have to pay competitive wages and other perks to attract and retain staff. How does this differ from the airline industry's current labor market?

Another influence on labor markets is the *cost of living*—the cost of a household's typical expenses, such as house payments, groceries, medical care, and gasoline. In some parts of the country, the cost of living is higher than in others, so the local labor markets there will likely demand higher pay. Also, over time, the cost of living tends to rise. When the cost of living is rising rapidly, labor markets demand pay increases. The federal government

Did You Know?

Tech Workers Out-Earn Managers

Looking at broad occupational categories, people in technology-related jobs are some of the nation's top earners. The pay rates are for the *median* worker in each category (half the employees earn more and half earn less).

Source: U.S. Census Bureau, *Statistical Abstract of the United States: 2010,* Table 633, www.census.gov.

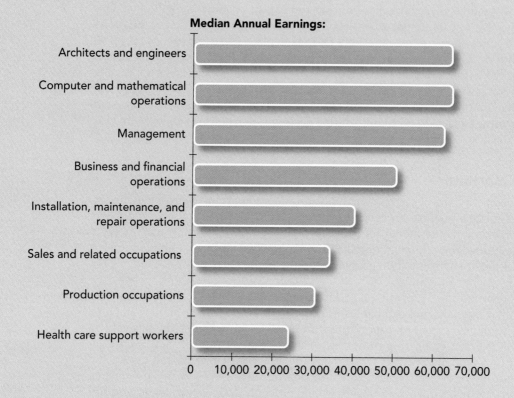

Median Annual Earnings:

tracks trends in the nation's cost of living with a measure called the Consumer Price Index (CPI). Following and studying changes in the CPI can help employers prepare for changes in the demands of the labor market.

Pay Level: Deciding What to Pay

Although labor and product markets limit organizations' choices about pay levels, there is a range within which organizations can make decisions.[10] The size of this range depends on the details of the organization's competitive environment. If many workers are competing for a few jobs, employers will have more choice. Similarly, employers can be more flexible about pay policies if they use technology and work design to get better results from employees than their competitors do.

When organizations have a broad range in which to make decisions about pay, they can choose to pay at, above, or below the rate set by market forces. Economic theory holds that the most profitable level, all things being equal, would be at the market rate. Often, however, all things are not equal from one employer to another. For instance, an organization may gain an advantage by paying above the market rate if it uses the higher pay as one means to attract top talent and then uses these excellent employees' knowledge to be more innovative, produce higher quality, or work more efficiently. For example, Costco has a practice of paying its employees higher wages and more generous benefits than Walmart pays employees of Costco's chief competitor, Sam's Club. In return for this apparent generosity, Costco enjoys a much lower rate of employee turnover, potentially saving the company hundreds of millions of dollars a year. Costco also earns higher profits per hourly employee and loses less to "shrinkage" (employee theft).[11]

This approach is based on the view of employees as resources. Higher pay may be an investment in superior human resources. Having higher labor costs than your competitors is not necessarily bad if you also have the best and most effective workforce, which produces more products of better quality. Pay policies are one of the most important human resource tools for encouraging desired employee behaviors and discouraging undesired behaviors. Therefore, organizations must evaluate pay as more than a cost, but also as an investment that can generate returns in attracting, retaining, and motivating a high-quality workforce. For this reason, paying above the going rate may be advantageous for an organization that empowers employees or that cannot closely watch employees (as with repair technicians who travel to customers). Those employers might use high pay to attract and retain top candidates and to motivate them to do their best because they want to keep their high-paying jobs.[12]

Gathering Information about Market Pay

To compete for talent, organizations use **benchmarking,** a procedure in which an organization compares its own practices against those of successful competitors. In terms of compensation, benchmarking involves the use of pay surveys. These provide information about the going rates of pay at competitors in the organization's product and labor markets. An organization can conduct its own surveys, but the federal government and other organizations make a great deal of data available already.

Benchmarking
A procedure in which an organization compares its own practices against those of successful competitors.

Pay surveys are available for many kinds of industries (product markets) and jobs (labor markets). The primary collector of this kind of data in the United States is the Bureau of Labor Statistics, which conducts an ongoing National Compensation Survey measuring wages, salaries, and benefits paid to the nation's employees. The "HR How To" box provides guidelines for using the BLS Web site as a source of wage data. The most widely used sources of compensation information include HR organizations such as WorldatWork and the Society for Human Resource Management.[13] In addition, many organizations, especially large ones, purchase data from consulting groups such as Mercer, Salary.com, and Hewitt. Consulting firms charge for the service but can tailor data to their clients' needs. Employers also should investigate what compensation surveys are available from any industry or trade groups their company belongs to.

Human resource professionals need to determine whether to gather data focusing on particular industries or on job categories. Industry-specific data are especially relevant for jobs with skills that are specific to the type of product. For jobs with skills that can be transferred to companies in other industries, surveys of job classifications will be more relevant.

GATHERING WAGE DATA AT THE BLS WEB SITE

A convenient source of data on hourly wages is the wage query system of the Bureau of Labor Statistics (BLS). This federal agency makes data available at its Web site on an interactive basis. The data come from the BLS's National Compensation Survey. The user specifies the category of data desired, and the BLS provides tables of data almost instantly. Here's how to use the BLS system.

Visit the BLS Web site (www.bls.gov), and click on the link to Pay & Benefits. Find and click on the link to the National Compensation Survey (NCS). On the NCS Web page, click on NCS Databases. You have a choice to use different tools to view various databases. The single-screen data search lets you define on one pop-up screen all the categories you want to include, while the multiscreen search asks you to specify one search category at a time, then click to open the next screen. The single-screen approach is faster, but as of this writing, that option was not yet available for the current NCS data, so these guidelines assume you are using the multiscreen search.

After you select Multi-Screen Data Search for NCS, the system presents you with a window in which to select either the entire United States or a single state. Click to highlight your choice and then click on Next Form. If you choose United States, your next choice is a Census region of the country; if you choose a state, the next option is a metropolitan region of the state.

On the next screen, select the occupation you wish to research. The survey data cover hundreds of occupations, grouped into more general categories. For example, at the most specific level, you could look at civil engineers. More broadly, you could look at all engineers, or at the larger grouping of architecture and engineering occupations. You should select the most specific grouping that covers the occupation you want to investigate. If you select occupation first, you can then select geographic areas for which the database includes data on that occupation.

After selecting an occupation, select a work level. This describes the level of such work features as knowledge required and the scope, complexity, and demands of the job. For instance, you could look only at data for entry-level or senior accountants, rather than all accountants. Some occupations, including artists, athletes, and announcers, are not classified by work level.

Click on the Retrieve Data link to submit the request to the BLS. The system immediately processes the request and presents the table (or tables) on your computer screen.

Source: Bureau of Labor Statistics Web site, www.bls.gov, accessed April 21, 2010.

LO4 Describe how employees evaluate the fairness of a pay structure.

Employee Judgments about Pay Fairness

In developing a pay structure, it is important to keep in mind employees' opinions about fairness. After all, one of the purposes of pay is to motivate employees, and they will not be motivated by pay if they think it is unfair.

Judging Fairness

Employees evaluate their pay relative to the pay of other employees. Social scientists have studied this kind of comparison and developed *equity theory* to describe how people make judgments about fairness.[14] According to equity theory, people measure outcomes such as pay in terms of their inputs. For example, an employee might think of her pay in terms of her master's degree, her 12 years of experience, and her 60-hour workweeks. To decide whether a level of pay is equitable, the person compares her ratio of outcomes and inputs with other people's outcome/input ratios, as shown in Figure 11.3. The person in the previous example might notice that an employee with

Equity: Pay Seems Fair

Inequity: Pay Seems Unfair

Figure 11.3

Opinions about Fairness: Pay Equity

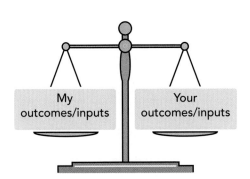

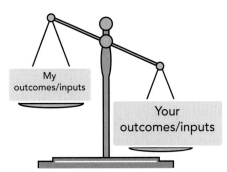

less education or experience is earning more than she is (unfair) or that an employee who works 80 hours a week is earning more (fair). In general, employees compare their pay and contributions against several yardsticks:

- What they think employees in other organizations earn for doing the same job.
- What they think other employees holding different jobs within the organization earn for doing work at the same or different levels.
- What they think other employees in the organization earn for doing the same job as theirs.

Employees' conclusions about equity depend on what they choose as a standard of comparison. The results can be surprising. For example, some organizations have set up two-tier wage systems as a way to cut labor costs without cutting employees' existing salaries. Typically, employers announce these programs as a way to avoid moving jobs out of the country or closing down altogether. In a two-tier wage system, existing employees continue on at their current (upper-tier) pay rate while new employees sign on for less pay (the lower tier). One might expect reaction among employees in the lower tier that the pay structure is unfair. But a study of these employees found that they were *more* satisfied than the top-tier employees.[15] The lower-tier employees were not comparing their pay with that of the upper-tier employees but with the other alternatives they saw for themselves: lower-paying jobs or unemployment.

The ways employees respond to their impressions about equity can have a great impact on the organization. Typically, if employees see their pay as equitable, their attitudes and behavior continue unchanged. If employees see themselves as receiving an advantage, they usually rethink the situation to see it as merely equitable. But if employees conclude that they are underrewarded, they are likely to make up the difference in one of three ways. They might put forth less effort (reducing their inputs), find a way to increase their outcomes (for example, stealing), or withdraw by leaving the organization or refusing to cooperate. Employees' beliefs about fairness also influence their willingness to accept transfers or promotions. For example, if a job change involves more work, employees will expect higher pay.

Communicating Fairness

Equity theory tells organizations that employees care about their pay relative to what others are earning and that these feelings are based on what the employees *perceive* (what they notice and form judgments about). An organization can do much to

HOBBY LOBBY INSPIRES WITH GOOD NEWS ABOUT PAY

The Hobby Lobby chain of crafts stores operates under a philosophy of service to others. Founder David Green says, "When we serve our employees well, we actually can serve our customers better." For compensation policy, this means the company pays its people as generously as it can in the low-margin world of retailing. As sales have increased, so have the wages paid to employees. Green sees this as a practical way to keep employees and to benefit from their experience: "I would rather have fewer people who have longevity," rather than more minimum-wage workers, because the experienced employees "are more valuable because they know how to answer all the thousands of questions that customers ask."

Hobby Lobby implements the pay policy in a way that is sure to get the attention of its employees. Two Aprils in a row, the company announced that because of its growth, it would increase the hourly wages of store employees. In 2009, the company granted raises to all full-time employees earning less than $13 per hour and set a $10-per-hour minimum for all full-time employees (up from as little as $6.55, which had been the national minimum wage). The initiative benefited more than one-third of the chain's workforce. A year later, the minimum was raised to $11, and the minimum for part-timers was raised to $8. The announcements meant that thousands of employees would get a raise all at the same time.

Store managers announced the changes to gatherings of their employees. Spreading good news in this way generated appreciation and excitement, especially considering that the raises came during years when other companies were instituting layoffs and pay cuts. At the Hobby Lobby store in Athens, Georgia, store manager Tom Lennon said employees' attitudes soared at the news of the first raise: "The associates actually showed more pride than they already did. We're very impressed with the ownership of the company." In Colorado Springs, assistant store manager Adam Garcia witnessed his employees' surprise and gratitude. Although the raise was granted to hourly employees, not managers, the impact was felt at the managerial level, too. Garcia, for example, said of the pay increase, "It gives you confidence—and makes you proud to work for such a good company. It makes you want to work harder."

Sources: Don Nelson, "Art, Craft Company Hikes Pay: Minimum Wage Boost," *Athens (Ga.) Banner-Herald,* April 17, 2010, Business & Company Resource Center, http://galenet.galegroup.com; Katharine Field, "A Matter of Principle," *Chain Store Age,* June 2009, Business & Company Resource Center, http://galenet.galegroup.com; Don Nelson, "Crafts Store Workers Get Good News," *Athens (Ga.) Banner-Herald,* May 3, 2009, Business & Company Resource Center, http://galenet.galegroup.com; and Becky Hurley, "Hobby Lobby Workers Elated about Across-the-Board Pay Hikes," *Colorado Springs Business Journal,* April 17, 2009, Business & Company Resource Center, http://galenet.galegroup.com.

contribute to what employees know and, as a result, what they perceive. If the organization researches salary levels and concludes that it is paying its employees generously, it should communicate this. If the employees do not know what the organization learned from its research, they may reach an entirely different conclusion about their pay. For example, to slow rapid growth in the wages it pays to U.S. workers, Toyota has shifted from using U.S. auto industry wages as its standard. The company now compares its wages with the prevailing wages in the state where each plant is located. Toyota has to educate its employees about this change and convince them that it is a fair way to compare wages.[16]

Employers must also recognize that employees know much more about what other employers pay now than they did before the Internet became popular. In the past, when gathering wage and salary data was expensive and difficult, employers had more leeway in negotiating with individual employees. Today's employees can go to websites like jobstar.org or salary.com to find hundreds of links to wage and salary data. For a fee, executive search firms such as Korn/Ferry provide data. Resources like these give employees information about what other workers are earning, along with the expectation that information will be shared. This means employers will face increased pressure to clearly explain their pay policies.

Managers play the most significant role in communication because they interact with their employees each day (see the "Best Practices" box for a positive example). The HR department should prepare them to explain why the organization's pay structure is designed as it is and to judge whether employee concerns about the structure indicate a need for change. A common issue is whether to reclassify a job because its content has changed. If an employee takes on more responsibility, the employee will often ask the manager for help in seeking more pay for the job.

Job Structure: Relative Value of Jobs

LO5 Explain how organizations design pay structures related to jobs.

Along with market forces and principles of fairness, organizations consider the relative contribution each job should make to the organization's overall performance. In general, an organization's top executives have a great impact on the organization's performance, so they tend to be paid much more than entry-level workers. Executives at the same level of the organization—for example, the vice president of marketing and the vice president of information systems—tend to be paid similar amounts. Creation of a pay structure requires that the organization develop an internal structure showing the relative contribution of its various jobs.

One typical way of doing this is with a **job evaluation,** an administrative procedure for measuring the relative worth of the organization's jobs. Usually, the organization does this by assembling and training a job evaluation committee, consisting of people familiar with the jobs to be evaluated. The committee often includes a human resource specialist and, if its budget permits, may hire an outside consultant.

Job Evaluation
An administrative procedure for measuring the relative internal worth of the organization's jobs.

To conduct a job evaluation, the committee identifies each job's *compensable factors*, meaning the characteristics of a job that the organization values and chooses to pay for. As shown in Table 11.1, an organization might value the experience and education of people performing computer-related jobs, as well as the complexity of those jobs. Other compensable factors might include working conditions and responsibility. Based on the job attributes defined by job analysis (discussed in Chapter 4), the jobs are rated for each factor. The rater assigns each factor a certain number of points, giving more points to factors when they are considered more important and when the job requires a high level of that factor. Often the number of points comes from one of the *point manuals* published by trade groups and management consultants. If necessary, the organization can adapt the scores in the point manual to the organization's situation or even develop its own point manual. As in the example in Table 11.1, the scores for each factor are totaled to arrive at an overall evaluation for each job.

Table 11.1

Job Evaluation of Three Jobs with Three Factors

| | COMPENSABLE FACTORS | | | |
JOB TITLE	EXPERIENCE	EDUCATION	COMPLEXITY	TOTAL
Computer operator	40	30	40	110
Computer programmer	40	50	65	155
Systems analyst	65	60	85	210

Popular actors, such as Leonardo DiCaprio, are evaluated by their impact on box office receipts and other revenues and then compensated based on these evaluations.

Job evaluations provide the basis for decisions about relative internal worth. According to the sample assessments in Table 11.1, the job of systems analyst is worth almost twice as much to this organization as the job of computer operator. Therefore, the organization would be willing to pay almost twice as much for the work of a systems analyst as it would for the work of a computer operator.

The organization may limit its pay survey to jobs evaluated as *key jobs*. These are jobs that have relatively stable content and are common among many organizations, so it is possible to obtain survey data about what people earn in these jobs. Organizations can make the process of creating a pay structure more practical by defining key jobs. Research for creating the pay structure is limited to the key jobs that play a significant role in the organization. Pay for the key jobs can be based on survey data, and pay for the organization's other jobs can be based on the organization's job structure. A job with a higher evaluation score than a particular key job would receive higher pay than that key job.

Pay Structure: Putting It All Together

As we described in the first section of this chapter, the pay structure reflects decisions about how much to pay (pay level) and the relative value of each job (job structure). The organization's pay structure should reflect what the organization knows about market forces, as well as its own unique goals and the relative contribution of each job to achieving the goals. By balancing this external and internal information, the organization's goal is to set levels of pay that employees will consider equitable and motivating. Organizations typically apply the information by establishing some combination of pay rates, pay grades, and pay ranges. Within this structure, they may state the pay in terms of a rate per hour, commonly called an **hourly wage;** a rate of pay for each unit produced, known as a **piecework rate;** or a rate of pay per month or year, called a **salary.**

Hourly Wage
Rate of pay for each hour worked.

Piecework Rate
Rate of pay for each unit produced.

Salary
Rate of pay for each week, month, or year worked.

Pay Policy Line
A graphed line showing the mathematical relationship between job evaluation points and pay rate.

Pay Rates

If the organization's main concern is to match what people are earning in comparable jobs, the organization can base pay directly on market research into as many of its key jobs as possible. To do this, the organization looks for survey data for each job title. If it finds data from more than one survey, it must weight the results based on their quality and relevance. The final number represents what the competition pays. In light of that knowledge, the organization decides what it will pay for the job.

The next step is to determine salaries for the nonkey jobs, for which the organization has no survey data. Instead, the person developing the pay structure creates a graph like the one in Figure 11.4. The vertical axis shows a range of possible pay rates, and the horizontal axis measures the points from the job evaluation. The analyst plots points according to the job evaluation and pay rate for each key job. Finally, the analyst fits a line, called a **pay policy line,** to the points plotted. (This can be done statistically on a computer, using a procedure called regression analysis.)

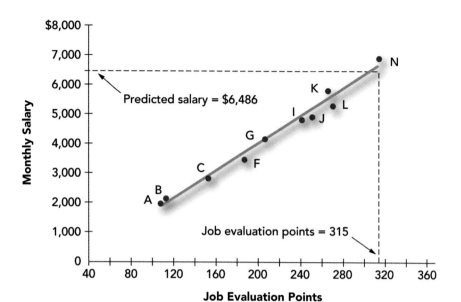

Figure 11.4

Pay Policy Lines

Mathematically, this line shows the relationship between job evaluation and rate of pay. Thus, the line slopes upward from left to right, and if higher-level jobs are especially valuable to the organization, the line may curve upward to indicate even greater pay for high-level jobs. Using this line, the analyst can estimate the market pay level for a given job evaluation. Looking at the graph gives approximate numbers, or the regression analysis will provide an equation for calculating the rate of pay. For example, using the pay policy line in Figure 11.4, a job with 315 evaluation points would have a predicted salary of $6,486 per month.

The pay policy line reflects the pay structure in the market, which does not always match rates in the organization (see key job F in Figure 11.4). Survey data may show that people in certain jobs are actually earning significantly more or less than the amount shown on the pay policy line. For example, some kinds of expertise are in short supply. People with that expertise can command higher salaries, because they can easily leave one employer to get higher pay somewhere else. Suppose, in contrast, that local businesses have laid off many warehouse employees. Because so many of these workers are looking for jobs, organizations may be able to pay them less than the rate that job evaluation points would suggest.

When job structure and market data conflict in these ways, organizations have to decide on a way to resolve the two. One approach is to stick to the job evaluations and pay according to the employees' worth to the organization. Organizations that do so will be paying more or less than they have to, so they will likely have more difficulty competing for customers or employees. A way to moderate this approach is to consider the importance of each position to the organization's goals.[17] If a position is critical for meeting the organization's goals, paying more than competitors pay may be worthwhile.

At the other extreme, the organization could base pay entirely on market forces. However, this approach also has some practical drawbacks. One is that employees may conclude that pay rates are unfair. Two vice presidents or two supervisors will expect to receive similar pay because their responsibilities are similar. If the differences between their pay are large, because of different market rates, the lower-paid employee will likely be dissatisfied. Also, if the organization's development plans include rotating managers through different assignments, the managers will be reluctant to participate if managers in some departments receive lower pay. Organizations therefore must weigh all the objectives of their pay structure to arrive at suitable rates.

Pay Grades

Pay Grades
Sets of jobs having similar worth or content, grouped together to establish rates of pay.

A large organization could have hundreds or even thousands of different jobs. Setting a pay rate for each job would be extremely complex. Therefore, many organizations group jobs into **pay grades**—sets of jobs having similar worth or content, grouped together to establish rates of pay. For example, the organization could establish five pay grades, with the same pay available to employees holding any job within the same grade.

A drawback of pay grades is that grouping jobs will result in rates of pay for individual jobs that do not precisely match the levels specified by the market and the organization's job structure. Suppose, for example, that the organization groups together its senior accountants (with a job evaluation of 255 points) and its senior systems analysts (with a job evaluation of 270 points). Surveys might show that the market rate of pay for systems analysts is higher than that for accountants. In addition, the job evaluations give more points to systems analysts. Even so, for simplicity's sake, the organization pays the same rate for the two jobs because they are in the same pay grade. The organization would have to pay more than the market requires for accountants or pay less than the market rate for systems analysts (so it would probably have difficulty recruiting and retaining them).

Pay Ranges

Pay Range
A set of possible pay rates defined by a minimum, maximum, and midpoint of pay for employees holding a particular job or a job within a particular pay grade.

Usually, organizations want some flexibility in setting pay for individual jobs. They want to be able to pay the most valuable employees the highest amounts and to give rewards for performance, as described in the next chapter. Flexibility also helps the organization balance conflicting information from market surveys and job evaluations. Therefore, pay structure usually includes a **pay range** for each job or pay grade. In other words, the organization establishes a minimum, maximum, and midpoint of pay for employees holding a particular job or a job within a particular pay grade. Employees holding the same job may receive somewhat different pay, depending on where their pay falls within the range.

A typical approach is to use the market rate or the pay policy line as the midpoint of a range for the job or pay grade. The minimum and maximum values for the range may also be based on market surveys of those amounts. Pay ranges are most common for white-collar jobs and for jobs that are not covered by union contracts. Figure 11.5 shows an example of pay ranges based on the pay policy line in Figure 11.4. Notice that the jobs are grouped into five pay grades, each with its own pay range. In this example, the range is widest for employees who are at higher levels in terms of their job evaluation points. That is because the performance of these higher-level employees will likely have more effect on the organization's performance, so the organization needs more latitude to reward them. For instance, as discussed earlier, the organization may want to select a higher point in the range to attract an employee who is more critical to achieving the organization's goals.

Usually pay ranges overlap somewhat, so that the highest pay in one grade is somewhat higher than the lowest pay in the next grade. Overlapping ranges gives the organization more flexibility in transferring employees among jobs, because transfers need not always involve a change in pay. On the other hand, the less overlap, the

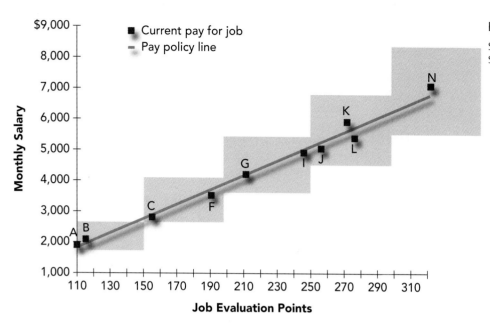

Figure 11.5

Sample Pay Grade Structure

more important it is to earn promotions in order to keep getting raises. Assuming the organization wants to motivate employees through promotions (and assuming enough opportunities for promotion are available), the organization will want to limit the overlap from one level to the next.

Pay Differentials

In some situations organizations adjust pay to reflect differences in working conditions or labor markets. For example, an organization may pay extra to employees who work the night shift, because night hours are less desirable for most workers. Similarly, organizations may pay extra to employees in locations where living expenses are higher. These adjustments are called **pay differentials.**

A survey of businesses in the United States found that almost three-quarters have a policy of providing pay differentials based on geographic location.[18] These differentials are intended as a way to treat employees fairly, without regard to where they work. The most common approach is to move an employee higher in the pay structure to compensate for higher living costs. For instance, the American Chamber of Commerce Research Association estimates that the cost of living in New York City is more than twice that of the average metropolitan area. An organization with employees in New York City and in an average U.S. city might pay its New York office manager substantially more than its office manager in the average city. This pay policy can become expensive for organizations that must operate in high-cost locations. Also, organizations need to handle the delicate issue of how to pay employees transferred to lower-cost areas.

Pay Differential
Adjustment to a pay rate to reflect differences in working conditions or labor markets.

Alternatives to Job-Based Pay

The traditional and most widely used approach to developing a pay structure focuses on setting pay for jobs or groups of jobs.[19] This emphasis on jobs has some limitations. The precise definition of a job's responsibilities can contribute to an attitude that some activities "are not in my job description," at the expense of flexibility,

LO6 Describe alternatives to job-based pay.

Night hours are less desirable for most workers. Therefore, some companies pay a differential for night work to compensate them.

Delayering
Reducing the number of levels in the organization's job structure.

Skill-Based Pay Systems
Pay structures that set pay according to the employees' levels of skill or knowledge and what they are capable of doing.

innovation, quality, and customer service. Also, the job structure's focus on higher pay for higher status can work against an effort at empowerment. Organizations may avoid change because it requires repeating the time-consuming process of creating job descriptions and related paperwork. Another change-related problem is that when the organization needs a new set of knowledge, skills, and abilities, the existing pay structure may be rewarding the wrong behaviors. Finally, a pay structure that rewards employees for winning promotions may discourage them from gaining valuable experience through lateral career moves.

Organizations have responded to these problems with a number of alternatives to job-based pay structures. Some organizations have found greater flexibility through **delayering,** or reducing the number of levels in the organization's job structure. By combining more assignments into a single layer, organizations give managers more flexibility in making assignments and awarding pay increases. These broader groupings often are called *broad bands.* In the 1990s, IBM changed from a pay structure with 5,000 job titles and 24 salary grades to one with 1,200 jobs and 10 bands. When IBM began using broad bands, it replaced its point-factor job evaluation system with an approach based on matching jobs to descriptions. Figure 11.6 shows descriptions of several job characteristics used by IBM. Job descriptions are assigned to the band whose characteristics best match those in the job description. Broad bands reduce the opportunities for promoting employees, so organizations that eliminate layers in their job descriptions must find other ways to reward employees.

Another way organizations have responded to the limitations of job-based pay has been to move away from the link to jobs and toward pay structures that reward employees based on their knowledge and skills.[20] **Skill-based pay systems** are pay structures that set pay according to the employees' level of skill or knowledge and what they are capable of doing. Paying for skills makes sense at organizations where changing technology requires employees to continually widen and deepen their knowledge. For example, modern machinery often requires that operators know how to program and monitor computers to perform a variety of tasks. Skill-based pay also supports efforts to empower employees and enrich jobs because it encourages employees to add to their knowledge so they can make decisions in many areas. In this way, skill-based pay helps organizations become more flexible and innovative. More generally, skill-based pay can encourage a climate of learning and adaptability and give employees a broader view of how the organization functions. These changes should help employees use their knowledge and ideas more productively. A field study of a manufacturing plant found that changing to a skill-based pay structure led to better quality and lower labor costs.[21]

Of course, skill-based pay has its own disadvantages.[22] It rewards employees for acquiring skills but does not provide a way to ensure that employees can use their new skills. The result may be that the organization is paying employees more for learning skills that the employer is not benefiting from. The challenge for HRM is to design work so that the work design and pay structure support one another. Also, if employees learn skills very quickly, they may reach the maximum pay level so quickly that it will become difficult to reward them appropriately. Skill-based pay does not necessarily provide an alternative to the bureaucracy and paperwork of traditional pay structures, because it requires records related to skills, training, and knowledge acquired.

Figure 11.6

IBM's New Job Evaluation Approach

Below is an abbreviated schematic illustration of the new—and simple—IBM job evaluation approach:

POSITION REFERENCE GUIDE

Band	Skills Required	Leadership/Contribution	Scope/Impact
1			
2			
3			
4			
5			
6			
7			
8			
9			
10			

Factors: Leadership/Contribution

Band 06: Understand the mission of the professional group and vision in own area of competence.

Band 07: Understand the departmental mission and vision.

Band 08: Understand departmental/functional mission and vision.

Band 09: Has vision of functional or unit mission.

Band 10: Has vision of overall strategies.

Both the bands and the approach are global. In the U.S., bands 1–5 are nonexempt; bands 6–10 are exempt. Each cell in the table contains descriptive language about key job characteristics. Position descriptions are compared to the chart and assigned to bands on a "best fit" basis. There are no points or scoring mechanisms. Managers assign employees to bands by selecting a position description that most closely resembles the work being done by an employee using an online position description library.

That's it!

SOURCE: From A. S. Richter, "Paying the People in Black at Big Blue," *Compensation and Benefits Review*, May–June 1998, pp. 51–59. Copyright © 1998 by Sage Publications, Inc. Reproduced with permission of Sage Publications via Copyright Clearance Center.

Finally, gathering market data about skill-based pay is difficult, because most wage and salary surveys are job-based.

Pay Structure and Actual Pay

L07 Summarize how to ensure that pay is actually in line with the pay structure.

Usually, the human resource department is responsible for establishing the organization's pay structure. But building a structure is not the end of the organization's decisions about pay structure. The structure represents the organization's policy, but what the organization actually does may be different. As part of its management responsibility, the HR department therefore should compare actual pay to the pay structure, making sure that policies and practices match.

A common way to do this is to measure a *compa-ratio*, the ratio of average pay to the midpoint of the pay range. Figure 11.7 shows an example. Assuming the organization has pay grades, the organization would find a compa-ratio for each pay grade: the average paid to all employees in the pay grade divided by the midpoint for the pay grade. If the average equals the midpoint, the compa-ratio is 1. More often, the compa-ratio is somewhat above 1 (meaning the average pay is above the midpoint for the pay grade) or below 1 (meaning the average pay is below the midpoint).

Figure 11.7

Finding a Compa-Ratio

Pay Grade: 1
Midpoint of Range: $2,175 per month

Salaries of Employees in Pay Grade

Employee 1	$2,306
Employee 2	$2,066
Employee 3	$2,523
Employee 4	$2,414

Compa-Ratio

$$\frac{\text{Average}}{\text{Midpoint}} = \frac{\$2,327.25}{\$2,175.00} = 1.07$$

Average Salary of Employees
$2,306 + $2,066 + $2,523 + $2,414 = $9,309
$9,309 ÷ 4 = $2,327.25

Assuming that the pay structure is well planned to support the organization's goals, the compa-ratios should be close to 1. A compa-ratio greater than 1 suggests that the organization is paying more than planned for human resources and may have difficulty keeping costs under control. A compa-ratio less than 1 suggests that the organization is underpaying for human resources relative to its target and may have difficulty attracting and keeping qualified employees. When compa-ratios are more or less than 1, the numbers signal a need for the HR department to work with managers to identify whether to adjust the pay structure or the organization's pay practices. The compa-ratios may indicate that the pay structure no longer reflects market rates of pay. Or maybe performance appraisals need to be more accurate, as discussed in Chapter 8.

Current Issues Involving Pay Structure

LO8 Discuss issues related to paying employees serving in the military and paying executives.

An organization's policies regarding pay structure greatly influence employees' and even the general public's opinions about the organization. Issues affecting pay structure therefore can hurt or help the organization's reputation and ability to recruit, motivate, and keep employees. Recent issues related to pay structure include decisions about paying employees on active military duty and decisions about how much to pay the organization's top executives.

Pay during Military Duty

focus on *social responsibility*

As we noted in Chapter 3, the Uniformed Services Employment and Reemployment Rights Act (USERRA) requires employers to make jobs available to their workers when they return after fulfilling military duties for up to five years. During the time these employees are performing their military service, the employer faces decisions related to paying these people. The armed services pay service members during their time of duty, but military pay often falls short of what they would earn in their civilian jobs. Some employers have chosen to support their employees by paying the difference between their military and civilian earnings for extended periods. First Data, which processes payments made with credit and debit cards, provides this type of differential pay to its employees during military deployment. The company also continues medical and life insurance benefits to employees serving in the military and their families. Besides providing this compensation-related support, First Data encourages its employees to support the troops with care packages and volunteer services at veterans' hospitals.[23]

Policies to make up the difference between military pay and civilian pay are costly. The employer is paying employees while they are not working for the organization, and it may have to hire temporary employees as well. This challenge has posed a significant hardship on some employers since 2002, as hundreds of thousands of Reservists and National Guard members have been mobilized. Even so, as the nation copes with this challenge, hundreds of employers have decided that maintaining positive relations with employees—and the goodwill of the American public—makes the expense worthwhile.

Pay for Executives

The media have drawn public attention to the issue of executive pay. The issue attracts notice because of the very high pay that the top executives of major U.S. companies have received in recent years. In recent years, the total compensation paid to executives of large companies was typically more than $6 million, of which about $2.5 million was in the form of salary plus bonus. Interestingly, at the five companies that had the highest shareholder returns in 2006, the median compensation was less than $5 million, and at the five companies with the lowest shareholder returns, CEOs earned more than $12 million.[24] Notice, however, that as shown in Figure 11.8, only a small share of the average compensation paid to CEOs is in the form of a salary. Most CEO compensation takes the form of performance-related pay, such as bonuses and stock; this variable pay is discussed in the next chapter.

Although these high amounts apply to only a small proportion of the total work-force, the issue of executive pay is relevant to pay structure in terms of equity theory. As we discussed earlier in the chapter, employees draw conclusions about the fairness of pay by making comparisons among employees' inputs and outcomes. By many comparisons, U.S. CEOs' pay is high. For example, when CEO pay is compared with the pay of the organization's lowest-level employees, the resulting ratio has been on the rise for more than two decades, surpassing 500:1 at large U.S. corporations in 2007. That ratio is greater in the United States than in other developed nations and was higher in 2007 than in any period measured before then.[25] To assess the fairness of this ratio, equity theory would consider not only the size of executive pay relative to pay for other employees but also the amount the CEOs contribute. An organization's executives potentially have a much greater effect on the organization's performance than its lowest-paid employees have. But if they do not seem to contribute 500 times

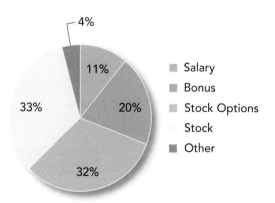

Figure 11.8

Average CEO Pay in S&P 500 Companies

SOURCE: Data for fiscal year 2008 from Edward E. Lawler III, "Fixing Executive Compensation: Right Time, Wrong Approach," *Chief Executive,* May/June 2009, pp. 30–41.

more, employees will see the compensation as unfair. Likewise, if CEOs in the United States don't contribute more to their organization than CEOs in other countries do, the difference would be perceived as unfair.

Top executives help to set the tone or culture of the organization, and employees at all levels are affected by behavior at the top. As a result, the equity of executive pay can affect more employees than, say, equity among warehouse workers or sales clerks. Recognizing the impact of his pay on his employees (and investors), John Mackey, founder and CEO of Whole Foods, reacted to poor financial results in 2007 by cutting his salary to $1 and taking no bonus or stock options. He donated his remaining compensation (from a previous bonus plan) to a charity, the Global Animal Partnership. Mackey has blamed the big pay gap between executives and employees on poor performance by demoralized workers.[26]

One study that investigated this issue compared the pay of rank-and-file employees and executives in various business units.[27] In business units where the difference in pay was greater, customer satisfaction was lower. The researchers speculated that employees thought pay was inequitable and adjusted their behavior to provide lower inputs by putting forth less effort to satisfy customers. To avoid this type of situation, organizations need to plan not only *how much* to pay managers and executives, but also *how* to pay them. In the next chapter, we will explore many of the options available.

thinking ethically

CAN THE BURDEN OF CUTBACKS BE SHARED EQUITABLY?

The downturn in the construction industry took a heavy toll on Aquapoint, a company based in New Bedford, Massachusetts, that makes systems for wastewater treatment. As builders delayed construction of new housing developments, revenues began to slow. When a big account, a retirement community, lost bank financing, Aquapoint's management knew the company wouldn't have enough cash to pay its bills.

Some companies might start with layoffs or pay cuts for employees, but Aquapoint's leaders thought they should share the pain. The top three executives cut their pay by half. Then they asked employees to accept a 10 percent pay cut. The next months were a struggle, but management thought the company would prosper as soon as the economy began to improve. They didn't want to lose valuable employees just before the next surge in business. For a few months, the executives cut

their pay again, down to zero. As the company passed the worst point, two of the executives began to work for 25 percent of their pay, and the executives hope they can eventually make up for the lost salaries with a bonus.

Questions

1. In your opinion, how fair was this approach to cutting pay when times got difficult at Aquapoint? Explain your reasoning.
2. As business improves, what approach should the company follow to restore the pay of the executives and the employees? Why?
3. How can Aquapoint ensure that its employees appreciate the leaders' willingness to share the pain of the recent economic downturn? Why is it important for employees to witness management's commitment to ethical conduct?

SOURCE: Based on Riva Richmond, "How to Cut Payroll Costs without Layoffs," *BusinessWeek*, April 3, 2009.

SUMMARY

LO1 Identify the kinds of decisions involved in establishing a pay structure.

Organizations make decisions to define a job structure, or relative pay for different jobs within

the organization. They establish relative pay for different functions and different levels of responsibility for each function. Organizations also must establish pay levels, or the average paid for the different jobs. These decisions are based on the organization's goals, market data, legal requirements, and principles of fairness. Together, job structure and pay level establish a pay structure policy.

LO2   Summarize legal requirements for pay policies.

To meet the standard of equal employment opportunity, employers must provide equal pay for equal work, regardless of an employee's age, race, sex, or other protected status. Differences in pay must relate to factors such as a person's qualifications or market levels of pay. Under the Fair Labor Standards Act (FLSA), the employer must pay at least the minimum wage established by law. Some state and local governments have established higher minimum wages. The FLSA also requires overtime pay—at one and a half times the employee's regular pay rate, including bonuses—for hours worked beyond 40 in each week. Managers, professionals, and outside salespersons are exempt from the overtime pay requirement. Employers must meet FLSA requirements concerning child labor. Federal contractors also must meet requirements to pay at least the prevailing wage in the area where their employees work.

LO3   Discuss how economic forces influence decisions about pay.

To remain competitive, employers must meet the demands of product and labor markets. Product markets seek to buy at the lowest price, so organizations must limit their costs as much as possible. In this way, product markets place an upper limit on the pay an employer can afford to offer. Labor markets consist of workers who want to earn as much as possible. To attract and keep workers, employers must pay at least the going rate in their labor markets. Organizations make decisions about whether to pay at, above, or below the pay rate set by these market forces. Paying above the market rate may make the organization less competitive in product markets but give it an advantage in labor markets. The organization benefits only if it can attract the best candidates and provide the systems that motivate and enable them to do their best work. Organizations that pay below the market rate need creative practices for recruiting and training workers so that they can find and keep enough qualified people.

LO4   Describe how employees evaluate the fairness of a pay structure.

According to equity theory, employees think of their pay relative to their inputs, such as training, experience, and effort. To decide whether their pay is equitable, they compare their outcome (pay)/input ratio with other people's outcome/input ratios. Employees make these comparisons with people doing the same job in other organizations and with people doing the same or different jobs in the same organization. If employees conclude that their outcome/input ratio is less than the comparison person's, they conclude that their pay is unfair and may engage in behaviors to create a situation they think is fair.

LO5   Explain how organizations design pay structures related to jobs.

Organizations typically begin with a job evaluation to measure the relative worth of their jobs. A job evaluation committee identifies each job's compensable factors and rates each factor. The committee may use a point manual to assign an appropriate number of points to each job. The committee can research market pay levels for key jobs, then identify appropriate rates of pay for other jobs, based on their number of points relative to the key jobs. The organization can do this with a pay policy line, which plots a salary for each job. The organization can combine jobs into several groups, called pay grades. For each pay grade or job, the organization typically establishes a pay range, using the market rate or pay policy line as the midpoint. Differences in working conditions or labor markets sometimes call for the use of pay differentials to adjust pay levels.

LO6   Describe alternatives to job-based pay.

To obtain more flexibility, organizations may reduce the levels in the organization's job structure. This process of delayering creates broad bands of jobs with a pay range for each. Other organizations reward employees according to their knowledge and skills. They establish skill-based pay systems, or structures that set pay according to the employees' level of knowledge and what they are capable of doing. This encourages employees to be more flexible and adapt to changing technology. However, if the organization does not also provide systems in which employees can apply new skills, it may be paying them for skills they do not actually use.

LO7   Summarize how to ensure that pay is actually in line with the pay structure.

The human resource department should routinely compare actual pay with the pay structure to see that policies and practices match. A common way to do this is to measure a compa-ratio for each job or pay grade. The compa-ratio is the ratio of average pay to the midpoint of the pay range. Assuming the pay structure supports the organization's goals, the compa-ratios should be close to 1. When compa-ratios are more or less than 1, the HR department should work with managers to identify whether to adjust the pay structure or the organization's pay practices.

LO8 Discuss issues related to paying employees serving in the military and paying executives.

The Uniformed Services Employment and Reemployment Rights Act requires employers to make jobs available to any of their employees who leave to fulfill military duties for up to five years. While these employees are performing their military service, many are earning far less. To demonstrate their commitment to these employees and to earn the public's goodwill, many companies pay the difference between their military and civilian earnings, even though this policy is costly. Executive pay has drawn public scrutiny because top executive pay is much higher than average workers' pay. The great difference is an issue in terms of equity theory. Chief executive officers have an extremely large impact on the organization's performance, but critics complain that when performance falters, executive pay does not decline as fast as the organization's profits or stock price. Top executives help to set the organization's tone or culture, and employees at all levels are affected by the behavior of the people at the top. Therefore, employees' opinions about the equity of executive pay can have a large effect on the organization's performance.

KEY TERMS

benchmarking, p. 335

delayering, p. 344

exempt employees, p. 331

Fair Labor Standards Act (FLSA), p. 330

hourly wage, p. 340

job evaluation, p. 339

job structure, p. 327

minimum wage, p. 330

nonexempt employees, p. 331

pay differential, p. 343

pay grades, p. 342

pay level, p. 327

pay policy line, p. 340

pay range, p. 342

pay structure, p. 327

piecework rate, p. 340

salary, p. 340

skill-based pay systems, p. 344

REVIEW AND DISCUSSION QUESTIONS

1. In setting up a pay structure, what legal requirements must an organization meet? Which of these do you think would be most challenging for a small start-up business? Why?

2. In gathering data for its pay policies, what product markets would a city's hospital want to use as a basis for comparison? What labor markets would be relevant? How might the labor markets for surgeons be different from the labor markets for nursing aides?

3. Why might an organization choose to pay employees more than the market rate? Why might it choose to pay less? What are the consequences of paying more or less than the market rate?

4. Suppose you work in the HR department of a manufacturing company that is planning to enrich jobs by having production workers work in teams and rotate through various jobs. The pay structure will have to be adjusted to fit this new work design. How would you expect the employees to evaluate the fairness of their pay in their redesigned jobs? In terms of equity theory, what comparisons would they be likely to make?

5. Summarize the way organizations use information about jobs as a basis for a pay structure.

6. Imagine that you manage human resources for a small business. You have recently prepared a report on the market rate of pay for salespeople, and the company's owner says the market rate is too high. The company cannot afford this level of pay, and furthermore, paying that much would cause salespeople to earn more than most of the company's managers. Suggest three possible measures the company might take to help resolve this conflict.

7. What are the advantages of establishing pay ranges, rather than specific pay levels, for each job? What are the drawbacks of this approach?

8. Suppose the company in Question 1 wants to establish a skills-based pay structure. What would be some advantages of this approach? List the issues the company should be prepared to address in setting up this system. Consider the kinds of information you will need and the ways employees may react to the new pay structure.

9. Why do some employers subsidize the pay of military reserve members called up to active duty? If the military instead paid these people the wage they command in the civilian market (that is, the salary they earn at their regular jobs), who would bear the cost? When neither the reserve members' employers nor the military pays reserve members their civilian wage, reserve members and their families bear the cost. In your opinion, who *should* bear this cost—employers, taxpayers, or service members (or someone else)?

10. Do you think U.S. companies pay their chief executives too much? Why or why not?

BUSINESSWEEK CASE

BusinessWeek Law Firms Slash First-Year Pay

Law firms including Cravath, Swaine & Moore LLP and Skadden, Arps, Slate, Meagher & Flom LLP cut year-end bonuses for first-year lawyers by as much as 71 percent, part of a plan to keep client costs down and ride out a recession that has forced structural changes in the industry. Bonuses dropped for first-year associates at many top-tier New York firms while staying the same or increasing for more experienced associates. Bonus reductions, along with overall pay cuts, signal a diminished role for junior lawyers at the larger U.S. firms, said consultant Bruce MacEwen.

The industrywide move to cut pay is "reflecting, frankly, the low value clients place on junior associates," MacEwen, who is based in New York, said in a phone interview.

Facing a slowdown in work due to the financial crisis, law firms fired thousands of associates this year and last, forced new hires to delay starting dates and cut hours in exchange for reduced salaries. Demand for legal services dropped 6.8 percent in the first nine months of 2009 compared with [2008], according to Citi Private Bank.

New York firms including Cleary Gottlieb Steen & Hamilton LLP, Sullivan & Cromwell LLP, Cravath, and Skadden Arps cut seniority-based bonuses from $17,500 to $5,000 for first-year associates. Other firms, such as San Francisco–based Morrison & Foerster LLP, Reed Smith LLP in Pittsburgh, and DLA Piper LLP in Chicago, cut starting salaries for first-year associates from $160,000 to as low as $130,000 this year. Firms in cities including New York, Washington, and San Francisco had adopted $160,000 as the industry standard beginning in January 2007.

Cleary's managing partner, Mark Walker, said the cuts aren't a reflection on the value of young associates at his firm. The best are traditionally offered partnerships after spending eight years as salaried associates. "The young lawyers today are the senior lawyers five years from now," Walker said.

Jeffrey Grossman, of the Legal Specialty Group at Well Fargo & Co., said U.S. law firms are cutting associate pay to temper their decline in profitability. Even partners are taking home less, he said.

Today's economic justification, however, may reap rewards for law firm bottom lines tomorrow when revenue increases. "It will be a future benefit," said Grossman. "It will change the cost structure for future years."

An additional consideration in paring pay, the law firm consultants said, is the need to address increased push-back from corporate clients seeking reduced hourly billing rates. Rates for the least experienced attorneys typically range from $250 to $350 an hour, MacEwen said, spurring some clients to complain they are paying top dollar for the training of young lawyers. The perception has existed for years and "bubbled to the surface" during the recession, Grossman said.

The bigger firms—which often move as a bloc in setting pay—still recognize they need to nurture top young lawyers. As a result, Grossman said, some have reconfigured compensation to reward high performance.

Orrick, Herrington & Sutcliffe LLP, based in San Francisco, this month said it would eliminate bonuses for first-year associates, while keeping salaries the same. It instituted a new system in which they get raises based on performance rather than seniority. The changes were made to align pay with performance and client needs, said Orrick CEO Ralph Baxter.

SOURCE: Excerpted from Carlyn Kolker, "Law Firms Slash First-Year Pay," *BusinessWeek*, December 21, 2009, www.businessweek.com.

Questions

1. Based on the information given, what issues have law firms considered in their decisions about their pay structure? (See Figure 11.1 for a summary of issues.)

2. Use the Bureau of Labor Statistics wage query system (at www.bls.gov) to look up information about compensation paid to lawyers. Compare the data you gathered with the information about compensation given in this case.

3. How would you expect first-year lawyers to perceive the fairness of the pay decisions described in this case? How could the decisions be communicated so that lawyers in these firms will see their pay as fair?

Case: How Fog Creek Software Pays Developers

When Joel Spolsky and Michael Pryor founded Fog Creek Software, their vision was of a company run by people whose technical backgrounds meant they understood what really motivates programmers. The company would hire the best, make them comfortable, pay them well, and then get out of the way so they could create great products.

Early on, Spolsky and Pryor set out to develop a pay structure that would be consistent with the company's mission. They decided that the system should be so objective that there would be no questioning or judgment calls about which employee earns how much. And the results would be so objective and fair that there would be no incentive to be secretive about what any employee earns.

Like any computer pro, Spolsky went online for ideas. He discovered that Construx, a software consulting firm, had posted online an outline for measuring levels of the software profession. Using this as a starting point, Spolsky created a job structure for Fog Creek. The structure is straightforward: every employee is assigned to a level between 8 (summer interns) and 16 (chief executive officer). Assignment to a level is not a judgment call but is based on a formula incorporating the employee's experience, skills, and scope of responsibility.

- Experience is measured as the number of years of full-time experience in the field of the employee's job at Fog Creek, counting only years after the employee finished school. At any given level, every employee earns the same salary.
- Skills are defined with descriptive statements along a continuum. For example, at the lowest level is a programmer "learning the basic principles of software engineering" who needs close supervision. At the other extreme would be someone who makes a unique contribution—a programmer who "has consistently had major success during participation in all aspects of small and large projects."
- Scope of responsibility ranges from primarily supporting another employee to running multiple projects.

Based on this job structure, Spolsky created a chart that is used for assigning each employee to a level.

Spolsky also created a chart that indicates the base salary for each level, based on market salaries obtained from sources such as Salary.com and Glassdoor.com. Each employee earns the amount specified by the chart. Every year, the company's managers review each employee's work to see if the employee should be assigned to a new level. Every employee who is reassigned then earns the amount associated with the new level. Employees also earn a bonus based on the company's profits for the year.

Fog Creek's system has been challenged by the stiff competition for programmer talent. If the company paid extra to lure in new employees at a higher rate, the existing employees would demand a raise or see their treatment as unfair. Rather than expect employees to accept the "salary inversion" of newer employees earning more than their more-experienced colleagues, Fog Creek has responded to talent crunches by raising the salaries of all employees at a given level to make them as high as the going market rate for that level. Spolsky believes that this solution is expensive but essential for maintaining equity and keeping talent.

SOURCES: Joel Spolsky, "Why I Never Let Employees Negotiate a Raise," *Inc.*, April 2009, www.inc.com; and Fog Creek Software, "Careers" and "About the Company," corporate Web site, www.fogcreek.com, accessed April 21, 2010.

Questions

1. How well does Fog Creek Software's pay structure meet (a) the legal requirement of equal pay for equal work; (b) the conditions of product markets; and (c) the conditions of labor markets?
2. Joel Spolsky set out to create a pay structure that is objective. Based on the information given, how objective would you say Fog Creek's system is? What other qualities besides objectivity do you think Fog Creek's employees might care about?
3. Fog Creek is a small company with a few dozen technical employees. How might its pay structure need to change (if at all) if the company grows to hundreds of employees? Would these changes likely appeal to the employees?

IT'S A WRAP!   Mc Graw Hill **connect**

www.mhhe.com/noefund4e is your source for Reviewing, Applying, and Practicing the concepts you learned about in Chapter 11.

Review
- Chapter learning objectives

Application
- Manager's Hot Seat segment: "Negotiation: Thawing the Salary Freeze"
- Video case and quiz: "Gender Gap: Why Do Women Make Less than Men?"
- Self-Assessment: Test your expectation of salary brackets
- Web Exercise: Experiment with salary calculators
- Small-business case: Changing the Pay Level at Eight Crossings

Practice
- Chapter quiz

NOTES

1. Kellie Schmitt, "Luce Rethinks Associate Pay System," *Recorder,* January 14, 2008, downloaded from General Reference Center Gold, http://find.galegroup.com.

2. U.S. Census Bureau, American FactFinder, "Geographic Area Series: Economywide Key Statistics, 2007," 2007 Economic Census, release date April 13, 2010, http://factfinder.census.gov.

3. Bureau of Labor Statistics, "Women's Earnings as a Percentage of Men's, 2008," *The Editor's Desk,* October 14, 2009, http://data.bls.gov; and Bureau of Labor Statistics, "Earnings of Women and Men by Race and Ethnicity," *The Editor's Desk,* October 30, 2008, http://data.bls.gov.

4. B. Gerhart, "Gender Differences in Current and Starting Salaries: The Role of Performance, College Major, and Job Title," *Industrial and Labor Relations Review* 43 (1990), pp. 418–33; G. G. Cain, "The Economic Analysis of Labor Market Discrimination: A Survey," in *Handbook of Labor Economics,* eds. O. Ashenfelter and R. Layard (New York: North-Holland, 1986), pp. 694–785; and F. D. Blau and L. M. Kahn, "The Gender Pay Gap: Have Women Gone as Far as They Can?" *Academy of Management Perspectives,* February 2007, pp. 7–23.

5. S. L. Rynes and G. T. Milkovich, "Wage Surveys: Dispelling Some Myths about the 'Market Wage,'" *Personnel Psychology* 39 (1986), pp. 71–90; and G. T. Milkovich, J. M. Newman, and B. Gerhart, *Compensation,* 10th ed. (New York: McGraw-Hill/Irwin, 2010).

6. Mary Swanton, "Clock Work," *Inside Counsel,* March 2010, Business & Company Resource Center, http://galenet.galegroup.com.

7. M. M. Clark, "Step by Step," *HRMagazine,* February 2005, downloaded from Infotrac at http://web6.infotrac.galegroup.com.

8. U.S. Department of Labor, "Hours Restrictions" and "Prohibited Occupations for Nonagricultural Employees," *eLaws: Fair Labor Standards Act Advisor,* http://www.dol.gov/elaws/flsa.htm, accessed April 21, 2010; and U.S. Department of Labor, "Compliance Assistance: Employers," *YouthRules,* http://www.youthrules.dol.gov/employers/default.htm, accessed April 21, 2010.

9. J. McCracken, "Desperate to Cut Costs, Ford Gets Union's Help," *Wall Street Journal,* March 2, 2007; and J. Green, "GM UAW Savings Said to Be Double Ford's $500 Million," *Bloomberg.com,* March 11, 2009, www.bloomberg.com.

10. B. Gerhart and G. T. Milkovich, "Organizational Differences in Managerial Compensation and Financial Performance," *Academy of Management Journal* 33 (1990), pp. 663–91; and E. L. Groshen, "Why Do Wages Vary among Employers?" *Economic Review* 24 (1988), pp. 19–38.

11. W. F. Cascio, "The High Cost of Low Wages," *Harvard Business Review* 84 (December 2006), p. 23; and J. Chu and K. Rockwood, "CEO Interview: Costco's Jim Sinegal," *Fast Company,* October 13, 2008.

12. G. A. Akerlof, "Gift Exchange and Efficiency-Wage Theory: Four Views," *American Economic Review*

74 (1984), pp. 79–83; and J. L. Yellen, "Efficiency Wage Models of Unemployment," *American Economic Review* 74 (1984), pp. 200–5.

13. IOMA, "HR Uses Many Sources to Set Pay Levels, Salary Budgets," *Report on Salary Surveys*, October 2009, pp. 1, 5–7, available at www.ioma.com/hr.

14. J. S. Adams, "Inequity in Social Exchange," in *Advances in Experimental Social Psychology*, ed. L. Berkowitz (New York: Academic Press, 1965); P. S. Goodman, "An Examination of Referents Used in the Evaluation of Pay," *Organizational Behavior and Human Performance* 12 (1974), pp. 170–95; J. B. Miner," *Theories of Organizational Behavior* (Hinsdale, IL: Dryden Press, 1980); M. M. Harris, F. Anseel, and F. Lievens, "Keeping Up with the Joneses: A Field Study of the Relationships among Upward, Lateral, and Downward Comparisons and Pay Level Satisfaction," *Journal of Applied Psychology* 93, no. 3 (May 2008), pp. 665–73; and Gordon D. A. Brown, Jonathan Gardner, Andrew J. Oswald, and Jing Qian, "Does Wage Rank Affect Employees' Well-Being?" *Industrial Relations* 47, no. 3 (July 2008), p. 355.

15. P. Capelli and P. D. Sherer, "Assessing Worker Attitudes under a Two-Tier Wage Plan," *Industrial and Labor Relations Review* 43 (1990), pp. 225–44.

16. J. Roberson, "Toyota Sweats U.S. Labor Costs," *Detroit Free Press*, February 8, 2007.

17. J. P. Pfeffer and A. Davis-Blake, "Understanding Organizational Wage Structures: A Resource Dependence Approach," *Academy of Management Journal* 30 (1987), pp. 437–55.

18. Culpepper, "Geographic Pay Differential Practices," *eBulletin*, December 2009, www.culpepper.com.

19. This section draws freely on B. Gerhart and R. D. Bretz, "Employee Compensation," in *Organization and Management of Advanced Manufacturing*, eds. W. Karwowski and G. Salvendy (New York: Wiley, 1994), pp. 81–101.

20. E. E. Lawler III, *Strategic Pay* (San Francisco: Jossey-Bass, 1990); G. E. Ledford, "Paying for the Skills, Knowledge, Competencies of Knowledge Workers," *Compensation and Benefits Review*, July–August 1995, p. 55; G. Ledford, "Factors Affecting the Long-Term Success of Skill-Based Pay," *WorldatWork Journal*, First Quarter 2008, pp. 6–18; and E. C. Dierdorff and E. A. Surface, "If You Pay for Skills, Will They Learn? Skill Change and Maintenance under a Skill-Based Pay System," *Journal of Management* 34 (2008), pp. 721–43.

21. B. C. Murray and B. Gerhart, "An Empirical Analysis of a Skill-Based Pay Program and Plant Performance Outcomes," *Academy of Management Journal* 41, no. 1 (1998), pp. 68–78.

22. Ibid.; N. Gupta, D. Jenkins, and W. Curington, "Paying for Knowledge: Myths and Realities," *National Productivity Review*, Spring 1986, pp. 107–23; and J. D. Shaw, N. Gupta, A. Mitra, and G. E. Ledford, "Success and Survival of Skill-Based Pay Plans," *Journal of Management* 31 (2005), pp. 28–49.

23. "First Data Recognized for Exceptional Support of Military Employees and Families," *Investment Weekly News*, October 3, 2009, Business & Company Resource Center, http://galenet.galegroup.com.

24. Joann S. Lublin, "The Pace of Pay Gains: A Survey Overview," *Wall Street Journal*, April 9, 2007, http://online.wsj.com.

25. Edward E. Lawler III, "Fixing Executive Compensation: Right Time, Wrong Approach," *Chief Executive*, May/June 2009, pp. 30–41.

26. Courtney Rubin, "Whole Foods CEO Donates Half of Pay to Charity," *Inc.*, January 26, 2010, www.inc.com.

27. D. M. Cowherd and D. I. Levine, "Product Quality and Pay Equity between Lower-Level Employees and Top Management: An Investigation of Distributive Justice Theory," *Administrative Science Quarterly* 37 (1992), pp. 302–20.

Recognizing Employee Contributions with Pay

What Do I Need to Know?

After reading this chapter, you should be able to:

LO1 Discuss the connection between incentive pay and employee performance.

LO2 Describe how organizations recognize individual performance.

LO3 Identify ways to recognize group performance.

LO4 Explain how organizations link pay to their overall performance.

LO5 Describe how organizations combine incentive plans in a "balanced scorecard."

LO6 Summarize processes that can contribute to the success of incentive programs.

LO7 Discuss issues related to performance-based pay for executives.

Introduction

The 7,500 employees of Jamba Juice Company know how to earn more money. They know that their pay raises depend on how well they performed their jobs the previous year. Supervisors rank employees according to whether their performance was outstanding, above requirements, meeting requirements, or below requirements. Those in the top category receive the largest raises. Those rated as performing below requirements receive no raise at all, and they don't have a chance to earn a bonus. According to Russ Testa, Jamba Juice's vice president of human resources, this pay system is a practical matter of allocating the company's money to the company's best employees: "If you're devoting dollars to underperformers, that simply means you're taking away from your high performers."[1] Employees consider the process fair because they understand how their performance will be measured and how it will affect their pay.

The pay earned by each Jamba Juice employee depends on the starting pay for a particular job (the topic of the preceding chapter) and pay raises tied to the employee's performance. In this chapter we focus on using pay to recognize and reward employees' contributions to the organization's success. Employees' pay does not depend solely on the jobs they hold. Instead, organizations vary the amount paid according to differences in performance of the individual, group, or whole organization, as well as differences in employee qualities such as seniority and skills.[2]

Incentive Pay
Forms of pay linked to an employee's performance as an individual, group member, or organization member.

In contrast to decisions about pay structure, organizations have wide discretion in setting performance-related pay, called **incentive pay.** Organizations can tie incentive pay to individual performance, profits, or many other measures of success. They select incentives based on their costs, expected influence on performance, and fit with the organization's broader HR and company policies and goals. These decisions are significant. A study of 150 organizations found that the way organizations paid employees was strongly associated with their level of profitability.[3]

This chapter explores the choices available to organizations with regard to incentive pay. First, the chapter describes the link between pay and employee performance. Next, we discuss ways organizations provide a variety of pay incentives to individuals. The following two sections describe pay related to group and organizational performance. We then explore the organization's processes that can support the use of incentive pay. Finally, we discuss incentive pay for the organization's executives.

LO1 Discuss the connection between incentive pay and employee performance.

Incentive Pay

Along with wages and salaries, many organizations offer *incentive pay*—that is, pay specifically designed to energize, direct, or control employees' behavior. Incentive pay is influential because the amount paid is linked to certain predefined behaviors or outcomes. For example, as we will see in this chapter, an organization can pay a salesperson a *commission* for closing a sale, or the members of a production department can earn a *bonus* for meeting a monthly production goal. Usually, these payments are in addition to wages and salaries. Knowing they can earn extra money for closing sales or meeting departmental goals, the employees often try harder or get more creative than they might without the incentive pay. In addition, the policy of offering higher pay for higher performance may make an organization attractive to high performers when it is trying to recruit and retain these valuable employees.[4] For reasons such as these, the share of companies offering variable pay rose in less than two decades from about half of companies to 9 out of 10.[5]

For incentive pay to motivate employees to contribute to the organization's success, the pay plans must be well designed. In particular, effective plans meet the following requirements:

- Performance measures are linked to the organization's goals.
- Employees believe they can meet performance standards.
- The organization gives employees the resources they need to meet their goals.
- Employees value the rewards given.
- Employees believe the reward system is fair.
- The pay plan takes into account that employees may ignore any goals that are not rewarded.

The "HR How To" box provides some additional ideas for creating and implementing an effective incentive-pay plan even when resources are limited.

Since incentive pay is linked to particular outcomes or behaviors, the organization is encouraging employees to demonstrate those chosen outcomes and behaviors. As obvious as that may sound, the implications are more complicated. If incentive pay is extremely rewarding, employees may focus on only the performance measures rewarded under the plan and ignore measures that are not rewarded. Suppose an organization pays managers a bonus when employees are satisfied; this policy may interfere with other management goals. A manager who doesn't quite know how to inspire employees to do their best might be tempted to fall back on overly positive performance

HR How To

STRETCHING INCENTIVE-PAY DOLLARS

One advantage of incentive pay is that, because it is targeted to reinforcing desired behaviors and outcomes, there are ways to get a lot of benefits out of it even when budgets are tight. Here are some ideas for getting the most out of an incentive-pay plan:

- Be very clear about what behavior or outcomes you want to encourage. Many options are available, from delighting customers to preventing accidents to selling the products that have the biggest profit margins. Direct most or all of the incentive pay to rewarding performance on the measurements that will have the most impact on the organization's success.
- Set up objective ways to measure whether the individual or group earns the incentive, so that rewards don't become a popularity contest or lottery.

The measurement should include a minimum level of performance required for receiving part or all of the reward.

- Communicate with employees. Especially if money is tight, be honest about the company's resources. Invite ideas about what employees would appreciate receiving, so that you'll be spending on what matters most.
- Combine the forms of incentive pay with nonmonetary rewards such as thank-you notes and public recognition for group and individual accomplishments. In some cases, employees may be wowed by a chance to have breakfast with the boss or attend a meeting with a company expert.
- When delivering the reward, communicate what accomplishment led to the award, so

employees see the connection— and that they see that the company also notices what they have contributed.

- Consider giving managers a pool of money to use for granting bonuses when individuals or groups exhibit the desired performance or exceed objectives.
- Grant bonuses or other incentives frequently. Smaller payouts delivered more frequently can keep excitement higher for the same amount of money as the organization would have spent on an annual bonus.

Sources: "How to Reward Employees on a Budget," *Inc.*, April 19, 2010, www.inc.com; and "Try Two Bonus Tactics Suited for Tough Times," *HR Specialist: Compensation & Benefits,* March 2010, Business & Company Resource Center, http://galenet.galegroup.com.

appraisals, letting work slide to keep everyone happy. Similarly, many call centers pay employees based on how many calls they handle, as an incentive to work quickly and efficiently. However, speedy call handling does not necessarily foster good customer relationships. As we will see in this chapter, organizations may combine a number of incentives so employees do not focus on one measure to the exclusion of others.

Attitudes that influence the success of incentive pay include whether employees value the rewards and think the pay plan is fair. Some observers of today's workplace have found that young workers typically want frequent encouragement, and creative managers have developed incentives that get this type of worker excited. A beverage wholesaler, for example, began awarding its employees "points." For every routine and extra task involved in running the warehouse, employees earn points, and those points can be exchanged for extra pay or time off. Employees see a connection between hard work and immediate rewards (points), so they work harder. Similarly, a manager of an ad agency discovered that a young employee was so delighted to learn she had been awarded "extra points" for going above and beyond her usual duties that the agency began awarding points to all employees for beating deadlines and turning in exceptional work. The agency counts up the points and converts them into bonus pay.[6]

Although most, if not all, employees value pay, it is important to remember that earning money is not the only reason people try to do a good job. As we discuss in other chapters (see Chapters 4, 8, and 13), people also want interesting work, appreciation for their efforts, flexibility, and a sense of belonging to the work group—not to mention the inner satisfaction of work well done. Therefore, a complete plan for motivating and compensating employees has many components, from pay to work design to developing managers so they can exercise positive leadership.

With regard to the fairness of incentive pay, the preceding chapter described equity theory, which explains how employees form judgments about the fairness of a pay structure. The same process applies to judgments about incentive pay. In general, employees compare their efforts and rewards with other employees', considering a plan to be fair when the rewards are distributed according to what the employees contribute.

The remainder of this chapter identifies elements of incentive pay systems. We consider each option's strengths and limitations with regard to these principles. The many kinds of incentive pay fall into three broad categories: incentives linked to individual, group, or organizational performance. Choices from these categories should consider not only their strengths and weaknesses, but also their fit with the organization's goals. The choice of incentive pay may affect not only the level of motivation but also the kinds of employees who are attracted to and stay with the organization. For example, there is some evidence that organizations with team-based rewards will tend to attract employees who are more team-oriented, while rewards tied to individual performance make an organization more attractive to those who think and act independently, as individuals.[7] Given the potential impact, organizations not only should weigh the strengths and weaknesses in selecting types of incentive pay but also should measure the results of these programs (see "Did You Know?").

LO2 Describe how organizations recognize individual performance.

Pay for Individual Performance

Organizations may reward individual performance with a variety of incentives:

- Piecework rates
- Standard hour plans
- Merit pay
- Individual bonuses
- Sales commissions

Piecework Rates

Piecework Rate
A wage based on the amount workers produce.

Straight Piecework Plan
Incentive pay in which the employer pays the same rate per piece, no matter how much the worker produces.

As an incentive to work efficiently, some organizations pay production workers a **piecework rate,** a wage based on the amount they produce. The amount paid per unit is set at a level that rewards employees for above-average production volume. For example, suppose that on average, assemblers can finish 10 components in an hour. If the organization wants to pay its average assemblers $8 per hour, it can pay a piecework rate of $8/hour divided by 10 components/hour, or $.80 per component. An assembler who produces the average of 10 components per hour earns an amount equal to $8 per hour. An assembler who produces 12 components in an hour would earn $.80 × 12, or $9.60 each hour. This is an example of a **straight piecework plan,** because the employer pays the same rate per piece, no matter how much the worker produces.

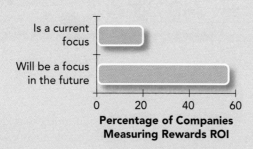
A variation on straight piecework is **differential piece rates** (also called *rising* and *falling differentials*), in which the piece rate depends on the amount produced. If the worker produces more than the standard output, the piece rate is higher. If the worker produces at or below the standard, the amount paid per piece is lower. In the preceding example, the differential piece rate could be $1 per component for components exceeding 12 per hour and $.80 per component for up to 12 components per hour.

In one study, the use of piece rates increased production output by 30 percent—more than any other motivational device evaluated.[8] An obvious advantage of piece rates is the direct link between how much work the employee does and the amount the employee earns. This type of pay is easy to understand and seems fair to many people, if they think the production standard is reasonable. In spite of their advantages, piece rates are relatively rare for several reasons.[9] Most jobs, including those of managers, have no physical output, so it is hard to develop an appropriate performance measure. This type of incentive is most suited for very routine, standardized jobs with output that is easy to measure. For complex jobs or jobs with hard-to-measure outputs, piecework plans do not apply very well. Also, unless a plan is well designed to include performance standards, it may not reward employees for focusing on quality or customer satisfaction if it interferes with the day's output. In Figure 12.1, the employees quickly realize they can earn huge bonuses by writing software "bugs" and then fixing them, while writing bug-free software affords no chance to earn bonuses. More seriously, a bonus based on number of faucets produced gives production workers no incentive to stop a manufacturing line to correct a quality-control problem. Production-oriented goals may do nothing to encourage employees to learn new skills or cooperate with others. Therefore, individual incentives such as these may be a poor incentive in an organization that wants to encourage teamwork. They may not be helpful in an organization with complex jobs, employee empowerment, and team-based problem solving.

Differential Piece Rates
Incentive pay in which the piece rate is higher when a greater amount is produced.

Figure 12.1

How Incentives Sometimes "Work"

SOURCE: DILBERT: © Scott Adams/Dist. By United Feature Syndicate, Inc.

Standard Hour Plans

Standard Hour Plan
An incentive plan that pays workers extra for work done in less than a preset "standard time."

Another quantity-oriented incentive for production workers is the **standard hour plan,** an incentive plan that pays workers extra for work done in less than a preset "standard time." The organization determines a standard time to complete a task, such as tuning up a car engine. If the mechanic completes the work in less than the standard time, the mechanic receives an amount of pay equal to the wage for the full standard time. Suppose the standard time for tuning up an engine is 2 hours. If the mechanic finishes a tune-up in 1½ hours, the mechanic earns 2 hours' worth of pay in 1½ hours. Working that fast over the course of a week could add significantly to the mechanic's pay.

In terms of their pros and cons, standard hour plans are much like piecework plans. They encourage employees to work as fast as they can, but not necessarily to care about quality or customer service. Also, they only succeed if employees want the extra money more than they want to work at a pace that feels comfortable.

Merit Pay

Merit Pay
A system of linking pay increases to ratings on performance appraisals.

Almost all organizations have established some program of **merit pay**—a system of linking pay increases to ratings on performance appraisals. (Chapter 8 described the content and use of performance appraisals.) To make the merit increases consistent, so they will be seen as fair, many merit pay programs use a *merit increase grid*, such as the sample for Merck, the giant drug company, in Table 12.1. As the table shows, the decisions about merit pay are based on two factors: the individual's performance rating and the individual's compa-ratio (pay relative to average pay, as defined in Chapter 11). This system gives the biggest pay increases to the best performers and to those whose pay is relatively low for their job. At the highest extreme, an exceptional employee earning 80 percent of the average pay for his job could receive a 15 percent merit raise. An employee rated as having "room for improvement" would receive a raise only if that employee was earning relatively low pay for the job (compa-ratio of .95 or less).

By today's standards, all of these raises are large, because they were created at a time when inflation was strong and economic forces demanded big pay increases to keep up with the cost of living. The range of percentages for a policy used today would be lower. Organizations establish and revise merit increase grids in light of changing economic conditions. When organizations revise pay ranges, employees have new compa-ratios. A higher pay range would result in lower compa-ratios, causing employees to

Table 12.1

Sample Merit Increase Grid

PERFORMANCE RATING		SUGGESTED MERIT INCREASE PERCENTAGE			
		COMPA-RATIO 80.00–95.00	COMPA-RATIO 95.01–110.00	COMPA-RATIO 110.01–120.00	COMPA-RATIO 120.01–125.00
EX	(Exceptional within Merck)	13–15%	12–14%	9–11%	To maximum of range
WD	(Merck Standard with Distinction)	9–11	8–10	7–9	—
HS	(High Merck Standard)	7–9	6–8	—	—
RI	(Merck Standard Room for Improvement)	5–7	—	—	—
NA	(Not Adequate for Merck)	—	—	—	—

SOURCE: K. J. Murphy, "Merck & Co., Inc. (B)," Boston: Harvard Business School, Case 491-006. Copyright © 1990 by the President & Fellows of Harvard College. Reprinted with permission.

become eligible for bigger merit increases. An advantage of merit pay is therefore that it makes the reward more valuable by relating it to economic conditions.

A drawback is that conditions can shrink the available range of increases. During recent years, budgets for merit pay increases were about 3 to 5 percent of pay, so average performers could receive a 4 percent raise, and top performers perhaps as much as 6 percent. The 2-percentage-point difference, after taxes and other deductions, would amount to only a few dollars a week on a salary of $40,000 per year. Over an entire career, the bigger increases for top performers can grow into a major change, but viewed on a year-by-year basis, they are not much of an incentive to excel.[10] As Figure 12.2 shows, companies typically spread merit raises fairly evenly across all employees. However, experts advise making pay increases twice as great for top performers as for average employees—and not rewarding the poor performers with a raise at all.[11] Imagine if the raises given to the bottom two categories in Figure 12.2 instead went toward 7 percent raises for the top performers. This type of decision signals that excellence is rewarded.

Average Pay Increase

Figure 12.2

Ratings and Raises: Underrewarding the Best

Note: Experts advise that the top category should receive twice as much as the middle category.

Another advantage of merit pay is that it provides a method for rewarding performance in all of the dimensions measured in the organization's performance management system. If that system is appropriately designed to measure all the important job behaviors, then the merit pay is linked to the behaviors the organization desires. This link seems logical, although so far there is little research showing the effectiveness of merit pay.[12]

A drawback of merit pay, from the employer's standpoint, is that it can quickly become expensive. Managers at a majority of organizations rate most employees' performance in the top two categories (out of four or five).[13] Therefore, the majority of employees are eligible for the biggest merit increases, and their pay rises rapidly. This cost is one reason that some organizations have established guidelines about the percentage of employees that may receive the top rating, as discussed in Chapter 8. Another correction might be to use 360-degree performance feedback (discussed in Chapter 9), but so far, organizations have not used multisource data for pay decisions.[14]

Another drawback of merit pay is that it makes assumptions that may be misleading. Rewarding employees for superior performance ratings assumes that those ratings depend on employees' ability and motivation. But performance may actually depend on forces outside the employee's control, such as managers' rating biases, the level of cooperation from co-workers, or the degree to which the organization gives employees the authority, training, and resources they need. Under these conditions, employees will likely conclude that the merit pay system is unfair.

Quality guru W. Edwards Deming also criticizes merit pay for discouraging teamwork. In Deming's words, "Everyone propels himself forward, or tries to, for his own good, on his own life preserver. The organization is the loser."[15] For example, if employees in the purchasing department are evaluated based on the number or cost of contracts they negotiate, they may have little interest in the quality of the materials they buy, even when the manufacturing department is having quality problems. In reaction to such problems, Deming advocated the use of group incentives. Another alternative is for merit pay to include ratings of teamwork and cooperation. Some employers ask co-workers to provide such ratings.

Performance Bonuses

Like merit pay, performance bonuses reward individual performance, but bonuses are not rolled into base pay. The employee must re-earn them during each performance period. In some cases, the bonus is a one-time reward. Bonuses may also be linked to objective performance measures, rather than subjective ratings.

Bonuses for individual performance can be extremely effective and give the organization great flexibility in deciding what kinds of behavior to reward. Examples include the companies described in the "Best Practices" box and Continental Airlines, which pays employees a quarterly bonus for ranking in the top three airlines for on-time arrivals, a measure of service quality. In many cases, employees receive bonuses for meeting such routine targets as sales or production numbers. Such bonuses encourage hard work. But an organization that focuses on growth and innovation may get better results from rewarding employees for learning new skills than from linking bonuses to mastery of existing jobs. Similarly, bonuses make up a large part of compensation packages in the financial industry, and when that industry nearly collapsed in 2008, some observers questioned the basis for awarding the bonuses. Were investment banks, for example, really rewarding the right behaviors if bonuses were falling

Best Practices

INCENTIVES FOR INNOVATION

Some companies tie bonuses to activities that foster innovation. Two good examples come from entirely different industries: candy making and survey research.

Hammond's Candies pays workers at its Denver factory a $50 bonus for any idea they provide that succeeds in driving down costs. This idea for incentive pay occurred to the company's new owner, Andrew Schuman, after he learned that one of Hammond's popular products, ribbon snowflake candy, was the idea of a worker on the assembly line. Schuman concluded that the people who actually made and packed the candy would have the best insight into possible improvements. The production processes involve a high degree of handwork, so employees are skilled at and involved in their work. In the first year of the incentive program,

the company paid out more than $500 in bonuses for ideas such as reducing breakage of candy canes with new packaging and improving the efficiency of an assembly line by adjusting a machine gear. The changes have helped the once-struggling company return to profitability.

Infosurv, a marketing research firm based in Atlanta, asks employees to offer business ideas. Once a quarter, managers pick the best business idea and award a $150 restaurant gift card to the employee who submitted that idea. Jared Heyman, Infosurv's founder, estimates that in the program's first five years, it has delivered hundreds of thousands of dollars' worth of cost savings and additional revenue. Building on this success, Infosurv added a group incentive, a challenge to the com-

pany's 15 employees to suggest 100 innovative ideas in 100 days. If they succeed, everyone will receive a $100 bonus. Given that most of the employees are research and information technology experts, the one expectation that seems certain is that great ideas will flow. The incentives add excitement and a sense of urgency to the kinds of creative thinking a company like Infosurv would need as part of its daily business.

Sources: Teri Evans, "Entrepreneurs Seek Ways to Draw Out Workers' Ideas," *Wall Street Journal,* December 21, 2009, http://online.wsj.com; Hammond's Candies, "About Us," corporate Web site, www.hammondscandies.com, accessed April 26, 2010; and Infosurv, "About Infosurv," corporate Web site, www.infosurv.com, accessed April 26, 2010.

less than 50 percent or holding steady during a period when government funds were needed to keep the companies alive?[16]

Adding to this flexibility, organizations also may motivate employees with one-time bonuses. For example, when one organization acquires another, it usually wants to retain certain valuable employees in the organization it is buying. Therefore, it is common for organizations involved in an acquisition to pay *retention bonuses*—one-time incentives paid in exchange for remaining with the company—to top managers, engineers, top-performing salespeople, and information technology specialists. When Chattem, a Chattanooga, Tennessee company that makes health and beauty products, was acquired by pharmaceutical company Sanofi-Aventis, the deal included retention bonuses for Chattem's chief executive officer, president, general counsel, and chief financial officer in exchange for them staying with the company for several more years.[17]

Sales Commissions

A variation on piece rates and bonuses is the payment of **commissions,** or pay calculated as a percentage of sales. For instance, a furniture salesperson might earn commissions equaling 6 percent times the price of the furniture the person sells during the period. Selling a $2,000 couch would add $120 to the salesperson's commissions

Commissions
Incentive pay calculated as a percentage of sales.

Many car salespeople earn a straight commission, meaning that 100% of their pay comes from commission instead of a salary. What type of individual might enjoy a job like this?

for the period. Commission rates vary tremendously from one industry and company to another. Examples reported include an average rate between 5.0 and 5.5 percent for real estate, 30 percent up to 90 percent of first year's premiums on life insurance (then dropping to as low as 4 percent in subsequent years of the policy), and 20 to 30 percent of *profits* for auto sales.[18]

Some salespeople earn a commission in addition to a base salary; others earn only commissions—a pay arrangement called a *straight commission plan.* Straight commissions are common among insurance and real estate agents and car salespeople. Other salespeople earn no commissions at all, but a straight salary. Paying most or all of a salesperson's compensation in the form of salary frees the salesperson to focus on developing customer goodwill. Paying most or all of a salesperson's compensation in the form of commissions encourages the salesperson to focus on closing sales. In this way, differences in salespeople's compensation directly influence how they spend their time, how they treat customers, and how much the organization sells.

The nature of salespeople's compensation also affects the kinds of people who will want to take and keep sales jobs with the organization. Hard-driving, ambitious, risk-taking salespeople might enjoy the potential rewards of a straight commission plan. An organization that wants salespeople to concentrate on listening to customers and building relationships might want to attract a different kind of salesperson by offering more of the pay in the form of a salary. Basing part or all of a salesperson's pay on commissions assumes that the organization wants to attract people with some willingness to take risks—probably a reasonable assumption about people whose job includes talking to strangers and encouraging them to spend money.

Pay for Group Performance

LO3 Identify ways to recognize group performance.

Employers may address the drawbacks of individual incentives by including group incentives in the organization's compensation plan. To win group incentives, employees must cooperate and share knowledge so that the entire group can meet its performance targets. Common group incentives include gainsharing, bonuses, and team awards.

Gainsharing

Gainsharing
Group incentive program that measures improvements in productivity and effectiveness and distributes a portion of each gain to employees.

Organizations that want employees to focus on efficiency may adopt a **gainsharing** program, which measures increases in productivity and effectiveness and distributes a portion of each gain to employees. For example, if a factory enjoys a productivity gain worth $30,000, half the gain might be the company's share. The other $15,000 would be distributed among the employees in the factory. Knowing that they can enjoy a financial benefit from helping the company be more productive, employees supposedly will look for ways to work more efficiently and improve the way the factory operates.

Gainsharing addresses the challenge of identifying appropriate performance measures for complex jobs. For example, how would a hospital measure the production of its nurses—in terms of satisfying patients, keeping costs down, or completing a number of tasks? Each of these measures oversimplifies the complex responsibilities involved in nursing care. Even for simpler jobs, setting acceptable standards and measuring performance can be complicated. Gainsharing frees employees to determine how to improve their own and their group's performance. It also broadens employees' focus beyond their individual interests. But in contrast to profit sharing, discussed later, it keeps the performance measures within a range of activity that most employees believe they can influence. Organizations can enhance the likelihood of a gain by providing a means for employees to share knowledge and make suggestions, as we will discuss in the last section of this chapter.

Gainsharing is most likely to succeed when organizations provide the right conditions. Among the conditions identified, the following are among the most common:[19]

- Management commitment.
- Need for change or strong commitment to continuous improvement.
- Management acceptance and encouragement of employee input.
- High levels of cooperation and interaction.
- Employment security.
- Information sharing on productivity and costs.
- Goal setting.
- Commitment of all involved parties to the process of change and improvement.
- Performance standard and calculation that employees understand and consider fair and that is closely related to managerial objectives.
- Employees who value working in groups.

A popular form of gainsharing is the **Scanlon plan,** developed in the 1930s by Joseph N. Scanlon, president of a union local at Empire Steel and Tin Plant in Mansfield, Ohio. The Scanlon plan gives employees a bonus if the ratio of labor costs to the sales value of production is below a set standard. To keep this ratio low enough to earn the bonus, workers have to keep labor costs to a minimum and produce as much as possible with that amount of labor. Figure 12.3 provides an example. In this example, the standard is a ratio of 20/100, or 20 percent, and the workers produced parts worth $1.2 million. To meet the standard, the labor costs should be less than 20 percent of $1.2 million, or $240,000. Since the actual labor costs were $210,000, the workers will get a gainsharing bonus based on the $30,000 difference between the $240,000 target and the actual cost.

Typically, an organization does not pay workers all of the gain immediately. First, the organization keeps a share of the gain to improve its own bottom line. A portion of the remainder goes into a reserve account. This account offsets losses in any months when the gain is negative (that is, when costs rise or production falls). At the end of the year, the organization closes out the account and distributes any remaining surplus. If there were a loss at the end of the year, the organization would absorb it.

Scanlon Plan
A gainsharing program in which employees receive a bonus if the ratio of labor costs to the sales value of production is below a set standard.

Figure 12.3

Finding the Gain in a Scanlon Plan

Target Ratio: $\dfrac{\text{Labor Costs}}{\text{Sales Value of Production}} = \dfrac{20}{100}$

Sales Value of Production: $1,200,000

Goal: $\dfrac{20}{100} \times \$1,200,000 = \$240,000$

Actual: $210,000

Gain: $240,000 − $210,000 = $30,000

SOURCE: Example adapted from B. Graham-Moore and Timothy L. Ross, *Gainsharing: Plans for Improving Performance* (Washington, DC: Bureau of National Affairs, 1990), p. 57.

Group Bonuses and Team Awards

In contrast to gainsharing plans, which typically reward the performance of all employees at a facility, bonuses for group performance tend to be for smaller work groups.[20] These

HR Oops!

Programs That Discourage Safety

The Occupational Health and Safety Administration has expressed concern that when companies set up programs to reward safety, they sometimes end up *discouraging* safe behavior. The problem occurs when companies offer incentives for low reports of injuries and illnesses—for example, giving a bonus if all the workers during a shift at a facility "work safely" with no accidents during a year. Under that type of program, if a worker does get hurt, the worker might feel bad about reporting the injury, or co-workers might discourage the worker from reporting the injury, because the injury report would cause them to lose the bonus.

Failure to report injuries can lead to future problems. For example, the failure to report could make it harder to identify and correct safety hazards. Also, a minor injury such as a repetitive-stress injury might keep getting worse until the employee can no longer bear to keep it a secret. In that case, the individual employee and company would have been better off if the employee had reported the injury sooner.

One alternative that has been suggested is for companies to reward employees for engaging in practices that increase safety rather than reward them for the absence of injury and illness reports.

Questions

1. What performance measures could a company use to identify and reward safe behavior in addition to counting injuries and illnesses?
2. Are the measures you identified in question 1 suitable for group bonuses, individual bonuses, or both? What are the advantages of rewarding safety at the group level? At the individual level?

Source: Based on Jennifer Stroschein, "OSHA Is Watching," *Industrial Safety & Hygiene News*, October 2009, Business & Company Resource Center, http://galenet.galegroup.com.

Group members that meet a sales goal or a product development team that meets a deadline or successfully launches a product may be rewarded with a bonus for group performance. What are some advantages and disadvantages of group bonuses?

bonuses reward the members of a group for attaining a specific goal, usually measured in terms of physical output. Team awards are similar to group bonuses, but they are more likely to use a broad range of performance measures, such as cost savings, successful completion of a project, or even meeting deadlines.

Both types of incentives have the advantage that they encourage group or team members to cooperate so that they can achieve their goal. However, depending on the reward system, competition among individuals may be replaced by competition among groups. Competition may be healthy in some situations, as when groups try to outdo one another in satisfying customers. On the downside, competition may also prevent necessary cooperation among groups. To avoid this, the organization should carefully set the performance goals for these incentives so that concern for costs or sales does not obscure other objectives, such as quality, customer service, and ethical behavior (see "HR Oops!").

LO4 Explain how organizations link pay to their overall performance.

Pay for Organizational Performance

Two important ways organizations measure their performance are in terms of their profits and their stock price. In a competitive marketplace, profits result when an organization is efficiently providing products that customers want at a price they are willing to pay. Stock is the owners' investment in a corporation; when the stock price is rising, the value of that investment is growing. Rather than trying to figure out what performance measures will motivate employees to do the things that generate high profits and a rising stock price, many organizations offer incentive pay tied to those organizational performance measures. The expectation is that employees will focus on what is best for the organization.

These organization-level incentives can motivate employees to align their activities with the organization's goals. At the same time, linking incentives to the organization's profits or stock price exposes employees to a high degree of risk. Profits and stock price can soar very high very fast, but they can also fall. The result is a great deal of uncertainty about the amount of incentive pay each employee will receive in each period. Therefore, these kinds of incentive pay are likely to be most effective in organizations that emphasize growth and innovation, which tend to need employees who thrive in a risk-taking environment.[21]

Profit Sharing

Under **profit sharing,** payments are a percentage of the organization's profits and do not become part of the employees' base salary. For example, General Motors provides for profit sharing in its contract with its workers' union, the United Auto Workers. Depending on how large GM's profits are in relation to its total sales for the year, at least 6 percent of the company's profits are divided among the workers according to how many hours they worked during the year.[22] The formula for computing and dividing the profit-sharing bonus is included in the union contract.

> **Profit Sharing**
> Incentive pay in which payments are a percentage of the organization's profits and do not become part of the employees' base salary.

Organizations use profit sharing for a number of reasons. It may encourage employees to think more like owners, taking a broad view of what they need to do in order to make the organization more effective. They are more likely to cooperate and less likely to focus on narrow self-interests. Also, profit sharing has the practical advantage of costing less when the organization is experiencing financial difficulties. If the organization has little or no profit, this incentive pay is small or nonexistent, so employers may not need to rely as much on layoffs to reduce costs.[23]

Does profit sharing help organizations perform better? The evidence is not yet clear. Although research supports a link between profit-sharing payments and profits, researchers have questioned which of these causes the other.[24] For example, Ford, Chrysler, and GM have similar profit-sharing plans in their contracts with the United Auto Workers, but the payouts are not always similar. In one year, the average worker received $4,000 from Ford, $550 from GM, and $8,000 from Chrysler. Since the plans are similar, something other than the profit sharing must have made Ford and Chrysler more profitable than GM.

Differences in payouts, as in the preceding example, raise questions not only about the effectiveness of the plans, but about equity. Assuming workers at Ford, Chrysler, and GM have similar jobs, they would expect to receive similar profit-sharing checks. In the year of this example, GM workers might have seen their incentive pay as highly inequitable unless GM could show how Chrysler workers did more to earn their big checks. Employees also may feel that small profit-sharing checks are unfair because they have little control over profits. If profit sharing is offered to all employees but most employees think only management decisions about products, price, and marketing have much impact on profits, they will conclude that there is little connection between their actions and their rewards. In that case, profit-sharing plans will have little impact on employee behavior. This problem is even greater when employees have to wait months before profits are distributed. The time lag between high-performance behavior and financial rewards is simply too long to be motivating.

An organization setting up a profit-sharing plan should consider what to do if profits fall. If the economy slows and profit-sharing payments disappear along with profits, employees may become discouraged or angry. Andersen Corporation, maker of doors and windows, recently faced this problem. The company has included profit sharing in its compensation since 1914. In 2007, Andersen had been able to pay its employees profit sharing equal to 22.5 percent of their salaries. A year later, the company paid out just 6.5 percent of salaries in profit sharing, and in 2009, for the first time since the Great Depression, there were no profit-sharing checks at all.[25] Management communicated with employees frankly about the company's appreciation of their efforts and the difficulty of the economic environment, in which construction has been hit especially hard. The hope is that employees' recognition of the role the economy plays in cyclical industries such as construction will enable them to see the compensation as fair, even if they are disappointed in the year's results.

Given the limitations of profit-sharing plans, one strategy is to use them as a component of a pay system that includes other kinds of pay more directly linked to individual behavior. This increases employees' commitment to organizational goals while addressing concerns about fairness.

Stock Ownership

While profit-sharing plans are intended to encourage employees to "think like owners," a stock ownership plan actually makes employees part owners of the organization. Like profit sharing, employee ownership is intended as a way to encourage employees to focus on the success of the organization as a whole. The drawbacks of stock ownership as a form of incentive pay are similar to those of profit sharing. Specifically, it may not have a strong effect on individuals' motivation. Employees may not see a strong link between their actions and the company's stock price, especially in larger organizations. The link between pay and performance is even harder to appreciate because the financial benefits mostly come when the stock is sold—typically when the employee leaves the organization.

Ownership programs usually take the form of *stock options* or *employee stock ownership plans*. These are illustrated in Figure 12.4.

Stock Options

Stock Options
Rights to buy a certain number of shares of stock at a specified price.

One way to distribute stock to employees is to grant them **stock options**—the right to buy a certain number of shares of stock at a specified price. (Purchasing the stock is called *exercising* the option.) Suppose that in 2005 a company's employees received options to purchase the company's stock at $10 per share. The employees will benefit

Figure 12.4

Types of Pay for Organizational Performance

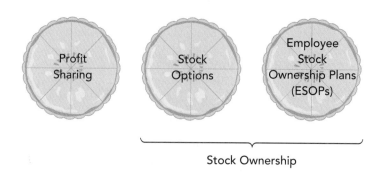

Stock Ownership

if the stock price rises above $10 per share, because they can pay $10 for something (a share of stock) that is worth more than $10. If in 2010 the stock is worth $30, they can exercise their options and buy stock for $10 a share. If they want to, they can sell their stock for the market price of $30, receiving a gain of $20 for each share of stock. Of course, stock prices can also fall. If the 2010 stock price is only $8, the employees would not bother to exercise the options.

Traditionally, organizations have granted stock options to their executives. During the 1990s, many organizations pushed eligibility for options further down in the organization's structure. Walmart and PepsiCo are among the large companies that have granted stock options to employees at all levels. Stock values were rising so fast during the 1990s that options were extremely rewarding for a time.

Some studies suggest that organizations perform better when a large percentage of top and middle managers are eligible for long-term incentives such as stock options. This evidence is consistent with the idea of encouraging employees to think like owners.[26] It is not clear whether these findings would hold up for lower-level employees. They may see much less opportunity to influence the company's performance in the stock market.

Recent scandals have drawn attention to another challenge of using stock options as incentive pay. As with other performance measures, employees may focus so much on stock price that they lose sight of other goals, including ethical behavior. Ideally, managers would bring about an increase in stock price by adding value in terms of efficiency, innovation, and customer satisfaction. But there are other, unethical ways to increase stock price by tricking investors into thinking the organization is more valuable and more profitable than it actually is. Hiding losses and inflating the recorded value of revenues are just two of the ways some companies have boosted stock prices, enriching managers until these misdeeds come to light. Also, officials at some companies, including K B Homes and United Healthcare, have been charged with "backdating" options granted to executives. This practice involves changing the date and/or price in the original option agreement so that the option holder can buy stock at a bargain price—making the backdated option profitable or more profitable. At the same time, backdating eliminates or reduces the incentive to improve the stock's performance. If backdating of options is kept secret, those who do it may be guilty of falsifying financial statements, which is unethical and may be illegal.[27]

Employee Stock Ownership Plans

While stock options are most often used with top management, a broader arrangement is the **employee stock ownership plan (ESOP).** In an ESOP, the organization distributes shares of stock to its employees by placing the stock into a trust managed on the employees' behalf. Employees receive regular reports on the value of their stock, and when they leave the organization, they may sell the stock to the organization or (if it is a publicly traded company) on the open market.

Employee Stock Ownership Plan (ESOP)
An arrangement in which the organization distributes shares of stock to all its employees by placing it in a trust.

ESOPs are the most common form of employee ownership, with the number of employees in such plans increasing from over 3 million in 1980 to more than 12 million in the past few years in the United States.[28] Figure 12.5 shows the growth in the number of ESOPs in the United States. One reason for ESOPs' popularity is that earnings of the trust holdings are exempt from income taxes.

ESOPs raise a number of issues. On the negative side, they carry a significant risk for employees. By law, an ESOP must invest at least 51 percent of its assets in the company's own stock (in contrast to other kinds of stock funds that hold a wide diversity of companies). Problems with the company's performance therefore can

Figure 12.5

Number of Companies with ESOPs

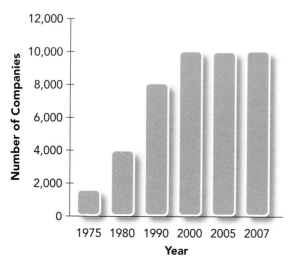

SOURCE: National Center for Employee Ownership, "A Statistical Profile of Employee Ownership," NCEO Web site, updated March 2010, www.nceo.org.

take away significant value from the ESOP. Many companies set up ESOPs to hold retirement funds, so these risks directly affect employees' retirement income. Adding to the risk, funds in an ESOP are not guaranteed by the Pension Benefit Guarantee Corporation (described in Chapter 13). Sometimes employees use an ESOP to buy their company when it is experiencing financial problems; this is a highly risky investment.

Still, ESOPs can be attractive to employers. Along with tax and financing advantages, ESOPs give employers a way to build pride in and commitment to the organization. Employees have a right to participate in votes by shareholders (if the stock is registered on a national exchange, such as the New York Stock Exchange).[29] This means employees participate somewhat in corporate-level decision making. Still, the overall level of participation in decisions appears to vary significantly among organizations with ESOPs. Some research suggests that the benefits of ESOPs are greatest when employee participation is greatest.[30]

Balanced Scorecard

LO5 Describe how organizations combine incentive plans in a "balanced scorecard."

Balanced Scorecard
A combination of performance measures directed toward the company's long- and short-term goals and used as the basis for awarding incentive pay.

As the preceding descriptions indicate, any form of incentive pay has advantages and disadvantages. For example, relying exclusively on merit pay or other individual incentives may produce a workforce that cares greatly about meeting those objectives but competes to achieve them at the expense of cooperating to achieve organizational goals. Relying heavily on profit sharing or stock ownership may increase cooperation but do little to motivate day-to-day effort or to attract and retain top individual performers. Because of this, many organizations design a mix of pay programs. The aim is to balance the disadvantages of one type of incentive pay with the advantages of another type.

One way of accomplishing this goal is to design a **balanced scorecard**—a combination of performance measures directed toward the company's long- and short-term goals and used as the basis for awarding incentive pay. A corporation would have financial goals to satisfy its stockholders (owners), quality- and price-related goals to satisfy its customers, efficiency goals to ensure better operations, and goals related to acquiring skills and knowledge for the future to fully tap into employees' potential. Different jobs would contribute to those goals in different ways. For example, an engineer could develop products that better meet customer needs and can be produced more efficiently. The engineer could also develop knowledge of new technologies in order to contribute more to the organization in the future. A salesperson's goals would include measures related to sales volume, customer service, and learning about product markets and customer needs. Organizations customize their balanced scorecards according to their markets, products, and objectives. The scorecards of a company that is emphasizing low costs and prices would be different from the scorecards of a company emphasizing innovative use of new technology.

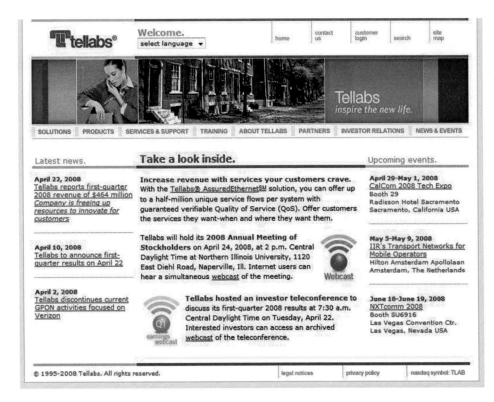

Tellabs is one company that uses a balanced scorecard. The company conducts quarterly meetings at which employees learn how their performance will be evaluated according to the scorecard. The company also makes this information available on the intranet.

Table 12.2 shows the kinds of information that go into a balanced scorecard. This sample scorecard is similar to one used for Blue Ridge Electric Membership Corporation, a cooperative that delivers electricity to its member-owners in North Carolina. The company gathers input from all levels of employees to create goals for member (customer) service, financial performance, safety, and innovation and learning. These are communicated to all employees, and all employees receive incentive pay based on whether the company meets its base, target, or stretch goals in each area. For example, employees earn 2 percent of their salary as incentive pay if the organization meets all of its base goals, including power interruptions lasting no longer than 140 minutes on average and operating expenses held to 4.03 cents per kilowatt-hour generated. If the company reaches the target or stretch goals, then the incentive pay will be 3 percent or 5 percent, respectively. If the company meets some of the goals but not others, the incentive pay is calculated as a portion of the total incentive. For example, each of the member service goals is worth 20 percent of the total incentive pay, so meeting both of these goals contributes 40 percent of an employee's incentive pay. Since Blue Ridge started using the balanced scorecard in the 1990s, it has increased its member satisfaction score, reduced its cost of service, improved reliability, and earned the best safety record among North Carolina's power distribution companies.[31]

Not only does the balanced scorecard combine the advantages of different incentive-pay plans, it helps employees understand the organization's goals. By communicating the balanced scorecard to employees, the organization shows employees information about what its goals are and what it expects employees to accomplish. In Table 12.2, for example, the organization indicates not only that the manager should meet the four performance objectives but also that it is especially concerned with the financial target, because half the incentive is based on this one target.

focus on
*social
responsibility*

Table 12.2

Sample Balanced Scorecard for an Electric Cooperative

PERFORMANCE CATEGORY	CRITICAL SUCCESS FACTORS	GOALS		
		BASE (2%)	TARGET (3%)	STRETCH (5%)
Member service (40% of incentive pay)	Reliability (average interruption duration)	140 min.	130 min.	120 min.
	Customer satisfaction (index from quarterly survey)	9.0	9.1	9.2
Financial performance (25% of incentive pay)	Total operating expenses (¢/kilowatt-hour)	4.03¢	3.99¢	3.95¢
	Cash flow (% of investment)	75%	80%	85%
Internal processes (20% of incentive pay)	Safety (safety index based on injury rate and severity)	4.6	3.6	2.6
Innovation and learning (15% of incentive pay)	Member value (revenue/kWh sold)	Budget	−10% state median	−13% state median
	Efficiency and effectiveness (total margins/no. employees)	$534,400	$37,200	$40,000

SOURCE: Adapted from Tim Sullivan and Henry Cano, "Introducing a Balanced Scorecard for Electric Cooperatives: A Tool for Measuring and Improving Results," *Management Quarterly*, Winter 2009, Business & Company Resource Center, http://galenet .galegroup.com.

LO6 Summarize processes that can contribute to the success of incentive programs.

Processes That Make Incentives Work

As we explained in Chapter 11, communication and employee participation can contribute to a belief that the organization's pay structure is fair. In the same way, the process by which the organization creates and administers incentive pay can help it use incentives to achieve the goal of motivating employees. The monetary rewards of gainsharing, for example, can substantially improve productivity,[32] but the organization can set up the process to be even more effective. In a study of an automotive parts plant, productivity rose when the gainsharing plan added employee participation in the form of monthly meetings with managers to discuss the gainsharing plan and ways to increase productivity. A related study asked employees what motivated them to participate actively in the plan (for example, by making suggestions for improvement). According to employees, other factors besides the pay itself were important—especially the ability to influence and control the way their work was done.[33]

Participation in Decisions

Employee participation in pay-related decisions can be part of a general move toward employee empowerment. If employees are involved in decisions about incentive pay plans and employees' eligibility for incentives, the process of creating and administering these plans can be more complex.[34] There is also a risk that employees will make decisions that are in their interests at the expense of the organization's interests.

However, employees have hands-on knowledge about the kinds of behavior that can help the organization perform well, and they can see whether individuals are displaying that behavior.[35] Therefore, in spite of the potential risks, employee participation can contribute to the success of an incentive plan. This is especially true when monetary incentives encourage the monitoring of performance and when the organization fosters a spirit of trust and cooperation.

Communication

Along with empowerment, communicating with employees is important. It demonstrates to employees that the pay plan is fair. Also, when employees understand the requirements of the incentive pay plan, the plan is more likely to influence their behavior as desired.

It is particularly important to communicate with employees when changing the plan. Employees tend to feel concerned about changes. Pay is a frequent topic of rumors and assumptions based on incomplete information, partly because of pay's importance to employees. When making any changes, the human resource department should determine the best ways to communicate the reasons for the change. Some organizations rely heavily on videotaped messages from the chief executive officer. Other means of communication include brochures that show examples of how employees will be affected. The human resource department may also conduct small-group interviews to learn about employees' concerns, then address those concerns in the communications effort. The "eHRm" box describes how companies use Web sites to help, provide employees with more ways to effectively understand and manage their pay.

Incentive Pay for Executives

LO7 Discuss issues related to performance-based pay for executives.

Because executives have a much stronger influence over the organization's performance than other employees do, incentive pay for executives warrants special attention. Assuming that incentives influence performance, decisions about incentives for executives should have a great impact on how well the executives and the organization perform. Along with overall pay levels for executives (discussed in Chapter 11), organizations need to create incentive plans for this small but important group of employees.

To encourage executives to develop a commitment to the organization's long-term success, executive compensation often combines short-term and long-term incentives. *Short-term incentives* include bonuses based on the year's profits, return on investment, or other measures related to the organization's goals. Sometimes, to gain tax advantages, the actual payment of the bonus is deferred (for example, by making it part of a retirement plan). *Long-term incentives* include stock options and stock purchase plans. The rationale for these long-term incentives is that executives will want to do what is best for the organization because that will cause the value of their stock to grow.

Each year *BusinessWeek* publishes a list of top executives who did the most for their pay (that is, their organizations performed best) and those who did the least. The performance of the latter group has prompted much of the negative attention that executive pay has received. The problem seems to be that in some organizations, the chief executive's pay is high every year, regardless of the organization's profitability or performance in the stock market. In terms of people's judgments about equity, it seems fairer if high-paid executives must show results to justify their pay levels.

A corporation's shareholders—its owners—want the corporation to encourage managers to act in the owners' best interests. They want managers to care about the

FINANCIAL EDUCATION ONLINE

Employees get the most value from—and appreciation of—their benefits if they understand how to manage their financial assets. As employers are coming to appreciate this fact, they are also recognizing that online training is an efficient and convenient way to deliver a financial education.

For example, the insurance company Axa set up a financial-education program for employees on a Web page titled "My Budget Day." Each employee is given one hour a month of paid work time to visit "My Budget Day" and use its interactive tools to calculate the costs and benefits of various spending and saving decisions. They can learn about creating a family budget and a retirement plan. The setup gives employees flexibility and convenience, and they report feeling "more in control of their finances."

Along with recorded training presentations on DVDs and podcasts, online training offers the power of the computer for showing employees how to get the most out of their earnings. Online modeling tools can show employees how the value of their stock can grow over time if they don't sell it immediately. Or employees can see how the power of compound interest can make their bonus or profit-sharing check grow if they invest it in various ways.

Sources: "Financial Education: Axa Ensures Engagement with Online Facility," *Employee Benefits*, April 1, 2010, Business & Company Resource Center, http://galenet.galegroup.com; "Best Practice: Face Up to Provision of Multi-Site Financial Education," *Employee Benefits*, February 8, 2008; and "Financial Education: Cache of Literacy," *Employee Benefits*, October 8, 2007, both downloaded from General Reference Center Gold, http://find.galegroup.com.

company's profits and stock price, and incentive pay can encourage this interest. One way to achieve these goals is to tie a large share of executives' pay to performance. In a *BusinessWeek* survey, almost 80 percent of chief executives' pay came in the form of stock options and other incentive pay based on long-term performance objectives. Another study has found that relying on such long-term incentives is associated with greater profitability.[36]

Performance Measures for Executives

The balanced-scorecard approach is useful in designing executive pay. Whirlpool, for example, has used a balanced scorecard that combines measures of whether the organization is delivering value to shareholders, customers, and employees. These measures are listed in Table 12.3. Rewarding achievement of a variety of goals in a balanced scorecard reduces the temptation to win bonuses by manipulating financial data.

Regulators and shareholders have pressured companies to do a better job of linking executive pay and performance. The Securities and Exchange Commission (SEC) has required companies to more clearly report executive compensation levels and the company's performance relative to that of competitors. These reporting requirements shine a light on situations where executives of poorly performing companies receive high pay, so companies feel more pressure to link pay to performance. Some forms of incentive pay also have tax advantages. Under the

Warren Buffett must be doing something right. The billionaire once was ranked by *BusinessWeek* magazine as being the top executive who gave shareholders the most for their pay.

Table 12.3

Balanced Scorecard for Whirlpool Executives

TYPE OF VALUE CREATION	MEASURES
Shareholder value	Economic value added
	Earnings per share
	Cash flow
	Total cost productivity
Customer value	Quality
	Market share
	Customer satisfaction
Employee value	High-performance culture index
	High-performance culture deployment
	Training and development diversity

SOURCE: E. L. Gubman, *The Talent Solution* (New York: McGraw-Hill, 1998).

Omnibus Budget Reconciliation Act of 1993, companies may not deduct executive pay that exceeds $1 million, but performance-related pay (including stock options) is exempt, so it is deductible even over $1 million.

Ethical Issues

Incentive pay for executives lays the groundwork for significant ethical issues. When an organization links pay to its stock performance, executives need the ethical backbone to be honest about their company's performance even when dishonesty or clever shading of the truth offers the tempting potential for large earnings. As recent scandals involving WorldCom, Enron, Global Crossing, and other companies have shown, the results can be disastrous when unethical behavior comes to light.

Among these issues is one we have already touched on in this chapter: the difficulty of setting performance measures that encourage precisely the behavior desired. In the case of incentives tied to stock performance, executives may be tempted to inflate the stock price in order to enjoy bonuses and valuable stock options. The intent is for the executive to boost stock value through efficient operations, technological innovation, effective leadership, and so on. Unfortunately, individuals at some companies determined that they could obtain faster results through accounting practices that stretched the norms in order to present the company's performance in the best light. When such practices are discovered to be misleading, stock prices plunge and the company's reputation is damaged, sometimes beyond repair.

A related issue when executive pay includes stock or stock options is insider trading. When executives are stockholders, they have a dual role as owners and managers. This places them at an advantage over others who want to invest in the company. An individual, a pension fund, or other investors have less information about the company than its managers do—for example, whether product development is proceeding on schedule, whether a financing deal is in the works, and so on. An executive who knows about these activities could therefore reap a windfall in the stock market by buying or selling stock based on knowledge about the company's future. The SEC places strict limits on this "insider trading," but some executives have violated these limits. In the worst cases executives have sold stock, secretly knowing their company was failing, before the stock price collapsed. The losers are the employees, retirees, and other investors who hold the now-worthless stock.

As recent news stories have reminded us, linking pay to stock price can reward unethical behavior, at least in the short term and at least in the minds of a handful of executives. Yet, given the motivational power of incentive pay, organizations cannot afford to abandon incentives for their executives. These temptations are among the reasons that executive positions demand individuals who maintain the highest ethical standards.

thinking ethically

SHOULD EMPLOYEES GIVE BACK BONUSES AFTER BAILOUTS?

Disastrous trades made by the financial-products division of American International Group (AIG) nearly caused the insurance giant to go out of business in 2008, until the U.S. government moved in with money to keep the company afloat. With public funds invested in this private business, citizens were infuriated when they learned that AIG would pay its financial-products employees retention bonuses totaling $168 million in 2009 and again when the company announced $195 million would be paid in retention bonuses in 2010.

Under pressure from the Obama administration's "pay czar" Kenneth Feinberg, AIG asked employees in the financial-products group if they would be willing to take a cut in the amount of their 2010 bonuses in exchange for being paid ahead of schedule. In addition, the company asked the employees to give back some of the bonuses they had received a year earlier. Most of the employees—over 95 percent—agreed, and some of them offered to take a bigger cut than the 10 percent requested or to pay back some of the bonus money not repaid by others (including individuals who had left the company).

This situation unfolded as other financial companies were enduring criticism about their incentive pay. Banks such as Citigroup and Bank of America justified paying bonuses to their investment-banking employees on the grounds that these employees normally receive a sizable share of their pay in the form of bonuses, so eliminating or even scaling back bonuses would present a severe hardship to employees who were working hard to unravel the tangle of toxic assets.

Questions

1. If a company performs poorly, is it ethical for its employees to receive a performance bonus? Who wins and who loses if they do?
2. When, if ever, is it ethical for a company to ask its employees to give back part of a bonus they have already been paid?
3. What are the ethical risks, if any, of making incentive pay a large share of employees' total compensation? How should a company balance or reduce these risks?

SOURCES: Serena Ng and Joann S. Lublin, "AIG Gets Strong Response on Bonus Cuts," *Wall Street Journal*, January 29, 2010, http://online.wsj.com; David Enrich, Sara Schaefer Muñoz, and Aaron Lucchetti, "Banks See Way Past Limits," *Wall Street Journal*, January 28, 2010, http://online.wsj.com; and Susanne Craig, David Enrich, and Robin Sidel, "Banks Brace for Bonus Fury," *Wall Street Journal*, January 11, 2010, http://online.wsj.com.

SUMMARY

LO1   Discuss the connection between incentive pay and employee performance.

Incentive pay is pay tied to individual performance, profits, or other measures of success. Organizations select forms of incentive pay to energize, direct, or control employees' behavior. It is influential because the amount paid is linked to predefined behaviors or outcomes. To be effective, incentive pay should encourage the kinds of behavior that are most needed, and employees must believe they have the ability to meet the performance standards. Employees must value the rewards, have the resources they need to meet the standards, and believe the pay plan is fair.

LO2   Describe how organizations recognize individual performance.

Organizations may recognize individual performance through such incentives as piecework rates, standard hour plans, merit pay, sales commissions, and bonuses for meeting individual performance objectives. Piecework rates pay employees according to the amount they produce. Standard hour plans pay workers extra for work done in less than a preset "standard time." Merit pay links increases in wages or salaries to ratings on performance appraisals. Bonuses are similar to merit pay, because they are paid for meeting individual goals, but they are not rolled into base pay, and they usually are based on achieving a specific output, rather than subjective performance ratings. A sales commission is incentive pay calculated as a percentage of sales closed by a salesperson.

LO3   Identify ways to recognize group performance.

Common group incentives include gainsharing, bonuses, and team awards. Gainsharing programs, such as Scanlon plans, measure increases in productivity and distribute a portion of each gain to employees. Group bonuses reward the members of a group for attaining a specific goal, usually measured in terms of physical output. Team awards are more likely to use a broad range of performance measures, such as cost savings, successful completion of a project, or meeting a deadline.

LO4   Explain how organizations link pay to their overall performance.

Incentives for meeting organizational objectives include profit sharing and stock ownership. Profit-sharing plans pay workers a percentage of the organization's profits; these payments do not become part of the employees' base salary. Stock ownership incentives may take the form of stock options or employee stock ownership plans. A stock option is the right to buy a certain number of shares at a specified price. The employee benefits by exercising the option at a price lower than the market price, so the employee benefits when the company's stock price rises. An employee stock ownership plan (ESOP) is an arrangement in which the organization distributes shares of its stock to employees by placing the stock in a trust managed on the employees' behalf. When employees leave the organization, they may sell their shares of the stock.

LO5   Describe how organizations combine incentive plans in a "balanced scorecard."

A balanced scorecard is a combination of performance measures directed toward the company's long- and short-term goals and used as the basis for awarding incentive pay. Typically, it includes financial goals to satisfy stockholders, quality- and price-related goals for customer satisfaction, efficiency goals for improved operations, and goals related to acquiring skills and knowledge for the future. The mix of pay programs is intended to balance the disadvantages of one type of incentive with the advantages of another type. The balanced scorecard also helps employees to understand and care about the organization's goals.

LO6   Summarize processes that can contribute to the success of incentive programs.

Communication and participation in decisions can contribute to employees' feeling that the organization's incentive pay plans are fair. Employee participation in pay-related decisions can be part of a general move toward employee empowerment. Employees may put their own interests first in developing the plan, but they also have firsthand insight into the kinds of behavior that can contribute to organizational goals. Communicating with employees is important because it demonstrates that the pay plan is fair and helps them understand what is expected of them. Communication is especially important when the organization is changing its pay plan.

LO7   Discuss issues related to performance-based pay for executives.

Because executives have such a strong influence over the organization's performance, incentive pay for them receives special attention. Executive pay usually combines long-term and short-term incentives. By motivating executives, these incentives can significantly affect the organization's performance. The size of incentives should be motivating but also meet standards for equity. Performance measures should encourage behavior that is in the organization's best interests, including ethical behavior. Executives need ethical standards that keep them from insider trading or deceptive practices designed to manipulate the organization's stock price.

KEY TERMS

balanced scorecard, p. 370
commissions, p. 363
differential piece rates, p. 359
employee stock ownership plan
   (ESOP), p. 369

gainsharing, p. 364
incentive pay, p. 356
merit pay, p. 360
piecework rate, p. 358
profit sharing, p. 367

Scanlon plan, p. 365
standard hour plan, p. 360
stock options, p. 368
straight piecework plan, p. 358

REVIEW AND DISCUSSION QUESTIONS

1. With some organizations and jobs, pay is primarily wages or salaries, and with others, incentive pay is more important. For each of the following jobs, state whether you think the pay should emphasize base pay (wages and salaries) or incentive pay (bonuses, profit sharing, and so on). Give a reason for each.
   a. An accountant at a manufacturing company.
   b. A salesperson for a software company.
   c. A chief executive officer.
   d. A physician in a health clinic.

2. Consider your current job or a job that you have recently held. Would you be most motivated in response to incentives based on your individual performance, your group's performance, or the organization's overall performance (profits or stock price)? Why?

3. What are the pros and cons of linking incentive pay to individual performance? How can organizations address the negatives?

4. Suppose you are a human resource professional at a company that is setting up work teams for production and sales. What group incentives would you recommend to support this new work arrangement?

5. Why do some organizations link incentive pay to the organization's overall performance? Is it appropriate to use stock performance as an incentive for employees at all levels? Why or why not?

6. Stock options have been called the pay program that "built Silicon Valley," because of their key role as incentive pay for employees in high-tech companies. They were popular during the 1990s, when the stock market was rising rapidly. Since then, stock prices have fallen.
   a. How would you expect this change to affect employees' attitudes toward stock options as incentive pay?
   b. How would you expect this change to affect the effectiveness of stock options as an incentive?

7. Based on the balanced scorecard in Table 12.2, find the incentive pay for an employee earning a salary of $4,000 a month in each of the following situations.
   a. The company met all of its target goals for the year. (Multiply the percentage at the top of the table by the employee's salary.)
   b. The company met only its target goals for financial performance (25 percent of the total incentive pay) but none of the other goals.
   c. The company met its stretch goals for financial performance and its base goals in the other areas. (For each category of goals, multiply the percentages by the employee's salary, and then add the amounts together.)

8. Why might a balanced scorecard like the one in Question 7 be more effective than simply using merit pay for a manager?

9. How can the way an organization creates and carries out its incentive plan improve the effectiveness of that plan?

10. In a typical large corporation, the majority of the chief executive's pay is tied to the company's stock price. What are some benefits of this pay strategy? Some risks? How can organizations address the risks?

BUSINESSWEEK CASE

BusinessWeek BMW Aligns Executive Bonuses with Workers' Bonuses

BMW became the first major blue-chip German company to link the bonuses of its top managers to those of its assembly line workers, amid growing global criticism of executive compensation. The move sends a strong message to other firms also examining their compensation practices, as the world's largest banks in particular have come under fire from politicians, shareholders and the public over excessive bonuses during one of the worst economic crises the world has seen.

BMW plans to tie executive bonuses to those of its blue-collar workers, in a bid to create a fairer and sustainable compensation environment within the company.

Starting in 2010, the company will use a common formula to ascertain and award bonuses to its upper- and lower-level employees, based on the company's performance as measured by profit, sales and other factors. That means that upper-level management could potentially lose more money than their lower-level counterparts for bad performance, BMW said.

A spokesman for BMW said the company's goal was to create fair and transparent compensation practices and to prevent a gap between management and the workers, as the under class, from developing. "We don't just want to build sustainable cars. We also want to have sustainable personnel politics. We think this is good for the company culture," the spokesman told *Spiegel Online*. He declined to be more specific on how the formula will work.

Other companies may follow BMW's example as pressure grows on firms to curb excessive bonuses in the wake of the financial crisis. German Chancellor Angela Merkel has been outspoken about her dislike for excessive bonuses, calling them "inappropriate."

U.S. President Barack Obama has also been outspoken about excessive compensation. In June 2009, he appointed attorney Kenneth Feinberg to oversee compensation practices at seven companies that received bailout funds from the government. To that end, Feinberg has devised a plan to cut the total compensation for these companies in half.

Joseph Sorrentino, managing director with Steven Hall & Partners, a U.S.-based executive compensation consulting firm, said a combination of factors including political pressure, government bailouts, public pressure and the declining stock market has led to many companies re-examining their compensation practices to make sure they are effectively paying for performance and not encouraging excessive risk-taking.

"Companies are trying to make sure they balance the public outcry with what they need to make sure they are able to attract and retain their employees," Sorrentino told *Spiegel Online*. He added that often when big companies such as BMW change their compensation practices, other companies take notice.

To be sure, the BMW spokesman said the company has been discussing its compensation practices for months, and that its announcement has nothing to do with the larger debate over executive compensation circulating through governments currently.

However, Harald Krüger, BMW's human resources director, was critical of the bonus structure of banks and other businesses. "If employees need the money or bonuses for motivation, it encourages harmful developments inside a company," the executive told *Frankfurter Allgemeine Sonntagszeitung* newspaper.

SOURCE: Excerpted from Christopher Lawton, "BMW Links Exec Pay to Line Workers," *BusinessWeek*, October 27, 2009, www.businessweek.com.

Questions

1. Based on the information given, summarize the method(s) BMW intends to use for determining incentive pay. Are these rewards for individual, group, and/or company performance?

2. Explain BMW's claim that under the new bonus program, "upper-level management could potentially lose more money than their lower-level counterparts for bad performance." Does this sound like a system that would support BMW's business strategy? Why or why not?

3. BMW says that one motivation for the new bonus method is to establish "sustainable personnel politics" in which employees have a positive relationship with the company. Describe how you think employees would rate the fairness of tying executive bonuses to their bonuses. Describe how you think executives would rate the plan's fairness. Why is fairness an important quality of incentive pay?

Case: Incentive Pay Part of the Strategy at Nucor

Nucor is not your average steel company. Compared with its traditionally managed competitors, Nucor is aggressive about pushing decision making down to the lowest levels of the hierarchy, and it links two-thirds of pay to performance, specifically production levels. That strategy has opened the company up to employee-driven changes that have made the company efficient, flexible, and innovative. Its use of new technology in the form of electric arc furnaces lets the company shut down and start up operations faster to meet demand for its process of melting down scrap metal and shaping it to meet customers' needs.

Nucor's practices may be different, but the company resembles its competitors in one way: when building construction crashed to a halt and manufacturing orders dried up, Nucor joined other steel companies in facing a shocking drop-off in demand. As orders fell, so did output: in the last quarter of 2008, production went from 95 percent of capacity to 50 percent, and it continued to fall to 45 percent in 2009.

At that point, Nucor's reliance on incentive pay went from an advantage in motivating workers to a serious problem of how to keep morale up. As bonuses shrank, total compensation fell by up to 40 percent. The company looked at its overall performance in 2008, which included a modest profit despite the end-of-the-year downturn, and paid all its employees profit sharing totaling $270 million. In addition, the company awarded a special one-time bonus of up to $2,000. More recently, it began offering financial counseling and the option to withdraw funds from employees' profit-sharing accounts.

Of course, the pain is felt at the top as well. Incentive pay is the norm for executives at most companies, and here Nucor is no exception. Chief Executive Officer Dan DiMicco saw a 23 percent drop in his total compensation in 2008, for example. Much of the drop was caused by a 46 percent decline in the value of stock awarded to DiMicco.

One advantage of tying part of employees' pay to profits is that Nucor can afford to keep more workers on board during lean times. The company has avoided layoffs and assigned otherwise-idle workers to review safety programs, find ways to cut costs, carry out preventive maintenance, and even mow the lawns. If Nucor can't motivate workers with money, it can at least show them the company is trying to save their jobs.

Employees seem to appreciate the effort. CEO DiMicco told a reporter, "[Our employees] go further than we would ever think to ask. It makes you feel really good about being a leader in this company when you have that kind of support."

That positive attitude has helped management lead the company to prepare for growth even as employees endured hard times. It's a commitment that is likely to reap dividends as demand picks up and profits begin to roll in again. With production rising above 70 percent of capacity and expected to hit 90 percent in some mills, the future is again looking bright for Nucor and its employees.

SOURCES: Nanette Byrnes, "Pain, but No Layoffs at Nucor," *BusinessWeek*, March 26, 2009, www.businessweek.com; Adam Bell, "Nucor CEO DiMicco Sees Total Pay Drop 23 Percent in 2008," *Charlotte (N.C.) Observer*, March 26, 2009, Business & Company Resource Center, http://galenet.galegroup .com; Stella M. Hopkins, "Special Bonus, Profit-Sharing Options Aid Nucor Workers," *Charlotte (N.C.) Observer*, August 16, 2009, Business & Company

Resource Center, http://galenet.galegroup.com; and Edmond Lococo, "Nucor Posts Second Straight Profit as Shipments Rise," *BusinessWeek*, April 26, 2010, www.businessweek.com.

Questions

1. Nucor gives its employees a relatively great say in decision making along with compensation tied to performance. Discuss how incentive pay could be more effective when it is linked to greater authority and room to innovate.

2. When times are tough, incentive pay falls even if employees are trying hard. In that case, should companies find other ways to reward employees? Why or why not? Evaluate Nucor's use of a "special bonus" in this situation.

3. Cutting compensation by paying smaller production bonuses and no profit sharing when orders dried up might have helped Nucor avoid layoffs. Evaluate the fairness of this approach. Does the fact that the chief executive also earned less make the situation fairer? Would you rather work for a company that lays off employees in lean times or one that offers no incentive pay in lean times? Why?

 IT'S A WRAP!

www.mhhe.com/noefund4e is your source for Reviewing, Applying, and Practicing the concepts you learned about in Chapter 12.

Review
- Chapter learning objectives
- Test Your Knowledge: Reinforcement Theory

Application
- Video case and quiz: "A Motivation Convention in Chicago"
- Self-Assessment: Test your money-talk skills
- Web Exercise: Inform yourself on compensation and benefits management
- Small-business case: Employees Own Bob's Red Mill

Practice
- Chapter quiz

NOTES

1. S. J. Wells, "No Results, No Raise," *HRMagazine*, May 2005, downloaded from Infotrac at http://web6.infotrac .galegroup.com.

2. This chapter draws freely on several literature reviews: B. Gerhart and G. T. Milkovich, "Employee Compensation: Research and Practice," in *Handbook of Industrial and Organizational Psychology*, 2nd ed., eds. M. D. Dunnette and L. M. Hough (Palo Alto, CA: Consulting Psychologists Press, 1992), vol. 3; B. Gerhart and S. L. Rynes, *Compensation: Theory,*

Evidence, and Strategic Implications (Thousand Oaks, CA: Sage, 2003); B. Gerhart, "Compensation Strategy and Organization Performance," in *Compensation in Organizations: Current Research and Practice*, eds. S. L. Rynes and B. Gerhart (San Francisco: Jossey-Bass, 2000), pp. 151–94; and B. Gerhart, S. L. Rynes, and I. S. Fulmer, "Compensation," *Academy of Management Annals* 3 (2009).

3. B. Gerhart and G. T. Milkovich, "Organizational Differences in Managerial Compensation and Financial

Performance," *Academy of Management Journal* 33 (1990), pp. 663–91.

4. G. T. Milkovich and A. K. Wigdor, *Pay for Performance* (Washington, DC: National Academy Press, 1991); Gerhart and Milkovich, "Employee Compensation"; C. Trevor, B. Gerhart, and J. W. Boudreau, "Voluntary Turnover and Job Performance: Curvilinearity and the Moderating Influences of Salary Growth and Promotions," *Journal of Applied Psychology* 82 (1997), pp. 44–61; A. Salamin and P. W. Horm, "In Search of the Elusive U-Shaped Performance-Turnover Relationship: Are High Performing Swiss Bankers More Likely to Quit?" *Journal of Applied Psychology* 90 (2005), pp. 1204–16; and C. B. Cadsby, F. Song, and F. Tapon, "Sorting and Incentive Effects of Pay-for-Performance: An Experimental Investigation," *Academy of Management Journal* 50 (2007), pp. 387–405.

5. Hewitt Associates, "Hewitt Study: While Salary Increases in 2008 Remain Modest, Variable Pay Awards Reach Record High," news release, August 21, 2007, www.hewittassociates.com.

6. Bruce Tulgan, "Managing in the 'New' Workplace," *Financial Executive*, December 2009, pp. 50–53.

7. R. D. Bretz, R. A. Ash, and G. F. Dreher, "Do People Make the Place? An Examination of the Attraction-Selection-Attrition Hypothesis," Personnel Psychology 42 (1989), pp. 561–81; T. A. Judge and R. D. Bretz, "Effect of Values on Job Choice Decisions," *Journal of Applied Psychology* 77 (1992), pp. 261–71; and D. M. Cable and T. A. Judge, "Pay Performance and Job Search Decisions: A Person-Organization Fit Perspective," *Personnel Psychology* 47 (1994), pp. 317–48.

8. E. A. Locke, D. B. Feren, V. M. McCaleb, K. N. Shaw, and A. T. Denny, "The Relative Effectiveness of Four Methods of Motivating Employee Performance," in *Changes in Working Life*, eds. K. D. Duncan, M. M. Gruenberg, and D. Wallis (New York: Wiley, 1980), pp. 363–88.

9. Gerhart and Milkovich, "Employee Compensation."

10. E. E. Lawler III, "Pay for Performance: A Strategic Analysis," in *Compensation and Benefits*, ed. L. R. Gomez-Mejia (Washington, DC: Bureau of National Affairs, 1989); A. M. Konrad and J. Pfeffer, "Do You Get What You Deserve? Factors Affecting the Relationship between Productivity and Pay," *Administrative Science Quarterly* 35 (1990), pp. 258–85; J. L. Medoff and K. G. Abraham, "Are Those Paid More Really More Productive? The Case of Experience," *Journal of Human Resources* 16 (1981), pp. 186–216; and K. S. Teel, "Are Merit Raises Really Based on Merit?" *Personnel Journal* 65, no. 3 (1986), pp. 88–95.

11. F. Hansen, "Lackluster Performance," *Workforce Management*, November 5, 2007, pp. 38–45; Jack Welch and Suzy Welch, "Give Till It Doesn't Hurt," *BusinessWeek*, February 11, 2008, downloaded from General Reference Center Gold, http://find.galegroup .com, and Michelle Conlin, "Making the Case for Unequal Pay and Perks," *BusinessWeek*, March 12, 2009, www.businessweek.com.

12. R. D. Bretz, G. T. Milkovich, and W. Read, "The Current State of Performance Appraisal Research and Practice," *Journal of Management* 18 (1992), pp. 321–52; R. L. Heneman, "Merit Pay Research," Research in *Personnel and Human Resource Management* 8 (1990), pp. 203–63; and Milkovich and Wigdor, *Pay for Performance*.

13. Bretz et al., "Current State of Performance Appraisal Research."

14. S. L. Rynes, B. Gerhart, and L. Parks, "Personnel Psychology: Performance Evaluation and Compensation," *Annual Review of Psychology* (2005).

15. W. E. Deming, *Out of the Crisis* (Cambridge, MA: Center for Advanced Engineering Study, Massachusetts Institute of Technology, 1986), p. 110.

16. See, for example, Dan Fitzpatrick, "For BofA Investment Bankers, Bonuses Likely Close to 2007," *Wall Street Journal*, January 8, 2010, http://online.wsj .com; Deborah Solomon, Sara Schaefer Muñoz, and Alistair MacDonald, "Firms Face New Curbs on Pay," *Wall Street Journal*, December 10, 2009, http:// online.wsj.com; and Reuters, "Wall St. Bonuses Fall 44 Percent, Report Says," *New York Times*, January 28, 2009, www.nytimes.com.

17. Mike Pare, "Chattem Chiefs Get Paid to Stay," *Chattanooga Times/Free Press*, January 5, 2010, Business & Company Resource Center, http://galenet.galegroup .com.

18. U.S. Department of Justice, Antitrust Division, "Home Prices and Commissions over Time," Competition and Real Estate page, http://www.justice. gov/atr/public/real_estate/save.htm, accessed April 26, 2010; Sil Anderson, "How Much Can You Prosper as an Insurance Agent?" AMPM Insure, www. ampminsure.org/insuranceagents/agent-commission. html, accessed April 26, 2010; and "Confesssions of a Car Salesman, Part 3: Meeting, Greeting and Dealing," Buying Tips, Edmunds.com, www.edmunds. com, accessed April 26, 2010.

19. T. L. Ross and R. A. Ross, "Gainsharing: Sharing Improved Performance," in *The Compensation Handbook*, 3rd ed., eds. M. L. Rock and L. A. Berger (New York: McGraw-Hill, 1991).

20. T. M. Welbourne and L. R. Gomez-Mejia, "Team Incentives in the Workplace," in *The Compensation Handbook*, 3rd ed.

21. L. R. Gomez-Mejia and D. B. Balkin, *Compensation, Organizational Strategy, and Firm Performance* (Cincinnati: South-Western, 1992).

22. J. A. Fossum, *Labor Relations* (New York: McGraw-Hill, 2002).

23. This idea has been referred to as the "share economy." See M. L. Weitzman, "The Simple Macroeconomics of Profit Sharing," *American Economic Review* 75 (1985), pp. 937–53. For supportive research, see the following studies: J. Chelius and R. S. Smith, "Profit Sharing and Employment Stability," *Industrial and Labor Relations Review* 43 (1990), pp. 256S–73S; B. Gerhart and L. O. Trevor, "Employment Stability under Different Managerial Compensation Systems," working paper (Cornell University Center for Advanced Human Resource Studies, 1995); D. L. Kruse, "Profit Sharing and Employment Variability: Microeconomic Evidence on the Weitzman Theory," *Industrial and Labor Relations Review* 44 (1991), pp. 437–53.

24. Gerhart and Milkovich, "Employee Compensation"; M. L. Weitzman and D. L. Kruse, "Profit Sharing and Productivity," in *Paying for Productivity*, ed. A. S. Blinder (Washington, DC: Brookings Institution, 1990); D. L. Kruse, *Profit Sharing: Does It Make a Difference?* (Kalamazoo, MI: Upjohn Institute, 1993); and M. Magnan and S. St.-Onge, "The Impact of Profit Sharing on the Performance of Financial Services Firms," *Journal of Management Studies* 42 (2005), pp. 761–91.

25. Mary Divine, "Andersen Profit-Sharing at 6.5 Percent—a Year Ago It Was 22.5," *America's Intelligence Wire*, January 14, 2009, Business & Company Resource Center, http://galenet.galegroup.com; and Mary Divine, "Andersen Corp. Workers Won't Get Profit-Sharing Checks for First Time since Great Depression," *America's Intelligence Wire*, January 27, 2010, Business & Company Resource Center, http://galenet.galegroup.com.

26. Gerhart and Milkovich, "Organizational Differences in Managerial Compensation."

27. Greg Risling, "Ex-KB Home CEO Guilty on Four Counts," *Houston Chronicle*, April 22, 2010, Business & Company Resource Center, http://galenet.galegroup.com; David Nicklaus, "Scandal Left Both Sides Sullied," *St. Louis Post-Dispatch*, February 21, 2010, Business & Company Resource Center, http://galenet.galegroup.com; and Richard A. Booth, "Malfeasance, Misappropriation, Manipulation—or Not?" *Regulation*, Spring 2010, Business & Company Resource Center, http://galenet.galegroup.com.

28. National Center for Employee Ownership, "A Statistical Profile of Employee Ownership," NCEO Web site, updated March 2010, www.nceo.org.

29. M. A. Conte and J. Svejnar, "The Performance Effects of Employee Ownership Plans," in *Paying for Productivity*, pp. 245–94.

30. Ibid.; T. H. Hammer, "New Developments in Profit Sharing, Gainsharing, and Employee Ownership," in *Productivity in Organizations*, eds. J. P. Campbell, R. J. Campbell, et al. (San Francisco: Jossey-Bass, 1988); and K. J. Klein, "Employee Stock Ownership and Employee Attitudes: A Test of Three Models," *Journal of Applied Psychology* 72 (1987), pp. 319–32.

31. Tim Sullivan and Henry Cano, "Introducing a Balanced Scorecard for Electric Cooperatives: A Tool for Measuring and Improving Results," *Management Quarterly*, Winter 2009, Business & Company Resource Center, http://galenet.galegroup.com.

32. R. T. Kaufman, "The Effects of Improshare on Productivity," *Industrial and Labor Relations Review* 45 (1992), pp. 311–22; M. H. Schuster, "The Scanlon Plan: A Longitudinal Analysis," *Journal of Applied Behavioral Science* 20 (1984), pp. 23–28; and J. A. Wagner III, P. Rubin, and T. J. Callahan, "Incentive Payment and Nonmanagerial Productivity: An Interrupted Time Series Analysis of Magnitude and Trend," *Organizational Behavior and Human Decision Processes* 42 (1988), pp. 47–74.

33. C. R. Gowen III and S. A. Jennings, "The Effects of Changes in Participation and Group Size on Gainsharing Success: A Case Study," *Journal of Organizational Behavior Management* 11 (1991), pp. 147–69.

34. D. I. Levine and L. D. Tyson, "Participation, Productivity, and the Firm's Environment," in *Paying for Productivity*.

35. T. Welbourne, D. Balkin, and L. Gomez-Mejia, "Gainsharing and Mutual Monitoring: A Combined Agency–Organizational Justice Interpretation," *Academy of Management Journal* 38 (1995), pp. 881–99.

36. Gerhart and Milkovich, "Organizational Differences in Managerial Compensation." and Jessica Silver-Greenberg, Tara Kalwarski, and Alexis Leondis, "CEO Pay Drops, but . . . Cash Is King," *Business-Week*, March 25, 2010, www.businessweek.com.

Providing Employee Benefits

What Do I Need to Know?

After reading this chapter, you should be able to:

LO1 Discuss the importance of benefits as a part of employee compensation.

LO2 Summarize the types of employee benefits required by law.

LO3 Describe the most common forms of paid leave.

LO4 Identify the kinds of insurance benefits offered by employers.

LO5 Define the types of retirement plans offered by employers.

LO6 Describe how organizations use other benefits to match employees' wants and needs.

LO7 Explain how to choose the contents of an employee benefits package.

LO8 Summarize the regulations affecting how employers design and administer benefits programs.

LO9 Discuss the importance of effectively communicating the nature and value of benefits to employees.

Introduction

focus on
*social
responsibility*

Patagonia has a long and strong reputation for caring about the environment and helping customers enjoy nature while using its top-quality recreational gear and clothing. The Ventura, California–based company carries out its mission to build the best products while reducing its environmental impact through dedicated people who deliver results. Most are drawn to Patagonia by its mission. Pay rates are, at best, only slightly above the market rate, but generous benefits help to keep talented employees on board. All Patagonia employees, full- and part-time, receive a full health insurance package, and the headquarters boasts an on-site day care center. In addition, the company will pay employees for a sabbatical of up to two months that is spent working for environmental groups.[1]

Like Patagonia's employees, employees at almost every organization receive more than dollars and cents in exchange for their efforts. They also receive a package of **employee benefits**—compensation in forms other than cash. Besides the use of corporate fitness centers, examples include paid vacation time, employer-paid health insurance, and pension plans, among a wide range of possibilities.

Employee Benefits
Compensation in forms other than cash.

This chapter describes the contents of an employee benefits package and the way organizations administer employee benefits. We begin by discussing the important role of benefits as a part of employee compensation. The following sections define major types of employee benefits: benefits required by law, paid leave, insurance policies, retirement plans, and other benefits. We then discuss how to choose which of these alternatives to include in an employee benefits package so that it contributes to meeting the organization's goals. The next section summarizes the regulations affecting how employers design and administer benefits programs. Finally, we explain why and how organizations should effectively communicate with employees about their benefits.

LO1 Discuss the importance of benefits as a part of employee compensation.

The Role of Employee Benefits

As a part of the total compensation paid to employees, benefits serve functions similar to pay. Benefits contribute to attracting, retaining, and motivating employees. The variety of possible benefits also helps employers tailor their compensation to the kinds of employees they need. Different employees look for different types of benefits. Employers need to examine their benefits package regularly to see whether they meet the needs of today. At the same time, benefits packages are more complex than pay structures, so benefits are harder for employees to understand and appreciate. Even if employers spend large sums on benefits, if employees do not understand how to use them or why they are valuable, the cost of the benefits will be largely wasted.[2] Employers need to communicate effectively so that the benefits succeed in motivating employees. For an example of a company that gets its benefits program right, see the "Best Practices" box.

Employees have come to expect that benefits will help them maintain economic security. Social Security contributions, pensions, and retirement savings plans help employees prepare for their retirement. Insurance plans help to protect employees from unexpected costs such as hospital bills. This important role of benefits is one reason that benefits are subject to government regulation. Some benefits, such as Social Security, are required by law. Other regulations establish requirements that benefits must meet to obtain the most favorable tax treatment. Later in the chapter, we will describe some of the most significant regulations affecting benefits.

Even though many kinds of benefits are not required by law, they have become so common that today's employees expect them. Many employers find that attracting qualified workers requires them to provide medical and retirement benefits of some sort. A large employer without such benefits would be highly unusual and would have difficulty competing in the labor market. Still, the nature of the benefits package changes over time, as we will discuss at various points throughout the chapter.

Like other forms of compensation, benefits impose significant costs. On average, out of every dollar spent on compensation, 30 cents or more go to benefits. As Figure 13.1 shows, this share has grown over the past decades. These numbers indicate that an organization managing its labor costs must pay careful attention to the cost of its employee benefits.

Why do organizations pay a growing share of compensation in the form of benefits? It would be simpler to pay all compensation in cash and let employees buy their own insurance and contribute to their own savings plans. That arrangement would also give employees greater control over what their compensation buys. However, several forces have made benefits a significant part of compensation packages. One is that laws require employers to provide certain benefits, such as contributions to Social Security and unemployment insurance. Also, tax laws can make benefits favorable to employees. For example, employees do not pay income taxes on most benefits they

Best Practices

BENEFITS HELP MAKE SAS EMPLOYEES HAPPY

SAS, the largest privately owned software company, has made it onto *Fortune* magazine's list of Best Companies to Work For every year that list has been compiled. One of the notable reasons is a generous set of employee benefits. Employees can unwind with a swim, haircut, workout, or massage at the recreation and fitness center on the company's campus near Raleigh, North Carolina. A subsidized day care center and summer camp help employees ensure that their children are in good hands. Employees with errands to run can take care of them swiftly with on-site dry cleaning, car detailing, tax preparation, and a book exchange. The subsidized cafeteria offers takeout for any employee who wants to take dinner home for the family. The company has set up a lactation room where nursing mothers can settle into a recliner and listen to soft music while feeding their babies.

One of the most unusual benefits is one of the most generous: an on-site health care center for routine medical needs. Employees and their families can make appointments to see a doctor,

nurse practitioner, nurse, physical therapist, or psychologist. There's no charge to the employees (except for a missed appointment, which costs $10), but the company says the center saves money because employees don't need to take as much time off as they would to visit doctors elsewhere, they get routine needs met before they become serious problems, and the company runs the center efficiently.

Generous benefits aren't a form of charity for employees, but rather part of a strategy to hire and keep the best people without paying top dollar in salaries. Taking care of people is all about the numbers for CEO Jim Goodnight, who has a doctorate degree in statistics and as co-founder owns two-thirds of the company's stock. Compared with 22 percent employee turnover in the industry, SAS reports turnover of just 2 percent. The average employee has been at SAS for 10 years. Of the company's 4,200 employees, 300 have worked there for at least 25 years. And for every year SAS has been in business, Goodnight says, it has turned a profit.

Offering perks is just one way SAS treats employees well. Employees have flexibility in setting their schedules, and they typically work just 35 hours a week. In fact, the worker-friendly policies don't make SAS into some kind of country club. SAS keeps its workers comfortable so they can work creatively, without distractions. In Goodnight's experience, exhausted, stressed-out workers don't produce great work. Happy employees would agree. Bev Brown, who works in external communications, told a reporter, "People do work hard here, because they're motivated to take care of a company that takes care of them."

Sources: David A. Kaplan, "SAS: A New No. 1 Best Employer," *Fortune,* January 22, 2010, http://money.cnn.com; Leah Friedman, "Nursing Mothers Get a Break, Starting Now," *News & Observer (Raleigh, N.C.),* April 28, 2010, Business & Company Resource Center, http://galenet.galegroup.com; and Stefan Stern, "The Real Value of Managing Information and People," *Financial Times,* February 1, 2010, Business & Company Resource Center, http://galenet.galegroup.com.

receive, but they pay income taxes on cash compensation. Therefore, an employee who receives a $1,000 raise "takes home" less than the full $1,000, but an employee who receives an additional $1,000 worth of benefits receives the full benefits. Another cost advantage of paying benefits is that employers, especially large ones, often can get a better deal on insurance or other programs than employees can obtain on their own. Finally, some employers assemble creative benefits packages that set them apart in the competition for talent. For example, International Business Machines and Texas Instruments offer an online course that helps employees cope with the demands of being a caregiver for an ill family member, while Pitney Bowes and Marriott International offer insurance that pays the full cost of drugs for chronic conditions like asthma and high blood pressure.[3]

Figure 13.1

Benefits as a Percentage
of Total Compensation

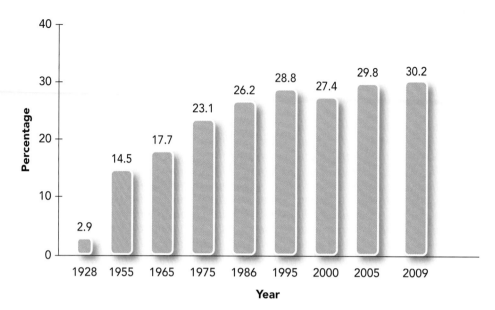

SOURCE: Bureau of Labor Statistics, "Employer Costs for Employee Compensation," http://data.bls.gov, accessed April 28, 2010.

LO2 Summarize the
types of employee
benefits required by
law.

Benefits Required by Law

The federal and state governments require various forms of social insurance to protect workers from the financial hardships of being out of work. In general, Social Security provides support for retired workers, unemployment insurance assists laid-off workers, and workers' compensation insurance provides benefits and services to workers injured on the job. Employers must also provide unpaid leave for certain family and medical needs. Because these benefits are required by law, employers cannot gain an advantage in the labor market by offering them, nor can they design the nature of these benefits. Rather, the emphasis must be on complying with the details of the law. Table 13.1 summarizes legally required benefits.

Social Security

In 1935 the federal Social Security Act established old-age insurance and unemployment insurance. Congress later amended the act to add survivor's insurance (1939), disability insurance (1956), hospital insurance (Medicare Part A, 1965), and

Table 13.1

Benefits Required by Law

BENEFIT	EMPLOYER REQUIREMENT
Social Security	Flat payroll tax on employees and employers
Unemployment insurance	Payroll tax on employers that depends on state requirements and experience rating
Workers' compensation insurance	Provide coverage according to state requirements. Premiums depend on experience rating
Family and medical leave	Up to 12 weeks of unpaid leave for childbirth, adoption, or serious illness
Health care	Provisions of 2010 law phased in through 2014

supplementary medical insurance (Medicare Part B, 1965) for the elderly. Together, the law and its amendments created what is now the Old Age, Survivors, Disability, and Health Insurance (OASDHI) program, informally known as **Social Security.** This program covers over 90 percent of U.S. employees. The main exceptions are railroad and federal, state, and local government employees, who often have their own plans.

Kathleen Casey-Kirschling was the first of the baby boomers to begin receiving Social Security benefits. The widening gap between those contributing to the system and those receiving benefits is a major concern.

Workers who meet eligibility requirements receive the retirement benefits according to their age and earnings history. If they elect to begin receiving benefits at full retirement age, they can receive full benefits, or if they elect to begin receiving benefits at age 62, they receive benefits at a permanently reduced level. The full retirement age rises with birth year: a person born in 1940 reaches full retirement age at 65 years and 6 months, and a person born in 1960 or later reaches full retirement age at 67. The benefit amount rises with the person's past earnings, but the level goes up very little after a certain level. In 2008, the maximum monthly benefit was $2,185. The government increases the payments each year according to the growth in the consumer price index. Also, spouses of covered earners receive benefits, even if they have no covered earnings. They receive either the benefit associated with their own earnings or one-half of the amount received by the covered earner, whichever is greater.

Benefits may be reduced if the worker is still earning wages above a maximum, called the *exempt amount*. In 2009, the exempt amount was $14,160 for beneficiaries under the full retirement age. A beneficiary in that age range who earns more than the exempt amount sees a reduction in his or her benefit. The amount of the reduction is $1 for every $2 the person earns above the exempt amount. For example a 63-year-old who earned $16,160 in 2009 would have earned $2,000 above the exempt amount, so the person's Social Security benefits would be reduced by $1,000. During the year a worker reaches full retirement age, the maximum untaxed earnings are $37,680 (in 2009), and benefits are reduced $1 for every $3 in earnings. Beginning in the month they reach full retirement age, workers face no reduction in benefits for earning above the exempt amount. For workers below that age, the penalty increases the incentive to retire or at least reduce the number of hours worked. Adding to this incentive, Social Security benefits are free from federal income taxes and free from state taxes in about half the states.

Employers and employees share the cost of Social Security through a payroll tax. The percentage is set by law and has changed from time to time. In 2009, employers and employees each paid a tax of 7.65 percent on the first $106,800 of the employee's earnings, with 6.2 percent of earnings going to OASDI and 1.45 percent going to Medicare (Part A). For earnings above $106,800, only the 1.45 percent for Medicare is assessed.

Social Security
The federal Old Age, Survivors, Disability, and Health Insurance (OASDHI) program, which combines old age (retirement) insurance, survivor's insurance, disability insurance, hospital insurance (Medicare Part A), and supplementary medical insurance (Medicare Part B) for the elderly.

Unemployment Insurance

Along with OASDHI, the Social Security Act of 1935 established a program of **unemployment insurance.** This program has four objectives related to minimizing the hardships of unemployment. It provides payments to offset lost income during involuntary unemployment, and it helps unemployed workers find new jobs. The payment of unemployment insurance taxes gives employers an incentive to stabilize

Unemployment Insurance
A federally mandated program to minimize the hardships of unemployment through payments to unemployed workers, help in finding new jobs, and incentives to stabilize employment.

employment. And providing workers with income during short-term layoffs preserves investments in worker skills because workers can afford to wait to return to their employer, rather than start over with another organization. Technically, the federal government left it to each state's discretion to establish an unemployment insurance program. At the same time, the Social Security Act created a tax incentive structure that quickly led every state to establish the program.

Most of the funding for unemployment insurance comes from federal and state taxes on employers. The federal tax rate is currently 0.8 percent of the first $7,000 of each employee's wages. The state tax rate varies. For a new employer, rates range from 1 percent to 6 percent, and the taxable wage base ranges from $7,000 to $32,200, so the amount paid depends a great deal on where the company is located.[4] Also, some states charge new employers whatever rate is the average for their industry, so the amount of tax paid in those states also depends on the type of business. In the severe recession of 2008–2009, layoffs were so widespread that unemployment insurance funds were drained and many states dramatically hiked premiums for unemployment insurance. In Hawaii, for example, the rate jumped from $90 per employee to an average around $1,000 per employee, with some employers paying as much as $2,040.[5]

No state imposes the same tax rate on every employer in the state. The size of the unemployment insurance tax imposed on each employer depends on the employer's **experience rating**—the number of employees the company laid off in the past and the cost of providing them with unemployment benefits. Employers with a history of laying off a large share of their workforces pay higher taxes than those with few layoffs. In some states, an employer with very few layoffs may pay no state tax. In contrast, an employer with a poor experience rating could pay a tax as high as 5.4 to 12.27 percent, depending on the state. The use of experience ratings gives employers some control over the cost of unemployment insurance. Careful human resource planning can minimize layoffs and keep their experience rating favorable.

Experience Rating
The number of employees a company has laid off in the past and the cost of providing them with unemployment benefits.

To receive benefits, workers must meet four conditions:

1. They meet requirements demonstrating they had been employed (often 52 weeks or four quarters of work at a minimum level of pay).
2. They are available for work.
3. They are actively seeking work. This requirement includes registering at the local unemployment office.
4. They were not discharged for cause (such as willful misconduct), did not quit voluntarily, and are not out of work because of a labor dispute (such as a union member on strike).

Workers who meet these conditions receive benefits at the level set by the state—typically about half the person's previous earnings—for a period of 26 weeks. States with a sustained unemployment rate above a particular threshold or significantly above recent levels also offer extended benefits for up to 13 weeks. Sometimes Congress funds emergency extended benefits. All states have minimum and maximum weekly benefit levels.

Workers' Compensation
State programs that provide benefits to workers who suffer work-related injuries or illnesses, or to their survivors.

Workers' Compensation

Decades ago, workers who suffered work-related injury or illness had to bear the cost unless they won a lawsuit against their employer. Those who sued often lost the case because of the defenses available to employers. Today, the states have passed **workers' compensation** laws, which help workers with the expenses resulting from job-related accidents and illnesses.[6] These laws operate under a principle of *no-fault liability*, meaning that an employee does not need to show that the employer was grossly negligent in order to receive compensation, and the employer is protected from lawsuits. The employer loses this protection if it intentionally contributes to a dangerous workplace. Employees are not eligible if their injuries are self-inflicted or if they result from intoxication or "willful disregard of safety rules."[7]

About 9 out of 10 U.S. workers are covered by state workers' compensation laws, with the level of coverage varying from state to state. The benefits fall into four major categories: (1) disability income, (2) medical care, (3) death benefits, and (4) rehabilitative services. The amount of income varies from state to state but is typically two-thirds of the worker's earnings before the disability. The benefits are tax free.

The states differ in terms of how they fund workers' compensation insurance. Some states have a single state fund. Most states allow employers to purchase coverage from private insurance companies. Most also permit self-funding by employers. The cost of the workers' compensation insurance depends on the kinds of occupations involved, the state where the company is located, and the employer's experience rating. Premiums for low-risk occupations may be less than 1 percent of payroll. For some of the most hazardous occupations, the cost may be as high as 100 percent of payroll. Costs also vary from state to state, so that one state's program requires higher premiums than another state's program. As with unemployment insurance, unfavorable experience ratings lead to higher premiums. Organizations can minimize the cost of this benefit by keeping workplaces safe and making employees and their managers conscious of safety issues, as discussed in Chapter 3.

Unpaid Family and Medical Leave

In the United States, unpaid leave is required by law for certain family needs. Specifically, the **Family and Medical Leave Act (FMLA)** of 1993 requires organizations with 50 or more employees within a 75-mile radius to provide as much as 12 weeks of unpaid leave after childbirth or adoption; to care for a seriously ill child, spouse, or parent, for an employee's own serious illness; or to take care of urgent needs that arise when a spouse, child, or parent in the National Guard or Reserve is called to active duty. In addition, if a family member (child, spouse, parent, or next of kin) is injured while serving on active military duty, the employee may take up to 26 weeks of unpaid leave under FMLA. Employers must also guarantee these employees the same or a comparable job when they return to work. The law does not cover employees who have less than one year of service, work fewer than 25 hours per week, or are among the organization's 10 percent highest paid. The 12 weeks of unpaid leave amount to a smaller benefit than is typical of Japan and most countries in Western Europe. Japan and West European nations typically require paid family leave.

Experience with the Family and Medical Leave Act suggests that a majority of those opting for this benefit fail to take the full 12 weeks. In about one out of four situations, employees take their leave intermittently, over periods of days or even hours, creating a significant record-keeping task.[8] Other employees, especially female executives, are simply keeping parental leaves under FMLA to a minimum, less than the available 12 weeks. Many are eager to return to their careers, and others fear that staying away for three months would damage their career opportunities.[9] Of course, another reason for not taking the full 12 weeks is that not everyone can afford three months without pay, especially when responsible for the expenses that accompany childbirth, adoption, or serious illness.

Family and Medical Leave Act (FMLA)
Federal law requiring organizations with 50 or more employees to provide up to 12 weeks of unpaid leave after childbirth or adoption; to care for a seriously ill family member, or for an employee's own serious illness; or to take care of urgent needs that arise when a spouse, child, or parent in the National Guard or Reserve is called to active duty.

When employees experience pregnancy and childbirth, employers must also comply with the Pregnancy Discrimination Act, described in Chapter 3. If an employee is temporarily unable to perform her job due to pregnancy, the employer must treat her in the same way as any other temporarily disabled employee. For example, the employer may provide modified tasks, alternative assignments, disability leave, or leave without pay.

Health Care Benefits

Patient Protection and Affordable Care Act
Health care reform law passed in 2010 that includes incentives and penalties for employers providing health insurance as a benefit.

In 2010, Congress passed the **Patient Protection and Affordable Care Act,** a complex package of changes in how health care is to be paid for, including requirements for insurance companies, incentives and penalties for employers providing health insurance as a benefit, expansion of public funding including Medicaid and community health centers, and creation of health insurance exchanges as an option for the sale of health insurance. Provisions of the law are being phased in between 2010 and 2014.

The first provisions of the law that take effect mainly involve requirements for insurance companies—for example, that they must cover children with pre-existing conditions and dependent children through age 26 and may not impose lifetime limits on coverage or end coverage for people when they get sick. Small-business employers (up to 25 employees) are affected by one change that takes effect in 2010: a tax credit equal to half the cost of providing health insurance benefits. In 2014, automatic enrollment in health insurance is required at companies with over 200 employees. Companies with more than 50 employees that do not provide health insurance will have to pay a penalty. Because the law is complex and details of implementation are still being worked out, HR departments must educate themselves about the requirements and communicate with employees, many of whom may be worried about how the law will affect them. A useful starting point is the government's health reform Web site, www.healthreform.gov.

Optional Benefits Programs

Other types of benefits are optional. These include various kinds of insurance, retirement plans, and paid leave. Figure 13.2 shows the percentage of full-time workers having access to the most common employee benefits. (Part-time workers often have access to and receive fewer benefits.) The most widely offered benefits are paid leave for vacations and holidays, life and medical insurance, and retirement plans. In general, benefits packages at smaller companies tend to be more limited than at larger companies.

Benefits such as health insurance often extend to employees' dependents. Traditionally, these benefits have covered employees, their spouses, and dependent children. Today, many employers also cover *domestic partners*, defined either by local law or by the companies themselves. Typically, a domestic partner is an adult nonrelative who lives with the employee in a relationship defined as permanent and financially interdependent. Some local governments provide for registration of domestic partners. Organizations offering coverage to domestic partners generally require that the partners sign a document stating they meet the requirements for a domestic partnership. Benefits provided to domestic partners do not have the same tax advantages as benefits provided to spouses. The partner's benefits are taxed as wages of the employee receiving the benefits.

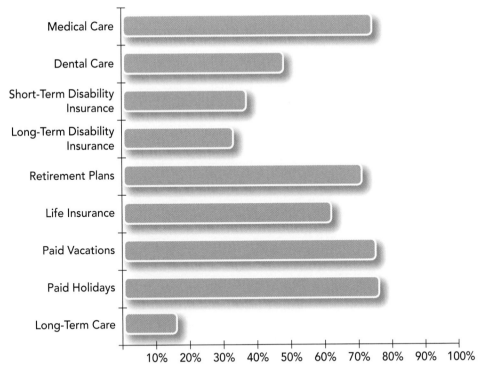

Figure 13.2

Percentage of Full-Time Workers with Access to Selected Benefit Programs

SOURCE: Bureau of Labor Statistics, "Employee Benefits in the United States, March 2009," news release, July 28, 2009, www.bls.gov; and Bureau of Labor Statistics, "Employee Benefits Survey," http://www.bls.gov/ncs/ebs/benefits/2009/, accessed April 30, 2010.

Paid Leave

The major categories of paid leave are vacations, holidays, and sick leave. Employers also should establish policies for other situations that may require time off. Organizations often provide for paid leave for jury duty, funerals of family members, and military duty. Some organizations provide for other paid leave, such as time off to vote or to donate blood. Establishing policies communicates the organization's values, clarifies what employees can expect, and prevents situations in which unequal treatment leads to claims of unfairness.

At first blush, paid vacation, holidays, sick leave, and other paid leave may not seem to make economic sense. The employer pays the employee for time spent not working, so the employer receives nothing in return for the pay. Some employers may see little direct advantage. This may be the reason that Western European countries require a minimum number of paid vacation days, with new employees receiving 30 days off in many countries. The United States, in contrast, has no such legal requirement. It is up to U.S. employers to decide whether paid leave has a payoff in recruiting and retaining employees. At U.S. companies, paid vacation is typically two weeks or less a year for the first few years (see the "Did You Know?" box). To receive as much vacation as European employees, U.S. workers must typically stay with an employer for more than 20 years.[10]

Paid holidays are time off on specified days in addition to vacation time. In Western Europe and the United States, employees typically have about 10 paid holidays each year, regardless of length of service. The most common paid holidays in the United States are New Year's Day, Memorial Day, Independence Day, Labor Day, Thanksgiving Day, and Christmas Day.

LO3 Describe the most common forms of paid leave.

U.S. and Japanese Workers Take Short Vacations

On average, workers in the United States reported receiving 13 vacation days but using only 11 of them. Japanese workers were even less willing to take time off: they reported receiving 15 days of vacation but taking only 7 of those days.

Source: Kenji Hall, "Can Vacation Reform Help Japan's Economy?" *BusinessWeek,* April 22, 2009, www.businessweek.com.

U.S. Vacations

Japanese Vacations

Sick leave programs pay employees for days not worked because of illness. The amount of sick leave is often based on length of service, so that it accumulates over time—for example, one day added to sick leave for each month of service. Employers must decide how many sick days to grant and whether to let them continue accumulating year after year. If sick days accumulate without limit, employees can "save" them in case of disability. If an employee becomes disabled, the employee can use up the accumulated sick days, receiving full pay rather than smaller payments from disability insurance, discussed later. Some employers let sick days accumulate for only a year, and unused sick days "disappear" at year-end. This may provide an unintended incentive to use up sick days. Some healthy employees may call in sick near the end of the year so that they can obtain the benefit of the paid leave before it disappears.

Employers may counter this tendency by paying employees for some or all of their unused sick days at year-end or when the employees retire or resign.

An organization's policies for time off may include other forms of paid and unpaid leave. For a workforce that values flexibility, the organization may offer paid *personal days*, days off that employees may schedule according to their personal needs, with the supervisor's approval. Typically, organizations offer a few personal days in addition to sick leave. *Floating holidays* are paid holidays that vary from year to year. The organization may schedule floating holidays so that they extend a Tuesday or Thursday holiday into a long weekend. Organizations may also give employees discretion over the scheduling of floating holidays.

Paid time off is a way for employees to enjoy time with their families and to refresh their bodies and spirits. Is paid time off an important criteria for you when accepting a position?

The most flexible approach to time off is to grant each employee a bank of *paid time off*, in which the employer pools personal days, sick days, and vacation days for employees to use as the need or desire arises. This flexibility is especially attractive to younger workers, who tend to rate work/life balance as one of the most important sources of job satisfaction. The flexibility also fits with the U.S. trend toward more frequent but shorter vacations. With these advantages, paid time off has become more widespread than traditional policies separating types of leave, according to a recent survey.[11]

Employers should also establish policies for leaves without pay—for example, leaves of absence to pursue nonwork goals or to meet family needs. Unpaid leave is an employee benefit because the employee usually retains seniority and benefits during the leave.

Group Insurance

As we noted earlier, rates for group insurance are typically lower than for individual policies. Also, insurance benefits are not subject to income tax, as wages and salaries are. When employees receive insurance as a benefit, rather than higher pay so they can buy their own insurance, employees can get more for their money. Because of this, most employees value group insurance. The most common types of insurance offered as employee benefits are medical, life, and disability insurance. As noted in the earlier discussion of benefits required under law, the U.S. government will require medium-sized and large businesses to offer health insurance or pay a penalty beginning in 2014; but until then, medical insurance is an optional benefit, and businesses continue to have many choices in the types of coverage they offer.

LO4 Identify the kinds of insurance benefits offered by employers.

Medical Insurance

For the average person, the most important benefit by far is medical insurance.[12] As Figure 13.2 shows, almost three-quarters of full-time employees receive medical benefits. The policies typically cover three basic types of medical expenses: hospital expenses, surgical expenses, and visits to physicians. Some employers offer additional coverage, such as dental care, vision care, birthing centers, and prescription drug programs. Under the Mental Health Parity Act of 1996, health insurance plans offered to employees must have the same maximum dollar benefits for covered mental illness as for other medical and surgical benefits. Some states have stricter requirements than the federal law. However, insurance plans can and do impose other restrictions on mental health care, such as limits on the number of days of hospitalization, and some employers avoid the restrictions by offering insurance without any mental health coverage.[13]

Consolidated Omnibus Budget Reconciliation Act (COBRA)
Federal law that requires employers to permit employees or their dependents to extend their health insurance coverage at group rates for up to 36 months following a qualifying event, such as a layoff, reduction in hours, or the employee's death.

Employers that offer medical insurance must meet the requirements of the **Consolidated Omnibus Budget Reconciliation Act (COBRA)** of 1985. This federal law requires employers to permit employees to extend their health insurance coverage at group rates for up to 36 months following a "qualifying event." Qualifying events include termination (except for gross misconduct), a reduction in hours that leads to loss of health insurance, and the employee's death (in which case the surviving spouse or dependent child would extend the coverage). To extend the coverage, the employee or the surviving spouse or dependent must pay for the insurance, but the payments are at the group rate. These employees and their families must have access to the same services as those who did not lose their health insurance.

As we will discuss later in the chapter, health insurance is a significant and fast-growing share of benefits costs at U.S. organizations, far outpacing the inflation rate and even the rise in the overall cost of health care in the United States.[14] Figure 13.3 shows that the United States spends much more of its total wealth on health care than other countries do. Most Western European countries have nationalized health systems, but the majority of Americans with coverage for health care expenses get it through their own or a family member's employer. As a result, a growing number of employees whose employers cannot afford this benefit are left without insurance to cover health care expenses.

Employers have looked for ways to control the cost of health care coverage while keeping this valuable benefit. They have used variations of managed care, employee-driven savings, and promotion of employee wellness:

- With *managed care*, the insurer plays a role in decisions about health care, aimed at avoiding unnecessary procedures. The insurer may conduct claims review, studying

Figure 13.3

Health Care Costs in Various Countries

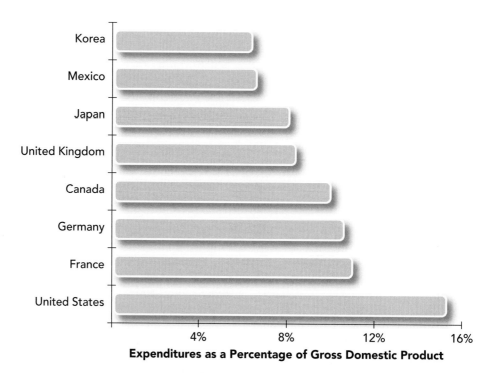

Expenditures as a Percentage of Gross Domestic Product

SOURCE: Organization for Economic Cooperation and Development, "Public Finance: Public Expenditure," *OECD Factbook 2009*, pp. 220–21, accessed at www.oecd.org.

claims to determine whether procedures are effective for the type of illness or injury. Patients may be required to obtain approval before hospital admissions, and the insurer may require alternatives to hospital stays—for example, outpatient surgery or home health care.

- A **health maintenance organization (HMO)** is a health care plan that requires patients to receive their medical care from the HMO's health care professionals, who are often paid a flat salary, and provides all services on a prepaid basis. In other words, the premiums paid for the HMO cover all the patient's visits and procedures, without an additional payment from the patient. By paying physicians a salary, rather than a fee for each service, the HMO hopes to remove any incentive to provide more services than the patients really need. HMO coverage tends to cost less than traditional health insurance. The downside is that employees sometimes complain cost-control incentives work so well that they are denied access to services they actually need.

- A **preferred provider organization (PPO)** is a health care plan that contracts with health care professionals to provide services at a reduced fee. Often, the PPO does not require employees to use providers in the network, but it pays a larger share of the cost of services from PPO providers. For example, the employee might pay 10 percent of the cost of a test by an in-network provider and 20 percent if the employee goes out of the PPO network. PPOs have quickly grown to become the most widely used health plan among U.S. employers. Recent data found that among workers with health insurance, about two-thirds were enrolled in a PPO; most of the remainder—almost one-fourth—were in an HMO.[15]

- With a **flexible spending account,** employees set aside a portion of pretax earnings to pay for eligible expenses. In particular, a *medical savings account* lets employees use their pretax savings to pay for qualified health care expenses (for example, payment of premiums). To avoid taxation, the money in the account must meet IRS requirements. Contributions to this account may not exceed $5,000 per year and must be designated in advance. The money in the account may be spent on health care expenses of the employee and employee's dependents during the plan year. At the end of the year, any remaining funds in the account revert to the employer. The major advantage of flexible spending accounts is that the money in the account is not taxed, so employees will have more take-home pay. But if they do not use all the money in the flexible spending account, they lose the amount they do not spend. Therefore, employees are most likely to benefit from a flexible spending account if they have predictable health care expenses, such as insurance premiums.

- *Consumer-driven health plans* (CDHPs) are intended to provide health coverage in a way that gets employees involved as consumers making decisions to lower costs. A CDHP typically brings together three elements: insurance with a high deductible, a medical savings account in which the employer contributes to employee-controlled accounts for paying expenses below the deductible, and health education aimed at helping employees improve their health and thus lower their need for health care. According to surveys, employees are at least initially less satisfied with CDHPs than with traditional health care plans. Employers should allow at least six months between introducing the plan and completing the enrollment process, so they can educate employees about how a CDHP can empower them in making decisions about their health and health care. Despite this challenge, the potential savings has led companies such as Humana and Black & Decker to offer

Health Maintenance Organization (HMO)
A health care plan that requires patients to receive their medical care from the HMO's health care professionals, who are often paid a flat salary, and provides all services on a prepaid basis.

Preferred Provider Organization (PPO)
A health care plan that contracts with health care professionals to provide services at a reduced fee and gives patients financial incentives to use network providers.

Flexible Spending Account
Employee-controlled pretax earnings set aside to pay for certain eligible expenses such as health care expenses during the same year.

Tom Johnson runs on a treadmill at the Western & Southern Financial Group headquarters building in Cincinnati. The company is encouraging employees to reduce their health risks as insurance costs climb. Can you think of firms that offer other unique benefits to reduce health risks?

Employee Wellness Program (EWP)
A set of communications, activities, and facilities designed to change health-related behaviors in ways that reduce health risks.

CDHPs. At Black & Decker, a key to success was to offer a large enough medical savings account to make the plan attractive to employees.[16]

- An **employee wellness program (EWP)** is a set of communications, activities, and facilities designed to change health-related behaviors in ways that reduce health risks. Typically, an EWP aims at specific health risks, such as high blood pressure, high cholesterol levels, smoking, and obesity, by encouraging preventive measures such as exercise and good nutrition. *Passive* programs provide information and services, but no formal support or motivation to use the program. Examples include health education (such as lunchtime courses) and fitness facilities. *Active* wellness programs assume that behavior change requires support and reinforcement along with awareness and opportunity. Such a program may include counselors who tailor programs to individual employees' needs, take baseline measurements (for example, blood pressure and weight), and take follow-up measures for comparison to the baseline. In general, passive health education programs cost less than fitness facilities and active wellness programs.[17] All these variations have had success in reducing risk factors associated with cardiovascular disease (obesity, high blood pressure, smoking, lack of exercise), but the follow-up method is most successful. The "eHRM" box describes how one company uses an online benefits portal as part of an effective wellness program.

Life Insurance

Employers may provide life insurance to employees or offer the opportunity to buy coverage at low group rates. With a *term life insurance* policy, if the employee dies during the term of the policy, the employee's beneficiaries receive a payment called the death benefit. In policies purchased as an employee benefit, the usual death benefit is twice the employee's yearly pay. The policies may provide additional benefits for accidental death and dismemberment (loss of a body part such as a hand or foot). Along with a basic policy, the employer may give employees the option of purchasing additional coverage, usually at a nominal cost.

Short-Term Disability Insurance
Insurance that pays a percentage of a disabled employee's salary as benefits to the employee for six months or less.

Long-Term Disability Insurance
Insurance that pays a percentage of a disabled employee's salary after an initial period and potentially for the rest of the employee's life.

Disability Insurance

Employees risk losing their incomes if a disability makes them unable to work. Disability insurance provides protection against this loss of income. Typically, **short-term disability insurance** provides benefits for six months or less. **Long-term disability insurance** provides benefits after that initial period, potentially for the rest of the disabled employee's life. Disability payments are a percentage of the employee's salary—typically 50 to 70 percent. Payments under short-term plans may be higher. Often the policy sets a maximum amount that may be paid each month. Because its limits make it more affordable, short-term disability coverage is offered by more employers. Fewer than half of employers offer long-term plans.

In planning an employee benefits package, the organization should keep in mind that Social Security includes some long-term disability benefits. To manage benefits costs, the employer should ensure that the disability insurance is coordinated with Social Security and any other programs that help workers who become disabled.

ONLINE BENEFITS PORTAL PUSHES WELLNESS EFFORT AT LEVITON

focus on *social responsibility*

Leviton Manufacturing Company helps its customers save energy by using its lighting management systems. So when the company built a new headquarters, it logically applied that commitment to the environment and constructed an eco-friendly building. Motion sensors turn off lights in areas that aren't being used, and blinds automatically raise and lower themselves to adjust for the sun's impact on heating and cooling needs. That commitment to the environment might not seem to apply to human resource management, but Fran Ruderman, Leviton's senior director of benefits and compensation, saw an opportunity.

Under Ruderman, the company committed to eliminating paper from its benefits system by putting all the information online. Employees access the information at a benefits portal called HR InTouch. Employees use HR InTouch to enroll in health care and retirement savings plans, update their personal and dependent information, and check the balance in their health savings account. Because not all employees have access to a computer on the job or at home, Ruderman had computer kiosks installed at each company location, so everyone can use the system conveniently.

An important application of HR InTouch has been getting employees more engaged with Leviton's wellness programs. Employees can log on to see interactive videos on a variety of health topics, including how to manage stress and how to eat wisely while traveling. During the company's open-enrollment period, when traffic to the site would be heavy, the company posted a video of Leviton's chief executive, Don Hendler, encouraging employees to take part in the wellness program.

A related effort is aimed at lowering health care expenses by encouraging employees with chronic conditions (for example, diabetes and high cholesterol) to be actively engaged in managing those conditions to prevent complications. Through that program, called Medication Dedication, the company encourages employees to use low-cost generic medicines or, if no generic is available, lowers the cost of the brand-name drugs these employees need. Medication Dedication and the wellness programs together have reduced costs by almost 8 percent among the employees responsible for most of the company's claims.

Sources: Joanne Wojcik, "Leviton Goes Green to Save Green," *Business Insurance,* November 30, 2009, Business & Company Resource Center, http://galenet.galegroup.com; and Joanne Wojcik, "Rising to the Benefits Challenge," *Business Insurance,* November 30, 2009, Business & Company Resource Center, http://galenet.galegroup.com.

Long-Term Care Insurance

The cost of long-term care, such as care in a nursing home, can be devastating. Today, with more people living to an advanced age, many people are concerned about affording long-term care. Some employers address this concern by offering long-term care insurance. These policies provide benefits toward the cost of long-term care and related medical expenses.

Retirement Plans

Despite the image of retired people living on their Social Security checks, Figure 13.4 shows that those checks amount to less than half of a retired person's income. Among persons over age 65, pensions provided a significant share of income in 2006. Employers have no obligation to offer retirement plans beyond the protection of Social Security, but most offer some form of pension or retirement savings plan. About half of employees working for private businesses (that is, nongovernment jobs) have employer-sponsored retirement plans. These plans are most common for

LO5 Define the types of retirement plans offered by employers.

397

Figure 13.4

Sources of Income for Persons 65 and Older

SOURCE: Based on Employee Benefit Research Institute, "Sources of Income for Persons Aged 55 and Over," Chapter 7, *EBRI Databook on Employee Benefits,* Chart 7.1b, updated March 2010, www.ebri.org.

Contributory Plan
Retirement plan funded by contributions from the employer and employee.

Noncontributory Plan
Retirement plan funded entirely by contributions from the employer.

Defined-Benefit Plan
Pension plan that guarantees a specified level of retirement income.

Employee Retirement Income Security Act (ERISA)
Federal law that increased the responsibility of pension plan trustees to protect retirees, established certain rights related to vesting and portability, and created the Pension Benefit Guarantee Corporation.

higher-earning employees. Among employees earning the top one-fourth of incomes, more than 80 percent participate in a retirement plan, and about one out of four employees in the bottom one-fourth have such plans.[18] Retirement plans may be **contributory plans,** meaning they are funded by contributions from the employer and employee, or **noncontributory plans,** meaning all the contributions come from the employer.

Defined-Benefit Plans

Employers have a choice of using retirement plans that define the amount to be paid out after retirement or plans that define the amount the employer will invest each year. A **defined-benefit plan** guarantees a specified level of retirement income. Usually the amount of this defined benefit is calculated for each employee based on the employee's years of service, age, and earnings level (for example, the average of the employee's five highest-earnings years). These calculations typically result in pension payments that range from 20 percent of final salary for an employee who is relatively young and has few years of service to 35 percent of the final salary of an older employee who has spent many years with the organization. Using years of service as part of the basis for calculating benefits gives employees an incentive to stay with the organization as long as they can, so it can help to reduce voluntary turnover.

Defined-benefit plans must meet the funding requirements of the **Employee Retirement Income Security Act (ERISA)** of 1974. This law increased the responsibility of pension plan trustees to protect retirees, established certain rights related to vesting (earning a right to receive the pension) and *portability* (being able to move retirement savings when changing employers), and created the **Pension Benefit Guarantee Corporation (PBGC).** The PBGC is the federal agency that insures retirement benefits and guarantees retirees a basic benefit if the employer experiences financial difficulties. To fund the PBGC, employers must make annual contributions of $33 per fund participant. Plans that are *underfunded*—meaning the employer does not contribute enough to the plan each year to meet future obligations—must pay an additional premium tied to the amount by which the plan is underfunded.[19] The PBGC's protection applies to the pensions of 44 million workers.

With a defined-benefit plan, the employer sets up a pension fund to invest the contributions. As required by ERISA, the employer must contribute enough for the plan to cover all the benefits to be paid out to retirees. Defined-benefit plans protect employees from the risk that the pension fund will not earn as much as expected. If the pension fund earns less than expected, the employer makes up the difference from other sources. If the employer experiences financial difficulties so that it must end or reduce employee pension benefits, the PBGC provides a basic benefit, which does not necessarily cover the full amount promised by the employer's pension plan. The PBGC establishes a maximum; in 2007, it was the lesser of $1/12$ of an employee's annual gross income or $3,712 per month.

Defined-Contribution Plans

An alternative to defined benefits is a **defined-contribution plan,** which sets up an individual account for each employee and specifies the size of the investment into that account, rather than the amount to be paid out upon retirement. The amount the retiree receives will depend on the account's performance. Many kinds of defined-contribution plans are available, including the following:

- *Money purchase plan*—The employer specifies a level of annual contributions (for example, 10 percent of salary). The contributions are invested, and when the employee retires, he or she is entitled to receive the amount of the contributions plus the investment earnings. ("Money purchase" refers to the fact that when employees retire, they often buy an annuity with the money, rather than taking it as a lump sum.)
- *Profit-sharing and employee stock ownership plans*—As we saw in Chapter 12, incentive pay may take the form of profit sharing and employee stock ownership plans (ESOPs). These payments may be set up so that the money goes into retirement plans. By defining its contributions in terms of stock or a share of profits, the organization has more flexibility to contribute less dollar value in lean years and more in good years.
- *Section 401(k) plans*—Employees contribute a percentage of their earnings, and employers may make matching contributions. The amount employees contribute is not taxed as part of their income until they receive it from the plan. The federal government limits the amount that may be contributed each year. The limit for 2007 and 2008 was $15,500; it may increase by up to $500 a year through 2010, depending on the inflation rate. The contribution limits are higher for persons 50 and older.[20]

These plans free employers from the risks that investments will not perform as well as expected. They put the responsibility for wise investing squarely on the shoulders of each employee. A defined-contribution plan is also easier to administer. The employer need not calculate payments based on age and service, and payments to the PBGC are not required. Considering the advantages to employers, it is not surprising that a growing share of retirement plans are defined-contribution plans. Three decades ago, the majority of workers with pension plans had defined-benefit plans, and less than one-fourth had defined-contribution plans. Today, following a steady decline in the number of defined-benefit plans and a steady rise in the number of defined-contribution plans, that pattern is reversed.[21] Still, many organizations offer both kinds of retirement plans.

When retirement plans make individual employees responsible for investment decisions, the employees need information about retirement planning. Retirement savings plans often give employees much control over decisions about when and how much to invest. Many employees do not appreciate the importance of beginning to save early in their careers. As Figure 13.5 shows, an employee who invests $3,000 a year ($250 a month) between the ages of 21 and 29 will have far more at age 65 than an employee who invests the same amount between ages 31 and 39. Another important lesson is to diversify investments. Based on investment performance between 1946 and 1990, stocks earned an average of 11.4 percent per year, bonds earned 5.1 percent, and bank savings accounts earned 5.3 percent. But in any given year, one of these types of investments might outperform the other. And within the categories of stocks and bonds, it is important to invest in a wide variety of companies. If one company performs poorly, the investments in other companies might perform better. However, studies of investment decisions by employees have found that many employees hold a sizable share of their retirement savings in stock of the company they work for, and few have followed basic guidelines for diversifying investments among stocks, bonds, and savings accounts according to their age and investment

Pension Benefit Guarantee Corporation (PBGC)
Federal agency that insures retirement benefits and guarantees retirees a basic benefit if the employer experiences financial difficulties.

Defined-Contribution Plan
Retirement plan in which the employer sets up an individual account for each employee and specifies the size of the investment into that account.

Figure 13.5

Value of Retirement Savings Invested at Different Ages

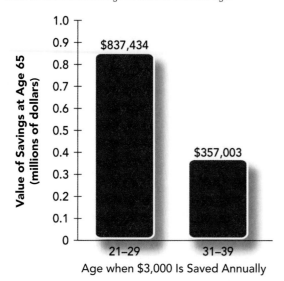

Note: Investment portfolio consists of 60 percent stocks, 30 percent bonds, and 10 percent cash (e.g., money-market funds, bank savings accounts), assuming average rates of return based on historical rates from 1946 to 1990.

Cash Balance Plan
Retirement plan in which the employer sets up an individual account for each employee and contributes a percentage of the employee's salary; the account earns interest at a predefined rate.

needs.[22] To help employees handle such risks, some organizations provide financial planning as a separate benefit, offer an option to have a professional invest the funds in a 401(k) plan, or direct funds into default investments geared toward the needs of employees at different life stages. For example, when a Portland, Oregon, developer called Classic American Homes found that its employees made poor investments, such as moving into risky real estate funds *after* real estate prices had been rising, the company began offering just one fund that combines 60 percent stocks and 40 percent bonds.

In spite of these challenges, defined-contribution plans also offer an advantage to employees in today's highly mobile workforce. They do not penalize employees for changing jobs. With these plans, retirement earnings are less related to the number of years an employee stays with a company.

Cash Balance Plans

An increasingly popular way to combine the advantages of defined-benefit plans and defined-contribution plans is to use a **cash balance plan.** This type of retirement plan consists of individual accounts, as in a 401(k) plan. But in contrast to a 401(k), all the contributions come from the employer. Usually, the employer contributes a percentage of the employee's salary, say, 4 or 5 percent. The money in the cash balance plan earns interest according to a predetermined rate, such as the rate paid on U.S. Treasury bills. Employers guarantee this rate as in a defined-benefit plan. This arrangement helps employers plan their contributions and helps employees predict their retirement benefits. If employees change jobs, they generally can roll over the balance into an individual retirement account.

A switch from traditional defined-benefit plans to cash balance plans, like any major change, requires employers to consider the effects on employees as well as on the organization's bottom line. Defined-benefit plans are most generous to older employees with many years of service, and cash balance plans are most generous to young employees who will have many years ahead in which to earn interest. For an organization with many experienced employees, switching from a defined-benefit plan can produce great savings in pension benefits. In that case, the older workers are the greatest losers, unless the organization adjusts the program to retain their benefits. After IBM switched to a cash-benefit plan, a group of employees filed an age discrimination lawsuit. IBM won the lawsuit on appeal, and the Pension Protection Act of 2006 seeks to clarify the legal requirements of such plans. As a result, some companies may renew their interest in cash balance plans, but IBM has decided to focus on its 401(k) plan.

Government Requirements for Vesting and Communication

Along with requirements for funding defined-benefit plans, ERISA specifies a number of requirements related to eligibility for benefits and communication with employees. ERISA guarantees employees that when they become participants in a pension plan and work a specified number of years, they earn a right to a pension upon retirement. These rights are called **vesting rights.** Employees whose contributions are *vested* have met the requirements (enrolling and length of service) to receive a pension at retirement age, regardless of whether they remained with the employer until that time. Employees' own contributions to their pension plans are always completely vested. In most cases, the vesting of employer-funded pension benefits must take place under one of two schedules selected by the employer:

1. The employer may vest employees after five years and may provide zero vesting until that time.
2. The employer may vest employees over a three- to seven-year period, with at least 20 percent vesting in the third year and at least an additional 20 percent in each year after the third year.

These two schedules represent minimum requirements. Employers may vest employees more quickly if they wish. Two less-common situations have different vesting requirements. One is a "top-heavy" pension plan, meaning pension benefits for *key employees* (such as highly paid top managers) exceed a government-specified share of total pension benefits. A top-heavy plan requires faster vesting for nonkey employees. Another exception from the usual schedule involves multiemployer pension plans. These plans need not provide vesting until after 10 years of employment.

The intent of vesting requirements is to protect employees by preventing employers from terminating them before they meet retirement age in order to avoid paying pension benefits. In addition, it is illegal for employers to transfer or lay off employees as a way to avoid pension obligations, even if these changes are motivated partly by business need.[23] One way employers may legally try to minimize pension costs is in choosing a vesting schedule. For example, if many employees leave after three or four years of employment, the five-year vesting schedule would minimize pension costs.

ERISA's reporting and disclosure requirements involve the Internal Revenue Service, the Department of Labor, and employees.[24] Within 90 days after employees enter a plan, they must receive a **summary plan description (SPD),** a report that describes the plan's funding, eligibility requirements, risks, and other details. If the employee requests one, the employer must also make available an individual benefit statement, which describes the employee's vested and unvested benefits. Many employers provide such information regularly, without waiting for employee requests. This type of communication helps employees understand and value their retirement benefits.

"Family-Friendly" Benefits

As employers have recognized the significance of employees' need to manage conflicts between their work and family roles, many have added "family-friendly" benefits to their employee benefits. These benefits include family leave policies and child care. The programs discussed here apply directly to the subset of employees with family responsibilities. However, family-friendly benefits often have spillover effects in the form of loyalty because employees see the benefits as evidence that the organization cares about its people.[25] The following types of benefits are typical:

- *Family leave*—Family or parental leave grants employees time off to care for children and other dependents. As discussed earlier in the chapter, federal law requires 12 weeks of unpaid leave. Companies may choose to offer more generous leave policies. Paid family leave remains rare in the United States, however, despite

Vesting Rights
Guarantee that when employees become participants in a pension plan and work a specified number of years, they will receive a pension at retirement age, regardless of whether they remained with the employer.

Summary Plan Description (SPD)
Report that describes a pension plan's funding, eligibility requirements, risks, and other details.

LO6 Describe how organizations use other benefits to match employees' wants and needs.

Figure 13.6

Percentage of Employees with Various Levels of Child Care Benefits

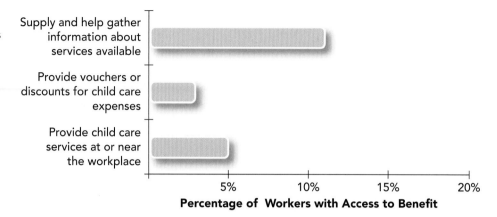

SOURCE: John E. Buckley, "Beyond Basic Benefits: Employee Access to Other Types of Benefits, 1979–2008," *Compensation and Working Conditions Online*, May 29, 2009, www.bls.gov.

some state laws. By contrast, more than 120 countries provide paid family leave by law. The norm in Western Europe is at least three to four months' maternity leave at 80 to 100 percent of pay, plus additional (often unpaid) parental leave for both parents.[26]

- *Child care*—Child care benefits may take several forms, requiring different levels of organizational involvement. As shown in Figure 13.6, the lowest level of involvement, offered by 19 percent of companies with at least 100 workers, is for the organization to supply and help employees collect information about the cost and quality of available child care. At the next level, organizations provide vouchers or discounts for employees to use at existing child care facilities. At the highest level of involvement, the employer provides child care at or near the work site. Staffing a child care facility is costly and involves important liability concerns. At the same time, the results of this type of benefit, in terms of reducing absenteeism and enhancing productivity, have been mixed.[27] When Providian Financial Corporation, a credit card company with headquarters in San Francisco, determined that for many of its employees, the big hurdle with child care and elder care was affordability, it set up flexible spending accounts for dependent care.[28]

- *College savings*—As workers' children grow up, their needs shift from maternity leave and child care to college tuition. Some organizations have supported this concern by sponsoring tax-favored *529 savings plans*. These plans, named after the section of the Internal Revenue Code that regulates them, let parents and other family members defer taxes on the earnings of their deposits into the 529 account. Some states also provide a (limited) tax deduction for these contributions. As an employee benefit, organizations can arrange with a broker to offer direct deposit of a portion of employees' paychecks into their accounts. Besides offering the convenience of direct deposit, employers can negotiate lower management fees. To support employee retention, United Supermarkets offers its employees a college-savings plan and matches contributions with a percentage that increases annually for four years.[29]

- *Elder care*—As the population of the nation's elderly grows, so do the demands on adult children to care for elderly parents, aunts, and uncles. When these people become ill or disabled, they rely on family or professional caregivers.

Responsibilities such as providing assistance, paying for professional caregivers, and locating services can be expensive, time consuming, and exhausting, often distracting employees from their work roles. In response, many employers have added elder care benefits. These benefits typically emphasize information and support, rather than direct financial assistance. For example, organizations may provide access to counseling, flexible schedules, and printed resources. An increasing popular benefit is referrals to health advocacy services, which can help employees pick Medicare Part D drug coverage, find long-term care facilities, or prepare a checklist of questions for a doctor visit.[30] Even companies that cannot afford to offer counseling or referral services can use intranets to provide links to helpful websites such as the National Alliance for Caregiving (www.caregiving.org), the National Council on Aging (www.benefitscheckup.org), and the federal government's benefits information site (govbenefits.gov).

Other Benefits

The scope of possible employee benefits is limited only by the imagination of the organization's decision makers. Organizations have developed a wide variety of benefits to meet the needs of employees and to attract and keep the kinds of workers who will be of value to the organization. Traditional extras include subsidized cafeterias, on-site health care for minor injuries or illnesses, and moving expenses for newly hired or relocating employees. Stores and manufacturers may offer employee discounts on their products.

To encourage learning and attract the kinds of employees who wish to develop their knowledge and skills, many organizations offer *tuition reimbursement* programs. A typical program covers tuition and related expenses for courses that are relevant to

In order to provide a relaxed environment for their employees, one of the perks at Neversoft Entertainment is allowing employees to bring their pets to work. What other unique benefits do companies offer their employees?

the employee's current job or future career at the organization. Employees are reimbursed for these expenses after they demonstrate they have completed an approved course.

Especially for demanding, high-stress jobs, organizations may look for benefits that help employees put in the necessary long hours and alleviate stress. Recreational activities such as on-site basketball courts or company-sponsored softball teams provide for social interaction as well as physical activity. Employers may reward hard-working groups or individuals with a trip for a weekend, a meal, or any activity employees are likely to enjoy. Some companies, including Minneapolis design agency Sevnthsin and Vancouver Web site designer Mezine, allow employees to bring their pets to work. Mezine cofounder Dean Gagnon explains the benefit: "It's almost impossible to have a bad day with a dog walking around the office."[31]

Selecting Employee Benefits

L07 Explain how to choose the contents of an employee benefits package.

Although the government requires certain benefits, employers have wide latitude in creating the total benefits package they offer employees.[32] Decisions about which benefits to include should take into account the organization's goals, its budget, and the expectations of the organization's current employees and those it wishes to recruit in the future. Employees have come to expect certain things from employers. An organization that does not offer the expected benefits will have more difficulty attracting and keeping talented workers. Also, if employees believe their employer feels no commitment to their welfare, they are less likely to feel committed to their employer.

The Organization's Objectives

A logical place to begin selecting employee benefits is to establish objectives for the benefits package. This helps an organization select the most effective benefits and monitor whether the benefits are doing what they should. Table 13.2 is an example of one organization's benefits objectives. Unfortunately, research suggests that most organizations do not have written benefits objectives.

focus on
social
responsibility

Among companies that do set goals, the most common objectives include controlling the cost of health care benefits and retaining employees.[33] The first goal explains the growing use of wellness programs and consumer-directed health plans. For the second goal, employers need to learn what employees care about. In some cases, the approach may be indirect, helping the company distinguish itself as an employer that certain kinds of employees will be attracted to and committed to. For example, a company that establishes itself as committed to the environment could offer benefits in line with that goal—say, bicycle storage for commuters and vouchers for taking the bus to work.[34] Employees with a passion for the environment would be especially engaged by such offerings.

Employees' Expectations and Values

Employees expect to receive benefits that are legally required and widely available, and they value benefits they are likely to use. For example, the "HR Oops!" box illustrates the value employees place on product discounts. To meet employee expectations about benefits, it can be helpful to see what other organizations offer. Employers can purchase survey information about benefits packages from private consultants. In addition, the Bureau of Labor Statistics gathers benefits data. The BLS Web site (www.bls.gov) is therefore a good place to check for free information about employee

Table 13.2

An Organization's Benefits Objectives

- To establish and maintain an employee benefit program that is based primarily on the employees' needs for leisure time and on protection against the risks of old age, loss of health, and loss of life.
- To establish and maintain an employee benefit program that complements the efforts of employees on their own behalf.
- To evaluate the employee benefit plan annually for its effect on employee morale and productivity, giving consideration to turnover, unfilled positions, attendance, employees' complaints, and employees' opinions.
- To compare the employee benefit plan annually with that of other leading companies in the same field and to maintain a benefit plan with an overall level of benefits based on cost per employee that falls within the second quintile of these companies.
- To maintain a level of benefits for nonunion employees that represents the same level of expenditures per employee as for union employees.
- To determine annually the costs of new, changed, and existing programs as percentages of salaries and wages and to maintain these percentages as much as possible.
- To self-fund benefits to the extent that a long-run cost savings can be expected for the firm and catastrophic losses can be avoided.
- To coordinate all benefits with social insurance programs to which the company makes payments.
- To provide benefits on a noncontributory basis except for dependent coverage, for which employees should pay a portion of the cost.
- To maintain continual communications with all employees concerning benefit programs.

SOURCE: Adapted from B. T. Beam Jr. and J. J. McFadden, *Employee Benefits*, 3rd ed. © 1992 by Dearborn Financial Publishing, Inc. Published by Dearborn Financial Publishing, Inc., Chicago. All rights reserved.

benefits in the United States. With regard to value, medical insurance is a high-value benefit because employees usually realize that surgery or a major illness can be financially devastating. Vision and dental care tend to be much less expensive, but many employees appreciate this type of coverage because so many people receive dental or vision care in the course of a year. As a result, many employers are finding that employees are even happy to pay the modest premiums for dental and vision coverage themselves because of the value they place on this benefit.[35]

Employers should also consider that the value employees place on various benefits is likely to differ from one employee to another. At a broad level, basic demographic factors such as age and sex can influence the kinds of benefits employees want. An older workforce is more likely to be concerned about (and use) medical coverage, life insurance, and pensions. A workforce with a high percentage of women of childbearing age may care more about disability or family leave. Young, unmarried men and women often place more value on pay than on benefits. However, these are only general observations; organizations should check which considerations apply to their own employees and identify more specific needs and differences. One approach is to use surveys to ask employees about the kinds of benefits they value. The survey should be carefully worded so as not to raise employees' expectations by seeming to promise all the benefits asked about at no cost to the employee.

The choice of benefits may influence current employees' satisfaction and may also affect the organization's recruiting, in terms of both the ease of recruiting and the kinds of employees attracted to the organization. For example, a benefits package that has strong medical benefits and pensions may be particularly attractive to older people or to those with many dependents. Such benefits may attract people with extensive

HR Oops!

Underestimating the Importance of Employee Discounts

Part of knowing what employees value is knowing what they don't want to lose. Brian Dunn learned that the hard way as an executive of Best Buy.

Dunn hoped to improve profitability by cutting costs, and he thought employees would accept a smaller employee discount. To be certain, the company monitored comments on its employee social-networking site, the Watercooler. The results were soon in: employees flooded the site with 54 pages of comments, most of them furious.

Just five days later, Dunn reviewed the reaction with senior management. The decision was easy: Best Buy backed down and restored the employee discount to its original level.

Questions

1. Are you surprised that employee discounts are a highly valued benefit at Best Buy? Why or why not? What kinds of employees would this benefit attract?
2. Suggest a way that Best Buy could have reduced the costs of benefits without sparking employee anger.

Source: Based on Matthew Boyle, "Look before You Chop Employee Perks," *BusinessWeek*, February 20, 2009, www.businessweek.com.

---

experience and those who wish to make a long-term commitment to the organization. This strategy may be especially beneficial when turnover costs are very high. On the other hand, offering generous health care benefits may attract and retain people with high health care costs. Thus, organizations need to consider the signals sent by their benefits package as they set goals for benefits and select benefits to offer.

Organizations can address differences in employees' needs and empower their employees by offering flexible benefits plans in place of a single benefits package for all employees. These plans, often called **cafeteria-style plans,** offer employees a set of alternatives from which they can choose the types and amounts of benefits they want. The plans vary. Some impose minimum levels for certain benefits, such as health care coverage; some allow better employees to receive money in exchange for choosing a "light" package; and some let employees pay extra for the privilege of receiving more benefits. For example, some plans let employees give up vacation days for more pay or to purchase extra vacation days in exchange for a reduction in pay.

Cafeteria-Style Plan
A benefits plan that offers employees a set of alternatives from which they can choose the types and amounts of benefits they want.

Cafeteria-style plans have a number of advantages.[36] The selection process can make employees more aware of the value of the benefits, particularly when the plan assigns each employee a sum of money to allocate to benefits. Also, the individual choice in a cafeteria plan enables each employee to match his or her needs to the company's benefits, increasing the plan's actual value to the employee. And because employees would not select benefits they don't want, the company avoids the cost of providing employees with benefits they don't value. Another way to control costs is to give employees incentives to choose lower-cost options. For example, the employee's deductible on a higher-cost health plan could be larger than on a relatively low-cost HMO.

A drawback of cafeteria-style plans is that they have a higher administrative cost, especially in the design and start-up stages. Organizations can avoid some of the higher cost, however, by using software packages and standardized plans that have been developed for employers wishing to offer cafeteria-style benefits. Another possible drawback is that employee selection of benefits will increase rather than decrease costs because employees will select the kinds of benefits they expect to need the most.

For example, an employee expecting to need a lot of dental work is more likely to sign up for a dental plan. The heavy use of the dental coverage would then drive up the employer's premiums for that coverage. Costs can also be difficult to estimate when employees select their benefits.

Benefits' Costs

Employers also need to consider benefits costs. One place to start is with general information about the average costs of various benefits types. Widely used sources of cost data include the Bureau of Labor Statistics (BLS), Employee Benefit Research Institute, and U.S. Chamber of Commerce. Annual surveys by the Chamber of Commerce state the cost of benefits as a percentage of total payroll costs and in dollar terms.

Employers can use data about costs to help them select the kinds of benefits to offer. But in balancing these decisions against organizational goals and employee benefits, the organization may decide to offer certain high-cost benefits while also looking for ways to control the cost of those benefits. The highest-cost items tend to offer the most room for savings, but only if the items permit choice or negotiation. Also, as we noted earlier, organizations can control certain costs such as workers' compensation by improving their experience ratings. Cost control is especially important—and difficult—when economic growth slows or declines.

In recent years, benefits related to health care have attracted particular attention because these costs have risen very rapidly and because employers have a number of options. Concern over costs has prompted many employers to shift from traditional health insurance to PPOs and CDHPs. Some employers shift more of the cost to employees. They may lower the employer's payments by increasing the amounts employees pay for deductibles and coinsurance (the employee's share of the payment for services). Or they may require employees to pay some or all of the difference in cost between traditional insurance and a lower-cost plan. Excluding or limiting coverage for certain types of claims also can slow the increase in health insurance costs. Employee wellness programs, especially when they are targeted to employees with risk factors and include follow-up and encouragement, can reduce risk factors for disease.[37]

Legal Requirements for Employee Benefits

LO8 Summarize the regulations affecting how employers design and administer benefits programs.

As we discussed earlier in this chapter, some benefits are required by law. This requirement adds to the cost of compensating employees. Organizations looking for ways to control staffing costs may look for ways to structure the workforce so as to minimize the expense of benefits. They may require overtime rather than adding new employees, hire part-time rather than full-time workers (because part-time employees generally receive much smaller benefits packages), and use independent contractors rather than hire employees. Some of these choices are limited by legal requirements, however. For example, the Fair Labor Standards Act requires overtime pay for nonexempt workers, as discussed in Chapter 11. Also, the Internal Revenue Service strictly limits the definition of "independent contractors," so that employees cannot avoid legal obligations by classifying workers as self-employed when the organization receives the benefits of a permanent employee. Other legal requirements involve tax treatment of benefits, antidiscrimination laws, and accounting for benefits.

Tax Treatment of Benefits

The IRS provides more favorable tax treatment of benefits classified as *qualified plans*. The details vary from one type of benefit to another. In the case of retirement plans, the advantages include the ability for employees to immediately take a tax deduction for the funds they contribute to the plans, no immediate tax on employees for the amount the employer contributes, and tax-free earnings on the money in the retirement fund.[38]

To obtain status as a qualified plan, a benefit plan must meet certain requirements.[39] In the case of pensions, these involve vesting and nondiscrimination rules. The nondiscrimination rules provide tax benefits to plans that do not discriminate in favor of the organization's "highly compensated employees." To receive the benefits, the organization cannot set up a retirement plan that provides benefits exclusively to the organization's owners and top managers. The requirements encourage employers to provide important benefits such as pensions to a broad spectrum of employees. Before offering pension plans and other benefits, organizations should have them reviewed by an expert who can advise on whether the benefits are qualified plans.

Antidiscrimination Laws

As we discussed in Chapter 3, a number of laws are intended to provide equal employment opportunity without regard to race, sex, age, disability, and several other protected categories. Some of these laws apply to the organization's benefits policies.

Legal treatment of men and women includes equal access to benefits, so the organization may not use the employee's gender as the basis for providing more limited benefits. That is the rationale for the Pregnancy Discrimination Act, which requires that employers treat pregnancy as it treats any disability. If an employee needs time off for conditions related to pregnancy or childbirth, the employee would receive whatever disability benefits the organization offers to employees who take disability leave for other reasons. Another area of concern in the treatment of male and female employees is pension benefits. On average, women live longer than men, so on average, pension benefits for female employees are more expensive (because the organization pays the pension longer), other things being equal. Some organizations have used this difference as a basis for requiring that female employees contribute more than male employees to defined benefit plans. The Supreme Court in 1978 determined that such a requirement is illegal.[40] According to the Supreme Court, the law is intended to protect individuals, and when women are considered on an individual basis (not as averages), not every woman outlives every man.

Age discrimination is also relevant to benefits policies. Two major issues have received attention under the Age Discrimination in Employment Act (ADEA) and amendments. First, employers must take care not to discriminate against workers over age 40 in providing pay or benefits. For example, employers may not set an age at which retirement benefits stop growing as a way to pressure older workers to retire.[41] Also, early-retirement incentive programs need to meet certain standards. The programs may not coerce employees to retire, they must provide accurate information about the options available, and they must give employees enough time to make a decision. In effect, employees must really have a choice about whether they retire.

When employers offer early retirement, they often ask employees to sign waivers saying they will not pursue claims under the ADEA. The Older Workers Benefit Protection Act of 1990 set guidelines for using these waivers. The waivers must be voluntary and understandable to the employee and employer, and they must spell out the employee's rights under the ADEA. Also, in exchange for signing the waiver, the employee must receive "compensation," that is, greater benefits than he or she would otherwise receive upon retirement. The employer must inform employees that they may consult a lawyer before signing, and employees must have time to make a decision about signing—21 days before signing plus 7 days afterward in which they can revoke the agreement.

The Americans with Disabilities Act imposes requirements related to health insurance. Under the ADA, employees with disabilities must have "equal access to whatever health insurance coverage the employer provides other employees." Even so, the terms and conditions of health insurance may be based on risk factors—as long as the employer does not use this basis as a way to escape offering health insurance to someone with a disability. From the standpoint of avoiding legal challenges, an employer who has risk-based insurance and then hires an employee with a disability is in a stronger position than an employer who switches to a risk-based policy after hiring a disabled employee.[42]

Accounting Requirements

Companies' financial statements must meet the many requirements of the Financial Accounting Standards Board (FASB). These accounting requirements are intended to ensure that financial statements are a true picture of the company's financial status and that outsiders, including potential lenders and investors, can understand and compare financial statements. Under FASB standards, employers must set aside the funds they expect to need for benefits to be paid after retirement, rather than funding those benefits on a pay-as-you-go basis. On financial statements, those funds must appear as future cost obligations. For companies with substantial retirement benefits, reporting those benefits as future cost obligations greatly lowers income each year. Along with rising benefits costs, this reporting requirement has encouraged many companies to scale back benefits to retirees.

Communicating Benefits to Employees

Organizations must communicate benefits information to employees so that they will appreciate the value of their benefits. This is essential so that benefits can achieve their objective of attracting, motivating, and retaining employees. Employees are interested in their benefits, and they need a great deal of detailed information to take advantage of benefits such as health insurance and 401(k) plans. It follows that electronic technology such as the Internet and supporting databases can play a significant role in modern benefit systems. Many companies are putting benefits information on their intranets. The "HR How To" box provides further suggestions for communicating effectively the value of the organization's benefits.

In actuality, employees and job applicants often have a poor idea of what benefits they have and what the market value of their benefits is. Research asking employees about their benefits has shown that employees significantly underestimate the cost and value of their benefits.[43] Probably a major reason for their lack of knowledge is a lack of communications from employers. Employees don't know what employers are spending for benefits, so many of them doubt employers' complaints about soaring costs and their impact on the company's future.[44] In one study, employees said their company neglected to tell them how to be better consumers of health care, and they would be willing to make changes in their lifestyle if they had a financial incentive to

LO9 Discuss the importance of effectively communicating the nature and value of benefits to employees.

HR How To

COMMUNICATING ABOUT BENEFITS

If benefits are aimed at increasing employees' satisfaction, making them feel more valued by and engaged with the organization, then employers defeat the purpose if they don't communicate. Research has shown that effective communication reinforces the value of the benefits and is associated with a positive attitude toward them. Here are some tips for getting out the word about the company's benefits:

- Communicate frequently, not just when it's time for employees to enroll in insurance and savings plans. Besides regular communications with all employees, the organization might consider personalized messages to employees at the time of major life events, such as marriage or the birth of a child, that may trigger different benefits needs or a fresh focus on finances.
- Use at least three different forms of communication: visual (for example, online videos or brochures with graphs and photos), auditory (for example, presentations at meetings or on podcasts), and hands-on (interactive tools such as calculators for comparing benefits options).
- Besides telling employees what the benefits *are,* provide information about how to get the most out of company benefits. For example, when employees saw their defined-contribution retirement funds shrink during the recent recession, they might have become discouraged about investing. That was an opportunity for employers to help younger workers take a long-term view and consider that continuing to invest when the market is down can deliver big returns later. Older employees might be interested in education about how to protect their investments and stretch their dollars in retirement.
- Make sure employees understand the message. Provide opportunities to ask questions online or in person. When a decision needs to be made, give employees plenty of time to review the options. One recent study found that employees need at least three weeks to review benefits options before making decisions.
- If employees do not all speak English as their primary language, provide materials in the languages employees are familiar with and consider providing access to bilingual customer service representatives to answer questions about the benefits.

Sources: Mike Simonds, "Better ROI from Benefits," *BusinessWeek,* January 8, 2010, www.businessweek .com; Anthony J. Nugent, "Measuring Up: The Strategic Use of Benchmarking and Voluntary Benefits," *Benefits Selling,* February 2010, Business & Company Resource Center, http://galenet .galegroup.com; and Joanne Sammer, "Rescuing Pension Plans," *HR Magazine,* May 2009, www.shrm.org.

do so. Such research suggests to employers that better communication, coupled with well-designed benefits plans, will pay off in practical terms.

Employers have many options for communicating information about benefits. To increase the likelihood that employees will receive and understand the messages, employers can combine several media, such as brochures, question-and-answer meetings, intranet pages, memos, and e-mail. Some other possible media include paycheck inserts, retirement or health coaching, training programs, and benefits fairs. An investment of creativity in communications to employees can reap great returns in the form of committed, satisfied employees.

thinking ethically

IS IT FAIR FOR EXECUTIVES' RETIREMENTS TO BE MORE SECURE?

Blame it on the economy? In 2009, according to Boston College's Center on Retirement Research, the 401(k) retirement plans of 50 million employees lost a total of $1 trillion or more when the value of their investments took a dive. But while most employees were hit hard, executives at some companies were protected. Because the Internal Revenue Service limits the amount of contributions to 401(k) plans, employers set up supplemental plans for their higher-paid employees. At some companies, these plans include less-risky fixed-income funds that deliver returns even when stock funds are declining.

In some cases, the differences were dramatic. Walmart's 401(k) retirement plan lost 18 percent of its value in 2009. Some employees did worse; manager Jacqueline D'Andrea says she lost 60 percent of the value in her plan. In contrast, Walmart's CEO enjoyed a $2.3 million gain in his supplemental retirement savings. Other companies with dramatic differences include Comcast, where executives' deferred-compensation accounts rose 12 percent while employees' 401(k)s

fell 29 percent, and McKesson, where executives enjoyed an 8 percent gain versus a 31 percent loss for employees.

SOURCE: Based on Ellen E. Schultz and Tom McGinty, "Executives Enjoy 'Sure Thing' Retirement Plans," *Wall Street Journal*, December 15, 2009, http://online.wsj.com.

Questions

1. Discuss whether it is fair for executives to receive larger retirement plans than employees in lower-ranking jobs. With more money to invest, should they have more investment options, such as fixed-income funds? Why or why not?

2. How, if at all, should employers help employees manage the risks of investing in defined-contribution retirement plans?

3. Assume you work in the HR division of Walmart. How would you communicate with employees about the performance of their retirement funds in a year when their value falls? How would you address the difference between employees' returns and executives' returns?

SUMMARY

LO1 Discuss the importance of benefits as a part of employee compensation.

Like pay, benefits help employers attract, retain, and motivate employees. The variety of possible benefits also helps employers tailor their compensation packages to attract the right kinds of employees. Employees expect at least a minimum level of benefits, and providing more than the minimum helps an organization compete in the labor market. Benefits are also a significant expense, but employers provide benefits because employees value them and many benefits are required by law.

LO2 Summarize the types of employee benefits required by law.

Employers must contribute to the Old Age, Survivors, Disability, and Health Insurance program known as Social Security through a payroll tax shared by employers and employees. Employers must also pay federal and state taxes for unemployment insurance, based on each employer's experience rating, or percentage of employees a company has laid off in the past. State laws require that

employers purchase workers' compensation insurance. Under the Family and Medical Leave Act, employees who need to care for a baby following birth or adoption or for an ill family member must be granted unpaid leave of up to 12 weeks. Under the Patient Protection and Affordable Care Act, employers need to prepare for future requirements to provide all employees with health insurance, as well as to educate themselves about other provisions such as insurance exchanges, tax rebates for small businesses, and broadened coverage from health insurers.

LO3 Describe the most common forms of paid leave.

The major categories of paid leave are vacations, holidays, and sick leave. Paid time off may seem uneconomical, which may be the reason U.S. employers tend to offer much less vacation time than is common in Western Europe. At large U.S. companies, paid vacation is typically 10 days. The typical number of paid holidays is 10 in both Western Europe and the United States. Sick leave programs often provide full salary replacement for a limited period of time, with the amount of sick leave usually based on length of service. Policies are needed to determine how the organization will handle unused sick days at the end of each year. Some organizations let employees roll over some or all of the unused sick days into the next year, and others let unused days expire at the end of the year. Other forms of paid leave include personal days and floating holidays.

LO4   Identify the kinds of insurance benefits offered by employers.

Medical insurance is one of the most valued employee benefits. Such policies typically cover hospital expenses, surgical expenses, and visits to physicians. Some employers offer additional coverage, such as dental care, vision care, birthing centers, and prescription drug programs. Under the Consolidated Omnibus Budget Reconciliation Act of 1985, employees must be permitted to extend their health insurance coverage at group rates for up to 36 months after they leave the organization. To manage the costs of health insurance, many organizations offer coverage through a health maintenance organization or preferred provider organization, or they may offer flexible spending accounts. Some encourage healthy behaviors through an employee wellness program. Life insurance usually takes the form of group term life insurance, with the usual benefit being two times the employee's yearly pay. Employers may also offer short-term and/or long-term disability insurance, with disability payments being a percentage of the employee's salary. Some employers provide long-term care insurance to pay the costs associated with long-term care such as nursing home care.

LO5   Define the types of retirement plans offered by employers.

Retirement plans may be contributory, meaning funded by contributions from employer and employee, or noncontributory, meaning funded only by the employer. These plans may be defined-benefit plans, which guarantee a specified level of retirement income, usually based on the employee's years of service, age, and earnings level. Benefits under these plans are protected by the Pension Benefit Guarantee Corporation. An alternative is to set up a defined-contribution plan, such as a 401(k) plan. The employer sets up an individual account for each employee and guarantees the size of the investment into that account, rather than the amount to be paid out on retirement. Because employees have control over investment decisions, the organization may also offer financial planning

services as an employee benefit. A cash balance plan combines some advantages of defined-benefit plans and defined-contribution plans. The employer sets up individual accounts and contributes a percentage of each employee's salary. The account earns interest at a predetermined rate, so the contributions and benefits are easier to predict.

LO6   Describe how organizations use other benefits to match employees' wants and needs.

Employers have responded to work-family role conflicts by offering family-friendly benefits, includ-ing paid family leave, child care services or referrals, college savings plans, and elder care information and support. Other employee benefits have traditionally included subsidized cafeterias, on-site health clinics, and reimbursement of moving expenses. Stores and manufacturers may offer discounts on their products. Tuition reimbursement encourages employees to continue learning. Recreational services and employee outings provide social interaction as well as stress relief.

LO7   Explain how to choose the contents of an employee benefits package.

A logical place to begin is to establish organizational objectives and select benefits that support those objectives. Organizations should also consider employees' expectations and values. At a minimum, organizations offer the benefits employees have come to view as basic; some organizations go so far as to match extra benefits to individual employees' needs and interests. Cafeteria-style plans are an intermediate step that gives employees control over the benefits they receive. Employers must also weigh the costs of benefits, which are significant.

LO8   Summarize the regulations affecting how employers design and administer benefits programs.

Employers must provide the benefits that are required by law, and they may not improperly classify employees as "independent contractors" to avoid paying benefits. Tax treatment of qualified plans is favorable, so organizations need to learn the requirements for setting up benefits as qualified plans—for example, ensuring that pension plans do not discriminate in favor of the organization's highly compensated employees. Employers may not use employees' gender as the basis for discriminating against anyone, as in pension benefits on the basis that women as a group may live longer. Nor may employers discriminate against workers over age 40 in providing pay or benefits, such as pressuring older workers to retire by limiting retirement benefits.

When employers offer early retirement, they must meet the requirements of the Older Workers Benefit Protection Act of 1990. Under the Americans with Disabilities Act, employers must give disabled employees equal access to health insurance. To meet the requirements of the Financial Accounting Standards Board, employers must set aside the funds they expect to need for retirement benefits ahead of time, rather than funding the benefits on a pay-as-you-go basis.

LO9 Discuss the importance of effectively communicating the nature and value of benefits to employees.

Communicating information about benefits is important so that employees will appreciate the value of their benefits. Communicating their value is the main way benefits attract, motivate, and retain employees. Employers have many options for communicating information about benefits, such as brochures, meetings, intranets, memos, and e-mail. Using a combination of such methods increases employees' understanding.

KEY TERMS

cafeteria-style plan, p. 406

cash balance plan, p. 400

Consolidated Omnibus Budget Reconciliation Act (COBRA), p. 394

contributory plan, p. 398

defined-benefit plan, p. 398

defined-contribution plan, p. 398

employee benefits, p. 383

Employee Retirement Income Security Act (ERISA), p. 398

employee wellness program (EWP), p. 396

experience rating, p. 388

Family and Medical Leave Act (FMLA), p. 389

flexible spending account, p. 395

health maintenance organization (HMO), p. 395

long-term disability insurance, p. 396

noncontributory plan, p. 398

Patient Protection and Affordable Care Act, p. 390

Pension Benefit Guarantee Corporation (PBGC), p. 398

preferred provider organization (PPO), p. 395

short-term disability insurance, p. 396

Social Security, p. 387

summary plan description (SPD), p. 401

unemployment insurance, p. 387

vesting rights, p. 401

workers' compensation, p. 388

REVIEW AND DISCUSSION QUESTIONS

1. Why do employers provide employee benefits, rather than providing all compensation in the form of pay and letting employees buy the services they want?

2. Of the benefits discussed in this chapter, list the ones you consider essential—that is, the benefits you would require in any job offer. Why are these benefits important to you?

3. Define the types of benefits required by law. How can organizations minimize the cost of these benefits while complying with the relevant laws?

4. What are some advantages of offering a generous package of insurance benefits? What are some drawbacks of generous insurance benefits?

5. Imagine that you are the human resource manager of a small architectural firm. You learn that the monthly premiums for the company's existing health insurance policy will rise by 15 percent next year. What can you suggest to help your company manage this rising cost?

6. In principle, health insurance would be most attractive to employees with large medical expenses, and retirement benefits would be most attractive to older employees. What else might a company include in its benefits package to appeal to young, healthy employees? How might the company structure its benefits so these employees can take advantage of the benefits they care about most?

7. What issues should an organization consider in selecting a package of employee benefits? How should an employer manage the trade-offs among these considerations?

8. How do tax laws and accounting regulations affect benefits packages?

9. What legal requirements might apply to a family leave policy? Suggest how this type of policy should be set up to meet those requirements.

10. Why is it important to communicate information about employee benefits? Suppose you work in the HR department of a company that has decided to add new benefits—dental and vision insurance plus an additional two days of paid time off for "personal days." How would you recommend communicating this change? What information should your messages include?

BUSINESSWEEK CASE

BusinessWeek GE Gets Radical with Health Benefits

It's been a hard year to work at General Electric. Salary freezes have hit its famously performance-driven employees, with some managers taking pay cuts. The price of GE stock, which once made millionaires out of even hourly workers, has gone nowhere as the rest of the market has risen. A 68 percent dividend cut—the first in 71 years—has stung execs who rely on a heavy dose of restricted shares.

And now GE is making changes that could deal another blow to morale. The company is forcing 75,000 salaried U.S. employees and 8,000 retirees under the age of 65 to choose what's known as a consumer-directed health plan, which includes deductibles that run as high as $4,000 a year. Traditional plans, where employees pay higher premiums in exchange for predictable co-pays up front, are no longer available for salaried workers. One employee says his colleagues "are looking at this as a cut in pay."

GE says the plan is being rolled out to make employees better health-care consumers and to coincide with its new "Healthymagination" strategy, a companywide initiative for health-care innovation. While GE says its future cost savings are unclear, people with knowledge of the situation estimate it could save $1 billion over the next decade or so. With three tiers of premiums and deductibles, GE spokesperson Sue Bishop notes, employees still have options. "It's not that different from their car insurance," she says. "You get to choose the amount of your premium, and that determines the amount of your deductible."

The total cost of care will depend, of course, on the individual. Consumer-driven plans can save money for healthy workers who rarely visit a doctor or shop around. Typically, employees have lower premiums and save pretax dollars in health-savings accounts to pay much higher deductibles, with companies providing contributions to offset expenses. (GE will fund up to $1,000 for two of the three tiers.) While GE's plans offer free preventive care, for the first time, it's making smokers pay an extra $625 a year.

Workplace experts say that while many companies are adopting consumer-directed plans—about half now offer one, according to consultancy Watson Wyatt Worldwide—most offer them as part of a broader menu. Wharton School professor Peter Cappelli argues that this isn't the year to be piling big changes on an already battered employee base. "There's the death-by-a-thousand-cuts issue," he says. Veteran recruiter Peter Crist adds that the health-care change could add to the grousing he hears from GE executives. "At the high end, it's not just the money," says Crist. "It's the aggravation."

Indeed, there are indications that many are anxious about their new benefits, even if they can take comfort in knowing GE's salary freeze will lift in 2010. Some are overwhelmed by the complexity of the new plans. GE is offering Web tools, town halls, and coaches to help. But James N. Cawse, a former staff scientist at GE Global Research, says: "I'm a statistical analysis guy and I finally had to draw up a spreadsheet to make any sense of it."

SOURCE: Reprinted from Jena McGregor, "Health Care: GE Gets Radical," *BusinessWeek*, November 19, 2009, www.businessweek.com.

Questions

1. Based on the discussion of health plans in the text and the description in this case, why do you think GE wanted to move all employees into consumer-driven health plans?
2. What are the risks of this change? How can GE decide whether those risks are worth taking?
3. What aspects of the plans would you expect employees to be worried or upset about? How could human resource management address those concerns?

Case: Employees Gobble Up the Benefits at General Mills

Number one on *Fortune*'s 2009 list of Best Companies to Work For. Voted by its employees as among the top five on Glassdoor.com's Best Places to Work. Placing on *Working Mother*'s list of 100 Best Companies *and* among the top five of its Best Companies for Multicultural Women. And finally, number one on *Computerworld*'s 2009 list of the 100 Best Places to Work in IT.

With all that praise, General Mills must be doing something right by its employees. And much of what people are talking about involves employee benefits at the company, whose products include Yoplait yogurt and Progresso soup.

Some of the benefits are flashy: the company's headquarters near Minneapolis boasts an on-site health clinic, fitness center, auto service center, and grocery, plus a concierge service to run errands for employees at the low cost of $6. Other benefits are practical for busy employees: flex-time, on-site infant care, and backup child care. Use of the infant day care is subsidized by the company. Still others are ideal for those with career ambitions: employees can take an educational leave for up to two years with tuition reimbursement or (in the case of R&D employees) an "innovation sabbatical" of up to six months of paid time to do research in their field.

General Mills sees the benefits as more than frills. According to the company's senior vice president of global human resources, Mike Davis, a flexible but challenging workplace "is critically tied to attracting and retaining top talent, driving innovation and, ultimately, connecting with customers around the world." Chief executive Ken Powell agrees, explaining that the company seeks to build a culture that is "performance-driven, where people work hard to achieve goals and are excited by the challenges of their jobs" but do not "lose sight of family and community"—a balance that, Powell says, helps the company keep "the best talent."

The benefits also are not simply a way to buy loyalty. The company's leaders see benefits as one expression of a company that cares about its people. Speaking of the intangible ways the company lives these values, Ken Charles, vice president of diversity and inclusion, says, "Inclusion is free, respect is free, having a manager who listens is free." One benefits objective, Charles explains, is to keep employees on board "for 35 years." Turnover among employees in the Twin Cities facilities is just 3 percent.

One of those dedicated employees is Karla Juarez, who joined General Mills as an intern earning a degree in computer science and stayed with the company, tackling one challenging assignment after another. Juarez told

Computerworld, "General Mills has done a good job of wanting to keep me here and given me enough support and benefits that I want to do just that." For information technology workers like Juarez, though (and perhaps for many of its other great people), what they appreciate most is not the fitness center, but rather the chance to do interesting work in a challenging environment with other talented people.

SOURCES: Suzanne Ziegler, "General Mills Is a Place Employees Come to Stay," *Minneapolis Star Tribune,* May 10, 2009, Business & Company Resource Center, http://galenet.galegroup.com; "Mayo Clinic, General Mills Make *Fortune*'s 'Best' List," *HR Specialist: Minnesota Employment Law,* April 2010, Business & Company Resource Center, http://galenet.galegroup.com; "Glassdoor.com Unveils Employees' Choice Award for Top 50 Best Places to Work for 2010," *Internet Wire,* December 16, 2009, Business & Company Resource Center, http://galenet.galegroup.com; "Working Mother 100 Best Companies 2009" and "Best Companies for Multicultural Women," *Working Mother,* www.workingmother.com, accessed April 29, 2010; and Julia King, "No. 1: General Mills, 'Company of Champions,'" *Computerworld,* June 8–15, 2009, pp. 24–25.

Questions

1. What employee benefits that are *not* described in this case would you expect to be important to employees at General Mills? Why do you think they aren't mentioned?
2. What evidence can you find in this case that benefits at General Mills are tied to benefits objectives and corporate objectives?
3. How can General Mills ensure that its benefits are not just luxurious expenses but also contribute to business success?

IT'S A WRAP!

www.mhhe.com/noefund4e is your source for **R**eviewing, **A**pplying, and **P**racticing the concepts you learned about in Chapter 13.

Review
- Chapter learning objectives

Application
- Video case and quiz: "Child Care Help"
- Self-Assessment: Will you find a job that offers the benefits you want?
- Web Exercise: Evaluate a company that helps businesses to set up intranets
- Small-business case: Babies Welcome at T3

Practice
- Chapter quiz

NOTES

1. S. Hamm, "A Passion for the Planet," *BusinessWeek,* August 21, 2006, www.businessweek.com; Patagonia Web site, www.patagonia.com, accessed March 11, 2008.

2. B. Gerhart and G. T. Milkovich, "Employee Compensation: Research and Practice," in *Handbook of Industrial and Organizational Psychology,* 2nd ed., eds.

M. D. Dunnette and L. M. Hough (Palo Alto, CA: Consulting Psychologists Press, 1992), vol. 3; and J. Swist, "Benefits Communications: Measuring Impact and Values," *Employee Benefit Plan Review*, September 2002, pp. 24–26.

3. S. Shellenbarger, "Companies Help Employees Cope with Caring for Parents," *Wall Street Journal*, June 21, 2007, http://online.wsj.com; and M. Freudenheim, "Some Employers Are Offering Free Drugs," *New York Times*, February 21, 2007, www.nytimes.com.

4. U.S. Department of Labor, Employment and Training Administration (ETA), "Unemployment Insurance Tax Topic," last updated July 31, 2007, http://workforcesecurity.doleta.gov; and ETA "Significant Provisions of State Unemployment Insurance Laws," January 2008, http://workforcesecurity.doleta.gov.

5. Lisa Jennings, "Employers Prepare for Hikes in Unemployment Tax Rates," *Nation's Restaurant News*, October 19, 2009, pp. 1, 16; and Sarah E. Needleman, "Feeling Blue about Pink-Slip Taxes," *Wall Street Journal*, April 6, 2010, http://online.wsj.com.

6. J. V. Nackley, *Primer on Workers' Compensation* (Washington, DC: Bureau of National Affairs, 1989); and T. Thomason, T. P. Schmidle, and J. F. Burton, *Workers' Compensation* (Kalamazoo, MI: Upjohn Institute, 2001).

7. B. T. Beam Jr. and J. J. McFadden, *Employee Benefits*, 6th ed. (Chicago: Dearborn Financial Publishing, 2000).

8. S. S. Muñoz, "A Good Idea, but … ," *Wall Street Journal*, January 24, 2005, p. R6.

9. P. Hardin, "Women Execs Should Feel at Ease about Taking Full Maternity Leave," *Personnel Journal*, September 1995, p. 19; U.S. Department of Labor Web site, www.dol.gov, 2000; and AAUW, "FMLA: Facts and Statistics," www.aauw.org, accessed April 29, 2010.

10. Economic Policy Institute, "U.S. Workers Enjoy Far Fewer Vacation Days than Europeans," *Snapshot*, August 24, 2005, www.epi.org; and Economic Policy Institute, "Unions Guarantee More Vacation," *Snapshot*, August 12, 2009, www.epi.org.

11. "How Does Your PTO Bank Measure Up?" *Managing Benefits Plans*, July 2009, Business & Company Resource Center, http://galenet.galegroup.com.

12. Paul Fronstin, "Sources of Health Insurance and Characteristics of the Uninsured: Analysis of the March 2009 Current Population Survey," *Issue Brief*, no. 334, September 2009, www.ebri.org.

13. J. D. Morton and P. Aleman, "Trends in Employer-Provided Mental Health and Substance Abuse Benefits," *Monthly Labor Review*, April 2005, pp. 25–35.

14. Catherine Arnst, "Survey: Company Health-Care Costs to Rise 9% in 2010," *BusinessWeek*, June 18, 2009, www.businessweek.com.

15. Employee Benefit Research Institute, "Typical Health Benefit Package in Private Industry," *Facts from EBRI*, April 2006, www.ebri.org.

16. Employee Benefit Research Institute, "How Satisfaction Levels Vary by Type of Health Plan," *Fast Facts*, no. 154, February 10, 2010, www.ebri.org; Elizabeth Galentine, "CDHPs: More than a Once-a-Year Investment," *Employee Benefit Adviser*, November 1, 2009, Business & Company Resource Center, http://galenet.galegroup.com; Joanne Wojcik, "CDHP Enrollment Growing Quickly," *Business Insurance*, July 27, 2009, Business & Company Resource Center, http://galenet.galegroup.com; and Robert J. Grossman, "Redirecting Health Coverage," *HR Magazine*, June 2009, Business & Company Resource Center, http://galenet.galegroup.com.

17. J. C. Erfurt, A. Foote, and M. A. Heirich, "The Cost-Effectiveness of Worksite Wellness Programs for Hypertension Control, Weight Loss, Smoking Cessation and Exercise," *Personnel Psychology* 45 (1992), pp. 5–27.

18. Bureau of Labor Statistics, "Employee Benefits in the United States, March 2009," news release, July 28, 2009, www.bls.gov.

19. Pension Benefit Guaranty Corporation, "Pension Insurance Premiums Fact Sheet," Key Resources: Fact Sheets, www.pbgc.gov, accessed March 4, 2008.

20. Internal Revenue Service, "Limitation on Elective Deferrals," Plan Sponsors section of *401(k) Resource Guide*, www.irs.gov/retirement/, accessed March 4, 2008.

21. Employee Benefit Research Institute, "Retirement Trends in the United States over the Past Quarter-Century," *Facts from EBRI*, June 2007, www.ebri.org.

22. Eleanor Laise, "Employers Grab Reins of Workers' 401(k)s," *Wall Street Journal*, April 25, 2007, http://online.wsj.com; and Dallas Salisbury, "The Future of Retirement Plans," *Wall Street Journal*, special advertising section, April 2, 2009.

23. "Supreme Court Lets Stand Third Circuit Ruling That Pension Avoidance Scheme Is ERISA Violation," *Daily Labor Report*, no. 234 (December 8, 1987), p. A-14, summarizing *Continental Can Company v. Gavalik*.

24. Beam and McFadden, *Employee Benefits*.

25. S. L. Grover and K. J. Crooker, "Who Appreciates Family Responsive Human Resource Policies: The Impact of Family-Friendly Policies on the Organizational Attachment of Parents and Non-parents," *Personnel Psychology* 48 (1995), pp. 271–88; M. A. Arthur,

"Share Price Reactions to Work-Family Initiatives: An Institutional Perspective," *Academy of Management Journal* 46 (2003), p. 497; and J. E. Perry-Smith and T. Blum, "Work-Family Human Resource Bundles and Perceived Organizational Performance," *Academy of Management Journal* 43 (2000), pp. 1107–17.

26. Department for Business Enterprise & Regulatory Reform (BERR), *International Review of Leave Policies and Related Research 2008*, Employment Relations Research Series No. 100 (BERR, July 2008), www.berr.gov.uk.

27. E. E. Kossek, "Diversity in Child Care Assistance Needs: Employee Problems, Preferences, and Work-Related Outcomes," *Personnel Psychology* 43 (1990), pp. 769–91.

28. B. Shutan, "Lending a Hand," *Human Resource Executive*, May 2, 2005, pp. 46–49.

29. Karen Smith Welch, "Job Market Still Good in Amarillo, Texas," *Amarillo Globe-News*, June 23, 2008, Business & Company Resource Center, http://galenet.galegroup.com.

30. Richard Stolz, "Advocacy Services: Partners in Caring," *Employee Benefit Adviser*, March 1, 2010, Business & Company Resource Center, http://galenet.galegroup.org.

31. Sarah E. Needleman, "Dogs, Cats and Squirrels, Oh My: Pet-Friendly Offices," *Wall Street Journal*, April 15, 2010, http://online.wsj.com.

32. R. Broderick and B. Gerhart, "Nonwage Compensation," in *The Human Resource Management Handbook*, eds. D. Lewin, D. J. B. Mitchell, and M. A. Zadi (San Francisco: JAI Press, 1996).

33. Michael Fradkin, "An Ounce of Prevention Also Can Cut Disability Costs," *National Underwriter Life & Health*, April 21, 2008, Business & Company Resource Center, http://galenet.galegroup.com.

34. Sarah Coles, "Package: Scratch Head at Start," *Employee Benefits*, January 14, 2008, Business & Company Resource Center, http://galenet.galegroup.com.

35. V. Colliver, "Balancing the Benefit Bite," *San Francisco Chronicle*, January 19, 2005, www.sfgate.com.

36. Beam and McFadden, *Employee Benefits*.

37. D. A. Harrison and L. Z. Liska, "Promoting Regular Exercise in Organizational Fitness Programs: Health-Related Differences in Motivational Building Blocks," *Personnel Psychology* 47 (1994), pp. 47–71; Erfurt et al., "The Cost-Effectiveness of Worksite Wellness Programs."

38. Beam and McFadden, *Employee Benefits*, p. 359.

39. For a description of these rules, see M. M. Sarli, "Nondiscrimination Rules for Qualified Plans: The General Test," *Compensation and Benefits Review* 23, no. 5 (September–October 1991), pp. 56–67.

40. *Los Angeles Department of Water & Power v. Manhart*, 435 U.S. S. Ct. 702 (1978), 16 E.P.D. 8250.

41. S. K. Hoffman, "Discrimination Litigation Relating to Employee Benefits," *Labor Law Journal*, June 1992, pp. 362–81.

42. Ibid., P. 375.

43. M. Wilson, G. B. Northcraft, and M. A. Neale, "The Perceived Value of Fringe Benefits," *Personnel Psychology* 38 (1985), pp. 309–20; H. W. Hennessey, P. L. Perrewe, and W. A. Hochwarter, "Impact of Benefit Awareness on Employee and Organizational Outcomes: A Longitudinal Field Experiment," *Benefits Quarterly* 8, no. 2 (1992), pp. 90–96; and MetLife, *Employee Benefits Benchmarking Report*, www.metlife.com, accessed June 24, 2007.

44. M. C. Giallourakis and G. S. Taylor, "An Evaluation of Benefit Communication Strategy," *Employee Benefits Journal* 15, no. 4 (1991), pp. 14–18; and Employee Benefit Research Institute, "How Readable Are Summary Plan Descriptions for Health Care Plans?" *EBRI Notes*, October 2006, www.ebri.org.

Meeting Other HR Goals

chapter 14
Collective Bargaining and Labor Relations

chapter 15
Managing Human Resources Globally

chapter 16
Creating and Maintaining High-Performance Organizations

PART FIVE

Collective Bargaining and Labor Relations

What Do I Need to Know?

After reading this chapter, you should be able to:

LO1 Define unions and labor relations and their role in organizations.

LO2 Identify the labor relations goals of management, labor unions, and society.

LO3 Summarize laws and regulations that affect labor relations.

LO4 Describe the union organizing process.

LO5 Explain how management and unions negotiate contracts.

LO6 Summarize the practice of contract administration.

LO7 Describe more cooperative approaches to labor-management relations.

Introduction

The costs of health care are skyrocketing. As we discussed in the previous chapter, individuals, insurance companies, and government agencies that pick up the tab are crying out that mounting increases must be slowed. So health care providers are looking for ways to improve efficiency. At many hospitals, cost control involves asking fewer workers to do more. Nurses and other workers are expected to handle more patients, perform more tasks, and work more hours. Often, health professionals are troubled by these changes. They worry that they will burn out and that patient care will suffer. Or they worry that their employer will control costs by laying them off or refusing pay increases. These changes and pressures have led some health care workers to join labor unions. Recently, union membership among professional and technical health care workers, such as registered nurses and laboratory technologists, increased by more than 10 percent.[1]

The presence of unions at a hospital changes some aspects of human resource management by directing more attention to the interests of employees as a group. In general, employees and employers share the same interests. They both benefit when the organization is strong and growing, providing employees with jobs and employers with profits. But although the interests of employers and employees overlap, they obviously are not identical. In the case of pay, workers benefit from higher pay, but high pay cuts into the organization's profits, unless pay increases are associated with higher productivity or better customer service. Workers may negotiate differences with their employers individually, or they may form unions to negotiate on their behalf. This chapter explores human resource activities in organizations where employees belong to unions or where employees are seeking to organize unions.

We begin by formally defining unions and labor relations, and then describe the scope and impact of union activity. We next summarize government laws and regulations affecting unions and labor relations. The following three sections detail types of activities involving unions: union organizing, contract negotiation, and contract administration. Finally, we identify ways in which unions and management are working together in arrangements that are more cooperative than the traditional labor-management relationship.

Role of Unions and Labor Relations

In the United States today, most workers act as individuals to select jobs that are acceptable to them and to negotiate pay, benefits, flexible hours, and other work conditions. Especially when there is stiff competition for labor and employees have hard-to-replace skills, this arrangement produces satisfactory results for most employees. At times, however, workers have believed their needs and interests do not receive enough consideration from management. One response by workers is to act collectively by forming and joining labor **unions,** organizations formed for the purpose of representing their members' interests and resolving conflicts with employers.

Unions have a role because some degree of conflict is inevitable between workers and management.[2] As we commented earlier, for example, managers can increase profits by lowering workers' pay, but workers benefit in the short term if lower profits result because their pay is higher. Still, this type of conflict is more complex than a simple trade-off, such as wages versus profits. Rising profits can help employees by driving up profit sharing or other benefits, and falling profits can result in layoffs and a lack of investment. Although employers can use programs like profit sharing to help align employee interests with their own, some remaining divergence of interests is inevitable. Labor unions represent worker interests and the collective bargaining process provides a way to manage the conflict. In other words, through systems for hearing complaints and negotiating labor contracts, unions and managers resolve conflicts between employers and employees.

As unionization of workers became more common, universities developed training in how to manage union-management interactions. This specialty, called **labor relations,** emphasizes skills that managers and union leaders can use to foster effective labor-management cooperation, minimize costly forms of conflict (such as strikes), and seek win-win solutions to disagreements. Labor relations involves three levels of decisions:[3]

1. *Labor relations strategy*—For management, the decision involves whether the organization will work with unions or develop (or maintain) nonunion operations. This decision is influenced by outside forces such as public opinion and competition. For unions, the decision involves whether to fight changes in how unions relate to the organization or accept new kinds of labor-management relationships.
2. *Negotiating contracts*—As we will describe later in the chapter, contract negotiations in a union setting involve decisions about pay structure, job security, work rules, workplace safety, and many other issues. These decisions affect workers' and the employer's situation for the term of the contract.
3. *Administering contracts*—These decisions involve day-to-day activities in which union members and the organization's managers may have disagreements. Issues include complaints of work rules being violated or workers being treated unfairly in particular situations. A formal grievance procedure is typically used to resolve these issues.

LO1 Define unions and labor relations and their role in organizations.

Unions
Organizations formed for the purpose of representing their members' interests in dealing with employers.

Labor Relations
Field that emphasizes skills that managers and union leaders can use to minimize costly forms of conflict (such as strikes) and seek win-win solutions to disagreements.

Figure 14.1

10 Largest Unions in the United States

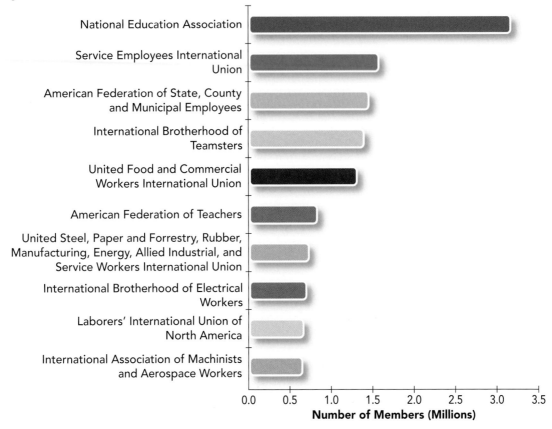

SOURCE: C. D. Gifford, *Directory of U.S. Labor Organizations* (Washington, DC: Bureau of National Affairs, 2008).

Later sections in this chapter describe how managers and unions carry out the activities connected with these levels of decisions, as well as the goals and legal constraints affecting these activities.

National and International Unions

Most union members belong to a national or international union. Figure 14.1 shows the membership of the 10 largest national unions in the United States. Half of these have memberships of over a million workers.

Craft Union
Labor union whose members all have a particular skill or occupation.

These unions may be either craft or industrial unions. The members of a **craft union** all have a particular skill or occupation. Examples include the International Brotherhood of Electrical Workers for electricians and the United Brotherhood of Carpenters and Joiners of America for carpenters. Craft unions are often responsible for training their members through apprenticeships and for supplying craft workers to employers. For example, an employer would send requests for carpenters to the union hiring hall, which would decide which carpenters to send out. In this way, craft workers may work for many employers over time but have a constant link to the union. A craft union's bargaining power depends greatly on its control over the supply of its workers.

In contrast, **industrial unions** consist of members who are linked by their work in a particular industry. Examples include the United Steelworkers of America and the Communication Workers of America. Typically, an industrial union represents many different occupations. Membership in the union is the result of working for a particular employer in the industry. Changing employers is less common than it is among craft workers, and employees who change employers remain members of the same union only if they happen to move to other employers covered by that union. Another difference is that whereas a craft union may restrict the number of skilled craftsmen—say, carpenters— to maintain higher wages, industrial unions try to organize as many employees in as wide a range of skills as possible.

Most national unions are affiliated with the **American Federation of Labor and Congress of Industrial Organizations (AFL-CIO).** The AFL-CIO is not a labor union but an association that seeks to advance the shared interests of its member unions at the national level, much as the Chamber of Commerce and the National Association of Manufacturers do for their member employers. Approximately 55 national and international unions are affiliated with the AFL-CIO. An important responsibility of the AFL-CIO is to represent labor's interests in public policy issues such as labor law, economic policy, and occupational safety and health. The organization also provides information and analysis that member unions can use in their activities. In 2005, several unions broke away from the AFL-CIO to form an alliance called Change to Win. This group includes seven unions representing a membership of 5 to 6 million workers. Since the split, both groups have increased national unions' focus on strategy and organizing.[4]

Dennis Van Roekel is president of the National Education Association, the nation's largest labor union with 3.2 million members.

Local Unions

Most national unions consist of multiple local units. Even when a national union plays the most critical role in negotiating the terms of a collective bargaining contract, negotiation occurs at the local level for work rules and other issues that are locally determined. In addition, administration of the contract largely takes place at the local union level. As a result, most day-to-day interaction between labor and management involves the local union.

Membership in the local union depends on the type of union. For an industrial union, the local may correspond to a single large facility or to a number of small facilities. In a craft union, the local may cover a city or a region.

Typically, the local union elects officers, such as president, vice president, and treasurer. The officers may be responsible for contract negotiation, or the local may form a bargaining committee for that purpose. When the union is engaged in bargaining, the national union provides help, including background data about other settlements, technical advice, and the leadership of a representative from the national office.

Individual members participate in local unions in various ways. At meetings of the local union, they elect officials and vote on resolutions to strike. Most of workers' contact is with the **union steward,** an employee elected by union members to represent them in ensuring that the terms of the contract are enforced. The union steward helps to investigate complaints and represents employees to supervisors and

Industrial Union
Labor union whose members are linked by their work in a particular industry.

American Federation of Labor and Congress of Industrial Organizations (AFL-CIO)
An association that seeks to advance the shared interests of its member unions at the national level.

Union Steward
An employee elected by union members to represent them in ensuring that the terms of the labor contract are enforced.

Figure 14.2

Union Membership Density among U.S. Wage and Salary Workers, 1973–2009

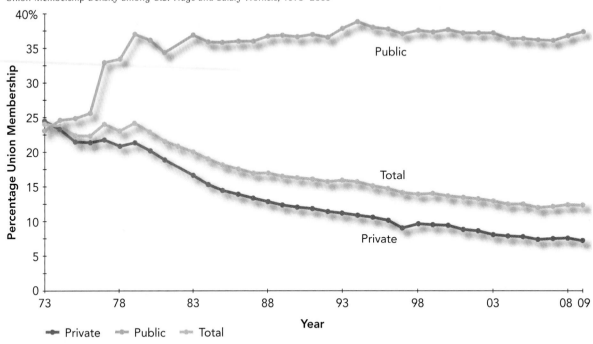

^a Percentage of total, private-sector, and public-sector wage and salary workers who are union members. Beginning in 1977, workers belonging to "an employee association similar to a union" are included as members.

SOURCE: Data for 1973–2001 from B. T. Hirsch and D. A. MacPherson, *Union Membership and Earnings Data Book 2001* (Washington, DC: Bureau of National Affairs, 2002), using data from U.S. Current Population Surveys. Data for 2002 through 2009 from Bureau of Labor Statistics, "Union Affiliation Data from the Current Population Survey," http://data.bls.gov, accessed May 3, 2010.

other managers when employees file grievances alleging contract violations.[5] When the union deals with several employers, as in the case of a craft union, a *business representative* performs some of the same functions as a union steward. Because of union stewards' and business representatives' close involvement with employees, it is to management's advantage to cultivate positive working relationships with them.

Trends in Union Membership

Union membership in the United States peaked in the 1950s, reaching over one-third of employees. Since then, the share of employees who belong to unions has fallen. It now stands at 12.1 percent overall and 7.5 percent of private-sector employment.[6] As Figure 14.2 indicates, union membership has fallen steadily since the 1980s. The decline has been driven by falling union membership in the private sector, while the share of government workers in unions has mostly held steady.

The decline in union membership has been attributed to several factors:[7]

- *Change in the structure of the economy*—Much recent job growth has occurred among women and older workers in the service sector of the economy, while union strength has traditionally been among urban blue-collar workers, especially middle-aged workers. Women have been less likely than men to belong to unions, and services industries such as finance, insurance, and real estate have lower union representation than manufacturing. Also, much business growth has been in the South, where workers are less likely to join unions.[8]

- *Management efforts to control costs*—On average, unionized workers receive higher pay than their nonunionized counterparts, and the pressure is greater because of international competition. In the past, union membership across an industry such as automobiles or steel resulted in similar wages and work requirements for all competitors. Today, U.S. producers must compete with companies that have entirely different pay scales and work rules, often placing the U.S. companies at a disadvantage.
- *Human resource practices*—Competition for scarce human resources can lead employers to offer much of what employees traditionally sought through union membership.
- *Government regulation*—Stricter regulation in such areas as workplace safety and equal employment opportunity leaves fewer areas in which unions can show an advantage over what employers must already offer.

As Figure 14.3 indicates, the percentage of U.S. workers who belong to unions is lower than in many other countries. More dramatic is the difference in "coverage"—the percentage of employees whose terms and conditions of employment are governed by a union contract, whether or not the employees are technically union members. In Western Europe, it is common to have coverage rates of 80 to 90 percent, so the influence of labor unions far outstrips what membership levels would imply.[9] Also,

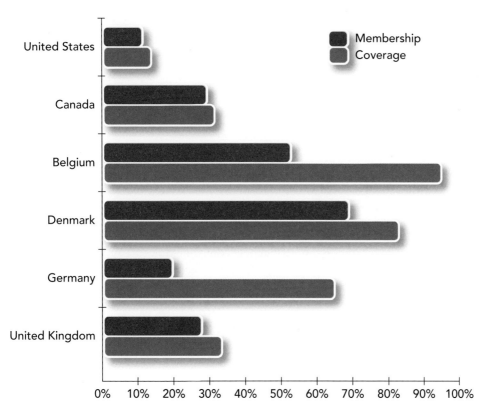

Figure 14.3

Union Membership Rates and Coverage in Selected Countries

Note: Data for 2007, except U.S. coverage rate for 2005.

SOURCES: Eurofund, "Industrial Relations Context," *European Industrial Relations Dictionary,* updated July 24, 2009, www.eurofund.europa.eu; Organization for Economic Cooperation and Development, "Trade Union Density (%) in OECD Countries 1960–2007," February 25, 2009, www.oecd.org; Statistics Canada, "Union Coverage Rates," modified November 25, 2008, www.statcan.gc.ca; and Lawrence Mishel, Jared Bernstein, and Sylvia Allegretto, *The State of Working America 2006/2007* (Ithaca, NY: ILR Press, 2007), Figure 3W, accessed at Economic Policy Institute's State of Working America Web site, www.stateofworkingamerica.org.

Did You Know?

Many Union Workers Hold Government Jobs

Compared with the overall U.S. workforce, union workers are more likely to have a government job and a college degree. They are less likely to have a manufacturing job and to be younger than 35. How well do the data fit your picture of a typical union worker?

Source: Data from John Schmitt and Kris Warner, *The Changing Face of Labor, 1983–2008* (Washington, DC: Center for Economic and Policy Research, November 2009), accessed at www.cepr.net.

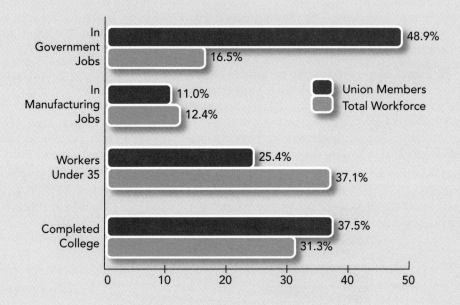

employees in Western Europe tend to have a larger formal role in decision making than in the United States. This role, including worker representatives on boards of directors, is often mandated by the government. But as markets become more and more global, pressure to cut labor costs and increase productivity is likely to be stronger in every country. Unless unions can help companies improve productivity or organize new production facilities opened in lower-wage countries, union influence may decline in countries where it is now strong.

Although union members are a smaller share of the U.S. workforce, they are a significant part of many industries' labor markets. Along with strength in numbers, large unions have strength in dollars. Union retirement funds, taken together, are huge. Unions try to use their investment decisions in ways that influence businesses. The "Did You Know?" box presents some statistics on union members.

Unions in Government

Unlike union membership for workers in businesses, union membership among government workers has remained strong. Union membership in the public sector grew during the 1960s and 1970s and has remained steady ever since. Over one-third of government employees are union members, and a larger share are covered by collective bargaining agreements. One reason for this strength is that government regulations and laws support the right of government workers to organize. In 1962 Executive Order 10988 established collective bargaining rights for federal employees. By the end of the 1960s, most states had passed similar laws.

An interesting aspect of union growth among government workers is that much of it has occurred in the service industry and among white-collar employees—groups that have been viewed as difficult to organize. The American Federation of State, County and Municipal Employees (AFSCME) has about 1.6 million members. Among them are nurses, park rangers, school librarians, corrections officers, and many workers in clerical and other white-collar occupations.[10]

Labor relations with government workers is different in some respects, such as regarding the right to strike. Strikes are illegal for federal workers and for state workers in most states. At the local level, all states prohibit strikes by police (Hawaii being a partial exception) and firefighters (Idaho being the exception). Teachers and state employees are somewhat more likely to have the right to strike, depending on the state. Legal or not, strikes by government workers do occur. Of the 39 strikes involving 1,000 or more workers in 2000, eight involved workers in state and local government.

Impact of Unions on Company Performance

Organizations are concerned about whether union organizing and bargaining will hurt their performance, in particular, unions' impact on productivity, profits, and stock performance. Researchers have studied the general relationship between unionization and these performance measures. Through skillful labor relations, organizations can positively influence outcomes.

There has been much debate regarding the effects of unions on productivity.[11] One view is that unions decrease productivity because of work rules and limits on workloads set by union contracts and production lost to such union actions as strikes and work slowdowns. At the same time, unions can have positive effects on productivity.[12] They can reduce turnover by giving employees a route for resolving problems.[13] Unions emphasize pay systems based on seniority, which remove incentives for employees to compete rather than cooperate. The introduction of a union also may force an employer to improve its management practices and pay greater attention to employee ideas.

Although there is evidence that unions have both positive and negative effects on productivity, most studies have found that union workers are more productive than nonunion workers. Still, questions remain. Are highly productive workers more likely to form unions, or does a union make workers more productive? The answer is unclear. In theory, if unions caused greater productivity, we would expect union membership to be rising, not falling as it has been.[14]

Even if unions do raise productivity, a company's profits and stock performance may still suffer if unions raise wage and benefits costs by more than the productivity gain. On average, union members receive higher wages and more generous benefits than nonunion workers, and evidence shows that unions have a large negative effect on profits. Also, union coverage tends to decline faster in companies with a lower return to shareholders.[15] In summary, companies wishing to become more competitive must continually monitor their labor relations strategy.

Harley-Davidson and the International Association of Machinists and Aerospace Workers have cooperated to produce good results. In general, though, companies wishing to become more competitive need to continually monitor their labor relations strategies.

The studies tend to look at the average effects of unions, not at individual companies or innovative labor relations. Some organizations excel at labor relations, and some have worked with unions to meet business needs. For example, even though U.S. manufacturers have outsourced or automated many jobs, a study by the National Association of Manufacturers found that 8 out of 10 had at least a moderate shortage of production workers, machinists, and craft workers. Many of these companies traditionally depended on unions to recruit and train new workers through apprenticeship programs. Some still do. Great River Energy in Bismarck, North Dakota, is one of the electric power companies that benefits from an apprenticeship program run by the North Central States Regional Council of Carpenters. A share of union members' dues funds the program for training carpenters and millwrights in trade and safety skills. Similarly, the companies that belong to the Mechanical Contractors Association of Chicago benefit from the skills taught to apprentices in the apprenticeship program of UA Pipefitters Local 597.[16]

Goals of Management, Labor Unions, and Society

L02 Identify the labor relations goals of management, labor unions, and society.

Resolving conflicts in a positive way is usually easiest when the parties involved understand each other's goals. Although individual cases vary, we can draw some general conclusions about the goals of labor unions and management. Society, too, has goals for labor and business, given form in the laws regulating labor relations.

Management Goals

Management goals are to increase the organization's profits. Managers tend to prefer options that lower costs and raise output. When deciding whether to discourage employees from forming a union, a concern is that a union will create higher costs in wages and benefits, as well as raise the risk of work stoppages. Managers may also fear that a union will make managers and workers into adversaries or limit management's discretion in making business and employment decisions.

When an employer has recognized a union, management's goals continue to emphasize restraining costs and improving output. Managers continue to prefer to keep the organization's operations flexible, so they can adjust activities to meet competitive challenges and customer demands. Therefore, in their labor relations managers prefer to limit increases in wages and benefits and to retain as much control as they can over work rules and schedules.

Labor Union Goals

In general, labor unions have the goals of obtaining pay and working conditions that satisfy their members and of giving members a voice in decisions that affect them. Traditionally, they obtain these goals by gaining power in numbers. The more workers who belong to a union, the greater the union's power. More members translates into greater ability to halt or disrupt production. Larger unions also have greater financial resources for continuing a strike; the union can help to make up for the wages the workers lose during a strike. The threat of a long strike—stated or implied—can make an employer more willing to meet the union's demands.

As we noted earlier, union membership is indeed linked to better compensation. In 2009, private-sector unionized workers received, on average, wages 19 percent higher than nonunion workers.[17] In addition, the impact of unionization on benefits packages was dramatic: Employer costs for benefits granted to union workers averaged almost 90 percent higher. Taking into account other influences, such as the greater ease with which unions are able to organize relatively highly paid, productive workers, researchers estimate that the total "union effect" on wages is about 10 to 15 percent.[18] In other words, a union worker would earn $1.10 to $1.15 for every dollar earned by a nonunion worker.

Unions typically want to influence the *way* pay and promotions are determined. Unlike management, which tries to consider employees as individuals so that pay and promotion decisions relate to performance differences, unions try to build group solidarity and avoid possible arbitrary treatment of employees. To do so, unions focus on equal pay for equal work. They try to have any pay differences based on seniority, on the grounds that this measure is more objective than performance evaluations. As a result, where workers are represented by a union, it is common for all employees in a particular job classification to be paid at the same rate.

The survival and security of a union depend on its ability to ensure a regular flow of new members and member dues to support the services it provides. Therefore, unions typically place high priority on negotiating two types of contract provisions with an employer that are critical to a union's security and viability: checkoff provisions and provisions relating to union membership or contribution.

Under a **checkoff provision,** the employer, on behalf of the union, automatically deducts union dues from employees' paychecks. Security provisions related to union membership are *closed shop, union shop, agency shop,* and *maintenance of membership.*

The strongest union security arrangement is a **closed shop,** under which a person must be a union member before being hired. Under the National Labor Relations Act, discussed later in this chapter, closed shops are illegal. A legal membership arrangement that supports the goals of labor unions is the **union shop,** an arrangement that requires an employee to join the union within a certain time (30 days) after beginning employment. A similar alternative is the **agency shop,** which requires the payment of union dues but not union membership. **Maintenance of membership** rules do not require union membership but do require that employees who join the union remain members for a certain period of time, such as the length of the contract. As we will discuss later in the chapter, some states forbid union shops, agency shops, and maintenance of membership.

All these provisions are ways to address unions' concern about "free riders"— employees who benefit from union activities without belonging to a union. By law, all members of a bargaining unit, whether union members or not, must be represented by the union. If the union must offer services to all bargaining unit members but some of them are not dues-paying union members, the union may not have enough financial resources to operate successfully.

Societal Goals

The activities of unions and management take place within the context of society, with society's values driving the laws and regulations that affect labor relations. As long ago as the late 1800s and early 1900s, industrial relations scholars saw unions as a way to make up for individual employees' limited bargaining power.[19] At that time, clashes between workers and management could be violent, and many people hoped that unions would replace the violence with negotiation. Since then, observers have expressed concern that unions in certain industries have become too strong,

---

Checkoff Provision
Contract provision under which the employer, on behalf of the union, automatically deducts union dues from employees' paychecks.

Closed Shop
Union security arrangement under which a person must be a union member before being hired; illegal for those covered by the National Labor Relations Act.

Union Shop
Union security arrangement that requires employees to join the union within a certain amount of time (30 days) after beginning employment.

Agency Shop
Union security arrangement that requires the payment of union dues but not union membership.

Maintenance of Membership
Union security rules not requiring union membership but requiring that employees who join the union remain members for a certain period of time.

achieving their goals at the expense of employers' ability to compete or meet other objectives. But even Senator Orrin Hatch, described by *BusinessWeek* as "labor's archrival on Capitol Hill," has spoken of a need for unions:

> There are always going to be people who take advantage of workers. Unions even that out, to their credit. We need them to level the field between labor and management. If you didn't have unions, it would be very difficult for even enlightened employers not to take advantage of workers on wages and working conditions, because of [competition from less-enlightened] rivals. I'm among the first to say I believe in unions.[20]

Senator Hatch's statement implies that society's goal for unions is to ensure that workers have a voice in how they are treated by their employers. As we will see in the next section, this view has produced a set of laws and regulations intended to give workers the right to join unions if they so wish.

LO3 Summarize laws and regulations that affect labor relations.

Laws and Regulations Affecting Labor Relations

The laws and regulations pertaining to labor relations affect unions' size and bargaining power, so they significantly affect the degree to which unions, management, and society achieve their varied goals. These laws and regulations set limits on union structure and administration and the ways in which unions and management interact.

National Labor Relations Act (NLRA)

National Labor Relations Act (NLRA) Federal law that supports collective bargaining and sets out the rights of employees to form unions.

Perhaps the most dramatic example of labor laws' influence is the 1935 passage of the Wagner Act (also known as the **National Labor Relations Act,** or **NLRA**), which actively supported collective bargaining. After Congress passed the NLRA, union membership in the United States nearly tripled, from 3 million in 1933 to 8.8 million (19.2 percent of employment) in 1939.[21]

Before the 1930s, the U.S. legal system was generally hostile to unions. The courts tended to view unions as coercive organizations that hindered free trade. Unions' focus on collective voice and collective action (such as strikes and boycotts) did not fit well with the U.S. emphasis on capitalism, individualism, freedom of contract, and property rights.[22] Then the Great Depression of the 1930s shifted public attitudes toward business and the free-enterprise system. Unemployment rates as high as 25 percent and a steep fall in production between 1929 and 1933 focused attention on employee rights and the shortcomings of the economic system of the time. The nation was in crisis, and President Franklin Roosevelt responded dramatically with the New Deal. On the labor front, the 1935 NLRA ushered in an era of public policy for labor unions, enshrining collective bargaining as the preferred way to settle labor-management disputes.

Section 7 of the NLRA sets out the rights of employees, including the "right to self-organization, to form, join, or assist labor organizations, to bargain collectively through representatives of their own choosing, and to engage in other concerted activities for the purpose of collective bargaining."[23] Employees also have the right to refrain from these activities, unless union membership is a condition of employment. The following activities are among those protected under the NLRA:

- Union organizing.
- Joining a union, whether recognized by the employer or not.
- Going out on strike to secure better working conditions.
- Refraining from activity on behalf of the union.

Most employees in the private sector are covered by the NLRA. However, workers employed under the following conditions are not covered:[24]

- Employed as a supervisor.
- Employed by a parent or spouse.
- Employed as an independent contractor.
- Employed in the domestic service of any person or family in a home.
- Employed as agricultural laborers.
- Employed by an employer subject to the Railway Labor Act.
- Employed by a federal, state, or local government.
- Employed by any other person who is not an employer as defined in the NLRA.

State or local laws may provide additional coverage. For example, California's 1975 Agricultural Labor Relations Act covers agricultural workers in that state.

In Section 8(a), the NLRA prohibits certain activities by employers as unfair labor practices. In general, employers may not interfere with, restrain, or coerce employees in exercising their rights to join or assist a labor organization or to refrain from such activities. Employers may not dominate or interfere with the formation or activities of a labor union. They may not discriminate in any aspect of employment that attempts to encourage or discourage union activity, nor may they discriminate against employees for providing testimony related to enforcement of the NLRA. Finally, employers may not refuse to bargain collectively with a labor organization that has standing under the act. For more guidance in complying with the NLRA, see the examples in the "HR How To" box.

When employers or unions violate the NLRA, remedies typically include ordering that unfair labor practices stop. Employers may be required to rehire workers, with or without back pay. The NLRA is not a criminal law, and violators may not be assigned punitive damages (fines to punish rather than merely make up for the harm done).

Laws Amending the NLRA

Originally, the NLRA did not list any unfair labor practices by unions. In later amendments to the NLRA—the Taft-Hartley Act of 1947 and the Landrum-Griffin Act of 1959—Congress established some restrictions on union practices deemed unfair to employers and union members.

Under the Taft-Hartley Act, unions may not restrain employers through actions such as the following:[25]

- Mass picketing in such numbers that nonstriking employees physically cannot enter the workplace.
- Engaging in violent acts in connection with a strike.
- Threatening employees with physical injury or job loss if they do not support union activities.
- During contract negotiations, insisting on illegal provisions, provisions that the employer may hire only workers who are union members or "satisfactory" to the union, or working conditions to be determined by a group to which the employer does not belong.
- Terminating an existing contract and striking for a new one without notifying the employer, the Federal Mediation and Conciliation Service, and the state mediation service (where one exists).

AVOIDING UNFAIR LABOR PRACTICES

The National Labor Relations Act prohibits employers and unions from engaging in unfair labor practices. For employers, this means they must not interfere with employees' decisions about whether to join a union and engage in union-related activities. Employers may not discriminate against employees for being involved in union activities or testifying in court about actions under the NLRA. Here are some specific examples of unfair labor practices that *employers must avoid:*

- Threatening employees with loss of their jobs or benefits if they join or vote for a union.
- Threatening to close down a plant if it is organized by a union.
- Questioning employees about their union membership or activities in a way that restrains or coerces them.
- Spying or pretending to spy on union meetings.

- Granting wage increases timed to discourage employees from forming or joining a union.
- Taking an active part in organizing a union or committee to represent employees.
- Providing preferential treatment or aid to one of several unions trying to organize employees.
- Discharging employees for urging other employees to join a union.
- Refusing to hire applicants because they are union members.
- Refusing to reinstate workers when job openings occur, on the grounds that the workers participated in a lawful strike.
- Ending operations at one facility and opening the same operations at another facility with new employees because employees at the first joined a union.

- Demoting or firing employees for filing an unfair labor practice complaint or testifying at an NLRB meeting.
- Refusing to meet with employees' representatives because the employees are on strike.
- Refusing to supply the employees' representative with cost and other data concerning a group insurance plan covering employees.
- Announcing a wage increase without consulting the employees' representative.
- Failing to bargain about the effects of a decision to close one of the employer's facilities.

Sources: National Labor Relations Board, *Basic Guide to the National Labor Relations Act* (Washington, DC: U.S. Government Printing Office, 1997); and National Labor Relations Board, "The National Labor Relations Board and You: Unfair Labor Practices," www.nlrb.gov, accessed May 4, 2010.

Right-to-Work Laws
State laws that make union shops, maintenance of membership, and agency shops illegal.

The Taft-Hartley Act also allows the states to pass so-called **right-to-work laws,** which make union shops, maintenance of membership, and agency shops illegal. The idea behind such laws is that requiring union membership or the payment of union dues restricts the employees' right to freedom of association. In other words, employees should be free to choose whether they join a union or other group. Of course, unions have a different point of view. The union perspective is that unions provide services to all members of a bargaining unit (such as all of a company's workers), and all members who receive the benefits of a union should pay union dues. Figure 14.4 indicates which states currently have right-to-work laws.

The Landrum-Griffin Act regulates unions' actions with regard to their members, including financial disclosure and the conduct of elections. This law establishes and protects rights of union members. These include the right to nominate candidates for union office, participate in union meetings and secret-ballot elections, and examine unions' financial records.

Figure 14.4

States with Right-to-Work Laws

SOURCE: National Right to Work Legal Defense Foundation, "Right to Work States," www.nrtw.org, accessed May 3, 2010.

National Labor Relations Board (NLRB)

Enforcement of the NLRA rests with the **National Labor Relations Board (NLRB).** This federal government agency consists of a five-member board, the general counsel, and 52 regional and other field offices. Because the NLRB is a federal agency, its enforcement actions are limited to companies that have an impact on interstate commerce, but as a practical matter, this extends to all but purely local businesses. For federal government workers under the Civil Service Reform Act of 1978, Title VII, the Federal Labor Relations Authority has a role similar to that of the NLRB. Many states have similar agencies to administer their laws governing state and local government workers.

The NLRB has two major functions: to conduct and certify representation elections and to prevent unfair labor practices. It does not initiate either of these actions but responds to requests for action.

The "HR Oops!" box shows how managers' comments and actions can be considered by the NLRB as illegally interfering with union organizing.

Representation Elections

The NLRB is responsible for ensuring that the organizing process follows certain steps, described in the next section. Depending on the response to organizing efforts, the NLRB conducts elections. When a majority of workers vote in favor of a union, the NLRB certifies it as the exclusive representative of a group of employees. The NLRB also conducts elections to decertify unions, following the same process as for representation elections.

The NLRB is also responsible for determining the appropriate bargaining unit and the employees who are eligible to participate in organizing activities. As we stated earlier, bargaining units may not include certain types of employees, such as agricultural laborers, independent contractors, supervisors, and managers. Beyond this, the NLRB attempts to group together employees who have a community of interest

National Labor Relations Board (NLRB)
Federal government agency that enforces the NLRA by conducting and certifying representation elections and investigating unfair labor practices.

HR Oops!

Thou Shalt Not Threaten

Community Health Center La Clinica is a nonprofit health clinic located in Pasco, a city in southeastern Washington State. Its employees are represented by the Office and Professional Employees International Union Local 8. La Clinica hired Carl Walters II to be its chief executive after several turbulent years marked by employee lawsuits and complaints of corruption.

Walters dedicated himself to getting La Clinica on a firmer financial foundation, and in so doing, he assembled employees to discuss the organization's current situation and future prospects. In one such meeting, Walters outlined the clinic's financial health and expressed concerns that the economic recession and cuts in state funding would make it necessary to find ways to cut its expenses. Among the possible actions, La Clinica would have to evaluate staffing levels and compensation, hoping to make cuts that would avoid layoffs.

Some of the unionized employees interpreted Walters's comments to mean he was threatening them that if they didn't agree to reduce their compensation or vote out the union, they would be laid off. The union complained to the NLRB that La Clinica was engaging in unfair labor practices by threatening employees. The NLRB found evidence to file a complaint and potentially a lawsuit but offered La Clinica a chance to settle instead. La Clinica agreed to the settlement, under which it does not admit wrongdoing but agrees to abide by and post a list of actions it will not take, including threats of job loss and creation of employee policies that should be the subject of collective bargaining.

Source: Based on Michelle Dupler, "La Clinica Settles over Union Complaints," *Tri-City Herald* (Kennewick, WA), March 13, 2010, Business & Company Resource Center, http://galenet .galegroup.com; Community Health Center La Clinica Web site, www. laclinicanet.org, accessed May 5, 2010.

Questions

1. How can a company communicate with unionized employees about its financial situation without seeming to issue threats?
2. How could HRM professionals at La Clinica help management avoid missteps such as the one described here?

---

in their wages, hours, and working conditions. A unit may cover employees in one facility or multiple facilities within a single employer, or the unit may cover multiple employers. In general, employees on the payroll just before the ordering of an election are eligible to vote, although this rule is modified in some cases, for example, when employment in the industry is irregular. Most employees who are on strike and who have been replaced by other employees are eligible to vote in an election (such as a decertification election) that occurs within 12 months of the onset of the strike.

Prevention of Unfair Labor Practices

The handling of complaints regarding unfair labor practices begins when someone files a charge. The deadline for filing a charge is six months after the alleged unfair practice. All parties must be served with a copy of the charge. (Registered mail is recommended.) The charge is investigated by a regional office. If, after investigating, the NLRB finds the charge has merit and issues a complaint, two actions are possible. The NLRB may defer to a grievance procedure agreed on by the employer and the union; grievances are discussed later in this chapter. Or a hearing may be held before an administrative law judge. The judge makes a recommendation, which either party may appeal.

The NLRB has the authority to issue cease-and-desist orders to halt unfair labor practices. It also can order the employer to reinstate workers, with or without back pay. The NLRB can set aside the results of an election if it believes either the union or the employer has created "an atmosphere of confusion or fear of reprisals."[26] If an employer or union refuses to comply with an NLRB order, the board has the authority to petition the U.S. Court of Appeals. The court may enforce the order, recommend it to the NLRB for modification, change the order itself, or set it aside altogether.

Union Organizing

Unions begin their involvement with an organization's employees by conducting an organizing campaign. To meet its objectives, a union needs to convince a majority of workers that they should receive better pay or other employment conditions and that the union will help them do so. The employer's objectives will depend on its strategy—whether it seeks to work with a union or convince employees that they are better off without union representation.

LO4 Describe the union organizing process.

The Process of Organizing

The organizing process begins with authorization cards, such as the example shown in Figure 14.5. Union representatives make contact with employees, present their message about the union, and invite them to sign an authorization card. For the organization process to continue, at least 30 percent of the employees must sign an authorization card.

If over half the employees sign an authorization card, the union may request that the employer voluntarily recognize the union. If the employer agrees, the NLRB certifies the union as the exclusive representative of employees. If the employer refuses, or if only 30 to 50 percent of employees signed cards, the NLRB conducts a secret-ballot election. The arrangements are made in one of two ways:

1. For a *consent election*, the employer and the union seeking representation arrive at an agreement stating the time and place of the election, the choices included on the ballot, and a way to determine who is eligible to vote.

YES, I WANT THE IAM

I, the undersigned employee of

(Company) _____

authorize the International Association of Machinists and Aerospace Workers (IAM) to act as my collective bargaining agent for wages, hours and working conditions. I agree that this card may be used either to support a demand for recognition or an NLRB election, at the discretion of the union.

Name (print)_____ Date _____

Home Address_____ Phone_____

City_____ State_____ Zip_____

Job Title_____ Dept._____ Shift _____

Sign Here X _____

Note: This authorization to be SIGNED and DATED in employee's own handwriting.
YOUR RIGHT TO SIGN THIS CARD IS PROTECTED BY FEDERAL LAW.

RECEIVED BY (Initial) _____

Figure 14.5

Authorization Card

SOURCE: From J. A. Fossum, *Labor Relations: Development, Structure and Process, 2002.* Copyright © 2002 The McGraw-Hill Companies, Inc. Reprinted with permission.

2. For a *stipulation election*, the parties cannot agree on all of these terms, so the NLRB dictates the time and place, ballot choices, and method of determining eligibility.

On the ballot, workers vote for or against union representation, and they may also have a choice from among more than one union. If the union (or one of the unions on the ballot) wins a majority of votes, the NLRB certifies the union. If the ballot includes more than one union and neither gains a simple majority, the NLRB holds a runoff election.

As noted earlier, if the NLRB finds the election was not conducted fairly, it may set aside the results and call for a new election. Conduct that may lead to an election result's being set aside includes the following examples:[27]

- Threats of loss of jobs or benefits by an employer or union to influence votes or organizing activities.
- A grant of benefits or a promise of benefits as a means of influencing votes or organizing activities.
- Campaign speeches by management or union representatives to assembled groups of employees on company time less than 24 hours before an election.
- The actual use or threat of physical force or violence to influence votes or organizing activities.

After certification, there are limits on future elections. Once the NLRB has certified a union as the exclusive representative of a group of employees, it will not permit additional elections for one year. Also, after the union and employer have finished negotiating a contract, an election cannot be held for the time of the contract period or for three years, whichever comes first. The parties to the contract may agree not to hold an election for longer than three years, but an outside party (another union) cannot be barred for more than three years.

Management Strategies

Sometimes an employer will recognize a union after a majority of employees have signed authorization cards. More often, there is a hotly contested election campaign. During the campaign, unions try to persuade employees that their wages, benefits, treatment by employers, and chances to influence workplace decisions are too poor or small and that the union will be able to obtain improvements in these areas. Management typically responds with its own messages providing an opposite point of view. Management messages say the organization has provided a valuable package of wages and benefits and has treated employees well. Management also argues that the union will not be able to keep its promises but will instead create costs for employees, such as union dues and lost income during strikes.

Employers use a variety of methods to oppose unions in organizing campaigns.[28] Their efforts range from hiring consultants to distributing leaflets and letters to presenting the company's viewpoint at meetings of employees. Some management efforts go beyond what the law permits, especially in the eyes of union organizers. Why would employers break the law? One explanation is that the consequences, such as reinstating workers with back pay, are small compared to the benefits.[29] If coercing workers away from joining a union saves the company the higher wages, benefits, and other costs of a unionized workforce, management may feel an incentive to accept costs like back pay.

Table 14.1

What Supervisors Should and Should Not Do to Discourage Unions

WHAT TO DO:

Report any direct or indirect signs of union activity to a core management group.

Deal with employees by carefully stating the company's response to pro-union arguments. These responses should be coordinated by the company to maintain consistency and to avoid threats or promises. Take away union issues by following effective management practices all the time:

Deliver recognition and appreciation.

Solve employee problems.

Protect employees from harassment or humiliation.

Provide business-related information.

Be consistent in treatment of different employees.

Accommodate special circumstances where appropriate.

Ensure due process in performance management.

Treat all employees with dignity and respect.

WHAT TO AVOID:

Threatening employees with harsher terms and conditions of employment or employment loss if they engage in union activity.

Interrogating employees about pro-union or anti-union sentiments that they or others may have or reviewing union authorization cards or pro-union petitions.

Promising employees that they will receive favorable terms or conditions of employment if they forgo union activity.

Spying on employees known to be, or suspected of being, engaged in pro-union activities.

SOURCE: From J. A. Segal, "Unshackle Your Supervisors to Stay Union Free," *HR Magazine*, June 1998. Copyright © 1998 by Society for Human Resource Management. Reproduced with permission of Society for Human Resource Management via Copyright Clearance Center.

Supervisors have the most direct contact with employees. Thus, as Table 14.1 indicates, it is critical that they establish good relationships with employees even before there is any attempt at union organizing. Supervisors also must know what *not* to do if a union drive takes place. They should be trained in the legal principles discussed earlier in this chapter.

Union Strategies

The traditional union organizing strategy has been for organizers to call or visit employees at home, when possible, to talk about issues like pay and job security. Local unions of the Teamsters have contacted dock workers at UPS Freight terminals in 11 states and invited them to sign authorization cards. When a majority of the workers at a terminal sign cards, UPS agrees to bargain with the Teamsters at that location.[30]

Beyond encouraging workers to sign authorization cards and vote for the union, organizers use some creative alternatives to traditional organizing activities. They sometimes offer workers **associate union membership,** which is not linked to an employee's workplace and does not provide representation in collective bargaining. Rather, an associate member receives other services, such as discounts on health and life insurance or credit cards.[31] In return for these benefits, the union receives membership dues and a broader base of support for its activities. Associate membership may be attractive to employees who wish to join a union but cannot because their workplace is not organized by a union.

Associate Union Membership
Alternative form of union membership in which members receive discounts on insurance and credit cards rather than representation in collective bargaining.

Corporate Campaigns
Bringing public, financial, or political pressure on employers during union organization and contract negotiation.

Another alternative to traditional organizing is to conduct **corporate campaigns**—bringing public, financial, or political pressure on employers during union organization and contract negotiation.[32] The Amalgamated Clothing and Textile Workers Union (ACTWU) corporate campaign against textile maker J. P. Stevens during the late 1970s was one of the first successful corporate campaigns and served as a model for those that followed. The ACTWU organized a boycott of J. P. Stevens products and threatened to withdraw its pension funds from financial institutions where J. P. Stevens officers acted as directors. The company eventually agreed to a contract with ACTWU.[33]

Another winning union organizing strategy is to negotiate employer neutrality and card-check provisions into a contract. Under a *neutrality provision*, the employer pledges not to oppose organizing attempts elsewhere in the company. A *card-check provision* is an agreement that if a certain percentage—by law, at least a majority—of employees sign an authorization card, the employer will recognize their union representation. An impartial outside agency, such as the American Arbitration Association, counts the cards. Evidence suggests that this strategy can be very effective for unions.[34]

Decertifying a Union

The Taft-Hartley Act expanded union members' right to be represented by leaders of their own choosing to include the right to vote out an existing union. This action is called *decertifying* the union. Decertification follows the same process as a representation election. An election to decertify a union may not take place when a contract is in effect.

When decertification elections are held, unions often do not fare well.[35] During the past few years, unions have lost between 54 and 64 percent of decertification elections. In another blow to unions, the number of decertification elections has increased from about 5 percent of all elections in the 1950s and 1960s to more than double that rate in recent years.

LO5 Explain how management and unions negotiate contracts.

Collective Bargaining

When the NLRB has certified a union, that union represents employees during contract negotiations. In **collective bargaining,** a union negotiates on behalf of its members with management representatives to arrive at a contract defining conditions of employment for the term of the contract and to resolve differences in the way they interpret the contract. Typical contracts include provisions for pay, benefits, work rules, and resolution of workers' grievances. Table 14.2 shows typical provisions negotiated in collective bargaining contracts.

Collective Bargaining
Negotiation between union representatives and management representatives to arrive at a contract defining conditions of employment for the term of the contract and to administer that contract.

Collective bargaining differs from one situation to another in terms of *bargaining structure*—that is, the range of employees and employers covered by the contract. A contract may involve a narrow group of employees in a craft union or a broad group in an industrial union. Contracts may cover one or several facilities of the same employer, or the bargaining structure may involve several employers. Many more interests must be considered in collective bargaining for an industrial union with a bargaining structure that includes several employers than in collective bargaining for a craft union in a single facility.

The majority of contract negotiations take place between unions and employers that have been through the process before. In the typical situation, management has come to accept the union as an organization it must work with. The situation can be

Establishment and administration of the agreement	Bargaining unit and plant supplements Contract duration and reopening and renegotiation provisions Union security and the checkoff Special bargaining committees Grievance procedures Arbitration and mediation Strikes and lockouts Contract enforcement	**Table 14.2** **Typical Provisions in Collective Bargaining Contracts**
Functions, rights, and responsibilities	Management rights clauses Plant removal Subcontracting Union activities on company time and premises Union–management cooperation Regulation of technological change Advance notice and consultation	
Wage determination and administration	General provisions Rate structure and wage differentials Allowances Incentive systems and production bonus plans Production standards and time studies Job classification and job evaluation Individual wage adjustments General wage adjustments during the contract period	
Job or income security	Hiring and transfer arrangements Employment and income guarantees Reporting and call-in pay Supplemental unemployment benefit plans Regulation of overtime, shift work, etc. Reduction of hours to forestall layoffs Layoff procedures; seniority; recall Worksharing in lieu of layoff Attrition arrangements Promotion practices Training and retraining Relocation allowances Severance pay and layoff benefit plans Special funds and study committees	
Plant operations	Work and shop rules Rest periods and other in-plant time allowances Safety and health Plant committees Hours of work and premium pay practices Shift operations Hazardous work Discipline and discharge	
Paid and unpaid leave	Vacations and holidays Sick leave Funeral and personal leave Military leave and jury duty	

(Continued)

Table 14.2

Concluded

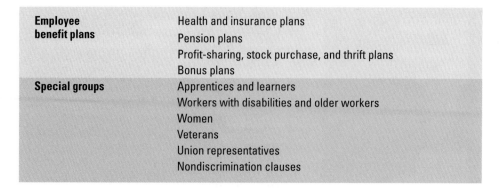

Employee benefit plans	Health and insurance plans
	Pension plans
	Profit-sharing, stock purchase, and thrift plans
	Bonus plans
Special groups	Apprentices and learners
	Workers with disabilities and older workers
	Women
	Veterans
	Union representatives
	Nondiscrimination clauses

SOURCE: T. A. Kochan, *Collective Bargaining and Industrial Relations* (Homewood, IL: Richard D. Irwin, 1980), p. 29. Original data from J. W. Bloch, "Union Contracts—A New Series of Studies," *Monthly Labor Review* 87 (October 1964), pp. 1184–85.

very different when a union has just been certified and is negotiating its first contract. In over one-fourth of negotiations for a first contract, the parties are unable to reach an agreement.[36]

Bargaining over New Contracts

Clearly, the outcome of contract negotiations can have important consequences for labor costs, productivity, and the organization's ability to compete. Therefore, unions and management need to prepare carefully for collective bargaining. Preparation includes establishing objectives for the contract, reviewing the old contract, gathering data (such as compensation paid by competitors and the company's ability to survive a strike), predicting the likely demands to be made, and establishing the cost of meeting the demands.[37] This preparation can help negotiators develop a plan for how to negotiate. Different situations and goals call for different approaches to bargaining, such as the following alternatives proposed by Richard Walton and Robert McKersie:[38]

- *Distributive bargaining* divides an economic "pie" between two sides—for example, a wage increase means giving the union a larger share of the pie.
- *Integrative bargaining* looks for win-win solutions, or outcomes in which both sides benefit. If the organization's labor costs hurt its performance, integrative bargaining might seek to avoid layoffs in exchange for work rules that improve productivity.
- *Attitudinal structuring* focuses on establishing a relationship of trust. The parties are concerned about ensuring that the other side will keep its part of any bargain.
- *Intraorganizational bargaining* addresses conflicts within union or management groups or objectives, such as between new employees and workers with high seniority or between cost control and reduction of turnover.

The collective bargaining process may involve any combination of these alternatives.

Negotiations go through various stages.[39] In the earliest stages, many more people are often present than in later stages. On the union side, this may give all the various internal interest groups a chance to participate and voice their goals. Their input helps communicate to management what will satisfy union members and may help the union achieve greater solidarity. At this stage, union negotiators often present a long list of proposals, partly to satisfy members and partly to introduce enough

Citing the strong potential for loss of jobs, union members protest Verizon's selling of its landline business to Frontier Communications in West Virginia.

issues that they will have flexibility later in the process. Management may or may not present proposals of its own. Sometimes management prefers to react to the union's proposals.

During the middle stages of the process, each side must make a series of decisions, even though the outcome is uncertain. How important is each issue to the other side? How likely is it that disagreement on particular issues will result in a strike? When and to what extent should one side signal its willingness to compromise?

In the final stage of negotiations, pressure for an agreement increases. Public negotiations may be only part of the process. Negotiators from each side may hold one-on-one meetings or small-group meetings where they escape some public relations pressures. A neutral third party may act as a go-between or facilitator. In some cases, bargaining breaks down as the two sides find they cannot reach a mutually acceptable agreement. The outcome depends partly on the relative bargaining power of each party. That power, in turn, depends on each party's ability to withstand a strike, which costs the workers their pay during the strike and costs the employer lost production and possibly lost customers.

When Bargaining Breaks Down

The intended outcome of collective bargaining is a contract with terms acceptable to both parties. If one or both sides determine that negotiation alone will not produce such an agreement, bargaining breaks down. To bring this impasse to an end, the union may strike, or the parties may bring in outside help to resolve their differences.

Strikes

Strike
A collective decision by union members not to work until certain demands or conditions are met.

A **strike** is a collective decision of the union members not to work until certain demands or conditions are met. The union members vote, and if the majority favors a strike, they all go on strike at that time or when union leaders believe the time is right. Strikes are typically accompanied by *picketing*—the union stations members near the worksite with signs indicating the union is on strike. During the strike, the union members do not receive pay from their employer, but the union may be able to make up for some of the lost pay. The employer loses production unless it can hire replacement workers, and even then, productivity may be reduced. Often, other unions support striking workers by refusing to cross their picket line—for example, refusing to make deliveries to a company during a strike. When the Writers Guild of America went on strike, production of television shows came to a standstill. The strike also affected the Golden Globe Awards, as actors and other union employees in the media industry refused to cross their picket lines.

The vast majority of labor-management negotiations do not result in a strike, and the number of strikes has plunged since the 1950s, as shown in Figure 14.6. In every year since 2000, the percentage of total working time lost to strikes each year has been 0.01 percent—that is, one-hundredth of 1 percent of working time—or even less. A primary reason strikes are rare is that a strike is seldom in the best interests of either party. Not only do workers lose wages and employers lose production, but the negative experience of a strike can make future interactions more difficult. During the Writers Guild of America strike, screenwriters won some compensation for their

Figure 14.6

Strikes Involving 1,000 or More Workers

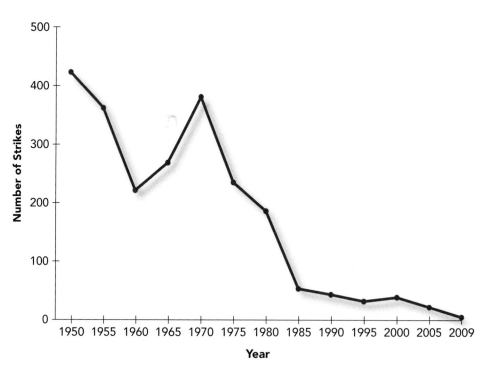

Note: Because strikes are most likely in large bargaining units, these numbers represent most lost working time in the United States.

SOURCE: Bureau of Labor Statistics, "Work Stoppages," http://data.bls.gov.

work that is distributed over the Internet. But while television shows switched to reruns, viewers were finding new, often free content online. That could ultimately damage network TV's future.[40] When strikes do occur, the conduct of each party during the strike can do lasting harm to labor-management relations. Violence by either side or threats of job loss or actual job loss because jobs went to replacement workers can make future relations difficult. Finally, many government employees do not have a right to strike, and their percentage among unionized employees overall has risen in recent decades, as we discussed earlier.

Alternatives to Strikes

Because strikes are so costly and risky, unions and employers generally prefer other methods for resolving conflicts. Three common alternatives rely on a neutral third party, usually provided by the Federal Mediation and Conciliation Service (FMCS):

- **Mediation** is the least formal and most widely used of these procedures. A mediator hears the views of both sides and facilitates the negotiation process. The mediator has no formal authority to dictate a resolution, so a strike remains a possibility. In a survey studying negotiations between unions and large businesses, mediation was used in almost 4 out of 10 negotiation efforts.[41]
- A **fact finder,** most often used for negotiations with governmental bodies, typically reports on the reasons for the dispute, the views and arguments of both sides, and (sometimes) a recommended settlement, which the parties may decline. The public nature of these recommendations may pressure the parties to settle. Even if

Mediation
Conflict resolution procedure in which a mediator hears the views of both sides and facilitates the negotiation process but has no formal authority to dictate a resolution.

Fact Finder
Third party to collective bargaining who reports the reasons for a dispute, the views and arguments of both sides, and possibly a recommended settlement, which the parties may decline.

Strikes such as this one between security officers and management of several office buildings in San Francisco are costly. Both unions and employees generally prefer to resolve contract conflicts in other ways.

they do not accept the fact finder's recommended settlement, the fact finder may identify or frame issues in a way that makes agreement easier. Sometimes merely devoting time to this process gives the parties a chance to reach an agreement. However, there is no guarantee that a strike will be avoided.

Arbitration
Conflict resolution procedure in which an arbitrator or arbitration board determines a binding settlement.

- Under **arbitration,** the most formal type of outside intervention, an arbitrator or arbitration board determines a settlement that is *binding,* meaning the parties have to accept it. In conventional arbitration, the arbitrator fashions the solution. In "final-offer arbitration," the arbitrator must choose either management's or the union's final offer for each issue or for the contract as a whole. "Rights arbitration" focuses on enforcing or interpreting contract terms. Arbitration in the writing of contracts or setting of contract terms has traditionally been reserved for special circumstances such as negotiations between unions and government agencies, where strikes may be illegal or especially costly. Occasionally, arbitration has been used with businesses in situations where strikes have been extremely damaging. However, the general opinion is that union and management representatives are in the best position to resolve conflicts themselves, because they are closer to the situation than an arbitrator can be.

Contract Administration

LO6 Summarize the practice of contract administration.

Although the process of negotiating a labor agreement (including the occasional strike) receives the most publicity, other union-management activities occur far more often. Bargaining over a new contract typically occurs only about every three years, but administering labor contracts goes on day after day, year after year. The two activities are linked, of course. Vague or inconsistent language in the contract can make administering the contract more difficult. The difficulties can create conflict that spills over into the next round of negotiations.[42] Events during negotiations—strikes, the use of replacement workers, or violence by either side—also can lead to difficulties in working successfully under a conflict.

Grievance Procedure
The process for resolving union-management conflicts over interpretation or violation of a collective bargaining agreement.

Contract administration includes carrying out the terms of the agreement and resolving conflicts over interpretation or violation of the agreement. Under a labor contract, the process for resolving these conflicts is called a **grievance procedure.** This procedure has a key influence on success in contract administration. A grievance procedure may be started by an employee or discharged employee who believes the employer violated the contract or by a union representative on behalf of a group of workers or union representatives.

For grievances launched by an employee, a typical grievance procedure follows the steps shown in Figure 14.7. The grievance may be settled during any of the four steps. In the first step, the employee talks to his or her supervisor about the problem. If this conversation is unsatisfactory, the employee may involve the union steward in further discussion. The union steward and employee decide whether the problem has been resolved and, if not, whether it is a contract violation. If the problem was not resolved and does seem to be a contract violation, the union moves to step 2, putting the grievance in writing and submitting it to a line manager. The union steward meets with a management representative to try to resolve the problem. Management consults with the industrial relations staff and puts its response in writing too at this second stage. If step 2 fails to resolve the problem, the union appeals the grievance to top line management and representatives of the industrial relations staff. The union may involve more local or international officers in discussions at this stage (see step 3 in Figure 14.7). The decision resulting from the appeal is put into writing. If the

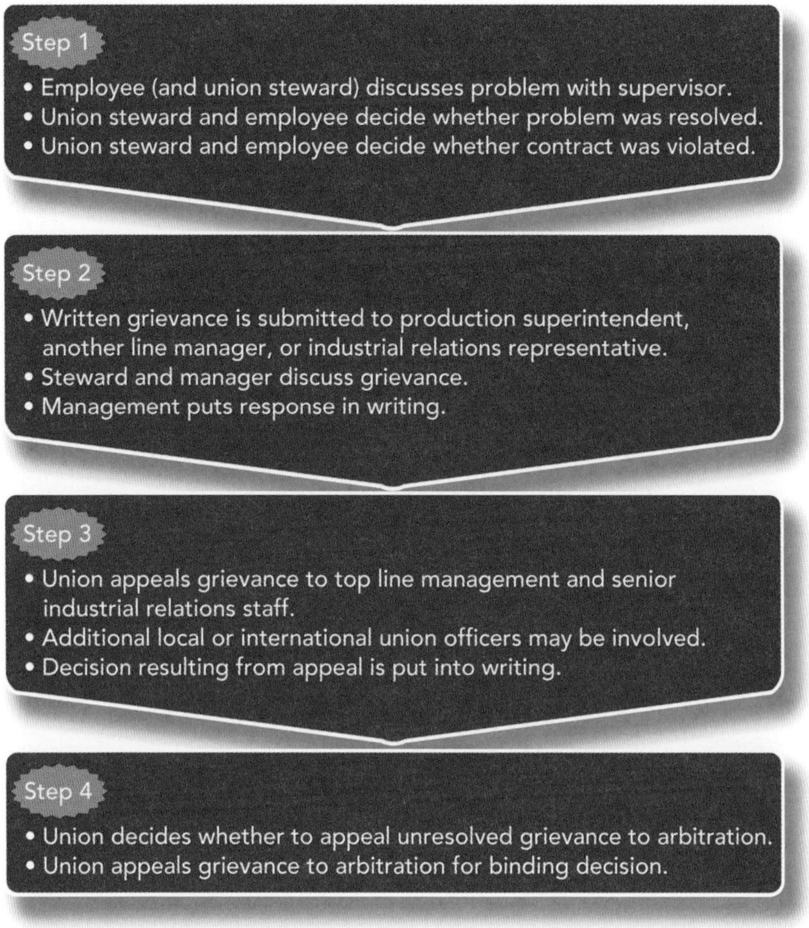

Figure 14.7

Steps in an Employee-
Initiated Grievance
Procedure

Step 1
- Employee (and union steward) discusses problem with supervisor.
- Union steward and employee decide whether problem was resolved.
- Union steward and employee decide whether contract was violated.

Step 2
- Written grievance is submitted to production superintendent, another line manager, or industrial relations representative.
- Steward and manager discuss grievance.
- Management puts response in writing.

Step 3
- Union appeals grievance to top line management and senior industrial relations staff.
- Additional local or international union officers may be involved.
- Decision resulting from appeal is put into writing.

Step 4
- Union decides whether to appeal unresolved grievance to arbitration.
- Union appeals grievance to arbitration for binding decision.

SOURCES: Adapted from T. A. Kochan, *Collective Bargaining and Industrial Relations* (Homewood, IL: Richard D. Irwin, 1980), p. 395; and J. A. Fossum, *Labor Relations* (Boston: McGraw-Hill/Irwin, 2002), pp. 448–52.

grievance is still not resolved, the union may decide (step 4) to appeal the grievance to an arbitrator. If the grievance involves a discharged employee, the process may begin at step 2 or 3, however, and the time limits between steps may be shorter. Grievances filed by the union on behalf of a group may begin at step 1 or step 2.

The majority of grievances are settled during the earlier steps of the process. This reduces delays and avoids the costs of arbitration. If a grievance does reach arbitration, the arbitrator makes the final ruling in the matter. Based on a series of Supreme Court decisions, courts generally avoid reviewing arbitrators' decisions and focus only on whether the grievance involved an issue that is subject to arbitration under the contract.[43]

Employers can judge a grievance procedure in terms of various criteria.[44] One consideration is effectiveness: how well the procedure resolves day-to-day contract questions. A second basic consideration is efficiency: whether it resolves issues at a reasonable cost and without major delays. The company also should consider how well the grievance procedure adapts to changing circumstances. For example, if sales drop off and the company needs to cut costs, how clear are the provisions related to layoffs and subcontracting of work? In the case of contracts covering multiple business units, the procedure should allow for resolving local contract issues, such as work rules at a particular facility. Companies also should consider whether the grievance procedure is fair—whether it treats employees equitably and gives them a voice in the process.

From the point of view of employees, the grievance procedure is an important means of getting fair treatment in the workplace. Its success depends on whether it provides for all the kinds of problems that are likely to arise (such as how to handle a business slowdown), whether employees feel they can file a grievance without being punished for it, and whether employees believe their union representatives will follow through. Under the National Labor Relations Act, the union has a *duty of fair representation,* which means the union must give equal representation to all members of the bargaining unit, whether or not they actually belong to the union. Too many grievances may indicate a problem—for example, the union members or line supervisors do not understand how to uphold the contract or have no desire to do so. At the same time, a very small number of grievances may also signal a problem. A very low grievance rate may suggest a fear of filing a grievance, a belief that the system does not work, or a belief that employees are poorly represented by their union.

What types of issues most commonly reach arbitration? According to data from the Federal Mediation and Conciliation Service, the largest share of arbitration cases involved discharge or other disciplinary actions.[45] Other issues that often reach arbitration involve wages, benefits, layoffs, work schedules, and management's rights. In reaching decisions about these and other issues, arbitrators consider a number of criteria, such as employees' understanding of the rules, the employer's consistency and fairness, and the employees' chance to present a defense and appeal a decision.[46]

Labor-Management Cooperation

L07 Describe more cooperative approaches to labor-management relations.

The traditional understanding of union-management relations is that the two parties are adversaries, meaning each side is competing to win at the expense of the other. There have always been exceptions to this approach. And since at least the 1980s, there seems to be wider acceptance of the view that greater cooperation can increase employee commitment and motivation while making the workplace more flexible.[47] Also, evidence suggests that employees who worked under traditional labor relations systems and then under the new, more cooperative systems prefer the cooperative approach.[48] For an example of a company where employees have enjoyed this difference, see the "Best Practices" box.

Cooperation between labor and management may feature employee involvement in decision making, self-managing employee teams, labor-management problem-solving teams, broadly defined jobs, and sharing of financial gains and business information with employees.[49] The search for a win-win solution requires that unions and their members understand the limits on what an employer can afford in a competitive marketplace.

Without the union's support, efforts at employee empowerment are less likely to survive and less likely to be effective if they do survive.[50] Unions have often resisted employee empowerment programs, precisely because the programs try to change workplace relations and the role that unions play. Union leaders have feared that such programs will weaken unions' role as independent representatives of employee interests. Indeed, the National Labor Relations Act makes it an unfair labor practice for an employer to "dominate or interfere with the formation or administration of any labor organization or contribute financial or other support to it."

Best Practices

UNION MEMBERS VALUED AT MIDWEST MECHANICAL

Midwest Mechanical started out as a family owned plumbing and heating contractor in Kansas City, Missouri. Under its third-generation owner, Tom Sanders, the company launched into a phase of tremendous growth, opening affiliates in New Jersey, Nevada, and Nebraska and tackling bigger, more complex projects. As so often happens during a period of rapid change, management responded with strict rules and tight controls. Unfortunately, that shifted the company's culture. Michael Kotubey, who joined the company in 2004 and eventually became its president, says Midwest Mechanical became a "stifling" environment where management "stopped believing in our people."

Fortunately, though, the unionized company changed its culture after performance began to suffer. Based on management's belief that "people will aspire to greatness if given the opportunity," the company began replacing strict rules with high expectations and active communication about the company's progress and performance. It encourages creativity and employee suggestions through its Innovator of the Year and Innovation of the Year awards. Recently, the winning innovators were plumbers in Midwest's fabrication shop who developed a series of process improvements. Tangible evidence of Midwest's commitment to communication is its new headquarters, designed to be energy efficient and to bring together the company's fabrication shop, office, and warehouse, along with a Gathering Room for meetings and celebrations.

Midwest Mechanical is committed to support for training of its employees, both in trade skills and in safety. Workers receive their training through the unions with which the company is affiliated. Various employees serve as trainers themselves in union-run training programs. That role provides a strong, positive connection between the company and its "union labor partners."

Finally, employees know that they have a real stake in the company's success. Employees, including union employees who are eligible, own shares of Midwest stock through its employee stock ownership plan (ESOP). Every employee who meets the eligibility requirements is automatically enrolled.

Efforts such as these are aimed at supporting the company's core values of integrity, teamwork, quality craftsmanship, and entrepreneurial spirit. Those qualities may sound difficult to promote in a company where many of the workers are union members, but Midwest Mechanical is making it work.

Sources: Katie Rotella, "2009 *PM's* Best Contractor to Work For: Midwest Mechanical Contractors, Kansas City, MO," *Plumbing & Mechanical*, January 2010, Business & Company Resource Center, http://galenet.galegroup.com; and Midwest Mechanical Contractors, corporate Web site, www.mmckc.com, accessed May 4, 2010.

Although employers must be careful to meet legal requirements, the NLRB has clearly supported employee involvement in work teams and decision making. For example, in a 2001 ruling, the NLRB found that employee participation committees at Crown Cork & Seal's aluminum-can factory did not violate federal labor law.[51] Those committees make and carry out decisions regarding a wide range of issues, including production, quality, training, safety, and certain types of discipline. The NLRB determined that the committees were not employer dominated. Instead of "dealing with" management, where employees make proposals for management to accept or reject, the committees exercise authority within boundaries set by management, similar to the authority of a first-line supervisor. In spite of the legal concerns, cooperative approaches to labor relations likely contribute to an organization's success.[52]

Beyond avoiding any taint of misuse of employee empowerment, employers build cooperative relationships by the way they treat employees—with respect and fairness, in the knowledge that attracting talent and minimizing turnover are in the employer's best interests. One company that does this is General Cable's Indianapolis Compounds plant, where teams of employees, represented by the International Brotherhood of Electrical Workers, continually seek ideas to improve quality and cut inefficiency. Terry Jones, a team coordinator and union representative, says these efforts reflect "a shared attitude that's driving the push for continuous improvement."[53]

thinking ethically

IS COMMUNICATING ENOUGH?

Recently, the *San Fernando Valley Business Journal* named Alma Quintero one of its Top Human Resources Professionals of the Year. A major reason she was nominated and received the prize had to do with her handling of her employer's relationship with its employees attempting to organize a union.

Quintero is director of human resources for the Hilton Los Angeles North–Glendale hotel. When she arrived at the organization, she found that workers were divided between some who wanted to be represented by the union, Unite Here Local 11, and others who were not interested in a union. Furthermore, union supporters were bitter about what they saw as unfair practices by the hotel. The union staged demonstrations and maintained a boycott of the hotel for almost two years.

While the hotel's management insisted that it was taking a neutral stance during the organizing effort, some employees complained that they felt harassed for their interest in a union. At one point, the National Labor Relations Board filed a complaint alleging intimidation, which the hotel settled. What one employee called "anti-union letters stapled to our paychecks," a Hilton spokesperson called an effort to help employees "get all the facts before they make their decisions."

Throughout that time, Quintero maintained an ongoing role in the negotiations and committed herself to communicating with employees frequently on what occurred during negotiations, trying to help them

"stay focused and do their job." Eventually, the sides reached a representation agreement, and the union's boycott ended.

SOURCES: Jeff Weiss, "Alma Quintero: Hilton Los Angeles North, Glendale," *San Fernando Valley Business Journal*, March 30, 2009, p. 39; "Hotel Workers Sign Contract," *San Fernando Valley Business Journal*, June 23, 2008, Business & Company Resource Center, http://galenet.galegroup.com; and Eugene Tong, "Union, Lawmakers Rally for Federal Labor Reforms," *Daily News (Los Angeles)*, February 23, 2007, Business & Company Resource Center, http://galenet.galegroup.com.

Questions

1. How does a union's organizing drive affect the interests of an organization's employees, owners, and customers? From an ethical perspective, which of these interests should the company's HR staff try to protect?
2. In this example, Alma Quintero was applauded for communicating with employees. What are some of the *ethical* requirements of communicating with employees during a union's organization effort? Which of these are also *legal* requirements?
3. In communicating with employees, Quintero says her goal was to give full information about the negotiations. What else would Quintero need to do to ensure that the hotel was treating workers fairly during this time—or is information all that Quintero owed the employees?

SUMMARY

LO1 Define unions and labor relations and their role in organizations.

A union is an organization formed for the purpose of representing its members in resolving conflicts with employers. Labor relations is the management specialty emphasizing skills that managers and union leaders can use to minimize costly forms of conflict and to seek win-win solutions to

disagreements. Unions—often locals belonging to national and international organizations—engage in organizing, collective bargaining, and contract administration with businesses and government organizations. In the United States, union membership has been declining among businesses but has held steady with government employees. Unionization is associated with more generous compensation and higher productivity but lower profits. Unions may reduce a business's flexibility and economic performance.

LO2 Identify the labor relations goals of management, labor unions, and society.

Management goals are to increase the organization's profits. Managers generally expect that unions will make these goals harder to achieve. Labor unions have the goal of obtaining pay and working conditions that satisfy their members. They obtain these results by gaining power in numbers. Society's values have included the hope that the existence of unions will replace conflict or violence between workers and employers with fruitful negotiation.

LO3 Summarize laws and regulations that affect labor relations.

The National Labor Relations Act supports the use of collective bargaining and sets out the rights of employees, including the right to organize, join a union, and go on strike. The NLRA prohibits unfair labor practices by employers, including interference with efforts to form a labor union and discrimination against employees who engage in union activities. The Taft-Hartley Act and Landrum-Griffin Act establish restrictions on union practices that restrain workers, such as their preventing employees from working during a strike or determining who an employer may hire. The Taft-Hartley Act also permits state right-to-work laws.

LO4 Describe the union organizing process.

Organizing begins when union representatives contact employees and invite them to sign an authorization card. If over half the employees sign a card, the union may request that the employer voluntarily recognize the union. If the employer refuses or if 30 to 50 percent of employees signed authorization cards, the NLRB conducts a secret-ballot election. If the union wins, the NLRB certifies the union. If the union loses but the NLRB finds that the election was not conducted fairly, it may set aside the results and call a new election.

LO5 Explain how management and unions negotiate contracts.

Negotiations take place between representatives of the union and the management bargaining unit.

The majority of negotiations involve parties that have been through the process before. The process begins with preparation, including research into the other side's strengths and demands. In the early stages of negotiation, many more people are present than at later stages. The union presents its demands, and management sometimes presents demands as well. Then the sides evaluate the demands and the likelihood of a strike. In the final stages, pressure for an agreement increases, and a neutral third party may be called on to help reach a resolution. If bargaining breaks down, the impasse may be broken with a strike, mediation, fact finder, or arbitration.

LO6 Summarize the practice of contract administration.

Contract administration is a daily activity under the labor agreement. It includes carrying out the terms of the agreement and resolving conflicts over interpretation or violation of the contract. Conflicts are resolved through a grievance procedure. Typically, the grievance procedure begins with an employee talking to his or her supervisor about the problem and possibly involving the union steward in the discussion. If this does not resolve the conflict, the union files a written grievance with a line manager, and union and management representatives meet to discuss the problem. If this effort fails, the union appeals the grievance to top line management and the industrial relations staff. If the appeal fails, the union may appeal the grievance to an arbitrator.

LO7 Describe more cooperative approaches to labor-management relations.

In contrast to the traditional view that labor and management are adversaries, some organizations and unions work more cooperatively. Cooperation may feature employee involvement in decision making, self-managing employee teams, labor-management problem-solving teams, broadly defined jobs, and sharing of financial gains and business information with employees. If such cooperation is tainted by attempts of the employer to dominate or interfere with labor organizations, however, such as by dealing with wages, grievances, or working conditions, it may be illegal under the NLRA. In spite of such legal concerns, cooperative labor relations seem to contribute to an organization's success.

KEY TERMS

agency shop, p. 429

American Federation of Labor and Congress of Industrial Organizations (AFL-CIO), p. 423

arbitration, p. 444

associate union membership, p. 437

checkoff provision, p. 429

closed shop, p. 429

collective bargaining, p. 438

corporate campaigns, p. 438

craft union, p. 422

fact finder, p. 443

grievance procedure, p. 444

industrial union, p. 423

labor relations, p. 421

maintenance of membership, p. 429

mediation, p. 443

National Labor Relations Act (NLRA), p. 430

National Labor Relations Board (NLRB), p. 433

right-to-work laws, p. 432

strike, p. 442

union shop, p. 429

union steward, p. 423

unions, p. 421

REVIEW AND DISCUSSION QUESTIONS

1. Why do employees join labor unions? Did you ever belong to a labor union? If you did, do you think union membership benefited you? If you did not, do you think a union would have benefited you? Why or why not?

2. Why do managers at most companies prefer that unions not represent their employees? Can unions provide benefits to an employer? Explain.

3. How has union membership in the United States changed over the past few decades? How does union membership in the United States compare with union membership in other countries? How might these patterns in union membership affect the HR decisions of an international company?

4. What legal responsibilities do employers have regarding unions? What are the legal requirements affecting unions?

5. Suppose you are the HR manager for a chain of clothing stores. You learn that union representatives have been encouraging the stores' employees to sign authorization cards. What events can follow in this process of organizing? Suggest some ways that you might respond in your role as HR manager.

6. If the parties negotiating a labor contract are unable to reach an agreement, what actions can resolve the situation?

7. Why are strikes uncommon? Under what conditions might management choose to accept a strike?

8. What are the usual steps in a grievance procedure? What are the advantages of resolving a grievance in the first step? What skills would a supervisor need so grievances can be resolved in the first step?

9. The "Best Practices" box near the end of the chapter gives an example of union-management cooperation at Midwest Mechanical. What does the company gain from this effort? What do workers gain?

10. What are the legal restrictions on labor-management cooperation?

BUSINESSWEEK CASE

BusinessWeek U.S. Labor Lobbies European Management

The Service Employees International Union [planned to] picket the annual meeting of French food-service group Sodexo in Paris on January 25 [2010] as U.S. unions take their organizing efforts abroad. Sodexo, which employs 380,000 people worldwide including 110,000 in the U.S., is "engaging in behavior around the world that would not be acceptable in their home country," says Mitch Ackerman, an SEIU executive vice-president who heads the Washington-based union's property services division.

With more than 5 million Americans now employed by foreign-owned companies, U.S. labor unions are starting to export their grievances. In industries ranging from food service to telecommunications, foreign companies are coming under attack in their home countries from American unions, which are teaming up with local labor groups to criticize the companies' U.S. labor practices.

The SEIU alleges that Sodexo's U.S. subsidiary has used "harsh" though legal anti-union tactics, such as requiring employees to attend meetings where managers try to dissuade them from unionizing. The union also alleges that some Sodexo employees have been punished for taking sick days, and that the company's health-insurance plan is too expensive for many workers, who hold kitchen and cleaning jobs in schools, hospitals, military bases, and other facilities.

Sodexo denies those allegations. "Sodexo respects unequivocally the rights of our employees to unionize or not to unionize, as they may so choose," the company says in a statement. "We will not discriminate against any employee for engaging in union organizing activities or otherwise supporting a union."

Sodexo provides paid sick leave for full-time employees, who account for 75 percent of its U.S. workforce, the company says. It says 60 percent of full-time U.S. employees have enrolled in Sodexo's health insurance plan, under which two-thirds of premiums are paid by the company. In a 2008 survey conducted for Sodexo by employee-benefits consulting group Hewitt, "Eighty-six percent of our American employees said our company compared favorably with our competitors," the company says.

According to Ackerman, SEIU is hoping its complaints will cause a stir in France, which offers universal public health insurance and guarantees the right to unionize and strike in its national constitution. "We want to tell our story to shareholders and to a larger public audience," he says.

Besides protesting at Sodexo's annual meeting, SEIU representatives will hold a press conference with French union members and representatives of UNISON, a British labor union. The British union represents hospital workers who staged a two-day strike this month against Sodexo in North Devon that resulted in the company's agreeing to better pay and benefits.

SEIU is one of at least three U.S. unions targeting foreign employers. The Washington-based Communications Workers of America, which is trying to organize U.S. employees of cellular provider T-Mobile, formed a partnership last November with German union Ver.di to exert pressure on T-Mobile's German owner, Deutsche Telekom. In Britain, retail chain Tesco has been targeted by the Washington-based United Food and Commercial Workers, which is attempting to organize employees of Tesco-owned Fresh & Easy markets in the western U.S.

When foreign companies set up shop in the U.S., Ackerman says, "We want to hold them accountable in their home countries."

SOURCE: Excerpted from Carol Matlack, "U.S. Labor Takes Its Case to European Bosses," *BusinessWeek*, January 22, 2010, www.businessweek.com.

Questions

1. How does the SEIU's plan give Sodexo's U.S. workers influence they might not have outside of a union? Do you think the effort described in this case will benefit these workers? Why or why not?

2. What do the SEIU's goals seem to be with regard to Sodexo? What would you expect Sodexo's goals to be in this situation?

3. Should Sodexo's U.S. employees receive benefits similar to benefits received by employees at the company's headquarters in France? Why or why not? Write a paragraph expressing your views to Sodexo's management, and then write a paragraph presenting these views to the SEIU.

Case: Boeing's Prickly Relationship with Its Unions

Boeing's headquarters is in Chicago, but until recently at least, the hub of its commercial-aircraft business was in the state of Washington. That changed when Boeing bought a South Carolina factory that had been making sections of the fuselage for Boeing's 787 Dreamliner, as well as a stake in an adjoining factory making 787 subassemblies. Eventually, amid talk that the South Carolina legislature would provide tax incentives worth $450 million, Boeing announced that it would be building a second 787 assembly line in South Carolina. It planned to start production in 2011.

Boeing has not been shy about saying the International Association of Machinists and Aerospace Workers, which represents workers at the Everett, Washington, assembly plant, bears much of the responsibility. During the past twenty years, the union has called several strikes. With the company way behind schedule in 2008, a strike by the Machinists set production back another eight weeks, costing Boeing $2 billion and leading some customers to

cancel their orders and buy from rival Airbus. In addition, the union recently refused to accept concessions in negotiating a new contract. The Machinists blame Boeing for presenting vague contract requirements, a charge the company denies. Boeing's Jim Proulx told reporters that strikes in Washington mattered: "Repeated labor disruptions have affected our performance in our customers' eyes. We have to show our customers we can be a reliable supplier to them."

With regard to bargaining, Boeing and the Machinists had different requirements for the contract. Among other demands, the union wanted wage increases of 3 percent per year plus cost-of-living raises, and it wanted a guarantee that future airplane construction would occur in Washington. Boeing was willing to grant pay raises of 2 percent per year and wouldn't commit to where future planes would be constructed. Boeing wanted union members to start sharing the cost of health insurance; the union said it would start to do so in 2018. The union claims Boeing wasn't clear about its requirements during bargaining, but only after announcing the move to South Carolina. Boeing's second-largest union, the Society of Engineering Employees in Aerospace (SPEEA), echoes that complaint. Boeing says the reason is that it had no complaints with the SPEEA.

Even without complaining about the Machinists, Boeing can cite economic advantages to employing workers in South Carolina. Most workers at the South Carolina plant will make roughly $14 to $15 per hour, compared with $26 for Machinists in Washington. One reason for the lower rate is that the South Carolina employees have less experience in the industry. Workers in Charleston also recently voted to decertify the Machinists as their union. Because South Carolina is a right-to-work state with one of the nation's lowest rates of unionization, the chance for future union organizing is not great. Together, these facts suggest that Boeing doesn't have to worry about strikes at its South Carolina facilities. The Machinists, for their part, say their highly skilled workers in Washington have been fixing problem after problem introduced by the company's suppliers, so using nonunion labor carries its own costs. In fact, Boeing did recently take control of operations at a subcontractor in Charleston that experienced delays and quality problems. Tom Wroblewski, president of Machinists district that represents Boeing workers, told a reporter, "If they continually offload and go into areas of nonskilled workers, they're just not going to have that quality product."

Perhaps the Machinists have a point, but Boeing seems to have the last word. The company recently announced layoffs of over a thousand workers, some of them in the Commercial Airplanes and Defense unit, which makes the 787. Under an agreement with the Machinists, some workers are eligible to volunteer to be laid off with benefits.

SOURCES: John Gillie, "Boeing Fallout to Take Time," *News Tribune* (Tacoma, WA), November 8, 2009, Business & Company Resource Center, http://galenet.galegroup.com; "S.C. May Benefit from Supplier Plan," *Post and Courier* (Charleston, S.C.), December 9, 2009, Business & Company Resource Center, http://galenet.galegroup.com; "Advantage Dixie; Aviation and the South," *The Economist*, January 9, 2010, Businesss & Company Resource Center, http://galenet.galegroup.com; Dean Foust and Justin Bachman, "Boeing's Flight from Union Labor," *BusinessWeek*, November 6, 2009, www.businessweek.com; and "Boeing Announces 1,020 Layoffs," *UPI NewsTrack*, February 20, 2010, Business & Company Resource Center, http://galenet.galegroup.com.

Questions

1. What are the advantages to Boeing of its non-union South Carolina workforce? Of its unionized Washington workforce?
2. If a Boeing human resource manager transferred from a Washington facility to a South Carolina facility, what differences could he or she expect in the department's work?
3. Could Boeing and the Machinists develop a more cooperative working relationship in Washington? Why or why not? What could Boeing do to encourage cooperation?

 IT'S A WRAP!   **connect**

www. mhhe.com/noefund4e is your source for Reviewing, Applying, and Practicing the concepts you learned about in Chapter 14.

Review
- Chapter learning objectives

Application
- Manager's Hot Seat segment: "Partnership: The Unbalancing Act"
- Video case and quiz: "Hollywood Labor Unions"
- Self-Assessment: Labor relations
- Web exercise: Understanding unions
- Small-business case: Republic Gets Serious

Practice
- Chapter quiz

NOTES

1. M. Evans, "Health Workers Saying, 'Union, Yes,'" *Modern Healthcare*, February 4, 2008, downloaded from General Reference Center Gold, http://find.galegroup.com.

2. J. T. Dunlop, *Industrial Relations Systems* (New York: Holt, 1958); and C. Kerr, "Industrial Conflict and Its Mediation," *American Journal of Sociology* 60 (1954), pp. 230–45.

3. T. A. Kochan, *Collective Bargaining and Industrial Relations* (Homewood, IL: Richard D. Irwin, 1980), p. 25; and H. C. Katz and T. A. Kochan, *An Introduction to Collective Bargaining and Industrial Relations*, 3rd ed. (New York: McGraw-Hill, 2004).

4. R. J. Grossman, "Reorganized Labor," *HRMagazine*, January 2008, downloaded from General Reference Center Gold, http://find.galegroup.com.

5. Whether the time the union steward spends on union business is paid for by the employer, the union, or a combination is a matter of negotiation between the employer and the union.

6. Bureau of Labor Statistics, "Union Affiliation Data from the Current Population Survey," http://data.bls .gov, accessed March 10, 2008; and J. Smerd, "Unions Reverse Decline," *Workforce Management*, February 4, 2008, downloaded from General Reference Center Gold, http://find.galegroup.com.

7. Katz and Kochan, *An Introduction to Collective Bargaining*, building on J. Fiorito and C. L. Maranto, "The Contemporary Decline of Union Strength," *Contemporary Policy Issues* 3 (1987), pp. 12–27; and G. N. Chaison and J. Rose, "The Macrodeterminants of Union Growth and Decline," in *The State of the Unions*, ed. G. Strauss et al. (Madison, WI: Industrial Relations Research Association, 1991).

8. Bureau of Labor Statistics Web site, www.bls.gov; Steven Greenhouse, "Survey Finds Deep Shift in the Makeup of Unions," *New York Times*, November 11, 2009, Business & Company Resource Center, http:// galenet.galegroup.com; and John Schmitt, *The Unions of the States* (Washington, DC: Center for Economic and Policy Research, February 2010), accessed at www.cepr.net.

9. C. Brewster, "Levels of Analysis in Strategic HRM: Questions Raised by Comparative Research," Conference on Research and Theory in HRM, Cornell University, October 1997; and Eurofund, "Industrial Relations Context," *European Industrial Relations Dictionary*, updated July 24, 2009, www.eurofund.europa.eu.

10. American Federation of State, County and Municipal Employees, "Jobs We Do," www.afscme.org, accessed May 3, 2010.

11. J. T. Addison and B. T. Hirsch, "Union Effects on Productivity, Profits, and Growth: Has the Long Run Arrived?" *Journal of Labor Economics* 7 (1989), pp. 72–105; and R. B. Freeman and J. L. Medoff, "The Two Faces of Unionism," *Public Interest* 57 (Fall 1979), pp. 69–93.

12. L. Mishel and P. Voos, *Unions and Economic Competitiveness* (Armonk, NY: M. E. Sharpe, 1991); Freeman and Medoff, "Two Faces"; and S. Slichter, J. Healy, and E. R. Livernash, *The Impact of Collective Bargaining on Management* (Washington, DC: Brookings Institution, 1960).

13. A. O. Hirschman, *Exit, Voice, and Loyalty* (Cambridge, MA: Harvard University Press, 1970); and R. Batt, A. J. S. Colvin, and J. Keefe, "Employee Voice, Human Resource Practices, and Quit Rates: Evidence from the Telecommunications Industry," *Industrial and Labor Relations Review* 55 (1970), pp. 573–94.

14. R. B. Freeman and J. L. Medoff, *What Do Unions Do?* (New York: Basic Books, 1984); Addison and Hirsch, "Union Effects on Productivity"; M. Ash and J. A. Seago, "The Effect of Registered Nurses' Unions on Heart-Attack Mortality," *Industrial and Labor Relations Review* 57 (2004), p. 422; and C. Doucouliagos and P. Laroche, "What Do Unions Do to Productivity? A Meta-Analysis," *Industrial Relations* 42 (2003), pp. 650–91.

15. B. E. Becker and C. A. Olson, "Unions and Firm Profits," *Industrial Relations* 31, no. 3 (1992), pp. 395–415; B. T. Hirsch and B. A. Morgan, "Shareholder Risks and Returns in Union and Nonunion Firms," *Industrial and Labor Relations Review* 47, no. 2 (1994), pp. 302–18; and Hristos Doucouliagos and Patrice Laroche, "Unions and Profits: A Meta-Regression Analysis," *Industrial Relations* 48, no. 1 (January 2008), p. 146.

16. Lauren Donovan, "Union Adds Training to Better Partner with Industry," *Bismarck (N.D.) Tribune*, January 17, 2010, Business & Company Resource Center, http://galenet.galegroup.com; and Jim Olsztynski, "Gone but Not Forgotten," *Plumbing & Mechanical*, January 2010, Business & Company Resource Center, http://galenet.galegroup.com.

17. Bureau of Labor Statistics, "Employer Costs for Employee Compensation—December 2009," news release, March 10, 2010, www.bls.gov.

18. S. B. Jarrell and T. D. Stanley, "A Meta-Analysis of the Union-Nonunion Wage Gap," *Industrial and Labor Relations Review* 44 (1990), pp. 54–67; L. Mishel and M. Walters, "How Unions Help All Workers," Economic Policy Institute Briefing Paper, August 2003, www.epinet.org; and McKinley L. Blackburn, "Are Union Wage Differentials in the United States Falling?" *Industrial Relations* 47, no. 3 (July 2008), p. 390.

19. S. Webb and B. Webb, *Industrial Democracy* (London: Longmans, Green, 1897); and J. R. Commons, *Institutional Economics* (New York: Macmillan, 1934).

20. "Why America Needs Unions, but Not the Kind It Has Now," *BusinessWeek*, May 23, 1994, p. 70.

21. E. E. Herman, J. L. Schwatz, and A. Kuhn, *Collective Bargaining and Labor Relations* (Englewood Cliffs, NJ: Prentice Hall, 1992).

22. Kochan, *Collective Bargaining and Industrial Relations*, p. 61.

23. National Labor Relations Board, *Basic Guide to the National Labor Relations Act* (Washington, DC: U.S. Government Printing Office, 1997).

24. National Labor Relations Board, "Employees/Employers Not Covered by NLRA," Workplace Rights, www.nlrb.gov, accessed March 12, 2008.

25. National Labor Relations Board, *Basic Guide.*

26. Ibid.

27. Ibid.

28. R. B. Freeman and M. M. Kleiner, "Employer Behavior in the Face of Union Organizing Drives," *Industrial and Labor Relations Review* 43, no. 4 (April 1990), pp. 351–65.

29. J. A. Fossum, *Labor Relations*, 8th ed. (New York: McGraw-Hill, 2002), p. 149.

30. J. Gallagher, "Driving to Organize," *Traffic World*, March 3, 2008; and "UPS Freight Teamsters Gain Steam," *Traffic World*, January 28, 2008, both downloaded from General Reference Center Gold, http://find.galegroup.com.

31. Herman et al., *Collective Bargaining*; and P. Jarley and J. Fiorito, "Associate Membership: Unionism or Consumerism?" *Industrial and Labor Relations Review* 43 (1990), pp. 209–24.

32. Katz and Kochan, *An Introduction to Collective Bargaining*; and R. L. Rose, "Unions Hit Corporate Campaign Trail," *Wall Street Journal*, March 8, 1993, p. B1.

33. Katz and Kochan, *An Introduction to Collective Bargaining.*

34. A. E. Eaton and J. Kriesky, "Union Organizing under Neutrality and Card Check Agreements," *Industrial and Labor Relations Review* 55 (2001), pp. 42–59.

35. National Labor Relations Board, N.L.R.B. Election Reports for 2006–2009, http://nlrb.gov, accessed May 4, 2010.

36. Chaison and Rose, "The Macrodeterminants of Union Growth and Decline."

37. Fossum, *Labor Relations*, p. 262.

38. R. E. Walton and R. B. McKersie, *A Behavioral Theory of Negotiations* (New York: McGraw-Hill, 1965).

39. C. M. Steven, *Strategy and Collective Bargaining Negotiations* (New York: McGraw-Hill, 1963); and Katz and Kochan, *An Introduction to Collective Bargaining.*

40. "The Show Will Resume," *Global Agenda*, February 12, 2008; and "Writer's Strike Ends, Viewers to Get Network Shows Again," *Information Week*, February 13, 2008, both downloaded from General Reference Center Gold, http://find.galegroup.com.

41. Kochan, *Collective Bargaining and Industrial Relations*, p. 272.

42. Katz and Kochan, *An Introduction to Collective Bargaining.*

43. *United Steelworkers v. American Manufacturing Company*, 363 U.S. 564 (1960); *United Steelworkers v. Warrior Gulf and Navigation Company*, 363 U.S. 574 (1960); and *United Steelworkers v. Enterprise Wheel and Car Corporation*, 363 U.S. 593 (1960).

44. Kochan, *Collective Bargaining and Industrial Relations*, p. 386; and John W. Budd and Alexander J. S. Colvin, "Improved Metrics for Workplace Dispute Resolution Procedures: Efficiency, Equity, and Voice," *Industrial Relations* 47, no. 3 (July 2008), p. 460.

45. Federal Mediation and Conciliation Service, "What We Do: Arbitration; Arbitration Statistics," www.fmcs.gov, accessed May 3, 2010.

46. J. R. Redecker, *Employee Discipline: Policies and Practices* (Washington, DC: Bureau of National Affairs, 1989).

47. T. A. Kochan, H. C. Katz, and R. B. McKersie, *The Transformation of American Industrial Relations* (New York: Basic Books, 1986), chap. 6; and E. Appelbaum, T. Bailey, and P. Berg, *Manufacturing Advantage: Why High-Performance Work Systems Pay Off* (Ithaca, NY: Cornell University Press, 2000).

48. L. W. Hunter, J. P. MacDuffie, and L. Doucet, "What Makes Teams Take? Employee Reactions to Work Reforms," *Industrial and Labor Relations Review* 55 (2002), pp. 448–472.

49. J. B. Arthur, "The Link between Business Strategy and Industrial Relations Systems in American Steel Minimills," *Industrial and Labor Relations Review* 45 (1992), pp. 488–506; M. Schuster, "Union Management Cooperation," in *Employee and Labor Relations*, ed. J. A. Fossum (Washington, DC: Bureau of National Affairs, 1990); E. Cohen-Rosenthal and C. Burton, *Mutual Gains: A Guide to Union-Management Cooperation*, 2nd ed. (Ithaca, NY: ILR Press, 1993); T. A. Kochan and P. Osterman, *The Mutual Gains Enterprise* (Boston: Harvard Business School Press, 1994); and E. Applebaum and R. Batt, *The New American Workplace* (Ithaca, NY: ILR Press, 1994).

50. A. E. Eaton, "Factors Contributing to the Survival of Employee Participation Programs in Unionized Settings," *Industrial and Labor Relations Review* 47, no. 3 (1994), pp. 371–89.

51. "NLRB 4–0 Approves Crown Cork & Seal's Use of Seven Employee Participation Committees," *HR News*, September 3, 2001.

52. Kochan and Osterman, *The Mutual Gains Enterprise*; W. N. Cooke, "Employee Participation Programs, Group-Based Incentives, and Company Performance: A Union-Nonunion Comparison," *Industrial and Labor Relations Review* 47, no. 4 (1994), pp. 594–609; C. Doucouliagos, "Worker Participation and Productivity in Labor-Managed and Participatory Capitalist Firms: A Meta-Analysis," *Industrial and Labor Relations Review* 49, no. 1 (1995), pp. 58–77; S. J. Deery and R. D. Iverson, "Labor-Management Cooperation: Antecedents and Impact on Organizational Performance," *Industrial and Labor Relations*

Review 58 (2005), pp. 588–609; James Combs, Yongmei Liu, Angela Hall, and David Ketchen, "How Much Do High-Performance Work Practices Matter? A Meta-analysis of Their Effects on Organizational Performance," *Personnel Psychology* 59, no. 3 (2006), pp. 501–28; Paul Osterman, "The Wage Effects of High Performance Work Organization in Manufacturing," *Industrial and Labor Relations Review* 59 (2006), pp. 187–204; and Robert D. Mohr and Cindy Zoghi, "High-Involvement Work Design and Job Satisfaction," *Industrial and Labor Relations Review* 61, no. 3 (April 2008), pp. 275–96.

53. J. Teresko, "Continuing a Winning Culture," *Industry Week*, January 2008, p. 42.

Managing Human Resources Globally

What Do I Need to Know?

After reading this chapter, you should be able to:

LO1 Summarize how the growth in international business activity affects human resource management.

LO2 Identify the factors that most strongly influence HRM in international markets.

LO3 Discuss how differences among countries affect HR planning at organizations with international operations.

LO4 Describe how companies select and train human resources in a global labor market.

LO5 Discuss challenges related to managing performance and compensating employees from other countries.

LO6 Explain how employers prepare managers for international assignments and for their return home.

Introduction

Students receiving their master's degrees from the top U.S. business schools are lining up for jobs in China, India, and Singapore as never before. The economies have been booming in those parts of the world, and the graduates want to be part of the excitement while gaining valuable expertise in what are likely to be some of the world's most important markets. The employers—including investment banks, consulting firms, and multinational corporations selling consumer products, high-tech goods, and health care—are looking for people who know about business principles and also about the language and culture of the country where they will be working. Those requirements can place U.S.-born candidates at a disadvantage, but some qualify. Joseph Kauffman, for example, learned to speak Mandarin in college and worked at Coca-Cola in China between earning his undergraduate degree and enrolling in business school. His language skills and work experience helped him land a summer job with Morgan Stanley in Hong Kong.[1] At the same time that Morgan Stanley and other U.S. companies are hiring employees for assignments in other countries, foreign companies are setting up operations in the United States. Today, human resource management truly takes place on an international scale.

This chapter discusses the HR issues that organizations must address in a world of global competition. We begin by describing how the global nature of business is affecting human resource management in modern organizations. Next, we identify how global differences among countries affect the organization's decisions about human resources. In the following sections we explore HR planning, selection, training, and compensation practices in international settings. Finally, we examine guidelines for managing employees sent on international assignments.

HRM in a Global Environment

LO1 Summarize how the growth in international business activity affects human resource management.

The environment in which organizations operate is rapidly becoming a global one. More and more companies are entering international markets by exporting their products, building facilities in other countries, and entering into alliances with foreign companies. At the same time, companies based in other countries are investing and setting up operations in the United States. Indeed, most organizations now function in the global economy.

What is behind the trend toward expansion into global markets? Foreign countries can provide a business with new markets in which there are millions or billions of new customers; developing countries often provide such markets, but developed countries do so as well. In addition, companies set up operations overseas because they can operate with lower labor costs—for example, the average *monthly* wage in China is about equal to the average *daily* wage in the United States.[2] Finally, thanks to advances in telecommunications and information technology, companies can more easily spread work around the globe, wherever they find the right mix of labor costs and abilities. Teams with members in different time zones can keep projects moving around the clock, or projects can be assigned according to regions with particular areas of expertise. Many high-tech companies have set up 20 percent or more of their research and development work in India and China, where engineers not only are well trained and affordable, but also are familiar with the needs of their fast-growing marketplace. In India, for example, Microsoft is developing software that translates text in 10 Indian languages, and Hewlett-Packard has been developing a Gesture Keyboard, which allows users to enter phonetic scripts used in the region. IBM has set up 86 software development centers around the world, many of them specializing in particular applications.[3]

Global activities are simplified and encouraged by trade agreements among nations. For example, most countries in Western Europe belong to the European Union and share a common currency, the euro. Canada, Mexico, and the United States have encouraged trade among themselves with the North American Free Trade Agreement (NAFTA). The World Trade Organization (WTO) resolves trade disputes among more than 100 participating nations.

As companies in the United States and Britain cut software jobs and outsource to other countries in order to drive down costs, countries such as India continue to see employment rates rise.

As these trends and arrangements encourage international trade, they increase and change the demands on human resource management. Organizations with customers or suppliers in other countries need employees who understand those customers or suppliers. Organizations that operate facilities in foreign countries need to understand the laws and customs that apply to employees in those countries. They may have to prepare managers and other personnel to take international assignments. They have to adapt their human resource plans and policies to different settings. Even if some practices are the same worldwide, the company now has to communicate them to its international workforce. A variety of international activities require managers to understand HRM principles and practices prevalent in global markets.

Employees in an International Workforce

Parent Country
The country in which an organization's headquarters is located.

When organizations operate globally, their employees are very likely to be citizens of more than one country. Employees may come from the employer's parent country, a host country, or a third country. The **parent country** is the country in which the organization's headquarters is located. For example, the United States is the parent country of General Motors, because GM's headquarters is in Michigan. A GM employee who was born in the United States and works at GM's headquarters or one of its U.S. factories is therefore a *parent-country national*.

Host Country
A country (other than the parent country) in which an organization operates a facility.

A **host country** is a country (other than the parent country) in which an organization operates a facility. Great Britain is a host country of General Motors because GM has operations there. Any British workers hired to work at GM's British facility would be *host-country nationals*, that is, employees who are citizens of the host country.

Third Country
A country that is neither the parent country nor the host country of an employer.

A **third country** refers to a country that is neither the parent country nor the host country. (The organization may or may not have a facility in the third country.) In the example of GM's operations in Great Britain, the company could hire an Australian manager to work there. The Australian manager would be a *third-country national* because the manager is neither from the parent country (the United States) nor from the host country (Great Britain).

Expatriates
Employees assigned to work in another country.

When organizations operate overseas, they must decide whether to hire parent-country nationals, host-country nationals, or third-country nationals for the overseas operations. Usually, they hire a combination of these. In general, employees assigned to work in another country are called **expatriates.** In the GM example, the U.S. and Australian managers working in Great Britain would be expatriates during those assignments.

The extent to which organizations use parent-country, host-country, or third-country nationals varies. In Venezuela, Pfizer's strategy to begin selling its medicines to clinics serving the poor included hiring residents of the slums and training them to call on doctors' offices. While it might seem easier to hire college graduates, Pfizer decided that training street-savvy local residents in biology would be more effective that training educated people to navigate the neighborhoods safely without losing samples to theft.[4] Companies face a different challenge with regard to management talent: the fastest economic growth has been occurring in Asia, where people with knowledge of business management have been scarce. U.S. companies have filled positions with parent-company and third-company nationals, but companies and governments in these countries have been ramping up their development of local management talent. Some U.S. companies have decided they need to be more involved, so they don't lose the war for local talent. For example, IBM worked with Boston's

focus on *social responsibility*

INNOVATION IS A GLOBAL AFFAIR AT CISCO

Cisco Systems, which develops and sells technology for computer networking, doesn't just hire people around the world. It also is committed to getting them fully engaged in the company's performance. As Cisco's CEO, John Chambers, sees it, high-tech companies can survive only as long as they keep ahead of developments in their industry. That means everyone has to be learning and creating new ideas.

Fundamentally, Cisco meets that goal with an organization that fosters collaboration, not control through some vast hierarchy. The company established an information-sharing tool it calls Ciscopedia, where employees are encouraged to share ideas with one another online.

Linking employees online is logical for a company with Internet-related products and customers spread around the globe. To connect with those customers, Cisco thinks beyond the conventional approach of staffing local offices with host-country nationals. The company serves clients in developing economies through a "second headquarters," established in Bangalore, India, the home of many engineers from India and other developing nations. With that talent pool to draw from, Cisco hires employees and assembles teams that travel to client sites in nations as far-flung as Russia and Chile. When the teams return, the company assigns them to expand what they learned into a client solution that could help other customers worldwide.

Cisco also has established training aimed at developing its multinational workforce. To develop managers, Cisco recruits employees with experience on at least two continents plus the ability to speak at least two languages and places them in its Global Talent Acquisition Program. These young managers and engineers undergo six months of training in sales and finance, coupled with mentoring. Cisco also provides resources to support local training programs in the areas where its customers operate. Cisco's commitment to local communities doesn't stop with training. The company has also set up a program called Cisco's Ready, which partners with 20 Red Cross chapters to train thousands of Cisco employees in emergency response skills.

This commitment to developing employees and communities must be serving Cisco well. Even at a time when other companies have been struggling, Cisco recently announced plans to hire 10,000 people in North Carolina and to maintain growth plans calling for 10,000 new employees in India.

Sources: Michael Useem, "Whether Up or Down, Always Innovating: John Chambers, CEO," *U.S. News & World Report*, November 1, 2009, Business & Company Resource Center, http://galenet.galegroup.com; Peter Burrows, "Cisco Builds a Local Workforce in Emerging Markets," *BusinessWeek*, March 12, 2009, www.businessweek.com; Cisco, "Just in Time for National Volunteer Week, Collaboration Creates Largest Corporate Disaster Response Volunteer Program in Red Cross History," news release, April 20, 2010, http://newsroom.cisco.com; John Murawski, "Cisco Hopes to Employ 10,000," *News and Observer (Raleigh, N.C.)*, March 5, 2010, Business & Company Resource Center, http://galenet.galegroup.com; and "Cisco's India Hiring Plan on Track: CEO," *Asia Pulse News*, March 15, 2010, Business & Company Resource Center, http://galenet.galegroup.com.

Northeastern University to set up an MBA training program for IBM employees in India.[5] To learn about another company that is developing employees in host countries, see the "Best Practices" box.

Employers in the Global Marketplace

Just as there are different ways for employees to participate in international business—as parent-country, host-country, or third-county nationals—so there are different ways for employers to do business globally, ranging from simply shipping products to customers in other countries to transforming the organization into a truly global one,

Figure 15.1

Levels of Global Participation

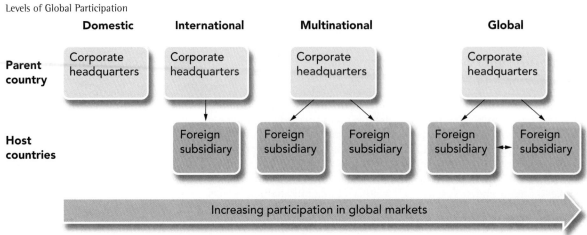

with operations, employees, and customers in many countries. Figure 15.1 shows the major levels of global participation.

Most organizations begin by serving customers and clients within a domestic marketplace. Typically, a company's founder has an idea for serving a local, regional, or national market. The business must recruit, hire, train, and compensate employees to produce the product, and these people usually come from the business owner's local labor market. Selection and training focus on employees' technical abilities and, to some extent, on interpersonal skills. Pay levels reflect local labor conditions. If the product succeeds, the company might expand operations to other domestic locations, and HRM decisions become more complex as the organization draws from a larger labor market and needs systems for training and motivating employees in several locations. As the employer's workforce grows, it is also likely to become more diverse. Even in small domestic organizations, a significant share of workers may be immigrants. In this way, even domestic companies are affected by issues related to the global economy.

As organizations grow, they often begin to meet demand from customers in other countries. The usual way that a company begins to enter foreign markets is by *exporting,* or shipping domestically produced items to other countries to be sold there. Eventually, it may become economically desirable to set up operations in one or more foreign countries. An organization that does so becomes an **international organization.** The decision to participate in international activities raises a host of HR issues, including the basic question of whether a particular location provides an environment where the organization can successfully acquire and manage human resources.

International Organization
An organization that sets up one or a few facilities in one or a few foreign countries.

Multinational Company
An organization that builds facilities in a number of different countries in an effort to minimize production and distribution costs.

While international companies build one or a few facilities in another country, **multinational companies** go overseas on a broader scale. They build facilities in a number of different countries as a way to keep production and distribution costs to a minimum. In general, when organizations become multinationals, they move production facilities from relatively high-cost locations to lower-cost locations. The lower-cost locations may have lower average wage rates, or they may reduce distribution costs by being nearer to customers. The HRM challenges faced by a multinational company are similar to but larger than those of an international organization, because more countries are involved. More than ever, the organization needs to hire managers

eHRM

THE INTERNET BRINGS TOGETHER P&G EMPLOYEES

With more than 138,000 employees working in more than 90 countries, Procter & Gamble is a massive global organization. Its global presence is massive as well: the company estimates that four billion consumers use its products already, and it hopes to add another billion over the next few years. Much of that growth is expected to come from developing nations such as China, India, and Mexico. To serve them, the company plans to add another 20 manufacturing facilities to its current operations.

How can so many employees in so many places share what they have learned about serving so many customers? The answer, of course, is to go online.

Procter & Gamble set up an online collaboration system for its employees. The system includes instant messaging, wikis (where users collaborate to post shared content), and high-definition videoconferencing. If someone needs help coming up with ideas or solving a problem, they can search the content or post requests. The system makes it far easier to find ideas, given that the best source could be in another city or even another continent.

The benefits quickly became evident to P&G's research and development groups. Researchers found that when they went online with these tools, they were discovering expertise from people through the company. Ultimately, says Laurie Heltsley, P&G's director of global business services, online collaboration means "work is not a place but something you do." Given the ferocious competition in the consumer products industry, that freedom from "place" is essential. What an employee learns about customers in, say, Mexico may be just the idea needed to solve a problem in China. That's why Heltsley calls this collaboration "an absolute necessity."

Sources: Matt Hamblen, "Finding the Stars with Bright Ideas," *Computerworld*, September 14, 2009, p. 10; Matthew W. Evans, "P&G Chief Targets Emerging Markets," *WWD*, October 14, 2009, Business & Company Resource Center, http://galenet.galegroup.com; and Procter & Gamble careers Web site, www.experiencepg.com, accessed May 10, 2010.

---

who can function in a variety of settings, give them necessary training, and provide flexible compensation systems that take into account the different pay rates, tax systems, and costs of living from one country to another.

At the highest level of involvement in the global marketplace are **global organizations.** These flexible organizations compete by offering top products tailored to segments of the market while keeping costs as low as possible. A global organization locates each facility based on the ability to effectively, efficiently, and flexibly produce a product or service, using cultural differences as an advantage. Rather than treating differences in other countries as a challenge to overcome, a global organization treats different cultures as equals. It may have multiple headquarters spread across the globe, so decisions are more decentralized. This type of organization needs HRM practices that encourage flexibility and are based on an in-depth knowledge of differences among countries. Global organizations must be able to recruit, develop, retain, and use managers who can get results across national boundaries. The "eHRM" box shows how Procter & Gamble uses online tools to keep its people connected on a global scale.

A global organization needs a **transnational HRM system**[6] that features decision making from a global perspective, managers from many countries, and ideas contributed by people from a variety of cultures. Decisions that are the outcome of a transnational HRM system balance uniformity (for fairness) with flexibility (to account for cultural and legal differences). This balance and the variety of perspectives should

Global Organization
An organization that chooses to locate a facility based on the ability to effectively, efficiently, and flexibly produce a product or service, using cultural differences as an advantage.

Transnational HRM System
Type of HRM system that makes decisions from a global perspective, includes managers from many countries, and is based on ideas contributed by people representing a variety of cultures.

work together to improve the quality of decision making. The participants from various countries and cultures contribute ideas from a position of equality, rather than the parent country's culture dominating.

LO2 Identify the factors that most strongly influence HRM in international markets.

Factors Affecting HRM in International Markets

Whatever their level of global participation, organizations that operate in more than one country must recognize that the countries are not identical and differ in terms of many factors. To simplify this discussion, we focus on four major factors:

- culture
- education
- economic systems
- political-legal systems

Culture

By far the most important influence on international HRM is the culture of the country in which a facility is located. *Culture* is a community's set of shared assumptions about how the world works and what ideals are worth striving for.[7] Cultural influences may be expressed through customs, languages, religions, and so on.

Culture is important to HRM for two reasons. First, it often determines the other three international influences. Culture can greatly affect a country's laws, because laws often are based on the culture's definitions of right and wrong. Culture also influences what people value, so it affects people's economic systems and efforts to invest in education.

Even more important for understanding human resource management, culture often determines the effectiveness of various HRM practices. Practices that are effective in the United States, for example, may fail or even backfire in a country with different beliefs and values.[8] Consider the five dimensions of culture that Geert Hofstede identified in his classic study of culture:[9]

1. *Individualism/collectivism* describes the strength of the relation between an individual and other individuals in the society. In cultures that are high in individualism, such as the United States, Great Britain, and the Netherlands, people tend to think and act as individuals rather than as members of a group. People in these countries are expected to stand on their own two feet, rather than be protected by the group. In cultures that are high in collectivism, such as Colombia, Pakistan, and Taiwan, people think of themselves mainly as group members. They are expected to devote themselves to the interests of the community, and the community is expected to protect them when they are in trouble.

2. *Power distance* concerns the way the culture deals with unequal distribution of power and defines the amount of inequality that is normal. In countries with large power distances, including India and the Philippines, the culture defines it as normal to maintain large differences in power. In countries with small power distances, such as Denmark and Israel, people try to eliminate inequalities. One way to see differences in power distance is in the way people talk to one another. In the high-power-distance countries of Mexico and Japan, people address one another with titles (Señor Smith, Smith-san). At the other extreme, in the United States, in most situations people use one another's first names—behavior that would be disrespectful in other cultures.

3. *Uncertainty avoidance* describes how cultures handle the fact that the future is unpredictable. High uncertainty avoidance refers to a strong cultural preference for structured situations. In countries such as Greece and Portugal, people tend to rely heavily on religion, law, and technology to give them a degree of security and clear rules about how to behave. In countries with low uncertainty avoidance, including Singapore and Jamaica, people seem to take each day as it comes.

4. *Masculinity/femininity* is the emphasis a culture places on practices or qualities that have traditionally been considered masculine or feminine. A "masculine" culture is a culture that values achievement, money making, assertiveness, and competition. A "feminine" culture is one that places a high value on relationships, service, care for the weak, and preserving the environment. In this model, Germany and Japan are examples of masculine cultures, and Sweden and Norway are examples of feminine cultures.

In Taiwan, a country that is high in collectivism, co-workers consider themselves more as group members instead of individuals.

5. *Long-term/short-term orientation* suggests whether the focus of cultural values is on the future (long term) or the past and present (short term). Cultures with a long-term orientation value saving and persistence, which tend to pay off in the future. Many Asian countries, including Japan and China, have a long-term orientation. Short-term orientations, as in the cultures of the United States, Russia, and West Africa, promote respect for past tradition and for fulfilling social obligations in the present.

Such cultural characteristics as these influence the ways members of an organization behave toward one another, as well as their attitudes toward various HRM practices. For instance, cultures differ strongly in their opinions about how managers should lead, how decisions should be handled, and what motivates employees. In Germany, managers achieve their status by demonstrating technical skills, and employees look to managers to assign tasks and resolve technical problems. In the Netherlands, managers focus on seeking agreement, exchanging views, and balancing the interests of the people affected by a decision.[10] Clearly, differences like these would affect how an organization selects and trains its managers and measures their performance.

Cultures strongly influence the appropriateness of HRM practices. For example, the extent to which a culture is individualist or collectivist will affect the success of a compensation program. Compensation tied to individual performance may be seen as fairer and more motivating by members of an individualist culture; a culture favoring individualism will be more accepting of great differences in pay between the organization's highest- and lowest-paid employees. Collectivist cultures tend to have much flatter pay structures.

Job design aimed at employee empowerment can be problematic in cultures with high "power distance." In a Mexican slipper-manufacturing plant, an effort to expand the decision-making authority of production workers stumbled when the workers balked at doing what they saw as the supervisor's proper responsibility.[11] Realizing they had moved too quickly, the plant's managers narrowed the scope of the workers' decision-making authority so they could adapt to the role. On the other hand, a factor in favor of empowerment at that plant was the Mexican culture's high collectivism. The workers liked discussing team-related information and using the information to benefit the entire team. As in this example, a culture does not necessarily rule out a particular HRM practice, such as employee empowerment, but it should be a consideration in deciding how to carry out the practice.

Finally, cultural differences can affect how people communicate and how they coordinate their activities. In collectivist cultures, people tend to value group decision making, as in the previous example. When a person raised in an individualistic culture must work closely with people from a collectivist culture, communication problems and conflicts often occur. People from the collectivist culture tend to collaborate heavily and may evaluate the individualistic person as unwilling to cooperate and share information with them. Cultural differences in communication affected the way a North American agricultural company embarked on employee empowerment at its facilities in t he United States and Brazil.[12] Empowerment requires information sharing, but in Brazil, high power distance leads employees to expect managers to make decisions, so they do not desire information that is appropriately held by managers. Empowering the Brazilian employees required involving managers directly in giving and sharing information to show that this practice was in keeping with the traditional chain of command. Also, because uncertainty avoidance is another aspect of Brazilian culture, managers explained that greater information sharing would reduce uncertainty about their work. At the same time, greater collectivism in Brazil made employees comfortable with the day-to-day communication of teamwork. The individualistic U.S. employees needed to be sold more on this aspect of empowerment. The "HR Oops!" box describes another example of miscommunication resulting from cultural differences.

Because of these challenges, organizations must prepare managers to recognize and handle cultural differences. They may recruit managers with knowledge of other cultures or provide training, as described later in the chapter. For expatriate assignments, organizations may need to conduct an extensive selection process to identify individuals who can adapt to new environments. At the same time, it is important to be wary of stereotypes and avoid exaggerating the importance of cultural differences. Recent research that examined Hofstede's model of cultural differences found that differences among organizations within a particular culture were sometimes larger than differences from country to country.[13] This finding suggests that it is important for an organization to match its HR practices to its values; individuals who share those values are likely to be interested in working for the organization.

Education and Skill Levels

Countries also differ in the degree to which their labor markets include people with education and skills of value to employers. As discussed in Chapter 1, the United States suffers from a shortage of skilled workers in many occupations, and the problem is expected to increase. For example, the need for knowledge workers (engineers, teachers, scientists, health care workers) is expected to grow almost twice as fast as the overall rate of job growth in the United States.[14] On the other hand, the labor markets in many countries are very attractive because they offer high skills and low wages.

Educational opportunities also vary from one country to another. In general, spending on education is greater per pupil in high-income countries than in poorer countries.[15] Poverty, diseases such as AIDS, and political turmoil keep children away from school in some areas. A concerted international effort to provide universal access to

Sometimes No One Reads between the Lines

Employees in the British division of an oil and gas company were frustrated. They carefully researched ideas for where to conduct exploration in the Persian Gulf. They wrote reports presenting their recommendations and sent them to the company's headquarters in Texas. But no matter what they recommended, the British division's ideas were turned down.

As it turned out, the British employees had a cultural problem. They were using the careful, understated language of their business culture. They started off each report by identifying the risks of the proposal. Next, they laid out historical background. Finally, at the end of the report, the writers presented the possible opportunities.

Back in Texas, management had the optimistic, can-do spirit typical of U.S. business culture. They were looking for the positives and expected proposal writers to actively sell them on exploration ideas. Without that message, the managers at headquarters concluded that the proposals must not be very attractive. When the British team learned to reorganize and rephrase their reports for an American audience, they started winning approvals.

Source: Based on Jill Rose, "Global Mindset," *American Executive*, January 2010, pp. 7–9.

Questions

1. In this example, who made a mistake—the writers of the proposal or the readers of the proposal? Why?
2. Imagine you are involved in recruiting a manager for a British facility of your company. Based on the example given here, what cultural differences in communication might you expect, and how might they affect your search for qualified candidates in Britain?

primary education has dramatically reduced the number and proportion of children without access to schooling. However, the problem persists in sub-Saharan Africa and is significant but declining in South Asia.[16]

Companies with foreign operations locate in countries where they can find suitable employees. The education and skill levels of a country's labor force affect how and the extent to which companies want to operate there. In countries with a poorly educated population, companies will limit their activities to low-skill, low-wage jobs. In contrast, India's large pool of well-trained technical workers is one reason that the country has become a popular location for outsourcing computer programming jobs.

Economic System

A country's economic system, whether capitalist or socialist, as well as the government's involvement in the economy through taxes or compensation, price controls, and other activities, influences human resource management practices in a number of ways.

As with all aspects of a region's or country's life, the economic system and culture are likely to be closely tied, providing many of the incentives or disincentives for developing the value of the labor force. Socialist economic systems provide ample opportunities for educational development because the education system is free to students. At the same time, socialism may not provide economic rewards (higher pay) for increasing one's education. In capitalist systems, students bear more of the cost of their education, but employers reward those who invest in education.

The health of an economic system affects human resource management. In developed countries with great wealth, labor costs are relatively high. Such differences show up in compensation systems and in recruiting and selection decisions.

Students at the University of Warsaw in Poland are provided with a government-supported education. In general, former Soviet bloc countries tend to be generous in funding education, so they tend to have highly educated and skilled labor forces. Capitalist countries such as the United States generally leave higher education up to individual students to pay for, but the labor market rewards students who earn a college degree.

In general, socialist systems take a higher percentage of each worker's income as the worker's income increases. Capitalist systems tend to let workers keep more of their earnings. In this way, socialism redistributes wealth from high earners to the poor, while capitalism apparently rewards individual accomplishments. In any case, since the amount of take-home pay a worker receives after taxes may thus differ from country to country, in an organization that pays two managers in two countries $100,000 each, the manager in one country might take home more than the manager in the other country. Such differences make pay structures more complicated when they cross national boundaries, and they can affect recruiting of candidates from more than one country.

Political-Legal System

A country's political-legal system—its government, laws, and regulations—strongly impinges on human resource management. The country's laws often dictate the requirements for certain HRM practices, such as training, compensation, hiring, firing, and layoffs. As we noted in the discussion of culture, the political-legal system arises to a large degree from the culture in which it exists, so laws and regulations reflect cultural values.

For example, the United States has led the world in eliminating discrimination in the workplace. Because this value is important in U.S. culture, the nation has legal safeguards such as the equal employment opportunity laws discussed in Chapter 3, which affect hiring and other HRM decisions. As a society, the United States also has strong beliefs regarding the fairness of pay systems. Thus, the Fair Labor Standards Act (discussed in Chapter 11), among other laws and regulations, sets a minimum wage for a variety of jobs. Other laws and regulations dictate much of the process of negotiation between unions and management. All these are examples of laws and regulations that affect the practice of HRM in the United States.

Similarly, laws and regulations in other countries reflect the norms of their cultures. In Western Europe, where many countries have had strong socialist parties, some laws have been aimed at protecting the rights and benefits of workers. Until recently, workers in Germany and France had 35-hour workweeks, but under growing pressure to adopt the "Anglo-Saxon model" emphasizing productivity, many have made concessions. The European Union's standard permits workweeks of up to 48 hours.[17]

An organization that expands internationally must gain expertise in the host country's legal requirements and ways of dealing with its legal system, often leading organizations to hire one or more host-country nationals to help in the process. Some countries have laws requiring that a certain percentage of the employees of any foreign-owned subsidiary be host-country nationals, and in the context of our discussion here, this legal challenge to an organization's HRM may hold an advantage if handled creatively.

Human Resource Planning in a Global Economy

As economic and technological change creates a global environment for organizations, human resource planning is involved in decisions about participating as an exporter or as an international, multinational, or global company. Even purely domestic companies may draw talent from the international labor market. As organizations consider decisions about their level of international activity, HR professionals should provide information about the relevant human resource issues, such as local market pay rates and labor laws. When organizations decide to operate internationally or globally, human resource planning involves decisions about where and how many employees are needed for each international facility.

Decisions about where to locate include HR considerations such as the cost and availability of qualified workers. In addition, HR specialists must work with other members of the organization to weigh these considerations against financial and operational requirements. For example, one reason that Toyota built manufacturing facilities in the United States was to address U.S. customers' concerns over U.S. jobs being lost to foreign auto companies. However, the company has tended to locate its factories in lower-wage areas of the United States (away from union strongholds) and also has facilities in Mexico, where it can serve North America as economically as possible.[18]

Other location decisions involve outsourcing, described in Chapter 2. Many companies have boosted efficiency by arranging to have specific functions performed by outside contractors. Many—but not all—of these arrangements involve workers outside the United States in lower-wage countries.

In Chapter 5, we saw that human resource planning includes decisions to hire and lay off workers to prepare for the organization's expected needs. Compared with other countries, the United States allows employers wide latitude in reducing their workforce, giving U.S. employers the option of hiring for peak needs, then laying off employees if needs decline. Other governments place more emphasis on protecting workers' jobs. European countries, and France in particular, tend to be very strict in this regard.

LO3 Discuss how differences among countries affect HR planning at organizations with international operations.

Selecting Employees in a Global Labor Market

Many companies such as Microsoft have headquarters in the United States plus facilities in locations around the world. To be effective, employees in the Microsoft Mexico operations in Mexico City must understand that region's business and social culture. Organizations often meet this need by hiring host-country nationals to fill most of their foreign positions. A key reason is that a host-country national can more easily understand the values and customs of the local workforce than someone from another part of the world can. Also, training for and transporting families to foreign assignments is more expensive than hiring people in the foreign country. Employees may be reluctant to take a foreign assignment because of the difficulty of moving overseas. Sometimes the move requires the employee's spouse to quit a job, and some countries will not allow the employee's spouse to seek work, even if jobs might be available.

Even so, organizations fill many key foreign positions with parent-country or third-country nationals. Sometimes a person's technical and human relations skills outweigh the advantages of hiring locally. In other situations, such as the shortage of

LO4 Describe how companies select and train human resources in a global labor market.

Qualities associated with success in foreign assignments are the ability to communicate in the foreign country, flexibility, enjoying a challenging situation, and support from family members. What would persuade you to take a foreign assignment?

U.S. knowledge workers, the local labor market simply does not offer enough qualified people. At organizations located where needed skills are in short supply, hiring immigrant employees may be part of an effective recruitment and selection strategy.[19] In the United States' largest metropolitan areas, where about two-thirds of immigrants live, these workers are distributed almost evenly among types of work and across income levels. In fact, in more than half of those cities, more immigrants hold white-collar positions than low-wage jobs.[20] The ability to tap this labor supply is limited by government paperwork and delays, which deter some immigrant workers, as well as by expanding opportunities in fast-developing nations such as China and India. Recent surveys have found that Chinese and Indian professionals returning home to work are most likely to say their reason is that they see better opportunities in their home country. In addition, as described in Chapter 6, U.S. employers must take care to hire employees who are eligible to work in the United States. Recently, Immigration and Customers Enforcement has been auditing the eligibility status of workers at hundreds of companies.[21]

Whether the organization is hiring immigrants or selecting parent-country or third-country nationals for foreign assignments, some basic principles of selection apply. Selection of employees for foreign assignments should reflect criteria that have been associated with success in working overseas:

- Competency in the employee's area of expertise.
- Ability to communicate verbally and nonverbally in the foreign country.
- Flexibility, tolerance of ambiguity, and sensitivity to cultural differences.
- Motivation to succeed and enjoyment of challenges.
- Willingness to learn about the foreign country's culture, language, and customs.
- Support from family members.[22]

In research conducted a number of years ago, the factor most strongly influencing whether an employee completed a foreign assignment was the comfort of the employee's spouse and family.[23] Personality may also be important. Research has found successful completion of overseas assignments to be most likely among employees who are extroverted (outgoing), agreeable (cooperative and tolerant), and conscientious (dependable and achievement oriented).[24]

Qualities of flexibility, motivation, agreeableness, and conscientiousness are so important because of the challenges involved in entering another culture. The emotions that accompany an overseas assignment tend to follow stages like those in Figure 15.2.[25] For a month or so after arriving, the foreign worker enjoys a

Figure 15.2

Emotional Stages Associated with a Foreign Assignment

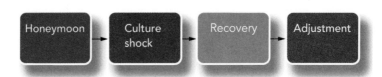

SOURCE: Adapted from Delia Flanja, "Culture Shock in Intercultural Communication," *Studia Europaea* (October 2009), Business & Company Resource Center, http://galenet.galegroup.com.

"honeymoon" of fascination and euphoria as the employee enjoys the novelty of the new culture and compares its interesting similarities to or differences from the employee's own culture. Before long, the employee's mood declines as he or she notices more unpleasant differences and experiences feelings of isolation, criticism, stereotyping, and even hostility. As the mood reaches bottom, the employee is experiencing **culture shock,** the disillusionment and discomfort that occur during the process of adjusting to a new culture and its norms, values, and perspectives. Eventually, if employees persist and continue learning about their host country's culture, they begin to recover from culture shock as they develop a greater understanding and a support network. As the employee's language skills and comfort increase, the employee's mood should improve as well. Eventually, the employee reaches a stage of adjustment in which he or she accepts and enjoys the host country's culture.

Culture Shock
Disillusionment and discomfort that occur during the process of adjusting to a new culture.

Training and Developing a Global Workforce

In an organization whose employees come from more than one country, some special challenges arise with regard to training and development: (1) Training and development programs should be effective for all participating employees, regardless of their country of origin; and (2) When organizations hire employees to work in a foreign country or transfer them to another country, the employer needs to provide the employees with training in how to handle the challenges associated with working in the foreign country.

Training Programs for an International Workforce

Developers of effective training programs for an international workforce must ask certain questions.[26] The first is to establish the objectives for the training and its content. Decisions about the training should support those objectives. The developers should next ask what training techniques, strategies, and media to use. Some will be more effective than others, depending on the learners' language and culture, as well as the content of the training. For example, in preparation U.S. employees might expect to discuss and ask questions about the training content, whereas employees from other cultures might consider this level of participation to be disrespectful, so for them some additional support might be called for. Language differences will require translations and perhaps a translator at training activities. Next, the developers should identify any other interventions and conditions that must be in place for the training to meet its objectives. For example, training is more likely to meet its objectives if it is linked to performance management and has the full support of management. Finally, the developers of a training program should identify who in the organization should be involved in reviewing and approving the training program.

The plan for the training program must consider international differences among trainees. For example, economic and educational differences might influence employees' access to and ability to use Web-based training. Cultural differences may influence whether they will consider it appropriate to ask questions and whether they expect the trainer to spend time becoming acquainted with employees or to get down to business immediately. Table 15.1 provides examples of how cultural characteristics can affect training design. For additional suggestions on providing effective training programs to an international workforce, see the "HR How To" box.

Table 15.1

Effects of Culture on Training Design

CULTURAL DIMENSION	IMPACT ON TRAINING
Individualism	Culture high in individualism expects participation in exercises and questioning to be determined by status in the company or culture.
Uncertainty avoidance	Culture high in uncertainty avoidance expects formal instructional environments. There is less tolerance for impromptu style.
Masculinity	Culture low in masculinity values relationships with fellow trainees. Female trainers are less likely to be resisted in low-masculinity cultures.
Power distance	Culture high in power distance expects trainer to be expert. Trainers are expected to be authoritarian and controlling of session.
Time orientation	Culture with a long-term orientation will have trainees who are likely to accept development plans and assignments.

SOURCE: Based on B. Filipczak, "Think Locally, Act Globally," *Training*, January 1997, pp. 41–48.

Cross-Cultural Preparation

Cross-Cultural Preparation
Training to prepare employees and their family members for an assignment in a foreign country.

When an organization selects an employee for a position in a foreign country, it must prepare the employee for the foreign assignment. This kind of training is called **cross-cultural preparation,** preparing employees to work across national and cultural boundaries, and it often includes family members who will accompany the employee on the assignment. The training is necessary for all three phases of an international assignment:

1. Preparation for *departure*—language instruction and an orientation to the foreign country's culture.
2. The *assignment* itself—some combination of a formal program and mentoring relationship to provide ongoing further information about the foreign country's culture.
3. Preparation for the *return* home—providing information about the employee's community and home-country workplace (from company newsletters, local newspapers, and so on).

Methods for providing this training may range from lectures for employees and their families to visits to culturally diverse communities.[27] Employees and their families may also spend time visiting a local family from the country where they will be working. In the later section on managing expatriates, we provide more detail about cross-cultural preparation.

U.S.-based companies sometimes need to be reminded that foreign employees who come to the United States ("inpatriates") need cross-cultural preparation as much as do U.S. employees sent on foreign assignments.[28] In spite of the many benefits of living in the United States, relocation can be challenging for inpatriates. In fact, in the 2010 Global Relocation Trends Survey Report, the United States had the third highest rate of assignment failure, after China and India.[29] For example, inpatriates exposed to the United States through Hollywood and TV shows often worry about safety in their new homes. In many parts of the world, a middle manager or professional's lifestyle may include servants, and the cost of rental housing is far less. As with expatriates, organizations can prepare inpatriate employees by providing

HR How To

TRAINING PROGRAMS IN OTHER COUNTRIES

Training professionals offer the following ideas for preparing and delivering training programs to employees in other countries:

- To get training sessions off to a positive start, learn the other culture's customs for greeting people and making eye contact. Know how to treat others with respect, and know how to interpret reactions to the presentation. In some cultures, speaking up is a sign of interest; in other cultures, listening quietly is preferred, because it signals that the participants are thinking about what they are learning.
- Learn about the other culture's values related to humor. A hilarious joke in the United States might be puzzling or completely inappropriate somewhere else.

- Be aware that employees from different countries may be used to different learning methods. Trainees in the United States might expect to get involved in a group to practice concepts, whereas trainees in Africa or Asia might assume that good teaching involves a lecture from a person with authority. A mixture of learning activities can engage many kinds of learners.
- If the trainees are a multicultural group and are expected to engage in teamwork, don't leave them alone to flounder with cultural differences. The trainer should assign trainees to groups, rather than leaving them to divide up on their own, and then the trainee

should monitor group activities, watching for individuals who seem not to be participating and asking questions that bring them into the activity.
- Devise training exercises that are relevant to all the participants. The exercises should not favor one cultural group of participants over another—for example, by investigating an issue that will be familiar only to part of the group.

Sources: Aliah D. Wright, "Respect Cultural Differences When Training, Experts Say," *HR Magazine*, December 2009 (HR Trendbook supp.), pp. 19–20; and Wei-Wen Chang, "Is the Group Activity Food or Poison in a Multicultural Classroom?" *T+D*, April 2010, Business & Company Resource Center, http:// galenet.galegroup.com.

---

information about getting the resources they need to live safely and comfortably in their new surroundings. HR personnel may be able to identify local immigrant communities where their inpatriate employees can go to shop for familiar foods and hear their native language.

Global Employee Development

At global organizations, international assignments are a part of many career paths. The organization benefits most if it applies the principles of employee development in deciding which employees should be offered jobs in other countries. Career development helps expatriate and inpatriate employees make the transitions to and from their assignments and helps the organization apply the knowledge the employees obtain from these assignments.

Performance Management across National Boundaries

The general principles of performance management may apply in most countries, but the specific methods that work in one country may fail in another. Therefore, organizations have to consider legal requirements, local business practices, and national

LO5 Discuss challenges related to managing performance and compensating employees from other countries.

471

cultures when they establish performance management methods in other countries. Differences may include which behaviors are rated, how and the extent to which performance is measured, who performs the rating, and how feedback is provided.[30]

For example, National Rental Car uses a behaviorally based rating scale for customer service representatives. To measure the extent to which customer service representatives' behaviors contribute to the company's goal of improving customer service, the scale measures behaviors such as smiling, making eye contact, greeting customers, and solving customer problems. Depending on the country, different behaviors may be appropriate. In Japan, culturally defined standards for polite behavior include the angle of bowing as well as proper back alignment and eye contact. In Ghana and many other African nations, appropriate measures would include behaviors that reflect loyalty and repaying of obligations as well as behaviors related to following regulations and procedures.

The extent to which managers measure performance may also vary from one country to another. In rapidly changing regions, such as Southeast Asia, the organization may have to update its performance plans more often than once a year.

Feedback is another area in which differences can occur. Employees around the world appreciate positive feedback, but U.S. employees are much more used to direct feedback than are employees in other countries. In Mexico managers are expected to provide positive feedback before focusing the discussion on behaviors the employee needs to improve.[31] At the Thai office of Singapore Airlines, managers resisted giving negative feedback to employees because they feared this would cause them to have bad karma, contributing to their reincarnation at a lower level in their next life.[32] The airlines therefore allowed the managers to adapt their feedback process to fit local cultures.

focus on **social** *responsibility*

Compensating an International Workforce

The chapters in Part 4 explained that compensation includes decisions about pay structure, incentive pay, and employee benefits. All these decisions become more complex when an organization has an international workforce. In a recent survey of employers with international operations, 85 percent said they have a global compensation strategy to guide compensation decisions for employees at all levels and in all countries where they operate.[33] Still, HR specialists may need to make extra efforts to administer these systems effectively. In half of the companies surveyed, the person in charge of HRM in one country reports to the head of that company's operations, rather than to the leader of HRM at headquarters.

Pay Structure

As Figure 15.3 shows, market pay structures can differ substantially across countries in terms of both pay level and the relative worth of jobs. For example, compared with the labor market in Germany, the market in Mexico provides much lower pay levels overall. In Germany, bus drivers average higher pay than kindergarten teachers, while the relative pay of teachers is much greater in Mexico and South Korea. For all the types of jobs shown, the pay differences between jobs are much less dramatic in Germany than in the other two countries. One reason for such differences is the supply of qualified labor. In Nigeria and China, for example, the supply of management talent has not caught up to the demand, so in those countries there is a large gap between the pay for management jobs and the pay for clerical workers.[34]

Differences such as these create a dilemma for global companies: Should pay levels and differences reflect what workers are used to in their own countries? Or should they reflect the earnings of colleagues in the country of the facility, or earnings at the company headquarters? For example, should a German engineer posted to Bombay be

Figure 15.3

Earnings in Selected Occupations in Three Countries

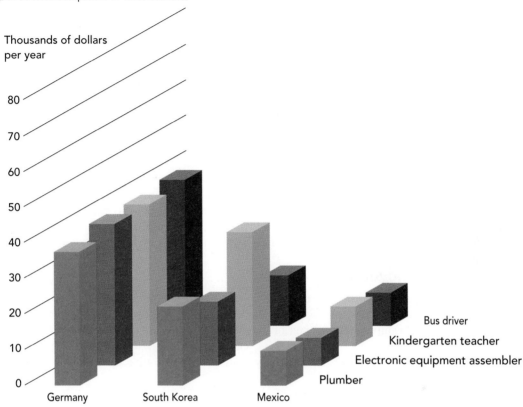

Note: Earnings are adjusted to reflect purchasing power.

SOURCE: Wage and hour data from International Labour Organization, LABORSTA Internet, http://laborsta.ilo.org, accessed May 7, 2010.

paid according to the standard in Frankfurt or the standard in Bombay? If the standard is Frankfurt, the engineers in Bombay will likely see the German engineer's pay as unfair. If the standard is Bombay, the company will likely find it impossible to persuade a German engineer to take an assignment in Bombay. Dilemmas such as these make a global compensation strategy important as a way to show employees that the pay structure is designed to be fair and related to the value that employees bring to the organization.

These decisions affect a company's costs and ability to compete. The average hourly labor costs in industrialized countries such as the United States, Germany, and Japan are far higher than these costs in newly industrialized countries such as Mexico, Hong Kong, and Brazil.[35] As a result, we often hear that U.S. labor costs are too high to allow U.S. companies to compete effectively unless the companies shift operations to low-cost foreign subsidiaries. That conclusion oversimplifies the situation for many companies. Merely comparing wages ignores differences in education, skills, and productivity.[36] If an organization gets more or higher-quality output from a higher-wage workforce, the higher wages may be worth the cost. Besides this, if the organization has many positions requiring highly skilled workers, it may need to operate in (or hire immigrants from) a country with a strong educational system, regardless of labor costs. Finally, labor costs may be outweighed by other factors, such as transportation costs or access to resources or customers. When a production process is highly automated, differences in labor costs may not be significant.

Cultural differences also play a role in pay structure. This became evident in the recent recession, when companies in many parts of the world, including the United States, were slashing payrolls. Even fast-growing India experienced some downsizing, but many of the cuts came from U.S.-based companies. India's business culture tends to be more "paternalistic," with managers feeling responsible for employees' well-being. So when business slowed, Indian companies were more likely to restructure, hold back on salary increases, and institute hiring freezes than to take actions like laying off employees or even reducing their hours.[37]

Incentive Pay

Besides setting a pay structure, the organization must make decisions with regard to incentive pay, such as bonuses and stock options. Although stock options became a common form of incentive pay in the United States during the 1990s, European businesses did not begin to embrace this type of compensation until the end of that decade.

However, the United States and Europe differ in the way they award stock options. European companies usually link the options to specific performance goals, such as the increase in a company's share price compared with that of its competitors.

Employee Benefits

As in the United States, compensation packages in other countries include benefits. Decisions about benefits must take into account the laws of each country involved, as well as employees' expectations and values in those countries. Some countries require paid maternity leave, and some countries have nationalized health care systems, which would affect the value of private health insurance in a compensation package.

Figure 15.4

Average Hours Worked in
Selected Countries

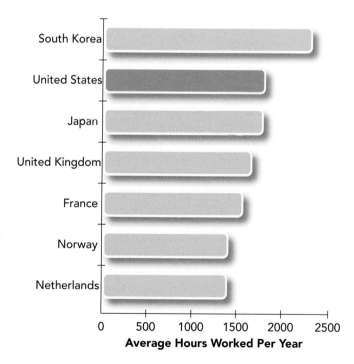

SOURCE: Data from Susan E. Fleck, "International Comparisons of Hours Worked: An Assessment of the Statistics," *Monthly Labor Review,* May 2009, pp. 3–31.

Pension plans are more widespread in parts of Western Europe than in the United States and Japan. Over 90 percent of workers in Switzerland have pension plans, as do all workers in France. Among workers with pension plans, U.S. workers are significantly less likely to have defined benefit plans than workers in Japan or Germany.

Paid vacation, discussed in Chapter 13, tends to be more generous in Western Europe than in the United States. Figure 15.4 compares the number of hours the average employee works in various countries. Of these countries, only in South Korea do workers put in more hours than U.S. workers. In the other countries, the norm is to work fewer hours than a U.S. worker over the course of a year.

International Labor Relations

Companies that operate across national boundaries often need to work with unions in more than one country. Organizations establish policies and goals for labor relations, for overseeing labor agreements, and for monitoring labor performance (for example, output and productivity).[38] The day-to-day decisions about labor relations are usually handled by each foreign subsidiary. The reason is that labor relations on an international scale involve differences in laws, attitudes, and economic systems, as well as differences in negotiation styles.

At least in comparison with European organizations, U.S. organizations exert more centralized control over labor relations in the various countries where they operate.[39] U.S. management therefore must recognize differences in how various countries understand and regulate labor relations. For example, in the United States, collective bargaining usually involves negotiations between a union local and an organization's management, but in Sweden and Germany, collective bargaining generally involves negotiations between an employers' organization and a union representing an entire industry's employees.[40] Legal differences range from who may form a union to how much latitude an organization is allowed in laying off workers. In China, for example, the government recently passed a law requiring employers to give new employees shorter probationary periods, consider workers' dependents in making layoff decisions, pay severance to fired workers, and give the Communist Party–run union more power in negotiating contracts and work rules.[41] In Germany, because labor representatives participate on companies' boards of directors, the way management handles labor relations can affect a broad range of decisions.[42] Management therefore has an incentive to build cooperative relationships.

International labor relations must also take into account that negotiations between labor and management take place in a different social context, not just different economic and legal contexts. Cultural differences that affect other interactions come into play in labor negotiations as well. Negotiators will approach the process differently depending on whether the culture views the process as primarily cooperative or competitive and whether it is local practice to negotiate a deal by starting with the specifics or agreeing on overall principles.[43] Working with host-country nationals can help organizations navigate such differences in negotiation style.

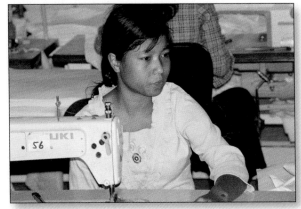

Due to the Multi Fibre Agreement which governs trade in the textile and clothing industry, the once prosperous clothing industry in Cambodia is falling to competitors in countries such as China. Many fear employees being laid off will be pushed to prostitution or become victims of human trafficking.

Managing Expatriates

At some point, most international and global organizations assign managers to foreign posts. These assignments give rise to significant human resource challenges, from selecting managers for these assignments to preparing them, compensating them, and helping them adjust to a return home. The same kinds of HRM principles that apply to domestic positions can help organizations avoid mistakes in managing expatriates: planning and goal setting, selection aimed at achieving the HR goals, and performance management that includes evaluation of whether the overseas assignment delivered value relative to the costs involved.[44]

Selecting Expatriate Managers

The challenge of managing expatriate managers begins with determining which individuals in the organization are most capable of handling an assignment in another country. Expatriate managers need technical competence in the area of operations, in part to help them earn the respect of subordinates. Of course, many other skills are also necessary for success in any management job, especially one that involves working overseas. Depending on the nature of the assignment and the culture where it is located, the organization should consider each candidate's skills, learning style, and approach to problem solving. Each of these should be related to achievement of the organization's goals, such as solving a particular problem, transferring knowledge to host-country employees, or developing future leaders for the organization.[45]

A successful expatriate manager must be sensitive to the host country's cultural norms, flexible enough to adapt to those norms, and strong enough to survive the culture shock of living in another culture. In addition, if the manager has a family, the family members must be able to adapt to a new culture. Adaptation requires three kinds of skills:[46]

1. Ability to maintain a positive self-image and feeling of well-being.
2. Ability to foster relationships with the host-country nationals.
3. Ability to perceive and evaluate the host country's environment accurately.

In a study that drew on the experience of people holding international assignments, expatriates told researchers that the most important qualities for an expatriate manager are, in order of importance, family situation, flexibility and adaptability, job knowledge and motivation, relational skills, and openness to other cultures.[47] To assess candidates' ability to adapt to a new environment, interviews should address topics such as the ones listed in Table 15.2. The interviewer should be certain to give candidates a clear and complete preview of the assignment and the host-country culture. This helps the candidate evaluate the assignment and consider it in terms of his or her family situation, so the employer does not violate the employee's privacy.[48]

Preparing Expatriates

LO6 Explain how employers prepare managers for international assignments and for their return home.

Once the organization has selected a manager for an overseas assignment, it is necessary to prepare that person through training and development. Because expatriate success depends so much on the entire family's adjustment, the employee's spouse should be included in the preparation activities. Employees selected for expatriate assignments already have job-related skills, so preparation for expatriate assignments often focuses on cross-cultural training—that is, training in what to expect from the host country's culture. The general purpose of cross-cultural training is to create an

Table 15.2

Topics for Assessing Candidates for Overseas Assignments

Motivation
- Investigate reasons and degree of interest in wanting to be considered.
- Determine desire to work abroad, verified by previous concerns such as personal travel, language training, reading, and association with foreign employees or students.
- Determine whether the candidate has a realistic understanding of what working and living abroad require.
- Determine the basic attitudes of the spouse toward an overseas assignment.

Health
- Determine whether any medical problems of the candidate or his or her family might be critical to the success of the assignment.
- Determine whether he or she is in good physical and mental health, without any foreseeable change.

Language ability
- Determine potential for learning a new language.
- Determine any previous language(s) studied or oral ability (judge against language needed on the overseas assignment).
- Determine the ability of the spouse to meet the language requirements.

Family considerations
- How many moves has the family made in the past among different cities or parts of the United States?
- What problems were encountered?
- How recent was the last move?
- What is the spouse's goal in this move?
- What are the number of children and the ages of each?
- Has divorce or its potential, or death of a family member, weakened family solidarity?
- Will all the children move? Why or why not?
- What are the location, health, and living arrangements of grandparents and the number of trips normally made to their home each year?
- Are there any special adjustment problems that you would expect?
- How is each member of the family reacting to this possible move?
- Do special educational problems exist within the family?

Resourcefulness and initiative
- Is the candidate independent; can he make and stand by his decisions and judgments?
- Does she have the intellectual capacity to deal with several dimensions simultaneously?
- Is he able to reach objectives and produce results with whatever personnel and facilities are available, regardless of the limitations and barriers that might arise?
- Can the candidate operate without a clear definition of responsibility and authority on a foreign assignment?
- Will the candidate be able to explain the aims and company philosophy to the local managers and workers?
- Does she possess sufficient self-discipline and self-confidence to overcome difficulties or handle complex problems?
- Can the candidate work without supervision?
- Can the candidate operate effectively in a foreign environment without normal communications and supporting services?

Adaptability
- Is the candidate sensitive to others, open to the opinions of others, cooperative, and able to compromise?
- What are his reactions to new situations, and efforts to understand and appreciate differences?
- Is she culturally sensitive, aware, and able to relate across the culture?
- Does the candidate understand his own culturally derived values?
- How does the candidate react to criticism?
- What is her understanding of the U.S. government system?
- Will he be able to make and develop contacts with peers in the foreign country?

(Continued)

Table 15.2   Concluded

- Does she have patience when dealing with problems?
- Is he resilient; can he bounce back after setbacks?

Career planning

- Does the candidate consider the assignment anything other than a temporary overseas trip?
- Is the move consistent with her progression and that planned by the company?
- Is his career planning realistic?
- What is the candidate's basic attitude toward the company?
- Is there any history or indication of interpersonal problems with this employee?

Financial

- Are there any current financial and/or legal considerations that might affect the assignment, such as house purchase, children and college expenses, car purchases?
- Are financial considerations negative factors? Will undue pressures be brought to bear on the employee or her family as a result of the assignment?

SOURCE: Excerpted with permission, pages 55–57 from *"Multinational People Management: A Guide for Organizations and Employees,"* by David M. Noer. Copyright © 1975 by the Bureau of National Affairs, Inc., Washington, DC 20037. Published by the Bureau of National Affairs, Inc., Washington, DC 20037. For copies of BNA Books publications call toll free 1-800-960-1220.

appreciation of the host country's culture so expatriates can behave appropriately.[49] Paradoxically, this requires developing a greater awareness of one's own culture, so that the expatriate manager can recognize differences and similarities between the cultures and, perhaps, home-culture biases. Consider, for example, the statements in Figure 15.5, which are comments made by visitors to the United States. Do you think these observations accurately describe U.S. culture?

On a more specific level, cross-cultural training for foreign assignments includes the details of how to behave in business settings in another country—the ways people behave in meetings, how employees expect managers to treat them, and so on. As an example, Germans value promptness for meetings to a much greater extent than do Latin Americans—and so on. How should one behave when first meeting one's business counterparts in another culture? The "outgoing" personality style so valued in the United States may seem quite rude in other parts of the world.[50]

Employees preparing for a foreign assignment also need information about such practical matters as housing, schools, recreation, shopping, and health care facilities in the country where they will be living. This is a crucial part of the preparation.

Communication in another country often requires a determined attempt to learn a new language. Some employers try to select managers who speak the language of the host country, and a few provide language training. Most companies assume that employees in the host country will be able to speak the host country's language. Even if this is true, host country nationals are not likely to be fluent in the home country's language, so language barriers remain. This is even true when employees move to a country that nominally speaks the same language. For example, a U.S. employee working in England might be surprised to discover that when a project suddenly goes awry, it has "hit the buffers," while if it is proceeding smoothly, it is "on cam." And a client who says, "Give me a bell," isn't requesting an unusual sort of gift, but rather a phone call.[51]

Along with cross-cultural training, preparation of the expatriate should include career development activities. Before leaving for a foreign assignment, expatriates should discuss with their managers how the foreign assignment fits into their career

Figure 15.5

Impressions of Americans: Comments by Visitors to the United States

"Americans seem to be in a perpetual hurry. Just watch the way they walk down the street. They never allow themselves the leisure to enjoy life; there are too many things to do."

—A visitor from India

"The American is very explicit; he wants a 'yes' or 'no.' If someone tries to speak figuratively, the American is confused."

—A visitor from Ethiopia

"The tendency in the United States to think that life is only work hits you in the face. Work seems to be the one type of motivation."

—A visitor from Colombia

"The first time . . . my [American] professor told me, 'I don't know the answer, I will have to look it up,' I was shocked. I asked myself, 'Why is he teaching me?' In my country, a professor would give the wrong answer rather than admit ignorance."

—A visitor from Iran

SOURCE: J. Feig and G. Blair, *There Is a Difference*, 2nd ed. (Washington, DC: Meridian House International, 1980), cited in N. Adler, *International Dimensions of Organizational Behavior*, 2nd ed. (Boston: PWS-Kent, 1991).

plans and what types of positions they can expect upon their return. This prepares the expatriate to develop valuable skills during the overseas assignment and eases the return home when the assignment is complete.

When the employee leaves for the assignment, the preparation process should continue.[52] Employees need a chance to discuss their experiences with other expatriates, so they can learn from their failures and successes. The organization may provide a host-country mentor or an executive coach with experience in the country to help expatriates understand their experiences. Successful expatriates tend to develop a bicultural or multicultural point of view, so as they spend more time in the host country, the value of their connections to other expatriates may actually increase.

Managing Expatriates' Performance

Performance management of expatriates requires clear goals for the overseas assignment and frequent evaluation of whether the expatriate employee is on track to meet those goals. Communication technology including e-mail and teleconferencing provides a variety of ways for expats' managers to keep in touch with these employees to discuss and diagnose issues before they can interfere with performance. In addition, before employees leave for an overseas assignment, HR should work with managers to develop criteria measuring the success of the assignment.[53] Measures such as productivity should take into account any local factors that could make expected performance different in the host country than in the company's home country. For example, a country's labor laws or the reliability of the electrical supply could affect the facility's output and efficiency.

Compensating Expatriates

One of the greatest challenges of managing expatriates is determining the compensation package. Most organizations use a *balance sheet approach* to determine the total amount of the package. This approach adjusts the manager's compensation so that it gives the manager the same standard of living as in the home country plus extra pay for the inconvenience of locating overseas. As shown in Figure 15.6, the balance sheet approach begins by determining the purchasing power of compensation for the same type of job in the manager's own country—that is, how much a person can buy, after taxes, in terms of housing, goods and services, and a reserve for savings. Next,

Figure 15.6

The Balance Sheet for Determining Expatriate Compensation

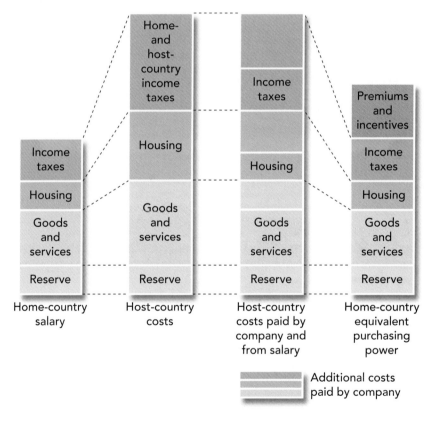

SOURCE: C. Reynolds, "Compensation of Overseas Personnel," in *Handbook of Human Resource Administration,* 2nd ed., ed. J. J. Famularo (New York: McGraw-Hill, 1986), p. 51. Reprinted with permission. Copyright © 1986 by The McGraw-Hill Companies, Inc.

Tokyo Tops Priciest Cities

Expatriates spend more for housing, transportation, food, clothing, and other living expenses in Tokyo than in any other major city, according to a survey by Mercer Human Resources Consulting. Mercer's list of the 50 most expensive cities includes seven in North America: New York, Los Angeles, White Plains, N.Y., San Francisco, Honolulu, Miami, and Chicago (which just barely made the list at number 50). The top five are shown in the figure below.

Source: Based on Mercer Human Resources Consulting, "Worldwide Cost of Living Survey 2009—City Ranking," July 7, 2009, www.mercer.com.

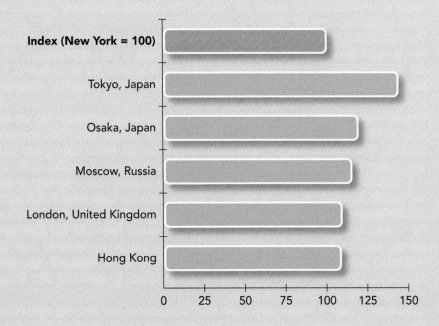

Index (New York = 100)

Tokyo, Japan

Osaka, Japan

Moscow, Russia

London, United Kingdom

Hong Kong

0   25   50   75   100   125   150

this amount is compared with the cost (in dollars, for a U.S. company) of these same expenses in the foreign country. In Figure 15.6, the greater size of the second column means the costs for a similar standard of living in the foreign country are much higher in every category except the reserve amount. This situation would be likely in one of the cities identified in the "Did You Know?" box. For the expatriate in this situation, the employer would pay the additional costs, as shown by the third column. Finally, the expatriate receives additional purchasing power from premiums and incentives. Because of these added incentives, the expatriate's purchasing power is more than what the manager could buy at home with the salary for an equivalent job. (Compare the fourth column with the first.) In practice, the total cost of an international assignment is roughly four times the employee's salary in the host country.[54] To restrain spending, some organizations are sending expatriates on shorter assignments. For instance, on an assignment of less than a year, an expatriate generally would not move his or her family, substantially reducing the cost of relocation and eliminating the need to cover children's education expenses.

After setting the total pay, the organization divides this amount into the four components of a total pay package:

1. *Base salary*—Determining the base salary is complex because different countries use different currencies (dollars, yen, euros, and so on). The exchange rate—the rate at which one currency may be exchanged for another—constantly shifts in response to a host of economic forces, so the real value of a salary in terms of dollars is constantly changing. Also, as discussed earlier, the base salary may be comparable to the pay of other managers at headquarters or comparable to other managers at the foreign subsidiary. Because many organizations pay a salary premium as an incentive to accept an overseas assignment, expatriates' salaries are often higher than pay for staying at headquarters.

2. *Tax equalization allowance*—Companies have different systems for taxing income, and in many countries, tax rates are much higher than in the United States. Usually, the employer of an expatriate withholds the amount of tax to be paid in the parent country, then pays all of the taxes due in the country where the expatriate is working.

3. *Benefits*—Most benefits issues have to do with whether an employee can use the same benefits in the foreign country. For example, if an expatriate has been contributing to a pension plan in the United States, does this person have a new pension in the foreign country? Or can the expatriate continue to contribute to the U.S. pension plan? Similarly, health benefits may involve receiving care at certain health facilities. While the person is abroad, does the same health plan cover services received in the foreign country? In one case, flying a manager back to the United States for certain procedures actually would have cost less than having the procedures done in the country where the person was working. But the company's health plans did not permit this alternative. An employer may offer expatriates additional benefits to address the problem of uprooting the spouse when assigning an employee overseas.

4. *Allowances to make a foreign assignment more attractive*—Cost-of-living allowances make up the differences in expenses for day-to-day needs. Housing allowances ensure that the expatriate can maintain the same standard of living as in the United States. Education allowances reimburse expatriates who pay tuition for their children to attend private English-speaking schools. Relocation allowances cover the expenses of making the move to the foreign country, including transportation, shipping or storage of possessions, and expenses for temporary housing until the employee can rent or purchase a home.

Figure 15.7 is an example of a summary sheet for an expatriate manager's compensation package, showing a variety of allowances.

Helping Expatriates Return Home

As the expatriate's assignment nears its end, the human resource department faces a final challenge: helping the expatriate make the transition back to his or her home country. The process of preparing expatriates to return home from a foreign assignment is called **repatriation.** Reentry is not as simple as it might sound. Culture shock takes place in reverse. The experience has changed the expatriate, and the company's and expatriate's home cultures have changed as well. Also, because of differences in economies and compensation levels, a returning expatriate may experience a decline in living standards. The standard of living for an expatriate in many countries includes maid service, a limousine, private schools, and clubs.

Repatriation
The process of preparing expatriates to return home from a foreign assignment.

John H. Doe		1 October 2010		
Name		**Effective date**		
Singapore		Manager, SLS./Serv. AP/ME		
Location of assignment		**Title**		
Houston, Texas	1234	202		202
Home base	**Emp. no.**	**LCA code**		**Tax code**

Reason for Change: _____ International Assignment _____

	Old	New
Monthly base salary		$5,000.00
Living cost allowance		$1,291.00
Foreign service premium		$ 750.00
Area allowance		-0-
Gross monthly salary		$7,041.00
Housing deduction		$ 500.00
Hypothetical tax		$ 570.00
Other		
Net monthly salary		$5,971.00

Prepared by	**Date**
Vice President, Human Resources	**Date**

Figure 15.7

International Assignment
Allowance Form

Companies are increasingly making efforts to help expatriates through this transition. Two activities help the process along: communication and validation.[55] Communication refers to the expatriate receiving information and recognizing changes while abroad. The more the organization keeps in contact with the expatriate, the more effective and satisfied the person will be upon return. The expatriate plays a role in this process as well. Expatriates should work at maintaining important contacts in the company and industry. Communication related to career development before and during the overseas assignment also should help the employee return to a position that is challenging and interesting. Validation means giving the expatriate recognition for the overseas service when this person returns home. Expatriates who receive praise and recognition from colleagues and top managers for their overseas service and future contribution have fewer troubles with reentry than those whose contributions are disregarded. Validation should also include planning for how the returning employee will contribute to the organization. What skills will this person bring back? What position will he or she fill?

Guardian Industries, a glass manufacturer based in Auburn Hills, Michigan, treats its returning expatriates as valuable employees who have made a sacrifice for the company. They are therefore placed first in line for key assignments. After Dana Partridge worked for Guardian in Saudi Arabia and Thailand for a total of 13 years, the company couldn't immediately give him the job he was prepared for, plant manager, but as soon as a position became available, Partridge was selected.[56]

thinking ethically

JOB LOCATION: IS IT ALL ABOUT THE MONEY?

A chief reason companies cite for locating operations in low-wage areas is to save money so they can meet customers' demands for low-priced products. That's what took Scovill Fasteners from Clarksville, Georgia, to China. Several years ago, management saw that customers who bought its snaps for baby clothes were making the clothes in China, and they expected that customers who bought its snaps to make blue jeans would soon be there as well. The company decided it would have to join them.

Scovill opened a factory in Shenzhen China, where it paid 500 workers an average of $2.20 per hour. The private equity firm that owns Scovill decided to keep all the profits instead of forming a partnership with Chinese business owners. To find English-speaking managers, it hired them in Hong Kong. The Shenzhen workers and Hong Kong managers distrusted each other, and no one could relate to the owners back in the United States.

With the difficult relationships came difficulty overseeing the work. Management back in the United States was unsure whether the factory's relationship with the Chinese government was proper. And when the lunar new year holiday occurred, headquarters was unprepared to see the Chinese workers leave en masse, many of them never to return.

Eventually, management concluded that the money-saving effort was actually expensive. The company considered setting up shop in a country where wages were even lower, but employees in Clarksville had agreed to cut their pay by 10 percent, and operations at home began looking like the most productive alternative. Scovill decided to keep 170 Georgia jobs on its payroll instead of outsourcing production.

SOURCE: Based on Dan Chapman, "Jobs Return from China," *Atlanta Journal-Constitution*, April 25, 2010, Business & Company Resource Center, http://galenet.galegroup.com.

Questions

1. Do companies have an ethical obligation to keep jobs in their home country? Why or why not?
2. In what ways, if at all, were Scovill's ethical obligations to its U.S. and Chinese workers different?
3. Scovill moved a sizable part of its operations to China, planning to move more, but workers accepted pay cuts, and Scovill moved back home. How would you rate the fairness of this situation from management's point of view? As a human resource manager, how would you communicate the decision to the workers?

SUMMARY

LO1 Summarize how the growth in international business activity affects human resource management.

More and more companies are entering international markets by exporting and operating foreign facilities. Organizations therefore need employees who understand customers and suppliers in other countries. They need to understand local laws and customs and be able to adapt their plans to local situations. To do this organizations may hire a combination of parent-country, host-country, and third-country nationals. They may operate on the scale of an exporter or an international, global, or multinational organization. A global organization needs a transnational HRM system, which makes decisions from a global perspective, includes managers from many countries, and is based on ideas contributed by people representing a variety of cultures.

LO2 Identify the factors that most strongly influence HRM in international markets.

By far the most important influence is the culture of each market—its set of shared assumptions about how the world works and what ideals are worth striving for. A culture has the dimensions of individualism/collectivism, high or low power distance, high or low uncertainty avoidance, masculinity/femininity, and long-term or short-term orientation. Countries also differ in the degree to which their labor markets include people with education and skills of value to employers. Another influence on international HRM is the foreign country's political-legal system—its government, laws, and regulations. Finally, a country's economic system, capitalist or socialist, as well as the government's involvement in the country's economy, such as through taxes and price controls, is a strong factor determining HRM practices.

LO3   Discuss how differences among countries affect HR planning at organizations with international operations.

As organizations consider decisions about their level of international activity, HR professionals should provide information about the relevant human resource issues. When organizations decide to operate internationally or globally, HR planning involves decisions about where and how many employees are needed for each international facility. Some countries limit employers' ability to lay off workers, so organizations would be less likely to staff for peak periods. Other countries allow employers more flexibility in meeting human resource needs. HRM professionals need to be conversant with such differences.

LO4   Describe how companies select and train human resources in a global labor market.

Many organizations with foreign operations fill most positions with host-country nationals. These employees can more easily understand the values and customs of the local workforce, and hiring locally tends to be less expensive than moving employees to new locations. Organizations also fill foreign positions with parent-country and third-country nationals who have human relations skills associated with success in foreign assignments. When sending employees on foreign assignments, organizations prepare the employees (and often their families) through cross-cultural training. Before the assignment, the training provides instruction in the foreign country's language and culture. During the assignment, there is communication with the home country and mentoring. For the return home the employer provides further training.

LO5   Discuss challenges related to managing performance and compensating employees from other countries.

Pay structures can differ substantially among countries in terms of pay level and the relative worth of jobs. Organizations must decide whether to set pay levels and differences in terms of what workers are used to in their own countries or in terms of what employees' colleagues earn at headquarters. Typically, companies have resolved this dilemma by linking pay and benefits more closely to those of the employee's country, but this practice may be weakening so that it depends more on the nature and length of the foreign assignment. These decisions affect the organization's costs and ability to compete, so organizations consider local labor costs in their location decisions. Along with the basic pay structure, organizations must make decisions regarding incentive pay, such as bonuses and stock options. Laws may dictate differences in benefit packages, and the value of benefits will differ if a country requires them or makes them a government service.

LO6   Explain how employers prepare managers for international assignments and for their return home.

When an organization has selected a manager for an overseas assignment, it must prepare the person for the experience. In cross-cultural training the soon-to-be expatriate learns about the foreign culture he or she is heading to, and studies her or his own home-country culture as well for insight. The trainee is given a detailed briefing on how to behave in business settings in the new country. Along with cross-cultural training, preparation of the expatriate should include career development activities to help the individual acquire valuable career skills during the foreign assignment and at the end of the assignment to handle repatriation successfully. Communication of changes at home and validation of a job well done abroad help the expatriate through the repatriation process.

KEY TERMS

cross-cultural preparation, p. 470
culture shock, p. 469
expatriates, p. 458
global organization, p. 461

host country, p. 458
international organization, p. 460
multinational company, p. 460
parent country, p. 458

repatriation, p. 482
third country, p. 458
transnational HRM system, p. 461

REVIEW AND DISCUSSION QUESTIONS

1. Identify the parent country, host country(ies), and third country(ies) in the following example: A global soft-drink company called Cold Cola has headquarters in Atlanta, Georgia. It operates production facilities in Athens, Greece, and in Jakarta, Indonesia. The company has assigned a manager from Boston to head the Athens facility and a manager from Hong Kong to manage the Jarkarta facility.

2. What are some HRM challenges that arise when a U.S. company expands from domestic markets by exporting? When it changes from simply exporting to operating as an international company? When an international company becomes a global company?

3. In recent years, many U.S. companies have invested in Russia and sent U.S. managers there in an attempt to transplant U.S.-style management. According to Hofstede, U.S. culture has low power distance, uncertainty avoidance, and long-term orientation and high individuality and masculinity. Russia's culture has high power distance and uncertainty avoidance, low masculinity and long-term orientation, and moderate individuality. In light of what you know about cultural differences, how well do you think U.S. managers can succeed in each of the following U.S.-style HRM practices? (Explain your reasons.)
   a. Selection decisions based on extensive assessment of individual abilities.
   b. Appraisals based on individual performance.
   c. Systems for gathering suggestions from workers.
   d. Self-managing work teams.

4. Besides cultural differences, what other factors affect human resource management in an organization with international operations?

5. Suppose you work in the HR department of a company that is expanding into a country where the law and culture make it difficult to lay off employees. How should your knowledge of that difficulty affect human resource planning for the overseas operations?

6. Why do multinational organizations hire host-country nationals to fill most of their foreign positions, rather than sending expatriates for most jobs?

7. Suppose an organization decides to improve collaboration and knowledge sharing by developing an intranet to link its global workforce. It needs to train employees in several different countries to use this system. List the possible cultural issues you can think of that the training program should take into account.

8. For an organization with operations in three different countries, what are some advantages and disadvantages of setting compensation according to the labor markets in the countries where the employees live and work? What are some advantages and disadvantages of setting compensation according to the labor market in the company's headquarters? Would the best arrangement be different for the company's top executives and its production workers? Explain.

9. What abilities make a candidate more likely to succeed in an assignment as an expatriate? Which of these abilities do you have? How might a person acquire these abilities?

10. In the past, a large share of expatriate managers from the United States have returned home before successfully completing their foreign assignments. Suggest some possible reasons for the high failure rate. What can HR departments do to increase the success of expatriates?

BUSINESSWEEK CASE

BusinessWeek Will Hardship Pay Survive the Downturn?

During hard times, a tempting target for cost cutters at multinational corporations might be hardship payments. Multinationals for years have paid these bonuses to managers who accept overseas assignments in difficult countries, usually in developing nations in Asia, Africa, Latin America, and the Middle East. Companies have calculated that, in order to have talented people in key locations, they need to sweeten the terms, with payments ranging from 5 percent to 30 percent of a manager's salary.

Despite the need to cut costs now, executives at the consultants that help companies calculate hardship bonuses argue companies are still going to pay managers extra for taking difficult posts. Cathy Loose, Asia-Pacific mobility leader for Mercer, the HR consulting firm that is part of the New York–based Marsh & McLennan Companies, expects demand for hardship payments to go up. "As companies expand into emerging markets, hardship allowances are actually still relevant," she says.

Economic growth continues in the big emerging markets, which will maintain their appeal to companies looking for new opportunities. With the shortage of experienced managerial talent in many of the emerging markets, multinationals will still need to find sweeteners for expatriates, says Robert Freedman, chief executive officer of ORC Worldwide, a New York–based human resource firm.

"Companies are trying to pare back where they can on some payments, but they absolutely need expats," he says. "We see the premiums for these difficult places continuing."

Even the fastest-growing emerging markets are suffering at the moment, though. Growth in India slumped to an annualized rate of 5.3 percent in the fourth quarter of 2008, compared to 7.6 percent in the previous quarter.

The expats won't necessarily be coming from the United States, Canada, or Western Europe. Companies now are trying to find managers from the same part of the world, finding someone from Singapore, for instance, to take a post in China. There are obvious cultural and language advantages to that strategy, and the costs can sometimes be lower.

HR experts don't recommend companies respond by phasing out hardship pay. The problems that make a city a hardship post—heavy pollution, risk of disease, high crime, poor sanitation, inadequate infrastructure—are the same for a manager from North America as they are for a manager from Asia, says Geoff Latta, ORC's executive vice-president. "Companies would be ill-advised to differentiate and say, 'You don't need a payment because you come from a terrible place in the first place.'"

Another way to cut costs is for a city to lose its status as a hardship post. For instance, both Prague and Budapest have fallen off ORC's list, a reflection of the improved quality of life in the former Soviet-bloc cities over the past decade.

SOURCE: Excerpted from Bruce Einhorn, "Will Hardship Pay Survive the Downturn?" *BusinessWeek*, March 4, 2009, www.businessweek.com.

Questions

1. For a company with operations in a "difficult country," what would be the advantages of hiring manager from that country? What would be the disadvantages?
2. What would be the advantages of sending managers from headquarters to lead the operations in the "difficult country"? What would be the advantages?
3. Suppose you work in HR for a company that needs to cut costs and is considering the elimination of hardship pay for managers sent to work in a "difficult country" where the company has an important facility. How can you measure whether the hardship pay is a worthwhile expense? Write a one-paragraph recommendation of how you think the company should handle the issue of hardship pay.

Case: How Roche Diagnostics Develops Global Managers

The health care company Roche has two operating divisions: a pharmaceuticals division and Roche Diagnostics, which applies research and development to identify ways that diagnostic tests can help patients manage their health with individualized care. At its main sites in Switzerland, Germany, and the United States, Roche Diagnostics conducts research by microbiologists, biochemists, geneticists, oncologists, and specialists in infectious diseases. Finding enough people with these skills is difficult, and managing them requires a special set of scientific and business expertise, as well as the ability to navigate the cultural differences of a diverse workforce.

In contrast to most of its competitors, Roche isn't focused on the most efficient way to conduct research in one or two centralized locations. Rather, the strategy is to have many different groups pursuing a variety of ideas, sharing what they learn so they create the most ideas. Thus, leadership requires a combination of technical strength and communication skill.

Roche develops the necessary management talent through a program of global rotation called the Perspectives Program. Employees who have completed their PhD or MBA and want to pursue an international career are eligible to participate. Participants are selected on the basis of geographic and functional needs. They are sent on four international assignments lasting six months each. Each assignment takes place in a different country—perhaps

one of the main facilities or another Roche laboratory in, say, China or New Zealand. Typically, employees who complete the program (95 percent finish it successfully) are assigned to positions as senior managers or directors. Many find that the experience has led their career in a new direction.

Before managers are sent on these assignments, the company briefs them on what to expect. The briefing includes benefits to seek, reasons why the company selected them and what it is investing, goals for the rotation, and success stories of prior participants.

Roche has run into some challenges in implementing the program. One is that some expats start to enjoy their assignments so much that they don't want to move on when the six-month period ends. Bringing candidates into the program is occasionally difficult because talented employees' managers don't want them to leave for a foreign assignment. The company also found that preparation was sometimes inadequate—either the participant or the manager of the international assignment wasn't fully prepared.

To address some of these problems, Roche is now more careful to lay out the plan for the rotation while preparing candidates, so they understand that the rotations will have a limited duration. Rather than simply saying their careers could take them to various places, the discussion now pinpoints locations where there is a need that matches the candidate's talents. The program also has more alternatives so some employees can take assignments for just a year.

For candidates who are deciding whether to participate, Roche lets them take their spouse or domestic partner with them on some trips to investigate the program. Although this adds to the program's expense, it helps to ensure that the participant will successfully complete the rotation. Candidates who are unsure also can shadow a current participant to see what the experience is like. One way Roche has lowered managers' resistance to losing top employees is to arrange swaps where a manager who lets a key employee participate in the rotation can be on the receiving end and get a top employee from another part of the world.

Recently, when a participant returned from a rotation in Japan, he could readily identify what aspect of the experience had made him a better businessperson. He said he learned to understand the typical decision-making process in Japan, which involves careful discussion in the office,

followed by a late evening out for dinner and further discussion, with key decisions occurring as late as midnight. Knowing the "after-hours" part of the workday is crucial for a company that has many interactions between colleagues in the United States and Japan.

SOURCE: Marilyn B. Leahy, "Making Global Rotation Work," *Research-Technology Management,* November–December 2009, pp. 38–41; and Arlene Weintraub, "Can Roche Leave Genentech Alone?" *BusinessWeek,* November 25, 2009, www.businessweek.com.

Questions

1. Based on the description in the case and the definitions in the text, would you characterize Roche Diagnostics as an *international, multinational,* or *global* organization? Explain.
2. Evaluate how Roche prepares employees for its global rotation program. What improvements or additions to the preparation would you recommend?
3. How could Roche evaluate the success of the global rotation program?

 IT'S A WRAP!

www.mhhe.com/noefund4e is your source for **R**eviewing, **A**pplying, and **P**racticing the concepts you learned about in Chapter 15.

Review
- Chapter learning objectives

Application
- Manager's Hot Seat segment: "Cultural Differences: Let's Break a Deal"
- Video case and quiz: "High Tech India"
- Self-Assessment: How much do you know about global HRM?
- Web Exercise: Compare labor statistics for different countries
- Small-business case: Is Translating a Global Business?

Practice
- Chapter quiz

NOTES

1. E. White, "For M.B.A. Students, a Good Career Move Means a Job in Asia," *Wall Street Journal,* May 10, 2005, http://online.wsj.com.
2. V. Masch, "A Radical Plan to Manage Globalization," *BusinessWeek Online,* February 14, 2007, downloaded from Business & Company Resource Center, http://galenet.galegroup.com.
3. "The Developer Matrix," *Financial Express,* April 12, 2010, Business & Company Resource Center, http://galenet.galegroup.com; and Steve Lohr, "Global Strategy Stabilized I.B . during Downturn," *New*

York Times, April 20, 2010, Business & Company Resource Center, http://galenet.galegroup.com.
4. Avery Johnson, "Drug Firms See Poorer Nations as Sales Cure," *Wall Street Journal,* July 7, 2009, http://online.wsj.com.
5. Claudio Fernández-Aráoz, "The Coming Fight for Executive Talent," *BusinessWeek,* April 20, 2010, www.businessweek.com; and Rebecca Knight, "IBM Goes the Distance for Its Key Indian Staff," *Financial Times,* May 25, 2009, Business & Company Resource Center, http://galenet.galegroup.com.

6. N. Adler and S. Bartholomew, "Managing Globally Competent People," *The Executive* 6 (1992), pp. 52–65.

7. V. Sathe, *Culture and Related Corporate Realities* (Homewood, IL: Richard D. Irwin, 1985); and M. Rokeach, *Beliefs, Attitudes, and Values* (San Francisco: Jossey-Bass, 1968).

8. N. Adler, *International Dimensions of Organizational Behavior,* 2nd ed. (Boston: PWS-Kent, 1991).

9. G. Hofstede, "Dimensions of National Cultures in Fifty Countries and Three Regions," in *Expectations in Cross-Cultural Psychology,* eds. J. Deregowski, S. Dziurawiec, and R. C. Annis (Lisse, Netherlands: Swets and Zeitlinger, 1983); and G. Hofstede, "Cultural Constraints in Management Theories," *Academy of Management Executive* 7 (1993), pp. 81–90.

10. Hofstede, "Cultural Constraints in Management Theories."

11. W. A. Randolph and M. Sashkin, "Can Organizational Empowerment Work in Multinational Settings?" *Academy of Management Executive* 16, no. 1 (2002), pp. 102–15.

12. Ibid.

13. B. Gerhart and M. Fang, "National Culture and Human Resource Management: Assumptions and Evidence," *International Journal of Human Resource Management* 16, no. 6 (June 2005): 971–86.

14. L. A. West Jr. and W. A. Bogumil Jr., "Foreign Knowledge Workers as a Strategic Staffing Option," *Academy of Management Executive* 14, no. 4 (2000), pp. 71–83.

15. Organization for Economic Cooperation and Development, *Education at a Glance 2007: Highlights,* http://www.oecd.org/dataoecd/36/5/39290975.pdf, accessed March 20, 2008.

16. World Bank, "The State of Education," *EdStats,* www.worldbank.org, accessed March 20, 2008.

17. European Union, "Organisation of Working Time," Employment Rights and Work Organisation: Health, Hygiene and Safety at Work, http://europa.eu, last updated July 24, 2007; and PriceWaterhouseCoopers, *Key Trends in Human Capital: A Global Perspective,* 2006, Publications, www.pwc.co.uk, accessed March 19, 2008.

18. N. Shirouzu, "Toyota's New U.S. Plan: Stop Building Factories," *Wall Street Journal,* June 20, 2007, http://online.wsj.com.

19. West and Bogumil, "Foreign Knowledge Workers as a Strategic Staffing Option."

20. Julia Preston, "Work Force Fueled by Highly Skilled Immigrants," *New York Times,* April 15, 2010, www.nytimes.com.

21. Neil A. Lewis, "Immigration Officials to Audit 1,000 More Companies," *New York Times,* November 20, 2009, www.nytimes.com; and Moira Herbst, "Skilled Immigrants on Why They're Leaving the U.S.," *BusinessWeek,* April 26, 2010, www.businessweek.com.

22. W. A. Arthur Jr. and W. Bennett Jr., "The International Assgnee: The Relative Importance of Factors Perceived to Contribute to Success," *Personnel Psychology* 48 (1995), pp. 99–114; and G. M. Spreitzer, M. W. McCall Jr., and J. D. Mahoney, "Early Identification of International Executive Potential," *Journal of Applied Psychology* 82 (1997), pp. 6–29.

23. J. S. Black and J. K. Stephens, "The Influence of the Spouse on American Expatriate Adjustment and Intent to Stay in Pacific Rim Overseas Assignments," *Journal of Management* 15 (1989), pp. 529–44.

24. P. Caligiuri, "The Big Five Personality Characteristics as Predictors of Expatriates' Desire to Terminate the Assignment and Supervisor-Rated Performance," *Personnel Psychology* 53 (2000), pp. 67–88.

25. Delia Flanja, "Culture Shock in Intercultural Communication," *Studia Europaea* (October 2009), Business & Company Resource Center, http://galenet.galegroup.com.

26. D. M. Gayeski, C. Sanchirico, and J. Anderson, "Designing Training for Global Environments: Knowing What Questions to Ask," *Performance Improvement Quarterly* 15, no. 2 (2002), pp. 15–31.

27. J. S. Black and M. Mendenhall, "A Practical but Theory-Based Framework for Selecting Cross-Cultural Training Methods," in *Readings and Cases in International Human Resource Management,* eds. M. Mendenhall and G. Oddou (Boston: PWS-Kent, 1991), pp. 177–204.

28. Kathleen Begley, "Managing across Cultures at Home," *HR Magazine,* September 2009, p. 115.

29. Brookfield Global Relocation Services, "The Global Recession Forced a Record Number of Companies to Cut Back on Overseas Assignments of Employees in 2009," news release, April 7, 2010, www.brookfieldgrs.com.

30. D. D. Davis, "International Performance Measurement and Management," in *Performance Appraisal: State of the Art in Practice,* ed. J. W. Smither (San Francisco: Jossey-Bass, 1998), pp. 95–131.

31. M. Gowan, S. Ibarreche, and C. Lackey, "Doing the Right Things in Mexico," *Academy of Management Executive* 10 (1996), pp. 74–81.

32. L. S. Chee, "Singapore Airlines: Strategic Human Resource Initiatives," in *International Human Resource Management: Think Globally, Act Locally,* ed. D. Torrington (Upper Saddle River, NJ: Prentice Hall, 1994), pp. 143–59.

33. "Global Compensation Strategies and HR," *HRMagazine,* May 2005, downloaded from Infotrac at http://web5.infotrac.galegroup.com.

34. Hay Group, "Hay Group Report Reveals Global Managers Spending Power and Pay Gaps," news release, December 8, 2009, www.haygroup.com.

35. Bureau of Labor Statistics, "International Comparisons of Hourly Compensation Costs in Manufacturing, 2007," news release, March 26, 2009, www.bls.gov.

36. See, for example, A. E. Cobet and G. A. Wilson, "Comparing 50 Years of Labor Productivity in U.S. and Foreign Manufacturing," *Monthly Labor Review,* June 2002, pp. 51–63; and Bureau of Labor Statistics, "International Comparisons of Manufacturing Productivity and Labor Cost Trends, 2008," news release, October 22, 2009, www.bls.gov.

37. "Job Cuts vs. Pay Cuts: In a Slowing Economy, What's Better for India?" *India Knowledge @ Wharton,* November 13, 2008, http://knowledge.wharton.upenn.edu/india/.

38. P. J. Dowling, D. E. Welch, and R. S. Schuler, *International Human Resource Management,* 3rd ed. (Cincinnati: South-Western, 1999), pp. 235–36.

39. Ibid.; J. La Palombara and S. Blank, *Multinational Corporations and National Elites: A Study of Tensions* (New York: Conference Board, 1976); A. B. Sim, "Decentralized Management of Subsidiaries and Their Performance: A Comparative Study of American, British and Japanese Subsidiaries in Malaysia," *Management International Review* 17, no. 2 (1977), pp. 45–51; Y. K. Shetty, "Managing the Multinational Corporation: European and American Styles," *Management International Review* 19, no. 3 (1979), pp. 39–48; and J. Hamill, "Labor Relations Decision-Making within Multinational Corporations," *Industrial Relations Journal* 15, no. 2 (1984), pp. 30–34.

40. Dowling, Welch, and Schuler, *International Human Resource Management,* p. 231.

41. D. Roberts, "Rumbles over Labor Reform," *BusinessWeek,* March 12, 2007, p. 57; Sarah Schafer, "Now They Speak Out," *Newsweek,* May 28, 2007, downloaded from General Reference Center Gold, http://find.galegroup.com; and "China Passes Workers' Rights Law," *UPI NewsTrack,* June 30, 2007, http://find.galegroup.com.

42. J. K. Sebenius, "The Hidden Challenge of Cross-Border Negotiations," *Harvard Business Review,* March 2002, pp. 76–85.

43. Ibid.

44. E. Krell, "Evaluating Returns on Expatriates," *HRMagazine,* March 2005, downloaded from Infotrac at http://web5.infotrac.galegroup.com.

45. Ibid.; and M. Harvey and M. M. Novicevic, "Selecting Expatriates for Increasingly Complex Global Assignments," *Career Development International* 6, no. 2 (2001), pp. 69–86.

46. M. Mendenhall and G. Oddou, "The Dimensions of Expatriate Acculturation," *Academy of Management Review* 10 (1985), pp. 39–47.

47. Arthur and Bennett, "The International Assignee."

48. J. I. Sanchez, P. E. Spector, and C. L. Cooper, "Adapting to a Boundaryless World: A Developmental Expatriate Model," *Academy of Management Executive* 14, no. 2 (2000), pp. 96–106.

49. P. Dowling and R. Schuler, *International Dimensions of Human Resource Management* (Boston: PWS-Kent, 1990).

50. Sanchez, Spector, and Cooper, "Adapting to a Boundaryless World."

51. Catherine Aman, "Horses for Courses," *Corporate Counsel,* December 15, 2008, Business & Company Resource Center, http://galenet.galegroup.com.

52. Javier Espinoza, "Location, Location, Location," *Wall Street Journal,* February 5, 2010, http://online.wsj.com; and David Everhart, "Preparing Execs for Asia Assignments," *BusinessWeek,* April 1, 2008, www.businessweek.com.

53. "How Can a Company Manage an Expatriate Employee's Performance?" *SHRM India,* www.shrmindia.org, accessed May 6, 2010.

54. Siobhan Cummins and Ed P. Hannibal, "Should Your Business Axe Overseas Assignments?" *BusinessWeek,* April 26, 2010, www.businessweek.com.

55. Adler, *International Dimensions of Organizational Behavior.*

56. Alice Andors, "Happy Returns," *HR Magazine,* March 2010, Business & Company Resource Center, http://galenet.galegroup.com.

16

Creating and Maintaining High-Performance Organizations

What Do I Need to Know?

After reading this chapter, you should be able to:

LO1 Define high-performance work systems, and identify the elements of such a system.

LO2 Summarize the outcomes of a high-performance work system.

LO3 Describe the conditions that create a high-performance work system.

LO4 Explain how human resource management can contribute to high performance.

LO5 Discuss the role of HRM technology in high-performance work systems.

LO6 Summarize ways to measure the effectiveness of human resource management.

Introduction

Does human resource management really help an organization meet its business goals? Joseph Nour would surely say yes. A few years ago, the chief executive officer of Protus IP Solutions was dealing with a terrible 60 percent employee turnover. Even worse, no one really knew why people were quitting. If the departing employees had an exit interview, the notes were simply filed away unread. For help in solving the problem, Nour hired Janice Vanderburg as director of human resources. Vanderburg discovered that HR practices had failed to keep pace with the start-up company's quick growth. She conducted surveys and learned that many employees had trouble communicating with managers, didn't know what was expected of them, and saw no clear career path at the company. Vanderburg began developing Protus's managers, helping them communicate with and develop their staff. She introduced performance management software that would help managers give employees better feedback and track their progress. She established a logical pay structure and made sure employees knew about all the benefits for which they are eligible. Now turnover at the 140-employee company is just 15 percent a year—far from ideal but a vast improvement for the technology company.[1]

The experience of Protus IP Solutions shows that high-tech products and rapid growth do not guarantee business success. Someone in the organization has to recognize how business activities, management style, and strategy changes will affect the organization's people. The organization must design work and performance management systems so that they bring out the best in the employees. These challenges are some of the most crucial responsibilities of human resource management.

491

This chapter summarizes the role of human resource management in creating an organization that achieves a high level of performance, measured in such terms as long-term profits, quality, and customer satisfaction. We begin with a definition of *high-performance work systems* and a description of these systems' elements and outcomes. Next, we identify the conditions that contribute to high performance. We explain how the various HRM functions can contribute to high performance. Finally, we introduce ways to measure the effectiveness of human resource management.

High-Performance Work Systems

LO1 Define high-performance work systems, and identify the elements of such a system.

High-Performance Work System
The right combination of people, technology, and organizational structure that makes full use of the organization's resources and opportunities in achieving its goals.

The challenge facing managers today is how to make their organizations into **high-performance work systems,** with the right combination of people, technology, and organizational structure to make full use of resources and opportunities in achieving their organizations' goals. To function as a high-performance work system, each of these elements must fit well with the others in a smoothly functioning whole. Many manufacturers use the latest in processes including flexible manufacturing technology, total quality management, and just-in-time inventory control (meaning parts and supplies are automatically restocked as needed), but of course these processes do not work on their own; they must be run by qualified people. Organizations need to determine what kinds of people fit their needs, and then locate, train, and motivate those special people.[2] According to research, organizations that introduce integrated high-performance work practices usually experience increases in productivity and long-term financial performance.[3]

Creating a high-performance work system contrasts with traditional management practices. In the past, decisions about technology, organizational structure, and human resources were treated as if they were unrelated. An organization might acquire a new information system, restructure jobs, or add an office in another country without considering the impact on its people.[4] More recently, managers have realized that success depends on how well all the elements work together. For instance, as health care providers feel increasing pressure to rein in costs, some are finding solutions in combinations of information technology, improved staffing, and the redesign of work processes. A Louisiana hospital chain began running a software system to analyze and fill staffing needs. Employees use the system to bid for the hours they want to work, and the system automatically assigns them to shifts, filling any empty positions with contract workers. Automating the staffing process saves money and frees managers from hours of paperwork each week. A health care chain based in Denver took technology use a step further with an enterprise resource planning system that links together decisions about patient needs, staffing, finances, and purchases of supplies.

Elements of a High-Performance Work System

As shown in Figure 16.1, in a high-performance work system, the elements that must work together include organizational structure, task design, people (the selection, training, and development of employees), reward systems, and information systems, and human resource management plays an important role in establishing all these.

Organizational structure is the way the organization groups its people into useful divisions, departments, and reporting relationships. The organization's top management makes most decisions about structure, for instance, how many employees report to each supervisor and whether employees are grouped according to the functions they carry out or the customers they serve. Such decisions affect how well

Figure 16.1

Elements of a High-Performance Work System

employees coordinate their activities and respond to change. In a high-performance work system, organizational structure promotes cooperation, learning, and continuous improvement.

Task design determines how the details of the organization's necessary activities will be grouped, whether into jobs or team responsibilities. In a high-performance work system, task design makes jobs efficient while encouraging high quality. In Chapter 4, we discussed how to carry out this HRM function through job analysis and job design.

The right *people* are a key element of high-performance work systems. HRM has a significant role in providing people who are well suited and well prepared for their jobs. Human resource personnel help the organization recruit and select people with the needed qualifications. Training, development, and career management ensure that these people are able to perform their current and future jobs with the organization.

Reward systems contribute to high performance by encouraging people to strive for objectives that support the organization's overall goals. Reward systems include the performance measures by which employees are judged, the methods of measuring performance, and the incentive pay and other rewards linked to success. Human resource management plays an important role in developing and administering reward systems, as we saw in Chapters 8 through 12.

The final element of high-performance work systems is the organization's *information systems*. Managers make decisions about the types of information to gather and the sources of information. They also must decide who in the organization should have access to the information and how they will make the information available. Modern information systems, including the Internet, have enabled organizations to share information widely. HR departments take advantage of this technology to give employees access to information about benefits, training opportunities, job openings, and more, as we will describe later in this chapter.

In a high-performance work system, all the elements—people, technology, and organizational structure—work together for success.

LO2 Summarize the outcomes of a high-performance work system.

Outcomes of a High-Performance Work System

Consider the practices of steel minimills in the United States. Some of these mills have strategies based on keeping their costs below competitors' costs; low costs let them operate at a profit while winning customers with low prices. Other steel minimills focus on "differentiation," meaning they set themselves apart in some way other than low price—for example, by offering higher quality or unusual product lines. Research has found that the minimills with cost-related goals tend to have highly centralized structures, so managers can focus on controlling through a tight line of command. These organizations have low employee participation in decisions, relatively low wages and benefits, and pay highly contingent on performance.[5] At minimills that focus on differentiation, structures are more complex and decentralized, so authority is more spread out. These minimills encourage employee participation and have higher wages and more generous benefits. They are high-performance work systems. In general, these differentiator mills enjoy higher productivity, lower scrap rates, and lower employee turnover than the mills that focus on low costs.

Outcomes of a high-performance work system thus include higher productivity and efficiency. These outcomes contribute to higher profits. A high-performance work system may have other outcomes, including high product quality, great customer satisfaction, and low employee turnover. Some of these outcomes meet intermediate goals that lead to higher profits (see Figure 16.2). For example, high quality contributes to customer satisfaction, and customer satisfaction contributes to growth of the business. Likewise, improving productivity lets the organization do more with less, which satisfies price-conscious customers and may help the organization win over customers from its competitors. Other ways to lower cost and improve quality are to

Figure 16.2

Outcomes of a High-Performance Work System

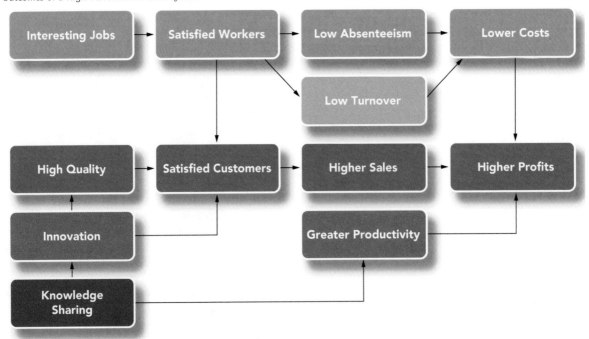

reduce absenteeism and turnover, providing the organization with a steady supply of experienced workers. In the previous example of minimills, some employers keep turnover and scrap rates low. Meeting those goals helps the minimills improve productivity, which helps them earn more profits.

In a high-performance work system, the outcomes of each employee and work group contribute to the system's overall high performance. The organization's individuals and groups work efficiently, provide high-quality goods and services, and so on, and in this way, they contribute to meeting the organization's goals. When the organization adds or changes goals, people are flexible and make changes as needed to meet the new goals.

Conditions That Contribute to High Performance

LO3 Describe the conditions that create a high-performance work system.

Certain conditions underlie the formation of a high-performance work system:[6]

- Teams perform work.
- Employees participate in selection.
- Employees receive formal performance feedback and are actively involved in the performance improvement process.
- Ongoing training is emphasized and rewarded.
- Employees' rewards and compensation relate to the company's financial performance.
- Equipment and work processes are structured, and technology is used to encourage maximum flexibility and interaction among employees.
- Employees participate in planning changes in equipment, layout, and work methods.
- Work design allows employees to use a variety of skills.
- Employees understand how their jobs contribute to the finished product or service.
- Ethical behavior is encouraged.

Practices involving rewards, employee empowerment, and jobs with variety contribute to high performance by giving employees skills, incentives, knowledge, autonomy—and satisfaction, another condition associated with high performance. Ethical behavior is a necessary condition of high performance because it contributes to good long-term relationships with employees, customers, and the public.

Teamwork and Empowerment

As we discussed in Chapter 2, today's organizations empower employees. They expect employees to make more decisions about how they perform their jobs. One of the most popular ways to empower employees is to design work so that it is performed by teams. On a work team, employees bring together various skills and experiences to produce goods or provide services. The organization may charge the team with making decisions traditionally made by managers, such as hiring team members and planning work schedules. Teamwork and empowerment contribute to high performance when they improve job satisfaction and give the organization fuller use of employees' ideas and expertise.

For empowerment to succeed, managers must serve in linking and coordinating roles[7] and provide the team with the resources it needs to carry out its work. The manager should help the team and its members interact with employees from other departments or teams and should make sure communication flows in both directions—the

It's important for companies to capture and share the knowledge of workers who have had years to learn their specialty.

manager keeps the team updated on important issues and ensures that the team shares information and resources with others who need them. At the Global Engineering Manufacturing Alliance (GEMA) plant in Dundee, Michigan, teamwork is designed to achieve the primary goal—to be the world's most productive engine plant. All employees, including the engineers, are either members or leaders of six-person teams. Groups of three employees work rotating shifts so that they know and work with one another around the clock. Team members are carefully selected to ensure they can handle the problem-solving responsibilities that GEMA has delegated to its teams. Technology such as large electronic display screens lets team members monitor productivity and delays, so they can identify when they are succeeding and when problems need to be resolved. All employees, not just managers or engineers, are empowered to solve problems. Employees who develop innovative solutions receive bonuses.[8]

Knowledge Sharing

Learning Organization
An organization that supports lifelong learning by enabling all employees to acquire and share knowledge.

For more than a decade, managers have been interested in creating a **learning organization,** that is, an organization in which the culture values and supports lifelong learning by enabling all employees to continually acquire and share knowledge. The people in a learning organization have resources for training, and they are encouraged to share their knowledge with colleagues. Managers take an active role in identifying training needs and encouraging the sharing of ideas.[9] An organization's information systems, discussed later in this chapter, have an important role in making this learning activity possible. Information systems capture knowledge and make it available even after individual employees who provided the knowledge have left the organization. Ultimately, people are the essential ingredients in a learning organization. They must be committed to learning and willing to share what they have learned.

A learning organization has several key features:[10]

Continuous Learning
Each employee's and each group's ongoing efforts to gather information and apply the information to their decisions in a learning organization.

- It engages in **continuous learning,** each employee's and each group's ongoing efforts to gather information and apply the information to their decisions. In many organizations, the process of continuous learning is aimed at improving quality. To engage in continuous learning, employees must understand the entire work system they participate in, the relationships among jobs, their work units, and the organization as a whole. Employees who continuously learn about their work system are adding to their ability to improve performance.
- Knowledge is *shared.* Therefore, to create a learning organization, one challenge is to shift the focus of training away from merely teaching skills and toward a broader focus on generating and sharing knowledge.[11] In this view, training is an investment in the organization's human resources; it increases employees' value to the organization. Also, training content should be related to the organization's goals. Human resource departments can support the creation of a learning organization by planning training programs that meet these criteria, and they can help to create both face-to-face and electronic systems for employee collaboration to create, capture, and share knowledge.
- *Critical, systematic thinking* is widespread. This occurs when organizations encourage employees to see relationships among ideas and to test assumptions and observe the results of their actions. Reward systems can be set up to encourage employees and teams to think in new ways.

- The organization has a *learning culture*—a culture in which learning is rewarded, promoted, and supported by managers and organizational objectives. This culture may be reflected in performance management systems and pay structures that reward employees for gathering and sharing more knowledge. A learning culture creates the conditions in which managers encourage *flexibility* and *experimentation*. The organization should encourage employees to take risks and innovate, which means it cannot be quick to punish ideas that do not work out as intended.
- *Employees are valued.* The organization recognizes that employees are the source of its knowledge. It therefore focuses on ensuring the development and well-being of each employee.

The experience of Lopez Foods shows that the qualities of a learning organization aren't limited just to high-tech industries. Lopez Foods, which makes beef and sausage patties, involved employees in making production more efficient. Working with consultants, Lopez managers and engineers diagrammed production processes on huge sheets of brown paper hung on the walls. They made sticky notes available so that any worker passing by could post notes correcting the information or making suggestions based on their day-to-day experience on the front lines. Not only did the practice improve the quality of information, but it also engaged workers in the improvement process so that they remain committed to making suggestions and helping their company become more efficient. The company also improved the communication of performance feedback, now posting hourly performance indicators, and it pays production workers modest but regular bonuses for exceeding productivity targets.[12]

Job Satisfaction

A condition underpinning any high-performance organization is that employees experience job satisfaction—they experience their jobs as fulfilling or allowing them to fulfill important values. Research supports the idea that employees' job satisfaction and job performance are related.[13] Higher performance at the individual level should contribute to higher performance for the organization as a whole. A study by CLC Genesee, an HR consulting firm, found that companies with a high level of employee engagement (which includes satisfaction with their jobs and the company) saw their revenues grow more than twice as fast as their competitors as well as profit growth three times higher.[14] The relationship between satisfaction and performance also relates to nonprofit and government organizations. In a survey by the Partnership for Public Service and American University, the Nuclear Regulatory Commission and Government Accountability Office showed the highest degrees of employee satisfaction, as the "Did You Know?" box shows. They far outranked the bottom agencies, the National Archives and Records Administration (56.0) and Department of Transportation (52.2).[15] How would you expect these differences to play out in terms of the agencies' effectiveness?

Chapter 10 described a number of ways organizations can promote job satisfaction. They include making jobs more interesting, setting clear and challenging goals, and providing valued rewards that are linked to performance in a performance management system that employees consider fair. For example, the Nuclear Regulatory Commission's top agency score for employee satisfaction is based partly on relatively high ratings for fair leadership, empowerment of employees by leaders, and rewards linked to performance. NRC employees also scored the agency very high on teamwork and matching employee skills to the agency's mission.[16]

Did You Know?

Satisfaction at Top Government Agencies Compares Favorably with Big Businesses

Federal government employees who rated their satisfaction with their job and work environment were most satisfied at the Nuclear Regulatory Commission. Employees in the highest-ranking agencies are at least as satisfied as the employees in large companies. On average, government employees are more satisfied with cooperation among co-workers and opportunities to improve skills, while private-sector employees are more satisfied with training, opportunities for advancement, and information sharing by management. The government has been improving in the past few years, but businesses have been improving faster.

Sources: Partnership for Public Service, "Welcome to the 2009 Best Places to Work Rankings," Best Places to Work, http://data.bestplacestowork.org, accessed May 12, 2010; and Partnership for Public Service, "Private Sector Comparison," Best Places to Work, http://bestplacestowork.org, accessed May 12, 2010.

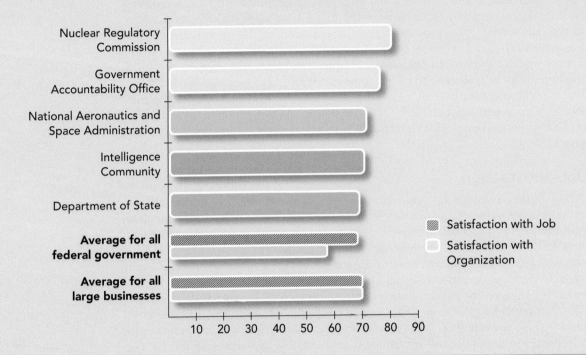

Some organizations are moving beyond concern with mere job satisfaction and are trying to foster employees' *passion* for their work. Passionate people are fully engaged with something so that it becomes part of their sense of who they are. Feeling this way about one's work has been called *occupational intimacy*.[17] People experience occupational intimacy when they love their work, when they and their co-workers care about one another, and when they find their work meaningful. Human resource managers have a significant role in creating these conditions. For example, they can select people who care about their work and customers, provide methods for sharing knowledge, design work to make jobs interesting, and establish policies and programs that show concern for employees' needs. Such efforts may become increasingly important as the business world increasingly uses employee empowerment, teamwork, and knowledge sharing to build flexible organizations.[18]

Ethics

In the long run, a high-performance organization meets high ethical standards. Ethics, defined in Chapter 1, establishes fundamental principles for behavior, such as honesty and fairness. Organizations and their employees must meet these standards if they are to maintain positive long-term relationships with their customers and their community.

Ethical behavior is most likely to result from values held by the organization's leaders combined with systems that promote ethical behavior. As Todd Linden worked his way up through housekeeping and maintenance jobs and the study of health care management to become chief executive of Grinnell Medical Center, he developed values based on the importance of making a difference in people's lives. Linden's conviction that "a hospital exists to make a difference in people's lives . . . often at a very difficult time" ensured that when financial difficulty required cutbacks, the burden was shared, with leaders expected to take more furlough days than rank-and-file workers. Similarly, Judy Rich, CEO of Tucson Medical Center, draws on her nursing career to demonstrate the values of putting the patient first and always telling the truth. That conviction leads to a requirement that any discussion of patient care or hospital business be conducted openly, which helps keep everyone clear and aligned about the values driving the decisions.[19]

A number of organizational systems can promote ethical behavior.[20] These include a written code of ethics that the organization distributes to employees and expects them to use in decision making. This type of guidance can be especially effective if developed with input from employees about situations they encounter. However, standards alone are not enough—the organization should reinforce ethical behavior. For example, performance measures should include ethical standards, and misdeeds should receive swift discipline, as described in Chapter 10. The organization should provide channels employees can use to ask questions about ethical behavior or to seek help if they are expected to do something they believe is wrong. Organizations also can provide training in ethical decision making, including training for supervisors in how to handle employees' concerns about ethical matters.

As these examples suggest, ethical behavior is a human resource management concern. The systems that promote ethical behavior include such HRM functions as training, performance management, and discipline policies. A reputation for high ethical standards can also help a company attract workers—and customers— who share those high standards. Keller Bros. Auto is committed to living out the business philosophy of its founder, Terry Keller: "Teach, never sell." The Littleton, Colorado, repair shop expects its employees to do more than fix cars; they educate customers about what options they have, giving them all the facts they need to make intelligent decisions. An employee might take the time to show a customer a relevant Web site or send out digital photos illustrating the need for a repair. Maintaining these values begins with hiring for people skills, not just technical skills. Chief operating officer David Rogers says employees can be trained in fixing cars, "but no one can train you to care about people," so he hires only "highly educated, considerate human beings" who have "a natural desire to help other people." To find such employees, Rogers conducts three interviews and administers a personality test before making hiring decisions. It's an approach that car owners seem to welcome: hundreds of them bring their cars to Keller Bros. every month.[21]

focus on
social
responsibility

LO4 Explain how human resource management can contribute to high performance.

HRM's Contribution to High Performance

Management of human resources plays a critical role in determining companies' success in meeting the challenges of a rapidly changing, highly competitive environment.[22] Compensation, staffing, training and development, performance management, and other HRM practices are investments that directly affect employees' motivation and ability to provide products and services that are valued by customers. Table 16.1 lists examples of HRM practices that contribute to high performance.

Research suggests that it is more effective to improve HRM practices as a whole than to focus on one or two isolated practices, such as the organization's pay structure or selection system.[23] Also, to have the intended influence on performance, the HRM practices must fit well with one another and the organization as a whole.[24]

Job Design

For the organization to benefit from teamwork and employee empowerment, jobs must be designed appropriately. Often, a high-performance work system places employees in work teams where employees collaborate to make decisions and solve problems. Individual employees also may be empowered to serve on teams that design jobs and work processes.

Job design emphasizing teamwork and empowerment is a fundamental piece of improving performance at nursing homes such as Mercy Nursing Facility and Beechwood Continuing Care, located near Buffalo, New York. Applying a philosophy known as "culture change," these nursing homes are moving toward giving residents more choices and personal attention in a homier atmosphere. Delivering this type of care requires less rigid job descriptions than have developed in the highly regulated nursing home industry. Mercy, Beechwood, and other facilities adopting culture change have structured work into teams of employees who are given greater flexibility and authority for how they carry out their jobs. Aides are assigned to groups of residents, rather than to a few specialized duties, so they can develop caring relationships with the residents.[25]

Recruitment and Selection

At a high-performance organization, recruitment and selection aim at obtaining the kinds of employees who can thrive in this type of setting. These employees are enthusiastic about and able to contribute to teamwork, empowerment, and knowledge sharing. Qualities such as creativity and ability to cooperate as part of a team

Table 16.1

HRM Practices That Can Help Organizations Achieve High Performance

- HRM practices match organization's goals.
- Individuals and groups share knowledge.
- Work is performed by teams.
- Organization encourages continuous learning.
- Work design permits flexibility in where and when tasks are performed.
- Selection system is job related and legal.
- Performance management system measures customer satisfaction and quality.
- Organization monitors employees' satisfaction.
- Discipline system is progressive.
- Pay systems reward skills and accomplishments.
- Skills and values of a diverse workforce are valued and used.
- Technology reduces time and costs of tasks while preserving quality.

may play a large role in selection decisions. High-performance organizations need selection methods that identify more than technical skills like ability to perform accounting and engineering tasks. Employers may use group interviews, open-ended questions, and psychological tests to find employees who innovate, share ideas, and take initiative.

Training and Development

When organizations base hiring decisions on qualities like decision-making and team-work skills, training may be required to teach employees the specific skills they need to perform the duties of their job. Extensive training and development also are part of a learning organization, described earlier in this chapter. And when organizations delegate many decisions to work teams, the members of those teams likely will benefit from participating in team development activities that prepare them for their roles as team members.

Training programs at Whirlpool have been aligned with the company's commitment to innovation. After the company defined the role innovation would play in the company's strategy, it trained 75 employees to be "Masters of Innovation"—experts in the qualities and processes that enable new ideas to contribute to Whirlpool's success. The Masters of Innovation are charged with training the rest of Whirlpool's employees to be innovative. Their lessons are supplemented by online and classroom training programs in innovation skills such as tapping into new resources and thinking about projects from various points of view. Employee development also focuses on knowledge sharing. Project teams complete five-question surveys that identify team members' networks of professional contacts. The results help the teams develop action plans for using their networks to come up with more creative and successful ideas.[26]

Performance Management

In a high-performance organization, employees know the organization's goals and what they must do to help achieve those goals. HR departments can contribute to this ideal through the design of the organization's performance management system. As we discussed in Chapter 8, performance management should be related to the organization's goals. Flagstar Bank, based in Troy, Michigan, develops goals for branch managers by using analytical software from Pitney Bowes. Pitney Bowes uses data about households in each branch's geographic area and comparative data about other bank branches, combined with Flagstar's customer data, to predict what each branch can achieve in terms of types of products sold, average balances in bank accounts, growth in the number of customers, and so on. The bank then sets goals that are achievable for the branch, given economic conditions and the needs of the clients in its area. This gets employees in the branches focused on the best opportunities available to them. Branch managers can see the criteria used to set their goals, so they are motivated by the fairness of the system.[27]

To set up a performance management system that supports the organization's goals, managers need to understand the process of employee performance. As shown in Figure 16.3, individual employees bring a set of skills and abilities to the job, and by applying a set of behaviors, they use those skills to achieve certain results. But success is more than the product of individual efforts. The organization's goals should influence each step of the process. The organization's culture and other factors influence

Figure 16.3

Employee Performance
as a Process

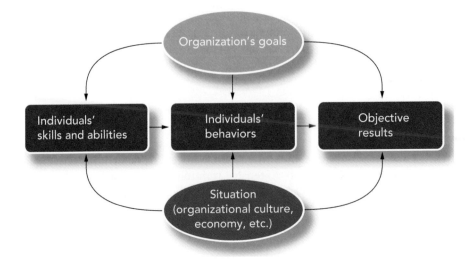

the employees' abilities, behaviors, and results. It mustn't be forgotten that sometimes uncontrollable forces such as the current economic conditions enter the picture—for example, a salesperson can probably sell more during an economic expansion than during an economic slowdown.

This model suggests some guidelines for performance management. First, each aspect of performance management should be related to the organization's goals. Business goals should influence the kinds of employees selected and their training, the requirements of each job, and the measures used for evaluating results. Generally, this means the organization identifies what each department must do to achieve

To develop future leaders, new IBM managers participate in IBM's Basic Blue program for an intensive nine-month training program. IBM is considered one of the best companies in the development of future leaders.

SETTING PERFORMANCE MEASURES IN NOT-FOR-PROFIT ORGANIZATIONS

In a business, profitability and the company's stock price provide some obvious measures of success. A nonprofit organization needs to apply and adapt some more creative measures of success.

- Performance measures for individuals and groups in the organization should support the achievement of the organization's mission. The mission is more than the products and services provided; it extends to the desired outcomes of those products and services—say, visiting a health clinic or participating in a tutoring program. These outcomes, in turn, should be associated with an impact on society, such as a reduction in the prevalence of a disease or the increase in the proportion of high school students who graduate.
- Financial measures, such as a cost reduction or improvement in efficiency, are important. However, they should be related to the organization's ability to fulfill its mission—for example, because they are needed for acquiring resources or carrying out activities associated with the desired outcomes and impact on society.
- When possible, measures should be expressed in monetary units (dollars in the United States). For example, if the organization places unemployed people in jobs, it can measure the decrease in public assistance paid by the government. Dollar measurements of success are useful because they can be tracked over time and clearly communicated to donors and other stakeholders.
- Other measurements can be expressed as percentages, such as the percent of the target population who participate in a program or the percent of participants who report achieving an organizational goal, such as earning a professional designation or discontinuing use of drugs or alcohol.

Source: Based on Marc J. Epstein and Adriana Rejc Buhovac, "Improving Performance Measurement: Not-for-Profit Organizations," *CMA Management,* November 2009, pp. 16–21.

---

the desired results, then defines how individual employees should contribute to their department's goals. More specifically, the following guidelines describe how to make the performance management system support organizational goals:[28]

- *Define and measure performance in precise terms*—Focus on outcomes that can be defined in terms of how frequently certain behaviors occur. Include criteria that describe ways employees can add value to a product or service (such as through quantity, quality, or timeliness). Include behaviors that go beyond the minimum required to perform a job (such as helping co-workers).
- *Link performance measures to meeting customer needs*—"Customers" may be the organization's external customers, or they may be internal customers (employees receiving services from a co-worker). Service goals for internal customers should be related to satisfying external customers.
- *Measure and correct for the effect of situational constraints*—Monitor economic conditions, the organization's culture, and other influences on performance. Measures of employees' performance should take these influences into account.

This approach gives employees the information they need to behave in ways that contribute to high performance. In addition, organizations should help employees identify and obtain the abilities they need to meet their performance goals. The "HR How To" box provides additional guidelines for performance management in nonprofit organizations.

Compensation

Organizations can reinforce the impact of this kind of performance management by linking compensation in part to performance measures. Chapter 12 described a number of methods for doing this, including merit pay, gainsharing, and profit sharing. Lincoln Electric has for decades paid its production workers a piecework rate. Not only does this motivate individual employees to look for the most efficient ways to do their jobs, but because the company is known for this compensation method, it attracts workers who value working hard in order to earn more. In addition, Lincoln has been paying all of its employees a profit-sharing bonus "every year since 1934," in the words of Lincoln's CEO John M. Stropki Jr.[29] Compensation systems also can help to create the conditions that contribute to high performance, including teamwork, empowerment, and job satisfaction. For example, as discussed in Chapter 12, compensation can be linked to achievement of team objectives.

Organizations can increase empowerment and job satisfaction by including employees in decisions about compensation and by communicating the basis for decisions about pay. When the organization designs a pay structure, it can set up a task force that includes employees with direct experience in various types of jobs. Some organizations share financial information with their employees and invite them to recommend pay increases for themselves, based on their contributions. Employees also may participate in setting individual or group goals for which they can receive bonuses. Research has found that employee participation in decisions about pay policies is linked to greater satisfaction with the pay and the job.[30] And as we discussed in Chapter 11, when organizations explain their pay structures to employees, the communication can enhance employees' satisfaction and belief that the system is fair.

HRM Technology

LO5 Discuss the role of HRM technology in high-performance work systems.

Human resource departments can improve their own and their organization's performance by appropriately using new technology (see the "HR Oops!" box). New technology usually involves *automation and collaboration*—that is, using equipment and information processing to perform activities that had been performed by people and facilitating electronic communication between people. Over the last few decades, automation has improved HRM efficiency by reducing the number of people needed to perform routine tasks. Using automation can free HRM experts to concentrate on ways to determine how human resource management can help the organization meet its goals, so technology also can make this function more valuable.[31] For example, information technology provides ways to build and improve systems for knowledge generation and sharing, as part of a learning organization. Among the applications are databases or networking sites where employees can store and share their knowledge, online directories of employee skills and experiences, and online libraries of learning resources, such as technical manuals and employees' reports from seminars and training programs.

HRM Applications

As computers become ever more powerful, new technologies continue to be introduced. In fact, so many HRM applications are developed for use on personal computers that publications serving the profession (such as *HR Magazine* and *Workforce Management*) devote annual issues to reviewing this software. Some of the technologies that have been widely adopted are transaction processing, decision support systems, and expert systems.[32]

HR Oops!

Inflexible without Technology

We know that companies use performance management systems because they want employees to do the things that will help their company succeed. And we know that the business environment is constantly changing, so companies need to be flexible in terms of their strategies and objectives. So logically, performance management systems should be flexible, too, adjusting goals as economic, social, competitive, and technological forces introduce risks and open up opportunities.

That may be logical, but according to a recent survey, it isn't what companies are actually doing. The Human Capital Institute recently found that 66 percent of midsized companies said their performance management system isn't set up to adjust goals; rather, employees see performance appraisals and get new goals once or twice a year.

Constant adjusting of goals could be complicated and confusing, but HRM technology exists to make flexibility part of the system. For example, Workscape Performance Manager is a Web-based HR application in which employees and their managers enter goals as the system prompts them through the process. Then employees log into the system to see a list of their goals, indicating the priorities, progress, and deadline for each, along with planned development activities and tasks related to performance appraisal. Users of the system can look up and alter details of the plans and their progress at any time.

Sources: "Aligning Employee Performance with Organizational Goals," *Financial Executive*, November 2009, p. 13; and Workscape, "Workscape Performance Manager," data sheet, www.workscape.com, accessed May 11, 2010.

Questions

1. What would hold back an employer from using HRM technology that was likely to improve performance? Which of these obstacles, if any, are reasonable barriers to using HRM technology, and which should HR managers try to overcome?

2. Suppose you are an HR manager who wants to encourage your organization to begin using Workscape Performance Manager or a similar system. How would you measure whether this system is a wise investment for your organization?

Transaction processing refers to computations and calculations involved in reviewing and documenting HRM decisions and practices. It includes documenting decisions and actions associated with employee relocation, training expenses, and enrollments in courses and benefit plans. Transaction processing also includes the activities required to meet government reporting requirements, such as filling out EEO-1 reports, on which employers report information about employees' race and gender by job category. Computers enable companies to perform these tasks more efficiently. Employers can fill out computerized forms and store HRM information in databases (data stored electronically in user-specified categories), so that it is easier to find, sort, and report.

Decision support systems are computer software systems designed to help managers solve problems. They usually include a "what if?" feature that managers can use to enter different assumptions or data and see how the likely outcomes will change. This type of system can help managers make decisions for human resource planning. The manager can, for example, try out different assumptions about turnover rates to see how those assumptions affect the number of new employees needed. Or the manager can test a range of assumptions about the availability of a certain skill in the labor market, looking at the impact of the assumptions on the success

Transaction Processing
Computations and calculations involved in reviewing and documenting HRM decisions and practices.

Decision Support Systems
Computer software systems designed to help managers solve problems by showing how results vary when the manager alters assumptions or data.

of different recruiting plans. Possible applications for a decision support system include forecasting (discussed in Chapter 5) and succession planning (discussed in Chapter 9).

Expert Systems
Computer systems that support decision making by incorporating the decision rules used by people who are considered to have expertise in a certain area.

Expert systems are computer systems that incorporate the decision rules used by people who are considered to have expertise in a certain area. The systems help users make decisions by recommending actions based on the decision rules and the information provided by the users. An expert system is designed to recommend the same actions that a human expert would in a similar situation. For example, an expert system could guide an interviewer during the selection process. Some organizations use expert systems to help employees decide how to allocate their money for benefits (as in a cafeteria plan) and help managers schedule the labor needed to complete projects. Expert systems can deliver both high quality and lower costs. By using the decision processes of experts, an expert system helps many people to arrive at decisions that reflect the expert's knowledge. An expert system helps avoid the errors that can result from fatigue and decision-making biases, such as biases in appraising employee performance, described in Chapter 8. An expert system can increase efficiency by enabling fewer or less-skilled employees to do work that otherwise would require many highly skilled employees.

In modern HR departments, transaction processing, decision support systems, and expert systems often are part of a human resource information system. Also, these technologies may be linked to employees through a network such as an intranet. Information systems and networks have been evolving rapidly; the following descriptions provide a basic introduction.

Human Resource Information Systems

A standard feature of a modern HRIS is the use of *relational databases*, which store data in separate files that can be linked by common elements. These common elements are fields identifying the type of data. Commonly used fields for an HR database include name, Social Security number, job status (full- or part-time), hiring date, position, title, rate of pay, citizenship status, job history, job location, mailing address, birth date, and emergency contacts. A relational database lets a user sort the data by any of the fields. For example, depending on how the database is set up, the user might be able to look up tables listing employees by location, rates of pay for various jobs, or employees who have completed certain training courses. This system is far more sophisticated than the old-fashioned method of filing employee data by name, with one file per employee.

The ability to locate and combine many categories of data has a multitude of uses in human resource management. Databases have been developed to track employee benefit costs, training courses, and compensation. The system can meet the needs of line managers as well as the HR department. On an oil rig, for example, management might look up data listing employee names along with safety equipment issued and appropriate skill certification. HR managers at headquarters might look up data on the same employees to gather information about wage rates or training programs needed. Another popular use of an HRIS is applicant tracking, or maintaining and retrieving records of job applicants. This is much faster and easier than trying to sort through stacks of résumés. With relational databases, HR staff can retrieve information about specific applicants or obtain lists of applicants with specific skills, career goals, work history, and employment background. Such information is useful for HR planning, recruitment, succession planning, and career development. Taking the process a step further, the system could store information related to hiring and terminations. By analyzing such data, the HR department could measure the long-term success of its recruiting and selection processes.

One of the most creative developments in HRIS technology is the **HR dashboard,** a display of a series of HR-related indicators, or measures, showing human resource goals and objectives and the progress toward meeting them. Managers with access to the HRIS can look at the HR dashboard for an easy-to-scan review of HR performance. For example, at Cisco Systems, employee development is a priority, so its HR dashboard includes a measure that tracks how many employees move and why.[33] By looking for divisions in which many employees make many lateral and upward moves, Cisco can identify divisions that are actively developing new talent.

HR Dashboard
A display of a series of HR measures, showing human resource goals and objectives and progress toward meeting them.

Human Resource Management Online: E-HRM

During the last decade or so, organizations have seen the advantages of sharing information in computer networks. At the same time, the widespread adoption of the Internet has linked people around the globe. As we discussed in Chapter 2, more and more organizations are engaging in e-HRM, providing HR-related information over the Internet. Because much human resource information is confidential, organizations may do this with an intranet, which uses Internet technology but allows access only to authorized users (such as the organization's employees). For HR professionals, Internet access also offers a way to research new developments, post job openings, trade ideas with colleagues in other organizations, and obtain government documents. In this way, e-HRM combines company-specific information on a secure intranet with links to the resources on the broader Internet.

As Internet use has increasingly taken the form of so-called Web 2.0 applications, e-HRM has moved in this direction as well (see the "eHRM" box). Generally speaking, Web 2.0 refers to tools that bring networks of people together to collaborate on projects, solve problems, or socialize. For instance, IBM applied social networking tools to its mentoring program. Any IBM employee interested in offering advice or getting help can participate by filling out an online profile in a directory called BluePages. Then when they want a mentor, they use a search engine to find the person with the necessary expertise. The program brings together employees from around the world and gives them personal control over the mentoring process.[34]

A benefit of e-HRM is that employees can help themselves to the information they need when they need it, instead of contacting an HR staff person. For example, employees can go online to enroll in or select benefits, submit insurance claims, or fill out employee satisfaction surveys. This can be more convenient for the employees, as well as more economical for the HR department.

Most administrative and information-gathering activities in human resource management can be part of e-HRM. For example, online recruiting has become a significant part of the total recruiting effort, as candidates submit résumés online.

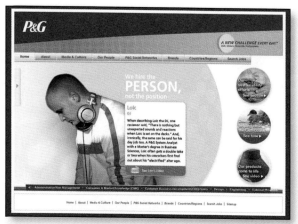

Online recruiting offers many benefits to the company and the potential employee. Companies are able to easily post job openings and retrieve résumés, while potential employees can research the company and submit their résumés. Procter & Gamble's Careers Web site incorporates Web 2.0 features such as links to P&G social networks, video clips of employee profiles, and a job search application with a choice of languages and countries.

WEB 2.0 FOR HUMAN RESOURCE MANAGEMENT

Many people had their introduction to Web 2.0 in their personal lives, posting and interacting with content on YouTube, MySpace, Facebook, Flickr, and Wikipedia. Other ways to use Web 2.0 include participating in discussion forums, playing virtual-reality games, and signing up for online newsfeeds. It hasn't taken long for HR professionals and other managers to see that Web 2.0 can bring together employees as effectively as it brings together people with other shared interests.

Web 2.0 can apply to any HR function that involves human interaction and collaboration, especially across many miles or when large numbers of people are involved. For example, networking tools can be useful for mentoring programs and for internal or external recruiting. Knowledge sharing today also generally involves Web 2.0 applications. Training programs might make a variety of downloadable options available online, and participants can be encouraged to sign into the company's training Web site to discuss what they are learning. Online registration for benefits can add a Web 2.0 component such as a button to click to chat with an HR representative.

Besides using Web 2.0 for its own functions, the role of human resource management may include helping the organization's top managers figure out the human dimensions of using these applications. Management may be rightly concerned that access to Web 2.0 tools at work will make information so widely available that there is a risk of breaching confidentiality. Internet users also sometimes (intentionally or unintentionally) spread rumors, errors, or offensive remarks that could hurt employees' effectiveness or the company's reputation. HR specialists therefore need to collaborate with IT specialists to ensure that security systems are in place to protect confidentiality where appropriate. They also should be involved in developing and communicating policies for appropriate use of the Internet by the company's employees.

IBM, for example, has published a policy describing appropriate online behavior for its employees when they are using blogs, wikis, social networks, virtual worlds, and social media. The guidelines acknowledge that the company's computer-savvy employees are going to be online, and it describes how to do so responsibly and professionally. Other employers should prepare, too, because whether or not they do, their employees are going to be online.

Source: Based on Anne Pauker Kreitzberg, "Building a Web 2.0–Friendly Culture," *People & Strategy,* June 2009, pp. 40–45.

Employers go online to retrieve suitable résumés from job search sites or retrieve information from forms they post at their own Web sites. For selection decisions, the organization may have candidates use one of the online testing services available; these services conduct the tests, process the results, and submit reports to employers. Aspects of job design can be automated; at United Parcel Service, for example, a software system maps out each day's route for drivers to minimize wasted time and gasoline.[35] Online appraisal systems can help managers make pay decisions consistent with company policies and employee performance. Many types of training can be conducted online, as we discussed in Chapter 7. Employees at Capital One can download podcasts of training modules in the financial service company's audio learning program.[36] Online surveys of employee satisfaction can be quick and easy to fill out. Besides providing a way to administer the survey, an intranet is an effective vehicle for communicating the results of the survey and management's planned response.

Not only does e-HRM provide efficient ways to carry out human resource functions, it also poses new challenges to employees and new issues for HR managers to address. The Internet's ability to link people anytime, anywhere has accelerated such trends as globalization, the importance of knowledge sharing within organizations, and the need for flexibility. These trends, in turn, change the work environment for employees. For example, employees in the Internet age are expected to be highly committed but flexible, able to move from job to job. Employees also may be connected to the organization 24/7. In the car, on vacation, in airports, and even in the bathroom, employees with handheld computers can be interrupted by work demands. Organizations depend on their human resource departments to help prepare employees for this changing work world through such activities as training, career development, performance management, and benefits packages that meet the need for flexibility and help employees manage stress.

Effectiveness of Human Resource Management

In recent years, human resource management at some organizations has responded to the quest for total quality management by taking a customer-oriented approach. For an organization's human resource division, "customers" are the organization as a whole and its other divisions. They are customers of HRM because they depend on HRM to provide a variety of services that result in a supply of talented, motivated employees. Taking this customer-oriented approach, human resource management defines its customer groups, customer needs, and the activities required to meet those needs, as shown in Table 16.2. These definitions give an organization a basis for defining goals and measures of success.

Depending on the situation, a number of techniques are available for measuring HRM's effectiveness in meeting its customers' needs. These techniques include reviewing a set of key indicators, measuring the outcomes of specific HRM activity, and measuring the economic value of HRM programs.

LO6 Summarize ways to measure the effectiveness of human resource management.

Human Resource Management Audits

An **HRM audit** is a formal review of the outcomes of HRM functions. To conduct the audit, the HR department identifies key functions and the key measures of business performance and customer satisfaction that would indicate each function is succeeding. Table 16.3 lists examples of these measures for a variety of HRM functions: staffing, compensation, benefits, training, appraisal and development, and overall effectiveness. The audit may also look at any other measure associated with successful management of human resources—for instance, compliance with equal employment opportunity laws, succession planning, maintaining a safe workplace, and positive labor relations. An HRM audit using customer satisfaction measures supports the customer-oriented approach to human resource management.

After identifying performance measures for the HRM audit, the staff carries out the audit by gathering information. The information for the key business indicators is

HRM Audit
A formal review of the outcomes of HRM functions, based on identifying key HRM functions and measures of business performance.

WHO ARE OUR CUSTOMERS?	WHAT DO OUR CUSTOMERS NEED?	HOW DO WE MEET CUSTOMER NEEDS?
Line managers	Committed employees	Qualified staffing
Strategic planners	Competent employees	Performance management
Employees		Rewards
		Training and development

Table 16.2

Customer-Oriented Perspective of Human Resource Management

Table 16.3

Key Measures of Success for an HRM Audit

BUSINESS INDICATORS	CUSTOMER SATISFACTION MEASURES
Staffing Average days taken to fill open requisitions Ratio of acceptances to offers made Ratio of minority/women applicants to representation in local labor market Per capita requirement costs Average years of experience/education of hires per job family	Anticipation of personnel needs Timeliness of referring qualified workers to line supervisors Treatment of applicants Skill in handling terminations Adaptability to changing labor market conditions
Compensation Per capita (average) merit increases Ratio of recommendations for reclassification to number of employees Percentage of overtime hours to straight time Ratio of average salary offers to average salary in community	Fairness of existing job evaluation system in assigning grades and salaries Competitiveness in local labor market Relationship between pay and performance Employee satisfaction with pay
Benefits Average unemployment compensation payment (UCP) Average workers' compensation payment (WCP) Benefit cost per payroll dollar Percentage of sick leave to total pay	Promptness in handling claims Fairness and consistency in the application of benefit policies Communication of benefits to employees Assistance provided to line managers in reducing potential for unnecessary claims
Training Percentage of employees participating in training programs per job family Percentage of employees receiving tuition refunds Training dollars per employee	Extent to which training programs meet the needs of employees and the company Communication to employees about available training opportunities Quality of introduction/orientation programs
Employee appraisal and development Distribution of performance appraisal ratings Appropriate psychometric properties of appraisal forms	Assistance in identifying management potential Organizational development activities provided by HRM department
Overall effectiveness Ratio of personnel staff to employee population Turnover rate Absenteeism rate Ratio of per capita revenues to per capita cost Net income per employee	Accuracy and clarity of information provided to managers and employees Competence and expertise of staff Working relationship between organizations and HRM department

SOURCE: Excerpted with permission, Chapter 1.5, "Evaluating Human Resource Effectiveness" (pp. 187–227) by Anne S. Tsui and Luis R. Gomez-Mejia from *Human Resource Management: Evolving Roles & Responsibilities*, edited by Lee Dyer. Copyright © 1988 by The Bureau of National Affairs, Inc., Washington, DC. For copies of BNA Books publications call toll free 1-800-960-1200.

usually available in the organization's documents. Sometimes the HR department has to create new documents for gathering specific types of data. The usual way to measure customer satisfaction is to conduct surveys. Employee attitude surveys, discussed in Chapter 10, provide information about the satisfaction of these internal customers. Many organizations conduct surveys of top line executives to get a better view of how HRM practices affect the organization's business success. To benefit from the HR profession's best practices, companies also may invite external auditing teams to audit specific HR functions. For example, the European Foundation of Management Development has audited management training at Novartis, which markets health care products.[37] In the United States, the American Society for Training and Development conducts similar assessments.

Of course, the benefits of the audit are only as great as the company's response to what it learns. The "Best Practices" box describes how consulting and accounting firm PricewaterhouseCoopers applied what it learned from gathering data on employee engagement.

Analyzing the Effect of HRM Programs

Another way to measure HRM effectiveness is to analyze specific programs or activities. The analysis can measure a program's success in terms of whether it achieved its objectives and whether it delivered value in an economic sense. For example, if the organization sets up a training program, it should set up goals for that program, such as the training's effects on learning, behavior, and performance improvement (results). The analysis would then measure whether the training program achieved the preset goals. Novartis analyzes the quality of its training programs by assessing whether they meet particular goals, such as preparing managers to meet leadership standards. As soon as a training program ends, participants are asked to rate the experience. Several months later, the training department measures whether participants' performance improved or behavior changed. Overall employee evaluations of company leadership also are measured against the use of management training.[38]

The analysis can take an economic approach that measures the dollar value of the program's costs and benefits. Successful programs should deliver value that is greater than the programs' costs. Costs include employees' compensation as well as the costs to administer HRM programs such as training, employee development, or satisfaction surveys. Benefits could include a reduction in the costs associated with employee absenteeism and turnover, as well as improved productivity associated with better selection and training programs.

In general, HR departments should be able to improve their performance through some combination of greater efficiency and greater effectiveness. Greater efficiency means the HR department uses fewer and less-costly resources to perform its functions. Greater effectiveness means that what the HR department does—for example, selecting employees or setting up a performance management system—has a more beneficial effect on employees' and the organization's performance. Employee turnover is a measure that can relate to both efficiency and effectiveness if an organization is spending money on recruiting, selection, and training because it loses people with valuable experience. When Ray Lieber became vice president of human resources at Superior Energy Services, he zeroed in on turnover and, for each job category, measured the revenue Superior lost per employee who quit. He also computed the turnover rate for each job category. Superior's managers were surprised when Lieber showed them that the highest turnover rates were not semiskilled workers, as they

PRICEWATERHOUSECOOPERS APPLIES THE DATA

Essentially, what Pricewaterhous-eCoopers (PwC) offers its clients is great people: experts at accounting and business management. But several years ago, following the merger of Price Waterhouse and Coopers & Lybrand, the firm's own employee turnover was appallingly high, costing the company tens of millions of dollars a year as it continually tried to replenish its ranks. The one path to promotion, a long road from hiring directly out of college and then positions as associate and senior manager, allowed only a select few to make it to partner. At each step of the way, turnover rates increased. Those who stayed on with the firm had to scramble to keep up with their workloads because team members kept quitting.

PwC's leaders decided the firm simply had to change. Twice-yearly surveys of employees provided a good starting point, but they showed only that employees were dissatisfied, not the root causes of the dissatisfaction. To learn more, the HR department hired the University of Southern California's Center for Effective Organizations to conduct an in-depth study of employee attitudes.

The center's study showed that only one out of five newly hired employees planned to make a long-term career at PwC. To develop commitment, employees were looking for a chance to do challenging work and develop their skills so they could advance in their careers. The compensation of their current jobs was less important than what they hoped to earn as their career progressed. And the main predictors of an employee leaving the firm were negative opinions of work/life balance, pay, and job satisfaction.

The information gave the firm ideas about where to improve as well as baseline data for measuring improvement. PwC applied the results to develop a strategy it called Unique People Experience. Under this strategy, the firm trained its partners in how to build stronger relations with staff, provide useful and timely feedback, and strengthen teamwork. Each office of the firm created an action plan targeting the main problems at that office. In one California office, employees were frustrated by a lack of performance feedback, so this office began scheduling regular meetings to discuss

progress. Partners were also assigned to employees for whom they were expected to provide coaching. Another practice reorganized work into "market teams." Each market team brings together a variety of functions to serve the clients in a particular market. As a result, the participants feel a greater sense of community with one another and a belief that what they do matters.

Throughout the process, HR professionals visited client sites, taught skills in coaching and delivering performance feedback, and helped managers develop employees through their assignments to engagements. Within a few years, PwC was seeing dramatic improvements. Turnover fell from far above to far below the industry average, and employee satisfaction has been rising every year.

Source: Based on Michael J. Fenlon and Susan Albers Mohrman, "Where Counting Counts," *HR Magazine,* January 2010, pp. 31–35.

had assumed, but skilled operators and supervisors. They gave him the go-ahead to develop a statistical model to predict which activities would have the greatest impact on turnover. Lieber learned that he could significantly lower turnover—and hence improve revenues and lower costs—by providing more coaching and training.[39]

HRM's potential to affect employees' well-being and the organization's performance makes human resource management an exciting field. As we have shown throughout the book, every HRM function calls for decisions that have the potential to help individuals and organizations achieve their goals. For HR managers to fulfill that potential, they must ensure that their decisions are well grounded. The field of human resource management provides tremendous opportunity to future researchers and managers who want to make a difference in many people's lives.

thinking ethically

CAN HRM MAKE ORGANIZATIONS MORE ETHICAL?

Ed Gubman, executive editor of *People & Strategy*, once received a proposed article from writers describing how their company had improved performance and leadership by using social networking applications. It was an inspiring story, except that it came from one of the financial institutions blamed for questionable practices leading to the recent near-meltdown of the financial services industry. Gubman was left to ponder what kind of "leadership" had resulted from the HR effort. Did the HR staff think it was fine to enable the company to become proficient at unethical conduct, or did they not understand what major parts of their company were doing?

The answers to these questions relate to the extent of HR professionals' knowledge and influence. The tools are available to provide an unprecedented level of guidance in how the company's HR practices affect business outcomes. If HRM is to promote ethical conduct, its practitioners must understand what their organization does, be committed to using goals and policies that reinforce ethical conduct, and be able to advocate for this effort. In practice—perhaps because

of the *human* focus of human resource management— top executives seem happy to leave decisions about ethics up to this department. The obvious risk is that if the HR director is the only executive thinking about ethics, then ethics is unlikely to be a true strategic priority.

SOURCES: Ed Gubman, "Where Is HR?" *People & Strategy*, September 2009, p. 3; and Stefan Stern, "Resources Are Limited and HR Must Raise Its Game," *Financial Times*, February 17, 2009, Business & Company Resource Center, http://galenet.galegroup.com.

Questions

1. If HR managers are the only managers charged with ensuring ethical conduct, then how much impact can they have on their organization's ethical behavior? Who else in an organization might an HR executive persuade to be an ally in advocating for ethics to be on the agenda?
2. Suppose you are an HR executive meeting with the company's board of directors. You have been asked to draft a code of ethics for the company. Make a business case for why other leaders should join you in this effort.

SUMMARY

LO1   Define high-performance work systems, and identify the elements of such a system.

A high-performance work system is the right combination of people, technology, and organizational structure that makes full use of the organization's resources and opportunities in achieving its goals. The elements of a high-performance work system are organizational structure, task design, people, reward systems, and information systems. These elements must work together in a smoothly functioning whole.

LO2   Summarize the outcomes of a high-performance work system.

A high-performance work system achieves the organization's goals, typically including growth, productivity, and high profits. On the way to achieving these overall goals, the high-performance work system meets such intermediate goals as high quality, innovation, customer satisfaction, job satisfaction, and reduced absenteeism and turnover.

LO3   Describe the conditions that create a high-performance work system.

Many conditions contribute to high-performance work systems by giving employees skills, incentives, knowledge, autonomy, and employee satisfaction. Teamwork and empowerment can make work more satisfying and provide a means for employees to improve quality and productivity. Organizations can improve performance by creating a learning organization, in which people constantly learn and share knowledge so that they continually expand their capacity to achieve the results they desire. In a high-performance organization, employees experience job satisfaction or even "occupational intimacy." For long-run high performance, organizations and employees must be ethical as well.

LO4   Explain how human resource management can contribute to high performance.

Jobs should be designed to foster teamwork and employee empowerment. Recruitment and selection should focus on obtaining employees who have the qualities necessary for teamwork, empowerment, and knowledge sharing. When the organization selects for teamwork and decision-making skills, it may have to provide training in specific job tasks. Training also is important because of its role in creating a learning organization. The performance management system should be related to the organization's goals, with a focus on meeting internal and external customers' needs. Compensation should include links to performance, and employees should be included in decisions about compensation. Research suggests that it is more effective to improve HRM practices as a whole than to focus on one or two isolated practices.

LO5 Discuss the role of HRM technology in high-performance work systems.

Technology can improve the efficiency of the human resource management functions and support knowledge sharing. HRM applications involve transaction processing, decision support systems, and expert systems, often as part of a human resource information system using relational databases, which can improve the efficiency of routine tasks and the quality of decisions. With Internet technology, organizations can use e-HRM to let all the organization's employees help themselves to the HR information they need whenever they need it.

LO6 Summarize ways to measure the effectiveness of human resource management.

Taking a customer-oriented approach, HRM can improve quality by defining the internal customers who use its services and determining whether it is meeting those customers' needs. One way to do this is with an HRM audit, a formal review of the outcomes of HRM functions. The audit may look at any measure associated with successful management of human resources. Audit information may come from the organization's documents and surveys of customer satisfaction. Another way to measure HRM effectiveness is to analyze specific programs or activities. The analysis can measure success in terms of whether a program met its objectives and whether it delivered value in an economic sense, such as by leading to productivity improvements.

KEY TERMS

continuous learning p. 496
decision support systems p. 505
expert systems p. 506

high-performance work system p. 492
HR dashboard p. 507
HRM audit p. 509

learning organization p. 496
transaction processing p. 505

REVIEW AND DISCUSSION QUESTIONS

1. What is a high-performance work system? What are its elements? Which of these elements involve human resource management?
2. As it has become clear that HRM can help create and maintain high-performance work systems, it appears that organizations will need two kinds of human resource professionals. One kind focuses on identifying how HRM can contribute to high performance. The other kind develops expertise in particular HRM functions, such as how to administer a benefits program that complies with legal requirements. Which aspect of HRM is more interesting to you? Why?
3. How can teamwork, empowerment, knowledge sharing, and job satisfaction contribute to high performance?
4. If an organization can win customers, employees, or investors through deception, why would ethical behavior contribute to high performance?

5. How can an organization promote ethical behavior among its employees?
6. Summarize how each of the following HR functions can contribute to high performance.
   a. Job design
   b. Recruitment and selection
   c. Training and development
   d. Performance management
   e. Compensation
7. How can HRM technology make a human resource department more productive? How can technology improve the quality of HRM decisions?
8. Why should human resource departments measure their effectiveness? What are some ways they can go about measuring effectiveness?

BUSINESSWEEK CASE

BusinessWeek How MasterCard and Others Are Keeping Employees Creative

MasterCard [recently hosted] a Webcast of PowerPoint slides and short videos on various directions the company could take once the U.S. economy turns up again. The online presentations [featured] findings from seven members of an internal, international scenario-planning "task force," which has been gathering ideas for months from MasterCard employees at all levels around the world.

In the recent past, such a production would have been reserved for senior management. But this Webcast will be open to all 5,500 employees of the credit card giant, from fresh-faced interns up to its 58-year-old chief executive, Robert Selander. The aim: invite anyone with an idea for new products, services, or internal processes to speak up, and encourage staff members to "bring their best selves to work" during the downturn, says Rebecca Ray, senior vice-president of MasterCard's Global Talent Management and Development Department.

MasterCard's initiative takes a page from innovation exercises at technology companies such as IBM, whose annual online "innovation jams" have, since 2006, allowed employees at all levels to submit ideas online during a 90-hour, round-the-clock brainstorming session. But the mission seems more critical today as companies grapple with keeping employees creative and motivated when job and budget cuts, declining revenue, and losses dominate the headlines. (While holding up relatively well, MasterCard reported that first-quarter earnings fell 18 percent, to $367.3 million, as revenue dipped 2 percent, to $1.2 billion.)

"I have seen more nontech companies get into Webcasts for all employees. In fact, I see them not using Webcasts for senior leaders as much," says Prasad Kaipa, a former Apple research fellow and now an innovation coach for such companies as Cisco, Ford, and PepsiCo.

For instance, accounting and consulting firm Deloitte offered a Webcast of PowerPoint slides, live polls, and live conversation hosted by John Kao, author of *Innovation Nation* and head of Deloitte's Institute for Large Scale Innovation. The Webcast, planned as the inaugural in a series, was open to Deloitte staff at various levels, as well as outside registrants. More than 550 people logged on; outside participants came from Kaiser Permanente, Coca-Cola, and ExxonMobil, among others.

Webcasts are attractive for another reason these days: They cost much less than flying employees to big-think conferences, especially as prices of high-speed broadband decline and technical capabilities rise.

Some companies are finding other ways to exploit new media tools to spread ideas. At Walt Disney, Luis Fernandez, a senior vice-president at Disney Consumer Products, is encouraging staff members to e-mail short video clips they create to one another, to share experiences at industry trade shows, conventions, or even museums.

Called "zip clips" internally, these mini-productions are meant to inspire fellow employees who might not have the same research and conference travel budgets they had in the past, says Fernandez. He adds that the self-help program is a direct result of the recession. "I'd be lying if I told you we didn't have budget cuts," he says. "[But] we do not question the value of innovation, even in a recession."

The smartest companies will continue with such brainstorming projects after the recession runs it course. "Even when the economy recovers, these practices are a good strategy," says executive coach Kaipa. "That's because the more hope, vision, and imagination employees experience, the more they feel they have the power and freedom to innovate."

SOURCE: Excerpted from Reena Jana and Damian Joseph, "Keeping Employees Creative in a Downturn," *BusinessWeek*, July 22, 2009, www.businessweek.com.

Questions

1. How do the innovation ideas described here support the creation and maintenance of a high-performance work system? What element(s) of a high-performance work system (shown in Figure 16.1) do these efforts relate to?
2. Describe one or two areas in which human resource management has benefited from recent innovations. Why is it important for HR professionals to be innovative in their field?
3. How might an HR department be involved with using Webcasts to promote innovation? What would this effort contribute to HR or organizational performance?

Case: Preparing for an Uncertain Future

In human resource management, as in all business functions, one of the most daunting challenges is that decisions and plans must be made about the future, in spite of all the uncertainties. And recently, the future of employee benefits has entered a stage of enormous uncertainty, at least with regard to health insurance benefits. At the time Congress passed the Patient Protection and Affordable Care Act, this comprehensive law gave rise to a whole host of hopes and fears. By the time you study this case, some of these possibilities may seem far more—or less—certain, but consider the situation facing HR professionals as they wondered about the details of regulations still to be drafted by the Department of Health and Human Services, as well as business responses.

As we discussed in Chapter 13, health insurance is one of the most widely offered benefits, and it is highly valued by employees, although they often do not appreciate its full cost to employers. Favorable tax treatment of health coverage made it an attractive way for employers to increase employees' compensation packages without increasing their pay. However, the rapid growth of health costs has made this benefit very expensive. Many employers expect that some of the early provisions of health reform to take effect, such as the extension of coverage to employees' children up to age 26 and the requirement that insurers not place lifetime limits on care, will cause the price of health insurance to rise even faster, at least in the early years under the law.

Some large employers have investigated their options under the health reform law by comparing the cost of continuing health insurance benefits versus discontinuing the benefits and paying the penalties to be imposed on employers beginning in 2014. If large companies do not provide their employees with health insurance, these individuals would have the option to buy health care through exchanges run by the states. Many of them would be eligible for subsidies from the federal government, and to offset the subsidies, the employers would pay a fee. One company that considered this as an alternative was Verizon. Hewitt Resources prepared a research report for Verizon saying the penalties would be "modest when compared to the average cost of health care." Internal memos and e-mail at Verizon, Deere, and Caterpillar indicate that managers at all three companies predicted increasing costs for health benefits. Documents at Caterpillar and AT&T also weighed the cost differences between the costs of the penalty and the costs of health benefits.

Further complicating the issue is the 40 percent excise tax to be charged on health policies costing more than $8,500 for an individual or $23,000 for a family, beginning in 2018. Employers are uncertain whether they can require employees to pay the full tax. In addition, the change poses complications for companies that include health care as a provision in collective bargaining agreements with unions. Depending on how the tax is paid, the law will affect the attractiveness of this benefit from the union's and the employer's perspectives.

The situation is different for small employers, which generally don't offer the pricier "Cadillac" health plans subject to the excise tax. Many of them are eligible for government tax credits in exchange for providing health coverage.

In response to questions about the possibility it would drop health benefits, Caterpillar issued a statement saying that after "considerable time evaluating the impact of the potential legislation to the company," the company is continuing to evaluate the law "and awaiting regulatory guidance to ensure full compliance with the new law," so it has not made any decisions.

SOURCES: Shawn Tully, "Documents Reveal AT&T, Verizon, Others Thought about Dropping Employer-Sponsored Benefits," *Fortune*, May 6, 2010, http://money.cnn.com; Rebecca Vesely, "A Lot More Paperwork," *Modern Healthcare*, April 5, 2010, Business & Company Resource Center, http://galenet.galegroup.com; and Paul Gordon, "Cat Weighs Future of Health Coverage," *Journal Star (Peoria, Il.)*, May 7, 2010, Business & Company Resource Center, http://galenet.galegroup.com.

Questions

1. What role do employee benefits play in creating and maintaining a high-performance work system? How well do you think health insurance has played that role for large companies in the United States?

2. If large companies stop offering health insurance as an employee benefit, the total compensation package paid to the average employee would be much smaller. How, if at all, do you think employers should make up for that reduction? What would be the impact of your recommendation on employees? On the government and taxpayers?

3. Suppose you work for a large company that is considering dropping health insurance and paying the penalty instead. What is your recommendation in each of the following situations? What other situations might occur?
   a. Most other large companies maintain health insurance benefits.
   b. Most other large companies drop health insurance benefits.
   c. You expect the government will respond by raising the penalties.

🖶 IT'S A WRAP!   connect™

www.mhhe.com/noefund4e is your source for Reviewing, Applying, and Practicing the concepts you learned about in Chapter 16.

Review	Application	Practice

Review
- Chapter learning objectives
- Test Your Knowledge: Levels of Strategy

Application
- Manager's Hot Seat segment: "Change: More Pain than Gain?"
- Video case and quiz: "HR in Alignment"
- Self-Assessments: Your Career in HR
- Web exercise: High Performance Work Systems
- Small-business case: Employees Make a Difference at Amy's Ice Creams

Practice
- Chapter quiz

NOTES

1. S. Covel, "Tech Company Stems Departures by Listening to Employees' Needs," *Wall Street Journal*, January 24, 2008, http://online.wsj.com.
2. S. Snell and J. Dean, "Integrated Manufacturing and Human Resource Management: A Human Capital Perspective," *Academy of Management Journal* 35 (1992), pp. 467–504.
3. M. A. Huselid, "The Impact of Human Resource Management Practices on Turnover, Productivity, and Corporate Financial Performance," *Academy of Management Journal* 38 (1995), pp. 635–72; U.S. Department of Labor, *High-Performance Work Practices and Firm Performance* (Washington, DC: U.S. Government Printing Office, 1993); and J. Combs, Y. Liu, A. Hall, and D. Ketchen, "How Much Do High-Performance Work Practices Matter? A Meta-Analysis of Their Effects on Organizational Performance," *Personnel Psychology* 59 (2006), pp. 501–28.
4. R. N. Ashkenas, "Beyond the Fads: How Leaders Drive Change with Results," *Human Resource Planning* 17 (1994), pp. 25–44; Ronald M. Katz, "OPTimize Your Workforce," *HR Magazine*, October 2009, p. 85; and Jim Catalino, "Software Solutions Can Trim Rising Costs," *Health Management Technology*, March 2010, pp. 10–11.
5. J. Arthur, "The Link between Business Strategy and Industrial Relations Systems in American Steel Minimills," *Industrial and Labor Relations Review* 45 (1992), pp. 488–506.
6. J. A. Neal and C. L. Tromley, "From Incremental Change to Retrofit: Creating High-Performance Work Systems," *Academy of Management Executive* 9 (1995), pp. 42–54; and M. A. Huselid, "The

Impact of Human Resource Management Practices on Turnover, Productivity, and Corporate Financial Performance," *Academy of Management Journal* 38 (1995), pp. 635–72.
7. D. McCann and C. Margerison, "Managing High-Performance Teams," *Training and Development Journal*, November 1989, pp. 52–60.
8. J. Marquez, "Engine of Change," *Workforce Management*, July 17, 2006, pp. 20–30.
9. D. Senge, "The Learning Organization Made Plain and Simple," *Training and Development Journal*, October 1991, pp. 37–44.
10. M. A. Gephart, V. J. Marsick, M. E. Van Buren, and M. S. Spiro, "Learning Organizations Come Alive," *Training and Development* 50 (1996), pp. 34–45.
11. T. T. Baldwin, C. Danielson, and W. Wiggenhorn, "The Evolution of Learning Strategies in Organizations: From Employee Development to Business Redefinition," *Academy of Management Executive* 11 (1997), pp. 47–58; J. J. Martocchio and T. T. Baldwin, "The Evolution of Strategic Organizational Training," in *Research in Personnel and Human Resource Management* 15, ed. G. R. Ferris (Greenwich, CT: JAI Press, 1997), pp. 1–46; and "Leveraging HR and Knowledge Management in a Challenging Economy," *HR Magazine*, June 2009, pp. S1–S9.
12. A. Hanacek, "Star Power," *National Provisioner*, February 2008, downloaded from General Reference Center Gold, http://find.galegroup.com.
13. T. A. Judge, C. J. Thoresen, J. E. Bono, and G. K. Patton, "The Job Satisfaction-Job Performance Relationship: A Qualitative and Quantitative Review,"

Psychological Bulletin 127 (2001), pp. 376–407; and R. A. Katzell, D. E. Thompson, and R. A. Guzzo, "How Job Satisfaction and Job Performance Are and Are Not Linked," *Job Satisfaction*, eds. C. J. Cranny, P. C. Smith, and E. F. Stone (New York: Lexington Books, 1992), pp. 195–217.

14. Corporate Executive Board, "'Involve Your Employees,' Says Google, CEB," *BusinessWeek*, December 11, 2009, www.businessweek.com.

15. Partnership for Public Service, "Overall Index Scores for Employee Satisfaction and Commitment," Best Places to Work, http://data.bestplacestowork.org, accessed May 12, 2010.

16. Partnership for Public Service, "Scores and Rankings: Nuclear Regulatory Commission," Best Places to Work, http://data.bestplacestowork.org, accessed May 13, 2010.

17. P. E. Boverie and M. Kroth, *Transforming Work: The Five Keys to Achieving Trust, Commitment, and Passion in the Workplace* (Cambridge, MA: Perseus, 2001), pp. 71–72, 79.

18. R. P. Gephart Jr., "Introduction to the Brave New Workplace: Organizational Behavior in the Electronic Age," *Journal of Organizational Behavior* 23 (2002), pp. 327–44.

19. Lee Ann Runy, "Leaders and Values in Uncertain Times," *H&HN Hospitals & Health Networks*, October 2009, Business & Company Resource Center, http://galenet.galegroup.com.

20. Wayne F. Cascio and Peter Cappelli, "Lessons from the Financial Services Crisis," *HR Magazine*, January 2009, Business & Company Resource Center, http://galenet.galegroup.com; Chris Petersen, "Thou Shalt Not . . . ," *Construction Today*, September 2009, p. 13; and Carolyn Hirschman, "Giving Voice to Employee Concerns," *HR Magazine*, August 2008, pp. 51–53.

21. Mike Taylor, "Ethics in Business Award: Keller Bros. Auto," *Colorado Biz*, March 2009, p. 47; Mike Cote, "Being the Best in Uncertain Times," *Colorado Biz*, August 2009, Business & Company Resource Center, http://galenet.galegroup.com; and Larry Silvey, "Trust Your Customers," *Motor Age*, June 2009, Business & Company Resource Center, http://galenet.galegroup.com.

22. W. F. Cascio, *Costing Human Resources: The Financial Impact of Behavior in Organizations*, 3rd ed. (Boston: PWS-Kent, 1991); and Gergana Markova, "Can Human Resource Management Make a Big Difference in a Small Company?" *International Journal of Strategic Management* 9, no. 2 (2009), pp. 73–80.

23. B. Becker and M. A. Huselid, "High-Performance Work Systems and Firm Performance: A Synthesis of Research and Managerial Implications," in *Research in Personnel and Human Resource Management* 16, ed. G. R. Ferris (Stamford, CT: JAI Press, 1998), pp. 53–101.

24. B. Becker and B. Gerhart, "The Impact of Human Resource Management on Organizational Performance: Progress and Prospects," *Academy of Management Journal* 39 (1996), pp. 779–801.

25. Henry Davis, "Adding Value to Late Years," *Buffalo (N.Y.) News*, April 12, 2010, Business & Company Resource Center, http://galenet.galegroup.com.

26. Gail Dutton, "Innovation Acceleration," *Training*, January 15, 2010, Business & Company Resource Center, http://galenet.galegroup.com.

27. Anne Rawland Gabriel, "Goal Tending," *Bank Systems + Technology*, June 1, 2009, Business & Company Resource Center, http://galenet.galegroup.com; and Pitney Bowes Business Insight, "Services," www.pbinsight.com, accessed May 12, 2010.

28. H. J. Bernardin, C. M. Hagan, J. S. Kane, and P. Villanova, "Effective Performance Management: A Focus on Precision, Customers, and Situational Constraints," in *Performance Appraisal: State of the Art in Practice*, ed. J. W. Smither (San Francisco: Jossey-Bass, 1998), p. 56.

29. M. Lewis Jr., "The Heat Is On," *Inside Business*, October 2007, downloaded from General Reference Center Gold, http://find.galegroup.com.

30. L. R. Gomez-Mejia and D. B. Balkin, *Compensation, Organizational Strategy, and Firm Performance* (Cincinnati: South-Western, 1992); and G. D. Jenkins and E. E. Lawler III, "Impact of Employee Participation in Pay Plan Development," *Organizational Behavior and Human Performance* 28 (1981), pp. 111–28.

31. S. Shrivastava and J. Shaw, "Liberating HR through Technology," *Human Resource Management* 42, no. 3 (2003), pp. 201–17.

32. R. Broderick and J. W. Boudreau, "Human Resource Management, Information Technology, and the Competitive Edge," *Academy of Management Executive* 6 (1992), pp. 7–17.

33. N. Lockwood, *Maximizing Human Capital: Demonstrating HR Value with Key Performance Indicators* (Alexandria, VA: SHRM Research Quarterly, 2006).

34. Steve Hamm, "IBM Reinvents Mentoring, via the Web," *BusinessWeek*, March 12, 2009, www.businessweek.com.

35. D. Foust, "How Technology Delivers for UPS," *BusinessWeek*, March 5, 2007, p. 60.

36. "Outstanding Training Initiatives: Capital One, Audio Learning in Stereo," *Training*, March 2006, p. 64.

37. K. Whitney, "Novartis: Using Analytics to Enhance Leadership Training," *Chief Learning Officer*, March 2007, www.clomedia.com.

38. Ibid.

39. Bill Roberts, "Analyze This!" *HR Magazine*, October 2009, pp. 35–41.

Glossary

Achievement Tests: Tests that measure a person's existing knowledge and skills.

Action Learning: Training in which teams get an actual problem, work on solving it and commit to an action plan, and are accountable for carrying it out.

Adventure Learning: A teamwork and leadership training program based on the use of challenging, structured outdoor activities.

Affirmative Action: An organization's active effort to find opportunities to hire or promote people in a particular group.

Agency Shop: Union security arrangement that requires the payment of union dues but not union membership.

Alternative Dispute Resolution (ADR): Methods of solving a problem by bringing in an impartial outsider but not using the court system.

Alternative Work Arrangements: Methods of staffing other than the traditional hiring of full-time employees (for example, use of independent contractors, on-call workers, temporary workers, and contract company workers).

American Federation of Labor and Congress of Industrial Organizations (AFL-CIO): An association that seeks to advance the shared interests of its member unions at the national level.

Apprenticeship: A work-study training method that teaches job skills through a combination of on-the-job training and classroom training.

Aptitude Tests: Tests that assess how well a person can learn or acquire skills and abilities.

Arbitration: Conflict resolution procedure in which an arbitrator or arbitration board determines a binding settlement.

Assessment: Collecting information and providing feedback to employees about their behavior, communication style, or skills.

Assessment Center: A wide variety of specific selection programs that use multiple selection methods to rate applicants or job incumbents on their management potential.

Associate Union Membership: Alternative form of union membership in which members receive discounts on insurance and credit cards rather than representation in collective bargaining.

Avatars: Computer depictions of trainees, which the trainees manipulate in an online role-play.

Balanced Scorecard: A combination of performance measures directed toward the company's long- and short-term goals and used as the basis for awarding incentive pay.

Behavior Description Interview (BDI): A structured interview in which the interviewer asks the candidate to describe how he or she handled a type of situation in the past.

Behavioral Observation Scale (BOS): A variation of a BARS which uses all behaviors necessary for effective performance to rate performance at a task.

Behaviorally Anchored Rating Scale (BARS): Method of performance measurement that rates behavior in terms of a scale showing specific statements of behavior that describe different levels of performance.

Benchmarking: A procedure in which an organization compares its own practices against those of successful competitors.

Benchmarks: A measurement tool that gathers ratings of a manager's use of skills associated with success in managing.

Bona Fide Occupational Qualification (BFOQ): A necessary (not merely preferred) qualification for performing a job.

Cafeteria-Style Plan: A benefits plan that offers employees a set of alternatives from which they can choose the types and amounts of benefits they want.

Calibration Meeting: Meeting at which managers discuss employee performance ratings and provide evidence supporting their ratings with the goal of eliminating the influence of rating errors.

Cash Balance Plan: Retirement plan in which the employer sets up an individual account for each employee and contributes a percentage of the employee's salary; the account earns interest at a predefined rate.

Checkoff Provision: Contract provision under which the employer, on behalf of the union, automatically deducts union dues from employees' paychecks.

Closed Shop: Union security arrangement under which a person must be a union member before being hired; illegal for those covered by the National Labor Relations Act.

Coach: A peer or manager who works with an employee to motivate the employee, help him or her develop skills, and provide reinforcement and feedback.

Cognitive Ability Tests: Tests designed to measure such mental abilities as verbal skills, quantitative skills, and reasoning ability.

Collective Bargaining: Negotiation between union representatives and management representatives to arrive at a contract defining conditions of employment for the term of the contract and to administer that contract.

Commissions: Incentive pay calculated as a percentage of sales.

Compensatory Model: Process of arriving at a selection decision in which a very high score on one type of assessment can make up for a low score on another.

Concurrent Validation: Research that consists of administering a test to people who currently hold a job, then comparing their scores to existing measures of job performance.

Consolidated Omnibus Budget Reconciliation Act (COBRA):   Federal law that requires employers to permit employees or their dependents to extend their health insurance coverage at group rates for up to 36 months following a qualifying event, such as a layoff, reduction in hours, or the employee's death.

Construct Validity: Consistency between a high score on a test and high level of a construct such as intelligence or leadership ability, as well as between mastery of this construct and successful performance of the job.

Content Validity: Consistency between the test items or problems and the kinds of situations or problems that occur on the job.

Continuous Learning: Each employee's and each group's ongoing efforts to gather information and apply the information to their decisions in a learning organization.

Contributory Plan: Retirement plan funded by contributions from the employer and employee.

Coordination Training: Team training that teaches the team how to share information and make decisions to obtain the best team performance.

Core Competency: A set of knowledges and skills that make the organization superior to competitors and create value for customers.

Corporate Campaigns: Bringing public, financial, or political pressure on employers during union organization and contract negotiation.

Corporate Social Responsibility: A company's commitment to meeting the needs of its stakeholders.

Craft Union: Labor union whose members all have a particular skill or occupation.

Criterion-Related Validity: A measure of validity based on showing a substantial correlation between test scores and job performance scores.

Critical-Incident Method: Method of performance measurement based on managers' records of specific examples of the employee acting in ways that are either effective or ineffective.

Cross-Cultural Preparation: Training to prepare employees and their family members for an assignment in a foreign country.

Cross-Training: Team training in which team members understand and practice each other's skills so that they are prepared to step in and take another member's place.

Culture Shock: Disillusionment and discomfort that occur during the process of adjusting to a new culture.

Decision Support Systems: Computer software systems designed to help managers solve problems by showing how results vary when the manager alters assumptions or data.

Defined Benefit Plan: Pension plan that guarantees a specified level of retirement income.

Defined Contribution Plan: Retirement plan in which the employer sets up an individual account for each employee and specifies the size of the investment into that account.

Delayering: Reducing the number of levels in the organization's job structure.

Development: The acquisition of knowledge, skills, and behaviors that improve an employee's ability to meet changes in job requirements and in customer demands.

Differential Piece Rates: Incentive pay in which the piece rate is higher when a greater amount is produced.

Direct Applicants: People who apply for a vacancy without prompting from the organization.

Disability: Under the Americans with Disabilities Act, a physical or mental impairment that substantially limits one or more major life activities, a record of having such an impairment, or being regarded as having such an impairment.

Disparate Impact: A condition in which employment practices are seemingly neutral yet disproportionately exclude a protected group from employment opportunities.

Disparate Treatment: Differing treatment of individuals, where the differences are based on the individuals' race, color, religion, sex, national origin, age, or disability status.

Diversity Training: Training designed to change employee attitudes about diversity and/or develop skills needed to work with a diverse workforce.

Downsizing: The planned elimination of large numbers of personnel with the goal of enhancing the organization's competitiveness.

Downward Move: Assignment of an employee to a position with less responsibility and authority.

Due-Process Policies: Policies that formally lay out the steps an employee may take to appeal the employer's decision to terminate that employee.

EEO-1 Report: The EEOC's Employer Information Report, which details the number of women and minorities employed in nine different job categories.

E-Learning: Receiving training via the Internet or the organization's intranet.

Electronic Human Resource Management (e-HRM): The processing and transmission of digitized HR information, especially using computer networking and the Internet.

Employee Assistance Program (EAP): A referral service that employees can use to seek professional treatment for emotional problems or substance abuse.

Employee Benefits: Compensation in forms other than cash.

Employee Development: The combination of formal education, job experiences, relationships, and assessment of personality and abilities to help employees prepare for the future of their careers.

Employee Empowerment: Giving employees responsibility and authority to make decisions regarding all aspects of product development or customer service.

Employee Retirement Income Security Act (ERISA): Federal law that increased the responsibility of pension plan trustees to protect retirees, established certain rights related to vesting and portability, and created the Pension Benefit Guarantee Corporation.

Employee Stock Ownership Plan (ESOP): An arrangement in which the organization distributes shares of stock to all its employees by placing it in a trust.

Employee Wellness Program (EWP): A set of communications, activities, and facilities designed to change health-related behaviors in ways that reduce health risks.

Employment at Will: Employment principle that if there is no specific employment contract saying otherwise, the employer or employee may end an employment relationship at any time, regardless of cause.

Equal Employment Opportunity (EEO): The condition in which all individuals have an equal chance for employment, regardless of their race, color, religion, sex, age, disability, or national origin.

Equal Employment Opportunity Commission (EEOC): Agency of the Department of Justice charged with enforcing Title VII of the Civil Rights Act of 1964 and other antidiscrimination laws.

Ergonomics: The study of the interface between individuals' physiology and the characteristics of the physical work environment.

Ethics: The fundamental principles of right and wrong.

Evidence-Based HR: Collecting and using data to show that human resource practices have a positive influence on the company's bottom line or key stakeholders.

Exempt Employees: Managers, outside salespeople, and any other employees not covered by the FLSA requirement for overtime pay.

Exit Interview: A meeting of a departing employee with the employee's supervisor and/or a human resource specialist to discuss the employee's reasons for leaving.

Expatriates: Employees assigned to work in another country.

Experience Rating: The number of employees a company has laid off in the past and the cost of providing them with unemployment benefits.

Experiential Programs: Training programs in which participants learn concepts and apply them by simulating behaviors involved and analyzing the activity, connecting it with real-life situations.

Expert Systems: Computer systems that support decision making by incorporating the decision rules used by people who are considered to have expertise in a certain area.

External Labor Market: Individuals who are actively seeking employment.

Externship: Employee development through a full-time temporary position at another organization.

Fact Finder: Third party to collective bargaining who reports the reasons for a dispute, the views and arguments of both sides, and possibly a recommended settlement, which the parties may decline.

Fair Labor Standards Act (FLSA): Federal law that establishes a minimum wage and requirements for overtime pay and child labor.

Family and Medical Leave Act (FMLA): Federal law requiring organizations with 50 or more employees to provide up to 12 weeks of unpaid leave after childbirth or adoption, to care for a seriously ill family member, or for an employee's own serious illness.

Feedback: Information employers give employees about their skills and knowledge and where these assets fit into the organization's plans.

Fleishman Job Analysis System: Job analysis technique that asks subject-matter experts to evaluate a job in terms of the abilities required to perform the job.

Flexible Spending Account: Employee-controlled pretax earnings set aside to pay for certain eligible expenses such as health care expenses during the same year.

Flextime: A scheduling policy in which full-time employees may choose starting and ending times within guidelines specified by the organization.

Forced-Distribution Method: Method of performance measurement that assigns a certain percentage of employees to each category in a set of categories.

Forecasting: The attempts to determine the supply of and demand for various types of human resources to predict areas within the organization where there will be labor shortages or surpluses.

Four-Fifths Rule: Rule of thumb that finds evidence of discrimination if an organization's hiring rate for a minority group is less than four-fifths the hiring rate for the majority group.

Gainsharing: Group incentive program that measures improvements in productivity and effectiveness objectives and distributes a portion of each gain to employees.

Generalizable: Valid in other contexts beyond the context in which the selection method was developed.

Glass Ceiling: Circumstances resembling an invisible barrier that keep most women and minorities from attaining the top jobs in organizations.

Global Organization: An organization that chooses to locate a facility based on the ability to effectively, efficiently, and flexibly produce a product or service, using cultural differences as an advantage.

Graphic Rating Scale: Method of performance measurement that lists traits and provides a rating scale for each trait; the employer uses the scale to indicate the extent to which an employee displays each trait.

Grievance Procedure: The process for resolving union-management conflicts over interpretation or violation of a collective bargaining agreement.

Health Maintenance Organization (HMO): A health care plan that requires patients to receive their medical care from the HMO's health care professionals, who are often paid a flat salary, and provides all services on a prepaid basis.

High-Performance Work System: An organization in which technology, organizational structure, people, and processes all work together to give an organization an advantage in the competitive environment.

Host Country: A country (other than the parent country) in which an organization operates a facility.

Hot-Stove Rule: Principle of discipline that says discipline should be like a hot stove, giving clear warning and following up with consistent, objective, immediate consequences.

Hourly Wage: Rate of pay for each hour worked.

HR Dashboard: A display of a series of HR measures, showing the measure and progress toward meeting it.

HRM Audit: A formal review of the outcomes of HRM functions, based on identifying key HRM functions and measures of business performance.

Human Capital: An organization's employees, described in terms of their training, experience, judgment, intelligence, relationships, and insight.

Human Resource Information System (HRIS): A computer system used to acquire, store, manipulate, analyze, retrieve, and distribute information related to an organization's human resources.

Human Resource Management (HRM): The policies, practices, and systems that influence employees' behavior, attitudes, and performance.

Human Resource Planning: Identifying the numbers and types of employees the organization will require in order to meet its objectives.

Immigration Reform and Control Act of 1986: Federal law requiring employers to verify and maintain records on applicants' legal rights to work in the United States.

Incentive pay: Forms of pay linked to an employee's performance as an individual, group member, or organization member.

Industrial Engineering: The study of jobs to find the simplest way to structure work in order to maximize efficiency.

Industrial Union: Labor union whose members are linked by their work in a particular industry.

Instructional Design: A process of systematically developing training to meet specified needs.

Interactional Justice: A judgment that the organization carried out its actions in a way that took the employee's feelings into account.

Internal Labor Force: An organization's workers (its employees and the people who have contracts to work at the organization).

International Organization: An organization that sets up one or a few facilities in one or a few foreign countries.

Internship: On-the-job learning sponsored by an educational institution as a component of an academic program.

Involuntary Turnover: Turnover initiated by an employer (often with employees who would prefer to stay).

Job: A set of related duties.

Job Analysis: The process of getting detailed information about jobs.

Job Description: A list of the tasks, duties, and responsibilities (TDRs) that a particular job entails.

Job Design: The process of defining how work will be performed and what tasks will be required in a given job.

Job Enlargement: Broadening the types of tasks performed in a job.

Job Enrichment: Empowering workers by adding more decision-making authority to jobs.

Job Evaluation: An administrative procedure for measuring the relative internal worth of the organization's jobs.

Job Experiences: The combination of relationships, problems, demands, tasks, and other features of an employee's job.

Job Extension: Enlarging jobs by combining several relatively simple jobs to form a job with a wider range of tasks.

Job Hazard Analysis Technique: Safety promotion technique that involves breaking down a job into basic elements, then rating each element for its potential for harm or injury.

Job Involvement: The degree to which people identify themselves with their jobs.

Job Posting: The process of communicating information about a job vacancy on company bulletin boards, in employee publications, on corporate intranets, and anywhere else the organization communicates with employees.

Job Rotation: Enlarging jobs by moving employees among several different jobs.

Job Satisfaction: A pleasant feeling resulting from the perception that one's job fulfills or allows for the fulfillment of one's important job values.

Job Sharing: A work option in which two part-time employees carry out the tasks associated with a single job.

Job Specification: A list of the knowledge, skills, abilities, and other characteristics (KSAOs) that an individual must have to perform a particular job.

Job Structure: The relative pay for different jobs within the organization.

Job Withdrawal: A set of behaviors with which employees try to avoid the work situation physically, mentally, or emotionally.

Knowledge Workers: Employees whose main contribution to the organization is specialized knowledge, such as knowledge of customers, a process, or a profession.

Labor Relations: Field that emphasizes skills that managers and union leaders can use to minimize costly forms of conflict (such as strikes) and seek win-win solutions to disagreements.

Leaderless Group Discussion: An assessment center exercise in which a team of five to seven employees is assigned a problem and must work together to solve it within a certain time period.

Leading Indicators: Objective measures that accurately predict future labor demand.

Learning Management System (LMS): A computer application that automates the administration, development, and delivery of training programs.

Learning Organization: An organization that supports lifelong learning by enabling all employees to acquire and share knowledge.

Long-Term Disability Insurance: Insurance that pays a percentage of a disabled employee's salary after an initial period and potentially for the rest of the employee's life.

Maintenance of Membership: Union security rules not requiring union membership but requiring that employees who join the union remain members for a certain period of time.

Management by Objectives (MBO): A system in which people at each level of the organization set goals in a process that flows from top to bottom, so employees at all levels are contributing to the organization's overall goals; these goals become the standards for evaluating each employee's performance.

Material Safety Data Sheets (MSDSs):   Forms on which chemical manufacturers and importers identify the hazards of their chemicals.

Mediation: Conflict resolution procedure in which a mediator hears the views of both sides and facilitates the negotiation process but has no formal authority to dictate a resolution.

Mentor: An experienced, productive senior employee who helps develop a less experienced employee (a protégé).

Merit Pay: A system of linking pay increases to ratings on performance appraisals.

Minimum Wage: The lowest amount that employers may pay under federal or state law, stated as an amount of pay per hour.

Mixed-Standard Scales: Method of performance measurement that uses several statements describing each trait to produce a final score for that trait.

Multinational Company: An organization that builds facilities in a number of different countries in an effort to minimize production and distribution costs.

Multiple-Hurdle Model: Process of arriving at a selection decision by eliminating some candidates at each stage of the selection process.

Myers-Briggs Type Indicator (MBTI):   Psychological inventory that identifies individuals' preferences for source of energy, means of information gathering, way of decision making, and lifestyle, providing information for team building and leadership development.

National Labor Relations Act (NLRA):   Federal law that supports collective bargaining and sets out the rights of employees to form unions.

National Labor Relations Board (NLRB):   Federal government agency that enforces the NLRA by conducting and certifying representation elections and investigating unfair labor practices.

Needs Assessment: The process of evaluating the organization, individual employees, and employees' tasks to determine what kinds of training, if any, are necessary.

Nepotism: The practice of hiring relatives.

Noncontributory Plan: Retirement plan funded entirely by contributions from the employer.

Nondirective Interview: A selection interview in which the interviewer has great discretion in choosing questions to ask each candidate.

Nonexempt Employees: Employees covered by the FLSA requirements for overtime pay.

Occupational Safety and Health Act (OSH Act):   U.S. law authorizing the federal government to establish and enforce occupational safety and health standards for all places of employment engaging in interstate commerce.

Occupational Safety and Health Administration (OSHA):   Labor Department agency responsible for inspecting employers, applying safety and health standards, and levying fines for violation.

Office of Federal Contract Compliance Procedures (OFCCP):   The agency responsible for enforcing the executive orders that cover companies doing business with the federal government.

Offshoring: Moving operations from the country where a company is headquartered to a country where pay rates are lower but the necessary skills are available.

On-the-Job Training (OJT):   Training methods in which a person with job experience and skill guides trainees in practicing job skills at the workplace.

Open-Door Policy: An organization's policy of making managers available to hear complaints.

Organization Analysis: A process for determining the appropriateness of training by evaluating the characteristics of the organization.

Organizational Behavior Modification (OBM):   A plan for managing the behavior of employees through a formal system of feedback and reinforcement.

Organizational Commitment: The degree to which an employee identifies with the organization and is willing to put forth effort on its behalf.

Orientation: Training designed to prepare employees to perform their jobs effectively, learn about their organization, and establish work relationships.

Outcome Fairness: A judgment that the consequences given to employees are just.

Outplacement Counseling: A service in which professionals try to help dismissed employees manage the transition from one job to another.

Outsourcing: Contracting with another organization (vendor, third-party provider, or consultant) to provide services.

Paired-Comparison Method: Method of performance measurement that compares each employee with each other employee to establish rankings.

Panel Interview: Selection interview in which several members of the organization meet to interview each candidate.

Parent Country: The country in which an organization's headquarters is located.

Patient Protection and Affordable Care Act: Health care reform law passed in 2010 that includes incentives and penalties for employers providing health insurance as a benefit.

Pay Differential: Adjustment to a pay rate to reflect differences in working conditions or labor markets.

Pay Grades: Sets of jobs having similar worth or content, grouped together to establish rates of pay.

Pay Level: The average amount (including wages, salaries, and bonuses) the organization pays for a particular job.

Pay Policy Line: A graphed line showing the mathematical relationship between job evaluation points and pay rate.

Pay Ranges: A set of possible pay rates defined by a minimum, maximum, and midpoint of pay for employees holding a particular job or a job within a particular pay grade.

Pay Structure: The pay policy resulting from job structure and pay level decisions.

Peer Review: Process for resolving disputes by taking them to a panel composed of representatives from the organization at the same levels as the people in the dispute.

Pension Benefit Guarantee Corporation (PBGC): Federal agency that insures retirement benefits and guarantees retirees a basic benefit if the employer experiences financial difficulties.

Performance Management: The process through which managers ensure that employees' activities and outputs contribute to the organization's goals.

Person Analysis: A process for determining individuals' needs and readiness for training.

Personnel Selection: The process through which organizations make decisions about who will or will not be allowed to join the organization.

Piecework Rate: Rate of pay for each unit produced.

Position: The set of duties (job) performed by a particular person.

Position Analysis Questionnaire (PAQ): A standardized job analysis questionnaire containing 194 questions about work behaviors, work conditions, and job characteristics that apply to a wide variety of jobs.

Predictive Validation: Research that uses the test scores of all applicants and looks for a relationship between the scores and future performance of the applicants who were hired.

Preferred Provider Organization (PPO): A health care plan that contracts with health care professionals to provide services at a reduced fee and gives patients financial incentives to use network providers.

Procedural Justice: A judgment that fair methods were used to determine the consequences an employee receives.

Profit Sharing: Incentive pay in which payments are a percentage of the organization's profits and do not become part of the employees' base salary.

Progressive Discipline: A formal discipline process in which the consequences become more serious if the employee repeats the offense.

Promotion: Assignment of an employee to a position with greater challenges, more responsibility, and more authority than in the previous job, usually accompanied by a pay increase.

Protean Career: A career that frequently changes based on changes in the person's interests, abilities, and values and in the work environment.

Psychological Contract: A description of what an employee expects to contribute in an employment relationship and what the employer will provide the employee in exchange for those contributions.

Readability: The difficulty level of written materials.

Readiness for Training: A combination of employee characteristics and positive work environment that permit training.

Realistic Job Preview: Background information about a job's positive and negative qualities.

Reality Check: Information employers give employees about their skills and knowledge and where these assets fit into the organization's plans.

Reasonable Accommodation: An employer's obligation to do something to enable an otherwise qualified person to perform a job.

Recruiting: Any activity carried on by the organization with the primary purpose of identifying and attracting potential employees.

Recruitment: The process through which the organization seeks applicants for potential employment.

Reengineering: A complete review of the organization's critical work processes to make them more efficient and able to deliver higher quality.

Referrals: People who apply for a vacancy because someone in the organization prompted them to do so.

Reliability: The extent to which a measurement is from random error.

Repatriation: The process of preparing expatriates to return home from a foreign assignment.

Right-to-Know Laws: State laws that require employers to provide employees with information about the health risks associated with exposure to substances considered hazardous.

Right-to-Work Laws: State laws that make union shops, maintenance of membership, and agency shops illegal.

Role: The set of behaviors that people expect of a person in a particular job.

Role Ambiguity: Uncertainty about what the organization expects from the employee in terms of what to do or how to do it.

Role Analysis Technique: A process of formally identifying expectations associated with a role.

Role Conflict: An employee's recognition that demands of the job are incompatible or contradictory.

Role Overload: A state in which too many expectations or demands are placed on a person.

Sabbatical: A leave of absence from an organization to renew or develop skills.

Salary: Rate of pay for each week, month, or year worked.

Scanlon Plan: A gainsharing program in which employees receive a bonus if the ratio of labor costs to the sales value of production is below a set standard.

Selection: The process by which the organization attempts to identify applicants with the necessary knowledge, skills, abilities, and other characteristics that will help the organization achieve its goals.

Self-Assessment: The use of information by employees to determine their career interests, values, aptitudes, and behavioral tendencies.

Self-Service: System in which employees have online access to information about HR issues and go online to enroll themselves in programs and provide feedback through surveys.

Sexual Harassment: Unwelcome sexual advances as defined by the EEOC.

Short-Term Disability Insurance: Insurance that pays a percentage of a disabled employee's salary as benefits to the employee for six months or less.

Simple Ranking: Method of performance measurement that requires managers to rank employees in their group from the highest performer to the poorest performer.

Simulation: A training method that represents a real-life situation, with trainees making decisions resulting in outcomes that mirror what would happen on the job.

Situational Interviews: A structured interview in which the interviewer describes a situation likely to arise on the job, then asks the candidate what he or she would do in that situation.

Skill-Based Pay Systems: Pay structures that set pay according to the employees' levels of skill or knowledge and what they are capable of doing.

Social Security: The federal Old Age, Survivors, Disability, and Health Insurance (OASDHI) program, which combines old age (retirement) insurance, survivor's insurance, disability insurance, hospital insurance (Medicare Part A), and supplementary medical insurance (Medicare Part B) for the elderly.

Stakeholders: The parties with an interest in the company's success (typically, shareholders, the community, customers, and employees).

Standard Hour Plan: An incentive plan that pays workers extra for work done in less than a preset "standard time."

Stock Options: Rights to buy a certain number of shares of stock at a specified price.

Straight Piecework Plan: Incentive pay in which the employer pays the same rate per piece, no matter how much the worker produces.

Strike: A collective decision by union members not to work until certain demands or conditions are met.

Structured Interview: A selection interview that consists of a predetermined set of questions for the interviewer to ask.

Succession Planning: The process of identifying and tracking high-potential employees who will be able to fill top management positions when they become vacant.

Summary Plan Description: Report that describes a pension plan's funding, eligibility requirements, risks, and other details.

Task Analysis: The process of identifying and analyzing tasks to be trained for.

Team Leader Training: Training in the skills necessary for effectively leading the organization's teams.

Teamwork: The assignment of work to groups of employees with various skills who interact to assemble a product or provide a service.

Technic of Operations Review (TOR): Method of promoting safety by determining which specific element of a job led to a past accident.

Third Country: A country that is neither the parent country nor the host country of an employer.

360-Degree Performance Appraisal: Performance measurement that combines information from the employee's managers, peers, subordinates, self, and customers.

Total Quality Management (TQM): A companywide effort to continuously improve the ways people, machines, and systems accomplish work.

Training: An organization's planned efforts to help employees acquire job-related knowledge, skills, abilities, and behaviors, with the goal of applying these on the job.

Transaction Processing: Computations and calculations involved in reviewing and documenting HRM decisions and practices.

Transfer: Assignment of an employee to a position in a different area of the company, usually in a lateral move.

Transfer of Training: On-the-job use of knowledge, skills, and behaviors learned in training.

Transitional Matrix: A chart that lists job categories held in one period and shows the proportion of employees in each of those job categories in a future period.

Transnational HRM System: Type of HRM system that makes decisions from a global perspective, includes managers from many countries, and is based on ideas contributed by people representing a variety of cultures.

Trend Analysis: Constructing and applying statistical models that predict labor demand for the next year, given relatively objective statistics from the previous year.

Unemployment Insurance: A federally mandated program to minimize the hardships of unemployment through payments to unemployed workers, help in finding new jobs, and incentives to stabilize employment.

Uniform Guidelines on Employee Selection Procedures: Guidelines issued by the EEOC and other agencies to identify how an organization should develop and administer its system for selecting employees so as not to violate antidiscrimination laws.

Union Shop: Union security arrangement that requires employees to join the union within a certain amount of time (30 days) after beginning employment.

Union Steward: An employee elected by union members to represent them in ensuring that the terms of the labor contract are enforced.

Unions: Organizations formed for the purpose of representing their members' interests in dealing with employers.

Utility: The extent to which something provides economic value greater than its cost.

Validity: The extent to which performance on a measure (such as a test score) is related to what the measure is designed to assess (such as job performance).

Vesting Rights: Guarantee that when employees become participants in a pension plan and work a specified number of years, they will receive a pension at retirement age, regardless of whether they remained with the employer.

Virtual Reality: A computer-based technology that provides an interactive, three-dimensional learning experience.

Voluntary Turnover: Turnover initiated by employees (often when the organization would prefer to keep them).

Work Flow Design: The process of analyzing the tasks necessary for the production of a product or service.

Workers' Compensation: State programs that provide benefits to workers who suffer work-related injuries or illnesses, or to their survivors.

Workforce Utilization Review: A comparison of the proportion of employees in protected groups with the proportion that each group represents in the relevant labor market.

Yield Ratio: A ratio that expresses the percentage of applicants who successfully move from one stage of the recruitment and selection process to the next.

Photo Credits

Name and Company Index

Subject Index